Writers

INC

A Student Handbook for College-and-Career Readiness

Houghton Mifflin Harcourt

Written and Compiled by
Patrick Sebranek, Dave Kemper, and **Verne Meyer**

Illustrated by
Chris Krenzke

ii

Acknowledgments

Writers INC **is a reality because of the help and advice of our team of students, educators, writers, editors, and designers:** Steve J. Augustyn, Chris Erickson, Tim Kemper, Lois Krenzke, Rob King, Mark Lalumondier, Janae Sebranek, Lester Smith, and Jean Varley.

Cover photographs: student © BlueSkyImage/Shutterstock; swirling letters (foreground) © EKS/Shutterstock

Printed in the United States of America

International Standard Book Number: 978-0-544-65200-2

5 6 7 8 9 10 DOC 20 19 18

4500702117   A B C D E F G

Writers

INC

A Student Handbook for College-and-Career Readiness

Writers INC is thoughtfully designed with college-and-career readiness in mind, starting with all facets of writing—from constructing sentences and paragraphs to developing academic essays. Explanatory essays and essays of argumentation are included, as are responses to literature and many narrative forms. In short, all phases and types of writing are presented with helpful models and guidelines.

As you know, writing is not carried out in isolation—it is often the result of thoughtful reading, speaking, and listening. So *Writers INC* addresses these essential strands of learning as well. Special attention is given to reading nonfiction texts, because they are such a critical source of information in all content areas.

But we don't stop there. Much high school writing and learning takes place outside the English classroom. So there is a special section for writing across the curriculum—from math to science to social studies. And writing involves research, so that, too, is addressed—from planning research projects to preparing and presenting your findings. Of course, academic research can't be conducted without using technology, so all aspects of electronic media are addressed.

What else do you need to know about *Writers INC*? Well, the handbook includes a special section on critical and creative thinking skills. You will also find guidelines for test taking plus a special grammar and language section—the Yellow Pages—to help you use the language correctly and effectively.

Here's what you won't find: There are no exercises in *Writers INC*, just page after page of useful information to help you become an effective writer and learner—someone with the high-level literacy skills needed to succeed in college and the workplace.

Using the Handbook

Your *Writers INC* handbook provides concise, easy-to-use guidelines, models, and strategies to help with your writing and learning needs in all of your classes. If that's not enough, you can also refer to our Web site, **www.thewritesource.com**, for more information. Here are some of the writing aids you will find on the Web site:

- Writing topics
- Links to publishing sites
- Writing samples, including an APA research paper
- MLA and APA documentation updates
- A sample multimedia report

Writers INC

Houghton Mifflin Harcourt.

A Student Handbook for College-and-Career Readiness

Your handbook guide . . .

The **Table of Contents** (starting on the next page) lists the major sections of the handbook and the chapters found in each. Use the table of contents when you're looking for a *general* topic.

The **Index** (starting on page 650) provides a thorough listing of the information covered in *Writers INC*. Use the index when you're looking for a *specific* topic.

The **Color Coding** used for the "Proofreader's Guide" (the Yellow Pages) makes this important section easy to find. The guide covers punctuation, capitalization, spelling, usage, grammar, and more.

The **Cross References** throughout the handbook tell you where to turn for more information about a topic. Some of these references are within the text. *Example:* (See page 190). Other cross-references are set off from the text because of their importance.

"Knowledge is of two kinds. We know a subject ourselves, or we know where we can find information upon it."

Samuel Johnson

Table of Contents

Writing About Literature

Narrative Writing

Creative Writing

Writing Across the Curriculum

Reading

Proofreader's Guide

Writers INC

The Process of Writing

Understanding Writing

You may feel that the information you find in your textbooks and class handouts is enough to handle. Add to that a whole library full of books, plus the sea of Internet sources, and it can all become overwhelming. However, with the right 21st century learning tools, you can be ready for this challenge.

Writing is one of these important tools because it helps you remember, analyze, and evaluate information. It also helps you demonstrate what you have learned and share your personal discoveries. In short, writing helps you gain control of information, turning it into knowledge. This chapter explores different reasons to write and introduces you to the writing process. Once you understand the scope and power of writing, you will appreciate what a valuable learning tool it truly is.

Learning Outcomes

Write to learn.
Write to share learning.
Use the writing process.
Write in personal journals or blogs.

"We're not in an information age anymore.
We're in the information management age."

Chris Hardwick

Writing to Learn

Gertrude Stein was a twentieth-century writer of great stature. The special place that writing held in her life echoes in Stein's own words: "To write is to write is to write is to write." For her, there was nothing more to say about the subject.

Why was Stein so taken by writing? Was it the recognition she received from it? Probably not. What Stein valued most was the special opportunity that writing offered her. It made her think, deepened her understanding of new subjects, and helped her to form interesting connections. In other words, writing helped Gertrude Stein to learn.

The Proper Approach

If you approach writing as just another assignment, you may miss its true value. Writing is actually a way to learn. Brief notes, a lengthy list, a series of questions about a topic—these are all meaningful forms of writing that connect you to the subjects you are studying. As you include writing in your learning routine, you will discover its value.

When you write to learn, write freely and naturally. Most writing-to-learn activities are short, spontaneous, exploratory, and almost never graded or shared with others. This kind of writing is not about showing how well you can write or how much you know. Instead, it is about increasing your understanding. Some educators believe that writing to learn is the key to mastering any subject—science or social studies, English or electronics.

The Payoff

Writing to learn offers these immediate, long-lasting benefits:

- **Deeper connection** with course work
- **Ability to understand** new concepts
- **Thinking at higher levels** (analyzing, evaluating)
- **Positive attitude** about course work
- **Lifelong learning technique**

"You must recognize that meaningful writing doesn't have to lead to an end product."

Todd Capewell

Keeping a Class Notebook

Keeping a class notebook, or learning log, is a good way to incorporate writing into your learning routine. You can take notes as well as reflect on new concepts and subjects. It is a place where you can dig deeper into what you have learned from letters, class discussions, group projects, and experiments. The free flow of ideas promotes true learning. Here are some specific ideas for using a class notebook.

Using a Class Notebook

- **Write a summary of a learning experience** (a lecture, a discussion, a project). Add your own conclusions, telling what information you found most valuable or interesting, what opinions you agreed with or disagreed with, and why.

- **Personalize new ideas and concepts.** Consider how this new information relates to what you already know.

- **Write about what you still want to know about a topic.** Then brainstorm ways to find this information.

- **Discuss your course work with a particular audience.** Write as if you were talking about these topics with a young child, a foreign exchange student, an alien from another planet, an object.

- **Question what you are learning.** How important are the concepts you are learning? One way to discover this is to write a dialogue.

- **Express ideas and information in pictures**, charts, and maps.

- **Start a glossary of important and interesting vocabulary words.** Use these words in your log entries.

- **Argue for or against a topic.** The topic can be anything that comes up in a discussion, in a lecture, or in your reading.

- **Write about how you are doing in a certain class.** Are you learning as much as you can, or doing as well as you had hoped? Is some of the material hard for you? What can you do to improve?

Sample Notebook Entries

The sample learning-log entries below were written in response to a science article and a chemistry lecture. Notice how both entries are personalized.

Response to a Science Article

I just read an article in a science magazine about mosquitoes and the diseases they can carry. I thought flies and mosquitoes were a pain just because they bite. But it turns out that you can get more than an itchy bump from a mosquito. They can carry viruses that cause serious diseases such as malaria and encephalitis. Doctors think that, in all of history, more people have died of malaria than any other disease. Malaria was even one of the reasons why the Roman Empire fell. In 1999, seven people in New York city died from encephalitis caused by mosquito bites. Health officials are very concerned about similar outbreaks in the future.

Response to a Chemistry Lecture

Save Edit   May 13

Noble Gases and the Hindenburg

Our teacher used the **Hindenburg** as an example of how noble gases are different from other elements. The **Hindenburg** was a zeppelin—a huge, cylinder-shaped, flying balloon that could carry passengers. It was filled with hydrogen—which is not a noble gas—and reacted with oxygen in the air, causing the zeppelin to burn. Thirty-six people died. If helium had been used instead, it also would have kept the zeppelin airborne, but it wouldn't have burned. This is because it is a noble gas, meaning it doesn't interact with other elements. That's why balloons and dirigibles use helium now, not hydrogen. This got me thinking about how what you don't know can hurt you. I guess chemistry can actually be useful in real life!

Writing-to-Learn Strategies

Writing to learn is essentially exploratory writing. What form it takes is strictly up to you, as long as it encourages thinking and learning. You may prefer free, nonstop writing, or you may decide to try some of the following strategies.

Debates ▪ Imagine yourself split into two persons. One of you defends an opinion about a topic, and the other disagrees with it. Keep the debate going as long as you can.

Dialogues ▪ Create an imaginary conversation between yourself and a character (perhaps a historical figure) or between two characters (perhaps from a novel).

First Thoughts ▪ In order to focus on a new topic, write down your immediate impressions about it.

Nutshelling ▪ Write in a nutshell (one sentence) the importance of something you've heard, seen, or read.

Predicting ▪ Stop at a key point in a book or lesson and write down what you think will happen next. Predicting works especially well with materials that have a strong cause-and-effect relationship.

Pointed Questions ▪ Keep asking yourself *why?* in your writing until you run out of answers.

Stop 'n' Write ▪ At any point in a reading assignment, stop and write about what you've just read. This allows you to evaluate your understanding of the topic.

Picture Outlines ▪ Instead of writing, organize the main points of a lecture or reading assignment into a picture outline.

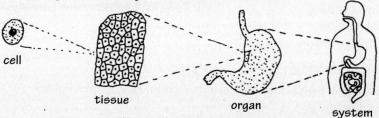

cell   tissue   organ   system

Writing to Share Learning

Another key function of writing is to share what you have learned. Explanatory essays and essays of argumentation are two examples of writing to share learning. Your audience may include an instructor, classmates, and others—perhaps online readers from around the world. Use the writing process to produce your best writing.

Improved Thinking

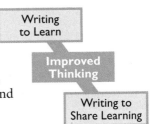

As this graphic shows, improved thinking is the link between writing to learn and writing to share learning. Once you've formed your initial thoughts, you can use improved thinking to clarify, complete, and share them.

▌Forms of Writing

The chart below displays many of the forms of writing to share covered in this handbook. Producing these different forms will expand your understanding of writing for different purposes and audiences.

Writing Arguments	(See pages 102–129.)
Supporting a Claim (*Judging the worth of something*)	Essays of Argumentation, Editorials, Commentaries, Problem-Solution Essays, Position Papers
Explanatory Writing	(See pages 130–157.)
Sharing Information (*Composing clear and complete messages*)	Explanatory Essays, Process Essays, Essays of Definition, Cause-Effect Essays, Comparison Essays, Classification Essays
Narrative Writing	(See pages 200–209.)
Remembering & Reflecting (*Exploring experiences*)	Journals, Personal Narratives, Personal Essays, Memoirs, Descriptive Writing
Writing About Literature	(See pages 158–199.)
Understanding & Interpreting (*Reacting to texts*)	Book Reviews, Mini-Reviews, Literary Analyses
Creative Writing	(See pages 210–231.)
Inventing & Imitating (*Reshaping ideas*)	Short Fiction, Play Scripts, Poetry

Using the Writing Process

At the start of her career, author Annie Dillard thought that in order to write anything, all she needed was "pen, paper, and a lap." She soon discovered that "in order to write even a sonnet [a 14-line poem], she needed a warehouse." In other words, Dillard learned that it took time—and numerous drafts—to produce effective writing, no matter what the length.

Think of the essays that you are most proud of. You probably worked hard to produce each one. If you had stopped writing after one draft, it is likely you would not have been happy with the end product. Writing must go through a series of steps before it is ready to share with an audience.

Previewing the Process

While no two writers work in exactly the same way, all writers appreciate the value of the writing process. Here's how author Walter Dean Myers works: "I rush through a first draft, and then I go back and rewrite because I can usually see what the problems are going to be. Rewriting is more fun for me than the writing is." Your own process will develop over time, but it generally includes these steps:

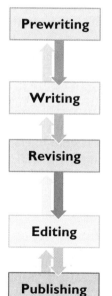

Prewriting　　At the start of a project, analyze the rhetorical situation (the purpose, audience, and form). Then select a writing idea, collect information about it, and devise a writing plan. (See pages 29–40.)

Writing　　Then develop a first draft, using your plan as a general guide. A first draft is your first look at a developing essay or article, so don't try to get everything exactly right. (See pages 41–46.)

Revising　　Next, review the rough draft, focusing first on your ideas, and then on your voice, word choice, and sentence style. Change any parts that are unclear or incomplete. (You may change some parts several times.) (See pages 47–60.)

Editing　　After making the necessary revisions, check your writing for correctness. Then produce a final copy and proofread it for errors. (See pages 61–67.)

Publishing　　Submit or post the finished product, following the required format/design.

Note: The graphic above shows how you can move back and forth between the steps in the writing process during a project. For example, after writing a first draft, you may decide to do more research before revising what you've written.

A Closer Look at the Process

To make each writing project a meaningful experience, keep the following points in mind.

Keep time on your side. Effective writing requires a lot of searching, planning, writing, reflecting, and revising. In order to do all of these things, you must give yourself plenty of time. If your teacher provides you with a timetable for your writing, make sure to follow it. Otherwise, create your own. (Always reserve plenty of time for revising.) As you probably know, waiting until the last minute takes all of the fun out of writing.

> *Remember:* Good writing takes time.

Limit your topic. It would be almost impossible to write an effective essay or report about a general subject such as photography. You wouldn't know where to begin or end. But if you limited this subject to a specific topic—let's say, the use of photography by investigative reporters—then you would find it much easier to manage your writing.

> *Remember:* Good writing has a focus, meaning that it stems from and is built around a limited topic.

Work from a position of authority. The more you know about your topic, the easier it is to write about it. So collect as much information as you can during prewriting—tapping into your own thoughts, asking other people for their ideas, consulting print material, surfing the Net, and so on.

> *Remember:* Good writing requires good information.

Pace yourself when you revise. Many of the pros believe that the real writing takes place when they revise—when they add, cut, rearrange, and rewrite different parts of their first drafts. They do not rush these changes or make them all at once. Instead, they pace themselves, working very patiently and methodically at times, making revisions until all of the parts seem clear and complete.

> *Remember:* Good writing usually requires a series of changes before it says exactly what you want it to say.

Take some risks. Don't be afraid to experiment in your writing. For example, you might share a personal story in an essay or develop an interview report in a question-and-answer format, much like you would find in many magazine articles. Then again, you might change the sequence of events in a narrative to add suspense. If one experiment doesn't work out, you can always try something else.

> *Remember:* Good writing is a process of discovery.

Writing in Personal Journals or Blogs

Writing to learn and writing to share learning are good reasons to write; but writing for yourself, to explore day-to-day experiences, thoughts, and feelings, is also important. Personal journal or blog writing is something you can do whenever and wherever you feel the need.

Becoming a regular journal writer takes you into the world of your inner thoughts. In time, you'll feel a little sharper, as if your senses have been fine-tuned. A squeaky car door will no longer go unnoticed. You'll wonder, "How long has it been squeaky, why hasn't anyone fixed it, and what else is squeaky in my life?" Your experiences and thoughts will become points of departure as you bend, stretch, and turn these initial ideas inside out to see them in new ways.

▌ Great Beginnings

Keeping a journal or blog doesn't require too much: a laptop or a notebook, and your commitment to write regularly. Most of your ideas will come from your everyday experiences, and when they don't inspire you to write, you can use the experiences of a friend or family member or browse the Web for ideas. If you are still drawing a blank, complete one of the following open-ended sentences and go from there.

▪ I wonder . . .	▪ I feel lucky to have . . .
▪ I wish I could tell someone about . . .	▪ I need help with . . .
▪ I've learned that . . .	▪ My life would be completely different if . . .
▪ If I could change one thing, I'd : . . .	▪ Everyone says . . . , but I think . . .
▪ I was once . . . , but now I am . . .	

▌ The Payoff

In the best of all worlds, journal writing will become one of your good habits, much like eating well or exercising. As you continue to journal, you'll find yourself showing an entry to a friend, or using it as a starting point for a personal narrative, poem, play, story, or blog posting. You'll discover that sharing your ideas with others can be exciting. However, even if you journal on a less than regular basis, it can help you feel more comfortable with writing and more confident in your ability to express yourself.

Sample Blog Entry

In the following blog post, a student talks about helping her mom plan a new menu for their potato-themed cafe. The post includes basic details about the experience but also reflects on its unique meaning.

Tater Patch blog

Home | Comments | Share

More Than a Menu

June 5th

So, Mom's working up a new menu for the Tater Patch, and she wants my help. Of course she does. I'm her best customer. After all, I eat dinner here every day, and I've tried everything on the menu.

I start by telling her to keep all the potato-crust pizzas. They taste awesome, and they were my idea to begin with. The open-faced potato sandwiches can stay, too, except for the beet special because beets are gross. Of course, we should keep the potato chowder and the minestrone, but the split pea soup ought to go, along with the leek soup. Who ever says, "I'd like some leek soup"?

Then Mom tells me we need to come up with dishes that make people's mouths water. More than that, each dish should promise a journey. Just like we've got pictures of Ireland up on the walls and Celtic music playing overhead, we've got to have foods that carry you to the Emerald Isle. So we'll replace the pot pie with "shepherd's pie," the beef soup with "mulligan stew," and the potato bread with "leprechaun gold." My mouth waters just thinking about the new menu.

We spend all night jotting ideas on a photocopy of the old menu, laughing about "brownie brownies" and "Irish muffins," and thinking about the old Tater Patch. I've grown up here. How many menus have we had? How many hours worth of homework have I done at the corner booth? It used to be that my feet didn't even reach the floor. Now I'm getting ready to go off to college. Who's going to help Mom rewrite the menus then?

She's right. The menu's not just a list of foods. It's an invitation to go to a special place. But that place isn't Ireland. It's our little corner restaurant, the place where I grew up, the food that fed me. The menu needs to be a "Welcome Home" sign for people who didn't even know they'd gotten lost.

That's what I tell Mom, and that's what we agree on. So we end up adding one more dish, a peasant dinner called the "Home Plate."

One Writer's Process

Each writer has his or her own unique way of working. Some writers need to talk about their writing, while others would rather keep their ideas to themselves. Some writers work things out in their heads, while others put everything on paper. For now, you are still forming your writing personality, but each new writing experience will move you toward your own particular way of working.

Professional writers understand that writing doesn't happen all at once. They know it is a process involving prewriting, writing, revising, and so on. And while they may approach the process differently, all writers understand that each step is important. This chapter shows you one writer's process. As you follow along, compare her approach with your own.

Learning Outcomes

Review the prewriting.
Read the first draft.
Review the revisions.
Check the editing.
Appreciate the final copy.

"There are a thousand ways to write, and each is as good as the other if it fits you."

Lillian Hellman

Review the Prewriting

▌ Selecting and Gathering

In a social studies class, Sarah Anne VanderPlaat's instructor gave this assignment:

> In a personal essay, reflect on one of your own experiences with health care, either as a caregiver, a person receiving care, or an interested observer. Conduct research as needed, but focus primarily on your own involvement.

1. **Analyzing the assignment . . .** To get started, Sarah identified the rhetorical elements (subject, purpose, audience, form) of the assignment.
   - **Subject:** Personal experience with health care
   - **Type of writing:** Personal essay
   - **Audience:** Instructor and classmates
   - **Purpose:** To reflect on (think about) an experience

2. **Selecting a topic . . .** Sarah thought about the times she had needed care, including just last month when she banged heads with an opponent in a soccer match. But in her own mind, Sarah's role as a caregiver far outweighed the times she had needed care herself. She is on the weekend staff in the dementia unit of the local nursing home, and she has strong feelings about this experience.

3. **Exploring her first thoughts . . .** To collect her initial thoughts, Sarah wrote freely about her topic. Here is a passage from that writing.

> Every Saturday at 7 a.m., I start my shift in the dementia unit at Country Nursing Home and try to make Jenny and Wilma and Steve and many others as comfortable as possible. These poor people are caught in a terrible trap, and there is no escape. Their lives are one big mess of confusion, anger, embarrassment, and loss of personal dignity. What makes my job doubly difficult is that a few of the patients are my neighbors. No, make that were my neighbors; they're not going home. In some ways the experience has hardened me; otherwise, how could I continue to clean up after these poor people. In other ways, I've become more caring and empathetic, someone who understands that all is not well for a growing number of our senior citizens. . . .

4. **Asking questions . . .** Sarah also planned to look at the current literature on the topic. She listed a few questions to guide her research.
   - What exactly is dementia?
   - Who is affected by it and what are the signs?
   - What is the current status of the problem?
   - What policies are in place to deal with the problem?
   - What might change in the future?

5. Carrying out the research . . . With these questions in mind, Sarah searched a few Web sites and read some periodical articles. She noted facts, statistics, findings, and references to experts. Here are some of those notes.

"Cost of Dementia Tops $157 Billion Annually in the United States." RAND Corporation. April 3, 2013.
- $157 billion actually low end of the amount, up to $215 billion
- more costly than two leading killers, heart disease and cancer
- greatest cost in institutional and long-term nursing home care rather than medical treatment
- by 2040 the costs could double because the population is becoming older
- "The economic burden of caring for people in the U.S. with dementia is large and growing larger," said Michael Hurd, the study's lead author.
- Hurd urges the fed. gov't. to develop coordinated plan to address growing impact of dementia

Span, Paula. "Studies Find Mixed Results for Dementia Units." New York Times Health Web site, May 10.
- 16% of nursing homes have memory care units
- designed for better care and support
- the findings of a study reported in The Journal of the American Medical Association--patients didn't really fare better in special units
- another study conducted in 2008 found otherwise:
  - fewer feeding tubes and bed rails
  - better use of bathroom
  - antipsychotic drugs used more

6. Forming a thesis . . . To guide her writing, Sarah crafted a thesis statement. After a few attempts, she finally landed on a statement that effectively captured her main idea.

Now that I understand more about the patients and their illness, I am better able to respond to them in a helpful way.

7. Planning the first draft . . . Sarah listed points from her research notes that she wanted to cover in her essay. She would use this information in addition to her reflections on personal experiences.

My Writing Plan

1. Defining dementia
2. Characteristics of the condition
3. Nature of the care
4. Care in the future

Reading the First Draft

In this essay, student writer Sarah Anne VanderPlaat discusses her experiences as a weekend employee working with dementia patients.

Understanding Dementia

The opening paragraph identifies the thesis.

When I first started work as a nursing-home housekeeper, the dementia patients freaked me out. I just didn't know. Now that I understand more about the patients and their illness, I am better able to respond to them in a helpful way.

What exactly is dementia? Dementia is a general term for a decline in mental ability severe enough to interfere with daily life. 60 to 80% of cases of dementia have Alzheimer's, a disease that can progress rapidly, whereas general dementia is different. What you see in many dementia patients can be scary, because the disease affects their language skills and actions.

The most common and noticable sign is memory loss. Patience in the early stages of dementia first experience short-term loss, as the illness advances, they begin to experience worse. One sign of memory loss is repetitiveness: Patients like to tell their stories over and over.

In addition to forgetting and repeating people with dementia may express some spooky idea. A patient named Wilma accused me of steeling from her. "You took it! You rottin thief!" she screamed.

The writer includes her personal experiences.

"What are you missing, Wilma?" I ask. She started to tell me, but then couldn't remember. Soon she had forgotten the episode altogether, although she was still spooked and very angry. This behavior can be caused by bout of schizophrenia.

Another symptom of dementia is related to language skills. While adults with healthy minds easily recall thousands of words patients with dementia struggle with this. A woman in the middle stages of the illness may recognize her son, but not be able to recall his name.

Then there's forgetting how to do simple tasks, like washing dishes. Another is forgetting to do basic things, like turning off the stove. Other

Each paragraph further examines dementia.

behavioral changes show a change in personality, for example, Wilma had been my next door neighbor who occasionally brought my family cookies. Wilma is one of the dementia patients who I take care of. As a neighbor she had been nice, but as a patient she gets very angry with anyone who enters her room.

What's the solution? Sadly, their is no cure for dementia. While nursing home staff can help patience with activities, and medication helps them cope with depression, nothing can stop the illness. Both the disease and the symptoms get worse.

Dementia can also leave people unable to care for themselves. They may have trouble dressing. This level of neediness causes two problems. First, the individual cannot do the act, and second, he or she often suffers from depression

Steve is a good example. When he entered the nursing home just 6 months ago, he was experiencing the early stages of dementia. Today, his illness is much more advanced. The stress of moving into this new environment and leaving his wife at home alone affected Steve deeply.

Steve was given stronger drugs to help with the depression. The medication seemed to work. But then Steve's dementia advanced again. Soon he was asking the same sad questions.

The writer cites a study about memory care units.

So what is the best way to care for people with dementia. Doctors who can prescribe medicine to provide temporary stabilization in some cases. Some nursing homes, including the one I work in, have memory care units set up specifically to address the needs of dementia patients. So far the reports on these units are mixed. A 2008 study, however, did see some positive developments. (Span)

The writer concludes with the one option for care.

So here we sit, spending more money on care for dementia patients than we do for any other disease or illness. At least $157 billion is spent annually on dementia patients and most of that money goes for institutional or home care rather than medical services. (Cost) Unless science can find a cure, care givers have only one option—to do whatever they can to keep their patients save and comfortable. That requires responding to their needs with patience.

Reviewing the Revisions for Content

Sarah took a break after finishing her first draft. When she was ready to review her work, she printed out a copy and looked carefully at the ideas in her essay. She wrote notes in the margin about parts that needed to be changed. Sarah also asked two peers to review her draft. (Their comments appear in the blue note boxes.)

Add more background.

What didn't you know?

Explain the difference.

What do you mean by worse?

Add definition.

Tell more about this symptom.

Understanding Dementia

"Hello, Jenny! It's Sarah. I'm going to clean your room." Saying her name . . ."

When I first started work as a nursing-home housekeeper, the *like Jenny* dementia patients freaked me out. I just didn't ~~know~~ *understand there words or behavior*. Now that I understand more about the patients and their illness, I am better able to respond to them in a helpful way.

What exactly is dementia? Dementia is a general term for a decline in mental ability severe enough to interfere with daily life. 60 to 80% of cases of dementia have Alzheimer's, a disease that can progress rapidly, whereas *patients often suffer from a gradual loss of functions* general dementia ~~is different.~~ What you see in many dementia patients can be scary, because the disease affects their language skills and actions.

The most common and noticable sign is memory loss. Patience in the early stages of dementia first experience short-term loss, as the illness *also* *long-term memory loss* advances, they ~~begin to~~ experience ~~worse.~~ One sign of memory loss is repetitiveness: Patients like to tell their stories over and over. *Jenny could recall countless . . .*

In addition to forgetting and repeating people with dementia may express some spooky idea. A patient named Wilma accused me of steeling from her. "You took it! You rottin thief!" she screamed.

"What are you missing, Wilma?" I ask. She started to tell me, but then couldn't remember. Soon she had forgotten the episode altogether, although she was still spooked and very angry. This behavior can be *, a psychotic disorder characterized by emotional outbursts* caused by bout of schizophrenia.

Another symptom of dementia is related to language skills. While adults with healthy minds easily recall thousands of words patients with *to name even common things and familiar people in there lives* dementia struggle ~~with this.~~ A woman in the middle stages of the illness *However, as the illness advances, she will loose the ability to recognize his face as well.* may recognize her son, but not be able to recall his name. *Patients with dementia also show behavioral changes. One common change is* ~~Then there's~~ forgetting how to do simple tasks, like washing dishes.

Another is forgetting to do basic things, like turning off the stove. Other

Cut unnecessary sentence.

behavioral changes show a change in personality, for example, Wilma had been my next door neighbor who occasionally brought my family cookies. ~~Wilma is one of the dementia patients who I take care of.~~ As a neighbor

Can you show Wilma's anger?

she had been nice, but as a patient she gets very angry with anyone who enters her room. *"Get out of here!" she yells with arms flailing. "You're not allowed here!"*

Reorder these paragraphs.

What's the solution? Sadly, their is no cure for dementia. While nursing home staff can help patience with activities, and medication helps them cope with depression, nothing can stop the illness. Both the disease and the symptoms get worse.

Dementia can also leave people unable to care for themselves. They may have trouble dressing. *, bathing, or using the bathroom* This level of needyness causes two problems. First, the individual cannot do the act, and second, he or she often suffers from depression

Steve is a good example. When he entered the nursing home just 6 months ago, he was experiencing the early stages of dementia. Today, his illness is much more advanced. The stress of moving into this new environment and leaving his wife at home alone affected Steve deeply. *When he first arrived, Steve often cried . . .*

Show how Steve was affected.

Painfully, I would explain, "Steve, this is your home." . . . Steve was given stronger drugs to help with the depression. The

What questions?

medication seemed to work. But then Steve's dementia advanced again. Soon he was asking the same sad questions. *"Where am I" and "Do you know what I am doing here?"*

So what is the best way to care for people with dementia. Doctors who can prescribe medicine to provide temporary stabilization in some cases. *In addition, 16 percent of* Some nursing homes, including the one I work in, have memory care units set up specifically to address the needs of dementia patients. So far the reports on these units are mixed. A 2008 study, however, did see some

What developments?

positive developments. (Span) *in terms of fewer feeding tubes and better use of the bathroom*

Add details for impact.

So here we sit, spending more money on care for dementia patients than we do for any other disease or illness. *, including cancer and heart disease* At least $157 billion is spent annually on dementia patients and most of that money goes for institutional or home care rather than medical services. (Cost) Unless science can find a cure, care givers have only one option—to do whatever they can to keep their patients save and comfortable. That requires

Add punch to last sentence.

responding to their needs with patience. *, kindness, and love*

Reviewing the Revisions for Style

After revising the draft for ideas, Sarah looked at her writing for voice, word choice, and sentences. She made her changes on a printout of her first revision. Here are the style revisions for the first pages of Sarah's essay.

Understanding Dementia

"Hello, Jenny! It's Sarah. I'm going to clean your room." Saying her

A rambling sentence is fixed.

name assured her that I know who she was and that I was friendly. As I made her bed I asked her another question, "How are your doing this morning, Jenny?"

Word choice improved.

"Oh, I'm good," she said. Than, after a pause, she *added* "My husband, Charlie, died in this room, you know."

I looked at her and saw the familiar tears. "I'm so sorry, Jenny," I answered. Than I held her hand and listened to the same details about Charlie that I had heard every week for the past year. Suddenly Jenny stopped, looks up, and asks, "Who are you"?

When I first started work as a nursing-home housekeeper, the

More-formal word improves voice.

dementia patients like Jenny *frightened me* I just didn't understand there words or behavior. Now that I understand more about the patients and their illness, I am better able to respond to them in a helpful way.

What exactly is dementia? Dementia is a general term for a decline in mental ability severe enough to interfere with daily life. 60 to 80% of cases

Ideas made parallel.

of dementia *patients* have Alzheimer's, a disease that can progress rapidly, whereas general dementia patients often suffer from a gradual loss of functions.

Word choice improved.

What you see in many dementia patients can be *disturbing* because the disease affects their language skills and actions.

A comma splice is fixed.

The most common and noticable sign is memory loss. Patience in the early stages of dementia first experience short-term loss, ~~as~~ but as the illness advances, they also experience long-term memory loss. One sign of memory loss is repetitiveness: Patients like to tell their stories over and over. Jenny could recall countless details about Charlies' death, something that happened 10 years earlier and repeated them often, but she could not remember my name—or even that I had entered her room.

Specific modifier, nouns, and transitional phrase added.

In addition to forgetting and repeating people with dementia may express ~~some spooky ideas~~ sudden fear and anger. At one point, A patient named Wilma accused me of steeling from her. "You took it! You rottin thief!" she screamed.

Word choice improved.

"What are you missing, Wilma?" I ask. She started to tell me, but then couldn't remember. Soon she had forgotten the episode altogether, although she was still ~~spooked~~ afraid and very angry. This behavior can be caused by bout of schizophrenia, a psychotic disorder characterized by emotional outbursts.

Specific modifier added.

Another symptom of dementia is ~~related to~~ diminished language skills. While adults with healthy minds easily recall thousands of words patients with dementia struggle to name even common things and familiar people in there lives. A woman in the middle stages of the illness may recognize her son, but not be able to recall his name. However, as the illness advances, she will loose the ability to recognize his face as well.

Changing the verb varies the word choice.

Sentence structure improved.

Patients with dementia also show behavioral changes. One common change is forgetting how to do simple tasks, like washing dishes. Another is ~~forgetting~~ neglecting to do basic things, like turning off the stove. Other behavioral changes show a change in personality; for example, Wilma, who had . . .

Checking the Editing

Finally, Sarah turned her attention to accuracy. She checked her paper for spelling, grammar, usage, and punctuation errors. She also made certain that she had documented her sources properly. Here are the editing corrections for the first part of Sarah's essay.

Understanding Dementia

Verb tense corrected.

Typo fixed.

Usage errors fixed.

"Hello, Jenny! It's Sarah. I'm going to clean your room." Saying her name assured her that I knew ~~know~~ who she was and that I was friendly. As I made her bed, I asked, "How are you ~~your~~ doing this morning, Jenny?"

"Oh, I'm good," she said. ~~Than,~~ Then after a pause, she added, "My husband, Charlie, died in this room, you know."

I looked at her and saw the familiar tears. "I'm so sorry, Jenny," I answered. ~~Than~~ Then I held her hand and listened to the same details about

Verb tense corrected.

Punctuation error fixed.

Charlie that I had heard every week for the past year. Suddenly Jenny stopped, ~~looks~~ looked up, and ~~asks,~~ asked "Who are you?"

When I first started work as a nursing-home housekeeper, the dementia patients like Jenny frightened me. I just didn't understand their ~~there~~ words or behavior. Now that I understand more about the patients and their illness, I am better able to respond to them in a helpful way.

Numbers correctly spelled out.

What exactly is dementia? Dementia is a general term for a decline in mental ability severe enough to interfere with daily life. ~~60 to 80%~~ Sixty to eighty percent of dementia patients have Alzheimer's, a disease that can progress rapidly, whereas general dementia patients often suffer from a gradual loss of

Source added.

functions (alz.org). What you see in many dementia patients can be disturbing, because the disease affects their language skills and actions.

Spelling errors corrected.

The most common and ~~noticable~~ *noticeable* sign is memory loss. ~~Patience~~ *Patients* in the early stages of dementia first experience short-term loss, but as the illness advances, they also experience long-term memory loss. One sign of memory loss is repetitiveness: Patients like to tell their stories over and

Source added.

over *("Understanding")*. Jenny could recall countless details about ~~Charlies~~ *Charlie's* death, something

Possessive form corrected.

that happened 10 years earlier, and repeated them often, but she could not remember my name—or even that I had entered her room.

Commas added to appositive and after introductory phrase.

In addition to forgetting and repeating, people with dementia may express sudden fear and anger. At one point, a patient named Wilma accused me of ~~steeling~~ *stealing* from her. "You took it! You ~~rottin~~ *rotten* thief!" she

Spelling errors corrected.

screamed.

"What are you missing, Wilma?" I ask. She started to tell me, but then couldn't remember. Soon she had forgotten the episode altogether, although she was still afraid and very angry. This behavior can be caused

Missing article added.

by *a* bout of schizophrenia, a psychotic disorder characterized by emotional outbursts *("Older")*.

Source added.

Another symptom of dementia is diminished language skills. While

Comma added after introductory clause.

adults with healthy minds easily recall thousands of words, patients with dementia struggle to name even common things and familiar people in

Usage errors fixed.

~~there~~ *their* lives. A woman in the middle stages of the illness may recognize her son, but not be able to recall his name. However, as the illness advances,

Spelling errors corrected.

she will ~~loose~~ *lose* the ability to recognize his face as well.

Patients with dementia also show behavioral changes. One common change is forgetting how to do simple tasks, like washing dishes. Another is neglecting to do basic things, like turning off the stove. . . .

Appreciating the Final Copy

Sarah produced a neat final copy of her essay. She proofread this copy before submitting it. Here is a portion of Sarah's first page. *Note:* Sarah included a works-cited page with her final copy.

Follow your instructor's direction for placement of name, class, date.

Sarah Anne VanderPlaat

Ms. Herman

Social Studies

January 20, 2015

Understanding Dementia

"Hello, Jenny! It's Sarah. I'm going to clean your room." Saying her name assured her that I knew who she was and that I was friendly. As I made her bed, I asked, "How are you doing this morning, Jenny?"

"Oh, I'm good," she said. Then, after a pause, she added, "My husband, Charlie, died in this room, you know."

I looked at her and saw the familiar tears. "I'm so sorry, Jenny," I answered. Then I held her hand and listened to the same details about Charlie that I had heard every week for the past year. Suddenly Jenny stopped, looked up, and asked, "Who are you?"

When I first started work as a nursing-home housekeeper, the dementia patients like Jenny frightened me. I just didn't understand their words or behavior. Now that I understand more about the patients and their illness, I am better able to respond to them in a helpful way.

What exactly is dementia? Dementia is a general term for a decline in mental ability severe enough to interfere with daily life. Sixty to eighty percent of dementia patients have Alzheimer's, a disease that can progress rapidly, whereas general dementia patients often suffer from a gradual loss of functions (alz.org). What you see in many dementia patients can be

Traits of Effective Writing

   Carpenters use the same basic materials whether they are building a model home or a chicken coop. This is also true for writers, who apply the same traits whether they are composing an academic essay or a text message. Their goal, too, remains fixed—to communicate a clear, effective message.

   To accomplish their goal of clear, effective writing, writers must understand what the qualities or traits of good writing are. The traits of writing include *ideas, organization, voice, word choice, sentence fluency,* and *conventions.* As a writer, you must pay proper attention to each one during every writing project. This chapter introduces you to the traits and shows you how they work together to produce good writing.

Learning Outcomes

Learn about the traits.
Review the traits in action.
Use a traits checklist.

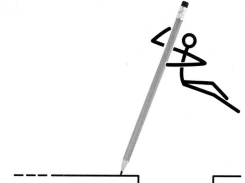

"This is my answer to the gap between ideas and action—I will write it out."

Hortense Calisher

Learning About the Traits

The traits of writing identify the main qualities or features found in all forms of writing.

▍ Ideas

Strong writing presents interesting, vital information about a specific topic. It has a clear purpose, "a controlling vision, which orders what is being said," as writer Donald Murray puts it. The main ideas and supporting details hold the reader's attention from start to finish.

▍ Organization

In terms of basic structure, good writing is always well organized. It has a beginning, a middle, and an ending and moves smoothly from one part to the next. The overall arrangement unifies the piece. Within the text, transitions are used to show relationships between ideas and tie them together.

▍ Voice

In the best writing, you can hear the writer's voice—his or her special way of expressing thoughts and feelings. Voice gives writing a personality and shows that the writer sincerely cares about the topic and the reader. A formal voice is appropriate for most academic writing.

▍ Word Choice

Strong writing uses specific nouns and verbs and a moderate number of vivid modifiers. Its overall level of language—whether informal, formal, or somewhere in between—sets an appropriate tone for the writing.

▍ Sentence Fluency

Effective writing flows smoothly from sentence to sentence. Fluent sentences lend a pleasing rhythm to writing, making it enjoyable to read. To achieve this trait, sentences must vary in length and begin in different ways.

▍ Convention

Strong writing follows the accepted standards of punctuation, mechanics, usage, and spelling. It is edited with care to ensure that the text is accurate and clear.

Help File

Presentation is also an important part of the writing process and is often included in the list of traits. A finished piece of writing should follow effective academic design. Any graphics used should be appropriate in terms of balance and scale.

Reviewing the Traits in Action

On the next few pages, the traits of writing are demonstrated in a number of writing samples. These samples show how the traits work together to produce quality writing.

Ideas and Organization

The excerpt below explains the physics behind a curveball—a topic of special interest to baseball fans and science buffs alike. The well-ordered information (main ideas and details) provides an engaging science lesson.

The Mechanics of a Curveball

Interesting background information introduces the main idea.

In 1671, long before home runs, no-hitters, and sacrifice bunts, Sir Isaac Newton wrote a paper on the fact that a spinning ball curves in flight. In 1852, German physicist Gustav Magnus, while studying the forces which act on the rotating blades of windmills, expanded on Newton's work and demonstrated that a spinning object moving through a fluid experiences a sideways force. Known as the Magnus effect, this phenomenon is not only the basis for a substantial amount of today's wind-generated energy but also for the fundamental principle behind the curveball.

Specific details explain the topic.

The Magnus force is actually not incredibly complicated—it's a relatively simple exercise in aerodynamics. The surface of an object traveling through the air interacts with the thin layer of air surrounding it; this layer of air is known as the boundary layer. For a spherical baseball (a very poor aerodynamic shape), the boundary layer peels off as the ball moves, creating a low pressure area, or wake, behind the ball. The pressure difference from front to back creates a force in the direction of the side with lower pressure. This force is the normal everyday air resistance or drag force that affects everything from cars to birds to rocket ships. When a baseball is traveling with no spin, its wake is symmetrical and the drag force and gravity are the only acting forces. But when the ball is spinning, the wake becomes symmetrical and a new force enters the picture. . . .

The details are arranged according to logical order.

The magnitude of the Magnus force depends on three factors: the rate of spin (faster spin, bigger force), the forward velocity of the ball (more velocity, more force), and the density of the air the ball travels through (higher density, higher Magnus force). In Denver, where the Colorado Rockies play, the air is much less dense and balls will not curve as much as in other cities. Not surprisingly, each year the Rockies are near the bottom of the league in pitching and near the top in hitting. . . .

▌Voice and Word Choice

In this review of *Tuesdays with Morrie*, the writer's word choice establishes a caring and sensitive voice. (See the words underlined in the text.) The quotations shared also reveal his understanding of the life-affirming aspects of Morrie's story. Finally, the writer maintains his strong voice in a thoughtful conclusion.

The Lessons of Death

"Once you learn how to die, you learn how to live" (82).

—Morrie Schwartz

In *Tuesdays with Morrie*, writer Mitch Albom shares a touching story about his former professor, Morrie Schwartz, who is dying from Lou Gehrig's disease. As Albom describes Schwartz's heart-wrenching decline, uplifting lessons about life are revealed.

Albom is a young college student in the 1970s when he has his first class with Morrie Schwartz. He is caught off guard by the friendliness and thoughtful concern of his professor. They regularly meet one-on-one during Albom's sophomore year. By the end of college, Albom finishes an honors thesis with Schwartz's help and encouragement. After graduation, Albom loses touch with his mentor.

It isn't until Albom sees a 1995 *Nightline* interview featuring Schwartz that former student and professor are reunited. Although it has been a long time, Morrie welcomes Albom with open arms. Always a teacher, Morrie wants to share what he is learning through the process of dying. Morrie points out the reality of life: "Everyone knows they're going to die, but nobody believes it" (81). Albom feels like a student again as Morrie shares his insights. The "final paper" is intended to be this book.

Morrie has plenty to say about matters of family, emotions, money, death, forgiveness, and fear of aging. As Albom says, "Morrie would walk that final bridge between life and death, and narrate the trip" (19). It is uplifting to note the tone in Morrie's thoughts. For example, Morrie says that one should put a daily limit on self-pity: "A little each morning, a few tears, and that's all" (57). Cry and then move on.

Morrie's powerful message is the key feature in the book. Through his experience with dying, Morrie finds incredible clarity in evaluating the major issues of life. Death may be a difficult topic, but somehow this story leaves the reader inspired rather than depressed. Readers should be prepared to laugh, to cry, and to learn.

The writer establishes a caring, sensitive voice.

This voice is maintained throughout the review.

▌ Sentence Fluency and Conventions

In the following article, the sentences vary in their beginning, length, and structure, which make them interesting to read. (When too many sentences sound the same, the writing can become monotonous.) Punctuation can also help establish an effective rhythm from sentence to sentence and within the longer sentences.

Farm Fresh

Sentence variety provides a pleasing flow of ideas.

    Buy local. Eat local. These core appeals direct sustainable and local food production. Sustainable farmers raise livestock on natural summer pasture grasses and winter hay, without artificial hormones, antibiotics, or animal by-products in their diet. Poultry are free to range for food to supplement their chemical-free diets. Fruits and vegetables are grown organically, or at least according to many organic principles.

    The farmers consider themselves stewards of the land and, as such, employ other small-farm practices. For example, to build up the soil, they rotate their crops or plant cover crops to manage pests, and they apply green manures or on-farm animal manures. To reduce water waste and slow erosion, some farmers use a drip irrigation system on vegetable plots. Sustainability is the mantra for these farmers: Serve the soil and the soil will continue to produce quality food.

    How, then, does this breed of farmers get products to market? Some use traditional roadside stands to sell their products when they are ready. In addition, many communities sponsor weekly farmers' markets. Some communities also have large food co-ops or small natural food stores that purchase and sell local foods. Then there are Community Supported Agriculture (CSA) programs in which consumer/investors buy annual shares in the farm and receive weekly boxes of fresh produce from the farm. Distribution services are the newest farm-to-consumer idea. These services buy local products and deliver them to food-buying clubs and to individual consumers. Home delivery is making a comeback.

Punctuation establishes an effective rhythm in the sentences.

    "Why should we buy local?" some consumers may ask. After all, local products often cost more than similar products in big-box stores. A sustainable farmer will tell you that the products really are not similar at all. Take, for example, a tomato—one grown locally and one grown on a huge corporate farm in Florida, California, or a completely different country. The former will be fresh, flavorful, and straight from the farm; the latter will be tough, tasteless, and straight out of a storage cooler. Is there actually anything here to compare . . . ?

Using a Traits Checklist

If a piece of writing meets the following standards, it exhibits the traits of effective writing. Check your work using these standards.

The writing . . .

Ideas

____ maintains a clear, specific focus or purpose.
____ thoroughly develops the topic, focus, or claim.
____ provides strong supporting evidence.
____ holds the reader's attention (and answers his or her questions about the topic).

Organization

____ forms a meaningful whole with a clear beginning, middle, and ending.
____ uses linking words and phrases to connect information.
____ follows a logical pattern of organization.

Voice

____ speaks in a tone appropriate for the purpose.
____ shows the writer's interest in the topic.

Word Choice

____ contains specific, clear nouns and verbs.
____ uses figurative techniques (if or when appropriate) to help explain complex ideas.
____ uses words with the appropriate level of formality or informality.

Sentence Fluency

____ flows smoothly from sentence to sentence.
____ uses sentences with an appropriate level of formality or informality.

Conventions

____ adhere to the rules of grammar, spelling, and punctuation.
____ follow established guidelines for presentation.

A Guide to Prewriting

Author Barry Lane says writers "continually move back and forth between the sea and the mountain" during a writing project. They begin in the "sea of experience," where they find memories, encounters, and information they will use in their writing. Then, as they think about a topic, writers start climbing the "mountain of perception."

Prewriting refers to the beginning of a writing project, when you're still at sea, searching for an idea and figuring out how to write about it. Prewriting can also refer to trips back to sea—when, for example, you decide to carry out additional research later in a project. If you give prewriting the proper attention, you will lay a solid foundation for all the other steps in the writing process.

Learning Outcomes

Learn about prewriting.
Select a topic.
Collect information.
Find a focus.
Organize your details.

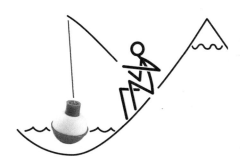

"As soon as you connect with your true subject, you will write."

Joyce Carol Oates

Learning About Prewriting

Analyze the rhetorical situation: To initiate a piece of writing, identify its rhetorical elements (*subject, purpose, audience, form*). You can do this by answering the **STRAP** questions (also see page 285).

Subject: What is my specific topic?

Type: What form should the writing take (*essay, report, letter*)?

Role: What is my position as the writer (*student, citizen, employee*)?

Audience: Who is the intended reader (*instructor, classmates, community members, employer*)?

Purpose: What is my goal (*to argue, to explain, to narrate, to describe*)?

Let's say your history instructor has given you this writing assignment:

In an essay, explain one of Franklin Delano Roosevelt's important presidential acts. Consider the reasons for the act, the manner in which it was carried out, its advocates and detractors, and its short- and long-term effects.

First you answer the **STRAP** questions about the assignment:

Subject: one of FDR's important presidential acts

Type: essay

Role: student

Audience: instructor and classmates

Purpose: to explain

Next you should begin planning your writing. (Referring to your **STRAP** analysis during the writing process will keep you focused on your intended purpose, audience, and so on.)

Understand your tasks: Next, you need to carry out the following tasks:

- **Select** a specific topic appropriate for the assignment.
- **Collect** information about it.
- **Establish** a thesis or focus.
- **Organize** your information for writing.

Consider the traits: The following traits are especially important during prewriting:

┌─ Traits ─

Ideas:	Collect as much information as you can. The more you know about your topic, the easier it will be to write about it.
Organization:	Decide on the best arrangement of the facts and details you have collected.
Voice:	Establish a voice that is appropriate for your audience and purpose.

Selecting a Topic

Often, a writing assignment will be related to a general subject in one of your classes. For example, in a health class, you may be asked to write about exercise and training; or, in a botany class, you may be asked to write about living green. Your first task is to narrow down that general subject to a specific topic.

General subject: Exercise and training   Living green

Specific topic: Aerobic spinning   Designing a rain garden

Help File

Consider the length of the assignment when choosing an appropriate topic. For example, running may be too broad a topic to cover in a two-page essay, while doing leg lifts may be too narrow.

Strategies for Selecting a Topic

The following strategies can be used to select a specific topic for your writing. Try them all to discover which strategies work best for you.

1. **Journal writing . . .** Write in a journal on a regular basis, exploring your thoughts and feelings about school and life. Underline ideas that you would like to explore further in assignments and in your personal writing.

2. **Freewriting . . .** Write nonstop for 5-10 minutes to discover possible writing ideas. Begin your writing with an idea that is related to your assignment.

3. **Clustering . . .** Choose a nucleus word related to your assignment. Then write ideas all around that word, circling each and drawing a line to connect it to the closest related idea.

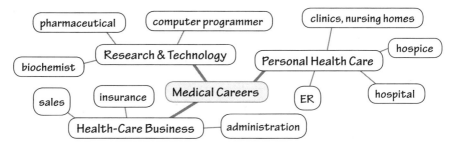

Help File

After 3 or 4 minutes, scan the cluster for potential writing topics or freewrite about one of the circled ideas to see if a topic emerges.

4. **Listing** . . . Begin with a thought or key word related to your assignment and freely list words and ideas as they come to mind. Listing ideas with a group of classmates (brainstorming) is also effective.

5. **Participating, listening, and reflecting** . . . Contribute to class discussions, assume an important role in group work, ask questions and take notes during lectures. Being actively involved in this way naturally brings topic ideas to mind.

6. **Metaphorical thinking** . . . Think about general subjects metaphorically by setting up an open-ended statement like the one below; then complete it in different ways.

> Civil rights is like . . .

Note: You can also connect two unrelated concepts (conceptual blending) to discover some interesting writing ideas. The following question demonstrates this type of metaphorical thinking.

> How is civil rights like a cruise ship?

7. **Using the essentials-of-life checklist** . . . This checklist—which lists a number of topics that are essential to a healthy, happy life—provides an effective starting point for a topic search.

Essentials of Life Checklist

clothing	communication	exercise/training
housing	purpose/goals	community
food	measurement	arts/music
education	machines	faith/religion
family	intelligence	trade/money
friends	agriculture	heat/fuel
love	environment	rules/laws
senses	plant life	science/technology
energy	land/property	work/occupation
entertainment	health/medicine	private/public life
recreation	literature/books	natural resources
personality	tools/utensils	freedom/rights

Consider how the category "energy" can lead to a number of different writing ideas:

- fracking
- geothermal energy
- solar energy
- wind turbines
- fuel-cell vehicles
- peat energy
- nuclear energy
- energy costs

Collecting Information

After selecting a topic, you must learn as much as you can about it. Writer Donald Murray says, "The writer writes with information [about a topic], and if there is no information, there will be no effective writing." To learn enough about your topic, you will probably need to use at least two of the collecting or gathering strategies listed in this section.

▌ Gathering Your First Thoughts

- **Freewriting and clustering** . . . Write freely or cluster about your topic to determine what you know and what you need to find out.

- **5 W's and H of writing** . . . Answer the 5 W's—*who? what? when? where? why?* and *how?*—to identify basic information about the topic.

- **Directed writing** . . . Consider your topic from different points of view by answering some (or all) of these questions:

> **Describe it.**
>   What do you see, hear, feel, smell, or taste?
>
> **Compare it.**
>   What is it similar to? What is it different from?
>
> **Apply it.**
>   What can you do with it? How can you use it?
>
> **Associate it.**
>   What connections between the topic and something else come to mind?
>
> **Analyze it.**
>   What parts does it have? How do they work together?
>
> **Argue for or against it.**
>   What do you like about it? What don't you like about it? What are its strengths and weaknesses?

- **Generating pointed questions** . . . Generate a list of questions that you want to answer about your topic.

- **Dialoguing** . . . Create an imaginary conversation between two people, using your topic as the focus. Keep writing as long as the ideas are flowing.

- **Categorizing** . . . Gather information about your topic by first placing it in the appropriate category (*Problems, Policies, Concepts*) and then answering the questions given in the chart below. For example, the topic *lead poisoning* is a "problem," *a system for grading* is a "policy," and *miniaturization* is a "concept." Your answers to the questions provide details about the *Description, Function, History,* and *Value* of the topic.

	Description	Function	History	Value
Problems	What is the problem? What are the signs of the problem?	Who or what is affected by it? What new problems may it cause in the future?	What is the current status of the problem? What or who caused it?	What is the significance? Why is it more (or less) important than other problems?
Policies	What type of policy is it? What are its most important features?	What is the policy designed to do? What is needed to make it work?	What brought this policy about? What are the alternatives to this policy?	Is the policy working? What are its advantages and disadvantages?
Concepts	What type of concept is it? Who or what is related to it?	Who has been influenced by this concept? Why is it important?	When did it originate? How has it changed over the years?	What practical value does it hold? What is its social worth?

Conducting Research

- **Reading** . . . Consult reliable Web sites, books, and periodicals to find new information about your topic. Follow your instructor's requirements concerning the number and types of resources you use.

- **Conducting other research techniques** . . . Interview experts; make observations; participate in chats, forums, or discussion groups; and take part in firsthand experiences.

- **Taking notes** . . . Record important facts, details, and quotations. Also take notes in the margin of the text if you are working with copies.

- **Using graphic organizers** . . . Use clusters, time lines, charts, and diagrams to collect information. (See the next page.)

- **Compiling a working bibliography** . . . Keep track of titles, dates, page numbers, authors' names, and so on, for documentation purposes. (See page 416.)

Graphic Organizers for Collecting Information

Cause/Effect Organizer

Use to collect and organize details for cause/effect essays.

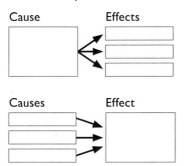

Problem/Solution Web

Use to map out problem/ solution essays.

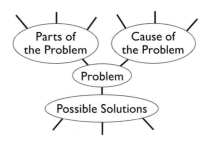

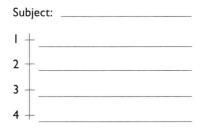

Time Line

Use for personal narratives to list actions or events in the order they occurred.

Subject: _____

1 _____
2 _____
3 _____
4 _____

Evaluation Collection Grid

Use to collect supporting details for essays of evaluation.

Subject: _____

Points to Evaluate	Supporting Details
1	
2	
3	
4	

Venn Diagram

Use to collect details to compare and contrast two topics.

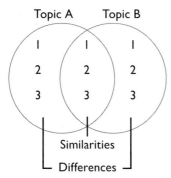

Line Diagram

Use to collect and organize details for basic explanatory essays.

Process (Cycle) Diagram

Use to collect details for science-related writing, such as how a process or cycle works.

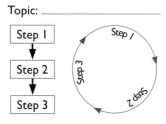

5 W's Chart

Use to collect the *who? what? when? where?* and *why?* details for personal narratives and news stories.

Subject: _____

Who?	What?	When?	Where?	Why?

Definition Diagram

Use to gather information for extended definition essays.

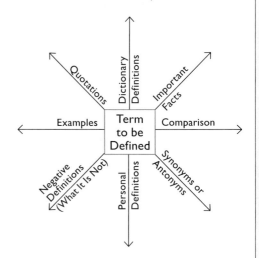

Sensory Chart

Use to collect details for descriptive essays and observation reports.

Subject: _____

Sights	Sounds	Smells	Tastes	Textures

Finding Your Focus

As you conduct your research, you will naturally begin to focus on a special feature, feeling, or opinion about the topic. This focus—the part of the topic that interests you the most—can become a **thesis statement**, or the controlling idea of your essay.

Write as many versions as it takes to come up with a thesis statement that sets the right tone and direction for your writing. An effective thesis will guide your writing, helping you to decide what information to include in your essay. Use the following formula to form your thesis statement.

Formula

> A specific topic
>
> **+** a particular feature, feeling, or opinion
> _____
> **=** an effective thesis statement.

Thesis Statement

> (specific topic) —— Young children exposed to low levels of lead poisoning
> (opinion) —— may face health problems later in life.

▌ Sample Thesis Statements

Writing Assignment: Essay on the Civil War
Specific Topic: General George McClellan
Thesis Statement: General George McClellan's overcautious tactics *(specific topic)* may have prolonged the war *(feeling)*.

Writing Assignment: Essay explaining a force of nature
Specific Topic: Tsunami
Thesis Statement: A tsunami *(specific topic)* occurs during the process of energy being transferred from the earth's crust to a body of water *(feature)*.

Writing Assignment: Essay related to dynamics of adolescence
Specific Topic: Youth violence
Thesis Statement: The problem of youth violence *(specific topic)* can be solved best through conflict resolution *(opinion)*.

Remember: A strong thesis statement tells the reader exactly what the essay will be about and it keeps the writer on track. If you try to cover too much ground or get off course, you will lose your reader.

Organizing Your Details

The facts and details that you use to support or develop your thesis must be clearly organized. To find the best method of organization, follow the steps below.

1. **Study your thesis statement.** It may suggest a logical method of organization. (See the next page.)

2. **Review your information,** identifying the facts and details that support your thesis. See if a particular plan of organization begins to emerge.

3. **Consider the different methods of organization.** (For more information on each method, see pages 86–88.)

Methods of Organization

Chronological order (*time*) is effective for sharing personal narratives, summarizing steps, and explaining events in the order in which they occurred.

Order of location (*spatial*) is useful for many types of descriptions. Details can be described from left to right, from right to left, from top to bottom, from edge to center, and so on.

Illustration (*deductive*) is a method of arrangement in which you first state a general idea (thesis statement) and follow with specific reasons, examples, and facts.

Climax (*inductive*) is a method of arrangement in which you present specific details that lead to a general statement or a conclusion.

Compare-contrast is a method of arrangement in which you show how one topic is different from and similar to another topic.

Cause-effect is a type of arrangement that helps you make connections between a result and the events that came before it. Usually, you begin with the cause of something, and then you discuss a number of specific effects.

Problem-solution is a type of arrangement in which you state a problem and explore possible solutions.

Order of importance organizes points from most important to least or from least important to most. This arrangement works well for argumentative and persuasive writing.

▌ **Letting the Thesis Guide You**

Notice how the thesis statements below suggest organizational patterns for the supporting details in each of the different types of essays.

Thesis (Illustration Essay)

General George McClellan's overcautious tactics prolonged the war.

Explanation: This thesis indicates that the writer is developing an illustration essay. She will discuss the tactics that illustrate her main point.

Thesis (Process Essay)

A tsunami occurs during the process of energy being transferred from the earth's crust to a body of water.

Explanation: This thesis indicates that the writer will explain step-by-step (chronologically) how a tsunami occurs.

Thesis (Problem-Solution Essay)

The problem of youth violence can be solved best through conflict resolution.

Explanation: This thesis indicates that the writer will discuss the problem of youth violence, probably touch on various solutions, and then present the best one.

Thesis (Comparison Essay)

My friends at both Riverview and Madison showed concern for my well-being, but I felt much more comfortable with the students at Madison.

Explanation: This thesis indicates that the writer will compare the treatment she received from students at two schools. She could discuss one subject completely and then the other, or both subjects concurrently (point by point).

Thesis (Cause-Effect Essay)

Formula One racing has experienced far fewer serious accidents because of improvements in driver safety.

Explanation: This thesis establishes a cause-effect pattern. The writer will likely explain the causes that prompted the improvements, and then discuss the improvements' effects.

Thesis (Essay of Argumentation)

Barbed hooks should be banned from fishing.

Explanation: This thesis suggests that the writer will employ order of importance to arrange his points against the use of barbed hooks for fishing.

Making a Plan

At this point, you should be ready to plan the arrangement of information for your writing. This plan will include your essay's main points and supporting details. Depending on the length and complexity of the essay, the plan can be anything from a brief list of main points to a detailed sentence outline.

Brief List

With this plan, you simply list the main points you want to cover. A list works well for a short piece of writing about a topic that you know very well.

> **Sample Brief List**
>
> • History of driver safety problems
> • Safety changes to cars
> • Safety changes to driver equipment
> • Modifications to racetrack

Outline

A **topic outline** uses words and phrases for main points and details, while a **sentence outline** uses complete sentences for these elements. (See the examples below.) Note that strict adherence to either of these formats is not as important as including all your main points and details in good order.

Use Roman numerals for main points.

Use capital letters for supporting details.

Use Arabic numerals (1, 2, 3) and lowercase letters for secondary details.

> **Sample Topic Outline**
>
> I. History of driver safety problems in Formula One
>   A. Bad accidents at start
>   B. Hazards due to the course
>   C. Hazards due to the cars
> II. Modifications to cars

> **Sample Sentence Outline**
>
> I. Driver safety wasn't always a primary concern in Formula One racing.
>   A. There is a history of bad accidents.
>   B. The courses have included hills and hairpin turns.
>   C. The cars are the fastest in the world and jockey for position.
> II. Many safety modifications have been made to cars.

A Guide to Drafting

Drafting refers to writing an early version of a document. The word *draft* comes from the Middle English word *draght*, akin to the Old English word *dragan*, which means "to draw." When you draw, you sketch a likeness of someone or something. Think of a first draft in the same way: You are creating a likeness of a person, place, thing, or idea—not a finished piece.

When you write a draft, you connect your ideas about a topic based primarily on your research and planning. But you should always be open to new ideas as they come to mind. Try to write your first draft in one sitting, while your thoughts are fresh in your mind. This chapter will help you develop first drafts from start to finish.

Learning Outcomes

Learn about drafting.
Write the opening.
Develop the middle part.
Write the closing.

"The first draft is the down draft—you just get it down."

Anne Lamott

Learning About Drafting

Purpose: Drafting is your first attempt at developing your writing idea. It allows you to get your thoughts about a topic down on paper.

Assess your readiness: You're ready to write a first draft after completing these three steps.

_____ Collect enough information about your topic.

_____ Establish a thesis (focus).

_____ Organize your supporting details.

Revisit the rhetorical situation: Consider again your audience, purpose, and role by reviewing your answers to the **STRAP** questions. (See page 30.)

Understand your tasks: As you develop your first draft, follow these tips.

> - **Concentrate on developing quality ideas**, not on producing an error-free draft. Do, however, strive for quality.
> - **Include as much detail as possible.**
> - **Continue writing until you've covered all your main points** or have come to a natural stopping point.
> - **Double-space your writing** to make room for revising later on.
>
> **Note:** Some writers give special attention to the opening before diving into the rest of a first draft. Once they are satisfied with the beginning, they find it easier to continue. Other writers put all of their thoughts on paper at once. Author John Steinbeck supported the second approach: "Write freely and rapidly as possible and throw the whole thing on paper."

Form: When drafting with pen and paper, write on every other line and use only one side of the paper. Double-space when using a computer. This will make revising much easier by hand.

Consider the traits: During the drafting process, pay special attention to ideas, organization, and voice.

Traits	
Ideas:	Present a strong thesis and support it with relevant facts and details.
Organization:	Use your prewriting plan as a general writing guide. Try to work logically through the opening, middle, and closing parts of your first draft.
Voice:	Speak honestly and sincerely to your audience.

Writing the Opening

For academic writing such as essays, reviews, and research papers, pay special attention to the opening. It should accomplish three things: (1) *introduce your topic,* (2) *gain your reader's attention,* and (3) *identify your thesis.* This will set the tone and establish the basic organization for your writing. Several techniques and specific examples for introducing a topic are listed here.

- **Begin with a telling quotation.**

  Barron's *Standard Press* quoted board president Thomas Anders as saying, "The school board needs to decide which music programs are necessary and which ones are not."

- **Start with a dramatic, eye-opening statement.**

  The tsunami of 2004 that struck Indonesia caused surges that traveled 500 miles per hour.

- **Open with an engaging story (anecdote).**

  During the first lap of a Grand Prix race in Melbourne, Australia, Martin Brundle's car hit another car at 185 miles per hour. Spinning into the air, Brundle's B & H Jordan broke into pieces, spraying debris across the track. The race was stopped as fragments of the car were cleared.

- **Share some thought-provoking details about the topic.**

  When someone uses the word *romance,* the images that come to mind are long-stemmed roses, soft music, and chocolates in heart-shaped boxes.

- **Identify the main points you plan to cover.**

  Canada's 29-30 million people can be divided into three main groups: founding people, descendants of Europeans, and recent immigrants.

Sample Opening Paragraph

This opening paragraph introduces the topic and provides the thesis (underlined) for an explanatory essay on Dr. Martin Luther King Jr.'s "I Have a Dream" speech. The writer uses a serious academic voice appropriate for the topic.

> Fifty years ago, on August 28, 1963, Dr. Martin Luther King Jr. stood in the shadow of the Lincoln Memorial and spoke words that have resonated down through the decades: "I have a dream. . . ." Dr. King's speech turned out to be one of the most recognizable orations of modern history, and it established him as one of the most important social and religious figures in the twentieth century. The speech summed up Dr. King's call for nonviolent, deep societal change and became a road map for the civil rights movement.

Developing the Middle Part

The middle paragraphs provide the evidence that supports your thesis. Use your planning notes as a general guide when you develop these paragraphs, and consider using different methods of support for adding details.

▌ Methods of Support

Explain: Provide important facts, details, and examples.

Narrate: Share a brief story (anecdote) or re-create an experience to illustrate or clarify an idea.

Describe: Tell how someone appears or how something works.

Summarize: Present a concise summary of the most important ideas.

Define: Identify or clarify the meaning of a specific term or idea.

Argue: Use logic and evidence to prove something is true.

Compare: Show how two things are alike or different.

Analyze: Examine the parts of something to better understand the whole.

Reflect: Express your thoughts or feelings about something.

Evaluate: Determine the value or worth of something.

FAQ How many methods of support should I use?

It all depends on the type of information that you have collected. For most academic essays, you should use at least two or three methods of support to develop your thesis. In an essay of definition, for example, you may provide one or two dictionary definitions, a comparison, a brief story, as well as some analysis and personal reflection. (See the sample middle paragraphs on the next page.)

▌ Levels of Support

Use different levels of detail to develop effective middle paragraphs. Clarifying details (level 2) and completing details (level 3) help explain or complete your main points. (The sentences below are from the second paragraph on the next page.)

Level 1: A controlling sentence names the main point.

Dr. King used a powerful rhetorical structure to get his point across.

Level 2: Clarifying sentences explain the main point.

He began by evoking the image of Lincoln, the Great Emancipator, who "five score years ago" freed the slaves.

Level 3: Completing sentences add details to finish the point.

Dr. King put that fact in perspective by pointing out that, one hundred years later, people of color were still not free.

▋ Sample Middle Paragraphs

The first middle paragraph below *explains* Dr. King's speech and *summarizes* his vision of a brighter future. By providing this information, the writer prepares the reader for a closer analysis in later paragraphs.

> Dr. King's speech was aimed at motivating and guiding a civil rights movement that required direction. The speech contained a general, idealistic outline of the rights and privileges that civil rights activists deemed inalienable to everyone. Dr. King's rhetoric showed what a world might look like in which skin color and ethnicity were nothing more than superficial characteristics. He broadly described a world where, for example, children of all races and ethnicities could live together as equals, and people would be judged based on their ability and character instead of the color of their skin (Harrison and Gilbert).

The next paragraph analyzes the speech by breaking it down into its parts and showing how they work together.

> Dr. King used a powerful rhetorical structure to get his point across. He began by evoking the image of Lincoln, who "five score years ago" freed the slaves. Dr. King put that fact in perspective by pointing out that, one hundred years later, people of color were still not free. Next, Dr. King called his people to action. He said his people could not be satisfied as long as discrimination and segregation continued, but he also told his followers, "We must not allow our creative protest to degenerate into physical violence" ("Dream"). After this, Dr. King delivered the famous "I Have a Dream" section of the speech, in which he laid out his vision of an ideal world in which these changes have been completed. By beginning in history, marching through the present, and looking to the future, Dr. King created a road map to civil rights that people still follow today.

In this paragraph, the author compares and contrasts Dr. King's approach to the strategies advocated by Malcolm X.

> Dr. King's road map may seem obvious now, but it was controversial even among civil rights leaders. For example, though Malcolm X attended King's March on Washington, he decried it as a "Farce on Washington" (Jenkins 371). While Dr. King spoke about the importance of integration, Malcolm X advocated "racial separation"—for blacks to willfully remove themselves from the systems of white oppression and colonialism that had enslaved them. Dr. King's nonviolent approach also did not sit well with Malcolm X, who advocated change "by any means necessary" and said that African Americans had to fight against those who fought against them (Jenkins 546–547).

Using Quotations

In this paragraph, the writer summarizes information from the speech and leads up to a famous quotation. Quotations can lend authority to an essay, but they should flow smoothly from the ideas that come before and after them.

> Dr. King's approach won out due to the timelessness of his ideas. He borrowed much of his language from ideas familiar to most Americans, quoting the Constitution, the Bible, and hymns and spirituals. Dr. King reinterpreted all of these familiar concepts but then moved on to create a new vision. One of his most enduring ideas came near the end of the speech: "I have a dream that my four little children will one day live in a nation where they will not be judged by the color of their skin but by the content of their character" ("Dream"). By referring to his children, Dr. King told his audience that he was working to improve life for the next generation.

Writing the Closing

Bring your writing to a natural stopping point with the strategies listed below. Generally, choose at least two of these to produce an effective closing.

- Restate your thesis.
- Reflect on its importance.
- Review the main supporting points or one point in particular.
- Answer any unresolved questions.
- Include a final thought-provoking idea.
- Make a call to action.

Sample Closing Paragraph

Here the writer *reflects* on the importance of Dr. King's speech 50 years after it was given.

> Dr. King's speech exemplifies the bravery of the men and women who endeavor to change the world for the better. His candor and brilliant description of the problems with equality in the United States are extremely admirable. Reformers like Dr. King have the power to reach back into the terrible past and help reshape the stormy present. It would be wonderful to say that Dr. King's dreams have been realized after 50 years, but that is not the case. Yes, many blacks have joined the middle class, but equality in terms of jobs, voting rights, medical care, and housing has not yet been realized. "I Have a Dream" rightfully stands the test of time, but surely Dr. King's dreams, for the most part, are still deferred.

A Guide to Revising

Revising is the process of making changes to your writing so that it says exactly what you want it to say. Author Ernest Hemingway changed one of his endings 27 times before he was satisfied with it. You may have neither the time nor the desire to rework any part of your writing 27 times, but you should always make as many improvements as possible before submitting your writing. You owe it to yourself and your reader.

Clearly, no writer gets it right the first time, not even professionals. In fact, very few get it right the second time. It may well take several go-rounds before you are satisfied with what you have. To be as efficient as possible, follow the guidelines in this chapter. Then ask a classmate or family member to respond to your writing as well. After all, you are writing this for others to read and enjoy, so find out what they think could be done to make it better.

Learning Outcomes

Learn about revising.
Review sample revisions.
Revise for the traits.
Learn to respond to writing.

"If [you] write a lot, that's good. If [you] revise a lot, that's even better."

Toni Morrison

Learning About Revising

Purpose: Revising is the process of improving the details that carry the meaning in your writing.

Assess your readiness: You're ready to revise after completing these tasks.

____ Complete a first draft.

____ Set the draft aside for a day or two (if possible).

____ Review your writing for strengths and weaknesses.

____ Ask at least one peer to respond to your writing.

Revisit the rhetorical situation: Consider again your audience, purpose, and role by reviewing your answers to the **STRAP** questions. (See page 30.)

Understand your tasks: As you revise your writing, follow these tips.

- **Add information to clarify** or complete an idea.
- **Delete information that doesn't support your thesis** or purpose.
- **Reorder material that is misplaced.**
- **Rewrite material that is confusing** or exhibits the wrong voice.

Work from whole to parts: Concentrate first on the big picture—the overall impact of your writing. Then examine the effectiveness of specific parts. Do not pay undue attention to spelling and punctuation too early in the process; otherwise, you may overlook ways to improve the content of your writing.

Consider the traits: When revising, pay special attention to the following traits.

Traits	
Ideas:	Consider your thesis and supporting information. Have you answered the reader's most pressing questions about the topic?
Organization:	Look at the beginning, middle, and ending to make sure each part adds to the overall strength of your writing.
Voice:	Determine whether your writing speaks to the reader in a way that is appropriate to your purpose.
Word choice:	Check your words for proper tone and exact meaning.
Sentence fluency:	Review your sentences, making certain they flow smoothly and hold the reader's interest.

Help File

Experiment with different types of revisions. The next thing that you try may truly energize your writing. If you need fresh ideas, refer to the prewriting strategies on pages 33–34.

Reviewing Sample Revisions

Remember, your basic revision tasks are adding, deleting, reordering, and rewriting information. An example of each task is shown in the following page of an essay about conflict resolution.

Grace Under Fire

Two friends have an argument that eventually becomes physical, even though neither one can point to the real cause of the situation. This situation plays itself out over and over in high schools across

This unnecessary detail was deleted.

the country, ~~even high schools in the greater Burlington area.~~ "Youth Violence," a report by the surgeon general, states: "In our country today, the greatest threat to the lives of children and adolescents is not disease or starvation or abandonment, but the terrible reality of violence." ~~Schools~~

The writer reworded this idea to give it an appropriate voice.

Given these findings, shouldn't schools address conflicts with as much vigor as ~~teach math and science and cheer on their sports teams, but what about~~ they address math, science, and athletics? ~~student conflicts?~~ The best way to address youth violence is to teach students strategies for conflict resolution.

To clarify the message, the writer moved a sentence to the beginning of the paragraph.

∧In fact, a United States Department of Justice report notes that most violent incidents begin with "a relatively minor affront that escalates from there." Conflicts may be unavoidable, but when people lose sight of the real issues, their arguments can become personal and spiral out of control. In other words, a fight could start about one student's choice for lunch, a peanut butter sandwich. Laughter over the sandwich can lead to insults, which in turn can lead to violence. The problem isn't the sandwich, but the way the students deal with the interchange of

This sentence was added to lend authority to the previous point.

comments. They need strategies for dealing with situations like this so that friendships aren't destroyed.∧ According to safeyouth.gov, "If resolved positively, conflicts can actually strengthen relationships and build greater understanding."

Revising for Ideas

Use these next two pages as a guide to revising the ideas in your writing. When you revise for ideas, you concentrate on your focus, thesis development, and level of detail.

Check the Overall Focus

After reviewing your essay about teen magazines, you notice that your opening paragraph lacks a specific focus. You revise the opening so that it builds to a main point about your topic (underlined).

> **Opening Paragraph** (Lacks focus or direction): Teen magazines are popular with young girls. These magazines contain a lot of how-to articles about self-image, fashion, and boy-girl relationships. Girls read these magazines for advice on how to act and how to look. There are many popular magazines to choose from, and girls who don't really know what they want are the most eager readers.
>
> **Revised Version** (Builds to a specific focus): Adolescent girls often see teen magazines as handbooks on how to be teenagers. These magazines influence the way they act and look. For girls who are unsure of themselves, these magazines can exert an enormous amount of influence. Unfortunately, the advice these magazines give about self-image, fashion, and boys may do more harm than good.

Check the Thesis (Main idea)

After reviewing your essay about Ulysses S. Grant, you realize that the opening paragraph lacks a thesis. You revise the opening so that it builds to a specific thesis.

> **Original Opening Paragraph** (Lacks a thesis): Ulysses S. Grant lived in Galena, Illinois, when the Civil War started. He was working at his father-in-law's leather good shop when he signed up to lead the Illinois Volunteers in the war. He fought in the Western theater, far from Washington, D.C. Fighting also went on near the nation's capital.
>
> **Revised Version** (Builds to a specific thesis): Ulysses S. Grant's improbable rise to power may be the most important story in the Civil War. At the start of the war, Grant was a lowly brigadier general of the Illinois Volunteers, completely unknown by the Union leaders in Washington. Yet by 1864, he was appointed by President Lincoln to lead the entire Union Army. In between, Grant earned this position by winning three important battles in the Western theater.

▌Check for Depth (Level of Detail)

Let's say you are writing a technical essay explaining how the healing process works, and you realize that a certain passage needs more support. To improve the passage, you add more details.

Original Passage (Too general): As soon as you receive a minor cut, the body's healing process begins to work. Blood from tiny vessels fills the wound and begins to clot. In less than 24 hours, a scab forms.

Revised Version (More specific): As soon as you receive a minor cut, the body's healing process begins to work. In a simple wound, the first and second layers of skin are severed along with tiny blood vessels called capillaries. As these vessels bleed into the wound, dislike structures called platelets help stop the bleeding by sticking to the edges of the cut and to one another, forming a plug. The platelets then release chemicals that react with certain proteins in the blood to form a clot. The blood clot, with its fiber network, begins to join the edges of the wound together. As the clot dries out, a scab forms, usually in less than 24 hours.

▌Check the Development of Each Paragraph

Suppose that one of the paragraphs in your essay skips around instead of developing a main point. You revise the paragraph so that it contains a topic sentence and clearly develops it.

Original Middle Paragraph (Unfocused): The Ogallala Aquifer is the largest "underground sponge" in the United States. The aquifer irrigates crops planted in the High Plains. These crops are the main food source for the country. Only a fraction of the water is ever replenished in the aquifer. Center-pivot irrigation has dramatically lowered the water level. The water pumps through the pipe and triggers a mechanism that causes the system to roll in a large circle (Opie 146). Irrigation continues to increase, and when there are droughts, farmers use more irrigation.

Revised Version (Fully develops the main idea): The water in the Qgallala Aquifer is being depleted at an alarming rate. In much of the Texas Panhandle, more than half the aquifer has gone dry (McGuire). The volume of water has decreased because the use of irrigation has increased so much since World War II. In 1949, 2.1 million acres were under irrigation. In 1980, the amount of irrigated land rose to 13.7 millions acres; and in 1997, it rose to 13.9 million acres (McGuire). The land presently under irrigation in the Texas Panhandle alone is equal to the size of New Jersey (Thorpe). Water for all of this land is supplied by irrigation wells, and the number of wells has exploded over the decades—from just 170 in 1930 to more than 150,000 today (Nebel and Wright 279).

Revising for Organization

Strong writing is structured, leading the reader logically from one point to the next. You may have great ideas to share, but if you don't organize them effectively, the reader will get lost. Organization involves four important features: an overall plan, the opening, the flow of ideas in the middle, and the closing.

Check the Overall Plan

Suppose a peer responder appreciates your topic but cannot follow what you are saying about it. When your essay has this kind of "big picture" organizational issue, ask these questions:

1. Have I included a focused, supportable thesis or position?
2. Do I express the main supporting points in clear topic sentences?
3. Have I developed these points with effective details?
4. Have I put the supporting paragraphs in good order—according to importance, logic, a problem-solution pattern, or so on?
5. Does my essay form a meaningful whole with beginning, middle, and ending parts?

Check the Opening

Suppose you are writing an essay about a topic you find truly interesting, but the opening paragraph just doesn't engage the reader. In the revised version, you get the reader's attention with a recent news story.

Original Opening (Doesn't create interest): Art is appreciated for its creativity and flair. Science is appreciated for its critical analyses and discoveries. The two disciplines appear to be polar opposites, but that isn't always true. For example, recent developments in physics, including the use of ion beams, can help art experts detect the authenticity of artwork.

Revised Version (Uses a news story to catch the reader's attention): New York news outlets recently reported that $80 million worth of counterfeit paintings have been sold during the past 15 years, including works purportedly created by famous artists such as Jackson Pollock and Willem de Kooning. Incredibly, all 63 of the forgeries were painted by an unknown artist in Queens, who was skilled enough to deceive reputable art dealers and gallery owners. Clearly, these art experts needed help to evaluate the authenticity of these paintings. Developments in physics, including the use of ion beams, may have an answer.

▌ Check the Flow of the Middle Paragraphs

Let's say that a peer reviewer cannot follow your description because you haven't linked the main points well enough. You revise the piece by adding spatial/location transitional phrases that lead the reader through your ideas.

Original Version (First sentences of middle paragraphs lack transitions):

There was a huge, steep hill . . .

Buffalo Creek ran . . .

A dense "jungle" covered . . .

Within walking distance from the house . . .

Revised Version (Transitional phrases added):

Behind the house, there was a huge, steep hill . . .

Across the road from the house, Buffalo Creek ran . . .

On the far side of the creek bank was a dense "jungle" covered . . .

Up the road, within walking distance from the house . . .

FAQ **How do I know how to arrange the details in my essay?**

There may be a specific method of organization that is best suited for each essay you write. Narratives are usually arranged by time; descriptions, by location. You may also customize or combine these methods to suit your particular needs. (See pages 86–88 for more information.)

▌ Check the Closing

Suppose you have written a book review, and the ending doesn't work. It neither summarizes the main points of your review nor makes a connection with the reader. In your revision, you address both points.

Original Closing (Too general): *Native Son* deals with a young man's struggle in a racist society. It shows the effects of prejudice in the United States and much more. Everyone living in this country should read this book.

Revised Version (More specific and relevant): *Native Son* deals with a young man's struggle in a racist society, but it deals with so much more. It also marks the challenges faced by the working poor. While trying to find their way out of their hard circumstances, an economic system controlled by a privileged few closes in on them. Anyone trying to better understand racism and economic inequality in America will benefit from this book.

Revising for Voice

Voice is the personality in a piece of writing. Generally, expressing your ideas sincerely will give your writing a strong voice. But you may need to adjust your writing to produce the right voice for a particular purpose or audience.

▌ Check Your Purpose

Imagine that you've written a personal narrative and reviewed the first draft. It's missing the storyteller's personality. You need to add more personal thoughts.

> **Original Passage** (Lacks personality): Cemeteries right in our own neighborhoods can teach us a lot about history. They can make history seem real because they contain many interesting stories. There is an old grave of a Revolutionary War veteran that I discovered . . .
>
> **Revised Version** (More personal, honest, and active): I've always had a special feeling for cemeteries, but not in a ghoulish way. It's hard to explain any further than that, except to say history never seems quite as real as it does when I walk between rows of old gravestones. One day I discovered the grave of a Revolutionary War veteran that . . .

▌ Check Your Audience

After reviewing your research paper, you realize that some parts are too casual. This is a formal report, so you change the casual parts to fit that requirement.

> **Original Excerpt** (Sounds too casual): At last, there are women in positions of leadership in different parts of the world. Germany, Chile, Liberia, and Finland all have women leaders. And the *Women in the World Foundation* Web site says that women make up 18.4 percent of parliamentarians. Here's another good sign: Some nations have a quota system to control the number of men and women in political positions. The Foundation says that the Rwanda parliament is 56.3 percent female! But should women be happy with this progress?
>
> **Revised Version** (Speaks more formally to the intended audience): It is true that women are assuming positions of leadership worldwide. For example, women lead Germany, Chile, Liberia, and Finland. According to the *Women in the World Foundation* Web site, 18.4 percent of parliamentarians are now women. Some nations are even adopting a quota system to control the number of men and women in political positions. The Foundation reports that Rwanda's parliament is 56.3 percent female. However, considering that women make up more than half of the world's population, they are far from being fairly represented in positions of authority.

Revising for Word Choice

To share your ideas clearly and establish an appropriate tone, you need to choose words and phrases carefully and check for common errors.

Check for Common Problems

Redundancy ▪ Words or phrases that are used together unnecessarily, because they mean the same thing

> **Original Sentence:** In May 2012, *PlanetSolar* became the first solar-electric vessel to circumnavigate around the world. ("Around" and the prefix "circum" mean the same thing.)
>
> **Revised Version:** In May 2012, *PlanetSolar* became the first solar-electric vessel to circumnavigate the world. ("Around" is deleted.)

General words ▪ Words that do not provide a specific picture for the reader

> **Original Sentence:** There are ("be" verb) 8.5 tons of batteries in the ship's two main parts (general noun).
>
> **Revised Version:** *PlanetSolar* houses 8.5 tons of batteries in its two hulls. (More specific words—an active verb and a specific noun—are used.)

Jargon ▪ Specialized words or phrases that are not adequately explained

> **Original Sentence:** The solar panels on *PlanetSolar* are rated 93 kW and are connected to electric motors. (The abbreviation *kW* may be unfamiliar.)
>
> **Revised Version:** The solar panels on *PlanetSolar* are rated 93 kW (kilowatts) and are connected to electric motors. A kilowatt is a unit of power equal to 1,000 watts. (The abbreviation is identified and explained.)

Check the Connotation of Your Words

In the editorial excerpt below, the writer changed some of the words to more accurately convey the feeling or connotation she was trying to achieve.

Original Passage: Newspapers should not put photographs of victims of crimes and tragedies on the front page. It's bad enough that these people are victims; to show them in their grief is wrong. It may even make things worse for them. (The words don't communicate the writer's strong feelings.)

Revision Version: Newspapers should not emblazon the front page with photographs of victims of crimes and tragedies. It's bad enough that these people have suffered; to have their grief so vividly displayed seems almost cruel. It may even deepen the hurt and unnecessarily delay their healing. (New words communicate the intended feelings.)

Revising for Sentence Fluency

Author E. B. White advises writers to "approach sentence style by way of simplicity, plainness, orderliness, and sincerity." That's good advice for everyone.

Check for Sentence Problems

After reviewing your essay, you realize that one passage has a series of short, choppy sentences. You combine these sentences into one longer, smoother sentence.

Original Passage: People involved in the smelting industry are at risk of exposure to lead. People in lead-battery manufacturing are at risk. Home-repair workers are also at risk. (Three short sentences)

Revised Version: People involved in the smelting industry, lead-battery manufacturing, and home repair are at risk of exposure to lead.
(One longer, smoother sentence)

You also notice a few sentences that use the passive voice, which creates a slow-moving, indirect style. You rewrite these in the active voice. (See pages 73 and 607.)

Original Sentence: Lead particles can be swallowed by curious toddlers. (Sentence in the passive voice)

Revised Version: Curious toddlers can swallow lead particles. (Sentence in the active voice)

You check your entire essay for misplaced modifiers after finding one in an early paragraph. (See page 622.2.)

Original Sentence: A young child risks any number of ill effects swallowing lead particles. (Misplaced modifying phrase)

Revised Version: Swallowing lead particles, a young child risks any number of ill effects. (Modifying phrase correctly placed)

Help File

Use the following strategy to add variety to your sentences:
- In one column on a piece of paper, list the opening words in each of your sentences. Then decide if you need to vary some beginnings.
- In another column, list the verbs. Then decide if you need to replace any overused "be" verbs (is, are, was) with more vivid ones (snap, stare, stir).
- In a third column, identify the number of words in each sentence. Then decide if you need to change the length of some of your sentences.

Learning to Respond to Writing

Peer responders can help you see both the strengths and the trouble spots in your writing. Their feedback is especially helpful when you are evaluating your first draft. These guidelines tell you how to conduct group-advising sessions.

Using Writing-Group Guidelines

The guidelines below will help you conduct effective group-advising sessions. (If you're just starting out, work in small groups of three or four classmates.)

Role of the Writer-Reader

- **Come prepared with a meaningful piece of writing.** Make a copy for each group member (if this is what the group usually does).
- **Introduce your writing.** However, don't say too much; let your writing do the talking.
- **Read your copy out loud.** Don't stop to comment on your writing; just read it as clearly as you can.
- **Listen and take notes as the group reacts to your writing.** Don't be defensive about your writing since this will stop some members from commenting honestly. Answer all of their questions.
- **Share your concerns with your fellow writers.** If, for example, you're not sure about your ending, ask your listeners to pay special attention to it. Asking for specific advice may help your peers open up.

Role of the Listener-Responders

- **Listen carefully and take notes as the writer reads.** Keep your notes brief so you don't miss any part of the reading. (Afterward, read the text silently if the writer has supplied individual copies.)
- **Imagine yourself as the intended audience.** If, for example, the writing was meant for younger readers, a business, or the writer's peers, react to it with that audience in mind.
- **Keep your comments positive and constructive.** Instead of saying, "Great job," make more meaningful comments: "Sharing the personal story in the opening really grabbed my attention."
- **Focus your comments on specific things you observe.** An observation such as "I notice that many of your sentences start in the same way" is more helpful than "Add style to your writing."
- **Ask questions of the author.** "What do you mean when you say . . . ?" "Where did you get your facts about . . . ?"

Group-Advising Strategies

This page provides two strategies that you can use in group-advising sessions. The next page provides a sample peer response sheet.

▌ Critiquing a Paper

Use the following checklist as a basic guide when you assess a piece of writing in progress.

_____ **Purpose:** Is it clear what the writer is trying to do—entertain, inform, persuade, describe? Explain.

_____ **Audience:** Does the writing address a specific audience? Will the readers understand and appreciate this subject? Why?

_____ **Ideas:** Does the writer develop the subject with enough information?

_____ **Organization:** Are the ideas arranged in the best way, making the main points clear to the readers?

_____ **Voice:** Does the writing sound sincere and honest? Does the writer speak to his or her audience? Explain.

_____ **Word Choice:** Does the writer include any technical terms? Are these terms defined? Does the level of language fit the audience and topic?

_____ **Sentence Fluency:** Do the sentences read smoothly from start to finish? Are the sentences varied in length and structure?

_____ **Purpose Again:** Does the writing succeed in making you smile, nod, or react in some other way? What is especially good about the writing?

▌ Reacting to Writing

Peter Elbow, in *Writing Without Teachers*, offers four types of reactions group members might have to a piece of writing:

- **Pointing** refers to a reaction in which a group member "points out" words, phrases, or ideas that impress her or him.

- **Summarizing** refers to a reader's general reaction to the writing—a list of main ideas or a single sentence that sums up the work.

- **Telling** refers to readers describing what happens in a piece of writing: first this happens, then this happens, later this happens, and so on.

- **Showing** refers to feelings expressed about the piece. Elbow suggests that readers express these feelings metaphorically. A reader might, for example, refer to something in the writing as if it were a voice quality, a color, a shape, a piece of clothing, and so on. ("Your writing has a neat, tailored quality.")

Peer Response Sheet

Consider using a response sheet like this one to make comments about a peer's writing. (Sample comments are included.)

Response Sheet

Responder's Name: Amber Hayward

Writer's Name: Jack O'Neill

Title: McKinley's Mighty Eleven

What I liked about your work:

- You use a lot of sensory details and descriptions, so now I know what it feels like to play soccer.
- You're obviously knowledgeable about your topic.
- It was really exciting the way you described, moment by moment, the final goal of the last game.
- Your metaphors were great! "Trevor made a jailbreak with the ball . . ." "Alex moved like quicksilver through the opposition . . ."

Changes I would suggest:

- There's too much here—describing the team, the season, and the last game. What if you just focus on the last game?
- While the play-by-play is exciting, I had trouble following parts of it.
- In the middle, your writing voice became more informational than storylike. Can you give us the info in the same tone as the rest of the piece?
- You use some soccer terms — "wingback," "sweeper," and a "Metodo defense"—that confused me.

Help File

Carefully review the feedback that you receive during peer-response sessions; then plan your revising accordingly. You may or may not agree with all of the suggestions that are made.

Responding Online

Many online programs and services are available for you to use when you are revising your writing.

- **Cloud Storage:** When you build a collaborative project, use cloud-storage programs such as wikis or Google Docs, which allow multiple contributors access to a single, evolving document.

- **Versioning:** When you make major changes to a document, save the revision with a new filename, for example by adding a version number: VicksburgSiege2.docx. Versioning lets you track the development of a document and return to previous versions if you change your mind.

- **Track Changes:** When you review a document, turn on the track-changes feature of your word-processing program. This feature shows alterations made by different reviewers at different times. Even if a responder has not used this feature, your program may allow you to "compare documents" to see changes.

- **Comments:** In doc and PDF files, you can insert a question or concern as a "Comment" anchored to a specific spot in the text. Reviewers can then view a list of comments and incorporate changes.

- **Fact Checking:** As you review a text, use Internet searches to confirm names, locations, dates, events, and other facts.

- **Readability Apps:** If you are concerned about the readability of a document, you can paste portions of it into a readability application such as Hemingway, which highlights over-long sentences and difficult words.

- **Plagiarism Checkers:** If you are concerned about the originality of material, you can upload material to a plagiarism checker to find similar or identical text. Remember that your instructors can do so, as well.

- **Thesauruses:** If you need to find synonyms for an overused word, check an online thesaurus.

- **Reference Generators:** For research projects, use reference generators to create references in MLA or APA format. These programs prompt you for information about sources and then automatically format it.

- **Spell Check and Grammar Check:** When you edit a document, run spell- and grammar-checks to root out lingering errors.

Track Changes

In her book *Mindset,* Researcher Carol Dweck shows that the ~~traditional~~ practice of telling students that they are "smart" and "talented" may actually work against them. These compliments create a "fixed mindset" in students. "Talented" students ~~, which makes learning harder. Those who are told they are smart or talented~~ relax, trusting their innate ability rather than pushing themselves to achieve. "Untalented" students quit trying altogether. ~~Those who are not told they are smart or talented believe a person is born with these traits rather than acquiring them.~~

A Guide to Editing and Proofreading

Editing and proofreading involve checking your writing for correctness. In her book *Woe Is I*, editor Patricia T. O'Conner says, "[You] come from the factory wired for language." Yes, language is something that you come by quite naturally, and at this point, you probably know quite a lot about using it correctly. Still, following the current conventions concerning language may require some reviewing and updating.

This chapter and the "Proofreader's Guide" will add to your understanding of the language and serve as an editing guide. Also keep other editing tools handy—a spell-checker, grammar-checker, dictionary, and thesaurus. With these aids, plus the help of your writing peers, you'll soon be editing your writing with confidence.

Learning Outcomes

Learn about editing.
Check for 10 common errors.
Use Standard English.
Review editing in action.
Use an editing and proofreading checklist.

"The best writers may not follow every rule every time, but they follow most of them most of the time."

Patricia T. O'Conner

Learning About Editing

Purpose: Editing and proofreading deal with the line-by-line changes you make to correct conventional errors. Your goal is to make your writing clear and accurate.

Assess your readiness: You're ready to edit after you complete these tasks.

_____ Revise your writing for its content.

_____ Set the writing aside for a day or two.

Consider the rhetorical situation: Once again, consider your audience, your purpose, and your role by reviewing your answers to the **STRAP** questions. (See page 30.)

Understand your tasks: As you edit your writing, follow these tips.

- **Check for errors** using the grammar- and spell-checkers, but remember that these tools are not foolproof.
- **Make the necessary changes**, print out a copy of the writing, and use the checklists in this chapter to do more editing.
- **Consider focusing on one type of error at a time.**
- **Ask a trusted editor to check your writing** for errors.
- **Proofread the final copy** for errors before submitting it.

Try different approaches: Here is another approach to editing: Print out your writing as a list of isolated sentences. Check each sentence first for capitalization, second for punctuation, and third for grammar. When checking for spelling and repeated words, try working backward—from the end of the piece to its beginning. That way you can focus on each word individually. Make your changes on the printout and then enter them on the computer. Save the edited copy so you have a record of your changes.

Consider the traits: Editing focuses on the conventions to produce writing that is free of errors.

Conventions

Punctuation:	Check all punctuation carefully; however, double-check your use of commas and apostrophes, which are commonly misused.
Usage:	Pay special attention to usage and commonly mixed pairs that electronic checkers often miss.
Grammar:	Check especially for subject-verb agreement and pronoun-antecedent agreement. (See pages 625–627.)

Checking for 10 Common Errors

Comprehensive studies have identified the most common errors, other than spelling, in academic writing. These two pages cover 10 of these errors. If you need more information about a particular error, follow the reference at the end of each explanation.

Problem	**Solution**
1. Missing Comma After Long Introductory Phrases	Place a comma after a long introductory phrase. (See page 556.4.)

> Because of the snowstorm‸school was canceled for the day.

| **2.** Confusing Pronoun Reference | Be sure the reader knows whom or what your pronoun refers to. (See page 622.1.) |

> When Angel talked with Samantha, ~~she~~ Angel said she would drive.

| **3.** Missing Comma in Compound Sentence | Use a comma between two independent clauses joined by a coordinating conjunction—*and, but, or, nor, so, for,* or *yet.* |

> I tried to call Jake this morning‸but his cell phone was turned off.

| **4.** Missing Comma(s) with Nonrestrictive Phrases or Clauses | Use commas to set off a phrase or clause that is not needed to understand the sentence. |

> I gave five dollars to my little brother‸who gave me a big smile.

| **5.** Comma Splices | When only a comma separates two independent clauses, add a conjunction or create two sentences. (See page 620.2.) |

> Javon is graduating from college on Sunday, so we're having a family party.

Common Errors (Cont.)

Problem	Solution

6. Subject-Verb Agreement Error — Verbs must agree in number with their subjects. (See page 625.)

> The ballots lists four candidates for class president.

7. Missing Comma in a Series — Use commas to separate individual words, phrases, or clauses in a series.

> Our van was cluttered with plastic bags, candy wrappers, and empty water bottles.

8. Pronoun-Antecedent Agreement Errors — A pronoun must agree in number with the word that the pronoun refers to. (See page 627.)

> her
> Either Rose or Emily brought their DVD's to Adrian's house.

9. Missing Apostrophe to Show Ownership — Use an apostrophe after a noun to show possession. (See page 564.)

> Jorges dream is to attend a World Series game.

10. Misusing Its and It's — *Its* is a possessive pronoun meaning "belong to it." *It's* is a contraction of "it is" or "it has."

> It's a fact that the distance from Earth's surface to its center is about 3,963 miles.

Remember: Reserve a section of your class notebook for examples of the errors that you most commonly make in your writing. Refer to these examples as you edit your writing assignments.

Using Standard English

Standard English, which is the English taught in school, is considered appropriate for academic, business, and government documents. Nonstandard English is considered inappropriate for such documents. The chart that follows shows the basic differences between the two dialects.

Differences in . . .	Nonstandard	Standard
1. Expressing plurals after numbers	10 mile	10 miles
2. Expressing habitual action	He always be early.	He always is early.
3. Expressing ownership	My friend car . . .	My friend's car . . .
4. Expressing the third-person singular verb	The customer ask . . .	The customer asks . . .
5. Expressing negatives	She doesn't never . . .	She doesn't ever . . .
6. Using reflexive pronouns	He sees hisself	He sees himself . . .
7. Using demonstrative adjectives	Them reports are . . .	Those reports are . . .
8. Using forms of *do*	He done it.	He did it.
9. Avoiding double subjects	My manager he . . .	My manager . . .
10. Using *a* or *an*	I need new laptop. She had angry caller.	I need a new laptop. She had an angry caller.
11. Using the past tense of verbs	Carl finish his . . .	Carl finished his . . .
12. Using *isn't* or *aren't* versus *ain't*	The company ain't . . .	The company isn't . . .

Reviewing Editing in Action

Review the corrections made in these paragraphs from a student essay. See the inside back cover of this book for an explanation of the editing symbols used.

Gender Equality

Should young women be grateful for their education? Absolutely. According to the united nations (UN), two-thirds of the world's illiterate people are female. Just as shocking is that two-thirds of the world's children who don't go to school are female. In point of fact, females in developing countries are disadvantaged in may aspects of life.

In September 2000, the UN set specific goals for the twenty-first century to address this problem. Eight goals were outlined in a resolution called the "United Nations Millennium Declaration." Two of the goals directly address promoting gender equality and primary education worldwide. The UN believes that placing more emphasis on education will have significant economic benefits. The organization's hope is that educated women will participate more fully in public and political life and break the cycle of poverty. A UN 2006 report shows the effort is slowly succeeding, but there is much more to be done.

The UN wants to eliminate gender (discrimenation) *discrimination* in all levels of education no later than 2015. The declaration states that "by 2015 children everywhere, boys and girls alike, will be able to complete a full *course* ~~coarse~~ of primary schooling and that girls and boys will have equal access to all levels of education."

A proper noun is capitalized.

A comma is placed after a transition.

A title is punctuated.

An apostrophe is added to show singular possession.

A spelling error is corrected.

A usage error is corrected.

Using an Editing and Proofreading Checklist

Use this checklist as a guide when you edit and proofread your writing. Also refer to pages 63–64. *Remember:* Edit your work only after you have revised it.

Conventions

Look at punctuation . . . (See pages 553–572.)

____ Do my sentences end with the proper punctuation?

____ Do I use commas correctly in compound sentences?

____ Do I use commas correctly in a series and after long introductory phrases or clauses?

____ Do I use apostrophes correctly?

____ Do I punctuate titles and dialogue correctly?

Look at mechanics . . . (See pages 573–588.)

____ Do I start my sentences with capital letters?

____ Do I capitalize proper nouns?

____ Have I checked for spelling errors (including those the spell-checker may have missed)?

Look at grammar . . . (See pages 616–634.)

____ Do the subjects and verbs agree in my sentences?

____ Do my sentences use correct and consistent verb tenses?

____ Do my pronouns agree with their antecedents?

____ Have I avoided any other usage errors or commonly mixed pairs?

Check for presentation . . . (See pages 385–392.)

____ Does the title effectively lead into the writing?

____ Are sources of information properly presented and documented?

____ Does my writing meet the standards of layout and design required for final presentation?

Writers INC

The Elements
of Writing

Writing Sentences

A well-written sentence is still the most effective way for a writer to get a point across. This is true in school, in business, and in life. Fortunately, you have been reading, writing, and thinking sentences long enough now that you use them almost automatically. You don't have to say, "I'll use a complex sentence here," or "I think a compound sentence would spice things up." Instead, you just write. There is a bit of mystery and magic going on because you're never exactly sure what you will come up with.

Of course, circumstances change when you review and revise your writing. Then you need to look closely at your sentences, especially those that for one reason or another are not clear or complete. This chapter helps you to think carefully about your sentences and improve those that need to be stronger.

Learning Outcomes

Consider the rhetorical situation.
Work with the basics.
Write natural sentences.
Write stylistic sentences.
Use different kinds of sentences.
Combine sentences.
Expand sentences.
Use a sentence checklist.

"Sentences are like just caught fish.
Spunky today, stinky tomorrow."

Max Lucado

Considering the Rhetorical Situation

Sentence structure and style vary according to the rhetorical situation—the audience, purpose, type of writing, and so on. Sentences in a research paper, for example, will be different from those in a personal blog.

In the first passage below, the sentences are formal and factual; in the second, they are informal and personal. Each style is matched to the writing's purpose and audience.

▌ Passage 1

This passage is taken from the science textbook *Living in the Environment*. Read it, paying special attention to the makeup of each sentence.

> Tropical rain forests are found near the earth's equator and contain an incredible variety of life. These lush forests are warm year-round and have high humidity and heavy rainfall almost daily. Although they cover only about 2% of the earth's land surface, studies indicate that they contain up to half of the world's known terrestrial plant and animal species. For these reasons, they make an excellent natural laboratory for the study of ecosystems—communities of organisms interacting with one another and with the physical environment of matter and energy in which they live.

Discussion: The sentences are formal in style, which means they are carefully worded, often complex in structure, and packed with details. The shortest sentence contains 16 words; the longest, 34. This style is well suited for a textbook.

▌ Passage 2

This passage comes from "Campus Racism 101," a personal essay written by writer and professor Nikki Giovanni.

> There is a bumper sticker that reads: TOO BAD IGNORANCE ISN'T PAINFUL. I like that. But ignorance is. We just seldom attribute the pain to it or even recognize it when we see it. Like the postcard on my corkboard. It shows a young man in a very hip jacket smoking a cigarette. In the background is a high school with the American flag waving. The caption says: "Too cool for school. Yet too stupid for the real world." Out of the mouth of the young man is a bubble enclosing the words "Maybe I'll start a band." There could be a postcard showing a jock in a uniform saying, "I don't need school. I'm going to the NFL or NBA."

Discussion: The sentences are informal in style, which means they are free flowing, varied, simple in structure, and personal. The shortest sentence contains 3 words; the longest, 19. The writer even uses fragments—"But ignorance is" and "Like the postcard on my corkboard." This style suits a personal essay.

Sentence Styles in Academic Writing

Academic essays and research papers explore ideas. They are generally loaded with facts, statistics, and specific details. The sentences used in academic writing are also pretty predictable. They are often of a certain length, type, and formality.

▪ **Length:** Long sentences are often used to *explain, examine,* and *illustrate* information. These examples are taken from a student essay:

> Prior to the graduated licensing laws (GDL), the National Highway Traffic Safety Administration found that 16-year-old drivers were twice as likely as adult drivers to be in fatal crashes.
>
> In nonfatal crashes, 16-year-olds had three times more accidents than 17-year-olds, five times more than 18-year-olds, and two times more than 85-year-olds.

▪ **Type:** Complex sentences can be used to discuss ideas and *show relationships between them.* A complex sentence contains one independent clause plus one or more subordinate clauses. In the examples below, the independent clause (main idea) is underlined. Additional or supporting information is included in the subordinate clause.

> <u>Insurance companies make young drivers pay very high rates</u> because, statistically, teenagers are much more likely to get involved in accidents than other drivers are.
>
> As more states establish strong GDL laws, <u>young drivers will likely pay more reasonable insurance rates.</u>

▪ **Formality:** Academic writing requires a formal style. Sentences are carefully structured and objective in voice. Contractions are seldom used, and informal expressions, such as *here's what I mean,* are avoided. The following examples illustrate a formal versus an informal treatment of identical ideas.

> **Formal:** It is never easy to wait for something important, but when it comes to a driver's license, the wait is necessary.
>
> **Informal:** It's never easy to wait for anything, but everyone knows that you have to wait forever to get a driver's license.

> **Formal:** Using drugs and alcohol is already illegal, but now, if a teenager gets caught using either of them, near a car or not, that teen's driver's license is revoked.
>
> **Informal:** Using drugs and alcohol are already big no-no's, but now, if a teenager gets caught, even with no car in sight, his license is toast.

Sentence Styles in Personal Writing

Personal essays, narratives, and blogs usually express an individual's thoughts and feelings about everyday life and topics of interest. The following features concerning length, type, and formality are typical of the sentences in these personal forms.

- **Length:** Sentences of varying lengths are used to express personal thoughts and feelings. Overall, however, they are often shorter than the information-packed sentences used in academic pieces. Here are a few examples taken from a personal essay:

> Everyone has to grow up, and for most people, the change from childhood to adulthood is gradual. Not for me.
>
> I remember the moment my childhood ended. It was right after a big basketball game. The parking-lot lights shone brightly as Jenna and I headed home. Suddenly, Jenna's cell phone rang.

- **Type:** All sentence types are used in personal writing, although simple and compound sentences may be dominant. Fragments are permitted in order to produce a conversational, free-flowing style, as you will notice in these examples:

> "I gotta get this," she said. She answered and listened, nodding solemnly. I could see her face go gray. "It's Mia," she said. "Mia's dead."
>
> I felt like I had been hit in the chest with a brick, and I could hardly breathe. I'd seen Mia in seventh hour. She had been making faces, crackin' me up. Now she was gone. No more basketball games. No more gab sessions. No more hugs.

- **Formality:** Personal writing exhibits an informal style. Sentences are casually structured and use a subjective or first-person voice to share the writer's thoughts and feelings. They often include contractions and informal expressions.

  Informal: I couldn't believe this was happening. In seventh hour, I just stared at Mia's desk and tried to imagine her there. God knows what the teacher was talking about.

  Informal: I always shared my deepest secrets with Mia. And just like that, everything had changed. Why didn't I tell Mia how I felt about her? I had to try, even now.

Working with the Basics

Your sentences work or don't work depending on the quality of the nouns and verbs that you use. Author Stephen King calls nouns and verbs "the indispensable part of writing." So you should know how to use them effectively.

Specific Nouns

Some nouns are **general** (*vegetable, pants, computers*) and give the reader a vague, uninteresting picture. Other nouns are more **specific** (*okra, corduroys, laptops*) and give the reader a clearer, more detailed picture. In the chart below, the nouns move from general to specific. The specific nouns are the ones you'll want to use in your writing.

	person	**place**	**thing**	**idea**
General	woman	landmark	drink	belief
	scientist	national landmark	coffee	strong belief
Specific	Marie Curie	Mount Rushmore	cappuccino	conviction

Vivid Verbs

Like nouns, verbs can be too general to create a vivid word picture. For example, the verb *looked* does not say the same thing as *stared, glared,* or *glanced.* ("Ms. Shaw *glared* at the two goof-offs.")

■ Whenever possible, use a verb that is strong enough to stand alone without the help of an adverb.

> **A verb and an adverb:** Water *moves forcefully* through a pipe, triggering the system's pumping mechanism.

> **A vivid verb:** Water *rushes* through a pipe, triggering the system's pumping mechanism.

■ Avoid overusing the "be" verbs (is, are, was, were). A better verb can often be made from another word in the sentence.

> **A "be" verb:** Irrigation *is* something that transformed the Great American Desert into the best farmland in the world.

> **A stronger verb:** Irrigation *transformed* the Great American Desert into the best farmland in the world.

■ Whenever possible, use active rather than passive verbs. (See page 607.)

> **A passive verb:** Wells *are drilled* by farmers in the High Plains to retrieve water from the Ogallala Aquifer.

> **An active verb:** Farmers in the High Plains *drill* wells to retrieve water from the Ogallala Aquifer.

Writing Natural Sentences

As a general rule, the best sentences sound honest and straightforward rather than artificial and fancy. The examples that follow demonstrate the difference between artificial-sounding sentences and ones that sound natural.

Deadwood ▪ Deadwood is wording that fills up lots of space but does not add anything important or new to the overall meaning.

> **Wordy:** At this point in time, I feel the study needs additional work before the subcommittee can recommend it be resubmitted for further consideration.
>
> **Concise:** The study needs more work.

Flowery Language ▪ Flowery language is writing that uses more or bigger words than needed. It often contains too many adjectives or adverbs.

> **Flowery:** The cool, fresh breeze, which came like a storm in the night, lifted me to exhilarating heights which had been previously suppressed by the stifling incandescent cloud in the learning center.
>
> **Concise:** The cool breeze was a refreshing change from the muggy classroom air.

Jargon ▪ Jargon is language used in a certain profession or by a certain group of people. It is usually very technical and not at all natural.

> **Jargon:** I'm having difficulty conceptualizing these employee mandates.
>
> **Natural:** I don't understand these work rules.

Euphemism ▪ A euphemism is a word or a phrase that is substituted for another because it is considered a less offensive way of saying something.

> **Euphemism:** I am so exasperated that I could expectorate.
>
> **Natural:** I am so mad I could spit.

Cliche ▪ A cliche is an overused word or phrase that springs quickly to mind but just as quickly bores the user and the audience. A cliche gives the reader nothing new or original to think about.

> **Cliche:** Her face turned as red as a beet.
>
> **Natural:** Her face turned a deep shade of red.

Trite Expression ▪ A trite expression is one that is overused and stale; as a result, it sounds neither sincere nor natural.

> **Trite:** It gives all of us a great deal of pleasure to present to you this plaque as a token of our thanks and appreciation.
>
> **Natural:** Please accept this plaque with our heartfelt thanks.

Writing Stylistic Sentences

Your sentences will always be in style if they are clear and correct. At times, however, you may need your sentences to do more. When that is the case, try one of the stylistic techniques explained below.

Using Metaphors

A metaphor compares an idea or an image in your writing to something new, bringing a basic idea to life for the reader.

To Create a Picture ▪ In the examples that follow, note how each of the basic ideas becomes a powerful picture when it is stated metaphorically.

> **Basic idea:** My performance was a real disappointment.
>
> **Metaphor:** My performance was a choke sandwich, all peanut butter and no jelly.
>
> **Basic idea:** The sunset changed the color of our river.
>
> **Metaphor:** Our river slowly turned into red and purple streaks of sunset.

To Expand an Idea ▪ Because a metaphor can unify ideas in a series of sentences, extending a metaphor can help you to expand and clarify your ideas. Note how the metaphor (comparing family relationships to fabric) is extended in the following passage.

> **Metaphor:** My family has always been a rich tapestry of personalities bound together by affection and respect.
>
> **Extended:** My family has always been a rich tapestry of personalities bound together by affection and respect. But that tapestry began to unravel last summer amid arguments and accusations surrounding my brother's divorce. People were taking sides, and the family tapestry was being tested. Relationships were frayed. It wasn't until we gathered for our annual reunion that people relented. One by one, they began the work of patching things up one piece at time—a simple conversation, a sincere thank you, a heartfelt hug. Whatever had pulled us apart was mended that day at the county park under a grove of red oak trees.

Help File

Make sure your metaphors are original and clear. And be careful when using extended metaphors. If "extended" too far, they may sound forced and unnatural.

Using Repetition

Repetition can add rhythm and emphasis to your sentences. Just remember to keep your words and ideas parallel, or "stated in the same way." As with any stylistic technique, repetition is effective when it is used selectively.

For Rhythm and Balance ▪ In the following sentences, notice how the repeated ideas flow smoothly from one to the next.

> At one time or another, the Austrians, the Russians, and the British fought against Napoleon's army.

> Jumal wants to graduate from college, become a volunteer medic, and work in the African sub-Sahara.

For Emphasis and Effect ▪ In the following passage, notice the intensity created by repeating the simple-sentence structure.

> "We shall fight on the beaches, we shall fight on the landing grounds, we shall fight in the fields and in the streets, we shall fight in the hills; we shall never surrender."
> —Winston Churchill

Using Long and Short Sentences

Incorporating a few very long and very short sentences can draw attention to key points.

Very Long Sentence ▪ A very long sentence can effectively hold lots of important information.

> Considering the dynamics of Lincoln's address at Gettysburg—the fact that he composed it on the train trip and in his boarding room, that he spoke for five minutes after another person's two-hour speech, and that he believed that "the world will little note nor long remember what we say here"—this speech should have simply slipped into obscurity.

Very Short Sentence ▪ A very short sentence can make a strong point.

> It did not.

Using Juxtaposition

Putting contrasting ideas together is called juxtaposition. When used effectively, juxtaposition can draw the reader's attention to an important idea.

Contrasting Ideas ▪ Contrasting ideas play off each other.

> For short-term muscle gain, some high school athletes risk a lifetime of health problems.

Using Different Kinds of Sentences

Primarily, you will use declarative sentences in your writing. Occasionally, however, you will want to use other kinds of sentences to get your reader's attention. For example you can ask a dramatic question, make a request, or express strong emotion.

Interrogative sentences ask questions.

> Did Jess Bezos, founder and CEO of Amazon.com, have a clear business plan in mind when he started out?

Imperative sentences make commands or requests.

> Consider what Stephen Hawking thinks about "string theory."

Exclamatory sentences communicate strong emotion.

> Television commercials drive me crazy!

Conditional sentences can express statements contrary to fact.

> If I had the power, I would ban television commercials.

Types of Sentences

If you were to analyze one of your academic essays, you might find that it contains a healthy mix of simple, compound, and complex sentences. If not, start using a variety of sentence types to improve the readability of your writing. (Also see page 78 for other combining techniques.)

Simple sentences contain one independent clause.

> An advertiser paid $9.00 for the very first television commercial.

Compound sentences contain two independent clauses.

> Vincent van Gogh died 120 years ago, but his fame and notoriety remain.

Complex sentences contain one independent clause (underlined) and one or more dependent clauses.

> As technological components have become smaller and smaller, they also have become more and more desirable to consumers.

Compound-complex sentences contain two or more independent clauses and one or more dependent clauses. The independent clauses are underlined in the example that follows.

> The Great Lakes are a magnificent freshwater resource, and local conservation groups are meeting to establish policies before water-starved regions start making withdrawal requests.

Combining Sentences

Sentence combining is one of the most effective techniques for improving the style of your sentences. When you combine your short, choppy sentences, your writing will read more smoothly and carry more meaning. Suppose a tornado struck a small town without warning, causing a great deal of damage, a number of injuries, and several deaths. Here are several sentences that express individual ideas about the tragedy:

There was a tornado.	The tornado caused a great deal of damage.
The tornado struck a small town.	The tornado caused a number of injuries.
The tornado struck without warning.	The tornado caused several deaths.

By combining some of the ideas, the writer not only provides all the necessary facts but also improves the sentence style. Here are some combining techniques.

Series ▪ Use a series to combine three or more similar ideas.

> The tornado struck the small town without warning, causing extensive damage, numerous injuries, and several deaths.

Relative Pronoun ▪ Use a relative pronoun (*who, whose, that, which*) to introduce the subordinate (less important) ideas.

> The tornado, which was completely unexpected, swept through the small town, causing extensive damage, numerous injuries, and several deaths.

Introductory Phrase ▪ Use an introductory phrase or clause for the less important ideas.

> Because the tornado was completely unexpected, it caused extensive damage, numerous injuries, and several deaths.

Participial Phrase ▪ Use a participial phrase (*-ing, -ed*) to begin or end a sentence.

> The tornado swept through the small town without warning, leaving a trail of death and destruction.

Key Word ▪ Repeat a key word or phrase to emphasize an idea.

> The unexpected tornado left a permanent scar on the small town, a scar of destruction, injury, and death.

Correlative Conjunctions ▪ Use correlative conjunctions (*not only, but also; either, or*) to compare or contrast two ideas in a sentence.

> The unexpected tornado inflicted not only immense property damage but also immeasurable human suffering.

Appositive ▪ Use an appositive (or an appositive phrase) for emphasis.

> A single incident, a tornado that came without warning, changed the face of the small town forever.

Expanding Sentences

Sentences of accomplished writers seem to overflow with interesting information. Follow the three steps below to learn how to create your own engaging sentences.

1. Become a regular and attentive reader, noticing the style as well as the content of the sentences. Over time, you will begin to internalize the structure of well-made sentences.

2. Carry out the necessary research about your topics. You'll need plenty of information to work with in order to write engaging sentences.

3. Practice sentence expanding by adding details to a basic idea. (See the information below about cumulative sentences.)

Cumulative Sentences

More than any other type of sentence, the cumulative sentence marks the work of good writers. In a cumulative sentence, the main idea is expanded with modifying words, phrases, and clauses. Here is a cumulative sentence that places the modifiers after the main clause, which is underlined. The modifiers expand the meaning of the sentence.

It is as if Gatsby is a theater director, gathering props and actors to stage a magnificent although artificial performance.

Here is another example with modifiers placed before and after the main clause (underlined). Again, the modifiers add meaning to the sentence.

Even with all the glitter and gold, Gatsby finds himself truly empty, devoid of any type of meaningful relationship to enrich his life.

As you practice writing cumulative sentences, you might try using the following modifying elements to expand your ideas.

Single words: Gatsby is seen strolling, purposelessly.

Prepositional phrases: Near the end, Gatsby is seen strolling, purposelessly, along his velvet lawn.

Participial (-ing or -ed) phrases: He searches the far shore of the bay, peering through the darkness.

Infinitive phrases: He searches the far shore of the bay, peering through the darkness to find Daisy's pier.

Using a Sentence Checklist

How can you make sure that your sentences are effective? Use the following checklist to stop and think about the sentences you are either reading or writing.

Sentence Checklist

Do I vary my sentence patterns?

____ Your writing will be interesting if you use a variety of sentence patterns. (See page 77.)

Does each sentence express a complete thought?

____ Your writing will be easy to follow if it has no sentence errors such as fragments and comma splices. (See pages 620.)

Are my sentences easy to understand?

____ Your writing will be clear if it is free of ambiguous wording and incomplete comparisons. (See page 621.)

Do my sentences sound honest and natural?

____ Your writing will sound natural if you avoid flowery language, jargon or technical language, deadwood, wordiness, euphemisms, and cliches. (See page 74.)

Do my sentences follow the rules of Standard English?

____ Your writing will reflect favorably on you if it is free of nonstandard language, double negatives, or shifts in construction. (See pages 623–624.)

Do I combine short, choppy sentences?

____ Your writing will read smoothly if you avoid using too many short, choppy sentences. (See page 78.)

Are my sentences stylistic?

____ Your writing will have style if you pay special attention to the sound and rhythm of your sentences. (See page 75.)

Do I expand basic ideas within sentences?

____ Your writing will also have style if you pay special attention to the ways in which you add specific details to your sentences. (See page 79.)

Writing Paragraphs and Essays

Have you ever seen a Russian nesting doll—a set of hollow wooden figurines that fit inside each other? The largest one is a hollow doll that holds a smaller version of the same doll, which holds a smaller one yet, and so on.

An essay works something like a nesting doll. Inside the framework of an essay are paragraphs; inside the paragraphs are sentences; inside the sentences are phrases, clauses, and words. But unlike a nesting doll, each part of the essay has to be exposed at the same time. Each part has to work together before any of it can make sense. This is especially true for paragraphs and essays, as you'll see in this chapter.

Learning Outcomes

Compare paragraphs and essays.
Develop a paragraph.
Use a variety of details.
Organize details.
Develop an essay.

"The paragraph [is] a mini-essay; it is also a maxi-sentence."

Donald Hall

Comparing Paragraphs and Essays

Writing paragraphs and essays provides two ways to organize your thinking. Depending on the topic, your ideas may fit into a single paragraph, or they may require a multi-paragraph essay. Paragraphs and essays have similar structures.

Paragraph Structure	Essay Structure
Topic Sentence ▪ Shares the main idea about a topic	**Opening Paragraph** ▪ Grabs the reader's attention ▪ Provides background information ▪ Leads to a thesis statement
Body Sentences ▪ Support the main idea	**Middle Paragraphs** ▪ Each supports the thesis statement ▪ Each has a topic sentence, body sentences, and a closing sentence
Closing Sentence ▪ Sums up the main idea about the topic	**Closing Paragraph** ▪ Revisits the thesis ▪ Provides a final thought for the reader

Why should I build paragraphs and essays this way?

You may have heard the following bit of advice about public speaking: "Tell me what you are going to tell me, then tell me, then tell me what you told me." Paragraphs and essays use the same plan: state the topic, develop the topic, and sum up the topic. This approach helps the reader grasp the ideas in paragraphs and essays.

Developing a Paragraph

Paragraphs are the building blocks of essays, so mastering the paragraph will naturally help you master the essay. As the graphic on the previous page shows, a paragraph consists of a topic sentence, body sentences, and a closing sentence.

Writing Topic Sentences

The topic sentence names the focus of the paragraph. To write an effective topic sentence, name the topic you will address and tell what you plan to say about it. Use the following formula:

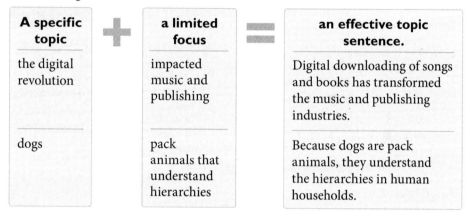

A specific topic		a limited focus		an effective topic sentence.
the digital revolution	✚	impacted music and publishing	═	Digital downloading of songs and books has transformed the music and publishing industries.
dogs		pack animals that understand hierarchies		Because dogs are pack animals, they understand the hierarchies in human households.

Writing Body Sentences

The body sentences in a paragraph provide the details that support the topic sentence. As you write your body sentences, use the guidelines below and those on the following pages.

- Use a **variety** of details.
- Use different **levels** of details.
- **Organize** details according to your purpose.
- Connect details using effective **transitions**.

Writing Closing Sentences

The closing sentence of a paragraph sums up the paragraph without repeating the topic sentence word for word. The best closing sentences revisit the ideas presented and often add a final thought for the reader to consider.

> Though dogs recognize the alphas, betas, and omegas in each household, they may disagree with their masters as to exactly who is in charge.

Using a Variety of Details

Paragraphs include many different types of details. Choose details that develop and support the main idea of your topic sentence.

Facts are details that can be proven. They connect ideas to reality.

> Originally built in 1797 and restored between 1927 and 1931, the tall ship USS *Constitution* is the world's oldest floating commissioned naval vessel.

Statistics are facts that include numbers. They quantify ideas.

> According to the FDA, a one-ounce bag of potato chips contains 10 grams of fat.

Definitions give the meaning of terms. They help the reader understand ideas.

> Medieval castle walls were topped with *battlements*, lines of stone blocks that provided cover for archers as they defended the castle against siege.

Examples are specific cases that illustrate a general point. They make abstract ideas concrete.

> Every year, the *Oxford English Dictionary* admits new words into the language. For example, the *OED* recently added the word *selfie*, which is a self-portrait photo taken by holding a camera at arm's length.

Anecdotes are brief stories that make a point. They connect ideas to life and create an emotional response in the reader.

> Many people who lived through the Great Depression never forgot the feeling of being hungry and barely scraping by. Even after becoming a millionaire many times over, Marc Damis continued to gather and hoard sugar and ketchup packets from local restaurants.

Quotations provide the exact words of an expert or a person involved in a situation. They let people speak for themselves.

> Education tends to drive creativity out of us. As artist Pablo Picasso once said, "Every child is born an artist. The problem is how to remain an artist once we grow up."

Reasons answer *why*. They help the reader understand cause and effect, and they also convince the reader to accept ideas.

> The discovery of the New World set off an age of European imperialism. Old World nations hungered for the resources of the Americas and set up colonies there. Soon Africa, India, and China were also colonized.

Explanations answer *how*. They talk about the way something is done or happens.

> At the base of every deciduous leaf is a ring of light-sensitive cells that sense when days are growing shorter. As darkness descends, these cells cause the leaf to cease photosynthesis, dry up, and break free of the branch.

Analyses break a whole into parts and show how the parts relate to each other.

> They help the reader explore a topic. The federal government divides power into three branches—the executive (President), which enforces laws; the legislative (Congress), which makes laws; and the judicial (the Supreme Court), which interprets laws.

Comparisons show how two topics are similar and different. They help the reader better understand both topics.

> The Statue of Liberty displays its hammered copper shell and hides its steel framework, while the Eiffel Tower exults the framework without a shell. Gustave Eiffel designed both steel frameworks. The first is a work of engineering that supports art, and the second is a work of engineering that has become art.

Elaborating Details

You can develop an idea by using a variety of details to explain it. Each detail provides greater clarity, additional information, or new depth. When you elaborate on an idea in this way, you and your reader think more deeply about it. The following progression of details elaborates on the idea of cooperation in nature.

Level 1: The main idea is stated.

Level 2: Three clarifying examples and an anecdote are provided.

Level 3: A completing point finishes the paragraph.

We tend to think that nature is driven by competition—a dog-eat-dog world of winners and losers—but cooperation plays a part as well. For example, many ants farm aphids, harvesting their honeydew while protecting them from predators. Coral reefs, the largest living structures in the world, are formed by a symbiotic relationship between algae and coral animals. Perhaps most amazing of all, the mitocondria that power our cells are actually bacteria with their own DNA and life cycle, living cooperatively within the cells. How did this miracle of cooperation come about? Long ago in some primordial sea, one cell tried to eat another but couldn't digest it. The engulfed cell lived on, benefiting its host. A failed attempt at competition turned into an ongoing collaboration that has made all plant and animal life possible. On the cellular level, we all are cooperatives.

Organizing Details

The way that you organize details in a paragraph depends mainly on your purpose for writing. The following pages discuss the most common organizational patterns.

Using Description

When you describe a person, a place, or an object, you organize details spatially (by location). Here are some options:

Describe the whole and then each part.

> The U.S. Capitol building is a stately structure of white limestone with a huge dome at its center, a chamber on one side for the Senate, and a chamber on the other side for the House of Representatives.

Move from top to bottom, front to back, or side to side.

> A wide set of stairs leads up to a stone colonnade. Above it rises the rotunda, a cylindrical structure ringed by another colonnade. The rotunda supports the massive dome, which is surmounted by the Statue of Freedom.

Follow a path through the space.

> Passing through a tall set of double doors, you enter the Senate chambers. Above you, a gallery of seats allows spectators to look down on the room. Before you, 100 desks descend in semicircles to the rostrum at the front of the chamber.

Transitions Used to Describe

above	around	between	inside	outside
across	behind	beyond	into	over
against	below	by	near	throughout
along	beneath	in back of	on top of	to the right
among	beside	in front of	onto	under

Using Classification

When you break down a topic into separate groups or parts, you organize details by categories or classes.

> There are two types of people in the world: one who believes there are two types of people in the world, and another who believes there aren't.

Key Words Used to Classify

category	form	kind	range	status
class	genus	level	rank	style
division	grade	order	set	type
family	group	phylum	sort	version

Using Chronological Order

When you want to tell how to do something or share an event or story, you organize details chronologically (by time). Here are three options:

Give commands for completing a task.

Begin by rolling out the piecrust dough on a floured board. Then lift it and lay it in the pie pan. Fill the lower crust with the filling. Afterward, lay the top crust over the mixture and crimp the edges to seal them.

Describe events in order.

The concert hall went dark except for chaser lights flitting across the stage. A bass began a thundering riff. Out stepped Geddy Lee, and the crowd erupted. Next, Alex Lifeson emerged, wailing on his electric guitar. Then rock legend Neil Peart rose like a dark wizard in the massive drum set.

Move back and forth through time as needed.

I walked slowly through the deserted playground. I paused at the base of the corkscrew slide where once I'd stood to catch Jack. I wandered to the dam where he'd broken the news that he'd enlisted. Water cascaded endlessly over the spillway. Maybe if I stared hard enough, I could freeze it in place. Maybe I could rewind time to a point before the email came from Afghanistan. . . .

Transitions Used to Show Time Order

about	during	later	second	today
after	finally	meanwhile	soon	tomorrow
as soon as	first	next	then	until
before	immediately	now	third	yesterday

Using Cause and Effect

When you discuss events and their results, you organize details according to their causal relationship.

A water molecule is shaped like a Mickey Mouse head, with hydrogen atoms as ears and an oxygen atom as the face. Because more electrons gather around the ears, they have a net negative charge, and the other end of the molecule has a net positive charge. This polarization causes molecules to pack tightly, creating surface tension and raising the water's boiling point.

Transitions Used to Show Causes and Effects

after	due to	in order that	then
as a result	for this reason	in order to	therefore
as a by-product	given that	since	when
because	if	so	whenever

Using Comparison

When you compare two topics, you organize details by their similarities and differences. There are three options you can use.

Subject by subject: Describe one topic fully, and then describe the other topic.

> Subject A has these features . . .
> Subject B has these features . . .

Similarities and differences: Describe how the topics are similar, and then describe how they are different.

> Subjects A and B are similar in many ways . . .
> Subjects A and B are also different in many ways . . .

Point by point: Discuss one point of comparison for both topics, then another, and so on.

> Subject A is reddish orange, while subject B is greenish brown . . .
> Subject A skitters quickly away, but subject B creeps slowly along . . .

Transitions Used to Compare and Contrast

also	but	however	otherwise
although	by contrast	like	similarly
as	even though	on the other hand	yet

Using Argumentation

When you share a position, you organize details to convince the reader.

Logos: Argue by establishing premises, drawing inferences, and stating conclusions.

> Given that life expectancy is increasing and that activity improves longevity, our society should raise the retirement age.

Ethos: Argue by presenting evidence from experts.

> The United States Bureau of Labor Statistics indicates that the retirement of baby boomers has created a shortage of highly skilled workers.

Pathos: Argue by appealing to emotion, empathy, or morality.

> Let's re-imagine Grandma from Bingo lady to high-powered CEO.

Transitions Used in Argumentation

again	as well	if . . . then	put simply
along with	besides	in fact	to emphasize
also	especially	it follows that	to repeat
another	for example	in summary	to sum up
assuming that	for instance	likewise	truly

Developing an Essay

An essay is basically an expanded paragraph. Just like a paragraph, the essay has a three-part structure:

- The **opening paragraph** introduces the topic and leads to the thesis statement.
- The **middle paragraphs** support the thesis statement with main points, which are in turn supported by details.
- The **closing paragraph** sums up what has been said in the essay and provides a strong final thought.

Writing Your Opening Paragraph

In your opening paragraph, you must grab the reader's attention. Here are some strategies to try:

Start with a surprising statement.

> For nearly 100 years, Chicago and Green Bay have been locked in an all-out war.

Ask an intriguing question.

> Why do we love football? Why does our own mood on any given Sunday depend so much on the position of a pigskin?

Use a thought-provoking quotation.

> Vince Lombardi once said, "Winning isn't everything. It's the only thing."

Tell a brief story (anecdote).

> Imagine you are an advertiser who has paid $3 million for a 30-second Super Bowl ad. After it airs, you check analytics—how many people saw it, what Twitter buzz it got, how it trended on Facebook. One statistic nettles you: the number of toilets that flushed during your ad. In the end, it's not about the ads, its about the game—it's about football.

Stating Your Thesis

After getting your reader's attention, lead up to your thesis statement. The thesis statement names the topic and limits the focus of your essay. Use the following formula to write effective thesis statements.

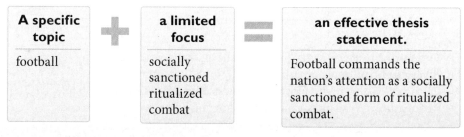

A specific topic		a limited focus		an effective thesis statement.
football	✚	socially sanctioned ritualized combat	=	Football commands the nation's attention as a socially sanctioned form of ritualized combat.

Writing the Middle Paragraphs

The middle paragraphs of your essay present the main points that support your thesis statement. Organize middle paragraphs based on the purpose of your essay.

▌ Descriptive Essays

An essay that describes a person, place, or thing is usually organized by location, using one or more of the following patterns.

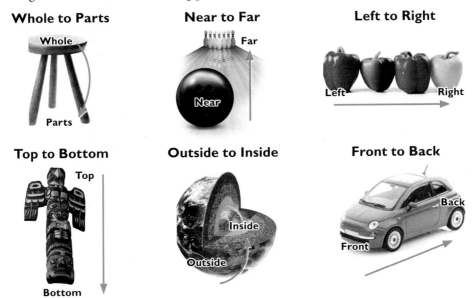

Whole to Parts

Whole

Parts

Near to Far

Far

Near

Left to Right

Left   Right

Top to Bottom

Top

Bottom

Outside to Inside

Inside

Outside

Front to Back

Back

Front

▌ Narrative Essays

An essay that tells a story—whether real or imagined—follows the classic story structure of exposition, rising action, climax, and resolution.

High

Level of Interest

Low

Exposition   Rising Action   Climax   Resolution

- **Exposition:** Set the scene, introduce the characters, and begin the action.
- **Rising action:** Depict a series of events with increasing interest.
- **Climax:** Reach a high point of interest, or turning point.
- **Resolution:** Wrap up the narrative, showing how the experience ends.

Explanatory Essays

An essay that explains a topic or shares information is usually organized in a hierarchical structure, moving from a general thesis, to main points, to supporting details.

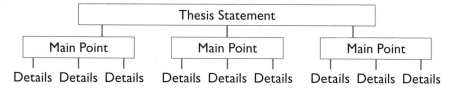

Cause-Effect Essays

An essay that traces the causes and effects of a certain situation follows a cause-focused or an effect-focused organization model. That means that either the causes are discussed first and then the overall effect, or the focus is on the effects rather than the causes.

Cause-Focused	**Effect-Focused**
Beginning	Beginning
Cause	Cause(s)
Cause	Effect
Cause	Effect
Effect(s)	Effect
Ending	Ending

Comparison-Contrast Essays

An essay that compares and contrasts two topics most often follows one of three organizational patterns.

Point-by-Point	**Subject-to-Subject**	**Similarities-Differences**
Beginning	Beginning	Beginning
Point 1 Subject 1 — Subject 2	Subject 1	Similarities
Point 2 Subject 1 — Subject 2	Subject 2	Differences
Point 3 Subject 1 — Subject 2		
Ending	Ending	Ending

Persuasive Essays

An essay that creates a logical argument or seeks to persuade the reader is organized according to how receptive or resistant the audience is to the position.

Receptive Audience	Resistant Audience
Beginning	Beginning
Most Important Reason	Objection and Answer
Less Important Reason	Less Important Reason
Objection and Answer	Most Important Reason
Ending	Ending

Problem-Solution Essays

An essay that presents a problem and argues for a specific solution follows one of two basic forms:

Solution-Focused	Problem-Focused
Introduce Solution	Introduce Problem
Outline Problem	Outline Problem
Outline Solution	Detail Problem
Promote Solution	Propose Solution
Enact Solution	Enact Solution

Writing the Closing Paragraph

The closing paragraph of your essay brings your ideas to a fitting conclusion. Use one or more of the following strategies:

Revisit your thesis statement.

> With its pageantry and rivalry, triumph and heartbreak, football allows us to indulge our taste for combat without actually declaring war. . . .

Sum up the information in the essay.

> Football is engineered to draw us together. Whether you view the spectacle in an oval stadium or in your own living-room theater, the game almost requires you to be surrounded by friends.

Leave the reader with a provocative final thought.

> If you still aren't convinced, consider this: Americans have so completely redesigned their favorite sport that it no longer resembles what the rest of the world calls "football."

Writer's Resource

Are you fearless in the face of writing assignments, ready to jump right in? Or are you worried by writing, looking for every excuse to put it off? In all probability, you fit somewhere in between these two writing personalities.

Actually, writing is work for everyone. It takes time. It involves searching, thinking, and attending to details. It is also one of the very best ways to discover, to think, to reveal who you are and what you know. In this chapter, you'll find answers to your questions about writing topics, techniques and terms, and the various forms of writing. It's a good place to look as you're wondering about that next writing assignment.

Preview

Review writing topics.
Consider writing techniques.
Examine writing terms.
Survey writing forms.

"There is nothing like looking, if you want to find something."

J. R. R. Tolkien, *The Hobbit*

Reviewing Writing Topics

When you need a writing topic, review the ideas on these two pages. Try one of the prompts below, select a topic from the facing page, or allow any one of these ideas to "suggest" some other topic to you.

Life and Times

My first memory
Getting my braces on/off
Meeting my friend
Saying good-bye
Learning a lesson
What family means
The last time I _____
A day to live over again
A night without sleep

Thoughts and Feelings

A scary dream
Most of all, I wish . . .
The future me
My invention
The definition of hope
Loneliness
Exhilaration
The meaning of respect

Best and Worst

The best meal I ever ate
The worst idea I ever had
My biggest accomplishment
My favorite season
The best email message
The most anticipated day

School Days

My favorite teacher
The big game
That unforgettable concert
The best field trip
Auditions for the play
How not to study
When I graduate . . .

People

My best friend
The stories of Uncle/Aunt _____
My next-door neighbor
My biggest inspiration
If I could trade lives with _____
Going to the doctor
My greatest hero/heroine
A female leader
My former self

Events

Last Thanksgiving
Homecoming
Prom
The big recital
The 4th of July
The wedding
Seeing _____ in concert
Mowing the lawn

Places

At the amusement park
A funny thing happened in . . .
My favorite vehicle
At the stadium
My escape
The spot that belongs to me

Questions

How can I be a good son/daughter?
What makes something funny?
Where would I most like to live?
How can we end hunger?
Who has helped me most?
Which are better pets, cats or dogs?
What new laws are needed?

Explanatory

How to . . . search the Internet, make spaghetti sauce, get a job, entertain a child, get in shape, study for a test, conserve energy, take a good picture

How to run . . . control . . . guide . . .
How to pick . . . tap . . . choose . . .
How to build . . . grow . . . create . . .
How to fix . . . clean . . . wash . . .
How to help . . . warn . . . save . . .

Causes of . . . climate change, snoring, inflation, shin splints, tornadoes, urban sprawl, poor grades, overpopulation

Kinds of . . . music, crowds, friends, teachers, love, rules, compliments, commercials, dreams, happiness, neighbors, pollution, heroes, vacations, pain

Definitions of . . . best friend, poverty, social networking, greed, loyalty, bioengineering, a team, literature, humor, courage, pressure, faith, personality, entertainment

Argumentation

School: study halls, final exams, a military career, teen centers, open lunch hours, girls on the football team, limiting the hours teens work during the school year

Community: curfews, volunteering, beautification projects, speed limits, planned development, teens in stores, church involvement

World: organ donation, capital punishment, gun control, courtroom television, political campaigns, political activism, Internet scams, Western imperialism, the War on Terror, systems of government

Narrative

In school: first memories, lunch hour, stage fright, learning to drive, odd field trips, asking for help, the big game, the school play, a school project

In life: just last week, on the bus, learning a lesson, a kind act, homesick, a big mistake, a reunion, getting lost, being late, Friday night, an embarrassing moment, staying overnight, getting hurt, success, a practical joke, being a friend, a family visit, on your own, moving, building a _____, the first day of _____, the last day of _____, a miserable time, cleaning up

Response to Readings and Art

Literature: a book I love, a book I'm supposed to love, a classic, the character I admire/despise most, the themes of _____, humor in _____, a haunting poem, the best novel to read on the beach (at home, on a train . . .)

Nonfiction: an article about discoveries in science, a report on the first _____, a convincing editorial, a strong rebuttal, an important law, the biography of a key person, a reliable study, an unreliable study

Film/play: the best films for _____, an amazing true-life play, dialogue vs. action, story vs. effects, an underrated film, a surprising documentary, a ground-breaking epic

Visual arts: a beautiful/tragic painting, a masterpiece of sculpture, my favorite artist, an influential movement, skyscrapers and skylines

Music: ten earworms, a tragic musician, the best song, how to write a hook, the playlist of my life

Considering Writing Techniques

Experiment with some of these techniques in your own stories and essays.

Allusion ▪ A reference to a familiar person, place, thing, or event

> I have feet that put Steven Spielberg's E.T. to shame. They are a tangle of toes held together by bunions.

Analogy ▪ A comparison of ideas or objects that are completely different but that are alike in one important way

> Benjamin Franklin witnessed the first successful balloon flight. When asked what good such an invention was, Franklin answered, "What good is a newborn baby?"

Anecdote ▪ A brief story used to illustrate or make a point

> In a passenger train compartment, a lady lit a cigarette, saying to Sir Thomas Beecham, a famous orchestra conductor, "I'm sure you don't object."
>
> "Not at all," replied Beecham, "provided you don't mind if I'm sick."
>
> "I don't think you know who I am," the lady pointed out. "I'm one of the railroad directors' wives."
>
> "Madam," said the conductor, "if you were the director's only wife, I should still be sick."

Antithesis ▪ Using opposite ideas to emphasize a point

> There was no possibility of being hired at the town's cotton gin or lumber mill, but maybe there was a way to make the two factories work for her.
> —Maya Angelou, *Wouldn't Take Nothing for My Journey Now*

Colloquialism ▪ A common word, phrase, or saying suitable for ordinary, everyday conversation but not for formal speech or writing

> Y'all listen up, now; it ain't over till it's over.

Exaggeration ▪ An overstatement or stretching of the truth to emphasize a point (See "Hyperbole" and "Overstatement.")

> The Danes are so full of *joie de vivre* [joy of life] that they practically sweat it.
> —Bill Bryson, *Neither Here nor There*

Flashback ▪ A technique in which a writer interrupts a story to go back and explain an earlier time or event for the purpose of making something in the present more clear

> In *The Outsiders*, readers first meet Ponyboy as he leaves a movie theater and is jumped by gang members. Later, the author goes back and explains what led up to the conflict.

Foreshadowing ▪ Hints or clues about what will happen next in a story

> Dulcie walked down the school steps and looked at the boiling sky. A voice inside her said, "Go back." She didn't, but two blocks later, she wished she had. Rain suddenly roared down ferociously from the swirling clouds, and the heavy drops pelted Dulcie as she ran. Then the rain stopped, and the air became deathly calm. "Get home," the voice said. "This is only the beginning." Then the voice went silent.

Hyperbole ▪ (hi-púr-bə-lē) Exaggeration used to emphasize a point (See "Exaggeration" and "Overstatement."

> We didn't need to [read] because my father has read everything . . . and people in town have said that talking to him about anything is better than reading three books.   —Cynthia Marshall Rich

Irony ▪ An expression in which the author says one thing but means just the opposite

> But then I was lucky enough to come down with the disease of the moment in the Hamptons, which was Lyme disease.   —Kurt Vonnegut

Juxtaposition ▪ Putting two words or ideas close together to create a contrasting of ideas or an ironic meaning

> Just remember, we're all in this alone.   —Lily Tomlin

Local color ▪ The use of details that are common in a certain place (The following passage lists foods common to small-town Southern life.)

> Folks had already brought over more cakes and pies, and platters of fried chicken and ham, and their good china bowls full of string beans, butter beans, okra, and tomatoes.   —Olive Ann Burns, *Cold Sassy Tree*

Metaphor ▪ A figure of speech that compares two things without using the words *like* or *as*

> Perfectionism is the voice of the oppressor, the enemy of the people.   —Anne Lamott, *Bird by Bird*

Overstatement ▪ An exaggeration or a stretching of the truth (See "Exaggeration" and "Hyperbole.")

> I bet you could set off dynamite in an A & P and the people would by and large keep reaching and checking oatmeal off their lists and muttering "Let me see, there was a third thing, began with an A, asparagus, no, ah, yes, applesauce!"   —John Updike, "A & P"

Oxymoron ▪ Connecting two words with opposite meanings

> jumbo shrimp   black light   controlled chaos

Paradox ▪ A true statement that says two opposite things

> The miniature, metal toy cars of the 1960s are no longer playthings.

Parallelism ▪ Repeating similar grammatical structures (words, phrases, or sentences) to give writing emphasis and rhythm

> All this waste happens before any lid is popped, any can is opened, or
> any seal is broken. —Allison Rozendaal, student writer

Personification ▪ A figure of speech in which a nonhuman thing is given human characteristics

> And what I remember next is how the moon, the pale moon with its one yellow
> eye . . . stared through the pink plastic curtains.
> —Sandra Cisneros, "One Holy Night"

Pun ▪ A phrase that uses words that sound the same in a way that gives them a funny effect

> I have come to believe that opposing gravity is something not to be
> taken—uh, lightly. —Daniel Pinkwater, "Why I Don't Fly"

Sensory details ▪ Details, experienced through the senses, that help readers see, feel, smell, taste, and hear what is being described

> I stood backstage, surrounded by giggles and rustling tulle. The smell
> of talcum powder, hairspray, and rosin rolled in from the stage. A familiar, acrid
> taste filled my mouth. The music rose, and the dancers swept onto the stage in a
> frothy swirl of pink and blue.

Simile ▪ A figure of speech that compares two things using the words *like* or *as*

> They [the old men] had hands like claws, and their knees were twisted like the
> old thorn trees. —William Butler Yeats

Symbol ▪ A concrete object used to represent an idea.

> hourglass = time passing   dove = peace

Synecdoche ▪ Using part of something to represent the whole.

> Idle hands are the devil's playground. (*Hands* represent the whole person.)

Understatement ▪ The opposite of *exaggeration*. By using very calm language, an author can bring special attention to an object or an idea.

> He [our new dog] turned out to be a good traveler, and except for an interruption
> caused by my wife's falling out of the car, the journey went very well.
> —E. B. White, "A Report in Spring"

Examining Writing Terms

The next two pages contain a glossary of terms used to describe different aspects of the writing process.

Argumentation: Writing or speaking in which a point of view is debated

Arrangement: The order in which details are placed in a piece of writing

Audience: Those people who read or hear what you have written

Balance: The even expression of ideas attained by using parallelism

Body: The main part that supports or develops the thesis statement in a piece of writing

Brainstorming: Collecting ideas by thinking freely about all the possibilities; used most often with groups

Case study: The in-depth story of one individual whose experiences speak for those of a larger group

Central idea: The main point of a piece of writing, often stated in a thesis statement or a topic sentence

Closing sentence: The sentence that summarizes the point being made in a paragraph

Coherence: The logical arrangement of ideas in writing

Deductive reasoning: A logical presentation of information, stating the main idea early in a piece of writing and following with supporting details

Description: Writing that paints a colorful picture of a topic

Details: Words used to describe a person, convince an audience, explain a process, and so on, often appealing to the senses

Editing: Checking your writing for the correct use of conventions

Emphasis: Highlighting the most important idea in a piece of writing by repeating it, giving it a prominent position, expanding upon it, and so on

Essay: A multiparagraph composition in which ideas on a special topic are presented, explained, argued for, or described

Explanatory writing: Writing that explains

Extended definition: Writing that offers an in-depth examination of a concept or term, including a personal definition, a negative definition (what it is not), example uses of the term, and so on

Figurative language: Language that goes beyond the actual meaning of the words being used

Focus: Concentrating on a specific aspect of a subject in writing, often called the *thesis*

Freewriting: Writing freely and rapidly, without any particular structure (**focused freewriting**: writing freely about a specific topic or angle)

Generalization: An idea emphasizing the general characteristics rather than the specific details of a subject

Grammar: The rules of a language for generating sentences; the system of inflections, syntax, and word formation

Idiom: A phrase or an expression that means something different from what the words actually say (using *over his head* for *didn't understand*)

Illustration: Using an experience to make a point or clarify an idea

Inductive reasoning: A logical presentation of information, stating specific examples and details early in a piece of writing and leading up to the main concluding idea

Inverted sentence: A sentence in which the normal word order is reversed or switched, usually placing the verb before the subject

Journal: Personal exploratory writing, often containing impressions and reflections and used as a source of ideas for other writing

Limiting the subject: Narrowing a general subject to a specific topic that is suitable for a writing assignment

Literal: The actual dictionary meaning of a word; language that means what it appears to mean

Loaded words: Words that are slanted for or against the subject

Logic: Correct reasoning; correctly using facts, examples, and reasons to support your point

Modifier: A word, phrase, or clause that limits or describes another word or group of words

Narration: Writing that tells a story or recounts an event

Objective: Relating information in an impersonal manner, without feeling or opinion (See "Subjective.")

Observation: Paying close attention to people, places, things, and events to collect details for later use

Overview: A general idea of what is or will be covered in a piece of writing.

Personal narrative: Writing that covers an event in the writer's life

Persuasion: Writing that is meant to change a reader's thinking or actions

Poetic license: The freedom a writer has to bend the rules of writing to achieve a certain effect

Point of view: The position or angle from which a story is told

Premise: A statement or central idea that serves as the basis of a discussion or a debate

Process: A method of doing something that involves several steps or stages

Profile: Writing that reveals an individual or re-creates a time period, using interviews and research

Proofreading: A final check for errors

Prose: Writing in the usual sentence form; as opposed to poetry, a condensed form that takes on rhyme and rhythm

Purpose: The specific reason or goal for a piece of writing

Reminiscence (Memoir): Writing that focuses on a memorable past experience

Report: An organized multiparagraph form of writing that contains facts about a topic

Revision: Changing a piece of writing to improve the content (ideas)

Subjective: Relating information in a personal way, including feelings, attitudes, and opinions (See "Objective.")

Syntax: The order and relationship of words within a sentence

Theme: The message in a piece of writing

Thesis statement: A statement of the purpose, intent, or main idea in an essay

Tone: The writer's attitude (serious, sarcastic, solemn, and so on) toward her or his subject

Topic: The specific subject of a writing assignment

Transitions: Words or phrases that tie ideas together

Unity: A sense of oneness in writing in which each sentence helps to develop the main idea

Universal: A topic or an idea that applies to everyone

Usage: The way in which words or phrases are used in a language, described as either standard (formal and informal) or nonstandard

Vivid details: Details that appeal to the senses and help the reader see, feel, smell, taste, or hear what the writer is describing

Voice: A writer's distinct, personal manner of expression

Surveying Writing Forms

The following chart classifies the forms of writing covered in this handbook. Experimenting with a variety of forms will broaden your understanding of writing.

Argument Writing (See pages 102–129.)

Arguing & Evaluating
(Judging the worth of something)
Reinforces critical thinking.

Essays of Argumentation ▪ Editorials
Essays of Opposing Ideas
Problem-Solution Essays
Position Papers

Explanatory Writing (See pages 130–157.)

Informing & Analyzing
(Sharing information)
Develops organizing skills.

Explanatory Essays ▪ Process Essays
Definition Essays ▪ Cause-Effect Essays
Comparison-Contrast Essays
Classification Essays ▪ Summaries
Research Papers

Writing About Literature (See pages 158–199.)

Understanding & Interpreting
(Reacting to texts)
Fosters critical reading.

Journal Entries ▪ Emails to an Author
Literature/Art Reviews ▪ Drama Reviews
Literary Analyses
Analyses of Informational Texts

Narrative Writing (See pages 200–209.)

Remembering & Sharing
(Exploring experiences)
Promotes writing fluency.

Journals ▪ Diaries ▪ Logs ▪ Notebooks
Personal Narratives and Essays
Freewriting ▪ Listing

Creative Writing (See pages 210–231.)

Inventing & Imitating
(Reshaping ideas)
Encourages creativity.

Stories ▪ Free Verse Poetry ▪ Sonnets
Haiku ▪ Plays

Writing in the Workplace (See pages 269–281.)

Questioning & Answering
(Writing to get a job done)
Builds real-world writing skills.

Request Letters ▪ Information Letters
Letters of Application ▪ Résumés
Email Messages ▪ Brochures

Writers INC

Argument Writing

Writing Essays of Argumentation

Developing essays of argumentation requires a thorough understanding of the topic and clear logical thinking. First you must learn all you can about your topic to establish a solid knowledge base. Then you must do these three things: (1) form a thoughtful opinion about the topic, (2) gather evidence to refine and support your opinion, and (3) analyze opposing points of view. Finally, you must connect all your thoughts in a convincing essay.

Your goal is to convince the reader to accept your point of view and rethink his or her ideas about the topic. With careful research and logical thought, that goal can be met. This chapter will show you how.

Learning Outcomes

Learn the basics.
Develop an essay of argumentation.
Avoid logical fallacies.
Read a sample essay.
Use an assessment rubric.

"The moment we want to believe something, we suddenly see all the arguments for it, and become blind to the arguments against it."

George Bernard Shaw

Learning the Basics

Recognize the parts of a formal argument: The elements listed below are defined according to their function in an essay of argumentation.

> The **main claim** is the controlling idea, or thesis, of the essay. You may argue that something is true, has value, or should be done.
>
> - **Reasons** are a claim's supporting points, which must be logical and strong enough to hold up to careful scrutiny.
> - **Evidence** includes details such as facts, statistics, examples, and definitions that illustrate and clarify the reasons.
> - **Opposing claims (arguments)** are worthy counterarguments that the writer can either **concede** or **counter**.
>   - To **concede** is to accept that an opposing claim has merit. (An effective concession can strengthen an argument.)
>   - To **counter** is to point out a critical flaw in an opposing claim. (An effective counter definitely strengthens an argument.)
> - A **call to action** is a request that the reader respond to the argument in a particular way, such as voting for a candidate or supporting a motion.

Understand the structure of a formal argument: Classic rhetoric is outlined below. Depending on your assignment, you may or may not follow this structure exactly. (Classical names for each part are given in *italics*.)

Beginning
- Introduce the subject and purpose of the writing. (*Exordium*)
- Set the scene for the argument. (*Narratio*)
- Offer your **claim**—the idea for which you will argue. (*Propositio*)

Middle
- Establish the rationale behind the claim and present logical **reasons** and **evidence** to support it. (*Confirmatio*)
- Address **opposing claims**—either **conceding** or **countering** them. (*Confutatio*)
- Return to your claim, refining or reinforcing it. (*Digressio*)

Ending
- Summarize the argument and, if appropriate, **call the reader to action**. (*Peroratio*)

Developing an Essay of Argumentation

When writing an argument, your goal is to help the reader understand and accept your position on an important topic. The quality of your argument depends on your ability to support your claim with relevant evidence and valid reasoning.

▌ Prewriting

1. Analyzing the rhetorical situation . . . To begin, identify the rhetorical elements for the assignment by answering the **STRAP** questions:

Subject: What is my subject and specific topic?

Type: What type or form of writing will I use (*editorial, position paper, project proposal*)?

Role: What role will I assume as writer (*teacher, student, citizen, employee*)?

Audience: Who is my intended audience (*instructor, classmates, general public*)?

Purpose: What is the goal or purpose of my writing (*to convince readers that something is true, has value, or needs to be done*)?

2. Selecting a topic . . . Often, you will be assigned to write an argument about a subject related to your course work. Choose a topic that is controversial (inspiring differing opinions) and specific enough to cover in an essay. The following chart shows the difference between topics that involve explanation alone and those that require argumentation.

Explanatory Essay Topics	Essay of Argumentation Topics
Factory farm operations	Importance of monitoring meat production in factory farms
Teaching English to immigrants via bilingual education	Benefits of bilingual education for both English language learners and mainstream students

3. Gathering information . . . Consult a variety of sources.

- **Books:** Your textbooks will provide a solid foundation, giving you the key facts about many topics.
- **Magazines and newspapers:** Newsmagazines (*Time, Newsweek, The Atlantic*) and newspapers will give you up-to-date information about current issues.
- **Web sites:** Refer to reliable sites on the Internet for information about your topic. (See page 366 for help.)
- **Personal resources:** Conduct surveys, carry out interviews, observe events, or attend conferences.

4. Forming a claim or position . . . After studying the information you have gathered, write a statement that establishes your position, the main claim of your argument. The following formula can help you form your main claim; your claim will serve as the thesis of your essay.

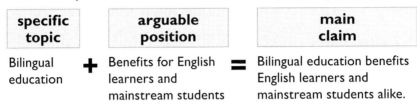

specific topic		**arguable position**		**main claim**
Bilingual education	**+**	Benefits for English learners and mainstream students	**=**	Bilingual education benefits English learners and mainstream students alike.

Claims fall into three main categories: claims of truth, claims of value, and claims of policy.

- **Claims of truth** state that an idea is or is not true.

  In the long run, bilingual students perform better in the classroom than students who receive English-only instruction.

- **Claims of value** state that something does or does not have worth.

  Bilingual education benefits English learners and mainstream students alike.

- **Claims of policy** state that something should or should not be done.

  Bilingual education should be promoted as the most appropriate form of education for English learners.

Help File

When you state your position, be certain you can effectively argue for it. For example, it may be hard to support an absolute position because few statements are always true in all circumstances. Qualifiers can make a position easier to support. Notice the difference between the following position statements.

Without bilingual education, English learners become overwhelmed and drop out of school.

Without bilingual education, **many** English learners become overwhelmed, and **some** drop out of school.

"Many" and "some" qualify the position, changing it from an all-or-nothing claim to one that is easier to support. Here are some other useful qualifiers:

almost	usually	maybe	probably
often	few	most	in most cases
if . . . then . . .	likely	may	frequently

5. Planning and organizing your thoughts . . .

After forming your position statement, decide on the best way to arrange your supporting details. You may use an outline or a graphic organizer for this purpose. The writer of the sample essay at the end of this chapter planned her essay with the sentence outline shown below. (The information is arranged in three main parts: background, reasons, and answers to opposing views.)

Sample Sentence Outline

Main claim Bilingual education benefits English learners and mainstream students.

Background

I. Bilingual education takes a variety of forms but has three main goals.
   A. Students should learn new academic skills.
   B. They should improve their native language skills.
   C. They should become proficient in English.

II. Bilingual education follows a clear process.
   A. Students begin learning in their native language.
   B. They next move to a sheltered classroom.
   C. When ready, students are mainstreamed.

Reasons

III. English learners deserve a fair chance.
   A. English-only classes make language acquisition difficult for English language learners.
   B. Holding students back sends the wrong message.

IV. Mainstream students benefit from bilingual education.
   A. Speaking two languages is highly valued.
   B. The United States is far behind in bilingual learning.

Answers to opposing views

V. Some see bilingual education as a threat.
   A. The goal of bilingual education is to move English learners into mainstream classrooms.
   B. Bilingualism is part of our heritage.

VI. Some people feel bilingual education sends the wrong message.
   A. However, immigrant parents feel it is essential that their children learn English.
   B. Bilingual education validates both English and native languages.

▌ Writing

6. Connecting your ideas . . . Create a beginning, a middle, and an ending for your essay. The structure shown below is based on the outline on the previous page. Consider using a similar pattern to guide your own writing.

Beginning Paragraph

- **Capture your reader's interest** and state your position or claim.

Middle Paragraphs

- **Explain your claim** and support it with reasons.
- **Provide evidence** to back up each reason.

- **Address important opposing arguments.** State the position and respond to it. (See "Help File.")
- Then **return to your claim.**

Ending Paragraph

- **Restate or summarize your argument** and offer final thoughts.

Help File

One way to strengthen your position is to address opposing viewpoints. You do so by stating these viewpoints and then responding to them. You can provide reasons that counter these opposing viewpoints, or you can concede some parts of them while supporting your own position. In the sample essay, the student writer counters one opposing viewpoint in this way:

> Some people are concerned that bilingual education is a threat to English and this country's traditions. This is not the case because . . .

The phrase "some people are concerned that" introduces the opposing point, and the information that follows provides an answer to it. Here are some useful expressions for addressing opposing views:

even though	I agree that	I accept the fact
while it is true that	admittedly	in some cases
I will admit	granted	occasionally

▌ Revising

7. Improving your writing . . . Carefully review your first draft. Ask a classmate to look over your essay as well. Then use the following questions to make changes that will strengthen your writing.

Traits

Ideas:	Have I selected a timely, controversial topic? Does my claim express a clear opinion? Have I provided reasons to support my position? Have I addressed other points of view? Have I used sound reasoning and avoided logical fallacies?
Organization:	Do I have a clear beginning, middle, and ending? Have I followed an effective organizational pattern? Have I used transitions to connect my ideas?
Voice:	Do I sound knowledgeable? Do I speak confidently, even when I consider other viewpoints?
Word choice:	Have I used specific nouns and active verbs? Have I used qualifiers to produce statements that can be supported?
Sentence fluency:	Do my sentences read smoothly? Have I varied my sentence beginnings and lengths?

▌ Editing and Proofreading

8. Checking for conventions . . . Check quotations and source citations for accuracy. Then ask yourself these questions:

Trait

Conventions:	Have I used punctuation and capitalization correctly throughout, especially with quotations? Have I checked for usage errors and other grammatical problems?

▌ Publishing

9. Finalizing your design . . . Ask yourself these questions:

Trait

Design:	Does my essay follow the design specifications from my instructor? Do I make effective use of margins, paragraphs, headings, typestyles, and graphics?

10. Preparing a final copy . . . Proofread your essay and share it with others. Did your argument change anyone's opinion about your topic?

Avoiding Logical Fallacies

To build a strong argument, you must draw logical conclusions from sound evidence. Learn to recognize and avoid these logical fallacies:

Appeal to Ignorance A person commits this fallacy by maintaining that because no one has ever proved a claim, it must be false. Appeals to ignorance unfairly shift the burden of proof to someone else.

> UFO's are real. There isn't a single scientific report that has ruled them out.

Appeal to Pity This fallacy may be used when a lawyer begs for leniency because his client's mother is ill, his brother is out of work, and so on. It can be heard in the classroom when a student says to the teacher, "May I have another day on this paper? I worked till my eyeballs fell out, but it's still not done."

> Imagine what it must have been like for him. If anyone deserves a break, he does.

Bandwagon Another form of false logic is the appeal to everyone's sense of wanting to belong or be accepted. By suggesting that everyone else is doing this or wearing that or going here or there, you can avoid the real question—"Is this idea or claim valid?"

> Everyone on the team wears brand X shoes. They must be the very best basketball shoes available.

Broad Generalization A broad generalization is a claim that is based on too little evidence and allows no exceptions. In jumping to a conclusion, the writer may use intensifiers such as *all*, *every*, or *never*.

> All teenagers spend too much time texting.

Circular Thinking This fallacy occurs when you assume the truth of the very point you are trying to prove. It takes the reader in circles without offering specific evidence.

> Mr. Baldwin's class is a great class because fundamentally it is one of the best classes there is. (But what's "great" about the class itself?)

Either-Or Thinking Either-or thinking consists of reducing a solution to two possible extremes: "America: Love it or leave it." "Put up or shut up." This logical fallacy eliminates all the possibilities in the middle.

> Either this community votes to build a new school, or the quality of education will drop dramatically.

False Cause This well-known fallacy confuses cause and effect. If *A* comes before *B*, *A* must have caused *B*. However, *A* may be one of several causes, or not a cause at all.

> Since that new community center opened, truancy has gone up in several schools. It should never have been built in the first place.

Half-Truths One of the most misleading forms of faulty thinking is telling only part of the truth. This is especially misleading because it leaves out "the rest of the story." Such a statement is partly true and untrue at the same time.

> Recycling is bad because it costs more than just dumping stuff in a landfill. (Maybe so; but recycling may also help save the environment.)

Oversimplification Beware of phrases like "It all comes down to . . . " or "It's a simple question of . . . " Almost no dispute is "a simple question." Anyone who believes, for example, that capital punishment "all comes down to" protecting society ought to question a doctor, an inmate on death row, the inmate's family, or a religious leader for other points of view.

> Capital punishment is a simple question of protecting society.

Red Herring This strange term comes from the practice of dragging a stinky fish across a trail to throw tracking dogs off the scent. In a similar way, readers can be distracted from the real issue when the writer interjects an unrelated or emotionally charged idea.

> Just as the infamous oil spill of the Exxon Valdez led to massive animal deaths and enormous environmental problems, drilling in the National Wildlife Refuge poses serious problems.

Slanted Language By choosing words that carry strong positive or negative connotations, a person can distract attention from the valid arguments being made.

> No one in his right mind would ever do anything that dumb.

Slippery Slope This fallacy suggests that if one thing happens, other things are sure to happen as well. In other words, one step begins an unstoppable chain of events.

> If we grant legal status to illegal immigrants, we'll have to pardon all kinds of other illegal things.

Straw Man In this fallacy, the writer exaggerates or misrepresents the opponent's position.

> Those who consider themselves caring people can't possibly approve of the death penalty.

Testimonial You can take Neil deGrasse Tyson's word on the composition of Saturn's rings, but the moment he starts promoting a product, watch out! If the testimonial or statement comes from a recognized authority in the field, great. If it comes from a person famous in another field, it may well be unreliable.

> This year's Super Bowl MVP recently said, "I've tried every cold medicine on the market, and—believe me—nothing works like No Cold."

Reading a Sample Essay

In this essay, student writer Noelle Green argues in favor of bilingual education. She follows the plan she outlined earlier.

Speaking in Two Worlds

The beginning introduces the topic and states the main claim, or position (underlined).

Getting a good education means being taught the skills that are needed to find success after graduation. A good education would never mean losing valuable skills. Unfortunately, that's what can happen to many immigrant students. They often lose their native language while they learn English. In an age in which knowing two languages is so valued, bilingual education is more important than ever. <u>Bilingual education benefits English learners and mainstream students alike.</u>

Background information is provided.

Bilingual education takes a variety of forms but has three main goals: to teach English learners new academic skills, to help them keep and improve their native language skills, and to ensure that they become proficient in English. This process can take anywhere from one to six years and can be carried out in many different ways. Initially, English learners can be taught in their native language while they take English-as-a-second-language classes. Then they move into "sheltered" classes where translation is used as needed. Once English learners become proficient, they are taught in mainstream English classes. It is important not to do this too quickly or students might lose their native language in the process. According to a recent study by the United States Department of Education, students perform better in the long run when they are fluent in both their native language and English (Ramirez et al. 9).

Main reasons in support of the position are provided.

All students deserve a fair chance to learn no matter what their background. The National Association for Bilingual Education (NABE) explains that alternatives like "English-only" classes or "sink-or-swim" methods are unfair. Immigrant students are often held back a grade or more—not because they aren't smart enough, but because they struggle to learn new academic skills and English at the same time. Many students become overwhelmed, and some drop out of school. High dropout rates have a negative impact on our whole society (Krashen).

Mainstream students in this country also can benefit from bilingual education. They have the opportunity to participate in sheltered classes with English learners to learn a second language. In today's global market, bilingual ability is highly valued. The United States falls far behind

other nations in terms of training students to be bilingual. This is partly because many immigrants feel pressure to learn English at the price of losing their native language. Why not use the foreign language resource immigrants bring to this nation to help all students learn a second language (Snow and Hakuta 386)?

The writer answers opposing viewpoints.

Some people are concerned that bilingual education is a threat to English language usage and this country's traditions. This is not the case because the ultimate goal is to teach English learners in mainstream English classes. James Crawford, author of *Hold Your Tongue*, writes that "bilingualism is as American as apple pie—and has been ever since this nation's beginnings." After all, members of the Continental Congress rejected John Adams's proposal to make English the national language because they felt it threatened democracy and freedom. They realized that what brought the people of this nation together was not race, culture, religion, or language, but a shared desire to live in a land of liberty and equality.

A direct quotation is cited. (The works-cited page is not shown.)

Another argument against bilingual education is that it sends the wrong message to immigrants. The claim is that immigrants will think they don't need to learn English. However, the American Civil Liberties Union cites a study in which "98% of Latinos surveyed said they felt it is 'essential' that their children learn to read and write English 'perfectly'" (qtd. in Fishman 82). Bilingual education provides the English education that immigrants want. At the same time, bilingual education validates their native language and gives them a sense of pride in their heritage.

The ending paragraph solidifies the writer's position.

The United States welcomes immigrants with the promise of opportunity, equality, freedom, and a better life. Bilingual education is the best way to fulfill that promise for immigrant students. It validates and celebrates the newcomers' cultures while teaching them the skills they will need to be successful in this country. At the same time, mainstream students in this country have the chance to attain highly valued bilingual skills, right from the source. Bilingual education teaches newcomers not only English but also the language of freedom and equality for all. That's a language everyone can understand.

Using an Assessment Rubric

Use this rubric as a checklist to evaluate your essays of argumentation. The rubric is arranged according to important standards of effective writing.

The writing . . .

Ideas

____ addresses a timely, debatable topic.

____ presents a clear claim and logical argument.

____ respectfully addresses opposing claims.

____ develops the argument with strong, reliable evidence.

Organization

____ follows a plan that logically presents claims, counterclaims, reasons, and evidence.

____ uses linking words and transitions to connect ideas.

Voice

____ speaks in an objective tone appropriate for the purpose.

____ demonstrates the writer's knowledge about the topic.

Word Choice

____ uses specific nouns and verbs.

____ uses words with the appropriate level of formality.

____ defines and explains unfamiliar terms.

Sentence Fluency

____ creates a smooth flow of ideas from sentence to sentence.

____ uses sentences with the appropriate level of formality.

Conventions

____ uses correct punctuation, capitalization, spelling, and grammar.

____ accurately quotes and cites sources.

Design

____ follows the specifications provided by the instructor.

____ makes good use of white space, headings, and graphics.

Other Forms of Argumentation

Some of the most meaningful movements in American history have begun with solidly built arguments. The ideas shared in Thomas Paine's *Common Sense* or Dr. Martin Luther King Jr.'s "I Have a Dream" speech certainly got America's attention. Because democracy depends on free speech and open debate, argumentation is essential to its success. And that's why it's important that you and all citizens, young and old, know how to write and speak effectively.

It's also important to understand that persuading people to change their minds on an important issue is not easy. Your argument needs to be clear, logical, practical, and—most of all—convincing. Knowing how to present your argument effectively will give you the persuasive edge you need.

Learning Outcomes

Write an editorial.
Develop a position paper.
Create an essay of opposing ideas.
Develop a problem-solution essay.
Respond to a prompt.

"Truth springs from argument amongst friends."
David Hume

Writing an Editorial

An editorial presents a brief essay of opinion about a timely and important topic. It may suggest a new course of action or a possible solution to a problem. When writing an editorial, state your position clearly and directly and provide solid reasons to support it.

Prewriting

1. **Analyzing the rhetorical situation** . . . Answer the **STRAP** questions (see page 30) to identify your **S**ubject, the **T**ype of writing (editorial), your **R**ole as a writer, your **A**udience, and your **P**urpose (to persuade).

2. **Selecting a topic** . . . If you don't already have a topic in mind, try reading a few stories in your local newspaper. You may also choose some general categories—school, sports, entertainment, environment—as headings and then list current topics under each. Finally, select one topic that you have strong feelings about.

3. **Gathering details** . . . Jot down everything you know and feel about your topic. Then do research to find additional information.

4. **Focusing your thoughts** . . . Review the details you have gathered and write an opinion statement telling how you feel about the topic. Then use a table diagram to list reasons that support your opinion. Also consider opposing arguments to counter.

Writing and Revising

5. **Connecting your ideas** . . . Build your argument in the most logical way. That may mean saving your best point for last. Remember that editorials published in a newspaper use a strong, to-the-point style and brief paragraphs.

6. **Improving your writing** . . . Review your first draft, paying special attention to ideas, organization, and voice. Ask yourself these questions: *Do I clearly state my opinion? Do I support it well? Do I sound sincere and confident?* Add, cut, and rearrange ideas as needed.

7. **Improving your style** . . . Consider your word choice and sentence fluency. Use the right words and vary your sentence lengths and beginnings to clearly communicate your opinion.

Editing and Proofreading

8. **Checking for conventions** . . . Check for errors in punctuation, mechanics, usage, and grammar. Use the rubric on page 114 as a final review of your revising and editing.

9. **Preparing a final copy** . . . Write or type a neat final copy of your essay and proofread it before sharing it.

Editorial

The writer of this editorial argues that art classes actually improve student performance in other areas. She cites several sources (works-cited page not shown).

Let There Be Art

The editorial opens with urgent news and a clear opinion (underlined).

The Clintondale School Board is proposing to eliminate art classes next year. Last week's *Clintondale Gazette* quotes the board president, Bill Howland, as saying, "The board needs to decide which programs are necessary and which ones are not" (A5). Superintendent Melvin Ambrose adds that the district should focus on preparing students for exit exams. These concerns are important, but the board should consider just how necessary art really is for students' success.

First of all, art improves visual literacy. The International Visual Literacy Association defines visual literacy as a group of competencies "fundamental to normal human learning" (Avgerinou). Art helps students better understand visual information presented in math, science, English, and social studies. Art also equips students to understand the images they see on TV and the Internet. In addition, art teaches students how to present their ideas in a visual way. Whether they are creating graphs for science or diagrams for social studies, students need art.

Middle paragraphs share supporting reasons.

Art also prepares students for business. The Business Circle for Arts Education in Oklahoma states the following: "Businesses understand that art education strengthens student problem-solving and critical-thinking skills . . ." ("Facts"). Art courses require students to solve problems in order to create a finished project. This project-based training is important in the real world, where employers ask workers to come up with creative solutions to problems.

What about those all-important tests? Who needs art to pass them? James Catterall, education professor at UCLA, says that students who are highly involved in the arts have higher standardized test scores than those who are not as involved. Results on college entrance exams like the SAT show a similar pattern. Dr. Catterall adds that this trend applies to students of all economic levels, including those from low-income backgrounds (Leroux and Grossman).

The closing personalizes and revisits the opinion.

My own experience in art supports what these experts are saying. I learn best by doing. Of course, the school board has to figure out how to stretch school funds, but it should be careful not to make cuts that will do more harm than good. Preserving art in the schools is a necessity.

Developing a Position Paper

Your goal in a position paper is to trace your particular line of thinking on an issue. Rather than argue for or against something, you will inform, explain, analyze, and speculate.

Prewriting

1. **Analyzing the rhetorical situation . . .** Answer the **STRAP** questions (see page 30) to identify your **Subject**, the **Type** of writing (position paper), your **Role** as a writer, your **Audience**, and your **Purpose** (to consider).

2. **Selecting a topic . . .** The best position papers deal with debatable issues. Current events, especially controversial ones, can provide excellent topic choices. Think about new trends in subject areas that interest you—science, technology, medicine, health, politics, fashion, music, or entertainment. Your topic must have at least two sides to debate.

3. **Gathering details . . .** Once you have selected a topic, look in books, newspapers, magazines, and on Web sites for information. Also watch news reports and documentaries about the topic and consider primary sources of information such as interviews, museum exhibits, and original documents.

4. **Focusing your thoughts . . .** Form a position statement, which is similar to an opinion statement, except that it emphasizes *ideas* rather than an *opinion*. Your position statement should (1) show knowledge of the topic and (2) provide a specific perspective.

Writing and Revising

5. **Connecting your ideas . . .** Create an opening paragraph that gets the reader's attention and states your position. Develop your middle paragraphs with main points and supporting details. Evaluate differing views and further establish your position. End your paper by expanding upon your position—stating it in a new way, applying it to life, or predicting the issue's implications for the future.

6. **Improving your writing . . .** Carefully review your first draft, paying special attention to ideas, organization, and voice. Ask yourself: *Do I have a clear position statement? Have I effectively supported my position?*

7. **Improving your style . . .** Check your word choice and sentence fluency to produce a clear, easy-to-read essay.

Editing and Proofreading

8. **Checking for conventions . . .** Review your writing for errors in punctuation, mechanics, and grammar.

9. **Preparing a final copy . . .** Finalize the essay's design and share a neat copy.

Position Paper

The following position paper appeared in the *New York Times* on August 9, 2010. At the time, Kennedy Odede, the executive director of Shining Hope for Communities, a social services organization, was a junior at Wesleyan University.

Slumdog Tourism

The opening introduces the concept and provides background.

Slum tourism has a long history—during the late 1800s, lines of wealthy New Yorkers snaked along the Bowery and through the Lower East Side to see "how the other half lives."

But with urban populations in the developing world expanding rapidly, the opportunity and demand to observe poverty firsthand have never been greater. The hot spots are Rio de Janeiro, Mumbai—thanks to "Slumdog Millionaire," the film that started a thousand tours—and my home, Kibera, a Nairobi slum that is perhaps the largest in Africa.

Slum tourism has its advocates, who say it promotes social awareness. And it's good money, which helps the local economy.

The fourth paragraph powerfully presents the position (underlined).

But it's not worth it. Slum tourism turns poverty into entertainment, something that can be momentarily experienced and then escaped from. People think they've really "seen" something—and then go back to their lives and leave me, my family and my community right where we were before.

I was 16 when I first saw a slum tour. I was outside my 100-square-foot house washing dishes, looking at the utensils with longing because I hadn't eaten in two days. Suddenly a white woman was taking my picture. I felt like a tiger in a cage. Before I could say anything, she had moved on.

The writer shares anecdotes that help the reader to understand.

When I was 18, I founded an organization that provides education, health and economic services for Kibera residents. A documentary filmmaker from Greece was interviewing me about my work. As we made our way through the streets, we passed an old man defecating in public. The woman took out her video camera and said to her assistant, "Oh, look at that."

For a moment I saw my home through her eyes: feces, rats, starvation, houses so close together that no one can breathe. I realized I didn't want her to see it, didn't want to give her the opportunity to judge my community for its poverty—a condition that few tourists, no matter how well intentioned, could ever understand.

Another anecdote captures a stark moment.

Other Kibera residents have taken a different path. A former schoolmate of mine started a tourism business. I once saw him take a group into the home of a young woman giving birth. They stood and watched as she screamed. Eventually the group continued on its tour, cameras loaded with images of a woman in pain. What did they learn? And did the woman gain anything from the experience?

To be fair, many foreigners come to the slums wanting to understand poverty, and they leave with what they believe is a better grasp of our desperately poor conditions. The expectation, among the visitors and the tour organizers, is that the experience may lead the tourists to action once they get home.

But it's just as likely that a tour will come to nothing. After all, looking at conditions like those in Kibera is overwhelming, and I imagine many visitors think that merely bearing witness to such poverty is enough.

The writer revisits the position statement.

Nor do the visitors really interact with us. Aside from the occasional comment, there is no dialogue established, no conversation begun. Slum tourism is a one-way street: They get photos; we lose a piece of our dignity.

Slums will not go away because a few dozen Americans or Europeans spent a morning walking around them. There are solutions to our problems—but they won't come about through tours.

Help File

Since your position statement is crucial to your paper, take extra time to get it right. This checklist can help you refine your statement. Keep working on it until you can check off each item.

Position Statement Checklist

My position statement . . .

_____ identifies a limited, specific topic.

_____ shows knowledge of the topic.

_____ provides a specific perspective.

_____ is stated clearly and directly.

_____ can be supported by facts and interpretations.

_____ meets the requirements of the assignment.

Creating an Essay of Opposing Ideas

An essay of opposing ideas explains two different points of view about an important issue. The essay shows both sides fairly, not arguing for one or the other, and works well to explain any controversy.

▌ Prewriting

1. **Analyzing the rhetorical situation . . .** Answer the **STRAP** questions (see page 30) to identify your **S**ubject, the **T**ype of writing, your **R**ole as a writer, your **A**udience, and your **P**urpose for writing.

2. **Selecting a topic . . .** In a small group or on your own, produce a list of some of the hottest topics in your world—grades, driving, college, underage drinking, relationships, the generation gap, culture clash, and so forth. Review your list for potential topics, choosing one that truly interests you.

3. **Gathering details . . .** After you choose a topic, collect information using this strategy: Fold a piece of paper in two, lengthwise. On the left side, list facts and details related to one point of view. On the right, list facts related to the other point of view.

4. **Focusing your thoughts . . .** Review your information and think about how to focus your essay. Ask yourself these questions: *How can I show both sides of the issue? How can I fairly balance the arguments? What message do I want to send?*

▌ Writing

5. **Connecting your ideas . . .** Create an opening paragraph that introduces the issue and states your thesis. Develop middle paragraphs that explain each main viewpoint. Write a closing paragraph that summarizes the topic and leaves the reader with a final thought.

▌ Revising

6. **Improving your writing . . .** Carefully review your first draft, paying special attention to ideas, organization, and voice. Ask yourself this question: *Have I addressed both viewpoints fairly and completely?* Revise as necessary.

7. **Improving your style . . .** Check your word choice and sentence fluency to produce a clear, easy-to-read essay.

▌ Editing and Proofreading

8. **Checking for conventions . . .** Review your writing for errors in punctuation, mechanics, usage, and grammar.

9. **Preparing a final copy . . .** Finalize the design of your essay and make a neat copy to share.

Essay of Opposing Ideas

In this essay, the writer examines a critical national debate—securing American borders against terrorism. Notice that the writer presents both sides of the debate in an evenhanded way. (The works-cited page is not shown.)

On the Border

The opening introduces the topic and states the thesis (underlined).

Terrorism is a relatively new threat in the United States. Before the first attack on the World Trade Center in 1993, foreign terrorists had not successfully attacked a target on United States soil. Other countries—including Russia, Spain, and the United Kingdom—have had decades of experience dealing with terrorists. But since the horrific second attack on the World Trade Center, defending our borders against terrorists has emerged as a key issue in America. However, some people are concerned that tighter security may jeopardize American freedoms. So a critical debate has developed between those individuals who want tighter immigration policies and those who are concerned about the negative effects such policies could have on the American way of life.

Points of agreement are identified.

Some basic reforms of the immigration system are clearly needed. For example, the United States should tighten its border security by providing border control with increased technology, infrastructure, and personnel. The immigration department also needs to document visiting aliens more closely and identify those foreign visitors known to have questionable intentions concerning the United States. Few people would dispute reforms like these.

One side of the debate is examined.

Such measures, however, don't go far enough for some people. An editorial in the *Chatterton Daily News* recently said that the threat of terror "demands that the United States completely revamp its immigration policy and restrict the rights of aliens to travel within this country" (Davis A23). Those who demand tighter security want immigrants to be required to show the proper paperwork to receive public services. They also back "English-only" laws that proclaim English as the only official language in this country. In what seems to be the ultimate restriction, some individuals are asking for a moratorium on all legal immigration.

Some of these proposed changes will affect the way that United States citizens go about their lives. A few states already require people to prove that they are citizens in order to register to vote. In addition, they require all voters to present an official picture ID every time they vote. If, as some people suggest, citizens are required to carry national photo IDs, the country would begin to resemble a police state rather than "the land of the free and the home of the brave."

The other side of the debate is examined.

Those concerned with maintaining the American way of life believe that such restrictions take away the freedoms of citizens and immigrants alike. The United States has always been a nation of immigrants. Severely restricting immigration simply seems un-American. Such folk argue that if terrorism forces the United States to surrender its free society, the terrorists will have won. Then there are those who suggest that tighter restrictions could harm the American economy. Tighter restrictions, they reason, would turn away legal foreign business partners, tourists, students, and honest immigrants. That is why Daniel Griswold from the Cato Institute suggests that we refrain from any drastic measures: "We should post a yield sign on the Statue of Liberty, not a stop sign." The economy in this country depends on open borders.

The United States Department of Homeland Security acknowledges that balancing immigration with the threat of terrorism is a challenge. The department's goal is "to secure our borders while respecting the privacy of our visitors . . . helping us demonstrate that we remain a welcoming nation and that we can keep America's doors open and our nation secure" ("US-VISIT"). In other words, terrorism must be prevented as much as freedom must be protected.

The closing puts the debate into perspective.

No one knows for sure how this debate will play itself out. But in time, measures will likely be enacted to protect our country as effectively as possible while still welcoming legitimate, productive immigrants— whether their names be Nguyen, O'Connor, Gonzales, or Al-Hewar. That would be the American way as established by our founders.

Developing a Problem-Solution Essay

A problem-solution essay provides the reader with a detailed analysis of a topic—from a clear statement of the problem to a full discussion of possible solutions. It is important to examine your topic from a number of different angles before proposing any solutions.

Prewriting

1. **Analyzing the rhetorical situation . . .** Answer the **STRAP** questions (see page 30) to identify your **S**ubject, the **T**ype of writing, your **R**ole as a writer, your **A**udience, and your **P**urpose for writing.

2. **Selecting a topic . . .** If your assignment is related to a specific course, review your text and class notes for possible topics. Otherwise, think about the things students complain about most: homework, school spirit, jobs, grades, and so on. Or consider problems that have come up recently in your neighborhood or in your personal life.

3. **Gathering details . . .** Write out your problem in a clear statement. Then research it thoroughly, collecting information about its history and causes. List possible solutions. Consider why different solutions may or may not work well.

4. **Focusing your thoughts . . .** Review your research to decide if the problem is manageable and if you have found enough information to write intelligently about it. (You may need to gather more facts and statistics.)

Writing

5. **Connecting your ideas . . .** Open your essay with background information that will help the reader grasp the subject. Continue to develop your first draft, discussing the problem and possible solutions clearly and completely.

Revising

6. **Improving your writing . . .** Review your first draft for ideas, organization, and voice. Ask yourself these questions: *Will the reader believe the problem is serious? Will the reader believe my solution will work? Do I sound knowledgeable?* Add, cut, and rework ideas as needed.

7. **Improving your style . . .** Check the sentences and words in your essay to make sure they communicate your ideas.

Editing and Proofreading

8. **Checking for conventions . . .** Check for errors in punctuation, mechanics, usage, and grammar. Use the rubric on page 114.

9. **Preparing a final copy . . .** Finalize your essay's design and make a neat copy to share.

Problem-Solution Essay

In this essay, student writer Terrance Masters discusses the very real problem of conflict and violence in schools. He tries to convince the reader of the seriousness of the problem and the value of his solution. (The works-cited page is not shown.)

A quotation helps the reader focus on the problem.

The opening identifies the problem and introduces the solution (underlined).

A key point from a report is paraphrased.

Another key point is quoted.

Grace Under Fire

"The passions are the same in every conflict, large or small."

—Mason Cooley

Two friends have an argument that breaks up their friendship forever, even though neither one can remember how the whole thing got started. This tragedy happens over and over in high schools across the country. Conflict may be unavoidable, but when people lose sight of the real issues, their arguments can become personal and spiral out of control. In fact, according to "Youth Violence," a report by the surgeon general, "In our country today, the greatest threat to the lives of children and adolescents is not disease or starvation or abandonment, but the terrible reality of violence" (2). Given that this is the case, why aren't students taught to manage conflict the way they are taught to solve math problems, drive cars, or stay physically fit? The best solution to the problem of youth violence is to teach students strategies for conflict resolution.

First of all, students need to realize that conflict is inevitable. In the report "Violence Among Middle School and High School Students," the United States Department of Justice indicates that most violent incidents between students begin with "a relatively minor affront but escalate from there" (2). In other words, a fight could start over the fact that one student eats a peanut butter sandwich each lunchtime. Laughter over the sandwich can lead to insults, which in turn can lead to violence. The problem isn't in the sandwich, but in the way students deal with the conflict. They need to learn that conflicts may be unavoidable, but they also can provide an opportunity to improve friendships. According to www.safeyouth.gov, "If resolved positively, conflicts can actually help strengthen relationships and build greater understanding."

Once students recognize that conflict is inevitable, they can practice the golden rule of conflict resolution: stay calm. Escalation begins with strong emotions. Pausing a moment to take a deep breath inflates the lungs and deflates the conflict. A person can also maintain control by intentionally relaxing his or her face and body. After all, in any conflict, it is better to look "cool" than "hot." Once the student feels calmer, he or she should choose words that will calm the other person down as well. Profanity, name-calling, accusations, and exaggerations only add fuel to the emotional fire. On the other hand, neutral words spoken at a normal volume can quench the fire before it explodes out of control.

The solution is carefully analyzed.

After both sides have calmed down, they can enact another key strategy for conflict resolution: listening. Listening allows the two sides to understand each other. One person should describe his or her side, and the other person should listen without interrupting. Afterward, the listener can ask nonthreatening questions to clarify the speaker's position. Then the two people should reverse roles.

Finally, students need to consider what they are hearing. This doesn't mean trying to figure out what's wrong with the other person. It means understanding what the real issue is and what both sides are trying to accomplish. For example, a shouting match over a peanut butter sandwich might happen because one person thinks the other person is unwilling to try new things. Students need to ask themselves questions such as these: *How did this start? What do I really want? What am I afraid of? How can this conflict be resolved?* As the issue becomes clearer, the conflict often simply fades away. Even if it doesn't, careful thought helps both sides figure out a mutual solution.

The closing revisits the problem and expands on the solution.

There will always be conflict in schools, but that doesn't mean there needs to be violence. When students in Atlanta instituted a conflict resolution program, "64 percent of the teachers reported less physical violence in the classroom; 75 percent of the teachers reported an increase in student cooperation; and 92 percent of the students felt better about themselves" (www.esrnational.org). Learning to resolve conflicts can help students deal with friends, teachers, parents, bosses, and coworkers. In that way, conflict resolution is a fundamental life skill that should be taught in schools across the country.

Responding to a Prompt

Argumentative prompts ask you to state and support a thesis about a timely, debatable topic. You may be asked to share your opinion about an issue, discuss your position on it, present a solution to a problem, and so on. The information you present must be logical, clear, and persuasive. Quickly work through the writing process to prepare your best response.

▌ Prewriting

    1. Analyzing the writing prompt . . . Answer the **STRAP** questions:

        Subject: What topic will I write about?

        Type: What form will my writing take?

        Role: What role will I assume as writer?

        Audience: Who will read my writing?

        Purpose: What is the goal of my writing?

    2. Outlining your response . . . Write down the main point of your answer and quickly list supporting details. Keep the purpose of your response in mind—sharing an opinion, presenting a solution, discussing your position, and so on. Use an appropriate organizational pattern.

▌ Writing

    3. Crafting an opening paragraph . . . Introduce your topic and lead up to your thesis statement.

    4. Building middle paragraphs . . . Write a topic sentence for each main point and include body sentences that support it.

    5. Using transitions . . . Connect paragraphs and sentences using transitions that indicate time, importance, cause and effect, and so on. (See pages 86–88.)

    6. Drafting a closing paragraph . . . Conclude your response by revisiting your thesis and leaving the reader with an interesting final thought.

▌ Revising

    7. Reviewing the prompt using STRAP . . . Reexamine your **STRAP** analysis to be certain you have accurately answered the prompt.

    8. Revising your answer . . . Check the ideas, organization, voice, words, and sentences of your writing. Make whatever improvements are necessary to strengthen your work.

▌ Editing

    9. Checking for conventions . . . Check your answer to eliminate errors in punctuation, capitalization, spelling, usage, and grammar.

Argumentative Prompt and Response

Prompt

Some students feel they can't make a positive difference in their communities. Think of problems in your own community. Write a letter to the editor of your local newspaper arguing for ways that fellow students can make a difference.

Outline

My fellow students and I need to make life better in our communities.
— Donate to homeless center.
— Care for the park.
— Being pleasant.
We're inheriting the world and need to show we're ready.

Response

The beginning catches the reader's interest and leads to the position (underlined).

Dear Editor:

    Americans like to complain. It's our right, enshrined in the First Amendment of the Constitution. It's our nature. Most of the first settlers of this country arrived here because of deep dissatisfaction with the way things were going in the old country. They were sick of religious persecution or of governmental tyranny or of lack of opportunity, and they got on a boat to change their world. They took their complaints and did something about them, something to make life better. <u>My fellow students and I know about the complaining part, and now it's time we do the "make life better" part.</u>

    Our city has a problem with homelessness. Students often complain about the people sleeping in doorways and begging on the corner, but how often do we do something to help? There are three shelters that need pantry donations. If each high school student gave something to the Student Council food drive this Friday, all the shelters would have enough to get through October. If one in ten students volunteered once a week to help at a shelter, the shortage of volunteers would be solved. Come on, people! The solutions aren't hard. It's just a matter of saying "yes."

Our city also has a problem with garbage in the park. Budgets for park maintenance were slashed two years ago, and Central Park has been declining ever since. Often, plastic bags and cigarette butts line the walkway, and someone even threw a picnic table into the lake. Here's the first way to help: Don't trash your own park! Throw your garbage in a garbage can, and don't vandalize. Here's a second way: Fix what problems you find. My friend Tom and I waded into the lake and pulled the table out, and more than once, I've righted a garbage can that someone had knocked over. Here's a third way: The city is having a park cleanup on the Saturday before Halloween. Just show up, and you'll get bags and gloves to help fix the spot for all of us. And you can apply those community-service hours toward graduation.

How else can we students make a difference in our community? How about by being pleasant? Greet people when you walk down the sidewalk. Wish them a good day. I've found that people who look at me suspiciously because I'm a teenager give me a different look after I've said, "Beautiful day." For those teens who feel they can't make a positive difference in the community, I ask, "Can you smile?" Sometimes, that's all it takes.

So, we can stop complaining about the world as it is and start changing it into the world we want it to be. After all, we're going to be in charge soon. Everything will be in our hands, the good and the bad. If we put in a little work now, the world we receive will be in better shape. And by putting in that work, we'll make the connections and learn the skills we need to succeed. We're the pioneers of our own futures.

Middle paragraphs suggest ways that students can make a difference.

The ending paragraph restates the position and connects it to the future.

Writers INC

Explanatory Writing

Writing Explanatory Essays

As a student, you will often be asked to do explanatory writing. It usually involves doing some research about a topic and then explaining what you have learned in writing. Anytime you inform, examine, discuss, or interpret, you are doing explanatory writing. You may write an essay or article, prepare a report, or explain a procedure.

Successful explanatory writing includes quality information from beginning to end. It offers a main idea, or thesis, which identifies an important aspect of the topic. Then it supports the thesis with a set of points, each of which is explained with details (statistics, quotations, paraphrases, and so on). This chapter will discuss how to do your best explanatory writing.

Learning Outcomes

Utilize details that explain.
Develop an explanatory essay.
Read a sample essay.
Use an assessment rubric.

"If you can't explain it simply, you don't understand it well enough."

Albert Einstein

Utilizing Details That Explain

Explaining ideas and information to your reader requires that you share a variety of details. The following detail types are often found in explanatory writing:

Facts are specific statements that can be proven to be true. Always cite the source of facts unless they are common knowledge. In the sample essay in this chapter, the writer mentions these facts about city life.

> Most innovators, entrepreneurs, and scientists live in cities, which are increasingly connected to each other—Chicago to Singapore to London to Cape Town.

Statistics are numerical facts. Always cite the source of statistics unless they are common knowledge. In the sample essay in this chapter, the writer uses statistics to show that America's love affair with the automobile may be on the decline.

> Ten years ago, 24 percent of cars were owned by young people. Now only 13 percent are (J.D. Powers).

Quotations are the exact words of experts or authorities. The source of a quotation must be cited. In the sample essay, the writer quotes a former beat cop who now lectures on safety in the Internet age.

> As Marc Goodman puts it, "All of the physical objects in our space are being transformed into information technologies. Criminals understand this. Terrorists understand this. If you control the code, you control the world" (NPR).

Paraphrases restate in your own words what someone else has said. The source of a paraphrase must still be cited. (See pages 438–441.) In the sample essay, the writer uses her own words to sum up an idea she read in an article.

> As our brains go from 300 million neurons to 300 billion or 300 trillion, we will develop whole new types of thinking—just as we created art, language, and science last time our frontal cortexes expanded (Kurzweil).

Anecdotes are brief stories that make a point. Cite the source of an anecdote, unless it comes from personal experience. In the sample essay, the writer provides an anecdote about the way medical technology will transform lives.

> In 2050, an average person will get rid of a cold by having nanorobots injected into her bloodstream. While they're at it, they'll destroy any cancer cells. Nanobots will also correct vision, create heart bypasses, . . . (Kornwitz).

Predictions tell what is likely to occur based on current conditions or plans. The essay in this chapter is full of such details.

> Google predicts that, by 2020, driverless cars will help remove human error from the roadway, saving many of the 32,000 Americans killed annually by traffic accidents (Kennedy).

Developing an Explanatory Essay

The primary purpose of an explanatory essay is to share information with your reader. You are not trying to change anyone's mind or influence opinions. Instead, you are attempting to pass on as much valuable information as you can about a topic. Before you begin, review the requirements of the assignment by completing these tasks:

- Analyze the assignment word for word. Locate any key terms (*define, compare, classify, etc.*) and know what they mean.
- Restate the assignment in your own words.
- Find out how your essay will be evaluated.

Prewriting

1. **Analyzing the rhetorical situation . . .** Answer the **STRAP** questions (see page 30) to identify your **S**ubject, the **T**ype of writing, your **R**ole as a writer, your **A**udience, and your **P**urpose for writing.

2. **Selecting a topic . . .** Usually, an explanatory writing assignment will give you a general subject related to your course work. First, you must narrow that subject to a specific topic. Topics that are too broad will give you too much information to handle in an essay-length assignment, and topics that are too narrow will not give you enough.

- After settling on an appropriate topic, look for a specific focus or angle for your paper. This focus will further limit your topic and help you plan your writing.

General Subject	The future	Democracy in action
Specific Topic	Population movements and technological trends	Women's suffrage in the 1800s
Limited Focus	How will technology shape our lives in the future?	How did Elizabeth Cady Stanton contribute to the women's suffrage movement in the 1800s?

3. **Gathering details . . .** Look for both print and online sources of information about your topic. Interview knowledgeable people, and make your own observations. (See pages 33–36 for strategies for gathering and organizing information.) Collect a variety of details—facts, statistics, anecdotes, quotations. (See the previous page.)

4. **Forming a thesis statement . . .** Use the formula below to write a statement that identifies your topic and focus. You may need to write two or three versions of your thesis statement before you are satisfied with it.

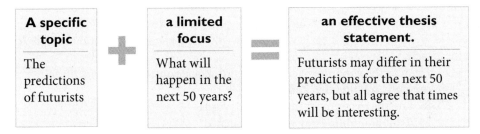

A specific topic		a limited focus		an effective thesis statement.
The predictions of futurists	**+**	What will happen in the next 50 years?	**=**	Futurists may differ in their predictions for the next 50 years, but all agree that times will be interesting.

5. **Selecting main points . . .** After you have written your thesis statement, review the information you've gathered and choose the main points you will use to support your thesis. Organizing your thoughts in a line diagram is one way to accomplish this task. The following line diagram corresponds to the essay on pages 138–139.

Line Diagram

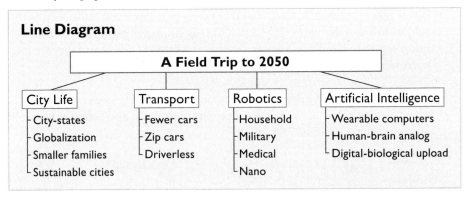

A Field Trip to 2050

City Life	Transport	Robotics	Artificial Intelligence
City-states	Fewer cars	Household	Wearable computers
Globalization	Zip cars	Military	Human-brain analog
Smaller families	Driverless	Medical	Digital-biological upload
Sustainable cities		Nano	

Help File

Three different levels of detail are often used to complete an idea or to make a point, as shown here:

Level 1: A main point is stated in the topic sentence of a paragraph.

▓ In our urbanized world, transportation also will change.

Level 2: Clarifying sentences support the main point.

▓ Public transportation will continue to grow, while cars will be deemphasized.

Level 3: Completing sentences add information (statistics, examples, quotations, etc.) to complete the explanation.

▓ Ten years ago, 24 percent of cars were owned by young people. Now only 13 percent are (J.D. Powers).

6. Creating an outline . . . After you have selected your main points, you are ready to create an outline for your essay. Topic outlines use phrases to state the main points and details, while sentence outlines use complete sentences. The beginning and ending paragraphs are usually not outlined.

Sample Topic Outline

I. Shift to cities
- A. Current demographics and population shift
- B. Deemphasized national borders
- C. Slowed population growth
- D. Sustainable cities

II. Changes to transportation
- A. Fewer cars, young ownership dropping 11 percent
- B. Zip cars and car sharing
- C. Driverless cars

III. Robotic use
- A. Household robotics by 2034
- B. Fully autonomous military soldiers by 2034
- C. Medical and nanorobots

Sample Sentence Outline

I. The future lies in cities.
- A. Currently 84 percent of Americans live in cities, and the world soon will follow.
- B. Globalization has deemphasized national borders.
- C. With urbanization, population growth will slow and top off at 10 billion by 2100.
- D. Sustainable cities are a necessity.

II. Transportation will also change.
- A. Millennials no longer think cars are cool.
- B. Zip cars and car sharing provide alternatives.
- C. Driverless cars eliminate human error.

III. Robots will become ubiquitous.
- A. Most households will have robots by 2034.
- B. Autonomous military robots will serve by 2034.
- C. Nanorobots will cure colds and cancer.

IV. Artificial intelligence will transform our lives.
- A. Wearable computers will provide constant connectivity.
- B. Computing power will reach and surpass humans.
- C. Brain uploads will occur by 2045.

▌ Writing

7. Connecting your ideas . . . As you write your first draft, focus on getting all of your ideas on paper. Each part of the draft—the beginning, middle, and ending—plays an important role. To develop your first draft, refer to the suggestions below and to the sample essay on pages 138–139.

Beginning

Your opening paragraph should capture the reader's interest and state your thesis. Here are some ways to get the reader's attention:

1. Tell a dramatic or exciting story (anecdote) about the topic.
2. Ask an intriguing question or two.
3. Provide a few surprising facts or statistics.
4. Provide an interesting quotation.
5. Explain your personal experience or involvement with the topic.

Middle

The middle paragraphs should support your thesis statement. Use them to provide the information that fully explains your thesis. For example, in the sample essay, the writer provides a combination of facts, statistics, quotations, anecdotes, and predictions to create a futuristic vision. You may also include graphs, charts, or photos.

Ending

Your closing paragraph should summarize your thesis and leave the reader with something to think about. Here are some strategies for creating a strong closing:

1. Review your main points.
2. Emphasize the special importance of one main point.
3. Answer any questions the reader may still have.
4. Put the information in perspective.
5. Share a final significant thought.

▌ Revising

8. Improving your writing . . . Carefully read your essay, looking for ways to improve it. Be prepared to do some adding, cutting, and rearranging. The following questions can guide your revision.

Traits

Ideas:	Does my thesis statement focus on an important part of the topic? Have I effectively supported the thesis? Should I add or delete any ideas or details?
Organization:	Does my essay contain clearly developed beginning, middle, and ending parts? Do my main points and details appear in the best possible order? Have I used transitions to connect my ideas?
Voice:	Do I sound knowledgeable about and interested in my topic?
Word choice:	Have I used specific nouns and verbs? Have I defined unfamiliar terms?
Sentence fluency:	Do my sentences read smoothly? Have I varied the sentence beginnings and lengths?

▌ Editing

9. Checking for conventions . . . After you have revised your essay, it's time to make sure your work is correct. The following questions can guide your editing.

Traits

Conventions:	Have I correctly cited information in my essay? Have I checked my use of end punctuation, commas, and quotation marks? Have I used correct capitalization for proper nouns, titles, and quoted material? Have I checked for spelling errors and watched for easily confused words (to, too, two)? **Note:** See the rubric on page 140 for a helpful guide for revising and editing your essay.
Design:	Have I included a title? Have I incorporated any photos or illustrations from the public domain? Have I used effective design features?

▌ Proofreading

10. Preparing a final copy . . . Write or type a neat final copy of your essay. Proofread it before sharing it.

Reading a Sample Essay

In this essay, student writer Lisa Posen reports on the predictions of futurists who speculate on how our world will change over the next 50 years.

The beginning captures the reader's interest and leads to the thesis statement (underlined).

Each middle paragraph focuses on one main point that supports the thesis statement.

A variety of details— facts, statistics, examples, anecdotes, quotations, and predictions— develop each main point.

A Field Trip to 2050

We all live in the present, that knife-edge where decisions shape the future. Some of us actively gaze into that future, though, imagining what will happen next. <u>Futurists may differ in their predictions for the next 50 years, but all agree that times will be interesting.</u>

To start, the future lies in cities. In the United States, 84 percent of the population already lives in urban areas, which produce 91 percent of the gross domestic product (US Census). By 2025, the world will have 37 megacities, each with more than 10 million people (Hirsh). Why this growth? Cities are where the action is. Most innovators, entrepreneurs, and scientists live in cities, which are increasingly connected to each other—Chicago to Singapore to London to Cape Town. Globalization has deemphasized national borders and reemphasized cities as players on the world stage. As people shift to cities, population growth will slow, reaching 9 billion by 2050 and topping off at 10 billion by 2100 (UN). To support that many people, the cities of the future will have to be sustainable, reducing their impact on the environment, especially in terms of carbon emissions.

In our urbanized world, transportation will also change. Public transportation will continue to grow, while cars will be deemphasized. Ten years ago, 24 percent of cars were owned by young people. Now only 13 percent are (J.D. Powers). As *USA Today* reports, for the Y-generation, "cars aren't cool anymore" (Millennials). The high price of gasoline, insurance, parking, and maintenance makes cars unattractive to urbanites, and Internet connectivity makes lugging one's physical body around less important. When people need cars, they'll increasingly resort to zip cars and car sharing, borrowing a vehicle for the cost of a bus ride (Getaround). Even those who own cars will be less likely to drive them, instead allowing vehicles to drive themselves. Google predicts that, by 2020, driverless cars will help remove human error from the roadway, saving many of the 32,000 Americans killed annually by traffic accidents (Kennedy). These cars could also reduce traffic jams by pacing vehicles more precisely, maintaining flow, and routing travelers around trouble spots (NPR).

Driverless cars are only one way in which robotics will become ubiquitous in our lives. TechCast predicts that by 2022, household robots will do routine chores in 30 percent of American homes, and iRobot predicts that these devices will be in most homes by 2034. The Department of Defense anticipates a similar increase in the military, with fully autonomous battle robots serving by 2034 (Defense). In medicine, robots already assist surgeons and should be able to perform low-invasive procedures autonomously by 2020. In 2050, an average person will get rid of a cold by having nanorobots injected into her bloodstream. While they're at it, they'll destroy any cancer cells. Nanobots will also correct vision, create heart bypasses, and monitor vat-grown organs devised from one's own stem cells (Kornwitz).

Sources of information are acknowledged in text or in parenthetical citations (works-cited list not shown).

These advances in robotics will parallel huge gains in artificial intelligence. We all will wear our computers. Computers stitched into our clothing will translate our speech into any language, monitor our health, and deliver information continuously to eyes, ears, and minds (Rex). Futurist Ray Kurzweil predicts that by 2040, a computer that the average person can afford will have a processing speed equal to a single human brain and by 2060, equal to all human brains. He says that our current always-on connectivity will only increase until our intelligence becomes a fusion of biological and nonbiological systems. "We do need a body— our intelligence is directed toward a body—but it doesn't have to be a biological body that is subject to all kinds of failure modes" (Howerton). As our brains go from 300 million neurons to 300 billion or 300 trillion, we will develop whole new types of thinking—just as we created art, language, and science last time our frontal cortexes expanded (Kurzweil). He goes on to predict that by 2045, it will be possible to fully upload a human consciousness, thereby achieving digital immortality.

The closing logically follows from the rest of the text.

All of these radical changes in our future create the opportunity for wonders and horrors in equal measure. For example, our tremendous reliance on computers can mean a woeful vulnerability to hackers. As Marc Goodman puts it, "All of the physical objects in our space are being transformed into information technologies. Criminals understand this. Terrorists understand this. If you control the code, you control the world" (NPR). That's why every advance must be accompanied by careful planning and safeguards. Online banking was unimaginable 20 years ago, but now it is commonplace and secure. If we anticipate and guard against abuses, we can avoid catastrophe and perhaps bring wonder. At least, it will be interesting.

Using an Assessment Rubric

Use this rubric as a checklist to evaluate your explanatory writing. The rubric is organized according to important standards of effective explanatory writing.

The writing . . .

Ideas

____ maintains a specific focus or purpose.

____ thoroughly develops the topic.

____ provides strong supporting evidence (facts, statistics, definitions, etc.).

Organization

____ forms a meaningful whole with a clear beginning, middle, and ending.

____ presents ideas in logically ordered paragraphs.

____ uses linking words and transitions to connect information.

Voice

____ speaks in an objective tone appropriate for the purpose.

____ shows the writer's investment in the topic.

Word Choice

____ contains specific nouns and active verbs.

____ defines and explains unfamiliar terms.

____ uses words with the appropriate level of formality.

Sentence Fluency

____ flows smoothly from one idea to the next.

____ uses sentences with an appropriate level of formality.

Conventions

____ adheres to the basic rules of writing.

Design

____ uses design features such as a title, white space, and, perhaps, illustrations and graphic devices to further explain the topic.

Other Forms of Explanatory Writing

Explanatory writing is a particularly effective way to learn. As you gather information about a topic, form a thesis, and explain and support it, you are increasing your understanding of new concepts and subjects.

The best explanations interpret and cite current research on a topic. With careful planning, writing, and revising, your writing will flow logically from one main point to the next. The specialized essays in this chapter represent several types of explanatory writing. Learning how to write these kinds of essays will improve your ability to analyze complex ideas and express them to others.

Learning Outcomes

Write a process essay.
Create a definition essay.
Develop a classification essay.
Produce a cause-effect essay.
Write a comparison-contrast essay.
Respond to a prompt.

"Don't be too clever for an audience. Make it obvious."

Billy Wilder

Writing a Process Essay

In a process essay, you explain how something works, how to do something, or how to make something. Your challenge is to explain the process clearly and completely. To do that, you must have a thorough understanding of your topic.

▌Prewriting

1. **Analyzing the rhetorical situation . . .** Answer the **STRAP** questions (see page 30) to identify your **S**ubject, the **T**ype of writing, your **R**ole as a writer, your **A**udience, and your **P**urpose for writing.

2. **Choosing a topic . . .** If your assignment is to explain how something works, review your class notes or text for ideas. For example, in a science class, you might explain how a cut heals or how a seed germinates. In a more general assignment, you might explain a certain job or chore, a hobby, or a special talent—like changing a flat tire or designing a Web site.

3. **Gathering information . . .** List facts and details about your topic as they come to mind, or freewrite an instant version of your essay. Either activity will tell you how much you already know about your topic . . . and how much you need to find out. Collect additional information as necessary.

4. **Planning and organizing . . .** Arrange the information about the process step-by-step (chronological order). Also write down the main point you want your audience to understand or appreciate.

▌Writing

5. **Connecting your ideas . . .** Write your first draft freely, working in details according to your prewriting and planning. As you develop your essay, cover all the steps in the process you are explaining, perhaps presenting them in a bulleted list.

▌Revising

6. **Improving your writing . . .** Review your first draft for ideas, organization, and voice. Fill in any missing information and check that all steps are in the correct order.

7. **Improving your style . . .** Check your word choice and sentence fluency so that all ideas are stated clearly and effectively.

▌Editing

8. **Checking for conventions . . .** Look for errors in punctuation, mechanics, and grammar. Use the rubric on page 140 to give your essay a final revising and editing review.

9. **Creating a final copy . . .** Make a neat final copy of your essay and proofread it before sharing it.

Process Essay

In the following process essay, the writer describes how one of nature's most devastating forces—a tsunami—develops.

The opening paragraph ends with the thesis statement (underlined).

Middle paragraphs introduce the process.

Details present the process step-by-step, in chronological order.

The closing shares key statistics about the topic.

Tsunami

On March 11, 2011, a level 9.0 earthquake shook the Pacific Ocean, and a huge tsunami struck Japan. A tsunami (the Japanese word for "harbor wave") is one of the most destructive forces in nature, and this tsunami caused $235 billion worth of damage (World Bank). Many people believe that a tsunami is simply a big wave that moves forward until it hits the shore, but the process is more complex than that. A tsunami is really a huge transfer of energy from the crust of the earth to a body of water.

Unlike typical ocean waves caused by wind and storms, a tsunami begins with a fault line in the seabed. Along such a fault, two or more of the earth's tectonic plates meet and grate against each other. An earthquake occurs when one plate suddenly slips. Beneath the ocean, if one tectonic plate thrusts up and over another, a tsunami begins to form.

When the underwater earthquake lifts the continental plate and all the water above it, tremendous energy is released. The force moves upward through the water until it nears the surface. There, the energy spreads out horizontally like ripples in a pool. This enormous energy is not apparent on the surface, however, and the outwardly spreading waves may be only a few feet high. The power of the tsunami is still under the surface, moving as fast as 500 miles per hour.

As the surge heads toward the shore, the immense energy does not have enough water to carry it. The water nearer the land is sucked back out to sea to feed the growing wave. People who witness tsunamis first notice that the ocean is suddenly receding, as it does at low tide. Then the wave rushes onshore in the form of a wall of water that can be a hundred feet high and several hundred miles wide. The power of this wall of water can be unbelievable.

The Japanese tsunami of 2011 resulted from the fifth largest earthquake since modern record keeping began. Taken together, the earthquake and tsunami released 9,320 gigatons of energy, which is 600 million times that of the Hiroshima atomic bomb. Many cities in Japan looked like they had suffered just such an attack.

Creating a Definition Essay

A definition essay provides a detailed explanation of a term or concept. The term may be complicated (*inflation, cancer, democracy*), or it may mean different things to different people (*love, courage, fairness*). The essay can include dictionary definitions, personal definitions, negative definitions (telling what the word does not mean), examples, comparisons, quotations, and anecdotes (stories).

▌ Prewriting

1. **Analyzing the rhetorical situation . . .** Answer the **STRAP** questions (see page 30) to identify your **S**ubject, the **T**ype of writing, your **R**ole as a writer, your **A**udience, and your **P**urpose for writing.

2. **Selecting a topic . . .** Select a term or concept that is complex enough to require some real thought on your part. If no topic comes to mind, write freely about your course work, current events, or your personal life. Also consider terms people misuse or use too often.

3. **Gathering details . . .** Collect information about your topic by referring to dictionaries, interviews, song lyrics, personal anecdotes, newspapers, the Internet, and so on.

4. **Focusing your thoughts . . .** Plan how you want to arrange the details. You may want to begin with a dictionary definition, include a quotation or two, follow with an important comparison, and so on. Fully explore the meaning of your word by providing a variety of details about it.

▌ Writing

5. **Connecting your ideas . . .** Write an opening that introduces your topic and states your thesis. Develop middle paragraphs that define the topic in different ways. Create a closing that thoughtfully sums up the topic.

▌ Revising

6. **Improving your writing . . .** Review your first draft, paying special attention to the ideas, organization, and voice. Add, cut, rearrange, and rewrite parts as necessary.

7. **Improving your style . . .** Focus next on your word choice and sentence fluency. Check that your words and sentences express your ideas in the best way.

▌ Editing

8. **Checking for conventions . . .** Review your revised copy for punctuation, mechanics, and grammar errors. Use the rubric on page 140 to check your revising and editing.

9. **Creating a final copy . . .** Finalize the design of your essay and create a neat copy to share.

Definition Essay

In this essay, student writer Mary Bruins defines the word *gullible*.

The Gullible Family

The first paragraph identifies the topic and provides the thesis statement (underlined).

The other day, my friend Loris fell for an old trick: "Hey, somebody wrote *gullible* on the ceiling!" Shortly after mocking "Gullible Loris" for looking up, I swallowed the news that Walmart sells popcorn that pops into the shapes of cartoon characters. And so, as "Gullible Mary," I decided to explore what our name means, and who else belongs to the Gullible family. What I learned is that our family includes both people and birds, related to each other by our willingness to "swallow."

A gullible person will swallow an idea or argument without questioning its truth. Similarly, the gull (a long-winged, web-footed bird) will swallow just about anything thrown to it. In fact, the word *gullible* comes from *gull*, and this word can be traced back to the Germanic word *gwel* (to swallow). Both *gull* and *gwel* are linked to the modern word *gulp,* which means "to swallow greedily or rapidly in large amounts." It's not surprising then that Loris and I, sisters in the Gullible family, both eagerly gulped (like gulls) the false statements thrown to us.

Each middle paragraph helps define the topic.

Swallowing things so quickly isn't too bright, and *gull* (when referring to a bird or a person) implies that the swallower is immature and foolish. For example, *gull* refers to an "unfledged" fowl, which the *Grolier Encyclopedia* describes as either "an immature bird still lacking flight feathers" or something that is "inexperienced, immature, or untried." These words describe someone who is fooled easily, and that's why *gull,* when referring to a human, means "dupe" or "simpleton." In fact, since 1550, *gullet*, which means "throat," has also meant "fooled."

To illustrate this usage, the *Oxford English Dictionary* quotes two authors who use *gull* as a verb meaning "to fool." "Nothing is so easy as to gull the public, if you only set up a prodigy," writes Washington Irving. William Dean Howells uses the word similarly when he writes, "You are perfectly safe to go on and gull imbeciles to the end of time, for all I care."

The closing focuses on more positive connotations for the word.

Both of these authors are pretty critical of gullible people, but does *gullible* have only negative connotations? Is there no hope for Gullibles like Loris and me? C. O. Sylvester Mawson's comments about *gullible* may give us some comfort. He links *gullible* to "credulous, confiding, and easily deceived." At first, these adjectives also sound negative, but *credulous* does mean "to follow implicitly." And the word *credit* comes from the Latin word *credo*, meaning "I believe." So what's bad about that? In other words, isn't wanting to believe other people a good thing? Why shouldn't Loris and I be proud of at least that aspect of our gull blood? We want to be positive—and we don't want to be cynics.

Developing a Classification Essay

A classification essay analyzes a topic by breaking it into groups or categories, exploring each, and showing how the categories relate to each other.

▌ Prewriting

1. **Analyzing the rhetorical situation** . . . Answer the **STRAP** questions (see page 30) to identify your **S**ubject, the **T**ype of writing, your **R**ole as a writer, your **A**udience, and your **P**urpose for writing.

2. **Selecting a topic** . . . Think about topics that include large groups and subgroups (such as Plains tribes), a hierarchy (such as offices in the Department of Defense), or a taxonomy (such as gliding mammals). Select a topic that interests you and satisfies the requirements of your assignment.

3. **Gathering information** . . . Research the topic, dividing it into groups or categories and collecting information about each. Gather facts, statistics, examples, anecdotes, quotations, and other details.

4. **Writing a thesis statement** . . . Name your overall topic and the categories or groups that you will examine.

▌ Writing

5. **Beginning your essay** . . . Write a beginning paragraph that captures your reader's interest and leads to your thesis statement.

6. **Developing middle paragraphs** . . . Focus on one group or category in each paragraph, fully explaining it. Show how the categories are distinct and also how they relate to each other.

7. **Closing your essay** . . . Write an ending paragraph that reviews the categories that you have analyzed and revisits the thesis.

▌ Revising

8. **Improving your essay** . . . Ask yourself these questions:

┌─ Traits ─

Ideas:	Is my thesis clear? Are my categories distinct and unified?
Organization:	Does the essay have a strong beginning, middle, and ending? Have I used transitions to connect my ideas?
Voice:	Does my voice connect to my audience? Do I sound confident about and interested in the topic?
Word choice:	Have I defined each category or group?
Sentence fluency:	Are my sentences complete and easy to read?

▌ Editing

9. **Checking for conventions** . . . Correct all mechanical errors.

10. **Creating a final copy** . . . Finalize the design and prepare a neat copy.

Classification Essay

The following classification essay discusses three types of black holes.

Sizes and Styles of Darkness

The opening introduces the topic and states the thesis (underlined).

Black holes grab our attention—voracious whirlpools from which even light cannot escape. A black hole forms whenever huge amounts of matter or energy become compacted into a single point. These cosmic vacuum cleaners come in three main varieties: stellar-mass black holes, supermassive black holes, and miniature black holes.

Stellar-mass black holes have about 10 times the mass of our sun and form when giant or supergiant stars reach the end of their life spans. When a star uses up its fuel, fusion reactions cease at its core, and the star collapses. The outer layers rush in to bounce off the incredibly dense core and then blast out in a supernova. The core continues to collapse until it occupies no space at all—a singularity, with no height, width, or depth. This point has an incredible amount of gravity, though. An event horizon forms around the singularity, the sphere where the escape velocity equals the speed of light. The event horizon of a stellar-mass black hole could be just 40 miles across, depending on the mass at the singularity.

Each middle paragraph explains one group or category.

A variety of details help to give a complete picture of each category.

Supermassive black holes are much larger and contain much more material. They are millions or billions times the mass of our sun, and their event horizons can be hundreds of millions of miles across. Our Milky Way galaxy has a supermassive black hole at its center, as do most galaxies. These black holes likely form through the collapse of large clouds of stars during galaxy formation, though scientists don't know how such a collapse could occur. When a supermassive black hole is "feeding off" stars and gas clouds, its accretion disk sends out jets of light called "quasars"—some of the brightest emissions in the universe.

A third type, miniature black holes, are theoretical. Astrophysicists conjecture that these singularities, containing Mount Everest-size masses, would have been created during the first moments of the Big Bang. Quantum physicists believe that miniature black holes could also be created in super-energetic collisions like those that occur at the Large Hadron Collider in Switzerland. However, such minuscule black holes would evaporate split seconds after forming, so they pose no risk.

The final paragraph provides another classification scheme and sums up the essay.

In addition to these categories based on mass, black holes can be classified by whether they are stationary (Schwarzschild) or rotating (Kerr) and by whether they have electromagnetic fields. So next time someone mentions black holes, you can tell them that darkness comes in three different sizes and in many different styles.

Producing a Cause-Effect Essay

In a cause-effect essay, you trace the reasons something happens and what results from it. Your essay can be cause-focused, effect-focused, or a combination of these.

Prewriting

1. **Analyzing the rhetorical situation . . .** Answer the **STRAP** questions (see page 30) to identify your **S**ubject, the **T**ype of writing, your **R**ole as a writer, your **A**udience, and your **P**urpose for writing.

2. **Selecting a topic . . .** Consider course-related topics, recent experiences, conversations, headlines, and events that have changed your life. Choose a topic that truly interests you.

3. **Gathering information . . .** Research your topic, using primary and secondary sources as appropriate.

4. **Focusing your thoughts . . .** Establish a thesis and choose one of the following organization patterns:

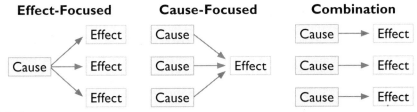

| Effect-Focused | Cause-Focused | Combination |

Writing

5. **Connecting your ideas . . .** Write an opening that introduces your topic and states your thesis (connecting the causes and effects).

6. **Building middle paragraphs . . .** Explain the causes and effects concerning the topic.

7. **Closing your essay . . .** Restate the thesis in an interesting way.

Revising

8. **Improving your writing . . .** Carefully examine your first draft for ideas, organizations, and voice. Ask at least one other person to react to your work as well. Add, cut, rearrange, or rewrite parts as necessary.

9. **Improving your style . . .** Check your word choice and sentence variety. Make any changes that ensure your essay reads smoothly and clearly.

Editing

10. **Checking for conventions . . .** Look for errors in punctuation, mechanics, and spelling in your revised writing. Use the rubric on page 140 as a final revising and editing guide.

11. **Creating a final copy . . .** Finalize your design and create a neat copy of your essay to share.

Cause-Effect Essay

In this essay, student writer Peter Hoelsema reviews the causes and effects of digital interconnectedness. (The works-cited page is not shown.)

Too Easy: Our Deepest Communication Need

An opening quotation introduces the topic, and the paragraph ends in the thesis (underlined).

"Dr. Watson, come here, I need you!" This exclamation, uttered by Alexander Graham Bell upon his invention of the telephone, began the age of electronic communication. We now live in the world Bell dreamed of, able to communicate with anyone from any distance, anytime. But it is also a world full of more loneliness than ever before. Has our connectedness actually caused us to separate? What has electronic communication done to face-to-face communication? How should we manage our communication? Electronic communication is very useful, but only to the extent that it increases face-to-face communication.

Quotations and paraphrases draw on the ideas of other writers.

In today's world, it is easy to be alone while still being connected. According to Sherry Turkle, "Technology redraws the boundaries between intimacy and solitude" (11). If one does not like the music playing in a car with a group of people, one can simply grab his or her headphones and listen to something else. If one is feeling lonely, one can log into Facebook or Twitter. If one is feeling awkward in a group of people, one can get out his or her phone and pretend to do something with it. Everyone will assume he or she is doing something important. We can be "alone together" (17); that is, via these technologies, we can be in the company of others while we are alone. We can be "there but not there" (14)—the image of a hermit happily sitting in a cave with headphones, a computer, and a cell phone comes to mind.

Each paragraph further explains the thesis, elaborating on it.

Being alone while we are together is especially attractive to guilty introverts. Introverts are those people who might not talk as much as others, who do their best work on their own, and who generally keep to themselves (Selles 18). Introverts are often not able to interact with others on the level that they would like, so they turn to electronic communication to fill in the gap. Often, if introverts meet with success in the electronic world, they will rely more and more on it and less and less on the face-to-face world. As Turkle says, their communication goes from "better than nothing to better than anything" (59), and eventually, they expect "more from technology and less from each other" (xii).

Introverts are not the only ones with an electronic communication addiction. All of us fear looking lonely or unpopular, and simultaneously fear intimate relationships in which we are fully open and vulnerable.

Turkle says "we are lonely but fearful of intimacy" (1). We both want and fear the closeness of a face-to-face relationship. We can have something close to intimacy without the fear, however, via electronic communication. It is far easier to ask and say intimate things when one is not looking another in the eye.

Thus, introversion, guilt, fear of intimacy, or a combination of the three can cause more electronic communication than face-to-face communication. Are texting, email, Facebook, and Twitter good solutions?

All these technologies shave communication down to near baldness; that is, they eliminate everything but words. They leave out voice inflections, gestures, facial expressions, and so on. In online chats and texting lingo, we have tried to substitute the sound of laughing with text-speak such as "haha" and "LOL"; and a smile with :-). But text is not nearly as contagious as the real thing. People laugh when they hear laughter, not when they read the word "haha." This stripped-down language is also open for misinterpretation. Without a face to put the words to, the meaning of words can wander.

Lying becomes very easy. It is easier to make oneself appear more interesting, more intelligent, and better looking via electronic communication than it is in person. After all, which is easier: to say I can bench press 300 pounds or to actually do it? According to Evgeny Morozov, "57% of college students believe social networking's purpose is self-promotion, narcissism, and attention seeking" (187). It may be convenient to be cooler via electronic communication than in reality, but how does it feel to know that everyone else can be fake as well? Fake interaction in order to promote oneself may occur in face-to-face communication as well, but it is harder to fake bicep size or IQ when you are looking someone in the eye.

Electronic communication lessens the responsibility of relationships. When technology becomes the only means of communication, it "offers the illusion of companionship without the demands of friendship" (Turkle 1). If we do not like what we hear, we can end the chat or text. An online relationship is "a companionship that can always be interrupted" (10). Exclusively electronic relationships make no sacrifices, make no promises, take no work, and can be ended at whim.

The intimate relationships that we long for take work and sacrifice.

Finding people and interacting via electronics is easy; in fact, it is too easy. Electronic interactions remove effort but also a sense of value. If a friend makes the effort to find time to meet with a person—face-to-face—that person feels valued. This sacrifice is even more meaningful in today's busy world, when taking the time to meet with someone probably means sacrificing money, giving up precious time, and maybe even driving several hours. Electronic communication can be "slactivism" (Morozov 191), or minimal sacrifice in a relationship.

The writer maintains an appropriate semiformal style.

The devises that we shape, shape us. The social architects who made electronic communication possible thought that it would make communication easier. It has, but it has also tempted us to neglect real communication. By allowing electronic communication to shape our relationships, "We lower our expectations of all relationships, including those with people," Turkle states. "In the process, we betray ourselves" (125).

The writer qualifies his position.

This is not to say that Facebook, Twitter, and Skype should not be used at all. In fact, these technologies are part of the solution to the problem of human loneliness. Facebook, email, Twitter, and Skype make it easy to set up face-to-face meetings, which are the meetings we really need. They also have value in that they make it easy to stay in contact with those who we could not otherwise because of distance. Skype and similar video technologies even allow a form of face-to-face communication with those separated by distance.

How then, are we to use electronic communication? We ought to manage our communication religiously. Leaders in India actually did this at a two-day meeting: "The clerics think it is necessary to set an edict on virtual networking, because this online relationship could lead to lust, which is forbidden in Islam" (Kirkpatrick 286). They concluded that "'Facebook is forbidden,' if it is used for gossiping, flirting, spreading lies, asking intimate questions, or vulgar behavior" (286). They felt that these things, if they have a place at all, have no place in the electronic world.

The closing paragraph connects with the thesis.

The solution to human loneliness is not electronic communication alone. Rather, it is electronic communication put to work to increase face-to-face communication. So go on Facebook. Check email, Skype, text, and tweet those you cannot see otherwise. These technologies are not meant to take the work out of relationships, but to put it back in. The right place for our deepest need of intimacy is face-to-face.

Writing a Comparison-Contrast Essay

A comparison-contrast essay examines the similarities and differences between two topics. For this kind of assignment, you may consider a wide range of categories—books, people, events, experiments, products, places, experiences—but the two topics must come from the same category and be worthy of comparison.

Prewriting

1. **Analyzing the rhetorical situation** . . . Answer the **STRAP** questions (see page 30) to identify your **Subject**, the **Type** of writing, your **Role** as a writer, your **Audience**, and your **Purpose** for writing.

2. **Selecting topics** . . . Unless you already have two topics in mind, review your class notes or text for ideas. You may also brainstorm ideas with classmates or write freely about your course work, noting potential topics.

3. **Gathering details** . . . Make a list of the similarities and differences between your topics. Decide whether you will emphasize similarities or differences.

4. **Writing a thesis statement** . . . Summarize the comparison.

Writing

5. **Opening your essay** . . . Write a paragraph that introduces your topics and states your thesis.

6. **Creating middle paragraphs** . . . Decide if you will fully describe one topic before addressing the other (subject-by-subject), if you will discuss the similarities of both topics before addressing the differences (similarities and differences), or if you will discuss one point for each topic before moving to the next point, and so on (point-by-point).

7. **Closing your essay** . . . Sum up the comparison with a final thought.

Revising

8. **Improving your writing** . . . Ask yourself these questions:

Traits	
Ideas:	Are the similarities and differences between my two topics clear?
Organization:	Does the arrangement help the reader grasp the main points?
Voice:	Do I sound knowledgeable and confident?

9. **Improving your style** . . . Check your word choice and sentence fluency.

Editing

10. **Checking for conventions** . . . Correct any mechanical errors.
11. **Creating a final copy** . . . Finalize your design and prepare a final copy.

Comparison-Contrast Essay

In the following essay, the student writer compares her relationship with friends at two different schools, in light of a difficult personal struggle.

If Only They Knew

The writer's personal story leads to the thesis statement (underlined).

Anorexia nervosa is an eating disorder that I struggled with for the majority of my middle school years and a portion of my high school years. My classmates at Riverview High School were aware of my disorder, and it greatly affected the way they treated me. At the start of my junior year, I transferred to Madison High School. I decided not to tell anyone at that school about my eating disorder since I was mostly recovered by that time. Even though my friends at Riverview and Madison all showed concern for my well-being, I felt much more comfortable with the students at Madison.

A point-by-point comparison is made in the essay, beginning with "lunchtime."

At Riverview, lunchtime was usually a nightmare for me. I would enter the cafeteria, and in my mind, all eyes would fix themselves on my gangly figure. I would take my place at a table full of friends and try to enjoy a "normal" lunch. The problem was that I would not always eat lunch, and that greatly concerned my friends. They would watch to make sure that I was eating, almost forcing food into my mouth. Sometimes I would pretend to eat and then drop pieces of food into a napkin and throw it out with the trash. When some of my friends found out, they were furious, which seemed to cause even more trouble. Lunch was obviously not my favorite time of the day, and it involved a lot of stress.

I stopped dreading lunch when I started at Madison. No one knew that I had an eating disorder, so they did not care what I ate. An enormous load of stress fell from my shoulders. I finally had the freedom to eat what I wanted without being harassed. It was still hard for me to eat in front of other people, which is common for anorexics, but I was able to put some of my fears aside. I began to enjoy lunch instead of disposing of it.

The second point focuses on "topics of conversation."

With my Riverview friends, instead of chatting about boys and other "girl things," we would discuss my disorder. Girls would follow me into the bathroom, and instead of fixing their hair, they would check to see if I was throwing up. We never got to gossip together like normal girls because we had to focus on anorexia instead. All I really wanted to talk about was how cute Mike Reynolds looked that day.

I was totally shocked to find that all the life-and-death conversations disappeared when I went to Madison. It was so much fun to talk about the little things that occurred in everyday life. The subject of eating disorders rarely came up, and when it did, I was not the focus. I loved having the freedom to go into the bathroom without being followed. High school is meant to be filled with frivolous chatter, and at Madison I participated in more than my fair share.

I found that the students at Riverview had made many generalizations about my character, and their behavior was guided by those generalizations. Their natural instincts told them to help me. I appreciated their concern, but they never took the time to find out who I was as a person. They knew me only as an anorexic. My friends cared about my health, but they failed to care about me. Truthfully, all I wanted was for them to love me for me and not to obsess over my shortcomings.

The people at Madison took the time to know who I really was. They had no idea that I had been an anorexic, so that particular stereotype did not color their opinions of me. I was finally recognized for my talents and achievements, not my failures. I was honored as a good student. I was also honored as a cheerleader, and no one cared how I looked in my skirt. I could finally be viewed as a real person. I liked the way that people saw me at Madison, and I was no longer afraid to show my true character and personality.

My days as an anorexic taught me many lessons that I would not trade for the world. They taught me about life and how to be a better friend. I learned about the joys of routine tasks such as eating lunch. I learned to appreciate the simple things in life, like the gossip shared by a group of teenage girls. I gained an understanding of what true character is. I hold no grudges against those who desperately tried to help me. In fact, I owe them a great debt. And I appreciate the people who helped me to see that there is much more to life than having an eating disorder.

> The third point interprets the "actions of each set of friends."

> The closing paragraph sums up what the writer has learned.

Point-by-Point	Subject-to-Subject	Similarities-Differences
Beginning	Beginning	Beginning
Point I	Subject I	Similarities
Subject I / Subject 2		
Point 2		
Subject I / Subject 2	Subject 2	Differences
Point 3		
Subject I / Subject 2		
Ending	Ending	Ending

Responding to a Prompt

Explanatory prompts ask you to state and support a thesis about some topic, providing information that helps the reader better understand it. You may be asked to explain an idea, compare and contrast two topics, define a term, outline a process, or trace causes and effects. Quickly work through the writing process to prepare your best response.

▌ Prewriting

1. Analyzing the writing prompt . . . Answer the **STRAP** questions:

Subject: What topic will I write about?

Type: What form will my writing take?

Role: What role will I assume as writer?

Audience: Who will read my writing?

Purpose: What is the goal of my writing?

2. Outlining your response . . . Write down the main idea of your answer and quickly list supporting points. Keep the purpose of your response in mind—to explain, outline, illustrate, demonstrate, define, and so on. Use an appropriate organizational pattern. (See pages 86–88.)

▌ Writing

3. Crafting an opening paragraph . . . Introduce your topic and lead up to your thesis statement.

4. Building middle paragraphs . . . Write a topic sentence for each main point and include body sentences that support it.

5. Using transitions . . . Connect paragraphs and sentences using transitions that indicate time, importance, cause and effect, and so on. (See pages 86–88.)

6. Drafting a closing paragraph . . . Conclude your response by revisiting your thesis and leaving the reader with an interesting final thought.

▌ Revising

7. Reviewing the prompt using STRAP . . . Revisit your **STRAP** analysis to be certain you have accurately answered the prompt.

8. Revising your answer . . . Check the ideas, organization, voice, words, and sentences of your writing. Make improvements.

▌ Editing

9. Checking for conventions . . . Check your answer to eliminate errors in punctuation, capitalization, spelling, usage, and grammar.

Explanatory Prompt and Response

Prompt

A recent survey shows that most teens would prefer to text someone rather than speak to the person on the phone. As a teen, write an essay explaining to older readers why your peers prefer texting to speaking on their cell phones.

Outline

Millennials have many reasons to prefer texting.
- --Real-time exchange
- --Time to think
- --Coolness factor
- --Few drawbacks

Millennials will keep preferring texting to talking.

Response

The beginning introduces the topic and leads to the thesis (underlined).

My friends and I in Generation-Y constantly text but rarely call on our cell phones, a fact that annoys moms and other Boomers. We're not doing it to be annoying, though. Texting has become one of our basic ways of communicating. Millennials have many reasons to prefer texting to talking.

First of all, texting allows a real-time exchange of ideas without interrupting everything else we are doing. We can be watching a game, doing homework, taking a walk, or having lunch and carrying on a text conversation at the same time. A phone call would completely interrupt what we were doing. Texting is silent, as well, so we don't disturb others in a room. I've been at a table with five people texting. The same table with five people talking on cell phones would be unbearable. Texting also is sort of secret, like passing notes. It happens on the sly, which makes you feel like you're getting away with something—and maybe you are!

Middle paragraphs provide many reasons supporting the thesis.

As a form of writing, texting has a lot of benefits over talking. For one thing, you get a chance to think about what you will say before you say it. Instead of getting off the phone and thinking, "I wish I hadn't said that," you can reread your text and think, "Maybe I won't send that." You can also get other opinions. For example, if a girl sends a flirty text, you can check with friends to see if they are reading it the same way, and you can ask them to "approve" your response before you send it. Texting also creates a record. Often, I'll show the thread of a conversation to someone so he or she knows what both sides said and understands what's going on. Finally, texting is more direct than talking. A phone conversation starts with a greeting, ends with a closing, and includes other social niceties about "your day." Texting gets right to the point without all that.

Finally, and most importantly, texting is cool. Whatever you text is automatically cooler than whatever you say on a phone. Being able to text puts you on the inside of modern communication. Knowing abbreviations and other text-speak shows that you aren't a relic in a phone booth using the Yellow Pages. It's how people communicate now, and it works.

Obviously, texting has some downsides. You shouldn't text and drive, which some people say is worse than driving under the influence. Often, you can't text your grandmother. And Auto Correct sometimes makes you look like a fool.

The ending paragraph restates the thesis and predicts the future.

Despite these drawbacks, texting works for most of us, and it's here to stay. Previous generations used to pass notes in class and in the hallways. That's basically the same as texting. They used to throw pebbles at a friend's window to get the person to look outside. That's texting, too. I wonder what new forms of communication the next generation will use. We'll probably shake our heads and wish that "kids these days" would see the value of writing a good, old-fashioned text message.

Writers INC

Writing About Literature

Writing About Informational Texts

Information arrives in many forms: articles on the Internet, videos on YouTube, chapters in your textbook, news reports on television, documentaries on Netflix, . . . Often, in class, you'll be asked to write about the information you learn from these sources.

You'll start by reading and engaging closely with a source, analyzing its thesis and development. You'll trace the argument presented and consider the creator's point of view. Finally, you'll write about what you have discovered, and, by doing so, author a new informational text that others can learn from.

Learning Outcomes

Analyze the ideas.
Analyze the medium.
Analyze the author.
Write an analysis of a graphic.
Develop an analysis of a speech.
Write an analysis of a documentary.
Develop a book analysis.

"Information is power."
Eric Schmidt

Analyzing the Ideas

When you write about nonfiction texts, focus mainly on what the writer says and why. Consider the central idea and its development.

▌Stating the Thesis

Start by identifying the central idea (thesis) of the text. Underline the thesis statement if you can find it. If not, write your own sentence that names the topic and expresses the writer's specific focus. Follow this formula:

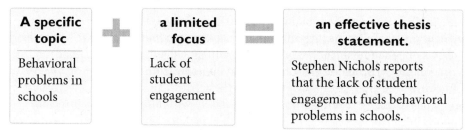

A specific topic	➕	a limited focus	▬▬ =	an effective thesis statement.
Behavioral problems in schools		Lack of student engagement		Stephen Nichols reports that the lack of student engagement fuels behavioral problems in schools.

▌Tracking the Development

After you have identified the thesis, track the way it is developed in the text. Start by annotating the text, underlining the main point of each paragraph and marking key details. Then write about the text, reporting the thesis, the main supporting points, and the key details. Explain how the writer develops the thesis and other main points.

> Nichols says that the question "Will this be on the test?" signals that students see little relevance in a piece of information beyond the next assessment. Once the test is over, students will quickly forget what they have learned because it is no longer useful.

▌Citing Evidence from the Text

As you consider the development of ideas, think about which details you want to include in your writing. Consider facts, statistics, definitions, examples, quotations, anecdotes, surveys, graphs, photos, and so on. Most often, you will paraphrase information, putting it in your own words. Other times, you may quote a source word for word. Either way, you must give credit to the source, either within the text of your report or in a parenthetical reference.

> According to Nichols, "Our brains use about 20 percent of our blood oxygen, a tremendous cost. As a result, the brain needs to be as efficient as possible and culls mental pathways that are disused. Students forget information not because they are lazy but because the information is not used—is not useful" (7).

Analyzing the Argument

When a text argues for a specific point, it not only assembles evidence but also uses logic and persuasive appeals to convince the reader. Your analysis of such a text must name the premises, inferences, and conclusions.

- **Premise:** A statement taken to be true as a starting point for an argument
- **Inference:** A statement derived from one or more previous statements
- **Conclusion:** The final inference made from previous statements

> Nichols' argument rests on the premise that students prefer real-world learning over academic learning. He infers that more authentic learning will increase engagement and reduce behavioral problems. However, shifting from academic to real-world learning may simply shift which part of the student population falls through the cracks.

In addition to logic, the writer may use emotional appeals. As you analyze an argument, note and comment on any supporting details that exude a strong emotional impact.

> Nichols includes a number of anecdotes about at-risk students who turned their grades and lives around due to their experience with community projects. These stories have a strong emotional impact, but are these students the exception rather than the rule?

▌ Argument Mapping

You can trace the flow of ideas in an argument by creating a map. Start with the central idea. Then track the supporting evidence, premises, inferences, and conclusions. Here is part of an argument map for the article about student engagement.

Thesis: Stephen Nichols reports that the lack of student engagement fuels behavioral problems in schools.

1st Paragraph

| **Premise:** Student engagement is key to learning. | **Anecdote:** "Will this be on the test?" | **Fact:** Retention is reduced after test. |

2nd Paragraph

| **Premise:** Students want learning that connects to their lives. | **Fact:** Mammals use play to practice skills. | **Statistic:** Brain uses 20 percent of blood oxygen. |

Analyzing the Medium

After analyzing what the text says, consider how it is said. Determine the overall structure, how the parts connect to each other, and what each part does.

- **Words:** Which words are critical to the writer's meaning? What are the technical definitions of these words? What are their connotations? What are the figurative meanings? How does word choice influence the meaning and tone of the work?
- **Sentences:** What controlling sentences (thesis statements and topic sentences) appear in the work? How are the body sentences arranged? What is the writer's sentence style? Are the sentences short and choppy, long and flowing, or something in between?
- **Paragraphs:** How does the writer build paragraphs? What organizational patterns are used? In what order do the paragraphs appear and what is their style? Are the paragraphs short, long, or something in between?
- **Sections:** What other divisions does the writer use in the text? How is the overall piece structured?

Analyzing Multimedia

When you are responding to a work that uses a variety of different media, pay attention to its formal structures.

- **Video:** Script, cast, setting, props, cuts, scenes, camera angles, visual effects
- **Audio:** Narration, dialogue, music, sound effects, cast
- **Web:** Pages, hierarchy, links, photos, video, audio
- **Performance:** Lines, blocking, costumes, set, props, speeches, music, lights
- **Graphics:** Organization, color, line, drawing, chart, photo, title, caption

Census 2000: Top US Ancestries by County

Ancestry with largest population in county

African American
Aleut/Eskimo
American
American Indian
Dutch
English
Finnish
French
German
Hispanic/Spanish
Irish
Italian
Mexican
Norwegian
Puerto Rican
Other

Source: U.S. Census Bureau, Census 2000 special tabulation. American Factfinder at factfinder.census.gov provides census data and mapping tools.

Analyzing the Author

In addition to analyzing the text, consider who created it and why. Do research to discover the author's position, background, purpose, and context in relation to the piece. The following research example provides key facts about Walt Whitman, writer of "The Great Army of the Sick."

- **Identity:** What is the author's name?

  - Walt Whitman

- **Position:** In what capacity was the author working to create this piece? Does the author speak for him- or herself or for a larger organization?

  - He was writing as a nurse in army hospitals during the Civil War.

- **Background:** What personal details influence the author? Are his or her nationality, heritage, political orientation, religious affiliation, gender, age, or other background information important to a full understanding of the work?

  - Whitman published *Leaves of Grass* in 1855, an important collection of Romantic poetry. He wrote "Beat! Beat! Drums!" to rally Northerners to fight the war, but later was horrified to see the carnage of the battlefield.

- **Purpose:** Why did the author write this piece? What did he or she hope to accomplish? Was the author trying to inform, direct, persuade, encourage, entertain, or inspire?

  - Whitman wrote "The Great Army of the Sick" to demonstrate war's tremendous cost in casualties and human suffering.

- **Context:** Where and when was the work created? What was happening in the author's life at the time? What was happening in the larger context of his or her home, city, and country? What came before this work? What came after?

  - Whitman was trying to establish himself as a major American poet and commentator at the same time that he was grappling with the meaning of the war. This report came out shortly after the Emancipation Proclamation near the end of the second year of the Civil War. The report preceded Lincoln's reelection campaign by a year and the 13th Amendment by two years.

Writing an Analysis of a Graphic

Graphics vary widely, from charts and diagrams to illustrations and photographs. Analyzing them involves describing them and discerning the ideas and facts that they convey. Focus on their appearance, their meaning, and the reason for their being displayed in a text or other medium.

▍Prewriting

1. **Analyzing the rhetorical situation . . .** Answer the **STRAP** questions (see page 30) to identify your **S**ubject (a graphic), the **T**ype of writing, your **R**ole as a writer, your **A**udience, and your **P**urpose for writing (to analyze).

2. **Selecting a graphic . . .** Find a graphic that relates to your school assignment, perhaps a map, chart, political cartoon, propaganda poster, or photograph. Choose an image that interests you.

3. **Analyzing the graphic . . .** Look at the overall graphic and write down its visual impact and meaning. Then consider each part of the graphic, determining what it signifies. Examine the use of colors, lines, images, icons, shapes, and other visual elements as well as words.

4. **Learning about the creator and context . . .** Find out who created the graphic and why. Discover when and where the graphic was made and displayed. Determine who was meant to see it.

▍Writing

5. **Drafting your analysis . . .** Write a beginning paragraph that introduces the graphic and leads to a thesis statement about it. Create middle paragraphs that focus on different parts of the graphic, describing them and indicating what they mean. Develop an ending paragraph that reflects on the graphic as a whole and wraps up the analysis.

▍Revising

6. **Improving your writing . . .** Review the first draft of your analysis. Your thesis must be clear and well supported in the middle paragraphs. Be certain you have described the graphic and explained what its parts mean. Check the structure of the analysis (beginning, middle, and ending) and of the individual paragraphs.

7. **Improving your style . . .** Check your word choice and sentences for clarity and effectiveness.

▍Editing

8. **Checking for conventions . . .** Look for and correct any errors in punctuation, mechanics, and grammar.

9. **Finalizing the design . . .** Make a neat final copy of your analysis, proofread it, and share it.

Graphic Analysis

The following document analyzes the cover of the Golden Record that was carried into space by the Voyager 1 spacecraft in 1977.

Listening to the Golden Record

The beginning paragraph leads to the thesis statement (underlined).

In 1977, NASA launched the Voyager 1 spacecraft. It carries a Golden Record that contains greetings in many languages, sounds of Earth such as whale and bird songs, music from Mozart to Chuck Barry, and encoded images. <u>An alien who wants to hear this record or see these photographs must first decipher the instructions on the record's cover.</u>

[Public domain], via NASA

Each middle paragraph describes part of the graphic.

The upper left corner of the cover shows a top-down view of the record and the enclosed stylus. Binary code around it indicates the speed at which the record should turn in 0.7 billionths of a second (the time for a hydrogen atom to shift states). A side view shows that overall playing time is about one hour.

Details help the reader understand the appearance and purpose of the graphic.

The upper right corner gives information about the photos on the record. The top illustration shows the wave form of the data, and the next illustrations show how to position the data in parallel vertical lines to form the picture. Below that is the first image—a circle, ensuring that the viewer has the correct resolution (is not seeing an ellipse).

On the bottom of the cover, the viewer can see where our sun is located in relation to 14 nearby pulsars. Each pulsar is identified according to how rapidly it pulses, again using 0.7 billionths of a second. This unit of time is defined in the lower right corner, where schematics show a hydrogen atom shifting from one form to another.

The ending paragraph reflects on the meaning of the graphic.

These well-meaning instructions most likely will never be read, given that Voyager 1 will take 40,000 years to reach the nearest star. Also, an average earthling might not be able to figure out the instructions, so one might wonder if aliens could. All of this assumes, too, that aliens have ears to hear and eyes to see, and that these senses are their main ways of understanding the world. The communication may, in the end, be lost on extra-terrestrial nonhumans. However, whether any creature ever listens and looks, the Golden Record and its instructions send a message of peace from the people of Earth.

Developing an Analysis of a Speech

Analyzing a speech involves capturing its main point and reviewing its development. If you witness the speech, you can analyze the speaker's appearance, delivery, tone of voice, and use of visuals. If you read the speech, you can focus on how the ideas unfold. In either case, you can follow these guidelines.

Prewriting

1. **Analyzing the rhetorical situation . . .** Answer the **STRAP** questions (see page 30) to identify your **S**ubject (a speech), the **T**ype of writing, your **R**ole as a writer, your **A**udience, and your **P**urpose for writing (to analyze).
2. **Selecting a speech . . .** Search for speeches that pertain to your class work. Check Web sites that host the text or video of famous historical speeches. Search for speeches given by scientists, educators, and other leaders. Choose a speech that interests you.
3. **Experiencing the speech . . .** Listen to a live speech, or review the text or video of a speech that has already taken place. If possible, read the transcript of the speech and take notes.
4. **Planning and organizing . . .** Write down the main idea of the speech and note supporting points or reasons. Create a thesis statement for your analysis and plan how you will organize your thoughts.

Writing

5. **Connecting your ideas . . .** In the beginning paragraph, introduce the topic and lead up to your thesis statement. In the middle paragraphs, support your thesis with information from the speech. In the ending paragraph, put the speech into context, reflecting on its overall meaning.

Revising

6. **Improving your writing . . .** Check your thesis and main supporting points for clarity and effectiveness. Be certain your analysis follows an appropriate pattern of organization.
7. **Improving your style . . .** Check your word choice and sentences for clarity and effectiveness.

Editing

8. **Checking for conventions . . .** Look for and correct any errors in punctuation, mechanics, usage, and grammar.
9. **Finalizing the design . . .** Check your use of white space, headings, paragraphs, and lists. If possible, provide a link to the speech so that readers can hear it for themselves.
10. **Creating a final copy . . .** Make a clean final copy and proofread it before sharing it.

Speech Analysis

This analysis explores Sojourner Truth's famous "Ain't I a Woman?" speech.

"Ain't I a Woman?"

The beginning paragraph provides background and the thesis statement (underlined).

A few male ministers showed up for the second day of the Women's Rights Convention in Akron, Ohio, in 1851. The men argued against women's rights, saying women were physically and intellectually weak, Christ was a man, and Eve brought evil into the world. A Pentecostal minister named Sojourner Truth rebutted these arguments, saying, "Ain't I a Woman?"

[Public domain], via Wikimedia Commons.

Middle paragraphs explore Truth's main points.

Quotations and other details help the reader understand the speech.

To start, Truth debunked the idea that women were physically weak. She said, "Look at my arm! I have ploughed and planted, and gathered into barns, and no man could head me! And ain't I a woman? I could work as much and eat as much as a man—when I could get it—and bear the lash as well! And ain't I a woman?" Truth had spent the first thirty years of her life as a slave and continued to work hard in her career. She was physically a match to a man.

Though Truth argued that women could be just as tough as men physically, she took a different tack regarding mental ability. She said that if women had pint-sized minds rather than quart-sized minds, who would deny that any mind should be filled to the brim? She calculated that the men wouldn't accept women as their intellectual equals but could not argue with their intellectual fulfillment. In this way, Truth showed herself more than an equal to the men in the room.

Truth next took on the claim that because Christ was a man, women were second-class citizens. She said that Christ was born from God and a woman, so no man had part in his creation. In this way, she elevated the role of women in connection to the Divinity.

The final claim stated that Eve brought sin into the world. Truth argued that if one woman was powerful enough to set the whole world on the wrong course, a gathering of women would be powerful enough to set it right. If these gathered women were asking to be treated equally, men should grant their request.

The ending comments on a surprising point of interest.

The speech quoted above was originally published in 1863. A version published in 1851 showed no features of southern dialect—no "Ain't I a Woman?" That version is probably more accurate since Truth was from New York. Though the later version probably was reworked, it is more fiery—the kind of speech we want Truth to have given. As a result, it is the version most often quoted.

Writing an Analysis of a Documentary

To analyze a documentary, look closely at the information that it provides and the argument that it makes. Documentaries include visual and auditory components. Often, a narrator reads a script, experts provide testimony, and location footage and computer-generated animation round out the message.

▌Prewriting

1. **Analyzing the rhetorical situation . . .** Answer the **STRAP** questions (see page 30) to reveal your **Subject** (a documentary), the **Type** of writing, your **Role** as a writer, your **Audience**, and your **Purpose** (to analyze).

2. **Choosing a documentary . . .** Search online or in television listings to find documentaries that deal with topics from your classes. Consider works offered by PBS, BBC, National Geographic, the Science Channel, and independent documentary filmmakers.

3. **Viewing the documentary . . .** Watch the program, taking careful notes as you do so. If possible, record the documentary so that you can review it as you write your analysis.

4. **Creating a thesis and organizing support . . .** Determine the focus of your analysis and write a thesis statement. Create a quick list or outline to plan your essay.

▌Writing

5. **Developing a beginning . . .** Name the documentary and the narrator, give background information, and provide your thesis.

6. **Writing middle paragraphs . . .** Create middle paragraphs, each focused on a main supporting point derived from the documentary. Write body sentences that elaborate on the topic sentence of each paragraph.

7. **Creating an ending . . .** Close by providing information that puts your ideas into context and leaves the reader with a strong final thought.

▌Revising

8. **Improving your writing . . .** Review your first draft, paying special attention to ideas, organization, and voice. Add, cut, rearrange, and rewrite parts as necessary.

9. **Improving your style . . .** Focus on word choice and sentence fluency to ensure the best expression of your ideas.

▌Editing

10. **Checking for conventions . . .** Review your revised copy for punctuation, mechanics, usage, and grammar errors.

11. **Creating a final copy . . .** Finalize the design, create a neat copy, proofread it, and share it.

Documentary Analysis

The following essay analyzes an episode of the documentary *Wonders of Life*.

The beginning paragraph identifies the documentary and provides the thesis statement (underlined).

"Endless Forms Most Beautiful"

Episode 3 of the BBC documentary series *Wonders of Life* begins with Brian Cox on the island of Madagascar. He and his crew seek the elusive aye-aye, a lemur that feeds by inserting a long, skinny middle finger into holes in tree trunks to pull out bugs. The aye-aye is a unique type of lemur, which is itself a unique type of primate that occurs only on Madagascar. Cox uses the idea of Madagascar in particular and islands in general to get at the central idea of natural selection.

Middle paragraphs explore main points from the documentary that support the thesis.

When a type of animal exists within a specific environment for a long time, the environment places selection pressure on the living thing. Individuals with traits advantageous for survival in the environment tend to live, reproduce, and thrive. Individuals with disadvantageous traits tend to die. When a population such as this is separated from others, say, by being on an island, that population tends to slowly diverge from other forms elsewhere and become a distinct type or group.

Cox shows that one of the mechanisms of change comes through the mutations caused by cosmic rays. He sets up a cloud chamber using a glass aquarium, duct tape, dry ice, and a blanket, and shows cosmic rays shooting through the space at a rate of a few per second. When such rays strike the DNA in our cells, mutations result. Some can cause cancer or disruption, but a few can lead to advantageous changes.

The writer cites evidence from the documentary, including demonstrations and analogies.

Cox shows that such changes over time in an isolated environment lead to distinct species. In fact, 90 percent of the plant and animal species on Madagascar are found nowhere else. But not all islands are literally chunks of land isolated by water. An ecological "island" exists anywhere species are separated from the larger ecosystem. In Africa, Cox explores termite mounds, which are "islands" that house a species of mushroom found nowhere else. These mushrooms, farmed by the termites, break down cellulose and lignin in woody material, freeing the carbon and forming a sugary substance that the termites can digest.

The ending focuses on a final interesting thought.

All living things on the planet take part in this carbon cycle. The cycle began with the creation of carbon inside massive stars. Dispersed by supernova explosions, the carbon infused the materials that coalesced to form our planet. Here on Earth, carbon dioxide in the air becomes glucose, cellulose, and lignin through the work of green plants, and in turn becomes part of our bodies through our diets. Cox points out that the carbon in us could have once been part of a T. rex's claw. So while ecological islands and separateness drive the diversification of species, the carbon cycle unites us all.

Developing a Book Analysis

Analyzing a nonfiction book requires you to not only summarize its contents but also show why the information is important in a larger context. It is also revealing to touch on who the author is and why he or she has written the book.

▌ Prewriting

1. **Analyzing the rhetorical situation . . .** Answer the **STRAP** questions (see page 30) to identify your **S**ubject (a book), the **T**ype of writing, your **R**ole as a writer, your **A**udience, and your **P**urpose for writing (to analyze).

2. **Selecting a nonfiction book . . .** Choose a book (other than your textbook) that relates to a topic you are studying. Check with your instructor or a librarian for recommended titles and select one that interests you.

3. **Reading the book . . .** Survey the book, noting its organization—table of contents, sections, chapters, index. Carefully read the book and take notes as you do. Review your notes.

▌ Writing

4. **Beginning your analysis . . .** Write a beginning paragraph that names the book and author and provides your thesis statement.

5. **Developing middle paragraphs . . .** Write middle paragraphs that support your thesis, each one dealing with a main point. Draw evidence from the text to explain your ideas.

6. **Ending your essay . . .** Write an ending paragraph that wraps up your analysis in a thoughtful way.

▌ Revising

7. **Improving your analysis . . .** Ask yourself these questions:

┌ Traits ───

Ideas:	Is my thesis clear? Do I provide effective support?
Organization:	Do I have a strong beginning, middle, and ending? Do I use transitions to connect my ideas?
Voice:	Is my voice welcoming? Do I sound confident and interested in the book that I am analyzing?
Word choice:	Are my nouns specific? Are my verbs active? Have I defined any unfamiliar words?
Sentence fluency:	Are my sentences complete and easy to read?

▌ Editing

8. **Checking for conventions . . .** Check your punctuation, mechanics, and spelling.

9. **Finalizing the design . . .** Prepare a neat copy to proofread and share.

Nonfiction Book Analysis

The following analysis explores Candice Millard's book *The River of Doubt*.

Journey Down the *River of Doubt*

The beginning introduces the topic and leads to the thesis statement (underlined).

When Theodore Roosevelt lost his reelection bid in 1912, he was crushed. Lesser men would have packed up their things and withdrawn from public life. Roosevelt instead packed up his things and launched into a perilous journey down an uncharted tributary of the Amazon River. As Candice Millard reports in her amazing book *The River of Doubt,* Roosevelt's journey through the Amazon proved to be the most harrowing adventure of his hard-fought life.

The middle paragraphs share facts from the book.

A variety of details makes the information come alive.

Despite his hearty later image, Roosevelt was a sickly child. He suffered from asthma and other ailments that should have kept him bedridden. However, determined to overcome his weaknesses, Roosevelt set himself a rigorous exercise regimen. He eventually became a Rough Rider, recruiting a diverse group of miners, cowboys, and law enforcement officials to fight beside him in the Spanish American War. Their famous charge up San Juan Hill made Roosevelt a household name and helped him get elected Vice President under William McKinley. When McKinley was assassinated, Roosevelt took office and began trust busting. Roosevelt served from 1901–1909, took a long African expedition, and returned to make another attempt at the White House in 1912. During a campaign stop in Milwaukee, Roosevelt was shot in the chest by an assassin. Instead of rushing to the hospital, though, he stood and delivered his speech, declaring, "It takes more than that to kill a Bull Moose." Despite his bravado, Roosevelt failed to win reelection, and the glory days seemed to be behind him.

Transitions connect paragraphs to paragraphs and sentences to sentences.

Instead of going quietly into retirement, Roosevelt cast around for the next big adventure. He decided that he would travel to South America to find the starting point of the River of Doubt and plot its course through the Amazon Rain Forest. He joined forces with Brazilian explorer Candido Rondon, who had led an expedition to string 800 miles of telegraph cable through the forest. Rondon was a great advocate of indigenous people and he saw the expedition not only as an opportunity to chart an uncharted river, but also as the chance to make first contact with some of the most isolated tribes along the river. These two men were joined on the expedition by Roosevelt's second son, Kermit, the exploitative Father Zahm, the rational George Cherrie, the volatile Julio, and a group of Brazilian porters and paddlers.

Right from the start, the expedition was poorly planned. Father Zahm organized the provisions, packing crates that were overloaded with delicacies rather than essentials. The arduous overland journey ended up killing many of their beasts of burden. On the river, the boats proved too unwieldy to navigate the tight passages and too heavy to port around rapids. As a result, the men had to create dugout canoes, which gradually became waterlogged as they made their way along. Worse yet, an argument among the men led to murder, and the expedition lost precious time trying to hunt down Julio to make him pay for his crime. In the end, they had to abandon him to the jungle.

The jungle and the river were a deadly pair. Oppressive heat, swarms of mosquitoes, giant snakes, prowling jaguars, and piranhas threatened the men on all sides. Despite the incredible diversity of the rain forest, there was very little to eat. After dumping the last of their meager supplies, the expedition had to hunt and eat monkeys to survive. Another threat came from the cannibalistic Cinta Larga, the native people along the river. Rondon's long experience in dealing with natives and his insistence that the expedition do nothing to threaten them allowed the group to move through the land without being slaughtered.

Rondon and Roosevelt eventually knocked heads, though. Rondon was determined to meticulously map the River of Doubt regardless of the lack of food and the terrible perils of the wilderness. Roosevelt was determined to get the expedition out of the rain forest before anyone else died. During one terrible day, Roosevelt suffered a minor leg injury that led to a wasting bacterial infection. He contemplated suicide and ordered the expedition to go on without him. Kermit refused, and Roosevelt realized that the only way to save his son was to allow his son to save him.

Roosevelt and his crew did make it out of the Amazon alive, only to return to deep skepticism and criticism from the National Geographic Society. Some members openly doubted that the journey had even taken place. The stature of Roosevelt and Rondon eventually won over even the worst detractors.

Millard's book is one part adventure novel, one part presidential history, and one part geographical treatise. She focuses on the men in the expedition and their experiences day by day, making the reader feel like another member of the party. Narrative chapters are occasionally punctuated by explanations of the geology, flora, fauna, and politics of the region. Rich details put readers directly in touch with the experience of this harrowing adventure. Millard did deep research for this project, not only unearthing journals and accounts long buried, but also traveling to the Amazon herself and interviewing the Cinta Larga. While flying over the rain forest, her plane stalled and dropped from the sky. If the pilot had been unable to restart the engine mid-flight, she too would have been claimed by the Amazon. These personal connections make Millard's book a vivid and real-life account of this amazing voyage.

Body sentences support the topic sentence in each paragraph.

The final paragraph reflects on the author's style and experiences while writing her book.

Writing a Literary Analysis

In a personal response, you explore your thoughts and feelings about a piece of literature. In a review, you discuss the merits of the piece, and in a literary analysis, you interpret it.

The starting point for a meaningful analysis is your honest response to the writing. You may like how the story line develops, find a character intriguing, or wonder why a writer returns so often to a particular image. Any one of these ideas, combined with careful reading and critical thought, can result in an effective analysis. Usually, you will present your analysis in an essay, supporting your ideas with specific references to the piece.

Learning Outcomes

Write a literary analysis.
Understand literary terms.
Use an assessment rubric.

"It must be remembered that no art lives by nature, only by acts of voluntary attention on the part of human individuals."

C. S. Lewis

Writing a Literary Analysis

A literary analysis may analyze a character in a novel, interpret an image in a poem, or examine the thesis in an essay. Follow these steps to write a literary analysis.

Prewriting

1. **Analyzing the rhetorical situation** . . . Answer the **STRAP** questions (see page 30) to identify your **S**ubject, the **T**ype of writing, your **R**ole as a writer, your **A**udience, and your **P**urpose for writing.

2. **Choosing a topic** . . . Your teacher may assign a piece of literature. If not, choose a book, story, or other work that has captured your interest.

3. **Finding a focus** . . . Zero in on what interests you most in the work—intriguing ideas, compelling characters, distinctive imagery. Freewrite about the text, if necessary, to focus your thoughts about it.

4. **Organizing your essay** . . . Write a sentence that states the thesis (focus) of your analysis. Then outline your main points and gather supporting details from the piece of literature.

Writing

5. **Connecting your ideas** . . . In the beginning, draw the reader into the analysis and identify your thesis. In the middle, explore your main points and support them with quotations, paraphrases, and other details from the text. End by restating the thesis, by emphasizing one main point, or by making a connection between the literature and life in general.

Revising

6. **Improving your writing** . . . Review your first draft and add, delete, move, or rework sections as needed. Use the following questions:

Traits

Ideas:	Have I selected an interesting piece of literature? Have I focused my analysis with a clear thesis statement? Have I included convincing support from the text?
Organization:	Does the beginning include the work's title, the author's name, and my thesis statement? Do my middle paragraphs thoroughly explore the thesis? Does the ending effectively conclude my analysis?
Voice:	Do I sound knowledgeable about the literature and use an appropriate voice for my audience?
Word choice:	Have I defined any unfamiliar terms? Is my word choice appropriate for the topic and for my audience?
Sentence fluency:	Do my sentences flow smoothly? Do they vary in length and structure?

▌ **Editing and Proofreading**

7. Checking for conventions . . . Check for punctuation, capitalization, spelling, and grammar errors. Also ask a classmate to help you look for errors. Use the rubric at the end of this chapter as a final review of your revising and editing.

8. Preparing a final copy . . . Create a clean final copy of your analysis and proofread it one last time before sharing it.

Supporting a Literary Analysis

It is important to support the ideas in your analysis with evidence from the piece of literature, as shown in the following examples.

- **Quotations** are word-for-word passages taken from a piece of literature. When only the author's exact words express the idea best, use them and enclose them in quotation marks.

  > Nancy Enright says that "both need to understand that skill in battle, though they have it to a high degree, is not enough for peace and wholeness. Together, they must find healing" (105).

- **Paraphrases** restate the author's ideas in your own words. Use paraphrasing to get to the point quickly when sharing information from the literary work.

  > When the dog's owner discovers him there, Christopher says he did not kill the dog, but he gets in a scuffle with the police and lands in jail.

- **Inferences** state assumptions based on facts or deductions. Use inferences to tell what is implied but not explicitly declared in a piece of literature.

  > Like most autistic people, Christopher has trouble reading even simple facial expressions. He describes people's clothing and hands, not their faces, as if it is too painful to look them in the eye.

- **Analyses** break information into parts, or details, and relate them to each other or the work of literature as a whole.

  > All these facts make Christopher alone in his social world, which demonstrates the very meaning of the word autism.

- **Interpretations** give a specific angle or view of the ideas in a piece of literature. Interpret the ideas in literature by applying them to life in general.

  > Haddon uses the theme of mystery to show how human expressions, language, and relationships can puzzle and confound a person with autism.

176

Literary Analysis of a Novel

In the following literary analysis, Becca Van Dam explores the character of Eowyn from *The Lord of the Rings*. (The works-cited page is not shown.)

The Transformation of Eowyn

The beginning names the book and author and introduces the thesis (underlined).

Many critics have noted the lack of female characters in J. R. R. Tolkien's *The Lord of the Rings* trilogy. Some attribute this fact to Tolkien's supposed sexism, while others argue that the shortage of women is merely a characteristic of the genre. In either case, it is important to notice that Eowyn, one of the few prominent females, also happens to be quite a complex character in the novels. In *The Return of the King,* especially, Eowyn undergoes a powerful transformation.

The analysis establishes starting points for the character.

In *The Two Towers*, Eowyn is established as a fiery shieldmaiden of Rohan. She longs to be part of the battle for Middle-earth and to achieve glory as her male counterparts have. Eowyn tries to convince Aragorn to let her go with him on the Paths of the Dead. In response to her declaration that she does "not fear either pain or death," Aragorn asks her what she does fear: "'A cage . . . to stay behind bars, until use and old age accept them, and all chance of doing great deeds is gone beyond recall or desire'" (977). Melissa McCrory Hatcher, author of "Finding Woman's Role in the *Lord of the Rings*," explains, "Eowyn feels that oblivion, not death, is the true fate to be feared" (47). It is partly because of this fear that Eowyn loves Aragorn. He embodies all that she longs to be part of and fight for. When Eowyn begs for Aragorn to let her come with him, he must reject her once more: "He kissed her hand, and sprang back into the saddle, and rode away, and did not look back; and only those who knew him well and were near to him saw the pain that he bore" (978). Aragorn cannot requite her love, adding insult upon injury to an already desperate woman.

The writer recounts a key event in the character's development.

Eowyn then decides to accompany her father and the rest of the Rohirrim to Gondor, disguised as a man. She and Merry ride together, two undesirables amidst the male dominated company of Rohan. Candice Fredrick and Sam McBride assert that Eowyn is forced to renounce her identity as a woman in order to fulfill her dream of attaining glory and renown (35). However, the events that unfold on the Fields of Pelennor contradict this statement. When Merry and Eowyn witness King Theoden's death, Eowyn responds by challenging the King of the Nazgul. He declares that "'No living man may hinder me!'" Eowen replies, "'But no living man am I! You look upon a woman. Eowyn I am, Eomund's daughter. You stand between me and my lord and kin. Begone, if you be not deathless! For living or dark undead, I will smite you, if you touch him'" (1047-48). Hatcher says, "It is important to

The writer shows how the character's transformation is not yet complete.

note that Eowyn fulfills the prophesy of the Ringwraith to her advantage. Her being a woman, not a woman disguised as a man, is crucial to slaying this monster" (49). This victory however, cannot be complete for Eowyn. Merry, as the only male witnessing the incident, views Eowyn's action with much of the same sentiment that Aragorn did in Dunharrow: "Pity filled his heart and great wonder, and suddenly the slow-kindled courage of his race awoke. He clenched his hand. She should not die, so fair, so desperate! At least she should not die alone, unaided" (1048).

After the battle, Aragorn cares for Eowyn and the rest of the wounded, acting as the Healer-King. "'Awake, Eowyn, Lady of Rohan!' said Aragorn again, and he took her right hand in his and felt it warm with life returning. 'Awake! The shadow is gone and all darkness is washed clean!'" (1081). Even though she is renewed to life, the shadow of her despair lingers. Both Eowyn and Faramir are left behind in the city when Aragorn and the others ride to meet the enemy at the Black Gate. Nancy Enright says that "both need to understand that skill in battle, though they have it to a high degree, is not enough for peace and wholeness. Together, they must find healing" (105). It is clear however, that Eowyn is far from this point: "'I do not desire healing . . . I wish to ride to war like my brother Eomer, or better like Theoden the king, for he died and has both honour and peace'" (1196). Faramir loves her immediately, despite her despair.

The character is physically healed, but needs spiritual healing.

Instead of finding healing when the ring is destroyed, Eowyn is thrown into more confusion. She does not answer her brother's plea to join him on the battlefield, and her health starts to deteriorate once more. It is when Faramir confronts her about this that the turning point and her healing occurs. Eowyn tells him that she desires "no man's pity" (1202). Faramir replies in a way that completely heals her: "'I do not offer you my pity. For you are a lady high and valiant and have won renown that shall not be forgotten . . . and I love you. Once I pitied your sorrow. But now, were you sorrowless, without fear or any lack, were you the blissful Queen of Gondor, still I would love you'" (1202). Hatcher comments that by calling her valiant, Faramir asserts that Eowyn has successfully avoided her fearful cage. "Faramir sees Eowyn as his equal, and he does not attempt to oppress her" (51). With this declaration of love, the shadow of her despair passes, and she is healed. Eowyn declares that she will be a shieldmaiden no longer. "'I will be a healer, and love all things that grow and are not barren'" (1203).

Only when she is accepted as an equal can the character truly heal.

The ending examines the character's complete transformation.

Fredrick and McBride again argue that Eowyn's healing comes at the cost of her freedom (35). However, as Enright says, this interpretation of the events is far too simple: "Her personal healing involves not only being open to love, but a movement from a desire for power and domination to the desire to heal and to help things grow" (105). At long last, Eowyn is fully appreciated for who and what she is. She is healed, and thereby transformed.

Short Literary Analysis of a Novel

In this short literary analysis, student writer Kyran Dasra explores the theme of materialism in F. Scott Fitzgerald's novel *The Great Gatsby*.

Glittering Outside but Empty Inside

The beginning paragraph identifies the thesis (underlined).

In F. Scott Fitzgerald's novel *The Great Gatsby*, Jay Gatsby gathers "enchanted objects" in a desperate attempt to fill the emptiness of his heart. <u>Although Gatsby seems fond of his sprawling mansion, splendid car, and exquisite wardrobe, his luxurious lifestyle does not bring him peace or satisfaction.</u>

The middle paragraphs use textual evidence to support the thesis.

As Fitzgerald introduces Gatsby, the reader is overwhelmed by descriptions of a lavish lifestyle. Elaborate weekend parties glitter late into the night. Most of the guests don't even know Gatsby, but they are happy to enjoy the festivities. Gatsby spends his time standing "alone on the marble steps and looking from one group to another with approving eyes" (51). It's as if Gatsby is a theater director, gathering props and actors to stage a magnificent although artificial performance.

Gatsby longs to be with his lost love, Daisy. In fact, he chose his mansion for its location across the bay from Daisy's home. After five years apart, Daisy and Gatsby are finally reunited. As he shows Daisy the mansion, he stares "around at his possessions in a dazed way, as though in her actual and astounding presence none of it was any longer real" (88). However, even Daisy is just another object to own, rather than a person to be embraced. Gatsby confides to his friend Nick, "Her voice is full of money" (115). The focus of Gatsby's hollow life has become possessions.

In the ending, the writer links the thesis with today's society.

On the outside, Gatsby is a distinguished figure with every luxury to gild his days, but on the inside, Gatsby finds himself to be truly empty, without any type of meaningful relationship. This point is made clear when Gatsby is seen strolling along his velvet lawn. He reaches into the darkness, straining to see the green light that marks the end of Daisy's dock—forever beyond his reach, forever just a dream. Even though this novel is set in the 1920s, it's easy to see the same story told today. When will people learn that all that glitters is not gold?

Help File

Can you find examples of quotations, paraphrases, and analyses in the essay above? By learning to recognize and understand these types of support, you'll be better equipped to use them in your own writing.

Short Analysis of an Essay

In this analysis, student writer David Foxx examines the main point in an essay by Richard Rodriguez.

To Turn Around Three Times

The beginning identifies the main point of the analysis (underlined).

"The teenage years are the best years of your life," my uncle once told me. My dad said he was crazy, that being a teenager can be a very difficult time. I think they both were right. In the essay "Growing Up in Los Angeles," Richard Rodriguez creates a compelling definition of adolescence and then extends the definition to refer to our whole culture.

Rodriguez defines adolescence using a series of contrasts. He contrasts being a child with having children, obeying adult rules with reinventing adult rules, battling for eternal youth with being overcome by "inevitabilities and consequences." According to Rodriguez, "The balancing trick of American adolescence is to stand in between—neither to be a child nor an adult" (348).

The middle analyzes the author's definition of adolescence.

He then extends this definition to apply to our whole culture. The first immigrants to this country "imagined themselves adolescent orphans" fleeing their fatherland to find a "land without history or meaning" (346). Those immigrants then wrote literature about their adolescent ideals, including books such as *The Adventures of Huckleberry Finn*. When the age of Hollywood dawned, the country began selling the ideal of eternal youth to the world, and the baby-boom generation "transformed youth into a lifestyle, a political manifesto, an aesthetic, a religion" (347). Our nation was born in adolescence and remains in it still.

The middle also interprets key ideas in the essay.

Our national obsession with youth has some less-than-positive results, though. Today's teenagers often have to take care of their siblings because their parents refuse to grow up. Adolescents in L.A. carry weapons because the streets are so dangerous. Gangs form to give kids the only real families they have ever known. Rodriguez describes today's youth as "tough and cynical as ancients." And he asks, "Have adults become the innocents?" (344). To a large extent, the answer has to be yes.

The ending provides a final intriguing thought.

Teenagers certainly aren't innocents, and youthful dangers aren't new. Think of Huck Finn, who had to escape an abusive, alcoholic father and flee with a runaway slave. Rodriguez believes these dangers have a purpose: "American teenagers are supposed to innovate, to improvise, to rebel, to turn around three times before they harden into adults" (344). In that way, the teenage years are simultaneously the best and worst years of a person's life—the dangerous, wonderful chance to grow up.

Understanding Literary Terms

The types and elements of literature are defined on the following pages. This information will help you to discuss and write about the novels, stories, and other literary works that you read.

Allegory is a story in which people, things, and actions represent an idea or a generalization about life; allegories often have a strong moral or lesson.

Allusion is a literary reference to a familiar person, place, thing, or event.

Analogy is a comparison of two or more similar objects, suggesting that if they are alike in certain respects, they will be alike in other ways as well.

Anecdote is a short account of an interesting event used to make a point. A number of anecdotes have been told about Abraham Lincoln, most related to what an honest man he was. One of them tells of a time when Abe was young and working as a clerk at a general store. After counting the day's receipts, he discovered that there were actually a few cents more in the cash drawer than there should have been. He then remembered that he had accidentally overcharged a woman who was in the store earlier that day. Abe took the pennies and set out toward her home, which was quite a distance away, to return the coins and make things right. This anecdote demonstrates that Abe was, indeed, an honest man. He would be known thereafter as "Honest Abe."

Antagonist is the person or force working against the protagonist, or hero, of the work.

Autobiography is an author's account of her or his own life.

Biography is the life story of one person written by another.

Caricature is a picture or an imitation of a person's features or mannerisms exaggerated in a comic or absurd way.

Character sketch is a short piece of writing that reveals or shows something important about a person or fictional character.

Characterization is the method an author uses to create believable people.

Climax is usually the most intense point in a story. A series of struggles or conflicts build a story or play toward the climax. (See "Plot line.")

Comedy is literature in which human errors or problems appear to be funny. Comedies end on a happy note.

Conflict is the problem or struggle in a story that triggers the action. There are five basic types of conflict:

- **Person vs. person:** One character in a story has a problem with one or more of the other characters.
- **Person vs. society:** A character has a problem with some element of society—the school, the law, the accepted way of doing things.
- **Person vs. self:** A character has trouble deciding what to do.
- **Person vs. nature:** A character has a problem with nature—heat, cold, a tornado, an avalanche, some other element of nature.
- **Person vs. fate (God):** A character must battle what seems to be an uncontrollable problem. Whenever the conflict is an unbelievable or strange coincidence, it can be attributed to fate or to an act of God.

Context is the set of facts or circumstances surrounding an event or a situation in a piece of literature.

Denouement is the final resolution or outcome of a play or story.

Dialogue is the conversation carried on by the characters in a literary work.

Diction is the overall effect of an author's words (preferably clear, correct, and appropriate).

- **Archaic words** sound old-fashioned: "I believe thee not."
- **Colloquialism** is an informal expression: "He's got game."
- **Jargon** is technical language used by specific groups: "override," "interface."
- **Profanity** shows disrespect for something sacred.
- **Slang** is informal language used by a particular group: "awesome," "chill."
- **Vulgarity** is language considered crude, low, and offensive.

Didactic literature instructs or presents a moral or religious statement.

Drama refers to plays; drama also refers to the type of serious play that is often concerned with the leading character's relationship to society.

Dramatic monologue is a literary work (or part of a literary work) in which a character is speaking about him- or herself as if another person were present. (See also "Soliloquy.")

Empathy is putting yourself in someone else's place and imagining how that person must feel. The question "What would you do if you were in my shoes?" is a request for one person to empathize with another.

Epic is a long narrative poem about the deeds and adventures of a hero.

Epigram is a brief saying or poem that often deals with a subject in a witty, satirical way:

"There never was a good war or a bad peace." —Ben Franklin

Epiphany is a sudden perception (moment of understanding) that causes a character to change or act in a certain way.

Epitaph is a short poem or verse written in memory of someone.

Epithet is a word or phrase used in place of a person's name: Alexander the Great, Material Girl, Ms. Know-It-All.

Essay is a piece of prose that expresses an individual's point of view; usually, it is a series of closely related paragraphs that combine to make a complete piece of writing.

Exaggeration is overstating or stretching the truth for special effect.
"My shoes are killing me!"

Exposition is writing that is intended to explain something that might otherwise be difficult to understand. In a play or novel, it is the portion that gives the background or situation surrounding the story.

Fable is a short fictional narrative that teaches a lesson. It usually includes animals that talk and act like people.

Falling action is the part of a play or story that leads from the climax or turning point to the resolution.

Farce is literature based on a humorous and improbable plot.

Figurative language is language used to create a special effect or feeling. (See "Figure of speech.")

Figure of speech is a literary device used to create a special effect or feeling by making an interesting or creative comparison.

■ **Antithesis** is an opposition, or contrast, of ideas:
"It was the best of times, it was the worst of times . . ."
—Charles Dickens, *A Tale of Two Cities*

■ **Hyperbole** (hī-pér-bə-lē) is an exaggeration or overstatement:
"I have seen this river so wide it had only one bank."
—Mark Twain, *Life on the Mississippi*

■ **Metaphor** is a comparison of two things in which no word of comparison (*as* or *like*) is used:
"A green plant is a machine that runs on solar energy."
—*Scientific American*

■ **Metonymy** (mə-tŏn-ə-mē) is the substituting of one word for another related word:
The White House has decided to create more public service jobs.
(*White House* is substituted for *president*.)

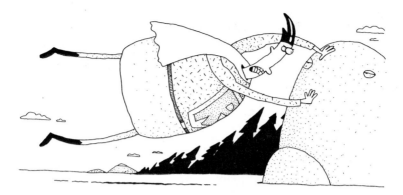

"The rock stubbornly refused to move."

- **Personification** is a literary device in which the author speaks of or describes an animal, object, or idea as if it were a person.

- **Simile** is a comparison of two things using the word *like* or *as*:

    "She stood in front of the altar, shaking like a freshly caught trout."
    —Maya Angelou, *I Know Why the Caged Bird Sings*

- **Understatement** is a way of emphasizing an idea by talking about it in a restrained manner:

    "Aunt Polly is prejudiced against snakes." (She was terrified of them.)
    —Mark Twain, *Adventures of Tom Sawyer*

Flashback is returning to an earlier time for the purpose of making something in the present more clear.

Foil is someone who serves as a contrast or challenge to another character.

Foreshadowing refers to hints of what is to come later in a story.

Genre refers to a category or type of literature based on its style, form, and content. The mystery novel is a literary genre.

Gothic novel is a type of fiction that is characterized by gloomy castles, ghosts, and supernatural happenings—creating a mysterious and sometimes frightening story. Bram Stoker's *Dracula* is probably the best known gothic novel still popular today.

Hubris, derived from the Greek word *hybris*, means "excessive pride." Hubris is often the flaw that leads to the downfall of the tragic hero.

Imagery is the use of sensory details to create a certain picture in the reader's mind:

    "The sky was dark and gloomy, the air was damp and raw, the streets were wet and sloppy."
    —Charles Dickens, *The Pickwick Papers*

Impressionism is the presentation of events or situations according to the writer's perception of them. Sensory details make such descriptions feel real.

Irony is using a word or phrase to mean the opposite of its literal or usual meaning. There are three kinds of irony:

- **Dramatic irony**—The audience sees a character's mistakes, but the character does not.
- **Verbal irony**—The writer says one thing and means another: "The best substitute for experience is being thirteen."
- **Irony of situation**—An action results in an opposite outcome.

Local color is the use of language and details that are common in a certain region or locale:

> "Memphis ain't a bad town, for them that like city life."
> —William Faulkner, *Light in August*

Malapropism is the type of pun, or play on words, that results when two words become jumbled: "Quick, grab the fire distinguisher!"

Melodrama is an exaggerated form of drama (as in television soap operas) awash in romance, suspense, and emotion.

Memoir is writing based on the writer's memory of a particular time, place, or incident. *Reminiscence* is another term for *memoir*.

Mood is the emotion created by a piece: happiness, peacefulness, sadness.

Moral is the particular value or lesson the author is trying to get across to the reader. The "moral of the story" is a common phrase in Aesop's fables.

Motif is the term for an often-repeated idea or theme in literature. In *The Adventures of Huckleberry Finn*, Huck is constantly in conflict with the "civilized" world. This conflict becomes a motif throughout the novel.

Myth is a traditional story that justifies a practice, belief, or phenomenon.

Narration is writing that relates an event or a series of events—a story.

Narrator is the person who is telling the story.

Naturalism is an extreme form of realism in which the author tries to show the relationship between a person and the environment or surroundings. Often, the author depicts the ugly or raw side of that relationship.

Novel is a lengthy fictional story with a plot that is revealed by the speech, action, and thoughts of the characters.

Novella is a prose work longer than the standard short story, but shorter and less complex than a full-length novel.

Oxymoron is a combination of contradictory terms, as in *jumbo shrimp, tough love,* or *cruel kindness.*

Parable is a short descriptive story that illustrates a particular belief or moral.

Paradox is a statement that seems contrary to common sense, yet may, in fact, be true: "The coach considered this a good loss."

Parody uses comic effect to mock a literary work or style.

Pathetic fallacy is a form of personification giving human traits to nature: *cruel sea, howling wind, dancing water.*

Pathos is a Greek root meaning "suffering" or "passion." It usually describes the part in a play or story that is intended to elicit pity or sorrow.

Picaresque novel is a work of fiction consisting of a lengthy string of loosely connected events. It usually features the adventures of a rogue living by his or her wits. *Mark Twain's Huckleberry Finn* is a picaresque novel.

Plot is the action or sequence of events in a story. It is usually a series of related incidents that build upon one another as the story develops. There are five basic elements in a plot line. (See below.)

Plot line is the graphic display of the action or events in a story: *exposition, rising action, climax, falling action,* and *resolution.*

Plot Line

Climax (Crisis)

Rising action (Complications)

Falling action

Exposition

Resolution (Denouement)

Poetic justice is a term that describes a character "getting what he deserves," often caught in his or her own trap.

Point of view is the vantage point of a story. First-person stories are told by one of the characters: "I turned sixteen that summer." Third-person stories are told by a narrator: "He turned sixteen that summer."

- **Omniscient** narrators share the thoughts and feelings of all characters.
- **Limited** narrators share the thoughts and feelings of one character.
- **Camera view** (objective) narrators record action without sharing the thoughts or feelings of any characters.

Protagonist is the main character or hero of the story.

Pseudonym (also known as a "pen name") means "false name" and applies to the name a writer uses in place of his or her given name. "Mark Twain" is a pseudonym for Samuel Langhorne Clemens.

Quest features a main character who is seeking to find something or achieve a goal. In the process, this character encounters and overcomes a series of obstacles, returning wiser and more experienced.

Realism is literature that attempts to represent life as it really is.

Renaissance, which means "rebirth," is the period of history following the Middle Ages. This period began late in the fourteenth century and continued through the fifteenth and sixteenth centuries. The term now applies to any period of time in which intellectual and artistic interest is revived or reborn.

Resolution, or denouement, is the portion of the play or story in which the problem is solved. It comes after the climax and falling action and is intended to bring the story to a satisfactory end. (See "Plot line.")

Rising action is the series of struggles that builds a story or play toward a climax. (See "Plot line.")

Romanticism is a literary movement with an emphasis on the imagination and emotions.

Sarcasm is the use of praise to mock someone or something, as in "She's a real winner" or "Charles is truly one of kind."

"Charles is truly one of kind."

Satire is a literary tone used to make fun of human vice or weakness, often with the intent of correcting or changing the subject of the attack.

Setting is the time and place in which the action of a literary work occurs.

Short story is a brief fictional work. It usually contains one major conflict and at least one main character.

Slapstick is a form of low comedy that often includes exaggerated, sometimes violent action. The "pie in the face" routine is a classic piece of slapstick.

Slice of life is a term that describes the type of realistic or naturalistic writing that accurately reflects what life is really like. This is done by giving the reader a sample, or slice, of experience.

Soliloquy is a speech delivered by a character when he or she is alone on stage. It is as though the character is thinking out loud.

Stereotype is a form that does not change. A "stereotyped" character has no individuality and fits the mold of that particular kind of person.

Stream of consciousness is a style of writing in which the thoughts and feelings of the writer are recorded as they occur.

Style is how the author uses words, phrases, and sentences to form his or her ideas. Style is also thought of as the qualities and characteristics that distinguish one writer's work from the work of others.

Symbol is a person, a place, a thing, or an event used to represent something else: the dove is a symbol of peace. Characters in literature may be symbols of good or evil.

Theme is the statement about life that a writer is trying to get across in a piece of writing. In most cases, the theme will be implied rather than directly spelled out.

Tone is the overall feeling, or effect, created by a writer's words. This feeling may be serious, humorous, or satiric.

Total effect is the general impression that a literary work leaves on the reader.

Tragedy is a literary work in which the hero is destroyed by some character flaw or by forces beyond his or her control.

Tragic hero is a character with a tragic flaw that causes an inner struggle and results in the character's fall or defeat.

Transcendentalism is a philosophy that requires human beings to go beyond (transcend) reason in their search for truth, arriving at it through spiritual insight.

Using an Assessment Rubric

Use this rubric to evaluate your literary analyses (fiction or nonfiction). It is arranged according to important standards of effective writing.

The writing . . .

Ideas

___ establishes a thesis based on one or more key literary elements (character, plot, theme, or setting) in fiction or the development of the main ideas in nonfiction.

___ draws evidence from the text to support the thesis.

Organization

___ includes an effective beginning, an informative and/or analytical middle part, and a strong conclusion.

___ presents the supporting evidence in an organized manner.

___ uses linking words and transitions to connect ideas.

Voice

___ speaks in an objective tone appropriate for the purpose.

___ reflects the writer's clear understanding of the text.

Word Choice

___ uses specific nouns and verbs.

___ uses words with the appropriate level of formality.

Sentence Fluency

___ flows smoothly from one idea to the next.

___ uses sentences with the appropriate level of formality.

Conventions

___ follows the standards of punctuation, grammar, and usage.

Design

___ uses design features such as titles, white space, and readable typeface.

Other Forms of Writing About Literature and Art

Have you ever seen a cave painting? Many involve a whole menagerie of creatures—galloping horses, snorting bulls, towering mammoths. In charcoal, ocher, and other natural pigments, ancient artists captured their world in images that fascinate us today. We can only imagine the purpose of these paintings. Were they part of a ritual? Did they commemorate a hunt? Or were they simply a medium for storytelling?

When you respond to a work of art—whether it's literature based, musical, or visual—you are encountering a human creation with many layers of meaning. By writing about your experience, you will better understand the art you encounter and be able to share it with others.

Learning Outcomes

Write a review of literature/art.
Craft an email to an author/artist.
Respond to a prompt.

"Every man's work, whether it be literature, or music or pictures or architecture or anything else, is always a portrait of himself."

Samuel Butler

Writing a Review of Literature/Art

In a review, you express your opinion about the value of a piece of literature or art. It's important to support your feelings with thoughtful explanations and specific evidence drawn from the piece itself. Use the following guidelines when you review books, short stories, poems, plays, movies, music, and so on.

▌Prewriting

1. **Analyzing the rhetorical situation . . .** Answer the **STRAP** questions (see page 30) to identify your **S**ubject, the **T**ype of writing (a review), your **R**ole as a writer, your **A**udience, and your **P**urpose for writing (analysis).

2. **Selecting a topic . . .** Think about the written, artistic, and musical works that have captured your attention. Consider titles you've recently read, viewed, or heard. Choose one that is still fresh in your mind to review.

3. **Gathering details . . .** Freewrite to collect your initial thoughts and feelings about your subject. Or, to work more systematically, create a T-bar chart, listing the work's strong points in the left column and its weak points in the right. Continue exploring and collecting ideas as needed.

4. **Focusing your thoughts . . .** Review the details you have gathered and consider how they connect with your main feeling/opinion about the piece. Choose the best details and use them to support your main point.

▌Writing

5. **Connecting your ideas . . .** In the beginning of your review, introduce the work and identify its creator. In the middle part, share the key actions or elements. If you are dealing with a work of fiction, avoid telling anything that would ruin the story for others who may want to read it for themselves. In the ending, recommend the piece to your reader.

▌Revising

6. **Improving your writing . . .** Review your first draft, focusing on ideas, organization, and voice. Consider these questions: Can the reader follow my ideas? Do I clearly explain how I feel about the piece and why? Revise your writing as necessary.

7. **Improving your style . . .** Check your word choice and sentences for clarity and effectiveness.

▌Editing

8. **Checking for conventions . . .** Look for and correct errors in punctuation, mechanics, usage, and grammar.

9. **Finalizing the design . . .** Ensure that your review makes good use of white space, headings, and paragraphs and uses a readable typeface. Make a neat final copy and proofread it before sharing it.

Book Review

The subject of Kya Hubble's review shown below is the novel *Girl with a Pearl Earring* by Tracy Chevalier.

Painted with Words

The beginning introduces the book and provides background information.

Inspired by the work of Dutch painter Johannes Vermeer, Tracy Chevalier creates the fascinating novel *Girl with a Pearl Earring*. Set in seventeenth-century Holland, the story comes to life through Chevalier's artistic use of historical details.

The book begins with the introduction of Griet, a 16-year-old girl living with her family. When two strangers come to the house, Griet listens to their conversation and thinks, "I could hear rich carpets in their voices, books and pearls and fur" (3). As a result of this meeting, Griet is hired to be a maid in the house of Johannes Vermeer, an artist.

Griet's daily tasks provide insight into what life was like for a servant, and she clearly understands her role. All the household clothing and linen have to be washed, dried, and ironed by hand. Groceries have to be bought every day from the local butchers, vegetable sellers, and bakers. Silver requires regular polishing to maintain its shine. Griet's life becomes consumed by her domestic duties: "I was new and young—it was to be expected I would have the hardest tasks" (21). Then Vermeer asks her to work in his studio, too.

The middle part highlights key features in the story.

As Vermeer's studio assistant, Griet learns about paints and painting. Paints are painstakingly mixed from ground natural materials: bones, white lead, madder (herb), and lapis lazuli (gemstone). Griet discovers "that the finer the materials were ground, the deeper the colour" (115). Explanations of the painting process reveal how much work goes into the creation of one piece.

Chevalier's use of imagery gives the book a strong sense of place and time. Griet and the Vermeer children "watched the boats go up and down the canal, full on their way to market with cabbages, pigs, flowers, wood, flour, strawberries, horseshoes" (46). As Griet does the daily shopping, she passes horses and carts rumbling past Town Hall, girls making lace, and shoppers making purchases in Market Square. These details help the reader envision Delft as it was in the mid-1600s.

The ending emphasizes the book's appeal.

This book weaves an imaginative tale about the story behind a Vermeer painting. Chevalier's imagery breathes beauty and believability into the *Girl with a Pearl Earring*. If you have ever looked at a painting and wondered about the story behind it, then you should read this book.

Drama Review

In the following review, student Anna Pitney analyzes a one-man play about life on the streets of Philadelphia.

Killadelphia

The beginning introduces key characters and then provides the thesis statement (underlined).

A man named Saul, living on the streets of Philadelphia and under the influence of drugs when he murdered the woman he loved; a radio announcer, describing the "war-like" violence of the city; a doctor, working in a hospital trauma center, comparing the brutality of Philadelphia to the war-torn deserts of Iraq: These and many more were the characters that Sean Christopher Lewis embodied when he performed *Killadelphia: Mixtape of a City* at the American College Theater Festival in Lawrence, Kansas, just a few weeks ago.

Middle paragraphs focus on the actor's techniques for depicting the many characters.

One of the challenges of doing a solo performance is having to impersonate and actually become several different people—taking on their particular styles of speaking and moving. These constant shifts in character occurred in a stronger accent or a simple movement. I felt I was watching a number of different people move about the stage. Lewis must have surely studied the people he impersonated, for he artfully captured their habitual gestures, slips of speech, and tones of voice. He wasn't Sean Christopher Lewis anymore; he was the convicted murderer Saul, one of the prison guards, the doctor who daily saw the pain of the city.

This paragraph analyzes the way that minimal props establish different settings.

Throughout Lewis's performance, he continually established and re-established the setting. He did this by using and rearranging a chair, a small table, a chalkboard, and a plastic crate. The lights dimmed, music sounded faintly, and Sean grabbed the piece he needed to continue, changing scenes, characters, ideas. Small adjustments allowed the audience to process what was just said and prepare for something different. Lewis carried the audience through many scenes. Though very few props occupied the stage, they were even more than what I needed to understand the performance. I could easily picture the prison yard's sharp, metal fence that Saul leaned against, or the table the opinionated radio announcer sat behind as he spoke. Lewis's words created many pictures that truly became real for me as I watched. He almost didn't need anything outside of himself to portray the story.

Throughout the performance, Lewis remained open to the audience. He used a lot of the space on stage but acted toward the audience. Doing so pulled me into the stories he shared. I couldn't help but watch him—his presence around the stage, the way he eased himself into the shifts in setting and personas, and the confidence that radiated from him. He held and captivated my attention for the whole performance.

Killadelphia: Mixtape of a City is more than a one-person show about the people of a city who are familiar with crime, violence, and poverty. Lewis doesn't just showcase or highlight those faces—he gives them back the voice they had lost. The hurting prisoners behind bars, the outsiders who can't seem to understand—Lewis captures these people and brings them into the light. His piece, done theatrically and artistically, is also a loud call for change. The forgotten people of Philadelphia have many important things to say, and Lewis's performance lets them speak.

> The ending paragraph sums up the performance and gives a final thought.

Music Review

The following review focuses on the song "Royals" by a sixteen-year-old from New Zealand.

We'll Never Be Royals

"Minimalistic" is how Lorde describes her work, especially her hit single "Royals." The song begins with Lorde's deep, bluesy, Adele-like voice, accompanied by a synthesized bass and snapping. This spare instrumentation does not change as the song progresses. Instead, Lorde's voice doubles and triples, becoming a soulful chorus of backup singers for herself. This unique sound comes from Lorde's creative process. She approaches songwriting as other 16-year-olds would approach poetry writing—something done privately in a journal. Since she was 12, though, Lorde's journal was a copy of GarageBand, a midi, and digital instruments that allowed her to accompany herself. The result is an intensely personal, powerfully confessional composition style. The lyrics to "Royals" deal with the teen experience of listening to rap music but being unable to achieve the wealthy rap lifestyle embodied in the videos. "That kind of lux just ain't for us. We crave a different kind of buzz." Lorde's work is simultaneously hip while being mature, fun while being poetic. Lorde's other single releases show an artist of tremendous potential at the beginning of her career.

> The writer identifies the artist and song.

> The review describes the song and the singer's style.

> Background information puts the song in context.

Crafting an Email to an Author/Artist

In an email, you can communicate directly with the person who created a work you care about. Show respect as you express your thoughts and feelings with an author or artist, and realize that you may or may not receive a response. A well-written email, however, improves your chances.

▌ Prewriting

1. **Analyzing the rhetorical situation . . .** Answer the **STRAP** questions (see page 30) to identify your **S**ubject, the **T**ype of writing (an email), your **R**ole as a writer, your **A**udience (a creator), and your **P**urpose for writing.
2. **Selecting an author or artist . . .** Think about books, plays, artwork, or music you've recently enjoyed. Choose one work and find its creator's email address, perhaps by contacting the publisher.
3. **Reviewing the piece . . .** Page through the book again, find clips from the play on YouTube, view the artwork online or in a museum, or listen again to the musical piece.
4. **Gathering your thoughts . . .** Freewrite about the work. Explore your overall feelings, focus on a specific part, or consider any questions you have.

▌ Writing

5. **Developing a beginning . . .** Create a respectful salutation and greet the person. Mention the piece that interests you and your reason for writing.
6. **Writing middle paragraphs . . .** Prepare middle paragraphs that share your connection to the work and provide observations and questions. Be polite and show your genuine interest.
7. **Creating an ending . . .** Close by thanking the author or artist for reading your email. Invite him or her to respond to any questions you may have posed. Restate your reasons for appreciating the piece.

▌ Revising

8. **Improving your writing . . .** Review your first draft, paying attention to ideas, organization, and voice. Add, cut, rearrange, and rewrite as necessary.
9. **Improving your style . . .** Focus on word choice and sentence fluency, making sure that you've expressed your ideas clearly.

▌ Editing

10. **Checking for conventions . . .** Review your revised copy for punctuation, mechanics, usage, and grammar errors.
11. **Creating a final copy . . .** Spell-check and proofread the message; press "send."

Email to an Author

In this email to the author, student writer Benjamin Draves shares his thoughts and feelings about Chinua Achebe's novel *Things Fall Apart*. Notice that Benjamin tells what he enjoyed about the book as well as what confused him.

The email begins with a formal salutation and a paragraph that identifies the novel and the student's reason for writing.

To: Chinua Achebe

From: Things Fall Apart

Dear Mr. Achebe:

Recently I finished reading *Arrow of God* in class, and I decided to also read *Things Fall Apart*. What I find unique about both of these novels is your strong insight into colonialism in Africa.

The writer explains what he enjoyed in the novel.

In *Things Fall Apart*, I especially enjoyed the character of Okonkwo. He is hardworking, strong, and respected, but at the same time he is fearful and angry and prone to making mistakes. This makes him a believable character, a kind of everyman that I can relate to. Okonkwo's extreme living conditions make me really care about him and make his life that much more tragic.

He shares a thoughtful question.

Mr. Achebe, there was one thing that I was confused about. Okonkwo, like most of the men in the Ibo society, views most women as weak and foolish. However, the priestess of Agbala is one of the most significant figures in the Ibo village. Her decisions have a great effect on Okonkwo's life throughout the book. Why is it that Okonkwo and the other men hold one woman in such high regard and have hardly any respect for their wives and daughters?

In the end, the writer tells what he has learned, thanks the author, invites a response, and includes a complimentary closing.

This book shows me that our greatest strengths can sometimes also be our greatest weaknesses. For example, Okonkwo does not show feelings other than anger because he does not want to appear fearful or weak. However, his fear of losing control in a changing society drives him to a tragic end. What you write shows that if we do not face our weaknesses and fears, everything we work for and believe in can fall apart.

Thanks for reading this email, and I would welcome any response you might like to make.

Sincerely,

Benjamin Draves

Responding to a Prompt

Prompts about literature or art ask you to state and support a thesis about a book, short story, poem, play, painting, or other work of art. Quickly work through the writing process to develop an effective response.

▌ Prewriting

    1. Analyzing the writing prompt . . . Answer the **STRAP** questions.

        Subject: What topic will I write about?

        Type: What form will my writing take?

        Role: What role will I assume as writer?

        Audience: Who will read my response?

        Purpose: What goal will my writing accomplish?

    2. Reviewing the work . . . Read the piece provided with the prompt, or reflect on a work you have already thoroughly considered.

    3. Outlining your response . . . Write down a thesis for your answer and quickly list supporting details.

▌ Writing

    4. Crafting a beginning paragraph . . . Identify the work, its author/ artist, and lead up to your thesis statement.

    5. Building middle paragraphs . . . Write a paragraph for each main point, stating it in a topic sentence and following with body sentences that support it.

    6. Drafting an ending paragraph . . . Conclude your response by revisiting your thesis and leaving the reader with an interesting final thought.

▌ Revising

    7. Reviewing the prompt using STRAP . . . Review your **STRAP** analysis to be sure you have accurately answered the prompt.

    8. Revising your answer . . . Check the ideas, organization, voice, words, and sentences in your writing. Make improvements to strengthen your work.

▌ Editing

    9. Checking for conventions . . . Eliminate errors in punctuation, capitalization, spelling, usage, and grammar.

Literature Prompt and Response

Prompt

In 1919, American poet Carl Sandburg wrote the brief poem below. This poem followed World War I (the War to End All Wars), which killed 16 million people, and the influenza pandemic of 1918, which killed 50 million. Read the poem, analyze its meaning, connect it to its context, and point out the poetic techniques used by Sandburg.

Grass
Carl Sandburg

Pile the bodies high at Austerlitz and Waterloo.
Shovel them under and let me work—
    I am the grass; I cover all.

And pile them high at Gettysburg
And pile them high at Ypres and Verdun.
Shovel them under and let me work.
Two years, ten years, and passengers ask the conductor:
    What place is this?
    Where are we now?

    I am the grass.
    Let me work.

Response

Let Me Work

Most of us don't think about grass. It is the green stuff that we walk on, the source of $10 after a summertime mow, the backdrop for clashing NFL teams. It carpets playgrounds, backyards, fields, golf courses. <u>In the poem "Grass," Carl Sandburg takes this most common plant and turns it into a symbol for human forgetfulness and self-deception.</u>

In the first stanza, grass speaks directly to the reader, giving commands—"pile" and "shovel" and "let." Grass is telling us what to do, letting us know that it is our partner, working with us. "I am the grass; I cover all." What is being covered? The bodies from the Battles of Austerlitz and Waterloo, one of Napoleon's greatest victories and one of his greatest defeats. The line sounds like the Internet meme that a good friend helps you move, and a best friend helps you move a body. The grass becomes a partner in covering up the carnage of war and helping us forget so that we can go on declaring more wars and killing more people. "Let me work."

The first stanza introduces this idea at a comfortable distance. The battles here are Napoleonic. The battlefields are grassy gardens, now. All those people died a long time ago, and half of them were French. This is a good place for a picnic. In the second stanza, though, Sandburg refers to more recent battles—first Gettysburg from the Civil War and then Ypres and Verdun from the War to End All Wars. These final battles were very fresh in Sandburg's mind, and the battlefields weren't yet green, grassy gardens. They were still torn up and horrible. Given two years or maybe ten, visitors to the spot will forget that they are standing atop tens of thousands of slain men. A walk through a green cemetery can be quite a peaceful journey until one remembers all the bodies in all the caskets.

Sandburg uses personification, having the grass speak to the reader and urge a partnership. The grass is eager to do its work—to cover all. If grass didn't do this, life would be pretty hard to live. After all, what is fertile topsoil but a layer of dead things underneath cushy grass? Sandburg also uses grass as a symbol for time and human forgetfulness. In time, visitors ask the conductor, "What place is this?" and "Where are we now?" These visitors represent new generations of human beings stumbling out over the healed earth where previous generations fought and died, not realizing that they are heading into yet another war.

The response draws evidence from the text to support the thesis.

Sandburg also uses repetition. The clause "I am the grass" appears twice, and the clause "let me work" appears three times. This repetition creates an insistence and inevitability. In this way, the grass isn't just a partner in human self-deception. It will do its work regardless of what humans do. All the limestone in the world has a similar origin, the accumulation of layer upon layer of dead marine animals, compressed together at the bottom of the ocean and then forced up onto continents, quarried by people, and built into great pyramids and other monuments. The grass, like the limestone, continues to cover over death until we don't notice it, right underfoot.

The ending paragraph reflects on the meaning of the poem.

Perhaps Sandburg is mocking us when he has us ask, "What place is this?" and "Where are we now?" But those questions help us dig into the past and remember what has happened there. Perhaps if more people had asked these questions at Ypres and Verdun, there would have been no Battle of Warsaw, no Auschwitz, no Hiroshima. Recently, a group of developers tried to turn part of the Battlefield at Gettysburg into a casino. How could anyone remember what had happened there over the flashing of the slot machines and the cascades of coins? Perhaps if human beings and grass weren't so efficient at forgetting one war, we would think longer before launching the next one. After all, just two decades after the War to End All Wars, we decided to re-up for World War II: "I am the grass. / Let me work."

Writers
INC

Narrative Writing

Writing Narrative Essays   201

Writing Narrative Essays

A personal narrative re-creates a specific experience or event in your life. The narrative can focus on a funny situation, a frightening experience, or a life-changing encounter. Whatever the focus, a narrative uses sensory details, specific action, and revealing dialogue to bring the experience to life.

Your personal narratives should invite the reader to share in your experiences, to feel the same things that you felt. You'll know your writing is a success when you can say, "That's just how it felt to lose the championship game," or "That's what life was really like with my friend Mia." As you write, be prepared to learn something new about the events, about others, and even about yourself. That's what writing personal narratives can do.

Learning Outcomes

Understand the narrative.
Write a narrative.
Review sample narratives.

"There is no longer any such thing as fiction or nonfiction; there's only narrative."

E. L. Doctorow

Understanding the Narrative

Narratives run the gamut from "What I did on summer vacation" to a dispatch from the front lines of a war to a Shakespearean play. Depending on the complexity of the story, narratives can include not only descriptive but also explanatory and argumentative elements.

In a way, we always want "the story"; we think "in narratives." And we find them in news stories, historical accounts, police reports, scientific documents, and more. Whether real-life or fictional, narratives include the following elements:

Using the 5 W's and H

Who — People: Narratives focus on what human beings are doing. A personal narrative tells about the writer's family, friends, and colleagues. A novel focuses on the lives of a group of characters. People are the *who* of a narrative.

What — Problems: Most narratives focus on a problem that occurs or on an obstacle to overcome. In fictional narratives, the problem that a character faces is called the conflict. Problems are part of the *what* of a narrative.
— Actions: Narratives tell what people do in response to the problems they face, showing how they act and interact. In fictional narratives, these actions are called the plot. Actions are also part of the *what* of a narrative.

Where — Places and times: Narratives tell what happens in one or more locations and at one or more times. Events usually take place in chronological (time) order. In a fictional narrative, the places and times are called the setting. Place and time are the *where* and *when* of a narrative.

When — Description: Narratives capture sights, sounds, smells, tastes, and sensations. News stories, historical narratives, memoirs, short stories, and myths all come to life by *showing* readers what happened rather than just *telling* them what happened.

Why — Meaning: Narratives interpret events to show their significance. A narrative is more than just a sequence of events. It means something, it is significant. A historical narrative, for example, shows why a specific event is important, and a fictional narrative develops themes that connect the story to life in general. Meaning is the *why* of a narrative.

How — Structure: Narratives have opening, middle, and closing parts, as do other forms of writing. Unlike the other forms, though, narratives establish dramatic tension early on and build toward a moment of truth, or climax. In the end, narratives show how events change the people involved. Structure is the *how* of a narrative.

Writing a Narrative

In a personal narrative, you re-create something that has happened to you over a short period of time—an uplifting event, a frightening encounter, a humorous incident, or some other memorable experience. Include enough specific details to make the experience real for the reader. If you cannot recall everything, fill in the gaps with details that fit the situation.

Prewriting

1. **Analyzing the rhetorical situation . . .** Answer the **STRAP** questions (see page 30) to identify your **S**ubject, the **T**ype of writing (personal narrative), your **R**ole as a writer, your **A**udience, and your **P**urpose for writing.

2. **Selecting a topic . . .** Think of a specific incident in your life that you think is worth sharing. (See page 94 for ideas.)

3. **Gathering ideas . . .** Imagine that you are sharing this event with a friend. What details would you include? Think about the specific actions related to the event. If any parts seem fuzzy, ask others who were involved what they remember. Focus on the following types of details:

   ▪ **Sensory details:** what you saw, heard, smelled, tasted, or touched
   ▪ **Reflective details:** what you thought and felt about the experience
   ▪ **Actions:** what people did or experienced
   ▪ **Dialogue:** what people said to each other

   To gather even more specific details for your narrative, complete a **sensory/reflective chart** like the one below.

Sensory/Reflective Chart

See	gray-tinted windows, waving parents, open farmlands, sun-bleached fields, woman in a housedress, Paradise Diner
Hear	clattering doors, hissing brakes, groaning bus, driver yelling into CB, muttering passengers, cursing man, words in Spanish
Smell	stale air, steaming engine, sweat, air conditioning
Taste	chocolate-vanilla twist ice cream
Touch	nosing into traffic, rusty minivan, hot bus, tight-packed people, blistering sun, searing blacktop, tugged sleeve, cool air
Think	never spent a week away from home, going to be a long trip, remembering my best friend and the Spanish he had taught me, pyramids in Mexico, beaches, family reunions, everybody seemed happier after breaking down, strangers becoming friends

▌Writing

4. Hooking your reader . . . Start your narrative right in the middle of the action. This will get your reader's attention.

5. Keeping the reader interested . . . Help the reader feel as if the experience is unfolding right before him or her. Show the reader your story; don't just tell it.

Use sensory details. Sensory details allow your reader to see, hear, smell, taste, and touch the same things you did.

> **Telling:** The turkey looked great.
>
> **Showing:** The skin of the turkey crackled as Uncle Bill carved it, and steam rose, curling out above mounds of sage dressing.

Share specific actions. Describe exactly what happened, using special details to help the reader visualize the scene.

> **Telling:** Our car went out of control and went into a ditch.
>
> **Showing:** Our car hit ice and fishtailed. Dad wrenched the wheel toward the skid, but it was too late. We slid sideways and tipped over into the ditch.

Include dialogue. Let the people in your narrative speak for themselves. Use words that reveal their unique voices.

> **Telling:** My friends Jana and Ella couldn't agree on what kind of pizza to order.
>
> **Showing:** "Anchovies?" Jana said. "You gotta be crazy. Who eats anchovies?"
>
> "I do," Ella replied. "But I could also go for a ham and pineapple."
>
> "Ham and pineapple!"
>
> "Or maybe mac and cheese. It's your call, Jana."

▌ Revising

6. Improving your writing . . . Read over your first draft (silently and aloud) to check for its overall effectiveness. Use the **traits** of writing to guide your revisions.

Traits

Ideas:	Do I focus on a specific event or experience? Do I use details and dialogue to show instead of tell? Does my narrative make the reader want to know what's next?
Organization:	Do I hook the reader in the beginning? Does my narrative flow smoothly, as if I were talking to a friend? Do I include events in the order that they occurred? Have I written a satisfying resolution or ending?
Voice:	Do I use a tone that fits the topic of my story? Does my personality come through in my writing?
Word choice:	Do I use specific, concrete nouns to create a clear picture? Do I use active verbs to tell what happens? Have I used words that have the right feeling (connotation)?
Sentence fluency:	Do I begin sentences in a variety of ways? Do I use sentences of different lengths?

▌ Editing

7. Checking for conventions . . . Once you have finished revising your narrative, make corrections so that it adheres to the standard rules of English.

Trait

Conventions:	Have I checked for punctuation, mechanics, and grammar errors?

▌ Proofreading

8. Preparing a final copy . . . Write or type a neat final copy of your narrative. Proofread it before sharing it.

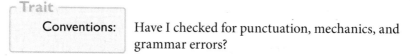

Help File

When you revise and edit your work, ask someone else to read it. As the writer, you're only guessing about what others know and need to know about your topic, so another person's perspective can be really helpful. Before you share your writing, however, step away from it for a time. Prepare yourself to listen to your reader's suggestions without feeling threatened by them.

Reviewing Sample Narratives

In this personal narrative, Lael Radde focuses on a day spent snowboarding.

The Day I Learned to Fly

The opening establishes the setting (place and time) and sets up the situation.

It's Christmas break, and I'm snowboarding with my good friend Dan. While we ride the lift, Dan describes the layout of the runs. "You see, this is Ullir Mountain, over there is Eagle Mountain, then Moose Mountain, and Mystery Mountain is to the left. Once we get going, we'll go to Moose Mountain. It has a lot of intermediate runs, and they're each about a mile long."

As I look down at the trees and slopes passing underneath us, Dan's words sink in. This is not a man-made hill, where you can only carve once before you reach the bottom of the hill. This is a mountain where the lift rides take over five minutes to make it to the top of the mile-long runs containing many steep drops, twists and turns, and the potential for a lot of pain. My heart rate is quickening; my skin is suddenly sweaty and clammy despite the chilly air.

Forget my insurance card; I should have brought my will.

The middle uses description and action to tell the story.

While the first run does involve some tumbling, a sore rear section, and a face full of snow, by the second and third attempts, my body remembers enough of what it is doing to complete the runs cleanly. Now, I am elated and ready to take on the next challenge.

Four hours of glorious snowboarding and one lunch break with the family later, we are now standing at the top of my favorite run. It is the run farthest out on Moose Mountain, so there are fewer people.

Sensory and reflective details make the narrative vivid.

We take off down the hill. The snow sprays off the edge of my snowboard as I cut across the hill. The air rushes across my face as I pick up speed. The exhilaration courses through my veins, making laps from my toes and fingers to my heart and back again. I want to yell and whoop as I chase Dan down the hill. We pass through a little tunnel of trees, breaking out to an open, sloping snow field. Dan glances back to check on me, but I must look as good as I feel, because he lets himself go faster, confident that I'll be fine for the last little bit of this trail. I cut heelside across the run, giving me a good view of everything downhill. The hill slightly crests, then heads more steeply downhill from there to the lift. As I come over the crest, I find myself heading down the side of the run where it slopes into the trees. I lean on my front foot and smoothly carve back to my toeside, where I can see up the hill behind me.

Except that I never get that view; instead, all I have time to see is a small child on skis blur right below my chin. Before I know what is happening, he rides over the front of my snowboard, shoving the back edge of my toeside snowboard into the hill. Forced to bite into the hill, the edge immediately halts the snowboard, and—WHAM—it catapults me.

I'm airborne, upside down. It's as if I'm snowboarding across the sky, headed downhill faster than I've done all day. Only one thought crosses through my mind: Crap.

I hit the hill in one glorious crash; my head and shoulder take the brunt of the fall as my legs jackhammer them into the hill. My helmet must have worked because I remain conscious enough to hear the resounding POP of my shoulder coming out of its socket. The sound and the searing pain are all I need to know the awful truth—I've dislocated my shoulder.

My momentum forces me to slide down the hill, but when I finally come to a halt, I wish I were still moving because now I'm very aware of my extreme pain. There is a fire burning in my shoulder, or rather, where my shoulder should be, for inside my roomy winter jacket, I feel the ball of my shoulder joint resting against the exterior of the socket. The tearing sensation of muscles stretched too far is multiplied a hundredfold as every muscle connecting my shoulder to my arm is protesting their new position by trying to yank my arm back into its proper spot. Despite those muscles' valiant efforts, my shoulder bone prevents my arm from sliding back into place. The pain overwhelms me, making it impossible to think.

As I sit up, a scream sounds in my ears, and it takes me a moment to realize—the person screaming is me. I lie back down. I'm just going to have to wait for help. Cold seeps through my jacket, my teeth chatter, and I think—tooootally worth it.

Eventually Dan and the ski patrol show up to rescue me from the hill and begin the painful process of relocation.

But it *is* worth it. The dislocated shoulder is a small price to pay for snowboarding across the sky. Whenever the chance comes to take another risk, a small part of me thinks, "Haven't you learned by now?" Another part always answers, "Nah." I'll continue to try, play, and dare my nerves with new feats. It's the risk I have to take if I want to learn to fly.

Strong descriptive details make the reader feel the injury.

The closing puts the event in context, showing how it affected the writer.

Sample Extended Personal Narrative

Some important experiences occur over an extended period of time. In this sample, Natalie Garcia focuses on looking for her father, a search that spanned a number of years. Note the "I remember . . ." details she includes.

Finding My Family

The opening provides important background information.

When I was four years old, I saw my dad all of the time. Although my parents were divorced, he used to drive all the way from Michigan just to see me. Sometimes he'd pick me up in his old blue pickup truck, and I'd travel back to his house, bumping along the potholed streets, listening to the radio.

I remember always waking up early in the morning, running into his room, and jumping on his bed to wake him. Soon after, I would smell homemade tortillas and eggs. Sometimes he even made breakfast burritos for a special treat. On other days, I just ate cereal.

I remember the sound of music from the ice-cream truck that would cruise through his neighborhood. We would run out of the house, and my dad would pick me up and hold me while I chose what I wanted. Sometimes I'd choose an orange push-up, but most of the time, I picked the green ice-cream frog on a stick with gum-ball eyes. It was my favorite.

My dad worked as a truck driver, and he'd often bring crates of produce home—bushels of bumpy brown potatoes, bright green peppers, and juicy orange-red tomatoes. I loved to eat the tomatoes whole, sprinkled with salt. I still do that now.

The writer shares deep feelings and concerns.

All of a sudden, my dad stopped visiting, and I was devastated. I wrote to him as many times as I could, but he never answered my emails. I thought that he didn't love me anymore. I asked my mom over and over why he didn't write to me. She said he probably didn't have the time. But how could someone not have enough time for his own child?

About a year ago, I finally received a return email from my dad. There was a phone number on the email, so I called. I asked about all of the emails he never answered, and he said, "I never got them." I didn't believe that, but I didn't care. I now had him back in my life, and that's all I wanted.

Then last year I came home from school and found an unexpected email. When I read it, I found out that I had an older half-sister, which really shocked me. (My family was suddenly growing.) She told me the real reason that my dad had never answered my emails: His English skills weren't very good. That, I understood, and I cried with joy after reading the email.

> " Then last year I came home from school and found an unexpected email. "

In the final paragraph, the writer shares the resolution to the problem.

I called my dad. During our conversation, for the first time since I was four years old, I heard him say, "I love you." I now know that I have family—here with Mom, of course, but now there's also Dad and a half-sister. My family may be scattered over three states, but knowing that everyone is out there is the best feeling in the world. It makes me feel like a hole in my heart has been filled.

Narrative Writing Tips

The following activities will help you find topics for personal narratives:

- **Page** through family photo albums.
- **Talk** to your parents, grandparents, aunts, and uncles.
- **Complete** a series of statements.
    "I was once . . ."
    "I remember . . ."
    "I wish I . . ."
    "Everyone says I'm . . ."
- **Brainstorm** a list of moments when you strongly felt these basic emotions: love, fear, sadness, joy.
- **Draw** a winding highway representing a map of your life. Note memorable experiences on the map.
- **Collect** writing ideas related to different periods in your life: early childhood, elementary school, holidays, and so on.
- **Introduce** yourself in writing to an imaginary stranger, starting with the phrase "I am the person I am today because of one very important experience . . ." Then describe the experience.
- **Write** a letter to the child that you once were, explaining how you have changed and why.

Writers INC

Creative Writing

Writing Stories and Plays

"What's the story?" You've probably heard this question from reporters, parents, and teachers as they try to get at the truth of a situation. You may ask the question yourself when you need to know what's really going on.

Lawyers tell the stories of their clients, scientists tell the stories of their theories, singer-songwriters tell the stories of their lives. And when you write a story or play, you are getting at the truth of what it's like to be alive. Even though fictional stories and plays are made-up, they share what is "true" about the experience of being human.

This chapter will help you understand how to write your own stories and plays, imagining events that never occurred or re-imagining events from another place and time.

Learning Outcomes

Learn about the story elements.
Develop a story or play.
Use an assessment rubric.

"The universe is made of stories, not atoms."
Muriel Rukeyser

Learning About the Story Elements

Whether you are reading stories or writing them, you'll be dealing with these basic elements: setting, character, conflict, plot, and theme. Each element is briefly explained below, and the following pages help you to work with them.

Setting ▪ Setting refers to the place and time of a story. Longer stories have multiple settings and can span many years. To help the reader get oriented, writers establish the setting at the beginning of each new scene.

Character ▪ A story centers on its characters—the people, animals, aliens, or machines that drive the action. Two key characters are explained here.
- **Protagonist:** This is the main character, the one the reader identifies with and likes. Sometimes the protagonist serves as the narrator, the person telling the story.
- **Antagonist:** This character opposes the protagonist and sometimes is called the villain. The antagonist can be a single person, a group, or even an idea.

Conflict ▪ Conflict arises when the plan or intent of one or more characters is opposed by other characters or situations. Conflict is central to a story and its characters. As a matter of fact, the words *protagonist* and *antagonist* have the same Greek root, *àgon*, which means "struggle." On page 214, you'll learn about different types of conflict.

Plot ▪ Plot is the overall structure of a story. The *exposition*, or beginning, introduces the setting, characters, and conflict. Then the *rising action*, a series of events, heightens the conflict, raising the tension as the story moves toward a *climax*. This is the point at which the protagonist faces the conflict directly and either overcomes it or is overcome by it. *Falling action* follows, moving toward a *resolution* that shows how the events of the story have changed the main character.

Theme ▪ Theme refers to the meaning of the story—what it has to say about life. Very rarely does a writer state a theme outright. Instead, the reader must infer the theme by analyzing the story and exploring its meaning. In the same way, a writer rarely sets out to write about a specific theme. Instead, by placing characters into critical situations, the writer discovers the theme as the story unfolds.

Developing Characters

Characters inhabit stories and plays. As a writer, you can base your characters on people that you know, or you can create all-new characters that no one has met. Include in each character a combination of strengths and weaknesses:

- **Strengths** make characters admirable. Perhaps the person can throw a football farther than anyone else in school. Or he or she volunteers on weekends to help the homeless. A character's strengths make us like him or her.
- **Weaknesses** make characters human. No one is perfect. Maybe the person who can throw the football is afraid of crowds. Maybe the person who helps the homeless has a terrible secret that no one else knows. A character's weaknesses make us care about him or her.

Describing Characters

When you create characters, give them multiple traits: species, gender, age, size, and so on. Here are a just a few of the possible adjectives you could use.

Physical

Species:	*Human, animal, alien, immortal, monstrous, ghostly*
Gender and age:	*Feminine, masculine; childish, teenage, adult, senior*
Size and strength:	*Hulking, beefy, wiry, svelte, scrawny*
Agility and dexterity:	*Graceful, plodding, quick, immovable*
Health and stamina:	*Robust, fainting, sickly, energetic*
Appearance and presence:	*Boyish, matronly, glowing, scowling*

Mental

Focus and drive:	*Persistent, organized, absentminded, determined*
Knowledge and skill:	*Talented, ingenious, capable, dull*
Attitude and outlook:	*Hopeful, pessimistic, desperate, committed*
Sociability and leadership:	*Outgoing, engaged, charismatic, shy*
Morality and ethics:	*Honest, conniving, compassionate, corrupt*
Wisdom and experience:	*Novice, seasoned, hardened, professional*

Understanding Wants and Fears

Define your characters by considering their desires, goals, dreams. Think about their fears, which will hint at the obstacles and challenges they'll face in the story. As you develop a character, complete the following sentences, possibly many times:

This character wants . . .

- to find a childhood friend.
- to build a sailboat.
- to overcome leukemia.
- to fit in at a new school.

This character fears . . .

- being left alone.
- a neighborhood dog.
- the final exam.
- what the email will say.

Working with Conflict

Once you understand the wants and fears of a character, you can begin to explore the conflicts that will drive your story. Conflict occurs when a person or other force opposes a character. There are six classic types of conflict.

- **Person versus self:** The character struggles with his or her own nature, thoughts, desires, or mind. This is an internal conflict.
- **Person versus person:** The character struggles against another character, as when the main character, or *protagonist*, is opposed by the *antagonist*.
- **Person versus society:** The character struggles against a particular group, an organization, or people in general.
- **Person versus nature:** The character struggles against natural phenomena such as rugged terrain, stormy conditions, wild animals, or desolate seas.
- **Person versus the supernatural:** The character struggles against destiny, magic, otherworldly creatures, or the divine.
- **Person versus machine:** The character struggles against computers, robots, technology, or other human creations.

Building Plot Structure

The conflict in a story provides the starting point for the plot: the character wants something but faces obstacles in getting it. As the story progresses, the struggle against the obstacles increases to a climactic point, when the character either succeeds or fails. After the climax, the action declines toward a resolution, showing how the character has changed or what she or he has learned. Here is the plot structure:

- **Exposition:** Setting is established, characters arrive, and conflict begins.
- **Rising Action:** Events intensify the conflict and increase the tension.
- **Climax:** The main character confronts the conflict head-on.
- **Falling Action and Resolution:** Events wrap up, and the characters move on, changed, perhaps wiser.

Writing Scenes

A scene is an event that occurs at a specific time and place. At the beginning of each new scene, your reader will have basic questions you must answer:

Reader asks . . .	Writer should . . .	Example
Where are we?	(Tell the location.)	On the front porch . . .
What's the time?	(Indicate time.)	as the sun quit the sky, . . .
Who's here?	(Tell who's involved.)	Rob and his grandfather . . .
What are they doing?	(Depict action.)	sat in folding chairs to talk away the evening.

Build your scenes paragraph by paragraph, each with a particular purpose, or focus. When the focus shifts, launch a new paragraph. And remember that you control the flow of information that reveals your story piece by piece. With that in mind, share details and actions to build suspense, making each scene a miniature of the overall plot structure.

Portraying Action

Action drives a story forward. The characters' actions can reveal to the reader most of the important details of a story.

▌ Showing Instead of Telling

You can *tell* your reader that a character is heroic, but if you *show* the character rescuing a child from the river, the reader will "see" and believe the heroism. Instead of telling the facts, show them through the characters' actions.

Don't Tell	Show
Joshua was incredibly strong and wouldn't hesitate to use his strength to solve a problem.	Joshua grappled the fallen log, hoisted it off his friend, and hurled it into a ditch.

▌ Sensory Details

Sensory details share the sights, sounds, smells, tastes, and textures of a story. By including these, you invite the reader to experience your story and live it vicariously. However, instead of telling us "Joe saw" or "Joe heard," show us what he saw and heard: "A bright flash lit up the room. Boom!"

▌ Specific Nouns and Active Verbs

Don't prop up imprecise nouns with adjectives (*yellow* fruit), but use specific nouns instead (*lemon*). Also avoid passive verbs (the night sky *was split* by lightning), but use active verbs instead (lightning *split* the night sky).

Creating Dialogue

Dialogue shares your characters' conversations. Each character should have a distinct way of speaking, revealing his or her personality and place in the story:

Identity: Use words that fit a character's personality, interests, thoughts, and desires, telling the reader who this character is.

> "Hey, the beach, yeah? A little sun. A little Frisbee. You in?"

> "Not me. See these freckles? I burst into flame when I step on sand."

Formality: For characters in positions of authority (judges, politicians, police), use formal language. For others, use casual language, or even slang.

> "Good afternoon, sir. Do you know why I pulled you over?"

> "Sure ain't for speeding seeing as this old tractor can't do but 30."

Vocabulary: For characters in a particular profession or social position, use the special vocabulary (jargon) of that group.

> "In your essays, I expect correct grammar, mechanics, and usage."

> "Man, I got no idea what you're talkin' 'bout."

Style: Vary the speaking style of characters. Some may get to the point with short, staccato sentences, while others may talk in long, flowing sentences.

> "Look! A bear. A bear! Oh no. What do we do?"

> "Just stand there and smile and look big. Stand and act natural. Smile, but don't wave."

Using Narrative Voice

The narrator of a story also has a distinctive voice. In your writing, experiment with narrative voice, choosing from first, second, or third person.

- **First person:** The narrator tells a story that includes him- or herself, using first-person pronouns such as *I, me, we, us,* and *our.*
- **Second person:** The narrator tells the story to the reader, using second-person pronouns such as *you, your,* and *yours.*
- **Third person:** The narrator tells the story about the characters, using third-person pronouns such as *she, he, they,* and *it.*

Help File

There are three types of third-person points of view.
1. Omniscient viewpoint shares the thoughts and feelings of all the characters.
2. Limited viewpoint shares the thoughts and feelings of one of the characters.
3. Objective viewpoint records action without sharing any of the characters' thoughts or feelings.

Developing a Story or Play

Story writing often begins with a question: "What's behind this image, memory, or feeling?" For example, a rickety old tree house may evoke a story about the children who built it. The memory of a former classmate may evolve into a story about losing a friend. Create your story with a few interesting characters, realistic dialogue, and believable action.

Prewriting

1. **Analyzing the rhetorical situation . . .** Answer the **STRAP** questions (see page 30) to identify the **S**ubject of your writing, the **T**ype of writing (a story or play), your **R**ole as a writer, your **A**udience, and your **P**urpose.
2. **Getting started . . .** Look for a seed, the starting point for your story or play. If you spent a lot of time playing near a river when you were young, that could be the setting for your story. Maybe you recall that both good and bad things happened there. Those memories could inspire your plot.
3. **Focusing your thoughts . . .** Organize your ideas. In most stories, there are people (*characters*) in a place (*setting*) doing something (*plot*) about a problem (*conflict*) and, in the process, they gain a new understanding about life (*theme*).
   - **Sensory details:** What characters see, hear, smell, taste, or touch
   - **Reflective details:** What they think and feel about the experience
   - **Actions:** What characters do or experience
   - **Dialogue:** What characters say to each other

Writing and Revising

4. **Connecting your ideas . . .** Write your first draft freely, guided by your prewriting plan. Start right in the middle of the action and let your characters tell the story by what they say and do.
5. **Improving your writing . . .** Make the changes necessary to create interesting characters and situations. Also, as the characters deal with the conflict, build the tension toward a climax. Keep the narrator's voice consistent.
6. **Improving your style . . .** Check that your word choice and sentences fit the story and create the right mood for your topic.

Editing and Proofreading

7. **Checking for conventions . . .** Edit your revised writing to correct any punctuation, mechanics, and grammar errors. Use the rubric on page 222 as a final check of your revising and editing.
8. **Preparing a final copy . . .** Make a clean copy and proofread it before sharing it.

Sample Short Story

The following short story tells about the education of a folding chair.

Frank Elem

The opening introduces the main character, sets the scene, and hooks the reader.

Frank Elem was a chair, but not just any chair. Most of the other folding chairs at his school lived on a trolley in a closet and came out only for events in the gym. But Frank worked every day. He was a band chair, a regular music supporter. For 30 years, he'd held up his end of the trombone section. Frank was built to last, with a black steel frame and a curved wooden seat and his name painted underneath: "Frank. Elem." They'd named him after Franklin Elementary School: That's how important he was.

A conflict drives the story forward.

This morning, though, a mom loaded him into a van and took him to the high school and used him to hold a box of T-shirts for a fund-raiser in the cafeteria. At the end of the day, she packed up everything else but left Frank behind.

Apparently, she thought he was ready for high school.

Frank couldn't believe it. At last, he'd graduated. A high-schooler! He felt a bit shaky but told himself he was ready for anything.

The only problem was, there *wasn't* anything. . . .

The cafeteria went dark. Everybody left. Frank stood alone among clusters of shiny Formica tables surrounded by chairs with molded plastic seats. He felt old-fashioned. None of the other furniture even looked at him. Frank stood there like that for a whole weekend.

Sensory details, thoughts, and actions make the story live.

Maybe Monday would be better. Maybe somebody would put him to use on Monday.

At last, the day came. The lights flashed on, and people started bustling through the cafeteria. Frank waited. Everybody walked right around him, though. A few students gathered at a nearby table and sat on the smooth plastic chairs, but nobody chose him. They talked and laughed like he wasn't even there.

Suddenly, a janitor grabbed his shoulder.

Dialogue enlivens the scene.

"Good morning!" Frank squeaked.

The man hauled him to one corner of the cafeteria, set him beside a wall, and stood on him to change a light bulb. At last, someone needed Frank.

But the janitor was heavy, and his boots pinched Frank's frame. He felt a terrible twinge. "You're really not supposed to stand on me," Frank groaned. "I sometimes get a hitch in my back and—"

Too late. Frank felt his frame give way, and he snapped shut, dropping the janitor and clamping around his legs like a crocodile. The man yelled and fell to one side. People came running.

"I'm all right. I'm all right," the janitor said. "Stupid chair."

Frank felt terrible. Why did he have to collapse like that? In front of everyone. And on his first day in high school.

The janitor snapped him shut and leaned him against the wall. Everybody went back to what they were doing. No one even spared Frank a second glance.

This whole thing had been a huge mistake. That one mom didn't know what she was doing. Frank wasn't ready for high school. After all, his last name was Elementary.

Just then, a student with long hair and a wispy beard walked up to Frank and stared at him. "Did you see what this chair did?"

A girl stepped up beside him and nodded at Frank. "Yeah. Totally snapped shut on that guy."

The boy clutched Frank's back, pulled him open, and slapped him closed. "Ha! Just like this."

"I've got a hitch in my back," Frank tried to explain. "You're not really supposed to stand on me."

"That chair could swallow a man, whole," the girl said.

"I-I-I-I—that's ridiculous. I've never swallowed anybody."

"It's perfect," said the kid with the beard. He hoisted Frank to his back and carried him out of the cafeteria and into the theater. The two students went backstage to a stripped-down chair trolley. "We'll fasten it on here, and this chair will be the frame for the crocodile's snapping jaws." He pumped Frank again, who snapped loudly.

"Perfect!" said the girl.

Frank was no longer a band chair. He was a theater chair. Chicken wire, foam, and papier-mache turned him into the Crocodile in *Peter Pan*. His performance made Captain Hook scream and the audience cheer. In the spring, Frank played a fender in *Greased Lightning*, and the next fall, he was a lead chair in *Twelve Angry Men*.

Frank was now a high school chair. He couldn't wait for college!

The details of the story are filtered through Frank's point of view.

The writer creates suspense by masking the intentions of the teens.

The closing completes the story arc of the main character, showing how he has changed.

Sample Fictionalized Journal Entry

A fictionalized journal entry is a first-person narrative told from the perspective of a participant in some important event. The excerpt below is the fictional account of one soldier's experience during the Battle of Gettysburg in the Civil War.

Journal of Color Sergeant Andrew J. Tozier

July 2, 1862: So, Old Abe dissolved the 2nd Maine Infantry after two years and sent most of the fellers home but sent me and about a hundred fifty more to join the 20th Maine. What a green company! Not a one of them'd seen action. Their rifles'd never been shot in anger, and I could get off three rounds before their fastest one could finish loading. Worst of all, though, I wasn't even carrying a rifle anymore since Colonel Chamberlain put me in charge of the regimental flag.

The opening gives the date and provides background information.

And this morning, without a gun in hand, I get thrust into the worst fighting I seen so far in this terrible war.

Colonel Chamberlain ran us and the rest of the 20th down south of Gettysburg on this boulder pile they call Little Round Top. We got shoved to the far left of the line and told to hold it at all cost.

The middle uses action and dialogue to tell the story.

Well, soon enough, we had ourselves a fight. General Hood brought his Alabama boys up against us, and boy could they fight! We had the high ground and the rocks to fire from, and the 20th Maine turned the air into flying lead. Still those Alabama boys advanced across the field. Minié balls split the air and bit chunks out of the regimental flag. I gripped the pole tight and could feel each bullet like a dog laying hold of the colors and yanking like to pull it from my grip, but nothing doing.

The narrator uses first-person pronouns.

"We're near out of ammo!" came a shout from below me. Sure enough, the cases by the shooters were lying almost empty. One private who'd run through his bullets was crouched down hurling rocks at the Rebs, they were so close. "They're coming up! We can't stop 'em!"

"Fix bayonets!" shouted Chamberlain.

He was ordering a charge! Well, at least that put me on even footing with the rest of the fellers. I figured I might not have a gun, but this flag pole of mine made about the biggest bayonet on the battlefield. I let out a whoop and charged downhill, my buddies from the 20th Maine all around me, into the teeth of the Southern line. . . .

Sensory details, precise nouns, and active verbs make history come alive.

Sample Play

A play is a story told by actors performing onstage, using dialogue and actions. The following excerpt shows how the beginning of the fictionalized journal entry on the facing page could be scripted for an onstage performance.

Title and playwright	<div align="center">**Color Sergeant Tozier** Zach Schmidt</div>
Cast of characters	**ANDREW TOZIER,** a sergeant in the 20th Maine Infantry **COLONEL CHAMBERLAIN,** leader of the 20th Maine Infantry **JOSH SORENSON,** a private in the 20th Maine Infantry **UNION** and **CONFEDERATE SOLDIERS**
Act and scene	**ACT I, SCENE 1**
Setting	**SETTING:** Little Round Top, a boulder-strewn hill south of Gettysburg, Pennsylvania, July 2, 1862.
Stage direction	*(TOZIER rushes onstage, carrying a heavy pack, two rifles, and two cases of minié ball bullets; SORENSON is right behind him, carrying a mortar. Other UNION SOLDIERS arrive with cases of artillery for the mortar, and all are hastily setting up defensive works.)*
Dialogue	**SORENSON:** 'Least we got here before the Rebs. **TOZIER:** Andrews, scout ahead! Make sure we've got this hillside to ourselves. **SOLDIER:** Yes, Sergeant. *(Exits with rifle.)* **TOZIER:** Sorenson, here's your rifle. **SORENSON:** Thanks, Serg. *(Pats the mortar.)* I'm hoping Betty'll convince them to stay behind the Mason-Dixon. **TOZIER:** It's not a matter of staying. They're already here. *(Points above the audience.)* *(Colonel Chamberlain arrives scowling, carrying the regimental flag.)* **CHAMBERLAIN:** This is everyone? **TOZIER:** The whole 20th Maine, sir, stretched from here to the ridge. **CHAMBERLAIN:** You're our left flank, Sergeant. General Hood's marched all the way from Alabama spoiling for a fight. **TOZIER:** We'll give him one, sir. **CHAMBERLAIN:** Not you, Tozier. You'll be the color sergeant. No matter how thick this gets, and it'll get thick, you keep this flag high. **TOZIER:** I'll use it as a bayonet if I have to, sir . . .

Using an Assessment Rubric

Use this rubric as a checklist to evaluate your fiction and script writing. It is arranged according to important standards of effective fiction writing.

The writing . . .

Ideas

____ clearly establishes a setting (place and time).
____ introduces interesting characters.
____ includes conflict, which builds toward a climax.

Organization

____ establishes setting, characters, and conflict in the opening (exposition).
____ builds tension in the middle (rising action).
____ reaches a high a point of excitement (climax).
____ leads to a closing (falling action and resolution).
____ builds scenes as miniature stories.
____ provides one focus per paragraph.

Voice

____ uses an effective storytelling voice.
____ includes dialogue that reflects who the characters are.
____ engages the reader with its use of language.

Word Choice

____ contains specific nouns and active verbs.
____ uses vocabulary that suits the setting and characters.

Sentence Fluency

____ flows smoothly from one idea to the next.
____ uses a variety of sentence lengths and structures.

Conventions

____ follows the rules of punctuation, mechanics, and grammar.
____ uses an effective design.

Writing Poetry

How would you define poetry? How would you describe it as a concept? Former Wisconsin Poet Laureate Bruce Dethlefsen says, "If a novel is winter, and a short story is a snow storm, then a poem is a snowball, squeezed." In other words, poetry is a smaller, more compressed type of writing. Every word, phrase, break, and even punctuation mark carries a great deal of weight.

By working with poetry, then, you can improve all your writing, as well as your reading comprehension. This chapter will prepare you to understand poems and to write your own.

Preview

Understand haiku.
Understand sonnets.
Understand free verse.
Understand poetic terms.

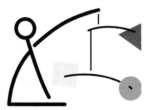

"Poetry is when an emotion has found its thought and the thought has found words."

Robert Frost

Understanding Haiku

You may know that a haiku is a poem of three lines, with five syllables in the first line, seven in the second, and five in the third. You may also be aware that this form originated in Japan and is traditionally about nature. But have you heard about the debate going on over the seemingly simple haiku in the English-speaking world?

The history of Japanese haiku is centuries old, with each new poem echoing earlier examples. Japanese haiku almost always contain seventeen syllables, a word to signify the season, and another to signal a thought shift at either the fifth or twelfth syllable. (See "Old Pond" below.)

The history of English haiku, on the other hand, is barely a century old. Some poets argue over how to best capture the Japanese form, and others adapt it to their own purposes, even omitting the nature theme. In addition, forming the seventeen-syllable English haiku, with our abundance of short words, may seem like cheating compared to crafting Japanese haiku, with that language's relatively long words.

Whatever you may think about the history and future of haiku, crafting an evocative poem with so few syllables is still good writing practice.

Sample Haiku

Bashō is Japan's most famous poet, and his most famous haiku is almost certainly "Old Pond." (Haiku are traditionally untitled.)

Bashō's "Old Pond" Haiku

Kanji version	Romaji version	Literal English	An English Paraphrase
古池や蛙飛こむ水のおと	Furuike ya kawazu tobikomu mizu no oto	Old pond . . . Frog dive Sound of water	A quiet old pond . . . suddenly a frog leaps in and water splashes.

 Search for other translations of "Old Pond" on the Web, as well as commentaries about the poem's importance.

"My Little Brother" Haiku

My little brother,
grinning, at my bedroom door.
What's he done this time?

—Bradley Schuerman

This haiku by a student writer focuses on a single image, with a sudden thought shift reflecting on that image. What one word might you use for this little brother?

Guidelines: Writing Haiku

Use the following guidelines to write your own haiku.

▌ Prewriting

1. Analyzing the rhetorical situation . . . Answer the **STRAP** questions (see page 30) to identify the **S**ubject of your writing, the **T**ype of writing (a haiku), your **R**ole as a writer, your **A**udience, and your **P**urpose.

2. Getting started . . . Jot down a list of striking images or other sensory impressions from nature, significant moments from your life, thoughts from a journal you may keep. Choose one idea from your list.

3. Focusing your thoughts . . . Ask yourself what makes this image, impression, memory, or thought significant. Isolate core details by freewriting about your chosen idea.

▌ Writing and Revising

4. Writing a first draft . . . Write your first draft freely as one, two, or three short sentences. Don't worry yet about syllable counts or line breaks. Just get your ideas down.

5. Improving your writing . . . Consider what you have written. Strive to describe the main idea of your poem without telling the reader what to think or how to feel about it. Look for ways to create a shift in thought at the end of line 1 or line 2.

6. Improving your style . . . Reconsider specific words and phrases to improve the impact of your haiku and to match a five/seven/five syllable pattern. Often, reworking a haiku to match that syllable count will reveal ways to improve the poem's rhythm and imagery. Don't rush this step; haiku may be short, but the best ones are polished over time.

▌ Editing and Proofreading

7. Checking for conventions . . . Edit your haiku for correct spelling, word usage, and punctuation. Haiku, like other poetry, may use punctuation creatively, but never carelessly.

8. Preparing a final copy . . . Make a clean final copy of your haiku.

▌ Publishing

9. Sharing your writing . . . Haiku make interesting Twitter posts. Just add slash marks to show line breaks (My little brother, / grinning at my bedroom door. / What's he done this time?) and add a hash tag like #haiku or #micropoetry. You may also post your haiku to a blog. Finally, look for a venue that hosts haiku recitals.

Understanding Sonnets

The sonnet is a rhymed poem of fourteen lines, typically using iambic pentameter (see "Foot" and "Verse" on pages 230–231). It is arguably the most widely used poetic form in the English language. Shakespeare himself wrote 154 of them, not counting those in his plays. Most sonnets in English follow either the Petrarchan pattern or the Shakespearean pattern, as in the examples below. (See "Sonnet" on page 231.)

Sample Sonnets

This famous sonnet follows the Petrarchan form. The first eight lines (octave) use an *abbaabba* rhyme scheme; the next six (sestet) are rhymed *cdcdcd*. Notice the subtle shift between the idealistic theme of the octave and the more realistic sestet.

How Do I Love Thee?

How do I love thee? Let me count the ways.
I love thee to the depth and breadth and height
My soul can reach, when feeling out of sight
For the ends of Being and ideal Grace.
I love thee to the level of everyday's
Most quiet need, by sun and candle-light.
I love thee freely, as men strive for Right;
I love thee purely, as they turn from Praise.
I love thee with a passion put to use
In my old griefs, and with my childhood's faith.
I love thee with a love I seemed to lose
With my lost saints, — I love thee with the breath,
Smiles, tears, of all my life! — and, if God choose,
I shall but love thee better after death.

—Elizabeth Barrett Browning

Video Games

Dry autumn nights would find my brother and me
gazing headlong into the digital
world of Mario or *Final Fantasy,*
hiding from Mom and Dad, pressing what little
freedom we had with plastic green and red
controllers in the small space of his room.
I remember sitting on his bedspread,
cross-legged together, adjusting the volume
to let us talk and laugh and forget
the fighting downstairs. *Don't take me away,*
we prayed, putting ourselves to bed at sunset,
saving our heartache for another day.
Primary dreams, silver streams of hall light,
a father-shaped shadow chokes out "Good night."

—Danielle Richards

This sonnet by a student uses the Shakespearean form of three quatrains and a couplet, with a rhyme scheme of *abab, cdcd, efef, gg.* A modern poem, it does not strictly follow iambic pentameter, but the "broken" rhythm suits the subject. Notice how each quatrain layers more details on the central idea, and how the couplet delivers a twist by sharing a new image.

Guidelines: Writing Sonnets

Use the following guidelines to write your own sonnet.

▌ Prewriting

1. **Analyzing the rhetorical situation . . .** Answer the **STRAP** questions (see page 30) to identify the **S**ubject of your writing, the **T**ype of writing (a sonnet), your **R**ole as a writer, your **A**udience, and your **P**urpose.

2. **Getting started . . .** Brainstorm to generate a topic for your poem. You may also choose to respond to an existing sonnet.

3. **Focusing your thoughts . . .** Make a list of ideas that reveal something about your topic. For a traditional Shakespearean sonnet, choose three parallel ideas—one for each quatrain—and a concluding idea for the couplet. For a traditional Petrarchan sonnet, separate your ideas into two groups: those that introduce and expand upon the topic in the octave, and those that respond to the topic in a new way in the sestet.

4. **Gathering rhymes . . .** Examine your ideas for words that suggest interesting rhymes and powerful line endings.

▌ Writing and Revising

5. **Writing a first draft . . .** Write your first draft freely, without worrying about exact line lengths, rhythms, and end rhymes. Jot new ideas in the margins of your paper as you draft. Tackle each section (quatrain, couplet, octave, or sestet) of the sonnet separately, without worrying about what comes after or before. Try different versions to see what you like best.

6. **Improving your writing . . .** Consider what you have written. Are the sensory impressions strong? Do the sentences make sense? Are the ideas in the best order? Does the sestet respond somehow to the octave? Does the couplet respond to the preceding quatrains? Rework any weak parts.

7. **Improving your style . . .** Have a friend read your poem aloud. Does the rhythm work? Do any rhymes seem either weak or heavy handed? Rework rough spots, using enjambment (see page 230) to avoid a singsong effect.

▌ Editing and Proofreading

8. **Checking for conventions . . .** Correct spelling and word usage and use effective punctuation.

9. **Preparing a final copy . . .** Make a clean final copy of your sonnet. Consider adding a title.

▌ Publishing

10. **Sharing your writing . . .** Submit your sonnet to poetry contests, print copies to share with family and friends, or post your sonnet online.

Understanding Free Verse

Originating as *vers libre* in France in the 1880s, free verse found its way into English-language poetry during the early 20th century, championed by poets like Ezra Pound and T. S. Eliot. Nowadays it is arguably the most common sort of poetry written.

Free verse follows no particular pattern: Its lines are uneven in length and their endings do not rhyme. Instead, each free-verse poem possesses its own internal structure, incorporating poetic techniques in new ways.

Sample Free Verse

The following poem written by a student demonstrates how free verse can incorporate the traditional techniques of rhyme, rhythm, and imagery while using untraditional line breaks to control the overall flow and emotional impact of the piece.

Home

Notice the rhyming *creak* and *sneak*, *dust*, *us*, and the nearly rhyming *stuff*.

The internal rhythm of the lines is controlled by word choice and punctuation.

Line breaks focus on interesting or powerful words.

Line breaks also affect the poem's pace, conveying ease or discomfort.

Repetition (*It's*) lends unity.

The last images convey a sense of finality, without telling the reader what to think or how to feel.

The words *window* and *mirror* complete the poem's message.

It's the third step to the living room
that, if I stay near the wall, will not creak
on Saturday mornings when I sneak down
for a muted Bugs Bunny. It's the counter
by the stove, collecting keys, mail,
loose change, dust—Mom asking us
Please take care of your own stuff.
It's not a hotel. It's afternoon summer sun
streaming through the bay window, flaming
up the curlicue copper wall molds,
setting the kitchen aglow. It's
my loss of breath
when Mom says *We've found*
something new; we're moving.
It's our living room—once comfy, close,
puffy furniture and afternoon movies—
now naked and bare. It's
the sound of the bright red door
Mom painted, to Dad's
consternation, closing.
It's a white house with blue
shutters, a stone pathway cutting
through a yard, Jake's tree leaning
for the kitchen window,
in a rearview mirror.

—Becca Van Dam

Guidelines: Writing Free Verse

Use the following guidelines to write your own free-verse poem.

Prewriting

1. **Analyzing the rhetorical situation . . .** Answer the **STRAP** questions (see page 30) to identify the **S**ubject of your writing, the **T**ype of writing (a free-verse poem), your **R**ole as a writer, your **A**udience, and your **P**urpose.

2. **Getting started . . .** Brainstorm or cluster a list of possible topics for a free-verse poem. Choose one that especially interests you.

3. **Focusing your thoughts . . .** Jot down details about your topic—as many as possible. Include sensory details (sight, sound, smell, touch, taste) as well as emotions and feelings about the topic. Choose which details to include and plan how to order them.

Writing and Revising

4. **Writing a first draft . . .** Write a first draft as if you were writing a descriptive paragraph. Don't concern yourself yet with line breaks, but get the strongest ideas down in good order.

5. **Improving your writing . . .** Review what you have written. Rearrange ideas for best impact. Break lines to focus on strong verbs and other interesting words and to control the flow.

6. **Improving your style . . .** Delete any unnecessary words or phrases. Replace weak or imprecise words and images with strong details. Read your poem aloud to hear and feel its rhythm; then fine-tune it by adjusting line breaks and wording.

Editing and Proofreading

7. **Checking for conventions . . .** Correct your spelling and word usage. Use intentional, effective punctuation, even if it is untraditional.

8. **Preparing a final copy . . .** Make a clean final copy of your free-verse poem. Add an interesting title.

Publishing

9. **Sharing your writing . . .** Submit your poem for publication, read it at a poetry event, perhaps a venue's open-mike night, or post it online. Your school's newspaper may accept creative writing, or your state may have a poetry organization that calls for student writing. Search online to discover what publishing options are available.

Understanding Poetic Terms

Alliteration is the repetition of initial consonant sounds in words:

"It is the happy heart that breaks."   —Sara Teasdale, "Moonlight"

Assonance is the repetition of vowel sounds without repeating consonants:

"Let the unknowable touch the buckle of my spine."
          —Mary Oliver, "Little Summer Poem Touching the Subject of Faith"

Ballad is a poem in verse form that tells a story.

Blank verse is an unrhymed form of poetry, normally written in iambic pentameter. (See "Foot" and "Verse.")

Caesura is a pause or sudden break in a line of poetry.

Canto is a main division of a long poem.

Consonance is the repetition of consonant sounds. Although it is similar to alliteration, consonance is not limited to the initial consonants of words:

"above his blond determined head the sacred flag of truth unfurled"
                              —e. e. cummings, "Two VIII"

Couplet is two lines of verse of the same length that usually rhyme.

Enjambment is letting a sentence or thought run from one line to another.

". . . with a puling infant's force
They sway'd about upon a rocking horse,
And thought it Pegasus."   —John Keats, "Sleep and Poetry"

Foot is the smallest repeated pattern of stressed and unstressed syllables in a poetic line. (See "Meter," "Rhythm," and "Verse.")

Iambic: an unstressed followed by a stressed syllable
Anapestic: two unstressed followed by a stressed syllable
Trochaic: a stressed followed by an unstressed syllable
Dactylic: a stressed followed by two unstressed syllables
Spondaic: two stressed syllables
Pyrrhic: two unstressed syllables

Free verse is poetry that does not have a regular meter or rhyme scheme.

Haiku is a form of Japanese poetry that has 17 syllables, with a shift in thought after either the 5th or 12th syllable. (In English, haiku are typically three lines long, with 5 syllables in the first, 7 in the second, and 5 in the third.) Traditionally, haiku have been about nature.

Heroic couplet (closed couplet) consists of two successive rhyming lines that constitute a complete thought.

Line break is an important element of free-verse poetry, affecting the poem's appearance on a page and causing the reader to pause at particular words.

Lyric is a short verse intended to express the emotions of the author.

Meter is the patterned repetition of stressed and unstressed syllables in a line of poetry. (See "Foot," "Rhythm," and "Verse.")

Onomatopoeia is the use of a word whose sound suggests its meaning, as in *clang, buzz,* and *twang.*

Refrain is the repetition of a line or phrase of a poem at regular intervals, especially at the end of each stanza.

Repetition is the repeating of a word or an idea for emphasis or for rhythmic effect: "someone gently <u>rapping</u>, <u>rapping</u> at my chamber door."

Rhyme is the similarity or likeness of sound in two words. *Sat* and *cat* are perfect rhymes because the vowel and final consonant sounds are exactly the same. *Stone* and *frown* are imperfect rhymes because the sounds that their vowels and final consonants make are similar but not identical.

- *End rhyme* is the rhyming of words at the ends of lines.
- *Internal rhyme* occurs when rhyming words appear within lines: "You break my <u>eyes</u> with a look that <u>buys</u> sweet cake."

Rhythm is the regular or random occurrence of sound in poetry. (See "Meter" and "Free verse.")

Sonnet is a poem of 14 lines, typically of iambic pentameter. (See "Foot" and "Verse.")

- The *Petrarchan* (Italian) sonnet has two parts: an octave (eight lines) and a sestet (six lines), usually rhyming *abbaabba, cdcdcd* or *cdecde.* Often, a theme is given in the octave and a response in the sestet.
- The *Shakespearean* (English or Elizabethan) sonnet consists of three quatrains (four lines) about the theme and a couplet (two lines) that responds. The rhyme scheme is usually *abab, cdcd, efef, gg.*

Spoken word is a type of performance poetry related to rap and hip-hop music. It involves both writing and dramatic speaking skills.

Stanza is a division of poetry named for the number of lines it contains:

Couplet: two-line stanza	*Sestet:* six-line stanza
Triplet: three-line stanza	*Septet:* seven-line stanza
Quatrain: four-line stanza	*Octave:* eight-line stanza
Quintet: five-line stanza	

Verse is a metric line of poetry. It is named according to the kind and number of feet composing it: iambic pentameter, for example. (See "Foot," "Meter," and "Rhythm.")

Monometer: one foot	*Pentameter:* five feet
Dimeter: two feet	*Hexameter:* six feet
Trimeter: three feet	*Heptameter:* seven feet
Tetrameter: four feet	*Octometer:* eight feet

Writers INC

Writing Across the Curriculum

Writing in Science

In 1687, Sir Isaac Newton published his book *Philosophiae Naturalis Principia Mathematica*, a work that redefined physics and helped usher in the age of reason. In 1916, Albert Einstein published *Relativity: The Special and General Theory*, a book that redefined Newtonian physics and helped usher in our modern age. For both of these great minds, writing was the key to exploring and expressing their ideas.

This chapter covers several types of science writing. It will help you remember and understand what you are learning, reflect on and develop new ideas, and express those ideas to others.

Learning Outcomes

Take notes.
Keep a learning log.
Write a summary.
Respond to a prompt.
Create a lab report.
Learn about other forms.

"Science is a way of thinking much more than it is a body of knowledge."

Carl Sagan

Taking Notes

Scientists take notes not just to record observations but also to think about concepts. Your science notes will help you remember what you learn, deepen your understanding, and study for tests. Follow these guidelines:

- **Reserve a spot for science notes** in a folder on your computer, a notebook, or a three-ring binder.
- **Date and title your entries** so you can easily find the information later.
- **Write down whatever your instructor writes on the board.**
- **Record and define new scientific terms.** Keep a science vocabulary list in a separate part of your notes.
- **Use your own words to explain new ideas.** Paraphrasing the information helps you to understand and remember it.
- **Draw pictures and create graphs** to visually represent ideas.
- **Link digital notes to Internet materials** that support the concepts you are studying.
- **Write down any questions that you have**; try to answer them later as you review your notes.

Sample Notes

Save   Edit   March 2

Exoplanet Search Methods

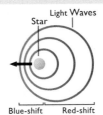

- **Wobble method**—Blue-/red-shift of star reveals movement toward/away from us. Period tells orbit time; shift intensity tells planet mass.

- **Transit method**—Dip in star's apparent magnitude reveals planet transit across star. Length of dip is time of transit/star diameter. Transition into dip is relative diameter of planet.

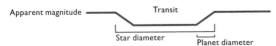

Exoplanet Types

- **Super-Jupiters:** Gas giants more massive than Jupiter
- **Jupiters/Neptunes:** Planets the mass of Jupiter or Neptune
- **Hot Jupiters:** Gas giants close to parent star
- **Super-Earths:** Potentially rocky planets up to 10 times Earth's size

Keeping a Learning Log

Writing in a learning log is a way of reflecting on what you are studying in class. It can deepen your understanding of the science concepts your instructor presents.

- **Set aside part of your science notebook or create a digital file** and store it in the same folder with your science notes.
- **Give each entry a date and title** so that you can connect it to your notes.
- **Freewrite about what you are learning in science.** Explore ideas without worrying about making every word correct. Ramble and discover.
- **Explain concepts as if you were talking to a friend** who wasn't in class. Often you learn the most when you teach the material to someone else.
- **Pose questions**, and then look for answers.
- **Do thought experiments.** Begin by answering, "What would happen if . . ." questions. Explore new ideas that occur to you.
- **Reflect on what you've learned** in each science unit to help you "lock down" the information.

Sample Learning Log Entry

| Save | Edit | March 2 |

Searching for Exoplanets

Today we talked about the search for extra-solar planets (exoplanets). The first thing that struck me was how much information scientists get from a little point of light. They can't see the exoplanets because they are too far away. Instead, they "see" the wobble of the star that the exoplanet goes around. But they can't actually see that either. What they actually see is how the light spectrum from the star shifts toward blue when the star is moving toward us and toward red when it is moving away. In other words, scientists aren't measuring the shift in miles or kilometers. They're measuring it in wavelengths of light. Talk about precise!

Mrs. Copeland told us that scientists now think our galaxy has about 15–30 billion earthlike planets. But hold on. What they mean by earthlike is a planet up to 10 times Earth's size and in the habitable zone around the star, not too hot or too cold for liquid water. Let's remember that in our own solar system, there are three earthlike planets—Venus, Earth, and Mars—but only one is habitable. So we can't expect all 30 billion earthlike planets to be habitable. And among the habitable ones, fewer still might actually have life started on them.

I hope we find habitable worlds beyond our solar system. I'd love to colonize another planet.

Writing a Summary

Every day, articles report new discoveries in science. By reading and summarizing such articles, you can better understand the latest scientific advancements.

▌ Prewriting

1. **Analyzing the rhetorical situation . . .** Answer the **STRAP** questions (see page 30) to identify your **S**ubject, the **T**ype of writing (summary), your **R**ole as a writer, your **A**udience, and your **P**urpose for writing.
2. **Choosing an article . . .** Check the Internet for reliable science news. Select an article that interests you and fits the requirements of the assignment.
3. **Surveying, questioning, and reading the article . . .** Look at headings, images, captions, and so on. Ask yourself questions about what you expect to learn. Then carefully read the article from start to finish.
4. **Reciting the main point and reviewing details . . .** State the main point of the article and then outline the details that support the main point.

▌ Writing

5. **Summarizing the article . . .** Write a topic sentence that captures the main point. Follow with body sentences that support this point with key details. End with a closing sentence that sums up the paragraph.

▌ Revising

6. **Improving the summary . . .** Ask yourself these questions:

┌─ Traits ──────
Ideas:	Have I clearly stated the main point? Have I supported it with key details?
Organization:	Are the ideas organized for easy accessibility? Do I use transitions to connect ideas?
Voice:	Have I used clear, objective terms?
Word choice:	Have I included key words from the article and used them correctly?
Sentence fluency:	Have I varied the beginnings and lengths of my sentences? Do they flow smoothly?

▌ Editing

7. **Checking for conventions . . .** Ask yourself these questions:

┌─ Traits ──────
Conventions:	Have I used correct punctuation, capitalization, and grammar? Have I spell-checked my work?
Design:	Do I use headings, graphics, and white space for readability?

8. **Preparing a final copy . . .** Proofread and prepare a final copy.

Science Article and Summary

The following science article focuses on Moore's Law and a computer-science breakthrough that could support it.

Article

Nanotubes Rescue Moore's Law
Charlie Broadhead

In 1965, Gordon E. Moore, cofounder of Intel, noted that for the past ten years, the number of transistors in integrated circuits had doubled every two years. He projected that this trend would continue for ten more years. As time passed, Moore's observation was adjusted to a doubling every 18 months and became Moore's Law. This trend has held strong for fifty years, describing many advances in technology, from microchip development to increased processing speed to increased pixelation in digital cameras.

Advances in microchip technology were beginning to slow recently due to some fundamentally limiting factors of silicon semiconductors. As microchips become smaller and more tightly packed, heat dissipation problems start to set bottom limits on further size reductions.

However, in 2013, a team of Stanford engineers created a rudimentary computer that used carbon nanotubes instead of silicon. These tubes can be as small as one nanometer in width (a billionth of a meter, or one ten-thousandth of a human hair). Using a mechanized process, the team created a proof-of-concept Turing machine that can perform simple calculations.

Though this mini-computer is not a production model, the use of nanotube technology could allow continued doubling of transistors, extending Moore's Law well into the future.

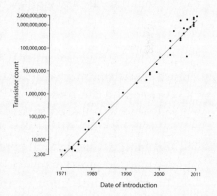

Microprocessor Transistor Counts 1971–2011 and Moore's Law

Student Summary

Let's Get Small: Nanotubes and Moore's Law

For sixty years, many fields of technology have experienced a growth rate that doubles every 18 months. This rate, known as Moore's Law, first applied only to the number of transistors on an integrated circuit. Since then, it has proven accurate in predicting advances in microchips, processing speed, pixelation, and other technologies. Recently, problems with heat dissipation threatened to end the doubling of transistors. However, in 2013, a team at Stanford created the first carbon nanotube computer, which uses circuits that are one ten-thousandth the width of a human hair. This advance could let the exponential trend of Moore's Law persist into the future. (Source: "Nanotubes Rescue Moore's Law," Broadhead)

Responding to a Prompt

Science prompts ask you to explain a scientific subject or use scientific data to argue for a specific position. When you respond to a test prompt, quickly work through the writing process to create the best answer.

▌Prewriting

1. **Analyzing the writing prompt . . .** Answer the **STRAP** questions:

Subject: What topic will I write about?
Type: What form will my writing take?
Role: What role will I assume as writer?
Audience: Who will read my writing?
Purpose: What is the goal of my writing?

2. **Creating a quick list or outline . . .** Jot down the main idea or thesis for your response and quickly list supporting points beneath it.

▌Writing

3. **Creating a beginning paragraph . . .** Introduce your topic and present a thesis statement.

4. **Developing the middle . . .** Provide support for your thesis in the middle paragraphs. Begin each with a topic sentence that presents a main point and follow with key supporting details.

5. **Including a visual . . .** If appropriate to the prompt, use a graph or drawing to express your ideas visually.

6. **Creating a closing paragraph . . .** Wrap up your response by providing any additional details, revisiting your thesis, and leaving the reader with an interesting final thought.

▌Revising

7. **Rereading the prompt . . .** Use the STRAP questions to check that your response accurately answers the prompt.

8. **Revising your response . . .** Check the ideas, organization, voice, words, and sentences in your writing. Make improvements to strengthen your work.

▌Editing

9. **Checking for conventions . . .** Check your response for errors in punctuation, capitalization, spelling, and grammar.

Science Prompt and Response

The following science prompt presents a scenario and asks the student to write an essay that explains scientific facts related to it.

Prompt

You and three friends donate blood at a blood drive. You discover that your blood is type O−, and your friends are A−, B+, and AB+. Write a brief essay explaining to your friends what these four blood types mean.

Response

Our blood types tell a lot about the biology we have inherited as well as how we have inherited it. Two systems categorize our blood—the ABO system, which gives a letter designation, and the Rh system, which gives a plus or minus.

The letter part of our blood type refers to the kinds of antigens that appear on the outside of our red blood cells. Type A has the A antigen, type B has the B antigen, type AB has both A and B antigens, and type O has no antigens. In fact, type O really is "type zero" because of its lack of antigens.

The plasma of each blood type guards against the antigen that the red blood cells lack. That means that type A plasma has anti-B, type B has anti-A, type AB has no antibodies, and type O has anti-A and anti-B.

Blood types include not just an ABO designation, but also a plus or minus designation, which indicates whether the D antigen is present. Those with the D antigen have a plus, and those without it have a minus.

All of these differences mean that blood types need to be matched. People with all blood types can receive their own type or O, as shown in the diagram. Negative blood types must receive negative blood, though positive can receive either type. Therefore, my O− blood makes me a universal donor, because anyone can receive my blood. My friend's AB+ blood makes her a universal recipient, because she can receive any blood type. These rules reverse for receiving plasma because of its opposite antibodies.

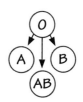

Blood types come from our parents, and different blood types predominate in different areas of the world. Differences in blood type most likely result from selection pressures caused by disease. For example, blood types that lack the Duffy antigen provide protection against malaria. As a result, our blood types tell about who we are as individuals and where we have come from as human beings.

Creating a Lab Report

A lab report outlines the procedure and results for a specific scientific experiment. It states a hypothesis, describes a method for testing it, provides observations, and draws conclusions. Follow these guidelines to create a lab report.

▌ Prewriting

1. **Analyzing the rhetorical situation** . . . Answer the **STRAP** questions (see page 30) to identify your **S**ubject, the **T**ype of writing (lab report), your **R**ole as a writer, your **A**udience, and your **P**urpose for writing.

2. **Choosing a topic** . . . Follow your science instructor's assignment or (if given a choice) select a topic that interests you.

3. **Organizing the experiment** . . . If your instructor provides directions, follow them. If you have designed the experiment, study your plan, gather materials, and carefully follow each step.

4. **Using the lab-report format** . . . Follow the format your instructor provides, or use the format shown on the facing page.

▌ Writing

5. **Opening your report** . . . Provide information for these sections:
   Purpose: Tell what the experiment is meant to determine.
   Materials: List equipment and materials.
   Variables: Indicate what variables you will test for and control.
   Hypothesis: Predict what will happen, writing a statement that can be proved or disproved.

6. **Developing the middle** . . . Describe the experiment in these sections:
   Procedure: Describe specific actions in step-by-step fashion.
   Observations: Record observations, giving exact measurements.

7. **Crafting a closing** . . . Draw inferences based on the observations.
   Conclusion: Discuss whether the hypothesis was proved or disproved and why.

▌ Revising

8. **Improving your report** . . . Check the ideas, organization, voice, words, and sentences of your lab report. Could another person use the report to replicate the experiment? Are your conclusions justified and clear?

▌ Editing

9. **Checking for conventions** . . . Check for punctuation, capitalization, spelling, and grammar errors.

10. **Preparing a final copy** . . . Create a neat final copy using the appropriate format and design.

Lab Report

This lab report describes an experiment about pendulum swing. It gives opening information, outlines the procedure and observations, and draws a conclusion.

Pendulum Lab

The opening states the purpose, materials, variables, and hypothesis.

PURPOSE: Determine what variables influence the period of a pendulum swing.

MATERIALS: String, paper clips, weights of 20 g, 100 g, and 200 g, ruler, protractor, stopwatch, paper, pencils

VARIABLES: Mass, release angle (amplitude), and string length

HYPOTHESIS: All three variables affect the period of the swing.

The middle details the procedure and the observations.

PROCEDURE: I attached a paper-clip hook to the drop ceiling and used it for attaching the string pendulum. I ran three sets of trials, each set testing for one of the variables:

- **Trial 1** tested 20 g, 100 g, and 200 g weights, controlling for string length (1 m) and release angle (45 degrees).
- **Trial 2** tested 15, 45, and 75 degree release angles, controlling for weight (100 g weight) and string length (1 m).
- **Trial 3** tested 1 m, 0.6 m, and 0.3 m string length, controlling for release angle (45 degrees) and weight (100 g).

OBSERVATIONS: Below, I have plotted averages for the three independent variables against the period of the pendulum swing.

Graphs visually demonstrate the relationship between variables.

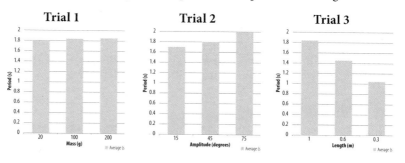

The conclusion explains that the hypothesis was disproved and tells why.

CONCLUSION: My hypothesis was incorrect. Though mass and release angle seemed to show very small effects on pendulum swing period, string length had a very large effect. The shorter the string, the faster the period.

Learning About Other Forms

Classification

Psychology—Research the Myers-Briggs personality profile and take a version of the test. Ask friends to do likewise. Write an essay reporting the results for yourself and your friends. Indicate what each category means and explore whether you agree with the profile.

Process

Chemistry—Write an essay that describes step-by-step how to conduct a specific experiment. Include the equipment and materials required, and note any cautions or warnings. Provide diagrams that can help others correctly conduct the experiment.

Definition

Earth/Space Science—Write a definition essay that fully explores an earth- or space-science term. For example, you might define "space-time" and how this concept came into being. Include public-domain illustrations or your own graphics.

Cause and Effect

Physics—Construct a miniature trebuchet or catapult. Safely launch payloads and track the results of each launch. Write an essay exploring the causes of increased or reduced distance and the effects of adjustments made to the device.

Compare and Contrast

Biology—Select two biological topics with some similarities and some differences, such as marsupial and placental mammals, or DNA and RNA. Write an essay that explores the similarities and differences between the two topics. Create and label diagrams that depict these similarities and differences.

Research

Any Science Class—Explore a science topic that interests you. Search secondary sources such as books and magazines, but also gather information from primary sources—experiments, interviews, surveys, and experiences. Write a research paper that reports what you have discovered. Document your sources.

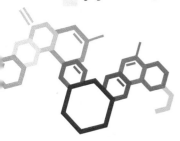

Writing in Social Studies

You've learned about prehistoric people, but did you ever wonder about the term *prehistoric*? How could people exist "before history"?

The answer is simple. Human history began, in a way, with the invention of writing. Prior to that, although people could talk about what was happening around them, no one could record it. After writing was invented, that problem was solved. Writing and history do go hand in hand.

When you write about social studies topics, you join a long line of people who have been writing since the dawn of human history. This chapter explores several forms that allow you to record and explore what is happening in your world.

Learning Outcomes

Take notes.
Keep a learning log.
Write a summary.
Create a current-events report.
Respond to a prompt.
Respond to document-based questions.
Learn about other forms.

"History is the interpretation of the significance that the past has for us."

Johan Huizinga

Taking Notes

Historians take notes to record events, make observations, and think about concepts. Your social studies notes will help you to remember key information, understand it, and review for tests. Follow these guidelines:

- **Reserve a place for notes** in a folder on your computer, in a notebook, or in a three-ring binder.
- **Date and title each entry** so that you can easily find the material later.
- **Record whatever your instructor writes on the board.**
- **Write down new vocabulary words and define them.** Keep a social studies word list in a separate part of your notes.
- **Use your own words,** explaining concepts to yourself as you write.
- **Draw pictures and create other visuals** to capture ideas.
- **Link digital notes to Internet sites** about the topics you are studying.
- **List any questions you have** and leave space to fill in answers later on.

Sample Notes

| Save | Edit | September 3 |

Berlin Wall separated West Berlin from East Berlin and rest of East Germany.

- Reinforced concrete, "Death Strip" of raked gravel, fence, guard towers, clear lines of fire, dogs, mines
- To stop East-West defections. Before wall, 3.5 million East Germans defected (20 percent of population).
- Symbol of Cold War/Iron Curtain: West used wall to show "failure of communism."

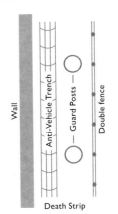

Defections after wall:

- 5,000 succeeded: climb, jump, run car through, use sewers, ride hot-air balloons, fly ultralights
- Another 136 killed trying to cross.

Major speeches:

- "Ich bin ein Berliner" (June 26, 1963) JFK declared Western solidarity with West Berlin.
- "Tear Down This Wall" (June 12, 1987) Reagan called for end of wall.
- "Rocking the Wall" (July 19, 1988) Bruce Springsteen calls for fall.

Fall, November 9, 1989: East Berlin party boss announces opening.

- People flock to wall to flood through.
- They celebrate, begin to tear down wall.

Keeping a Learning Log

A learning log lets you reflect on the ideas you encounter in class. Your entries can help you grasp new social studies content and deepen your thinking.

- **Use a digital folder or physical notebook for your learning log** and keep it separate from but nearby your regular notes.
- **Title and date the entries** so you can connect them with your notes.
- **Write freely** to explore what you are feeling and thinking about the material you are studying. Don't worry about producing error-free entries.
- **Explain concepts in your own words.** Then go beyond simple explanations and connect concepts to other subject areas.
- **Use PERSIA to think through ideas**—politics, economics, religion, society, intellect (the arts), and area (geography).
- **Write a summary at the end of each social studies unit**.
- **Review your learning log** before tests.

Sample Learning Log Entry

Save	Edit	September 3

Today's Berlin Wall

We learned today about the Berlin Wall, which kept East Germans from escaping to the West. For about 30 years, the wall was a symbol of the Cold War and the Iron Curtain across Europe.

Why didn't the Soviets realize how disastrous the wall would be to their international image? Their propaganda said that the wall was to prevent fascists in West Germany from meddling with the growth of communist East Germany, but nobody was buying it. West Berlin boomed economically while East Berlin lagged. The wall only highlighted this disparity, making capitalism seem the clear winner over communism. The Soviets could control media on their side of the wall but not everywhere else. That fact shows that totalitarian propaganda is always weak compared to public opinion in a free and open country.

What's happening now in North Korea seems similar. State-run media creates all kinds of propaganda about the greatness of the country, but outside observers see oppression, economic struggles, and state executions. Kim Jong-un has banned the Internet in his country, but everywhere else, people laugh at his country's propaganda.

Bullies can control what people say in their presence, but not what people say when they aren't around. The only way to get people to say nice things is to be nice to them. Oppression and lies go only so far. In the end, freedom and truth win out. That's what the fall of the Berlin Wall represents to me.

Writing a Summary

News reports provide the latest information about many social studies topics. Reading and summarizing news articles keeps you up to date with current events.

Prewriting

1. **Analyzing the rhetorical situation . . .** Answer the **STRAP** questions (see page 30) to identify your **S**ubject, the **T**ype of writing (a summary), your **R**ole as a writer, your **A**udience, and your **P**urpose for writing.

2. **Selecting an article . . .** Read newspaper and magazine articles and search the Internet for social studies news. Choose a reliable article that interests you and connects with a topic you are currently studying.

3. **Using SQ3R to closely read the article . . .** Survey headings, images, and captions. Ask questions as you go along. Read the material quickly from start to finish and then again, more carefully.

4. **Reciting main points and reviewing details . . .** Summarize the thesis and main points out loud, noting the key supporting details.

Writing

5. **Summarizing the article . . .** Write a topic sentence that names the article, its author, and the thesis. Create body sentences that support your topic sentence. Include a closing sentence that sums up the article.

Revising

6. **Improving the summary . . .** Ask yourself these questions:

Traits	
Ideas:	Have I stated the thesis? Have I captured the main points? Do I include only necessary details?
Organization:	Have I organized ideas to make them easy to grasp? Do transitions connect the ideas?
Voice:	Do I convey ideas objectively, matching the article's voice?
Word choice:	Do I use key words from the article correctly? Do I define unfamiliar terms?
Sentence fluency:	Have I crafted smooth-reading sentences? Do I use a variety of sentence lengths and beginnings?

Editing

7. **Checking for conventions . . .** Ask yourself these questions:

Trait	
Conventions:	Are my punctuation, capitalization, and grammar correct? Have I used the spell-checker?

8. **Creating a neat, final copy . . .** Proofread and prepare a final copy.

Social Studies Article and Summary

The following social studies article focuses on an ancient temple discovered in Turkey. The site requires historians to rethink their ideas about prehistoric people.

Article

Mysteries of Göbekli Tepe
Jason Devlin

Excavations at a temple in southeastern Turkey are changing our beliefs about prehistoric humans. The site, called Göbekli Tepe (or Potbelly Hill) consists of large T-shaped monoliths standing in circles, much like those at Stonehenge. Surprisingly, though, these stones were erected at least 6,000 years earlier.

This ancient temple site was built about 12,000 years ago, before writing, metallurgy, pottery, or the wheel. It predates agriculture and animal husbandry. Its builders weren't from city-states. They were hunter-gatherers.

Certainly, animals figure large in the temple complex itself. The walls contain carvings of what chief archaeologist Klaus Schmidt describes as a "stone-age zoo" with vultures, gazelles, donkeys, lions, snakes, bulls, insects, spiders, birds, boars, and foxes. A large stone crocodile slithers along between the stones, its teeth bared menacingly. The T-shapes themselves seem to be human analogs, with some having arms carved into them and others having loin cloths.

What was the purpose of this elaborate gathering of monoliths? After 20 years of excavation, Schmidt believes that Göbekli Tepe was not a dwelling. He has found no sign of continued habitation. Instead, the site seems a center for ancestor worship, with the T-stones representing the ancestors and the other carvings being animal guardians.

Perhaps most puzzling of all, the site was purposely backfilled with rubble around 8,000 B.C.E. The stones were not toppled but buried, as if to preserve them.

How could prehistoric people carve out and erect 6 m tall stones? Why would they do so? As of yet, these questions remain unanswered. What Göbekli Tepe does tell us is that, even prior to the Neolithic Revolution, our ancestors were capable of working together on vast projects over long periods. Primitive people were not so primitive as we once believed.

Student Summary

Turkey's Prehistoric Temple

In "Mysteries of Gobekli Tepe," Jason Devlin reports about a 12,000-year-old temple complex in Turkey that is changing our ideas about prehistoric people. The complex consists of circles of T-shaped monoliths, some up to 6 m in height, with many animal carvings around them. Chief archaeologist Klaus Schmidt believes the site to be a temple for ancestor worship, with the T-shaped monoliths representing the ancestors and animal carvings representing guardians. Around 8,000 B.C.E., the complex was intentionally backfilled, apparently to preserve the stones. The temple was built by people who did not have writing, agriculture, or the wheel. It changes our ideas of what hunter-gatherers could accomplish.

Creating a Current-Events Report

A current-events report tells the reader what is happening and why it is important by answering the 5 W's and H (who? what? where? when? why? and how?).

■ Prewriting

1. **Analyzing the rhetorical situation** . . . Answer the **STRAP** questions (see page 30) to identify your **S**ubject, the **T**ype of writing, your **R**ole as a writer, your **A**udience, and your **P**urpose for writing (to report events).

2. **Selecting a topic** . . . Check newspapers, journals, magazines, and Web services for articles. Consider current events that involve geography, archaeology, culture, politics, and art. Choose a topic that interests you.

3. **Gathering information** . . . Collect facts and details, and check the sources to ensure that your data is current and reliable.

4. **Writing a thesis statement** . . . Name your topic and tell what you want to say about it.

■ Writing

5. **Beginning your report** . . . Write an opening paragraph that captures your reader's interest and leads to your thesis statement.

6. **Building middle paragraphs** . . . Focus each paragraph on one point that supports your thesis.

8. **Answering the 5 W's and H** . . . Report *who? what? where? when? why?* and *how?* Answer any other questions you think the reader may have.

9. **Closing your report** . . . End with a paragraph that wraps up your ideas.

■ Revising

10. **Improving your report** . . . Ask yourself these questions:

Traits	
Ideas:	Is my thesis statement clear? Have I answered the 5 W's and H?
Organization:	Do I have a strong beginning, middle, and ending? Do I use transitions to connect my ideas?
Voice:	Do I sound confident about and interested in the topic?
Word choice:	Have I defined any unfamiliar terms?
Sentence fluency:	Are my sentences complete and easy to read?

■ Editing

11. **Checking for conventions** . . . Ask yourself these questions:

Trait	
Conventions:	Do I use correct punctuation, capitalization, and spelling?

12. **Creating a final copy** . . . Prepare a neat copy to share.

Current-Events Report

The following current-events report by Corporal Jahn R. Kuiper focuses on a Marine who has battled back from a devastating injury in order to rejoin his unit.

The beginning captures the reader's attention and introduces the main idea.

Marine Burn Victim Blazes Through Road to Recovery

After an improvised explosive device had one Marine burned, broken, and at death's doorstep, the sergeant did what any good Marine would: He battled back. Now he is on the verge of returning to active duty.

For Sgt. Isaac Gallegos, a 26-year-old native of Dulce, N.M., returning to his unit, the 3rd Light Armored Reconnaissance, has been on his mind since he stepped on that IED in the Al Anbar Province, Afghanistan.

Middle paragraphs answer the 5 W's and H of the situation.

Burned over 74 percent of his body, his jaw shattered into 37 pieces, and his left ulna broken, Gallegos maintained a core value of determination. "That's all I've been thinking about since I got injured," said Gallegos, an infantry scout. "I want to get back with my guys and get back to doing my job."

But before he can return to his unit, Gallegos has to prove he is fit for duty. After extensive physical therapy where therapists worked to stretch and break up the scar tissue, Gallegos got back into training his body. He even scored a 292 on the combat fitness test last December. But for Gallegos the more proof he can offer, the better. So the Marine Corps Trials has become another testament to his readiness.

Facts, anecdotes, quotations, and statistics support the main points of the report.

The Trials is a series of athletic competitions held by the Wounded Warrior Regiment, headquartered aboard Quantico, Virginia, and is designed to build morale. This year more than 150 participated at the Trials Feb. 21-26 at Marine Corps Base Camp Pendleton, California. The top 50 competitors will compete in the all-service Warrior Games on May 16-22 at Colorado Springs, Colorado.

"I knew some guys who were doing it, so I thought it would be fun to join in and see how far I've progressed as I compete against other guys," said Gallegos, who competed in the prone shooting competition, the 100- and 200-meter sprint, and the 400-meter relay sprint.

A final quotation sums up the experience of the Marine.

"I think I definitely proved to myself I'm capable of doing my work again," Gallegos said. "I'm ready."

Responding to a Prompt

Social studies prompts ask you to write about history, geography, politics, economics, or the arts. Some prompts, like the one on the facing page, ask you to write about what you have already learned. Others, called document-based questions (DBQs), provide articles, graphics, and other documents that you must read before forming your response. Quickly work through the writing process to prepare your best response.

▌Prewriting

1. Analyzing the writing prompt . . . Answer the **STRAP** questions:

Subject: What topic will I write about?
Type: What form will my writing take?
Role: What role will I assume as writer?
Audience: Who will read my writing?
Purpose: What is the goal of my writing?

2. Outlining your response . . . Write down the main idea, or thesis, of your answer and quickly list supporting points.

▌Writing

3. Crafting an opening paragraph . . . Introduce your topic and provide a thesis statement.

4. Building middle paragraphs . . . Begin each paragraph with a topic sentence that presents one of your main supporting points. Follow with body sentences that include supporting details.

5. Using transitions . . . Connect paragraphs and sentences using transitions that indicate time, importance, cause and effect, and so on. (See pages 86–88.)

6. Drafting a closing paragraph . . . Conclude your response by revisiting your thesis and leaving the reader with an interesting final thought.

▌Revising

7. Reviewing the prompt using STRAP . . . Revisit your **STRAP** analysis to be certain you have accurately answered the prompt.

8. Revising your answer . . . Check the ideas, organization, voice, words, and sentences of your writing. Make improvements to strengthen your work.

▌Editing

9. Editing for conventions . . . Check your answer to eliminate errors in punctuation, capitalization, spelling, and grammar.

Social Studies Prompt and Response

The following social studies prompt asks students to trace the causes and effects of the Battle of the Alamo.

Prompt

The Battle of the Alamo became a turning point for the Texas Revolution. In an essay, explain the causes that led up to the Battle of the Alamo and the effects that resulted from it. Draw evidence from your textbook to support your points.

Response

Many people consider the Battle of the Alamo a pivotal point in the Texas Revolution. Indeed, before and during the battle, the Mexican forces seemed to be winning the war, but after the Alamo, things changed. To understand how and why things changed, one must discover this battle's causes and effects.

The road to the Alamo started in 1821 after Mexico had won its independence from Spain. Because the new republic was bankrupted by the war, it encouraged local populations to create militias to defend themselves. The government also encouraged settlers from the United States as long as they declared allegiance to Mexico and didn't bring slaves. Settlers flooded in, bringing their slaves. Texans increasingly came to see themselves as separate from both Mexico and the United States and moved toward declaring their own independence. The Mexican government sent General Martin Perfecto de Cos northward with a small fighting band to quell the Texan rebellion. After a series of battles, though, his force was pushed back to the Alamo, where they were defeated in December of 1835 by Stephen Austin and his Texas army. The old Spanish mission became a Texan stronghold.

Determined to end the Texan Revolution, Mexican dictator and general Santa Anna marched an army north. On February 23 of 1836, Santa Anna and 1,500 Mexican troops surrounded the Alamo and lay siege. Over the next 13 days, they fought small-scale skirmishes as more Mexican troops arrived. On March 6, the Mexican army attacked the 200 or so Texan defenders, killing all, including Davie Crockett and Jim Bowie. Santa Anna was sure this decisive victory would cause the Texan resistance to fold quickly.

However, just the opposite happened. As the ragtag Texan army evaded Santa Anna's superior forces, news of the Alamo spread through Texas and brought many new recruits. Determined to capture the leaders of the Texas government, Santa Anna took an elite force of 700 men to chase them down. On April 21, Sam Houston met this force at San Jacinto and defeated them, capturing Santa Anna. This stunning reversal of fortune won Texas its independence from Mexico.

Responding to Document-Based Questions

Sometimes social studies prompts include a variety of sources—articles, maps, charts, photographs, and so on—related to a specific topic. You are asked to read the material and then respond to a question, using evidence you have gathered from the documents. The following prompt focuses on the worldwide need for freshwater.

Prompt

Though 70 percent of the earth is covered by water, only 2 percent of that water is fresh and drinkable. As the earth's human population continues to expand past 7 billion, access to freshwater is becoming a defining problem of the 21st century. Read the following texts and use them to respond to the question that follows them.

Document A

Water Shortages Now Suggest Future Crisis
Lisa Stephens

Seven billion people now share our planet, and each of those people needs freshwater to drink, to bathe, to grow crops, and to get rid of waste. As the human population has doubled, human water use has quadrupled. It's no wonder that areas of our world have come under great water stress.

The map below shows the areas of the world in which demand for water exceeds supply by more than 120 percent. As the population continues to expand, so, too, will these water-stressed areas.

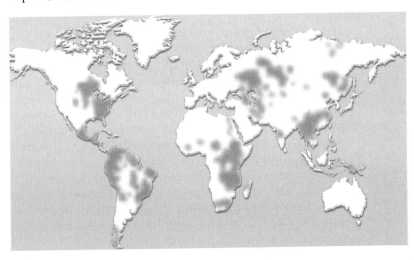

Document B

World Water Supplies
Derek Geldorf

We live on a water world, with 70 percent of the surface covered in the wet stuff. There is water, water everywhere, but little of it is fit to drink. In fact, 96.5 percent of the water on the planet is in the salty oceans. Our drinkable water comes from a variety of other sources.

Glaciers

By far the largest amount of freshwater on Earth is locked up in glaciers, ice caps, and snow. The poles, Greenland, and mountaintop glaciers hold 68.7 percent of the world's freshwater. Some nations have begun harvesting these resources, towing freshwater icebergs to areas in need of water.

Aquifers

Over 30 percent of freshwater on Earth comes from groundwater. Gravel, sand, and many types of stone are porous enough that water permeates them. The top of the water level in the ground is called the water table, and deeper stretches are called aquifers. People drill wells to pump water from these vast storehouses. Some aquifers are renewable resources, replenished by rains, but not all.

Lakes

Only 1.3 percent of Earth's freshwater appears on the surface of the planet, and 87 percent of that amount occurs in lakes. The Great Lakes by themselves hold 21 percent of the world's surface freshwater.

Wetlands

Marshes and swamps hold 11 percent of the surface freshwater. These bodies are the most biodiverse of all ecosystems, hosting a wide assortment of plant and animal life. They are thus most in need of protection from human exploitation.

Rivers

Rivers contain about 2 percent of the surface freshwater. These bodies flow from a source, such as a wetland or melting glacier, down to a lake or ocean. Along the way, they support a variety of plant and animal life. Many rivers these days are polluted, making them poor sources of water for humans.

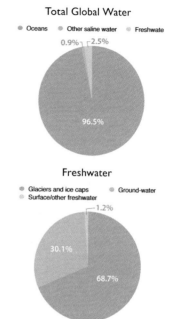

Total Global Water

- Oceans
- Other saline water
- Freshwate

0.9% 2.5%

96.5%

Freshwater

- Glaciers and ice caps
- Ground-water
- Surface/other freshwater

1.2%

30.1%

68.7%

Surface water and other freshwater

- Ground ice and permafrost
- Lakes
- Swamps, marshes
- Rivers
- Atmosphere
- Soil moistur
- Living things

0.49% 0.26%
2.6% 3.0%
3.8%
20.9%
69.0%

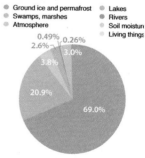

Document C

10 Ways You Can Conserve Water
Reggie Lewis

Water conservation helps all of us and the environment. These 10 simple tips make water conservation easy for everyone:
1. Take short showers rather than long ones.
2. Don't let the faucet run while brushing your teeth or shaving.
3. Run the dishwasher only when it is full.
4. When doing laundry, adjust the water level to the size of the load.
5. Water the lawn and garden in the morning or the evening.
6. Wash the car on the lawn and shut off the water between rinses.
7. Sweep sidewalks instead of washing them.
8. Install a low-flow toilet or place a pebble jar in your regular toilet tank.
9. Install a low-flow showerhead.
10. Collect rainwater and use it to water gardens and lawns.

Document D

Making Water Accessible and Drinkable
Trisha Riley-Clark

In many places across the globe, people lack access to safe, clean drinking water. In addition to shipping bottled water to these locations, relief workers can use a number of inventions that help people harness the water in the environment around them.

Rolling water drums are round plastic water containers that walkers roll behind them. These devices allow people to efficiently transport large quantities of water without risking neck injuries from balancing jugs atop their heads.

Rainwater harvesting systems gather rooftop runoff into barrels to store for later use. Portable systems shaped like umbrellas can harvest rain directly.

Filtration bottles remove waterborne particulates as small as 15 nanometers in diameter, which is smaller than the smallest virus. Straws, bottles, and drums purify water at its point of use rather than requiring shipments of sterile water.

Ultraviolet germicidal irradiation technologies use UV light to purify water, killing 99.9 percent of bacteria and viruses in it. These systems need to be used in combination with filtration.

Combined systems include filtration and ultraviolet components, with tubes and pumps drawing water from local sources. Some systems are portable while larger systems work in villages to provide continuous water purification.

Solar ovens harvest sunlight to cook food and to boil water, which kills bacteria and viruses, making it drinkable.

Document E

Water Crisis? What Water Crisis?

Document F

Improving Agricultural Efficiency
Terrance Williams

Crop irrigation accounts for about 70 percent of water usage worldwide. As the world's demand for food increases, so will the demand for water to grow the food. A number of measures can help farmers get the best use of the available water:

Catchment systems such as weirs and sand dams help farmers gather rain runoff to use for irrigation.

Separating storm water and sewer systems in cities allows for rainwater to be channeled to agricultural use rather than becoming tainted with sewage.

Treatment facility outflow, which by law must be cleaner than the rivers into which it is discharged, could be channeled to irrigation systems.

Anti-evaporation measures can vastly increase irrigation efficiency by delivering water beneath the ground rather than spraying it through the air, or by storing it in covered drums rather than in open reservoirs.

Crop selection can greatly reduce water use by favoring crops that are more efficient users of water. To produce a pound of beef requires 1,799 gallons of water, a pound of cheese requires 700 gallons, a pound of bread requires 400 gallons, and a pound of lettuce requires 13 gallons.

Water-pollution regulation prevents agricultural runoff and industrial waste from turning natural water sources into toxic dumps.

Document-Based Question and Response

Prompt

Imagine that you are working for a United Nations task force assigned to create a proposal for addressing current and future global water crises. Write your proposal below, drawing on the documents you have read.

Water for the Future

The beginning introduces the topic and leads to the thesis statement (underlined).

The earth's human population continues to expand past 7 billion people, and our water use expands at double the population-growth rate. In many places around the world, the demand for water has exceeded the supply. You may not be surprised that areas of North Africa, the Middle East, India, and China are suffering from water shortages, but the American plains states and desert southwest are also struggling to meet their water needs (Stephens). First-world and third-world nations alike need to take a more thoughtful approach to water. <u>A multiprong approach will help the world address current water shortages and prevent future water crises.</u>

Each middle paragraph starts with a topic sentence that names a main point.

First, our attention should turn to the people in greatest need. In many places throughout the developing world, people lack access to clean, safe water. The United Nations should partner with entrepreneurs worldwide to supply these people with water treatment systems. Rolling drums can help villagers transport large quantities of water from rivers and lakes to their homes. Solar stoves allow them to boil the water to destroy bacteria and viruses. Filtration bottles and straws can purify water at its point of use for individuals. Combined systems use filtration and UV light to provide pure water to villages and refugee camps (Riley-Clark). By making such technology available to water-stressed areas, the UN can reduce suffering and save lives.

Body sentences give a variety of details to support the main point of the paragraph.

As population has doubled, water use has quadrupled, showing that we are not using water efficiently (Stephens). As a result, the UN must promote water conservation across the globe. Efforts can start with individual consumers. For starters, people can reduce water use by installing low-flow toilets, faucets, and showerheads.

They can take shorter showers and not allow the water to run while brushing their teeth and shaving. Other water-saving methods include running the dishwasher only when it is full, matching the water level in the washing machine to the size of the load, and using a rain barrel to harvest rainwater from the rooftop for watering the garden and the lawn (Lewis).

> **Sources of information are cited using the author's last name in parentheses.**

Using water to grow our food accounts for 70 percent of global freshwater consumption, so we need to be far more efficient in this important area (Williams). Farmers in developing nations can create weirs, sand dams, and other catchment systems to gather rainwater for agricultural use. Farmers in industrialized nations can replace high-evaporation systems of water storage and irrigation with covered and underground systems. All around the world, farmers and consumers can switch from food crops that require a great deal of water, such as beef, to crops that require much less, such as grains and vegetables (Williams).

> **Transitions link paragraph to paragraph and sentence to sentence.**

As well as addressing current water crises and promoting ways to conserve water right now, the UN should advocate a number of approaches to ensure enough water for the future. One idea involves helping member states draft water-protection regulation that reduces pollution and agricultural runoff, thus maintaining the purity of natural water sources (Williams). Another plan is to help countries use the water in their aquifers to best advantage, ensuring that these water sources are not depleted by overuse. Regulations about drilling, fracking, and other practices could also help prevent contamination of these aquifers. Finally, the UN needs to explore water-harvesting techniques such as towing icebergs to places that need freshwater (Geldorf). With these steps, the UN can avert future water crises and ensure enough water for people around the globe.

> **The ending sums up the main points of the essay and provides a final thought.**

Water is life. Our bodies are composed mainly of water, and every living thing on the planet requires it. As a result, we must carefully preserve this precious resource. With an assortment of affordable systems, the UN can help people in water-stressed areas find and purify their own water. By advocating water conservation, the UN can inspire individuals, farmers, corporations, and nations to make more efficient use of water. And by helping nations manage their water now and into the future, the UN can save millions of lives and avert the inevitable conflicts that would result from global water shortages.

Learning About Other Forms

Cause and Effect

U.S. History—Select one of the wars that the United States has fought. Research the reasons for U.S. involvement in the war. Discover how the war impacted the U.S. Write a cause-effect essay that outlines the reasons for U.S. involvement and its results.

Process

Modern World History—Choose a country that you are currently studying and research how public officials are chosen in that country, perhaps through election, appointment, inheritance, or some other method. Write a process essay that shows step-by-step how a particular public office is filled.

Compare and Contrast

Ancient History—Choose two similar ancient civilizations. Research them. Write a comparison-contrast essay that describes how the civilizations were similar to and different from each other. Include visuals such as graphs, photos, or diagrams to illustrate the similarities and differences.

Problem and Solution

Current Events—Read news reports about problems that are occurring around the world. Note attempts to solve these problems. Choose one problem and suggest a solution. Write an essay that explains the problem and argues for your solution.

Research

Economics—Explore the types of energy that different countries rely upon. Discover where countries get their fuel, how much they use, what impact their fuel consumption has on the environment, and what innovations they are making to address future fuel needs. Write a research paper that reports your findings. Document sources.

Classification

Government—Survey the world's current governments. Separate them into distinct types, or categories. Write an essay that defines each category, providing examples of each and outlining its main features. Also evaluate the strengths and weaknesses of each type of government.

Writing in Math

One of the biggest innovations in math was "nothing." Nada. Zilch. Zip. The old goose egg. It might surprise you to find out that math was missing its zeros until about 1,100 years ago. That's when a sculptor in India etched a small circle in a temple wall, a circle that represented nothing, but changed everything.

After zero made its appearance, so did places—tens, hundreds, thousands, and so on. Plus, mathematicians could cross from positive numbers into negative numbers. The idea of *nothing* transformed the way in which people thought about *everything*. Writing about math can deepen your understanding of numbers and your world. This chapter will show you how.

Learning Outcomes

Take notes.
Keep a learning log.
Write a summary.
Respond to a prompt.
Develop a statistical argument.
Learn about other forms.

"Go down deep enough into anything and you will find mathematics."

Dean Schlicter

Taking Notes

Note taking helps you to understand and remember the concepts and processes presented in math class. Your notes can also serve as an excellent review before a test. To take effective math notes, follow these guidelines:

- **Reserve a spot for math notes** in a three-ring binder, a notebook, or a folder on your tablet.
- **Date each entry and title it.** Titles help you find the information you need during a review.
- **Write down any information your instructor puts on the board.**
- **Record and define new math terms.** Compile a vocabulary list of these terms for convenient reference.
- **Use your own words to explain new ideas to yourself.** You'll understand and remember the concepts better that way.
- **Represent ideas in multiple ways**—with words, equations, or figures.
- **Capture links, tutorial videos, and other Internet supports** if you are taking digital notes.
- **Write questions about ideas that confuse you.** Later, get answers from your instructor, your classmates, or sites on the Internet.

Sample Notes

Save Edit   Feb. 2

Transformations

Show that two geometric figures are congruent, similar, or dissimilar.
- **Congruent**—same angles and the same side lengths
- **Similar**—same angles and proportional side lengths
- **Dissimilar**—different angles and/or side lengths

Three Rigid Geometric Transformations

1. **Translation**—sliding a shape
2. **Rotation**—spinning a shape
3. **Reflection**—flipping a shape

1.    2.   3.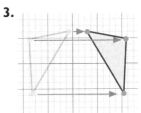

Keeping a Learning Log

A learning log is a space for writing about—and thinking about—what you are learning in class. Reflect on new math concepts and explore ideas more deeply by writing in your learning log. Follow these guidelines:

- **Dedicate a space for your learning log.** Keep it separate from but close to your regular notes. For example, use the final third of your notebook, or create a computer file and store it in the same folder with your regular notes.
- **Date and title each entry** so that you can cross-check it with your notes.
- **Write freely about what you are learning.** Put ideas in your own words, focusing on what you "get" and "don't get."
- **Summarize concepts** as if you were explaining them to someone else.
- **Ask questions** and then answer them, or highlight them for further discussion with your instructor.
- **Perform thought experiments.** Try out new ideas in entertaining ways. For example, use triangles to measure the closeness of friendships.
- **Sum up each math unit with a log entry** on what you have learned.
- **Review your learning log** when you are preparing for tests.

Sample Learning Log Entry

Save Edit   Feb. 2

Transforming Figures

Today we learned about transforming a figure to show whether it is the same as another figure.

One way is translation. You slide a shape sideways so it completely overlaps another shape. "Translation" is a weird word for this. Usually it means taking a foreign word and making it English, like "bon" in French means "good." But I guess that's the same idea. Translating a triangle onto another can show they "mean" the same thing—they have the same angles and side lengths.

Another way is reflection. You flip the shape over, like turning over a pancake on a griddle. So think of a pancake that's melded into the corner of the griddle. If you flip it over, the square corner is on the opposite side, but it's still the same pancake. So when you use reflection, you basically are showing that, whatever way a shape is flipped, it's still the same shape.

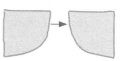

Writing a Summary

New articles often share numerical details, such as the average salary for various jobs or patients' recovery rates with different types of treatment. Summarizing a math article can help you grasp the key information.

▌Prewriting

1. **Analyzing the rhetorical situation . . .** Answer the **STRAP** questions (see page 30) to identify your **S**ubject, the **T**ype of writing (a summary), your **R**ole as a writer, your **A**udience, and your **P**urpose for writing.

2. **Reading the article . . .** Survey the article, looking at headings, images, and captions. Ask questions about what you may learn. Then read carefully.

3. **Reciting the main point and reviewing supporting facts . . .** Out loud, state the main point of the article. Include any numbers that are part of this main point. Then review the specific details that support the main point.

▌Writing

4. **Drafting your summary . . .** Start with a topic sentence that expresses the main idea in your own words. Support the topic sentence with key details. Create a visual—table, graph, chart—that can quickly summarize the math in the article. End with a clear closing sentence.

▌Revising

5. **Improving the summary . . .** Ask yourself these questions:

Traits	
Ideas:	Have I clearly stated the main point? Have I supported it with key details?
Organization:	Are the ideas in the best order?
Voice:	Have I used clear, objective terms?
Word choice:	Have I included key words from the article?
Sentence fluency:	Have I varied the beginnings and lengths of my sentences?

▌Editing

6. **Checking for conventions . . .** Ask yourself these questions:

Traits	
Conventions:	Have I used correct punctuation, capitalization, and grammar? Have I spell-checked my work?
Design:	Do I use headings, graphics, and white space for readability?

7. **Preparing a final copy . . .** Write or type a neat final copy of your summary and proofread it before sharing it.

Math Article and Summary

The following article reports the average costs of various college expenses. A student summarized the information, creating a table to make the details accessible.

Article

Calculating College Costs

Every year, the price of higher education creeps higher, so many students and parents experience sticker shock when they consider their college options. It helps to understand that the overall cost includes a number of subcategories: tuition and fees, room and board, books and supplies, and other living expenses.

Tuition is the money paid to attend a school, and it varies widely. Two-year schools average about $5,000 per year, four-year schools average $10,000 for in-state students and $23,000 for out-of-state students, and four-year private schools average $35,000 per year. Various fees add to these amounts.

Room expenses may involve a dorm room, an apartment, or living at home. Average room expense is about $9,000 per year. Board also varies, from home-cooked meals and sack lunches to dorm meal plans to restaurant dining. Board averages $4,000 per year.

Books, calculators, computers, software, pens, pencils, paper, and other necessary materials cost an average of $2,000 to $3,000 per year.

Miscellaneous expenses include the cost of laundry, Internet access, cell-phone plan, gasoline, parking, and whatever else students spend money on. These expenses average $1,000 to $2,000 per year.

So, a student who stays at home, commutes on foot to a two-year school, carries a sack lunch, and buys used textbooks can eek by for about $6,000 per year. One who attends a private university in a big city, has an apartment and a car, and eats out every night can easily spend $60,000 or more.

Student Summary

Affording College

The article "Calculating College Costs" shows that college can be as affordable or as expensive as you choose. This table summarizes average costs for four categories:

Tuition	
Two-year school	$5,000
Four-year school (in/out-of-state)	$10,000/$23,000
Four-year private school	$35,000
Room and board	
Dorm room/apartment space	$9,000
Board	$4,000
Books and supplies	$2,000 to $3,000
Miscellaneous expenses	$1,000 to $2,000

Staying at home and attending a two-year college can cost about one-tenth the price of renting an apartment in a big city and attending a private college there.

Responding to a Prompt

Math prompts present you with a word problem and ask you to respond in writing, showing the mathematical calculations you did to arrive at your answers. First analyze the prompt and decide what you are supposed to do. Then develop a response. Follow these guidelines.

Prewriting

1. **Analyzing the rhetorical situation . . .** Answer the **STRAP** questions (see page 30) to identify your **S**ubject, the **T**ype of writing (response to a prompt), your **R**ole as a writer, your **A**udience, and your writing **P**urpose.
2. **Reading the prompt . . .** Read the problem carefully, noting statements, conditionals, questions, and commands.
3. **Thinking of what you know . . .** Write down the key information that is given in the prompt.
4. **Thinking of what you need to find . . .** Look for questions and commands (sentences that begin with verbs) and note what you need to find.
5. **Gathering functions . . .** Think of the math functions (formulas) that you know that can lead you from the knowns to the unknowns.

Writing

6. **Representing the problem graphically . . .** Arrange the data in a table. Visualize geometric shapes by drawing a graph, or create a diagram and label it with measurements.
7. **Building your solution . . .** Work from the knowns to the unknowns. Calculate what you can. Then assess what you can do next to reach the answer. If you get stuck, work backward from that point and try again.
8. **Showing your work . . .** Include your calculations. Also label the parts of your solution so that the scorer can see what you are thinking.

Revising

9. **Rereading the prompt . . .** Check to make sure that you have correctly transferred the knowns from the prompt to your response and that you have found the required unknowns.
10. **Checking your math . . .** Trace through each step of the process to ensure that you have correctly calculated each part.

Editing

11. **Checking for conventions . . .** Check your response to eliminate errors in punctuation, capitalization, spelling, and grammar.
12. **Preparing a final copy . . .** Make a neat copy of your solution and proofread it.

Math Prompt and Response

The following math prompt focuses on a real-world problem. The first three sentences are statements that provide the knowns (givens). The final sentence is a question that indicates the unknown (the answer the student needs to find).

Prompt

29. A farmer wants to fill a silo with grain, but she is uncertain how much grain it can hold. The silo is a cylinder that is 6 m in diameter and 11 m tall. It has a conical roof that is the same diameter but rises an additional 5 m in height. How much grain can the farmer store in this silo if it is totally full?

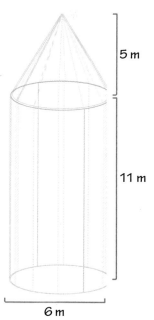

Knowns

The silo is a cylinder that is 6 m in diameter and 11 m tall. It has a conical roof that is 5 m tall.

Unknown

What is the total volume of the silo?

Functions

Radius = diameter ÷ 2

Cylinder volume = π × radius² × height

Cone volume = 1/3 × π × radius² × height

Silo volume = cylinder volume + cone volume

Calculations

Silo radius = 6 m ÷ 2 = 3 m

Cylinder volume = 3.1416 × 3² m × 11 m = 311.02 m³

Cone volume = 1/3 × 3.1416 × 3² m × 5 m = 47.12 m³

Silo volume = 311.02 m³ + 47.12 m³ = 358.14 m³

Answer

The farmer can store 358.14 cubic meters of grain in the silo if it is completely full.

5 m

11 m

6 m

Developing a Statistical Argument

Writers often use statistics to prove a point. Statistical arguments require you to gather accurate data and to use it fairly.

▌Prewriting

1. **Analyzing the rhetorical situation . . .** Answer the **STRAP** questions (see page 30) to identify your **S**ubject, the **T**ype of writing, your **R**ole as a writer, your **A**udience, and your **P**urpose for writing.

2. **Choosing a topic . . .** Select a topic that interests you and has patterns and trends about which you can form an opinion or position.

3. **Gathering data . . .** Research your topic, collecting facts and figures from reliable sources.

4. **Creating a position statement . . .** State your topic and your specific position concerning it. Try to capture your position in one or two sentences.

▌Writing

5. **Opening your argument . . .** Write an opening paragraph that introduces your topic and leads to your position statement.

6. **Developing the middle . . .** Create middle paragraphs that use statistics to support your position statement.

7. **Creating graphics . . .** Use a table, graph, histogram, or other visual representation to help the reader see the patterns in the numbers you present.

8. **Crafting a closing . . .** Write a final paragraph that restates your position.

▌Revising

9. **Improving your argument . . .** Ask yourself these questions:

Traits	
Ideas:	Is my position statement clear? Is my argument persuasive?
Organization:	Is my argument well ordered? Do I use transitions?
Voice:	Is my voice confident and convincing?
Word choice:	Have I defined any unfamiliar terms?
Sentence fluency:	Do my sentences flow smoothly?

▌Editing

10. **Checking for conventions . . .** Ask yourself these questions:

Traits	
Conventions:	Have I corrected any convention errors?
Math:	Have I double-checked all figures and calculations?
Design:	Are all visuals well created and clear?

11. **Preparing a final copy . . .** Create a neat final copy and proofread it.

Statistical Argument

In the following statistical argument, a student uses unemployment and earning figures to argue for the importance of higher education.

Earning with Your Degree

The opening introduces the topic and leads to the position statement (underlined).

One complaint that students have about school is that it doesn't make any difference in their lives. Statistically, that idea is false. The amount of schooling you receive has a direct impact on your earning potential and your likelihood to be unemployed.

Let's start with employment. Last year, the Bureau of Labor Statistics reported that median unemployment rates varied widely depending on education level. Those with professional degrees (dentistry, engineering, law, architecture, medicine, and so on) had the least unemployment at 2.1 percent, followed by those with masters (3.5) and bachelors (4.5). Those with only high school diplomas had 8.3 percent unemployment, and those with less had 12.4 percent (Bureau). *The Wall Street Journal* reports that the recession created a wide gap between groups, with unemployment for those without a high school degree increasing by 15 percent while rates for those with bachelors degrees remained constant (Lahart).

Middle paragraphs present statistical data and cite their sources.

The earnings also differed considerably depending on the level of education. Median weekly earnings for those with a professional degree were $1,735. Earnings were $1,300 for those with a masters and $1,066 for those with a bachelors. By contrast, those with just a high school diploma earned $652 (Bureau).

A graph makes supporting data visual.

Consider the average lifetime income levels for holders of different degrees. The graph here shows that those with higher degrees more than double their earning potential over those with less (Burnsed).

The final paragraph revisits the position statement.

The numbers don't lie. Degrees are money in the bank for those who have them. Why? Because education helps people become self-motivated, problem-solving, innovative workers. That's education you can bank on.

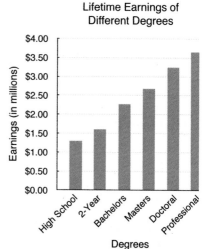

Lifetime Earnings of Different Degrees

Earnings (in millions): $4.00, $3.50, $3.00, $2.50, $2.00, $1.50, $1.00, $0.50, $0.00

Degrees: High School, 2-Year, Bachelors, Masters, Doctoral, Professional

Learning About Other Forms

Writing any of the following forms can help you improve your understanding of math concepts and how they apply to the real world.

Definition

Trigonometry—Write an explanatory essay that defines the terms *sine, cosine,* and *tangent*. Show how these concepts help mathematicians calculate angles and sides. Include diagrams to demonstrate your point.

Argument

Statistics—Write a position paper that uses statistics to argue for or against a certain governmental economic policy. Include graphs to make the statistics visual.

Narrative

Any Math Class—Write a narrative that tracks your day in terms of numbers. Include amounts of time, portions of food, number of songs, weight of backpack, number of steps, and so on. Create a table, graph, chart, or other visual that can help demonstrate some of the main patterns of math in your day.

Process

Algebra—Write a process paper that explains how to perform an algebraic calculation, such as working with the quadratic equation or factoring polynomials. Use commands in numbered lists to make steps clear, and provide examples to help the reader follow along.

Compare and Contrast

Geometry—Write a comparison-contrast paper that analyzes two geometrically interesting skyscrapers, focusing on the ways in which the shapes are similar and different. Discuss the overall function of the geometric forms present in each building. Include photographs, blueprints, or drawings to make your points clear.

Research

Any Math Class—Write a research paper that mathematically profiles a major natural disaster such as a hurricane, a volcanic eruption, an earthquake, or an asteroid impact. Gather many types of mathematical data in terms of speeds, intensities, damage, and other factors. Report these data in words and graphics that make them accessible and understandable to the reader.

Writing in the Workplace

People in the workplace write for many reasons, and their writing involves the same steps you take to write essays and reports in school. From considering the writing's purpose, audience, and topic to drafting, revising, and editing—workplace writers produce emails, letters, proposals, and more.

Today, school is your workplace, and much of your academic work can be done effectively with workplace documents. For example, this chapter can help you write a letter to gather information for a project, an email to update your instructor about an assignment, or a résumé to apply for an internship or a job. Good writing will help you succeed now and in the future.

Learning Outcomes

Learn about the parts of a letter.
Write a business letter.
Review letters.
Send a letter.
Write an email message.
Create a brochure.
Develop a résumé.

"In the workplace, you don't write for
a grade, you write for a living."
Jim Franken

Learn About the Parts of a Letter

A business letter presents information in the order below.

Heading

The heading gives the writer's address, either printed in the letterhead or typed out, and the date. (If the address is part of the letterhead, place only the date in the upper left-hand corner.)

Inside Address

The inside address gives the reader's name and address (including the company name). If you're not sure about the name of the person you want to address or how to spell it, call the company and ask. If the person's title is a single word or very short, place it after the name, separated by a comma. Longer titles go on a separate line.

Salutation

The salutation personalizes the letter. Use *Dear* with people only, not with company names. Place a colon after the name. (Also see "Avoiding Sexism" on page 633.)

Body

The body contains your message in single-spaced paragraphs (no indents) with double spacing between them. Your message is organized in three parts: (1) the beginning states why you are writing, (2) the middle provides the necessary details, and (3) the ending focuses on what should happen next.

Complimentary Closing

The closing politely ends the message with a parting word or phrase—*Sincerely, Yours sincerely, Yours truly,*—followed by a comma. Capitalize only the first word of complimentary closings.

Signature

The signature makes the letter official. It includes the writer's handwritten name and corresponding typed name.

Initials, Enclosures, Copies

- When someone types the letter for the writer, the typist's *lowercased initials* appear after the writer's capitalized initials, separated by a colon.
- If a document (brochure, form, copy) is enclosed with the letter, the word *Enclosure* or the abbreviation *Encl.* appears below the initials.
- If a *copy* of the letter is sent elsewhere, type *cc:* and follow with the name of the person or department receiving the copy.

▌ Sample Business Letter

Heading

Monroe Chamber of Commerce
105 East Bay Road
Monroe, LA 31404-1832
October 6, 2014

———————————————— Four to Seven Spaces ————————————————

Inside Address

Ms. Charlotte Williams, Manager
Belles Lettres Books
1617 Delta Mall Road
Monroe, LA 31404-0012

———————————— Double Space ————————————

Salutation

Dear Ms. Williams:

———————————— Double Space ————————————

Welcome to the Monroe business community. As the Chamber's executive director, I'd like to thank you for opening your store in the Delta Mall. Belles Lettres Books is a welcome addition to the town's economy, especially with the store's emphasis on Southern authors. I wish you success.

Body

I would like to invite you to join our Chamber of Commerce. Membership gives you a voice in your community and access to promotional materials.

If you decide to join, I could set up a ribbon-cutting ceremony, which would provide some useful news coverage. Call me at 944-0645 or email me at alein@chamber.org if you have any questions.

———————————— Double Space ————————————

Complimentary Closing

Sincerely,

Signature

Ardith Lein ———————— Four Spaces ————————

Ardith Lein

———————————— Double Space ————————————

Initials Enclosures Copies

AL:nk
Encl. membership brochure
cc: Peter Sanchez, Membership Chairperson

Writing a Business Letter

Prewriting

1. **Analyzing the rhetorical situation . . .** Answer the **STRAP** questions (see page 30) to identify your **S**ubject, the **T**ype of writing (a business letter), your **R**ole as a writer, your **A**udience, and your **P**urpose for writing.

2. **Considering your audience . . .** Who is your reader, and how will he or she feel about your message?

3. **Determining your purpose . . .** Jot down your reason for writing or what you want your reader to know or do.

4. **Gathering details . . .** Collect the information you will need for your letter. Think about the best way to organize and present it.

Writing and Revising

5. **Organizing the details . . .** Organize your letter in three parts.

Beginning	Introduce the message by stating the topic and purpose of your letter.
Middle	Present whatever information is appropriate for the kind of letter you are writing. Use a voice that fits your purpose—persuasive, informative, and so on.
Ending	Focus on the outcome. What do you want the reader to do, and when, and how? Is there an action you will take?

6. **Improving your writing . . .** Revise your draft by asking these questions:

   ┌─ Traits ─────
Ideas:	Is my main point clear? Are my details accurate and complete?
Organization:	Does each paragraph develop one main idea?
Voice:	Do I use a polite, respectful tone? (See pages 632–634.)

7. **Improving your style . . .** Ask yourself these questions:

   ┌─ Traits ─────
Word choice:	Do I use clear, natural words?
Sentence fluency:	Have I written smooth-flowing sentences?

Editing and Proofreading

8. **Checking for conventions . . .** Correct errors in punctuation, mechanics, and grammar.

9. **Preparing a final copy . . .** Check the design: *Is the message centered on the page? Are the margins even? Is the spacing correct and attractive?* Address the envelope, add correct postage, and mail your letter. (See page 275.)

Reviewing Letters: Informative Letter

4213 Minnow Lane
Medford, MA 02052
March 6, 2014

Geoffrey Gosbin
164 12th Street, NW
Somerville, MA 02044

Dear Geoffrey:

Beginning
Explain why you are writing.

Thanks for your letter praising our school's Web page! As for your request, I'd be happy to help you build a Web page for your school's Environmental Awareness Club.

First, you need a Web page-maker program. You may download one from the Internet or buy one separately.

Middle
Supply necessary details.

Second, you'll need a plan for your page. A good page has a clear, concise, and interesting design. Here are a few points to think about:
- Explain who you are and what you're about.
- Don't overdo the graphics; they can really slow things down.
- Include some links to sites that would interest visitors.
- Include a FAQ (frequently asked questions) section.

Ending
Establish a plan of action and end politely.

Let's get together next Wednesday in your computer lab at 3:30 p.m. I'll take you through a sample page. If you're ready with your design plan, we can dig right in.

Sincerely,

Brian Krygsman

Brian Krygsman
Tech Club President

Application Letter

326 Ash Boulevard
Florence, OR 97439-3216
March 21, 2014

Dr. Ray Peters
Communications Department Chair
St. Xavier College
32 Fountain Street
Omaha, NE 68102-6070

Dear Dr. Peters:

Beginning
Explain how you learned about the position.

In response to the brochure I received from St. Xavier College, I am applying for a position on the staff of the *Xavier News*. I have enclosed a recommendation from my high school English teacher as well as several articles that I wrote for my high school newspaper, the *Florence Flier*.

Middle
Describe your qualifications.

I have been on the staff of the *Florence Flier* for four years, and this year I am the editor. I have always enjoyed English, and I plan on majoring in journalism at St. Xavier College. I am an organized, creative person, and I have never missed a deadline. In addition to writing and editing, I do layout work.

Ending
Politely offer additional information and thank the reader.

If you would like more information, please let me know by calling 555-997-3205 anytime during the day or by emailing me at greensleeves@gmail.com. Thank you for considering my application. I look forward to hearing from you.

Sincerely,

Allison Emerson

Allison Emerson
Encl. recommendation and newspaper articles

Sending a Letter

▋ Addressing the Envelope

Address the envelope correctly so your letter can be delivered promptly. Place the return address (matching the letter's heading) in the upper left corner, the destination address (matching the letter's inside address) in the center, and the correct postage in the upper right corner.

ANDREA MCGRADY
2518 FOURTH AVE SW
COLUMBUS OH 43230

POSTAGE

MR TIM LINDON
1286 ELM ST NW
COLUMBUS OH 43230

Follow one of the two acceptable forms for addressing the envelope: the traditional form or the postal service form (preferred).

Traditional Form

Ms. Theresa Chang
Goodwill Industries
9200 Wisconsin Avenue
Bethesda, MD 20814-3896

Postal Service Form

MS THERESA CHANG
GOODWILL INDUSTRIES
9200 WISCONSIN AVE
BETHESDA MD 20814-3896

▋ Official USPS Envelope Guidelines

- Capitalize everything in the address and leave out all punctuation.
- Use the list of common abbreviations found in the *National ZIP Code Directory*. Use numerals rather than words for numbered streets and avenues (9TH AVE SE, 3RD ST NE).
- If you know the ZIP + 4 code, use it. You can get this information online or by phoning one of the postal service's ZIP-code information units.

Writing an Email Message

Electronic mail helps you send, receive, and store messages quickly through computer networks. In spite of email's delivery speed, it still takes time to write, edit, and design a good message. Follow the guidelines below.

▌ Prewriting

1. **Analyzing the rhetorical situation . . .** Answer the **STRAP** questions (see page 30) to identify your **S**ubject, the **T**ype of writing (an email), your **R**ole as a writer, your **A**udience, and your **P**urpose for writing.

2. **Considering your audience . . .** Think about your reader and your purpose for emailing this person.

3. **Gathering details . . .** Gather the details that your reader needs in order to understand and respond to your message.

▌ Writing and Revising

4. **Organizing the body . . .** Organize your email message in three parts:

Beginning	Complete your email header, supplying a subject line that clearly states your topic. Expand on the subject in the first sentences of your email, getting right to the point.
Middle	Fill in the details of your message, but keep all of your paragraphs short. Double-space between paragraphs. Try to limit your message to one or two screens and use numbers, lists, and headings to organize your thoughts.
Ending	Let your reader know what follow-up action is needed and when. Then end politely.

5. **Improving your writing . . .** Revise your email by asking these questions:

┌─ Traits ─
Ideas:	Is my message accurate, complete, and clear?
Organization:	Do I have an effective beginning, middle, and ending?
Voice:	Is my tone appropriate for the topic and the reader?

6. **Improving your style . . .** Ask yourself these questions:

┌─ Traits ─
Word choice:	Have I used clear, everyday language?
Sentence fluency:	Does my message read smoothly?
Design:	Does the format clearly display the message?

▌ Editing and Proofreading

7. **Checking for conventions . . .** Check your message for errors in punctuation, mechanics, and grammar.

▌ Sample Email

To: James Marcus

Subject: Update on My History Paper

Attachment: Hist_Proposal.doc

Hi Mr. Marcus:

Beginning
State your reason for writing.

Here's an update on my history paper about China. At first I had trouble finding information on my topic, but I've made this progress:

1. I went to the library, and Ms. Pate helped me use the computer for my search.

2. After I showed you my project proposal, I took your advice to look at either Chinese dating practices or wedding traditions, but not both.

Middle
Give the necessary details.

3. After researching both topics, I found several sources on Chinese wedding traditions, but only a few on dating practices. So I will write about present-day Chinese wedding customs.

4. I found a Web site with information about Chinese wedding traditions at www.travelchinaguide.com.

5. For my primary research, I interviewed Donna Sung, our foreign exchange student from Shanghai, about her experiences with weddings in China.

Ending
Focus on what should happen next.

I will finish my first draft by October 22 and will be on schedule for the deadlines I gave you in my project proposal (copy attached).

Thank you!

Danielle White

Creating a Brochure

A brochure is an effective tool for advertising a product or promoting a cause. Follow the guidelines below to produce an effective brochure.

▌ Prewriting

1. **Analyzing the rhetorical situation . . .** Answer the **STRAP** questions (see page 30) to identify your **S**ubject, the **T**ype of writing (a brochure), your **R**ole as a writer, your **A**udience, and your **P**urpose for writing.

2. **Selecting a topic . . .** Think of a service or product that you want to promote or sell and research the topic thoroughly.

3. **Considering your audience . . .** Consider who your audience is and what kind of brochure will effectively deliver your message.

4. **Gathering details . . .** Think about what your reader needs to know about this product or service in order to be convinced of its value.

▌ Writing and Revising

5. **Organizing the body . . .** Organize your brochure in three parts:

Beginning	State the main point in bold type, possibly as a question and an answer or as a large headline, at the top.
Middle	State your message fully, but concisely. Fill in the details using bulleted lists. Add visuals and testimonials to clarify and verify the quality of your product or service.
Ending	Include reader-response instructions, offering all the necessary names, addresses, and phone numbers.

6. **Designing your brochure . . .** Design your brochure with large headlines, attention-grabbing visuals, and interesting graphics.

7. **Improving your writing . . .** Revise by asking these questions:

Traits

Ideas:	Is my message clear, concise, and complete?
Organization:	Do I use headings, lists, and graphics effectively?
Voice:	Does my writing voice sound informed and persuasive?

8. **Improving your style . . .** Ask yourself these questions:

Traits

Word choice:	Have I chosen precise words to convey my message?
Sentence fluency:	Does my brochure read smoothly?

▌ Editing and Proofreading

9. **Checking for conventions . . .** Correct any mechanical errors.

10. **Checking the design . . .** Make sure the text and visuals convey a unified message.

▌Sample Brochure

The size of brochures can vary. This sample brochure was designed on a standard sheet of paper folded in half.

Note: See pages 393–395 for a sample brochure written to fulfill a research assignment.

Save a
**Life—
Give Blood**

Front
The main point
is stated boldly.

Your student council invites you to
help others by participating in our
school's blood drive.

Thursday
October 16, 2014

8–11 a.m. and **1–3 p.m.**
School Cafeteria

Inside
Bulleted lists
highlight details.

Why should you give?

- Accident victims, people who need surgery, and people with blood disorders need your help.
- Community blood banks must be resupplied because . . .
  - all types of blood are constantly in demand.
  - blood has a limited shelf life and must be replaced often.

When and where can you give?

- Thursday, October 16, in the school cafeteria from 8 to 11 a.m. or 1 to 3 p.m.
- Information about community blood-bank hours is available in the school office.

Who should donate?

- Any healthy person 17 or older
- Someone who hasn't donated within 60 days

Remember . . .

- Bring a signed parental-release form with you. They are available in the school office.
- Bring identification—driver's license or school I.D.
- Be prepared to fill out a medical questionnaire.
- Eat before and after your donation and drink plenty of fluids.
- Giving blood is . . .

**A Chance
To Help Others**

Ending
The writer gives
a final message.

Developing a Résumé

Your résumé presents you—your skills, knowledge, and experiences—to a prospective employer. There are two basic forms of résumés:

- A **chronological résumé** lists work experiences and education by date. Chronological résumés work best when you've held a number of jobs.
- A **functional résumé** lists skills you have acquired at home, at school, or on the job. Functional résumés are a good choice when you have limited work experience.

Prewriting

1. **Analyzing the rhetorical situation . . .** Answer the **STRAP** questions (see page 30) to identify your **S**ubject, the **T**ype of writing (a résumé), your **R**ole as a writer, your **A**udience, and your **P**urpose for writing.

2. **Gathering details . . .** Think about your immediate and long-term goals. Then list the following: (1) a job objective showing what kind of job you want; (2) your education, work experience, and activities, both extracurricular and volunteer; (3) responsibilities and related skills; (4) teachers, employers, and other people who could act as references for you.

Writing and Revising

3. **Organizing the body . . .** Organize your résumé in three parts:

Beginning	Provide personal data and a job objective.
Middle	Depending on whether you are preparing a chronological or a functional résumé, list your skills, achievements, education, and work experience in the appropriate way.
Ending	Either list the names and contact information of your references, or state that references are available upon request.

4. **Improving your writing . . .** Revise by asking these questions:

Traits

Ideas:	Have I used specific, accurate, and complete details?
Organization:	Does the format highlight my strengths?
Voice:	Have I used a serious, factual tone?
Word choice:	Have I considered each word carefully?
Sentence fluency:	Have I presented my ideas in a parallel way?

Editing and Proofreading

5. **Checking for conventions . . .** Check for errors in punctuation, mechanics, and grammar.

6. **Checking the design . . .** Consider whether the headings, lists, type choices, and other elements work together to feature your strengths.

▌ **Sample Functional Letter Résumé**

Adam Thoral
567 West Highland Road
Tiewing, FL 34207-2367
Phone: (111) 943-7125
Email: a_thoral@tiewing.net

Job Objective: Participate in a summer environmental studies program.

Environmental Science Skills:
- Wrote three research papers based on environmental issues: "Effects of Gulf War on Nature"; "Rain Forests: Why Do We Need Them?"; and "North American Environmental Disasters"
- Subscribe to the following environmental magazines: *Earth Awareness; Endangered Environment*
- Completed wilderness-survival training through Boy Scouts

Communication Skills:
- Team worker: Led group projects at school, participated in Scouting events, served as crew leader at fast-food restaurant
- Well acquainted with writing memos, letters, and email
- Worked to promote environmental bills (Bills 104, 235)

Organizational Skills:
- Organized an Earth Day community cleanup at school
- Helped set up a school recycling program
- Assisted Mr. Carper, my biology teacher, in lab preparations

Education:
- 11th grader, Tiewing High School
- Course work: Environmental Science, Biology, Chemistry

Awards/Activities:
- Boy Scouts (2009–present)
- Peer tutor at Tiewing High School (2012–2014)
- First aid and CPR certification—Tiewing Hospital (2014)

Work History:

2013 (Summer)	Internship in environmental studies and public relations at Landzone Industries in Tiewing
2013–2014	Restaurant crew leader—supervised three workers

References available upon request.

Writers INC

Reading

Critical Reading Strategies

Kyudo, which means "the way of the bow" in Japanese, is the Zen martial art of archery. It is regarded as one of the most intensive martial arts in existence, taking an estimated 30 years to master. If that introduction piques your interest, you could check online and find several sources of information about Kyudo. And if you're a critical reader, you'll know how to read each one of them.

A critical reader applies a thoughtful reading process to gain new information and understanding from a text. He or she knows not only how to read a text, but also how to utilize the information. The guidelines and strategies in this chapter will help you develop your critical reading skills.

Learning Outcomes

Understand reading and thinking.
Identify the key features in a text.
Learn about the critical-reading process.
Use critical reading strategies.
Interact with a text.

"The eye sees only what the mind is prepared to comprehend."

Henri Bergson

"You should never read just for 'enjoyment.' Read to make yourself smarter! Less judgmental. More apt to understand your friends' insane behavior, or better yet, your own."

John Waters

Understanding Reading and Thinking

Reading may seem automatic to you, like riding a bike or making a PB & J sandwich. You probably pick up a favorite magazine and dig in to the first article that interests you, never considering the kinds of thinking your reading will require. In fact, the article may contain details you want to *remember*, descriptions that prompt *comparisons*, or new ideas that cause you to *evaluate* your own thoughts about the topic. The complexity of the material as well as your purpose for reading it will determine which levels of thinking you use. That is especially true for academic reading assignments, which will often require several levels of thinking.

Bloom's New Taxonomy

The chart below lists different levels of thinking according to Bloom's new taxonomy. Beginning with basic *remembering*, it progresses through ever more challenging levels of thought. The second column of the chart describes what each level of thinking involves. When you read critically, you will employ most of these levels of thinking.

You are . . .	When you read to . . .
Remembering	note basic information about the topic and remember main points.
Understanding	follow the general meaning of a text.
Applying	identify the specific parts, including the main idea (thesis) and supporting details.
Analyzing	carefully examine the text—making comparisons, looking for causes and effects, classifying, etc.
Evaluating	judge the value of the information, identify the text's strengths and weaknesses, and argue for or against its main claim.
Creating	develop something new from what you have learned.

Identifying the Key Features in a Text

Answering the **STRAP** questions about a text's *subject, type of text, role of the writer, audience,* and *purpose* will identify the rhetorical features that shape the piece. Knowing these features, especially if you are doing research, will help you select the best text for your purpose. For example, a medical report about a certain health product would offer more trustworthy information about the product's benefits than would a marketing report aimed at selling the product. (You can also use the **STRAP** strategy to identify the rhetorical features of writing assignments.)

Subject:	What topic does the reading address?
Type of Writing:	What is the form (*essay, textbook chapter, article, nonfiction book, Web site, . . .*)?
Role:	What role or position (*expert, participant, journalist, . . .*) does the author assume?
Audience:	Who is the intended reader (*general audience, fellow students, older adults, professionals, . . .*)?
Purpose:	What is the goal (*to inform, to persuade, to recall, to describe, to entertain, . . .*)?

How the Strategy Works

Suppose you are about to read a commentary in your social studies class entitled "The United States Postal Service: Slow and Slower." You found the article online, but it first appeared in a newspaper. Here are the answers to the **STRAP** questions for this reading selection:

Subject:	The United States Postal Service
Type of Writing:	Personal column or commentary
Role:	Columnist or commentator
Audience:	General readers of the newspaper
Purpose:	To share a personal viewpoint

Or suppose you've been assigned to read an informative essay in your science class entitled "Causes of Tropical Deforestation." Here are the answers to the **STRAP** questions for this selection:

Subject:	Tropical deforestation
Type of Writing:	Cause-effect essay
Role:	Science writer
Audience:	Science students
Purpose:	To inform

Learning About the Critical Reading Process

Critical reading requires your full attention before, during, and after reading. By immersing yourself completely, you will become an effective critical reader.

Before you read . . .

- **Skim the selection:** For essays, articles, and chapters—pay attention to the title, headings, bold words, beginning and ending parts, graphics, and side notes. For books—preview the title, preface or introduction, opening chapter, chapter headings, graphics, and author notes.
- **Apply the STRAP strategy:** Identify the subject, purpose, audience, role, and kind of text you are reading.
- **Use a reading strategy:** KWL and SQ3R are two possibilities. (See pages 287 and 288.) KWL works well for short texts about familiar topics; SQ3R works well for longer complex texts.
- **Focus your thinking:** When using KWL, identify what you already know about the topic (the K) and what you want to find out (the W). When using SQ3R, list questions you want to answer about the topic (the Q). Otherwise, simply predict what you expect to learn.

As you read . . .

- **Annotate or highlight as you read,** but only if you own the text or are reading a photocopy.
- **Take notes.**
- **Recite out loud what you are learning from your reading** if you are using the SQ3R strategy. (See page 288.)
- **Interact in other ways:** Predict what you expect to learn next; also stop from time to time and write freely about the text.
- **Reread parts as needed:** Challenging parts or sections that contain especially important ideas deserve second and third readings.

After you read . . .

- **Review what you have learned.** Summarizing the text is one way to do this. (See page 294.)
- **Discuss the reading with classmates.**
- **Write freely about your reading experience:** Consider what you like about the text, what bothers you about it, and how you will use the information.
- **Compare the text to others** that cover the same topic.
- **Identify questions about the topic** that you still need to answer.

Using Critical Reading Strategies

Critical reading is more than moving your eyes across the page, taking in words and ideas one after another, and forgetting them just as quickly. Instead, it is the thoughtful process of engaging with the text. KWL and SQ3R are two strategies that promote critical reading.

▌ KWL

This strategy works well for short texts about familiar topics. **KWL** stands for "what I **k**now," "what I **w**ant to know," and "what I **l**earned." You can use a chart like the one below to record information. (The information in the chart is based on a May 2013 *Scientific American* article entitled "Good Bacteria for Bad Breath.")

"Good Bacteria for Bad Breath"

K What do I know?	W What do I want to know?	L What did I learn?
People get bad breath when their mouths become dry, after sleeping, and after eating strong-smelling foods. People use toothpaste and mouthwash to combat bad breath.	What do bacteria have to do with the problem? Are some people more prone to bad breath than others? What is the best way to deal with the problem?	Brushing, flossing, and rinsing may not be enough for people with "problem" breath. Scraping the tongue is another temporary fix. Diet, stress, and illness are contributors to the bacterial community in people's mouths. Gram-negative bacteria on the tongue may cause bad breath. A strain of gram-positive bacteria has been shown to deter gram-negative bacteria.

How to Use a KWL Chart

1. Divide a sheet of paper into three columns. Label them *K, W, L.*
2. Write the appropriate question under each letter. (See the chart above.)
3. Identify what you know about the topic in the first column.
4. List the questions you want answered in the second column.
5. State what you learned (and may still want to learn) in the third column.

▌SQ3R

An effective reading technique for all types of nonfiction is the **SQ3R** method. **SQ3R** stands for the five steps in this reading process: *survey, question, read, recite,* and *review.* Using **SQ3R** when you read textbooks in particular will make you a more effective critical reader.

Before you read . . .

Survey ▪ The first step in the SQ3R study method is "survey." When you survey a reading assignment, you try to get a general idea of what the assignment is about. You look briefly at each page, paying special attention to the headings, chapter titles, illustrations, and boldfaced type. It is also a good idea to read the first and last paragraphs.

Question ▪ As you do your survey, you should begin to ask questions about the material—questions that you hope to find the answers to as you read. One quick way of doing this is to turn the headings and subheadings into questions. Asking questions will make you an "active" rather than a "passive" reader, keeping you involved and thinking about what is coming up next.

As you read . . .

Read ▪ Read the material carefully from start to finish. Look for main ideas in each paragraph or section. Take notes as you read. (See the next page.) Read the difficult parts slowly. (Reread them if necessary.) Use context to help you figure out the most difficult passages. (See page 342.) Look up unfamiliar words or ideas and imagine the events, people, places, or things you are reading about.

Recite ▪ One of the most valuable parts of the SQ3R method is the reciting step. It is very important that you recite out loud what you have learned from your reading. Stop at the end of each page, section, or chapter to answer *who? what? when? where? why?* and *how?* about the information. This step is a way of testing yourself on how well you understand what you have read. You may then reread if necessary.

After you read . . .

Review ▪ The final step is to review. If you have some questions about the assignment, answer them immediately. If you have no questions, summarize the assignment in a short writing. You may also make an outline, note cards, flash cards, and illustrations to help you review and remember what you have read.

Interacting with a Text

If you would like to enrich your reading experience and enhance your understanding of the material, use one or more of the methods on the next eight pages.

Annotating

Annotating allows you to react to ideas as you read. The term annotate means "to add comments or make notes in a text." Use this method only if you are reading a photocopy or own the text. Here are several ways to annotate a reading selection.

- Write questions in the margins.
- Underline or highlight important points and comment on them in the margin.
- Circle new terms and define them in the margin.
- Make connections to other parts by drawing arrows.
- Add personal comments or reminders.

Annotating in Action

Pay As You Go

Why not?

If you live on the East Coast, you may know about turnpikes, but that will not be the case if you reside elsewhere. Either way, the word has an interesting history. According to the Free Online Dictionary, the word *turnpike* comes from the Middle English word *turnepike*, which is a combination of *turnen* meaning "to turn" and *pike* meaning "sharp point." Between the mid-16th and late-19th centuries, a turnpike in Great Britain was a gate or some other barrier across a road. The barrier prohibited passage until a toll was paid. Webster.dictionary.net describes the barrier as consisting of two bars at right angles spinning on a post. In some cases, the barrier was used to allow humans but not beasts of burden to progress along the road. This structure was similar to the turnstyles used to enter subway platforms today. The British writer and actor Ben Jonson (1572-1637) made reference to a spinning turnpike in this line: "I move upon an axle like a turnpike."

Check this site for a picture.

How exactly is the money used?

The money collected from a turnpike was, and still is, intended to keep the road in good repair. It certainly makes sense that residents of the East Coast today call the roads that they "pay for as they go" turnpikes. One can only assume that the roads remain in good repair with all the money that is collected. People in other parts of the country may be more familiar with the term *toll road* or *tollway*, either one being a synonym for *turnpike*. The opposite of a turnpike is a freeway, because a freeway is "free" of tolls, and the motorist is free to travel without stopping.

Contrast an apt name.

Taking Notes

Taking notes changes information that you have merely read into information that you have thought about and written down. Note taking is especially useful when the reading contains many important or complex facts and ideas. With notes, you can keep track of information and use it later for projects, in essays, and on tests.

- **Use your own words** as much as possible.
- **Record key terms, facts, and ideas** as simply as possible.
- **Note information from charts, graphs, and photographs** as well as from the main text.
- **Decide on a system for organizing your notes.** (The two-column Cornell method is shown below.)
- **Use abbreviations and symbols** to save time (# for *number*, & for *and*, = for *equals*, a hyphen [-] before each new detail, etc.).

Active Note Taking

Note taking can be more than simply recording what you read. Make it an active process by responding to the information, using a two-column system. Reserve one column (two-thirds of the page) for your main notes and another column (one-third of the page) for questions and key terms. Fill in the latter column after you've finished taking the main notes. Also save space at the bottom of the page to summarize your notes later.

Two-Column Notes (Cornell Method)

February 3

Meeting James A. Garfield

Questions and Key Terms	Main Notes
Who was the first?	- last president born in a log cabin
	- no official schooling until a young man
	- paid own expenses working as a carpenter
	- knew 7 languages
What are "ancient languages"?	- professor of ancient languages in early 20s
	- delivered spellbinding sermons, studied law
distinction=high quality, excellence	- served with distinction in Civil War
Who did he run against?	- 1st candidate to campaign in 2 languages, English & German (1880)

Using Graphic Organizers

As you read, consider using a graphic organizer to help you visualize the relationship between ideas. The following examples show how graphic organizers work for nonfiction selections that follow these patterns: chronological order, comparison-contrast, and cause-effect. Key ideas are listed in the time line.

Chronological Order

When a selection relates information in chronological order, you can use a time line to help you take notes. A time line lists events in the order in which they happen.

Today when we think of technology, we think of things like computers and satellites. But the story of technology begins at least 12,000 years ago (in about 10,000 B.C.E.). That's when people first began to use metal to make tools and utensils. The first metal to be used was copper. It was a big improvement over stone because coppersmiths could heat it and mold it into any needed shape.

The earliest evidence of people combining copper with tin to make bronze dates from about 4500 B.C.E. in Thailand. Bronze was much harder than copper and could be shaped into a sharp edge. With the invention of bronze, people were able to make knives, swords, and other weapons.

Around 3000 B.C.E., iron became the metal of choice. It was even harder than bronze and easier to come by because there was plenty of it near the earth's surface. The process of making steel—a strong, hard, flexible alloy (mixture) of iron and carbon—was first developed around 1400 but wasn't perfected until the 1800s.

Time Line

History of Modern Metals

10,000 B.C.E.	Copper was the first metal to be used for tools.
4500 B.C.E.	In Thailand, copper and tin were combined to make bronze, a harder metal than copper.
3000 B.C.E.	Iron was used because it was harder and more plentiful.
1400 C.E.	Early steelmaking technology combined iron and carbon.
1800 C.E.	Steelmaking was perfected.

▌ Comparison/Contrast

The comparison/contrast pattern introduces two (or more) topics and then tells how they are the same and how they are different. A Venn diagram is a helpful way to organize comparison/contrast notes.

There are many similarities between the two world wars, but also some important differences. In both wars, Great Britain, France, and Russia (the Soviet Union in World War II) were the main Allies until the United States joined them late in the conflict. In both wars, Germany was the primary adversary. In World War I, Germany was joined by Austria-Hungary, Turkey, and Bulgaria; in World War II, Germany's partners were Japan and Italy. (Italy had been an Allied nation in World War I.) Germany and its partners lost both wars.

WW II caused about four times as many deaths as WW I (about 55 million compared to about 14 million) and had a far greater impact on world politics, leaving the United States and Soviet Union as powerful leaders.

Venn Diagram

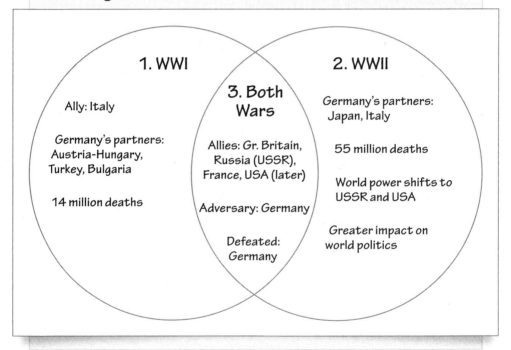

1. WWI

Ally: Italy

Germany's partners:
Austria-Hungary,
Turkey, Bulgaria

14 million deaths

3. Both
Wars

Allies: Gr. Britain,
Russia (USSR),
France, USA (later)

Adversary: Germany

Defeated:
Germany

2. WWII

Germany's partners:
Japan, Italy

55 million deaths

World power shifts to
USSR and USA

Greater impact on
world politics

Note: If you need to compare or contrast three things or ideas, add a third circle overlapping the other two.

Cause and Effect

The cause-and-effect pattern shows the relationships between two or more events or situations. Cause-and-effect relationships can take on a variety of forms: one cause with many effects, many causes that create one final effect (as in the excerpt below), and other variations. When a selection features cause-and-effect relationships, you can use an organizer like the one below to help you take notes.

Economic, political, and philosophical causes combined to bring about the French Revolution. France was in financial crisis because of war expenditures (including loans to American revolutionaries) and luxury-loving kings and queens. The middle class and peasants were taxed heavily, while the clergy and wealthy nobility paid nothing. Although the common people made up four-fifths of the population, they had only one-third of the vote in the French legislature. Therefore, they had no political power to change the tax laws. Dissatisfaction with this state of affairs was fueled by philosophers throughout Europe who were promoting philosophical ideas such as "government by majority rule" and "the inalienable rights of all human beings, regardless of their social or economic status." When efforts to reform the French government failed, a full-scale revolt began.

Cause-and-Effect Organizer

Subject: The French Revolution

Causes:	Effects:

Economic Crisis
    common people—heavily taxed for
    war debts
	resentment of luxury-loving royalty and
	untaxed clergy and nobility

Political Power
    common people—no power to make
    changes (4/5 of population with 1/3
    of vote)
	dissatisfaction over inability to change
	tax laws

Philosophical Ideas inalienable rights, majority rule	attempts to reform fail
	Final Effect: Revolution

Writing a Summary

Writing an effective summary is an excellent way to understand and remember what you have read. Summarizing is the process of condensing a text using your own words. Generally, a summary is no more than one-third the length of the original piece. Follow the guidelines below and read through the model on the next page.

▌ Writing Guidelines

1. **Skim the selection** first to get the overall meaning.

2. **Read the selection carefully,** paying particular attention to key words and phrases. (Check the meaning of any words you're unsure of.)

3. **List the main ideas** on your own paper—without looking at the selection.

4. **Review the selection** a final time so that you have the overall meaning clearly in mind as you begin to write.

5. **Write a summary** of the major ideas, using your own words except for those few words in the original that cannot be changed. Keep the following points in mind as you write:

   ▪ Your opening (topic) sentence should be a clear statement of the main idea of the original selection.

   ▪ Stick to the essential information. Names, dates, times, places, and similar facts are usually essential. Examples, descriptive details, and adjectives are usually not needed.

   ▪ Try to state each important idea in one clear sentence.

   ▪ Use a concluding sentence that ties all of your thoughts together and brings the summary to an effective end.

6. **Check your summary** for accuracy and conciseness. Ask yourself the following questions:

   ▪ Have I included all of the main ideas?

   ▪ Have I cut or combined most of the descriptive details? (Your summary should be about one-third the length of the original.)

   ▪ Will another person understand the main points simply by reading my summary?

Help File

To write a *précis* (a special form of summary), do the following:

▪ Keep the same voice and perspective as the original.

▪ Use paraphrases instead of direct quotations.

▪ Be brief and *precise.*

▌ Sample Summary

Notice that the opening sentence of the summary at the bottom of the page contains both a definition of the topic and the main point of the summary. The writer then lists the key details and concludes with a summarizing statement.

Original Text

"Acid rain" is precipitation with a high concentration of acids. The acids are produced by sulfur dioxide, nitrogen oxide, and other chemicals that are created by the burning of fossil fuels. Acid rain is known to have a gradual destructive effect on plant and aquatic life.

The greatest harm from acid rain is caused by sulfur dioxide, a gas produced from coal. As coal is burned in large industrial and power plant boilers, the sulfur it contains is turned into sulfur dioxide. This invisible gas is funneled up tall smokestacks and released into the atmosphere some 350–600 feet above the ground. As a result, the effects of the gas are seldom felt immediately. Instead, the gas is carried by the wind for hundreds and sometimes thousands of miles before it floats back down to earth. For example, sulfur dioxide produced in Pennsylvania at noon on Monday may not show up again until early Tuesday when it settles into the lakes and soil of rural Wisconsin.

Adding to the problem is the good possibility that the sulfur dioxide has undergone a chemical change while in flight. By simply taking on another molecule of oxygen, the sulfur dioxide could be changed to sulfur trioxide. Sulfur trioxide, when mixed with water, creates sulfuric acid—a highly toxic acid. If the sulfur trioxide enters a lake or stream, the resulting acid can kill fish, algae, and plankton. This, in turn, can interrupt the reproductive cycle of other life-forms, causing a serious imbalance in nature. If the sulfuric acid enters the soil, it can work on metals such as aluminum and mercury and set them free to poison both the soil and water.

Summary

"Acid rain," the term for precipitation that contains a high concentration of harmful chemicals, is gradually damaging our environment. The greatest harm from acid rain is caused by sulfur dioxide, a gas produced from the burning of coal. This gas, which is released into the atmosphere by industries using coal-fired boilers, is carried by the wind for hundreds of miles. By the time this gas has floated back to earth, it has often changed from sulfur dioxide to sulfur trioxide. Sulfur trioxide, when mixed with water, forms sulfuric acid. This acid can kill both plant and aquatic life and upset the cycle of life.

Forming Personal Responses

Taking notes is a good way to identify the important information in a reading selection, but writing a personal response actually connects you to the information. In a response, you can agree with what you've read, question it, or relate it to other things you know. Follow these guidelines to get started:

- **Reserve part of a notebook** or create a file for personal responses.
- **Respond before, during, and after reading.**
- **Write nonstop for 3-5 minutes**, freely exploring your thoughts about the material.
- **Pay attention to ideas that confuse you.** Writing about difficult concepts can help you sort them out.
- **Label and date your responses** to keep track of them.
- **Share your thoughts.** Personal responses can serve as conversation starters in classroom discussions.

Ways to Respond

Predict: State what you think will happen next and why.

Discuss: "Talk with the author" at different points during your reading.

React: Explore your thoughts and feelings about something you have just read.

Answer: Answer the questions *why?* or *what if?* at different points during your reading.

Connect: Relate your own experiences to something you have read.

Sample Personal Response

Here is how one reader reacted to an article in the May 2013 issue of *Scientific American* entitled "Good Bacteria for Bad Breath."

Leave it to science to "investigate" a problem that plagues mankind: bad breath. Apparently toothpaste, mouthwashes, and rinses are not enough, at least for those people who suffer from chronic bad breath. Even a brisk tongue scraping (no thanks) won't help those unfortunate folks. So science has identified a "gram-negative bacteria" (the problem) as well as a "gram-positive bacteria" that deters the growth of the former. I suppose some company will make a fortune with a "gram positive" mouthwash. If only a cure for cancer or dementia could be found so easily. . . .

Reading Informational Texts

You can thank computer technology for many things, including Facebook, YouTube, and personal learning networks (PLNs). You can also thank it for the incredible number of articles, essays, and books now available online. Having the skill and confidence to read all these informational texts is an important part of being college and workplace ready.

This chapter will help you identify and analyze the key elements of a text, including its *ideas, organization, voice, word choice,* and *sentence fluency.* This kind of analysis can turn the information you read into knowledge you can use.

Learning Outcomes

Use the traits for analysis.
Read for ideas.
Read for organization.
Read for voice and point of view.
Read for word choice and sentences.

"Books and movies are like apples and oranges.
They both are fruit, but taste completely different."

Stephen King

Using the Traits for Analysis

The traits focus on the essential elements in a reading selection—ideas, organization, voice, word choice, and sentence fluency. These traits are reviewed in the chart below and addressed in more detail on the following pages.

When reading for . . .	Identify and analyze . . .
Ideas	the topic, main idea (thesis), and evidence (supporting details).
Organization	the beginning, middle, and ending parts and the arrangement of evidence.
Voice (Tone)	the writer's personality, level of interest, and knowledge of the topic.
Word Choice	the use of specific vs. general nouns, active vs. passive verbs, sensory details, figurative language, and overall word choice.
Sentence Fluency	the flow and clarity of the sentences.

Developing Your Reading Skills

Your thoughtful analysis for each trait is an important first step in building your reading skills. With experience, you will begin to see relationships between the traits—how ideas and organization work together, and how voice is connected to word choice and sentence fluency. The more connections you make, the better you will understand what you are reading.

The traits cover the major elements that your instructors expect you to identify and understand when you read academic texts. And when you take high school exit exams as well as college entrance and placement exams, questions related to readings will focus on the traits. For example, these exams will ask you to . . .

- identify central ideas,
- locate relevant support evidence,
- analyze the text's structure or organization,
- interpret words, phrases, and figurative language, and
- assess tone and point of view.

Reading for Ideas

All reading material begins and ends with ideas. The author develops a main idea (thesis, claim) with supporting facts and details (evidence). Your number one task when reading nonfiction material is to identify the main idea and analyze its development.

Understanding Main Ideas

The main idea serves as the conductor in a piece of writing, directing all the information that follows. It is usually included in the topic sentence of a paragraph and in the thesis statement or claim of an article or essay. The following examples from various sources show how main ideas are formed. Each one names a topic and identifies some special feature about it, perhaps a part of the topic or a feeling about it, that the author will develop.

History textbook:

"Throughout their long history, Native American groups have moved
                                           (topic)
from region to region."
      (feature)

Health textbook:

"A study shows that many US presidents actually lived longer than their peers."
                       (topic)   **(feature)**

Newspaper:

"For all the criticism and new legal bans, texting while driving is still a problem,
                                           (topic)
especially among younger motorists."
         (feature)

Web sites:

[**Science**] "Is a giant, cloaked spaceship orbiting around Mercury?"
                        (topic)   **(feature)**
[**Technology**] "Creating software for smartphones and tablets isn't just for
                                           (topic)
professionals anymore."
       (feature)
[**Travel**] "If your tastes run to the offbeat and quirky, these top five weirdest
                                           (topic)
natural formations should be on your list of places to visit."
         (feature)

Note: A writer may need more than one sentence to state a main idea:

"Some Beijing residents are recording pollution levels and posting them online.
                                           (topic)
It's an act that borders on subversion."
       (feature)

▌ Identifying Main Ideas

In most texts, the main idea is stated (or implied) within the first or second paragraph. These guidelines will help you find the main idea in most texts:

1. Skim the text, reading the title, any headings, and the first few paragraphs.
2. Look for one sentence (often at the end of one of the opening paragraphs) that seems to control the writing.
3. If you can't find such a sentence, express the main idea in your own words.
4. Then, during your first complete reading, decide if this idea actually does control the writing. If not, look further for the main idea.

Example 1

Artist Finds New Hidden Images in *Mona Lisa* Painting

An artist in New York has found a series of hidden images in Leonardo da Vinci's masterpiece, the *Mona Lisa*. Artist Ron Piccirillo says that if you turn the painting sideways, you can see an outline of a lion, an ape, and a buffalo around Mona Lisa's head, and a crocodile and snake coming out of her body. So what's the meaning behind the images? Well, Piccirillo studied da Vinci's journals and says the painting is a representation of jealousy. The telltale journal passage reads, "Give her a leopard's skin, because this creature kills the lion out of envy and by deceit," and that's when he made the connection to the lion's head, hovering above her head. . . .

Explanation: The first sentence in this paragraph essentially repeats the idea stated in the title. This clearly identifies the first sentence as the topic sentence. The remaining sentences in the paragraph develop this idea.

Example 2

from *The Autobiography of Benjamin Franklin*

My list of virtues contain'd at first but twelve; but a Quaker friend having kindly informed me that I was generally thought proud; that my pride show'd itself frequently in conversation; that I was not content with being in the right when discussing any point, but was overbearing, and rather insolent, of which he convinc'd me by mentioning several instances; I determined endeavoring to cure myself, if I could, of this vice or folly among the rest, and I added Humility to my list giving an extensive meaning to the word.

Explanation: The background information that begins this passage naturally leads to the main idea, or thesis, which is underlined. The two topic sentences that follow show that the virtue of humility is discussed and developed in the next paragraphs.

Understanding Evidence

The supporting evidence in a text explains and develops the main idea. To share a clear and complete message, an essay, article, or report needs strong evidence.

▌ Types of Evidence

Different texts use different types of evidence. The following list identifies the types of evidence used most often.

Facts and statistics provide specific details based on reliable information.

> According to the Environmental Defense Fund, fine particle pollution from U.S. power plants causes nearly 24,000 premature deaths each year.

Explanations expound on or clarify a key point.

> The closer people live to these power plants, the more susceptible they are to the plants' emissions.

Examples show or reveal something.

> Burning coal, for example, emits soot, or fly ash, which can cause chronic bronchitis and aggravated asthma.

Descriptions show how something or someone appears.

> Fine particle pollutants are tiny particles of dust, soot, and smoke about 1/30 the width of a strand of human hair.

Reasons answer the question *why?* in a text.

> Some people may ask why our city doesn't simply shut down certain power plants. Indiana's dependence on burning fossil fuels for energy is one answer.

Quotations provide the exact words of someone knowledgeable about the topic.

> "The greatest health risk, in my opinion, in this city is fine particulate matter," said Dick Van Frank, who served on Indiana's Air Pollution Control Board for six years.

Reflections express the writer's feelings.

> Facilities like Covanta Energy give Indianapolis hope for cleaner air in the future. Still, a citywide effort is necessary to reduce air pollutant emissions.

Analysis reveals the writer's critical thinking on the topic.

> The power for change, though, really resides in the citizens themselves. They need to recycle, carpool, and educate themselves about clean-air issues. Clean air is vital for a healthy, sustainable Indianapolis.

Analogies compare something unfamiliar with something familiar.

> Holladay compares a pollution control device called a baghouse to a Brita filter for household water, because it filters 99.9 percent of particulate matter from flue gas.

Definitions explain unfamiliar terms.

> "Criteria pollutants" are a set of principal air pollutants (including particulate matter, sulfur dioxide, and others) that are harmful to people.

Evidence in Action

Generally, the evidence in a text will appear soon after the main idea. In a paragraph, the sentences following the topic sentence will contain evidence. And in essays and articles, the paragraphs following the thesis statement will provide evidence.

Evidence in a Paragraph

from "History of Medieval Tapestries"

From time immemorial, man has expressed a wish or desire to capture pictures in a preservable or permanent form. Cavemen drew scenes of hunts and food gathering, of fire and their homes, on the walls of caves using ocher or animal blood and sap. The Renaissance saw portraits and artwork come alive, with the paintings of da Vinci and Michelangelo. The advent of photography did not diminish this creative streak. Instead, artists took interesting and varied photographs depicting the situations and styles of their period.

Explanation: The evidence consists of a series of brief *examples* of man's "wish or desire to capture pictures in a preservable or permanent form."

Evidence in an Essay

Tsunami

On March 11, 2011, a level 9.0 earthquake shook the Pacific Ocean, and a huge tsunami struck Japan. A tsunami (the Japanese word for "harbor wave") is one of the most destructive forces in nature, and this tsunami caused $235 billion worth of damage (World Bank). Many people believe that a tsunami is simply a big wave that moves forward until it hits the shore, but the process is more complex than that. A tsunami is really a huge transfer of energy from the crust of the earth to a body of water.

Unlike typical ocean waves caused by wind and storms, a tsunami begins with a fault line in the seabed. Along such a fault, two or more of the earth's tectonic plates meet and grate against each other. An earthquake occurs when one plate suddenly slips. Beneath the ocean, if one tectonic plate thrusts up and over another, a tsunami begins to form.

When the underwater earthquake lifts the continental plate and all the water above it, tremendous energy is released. The force moves upward through the water until it nears the surface. There, the energy spreads out horizontally like ripples in a pool. This enormous energy is not apparent on the surface, however, and the outwardly spreading waves may be only a few feet high. The power of the tsunami is still under the surface, moving as fast as 500 miles per hour.

As the surge heads toward the shore, the immense energy does not have enough water to carry it. The water nearer the land is sucked back out to sea to feed the growing wave. People who witness tsunamis first notice that the ocean is suddenly receding, as it does at low tide. Then the wave rushes onshore in the form of a wall of water that can be a hundred feet high and several hundred miles wide. The power of this wall of water can be unbelievable.

The Japanese tsunami of 2011 resulted from the fifth largest earthquake since modern record keeping began. Taken together, the earthquake and tsunami released 9,320 gigatons of energy, which is 600 million times that of the Hiroshima atomic bomb. Many cities in Japan looked like they had suffered just such an attack.

Explanation: In this essay, the writer's evidence explains the thesis statement (underlined) with a definition, facts, statistics, explanations, and analysis.

Judging the Reliability of Evidence

Unfortunately, not every text contains reliable, dependable information. Skilled readers can usually detect questionable texts. Until you get to that point, answering questions like the ones that follow will help you check for a text's reliability. Also consult with an instructor or media specialist as needed.

- **Consider the source:** Does the text come from a respected periodical, a well-known publisher, or a Web site with a reliable domain such as *.edu*, *.org*, or *.gov*?

- **Consider the author:** What is the author's background? Does the text deal with his or her field of expertise? What else has the author written? Is the author promoting a particular point of view or bias?

- **Consider the information:** Is the topic covered thoroughly? Is the information balanced? Current? Trustworthy? Are the conclusions logical? Does the text contain any errors? How does the information compare to other texts that address the same topic?

- **Consider your position:** Is the text too simple or too challenging for you? Are you too accepting of the author's point of view, or too skeptical? Does the author's voice (writing personality) distract you or prevent you from reading the text thoughtfully?

▌An Unreliable Text

What follows is a completely **fictitious** and thoroughly flawed electronic article. Reviewing its flaws will tell you what to look for whenever you have questions about the reliability of a more legitimate text.

bublout.com

Say No to Clean Clothes

Washing your cloths can be dangerous to your health. As crazy as this may sound, it is true because laundry detergents contain so many harmful chemicals. You may have heard about phosphates, but there are also things like sulfuric dexterozine (SDO) and nonptenzine preconital (NPP). Studies have shown they may cause cancer-like conditions in rats and mice.

The Council for Skin Care (CSC) warns consumers that SDO can go by other names such as . . .
- bicandle corzine (BCC)
- ziroxital butin (ZB)
- geroutal fennix (GF)

NPP can also be called . . .
- memindal ozenahal (M0)
- systax sansibical (SSS)
- virtol dtoxicant (VD)

A typical family does up to 100 pounds of laundry each week! Multiply that figure by 52 and you get 52,000 pounds of wash for a year. Multiply that figure by the number of families and you soon see the severity of the problem—with the dangerous chemicals on our clothes, in our water, and floating around in the air.

The Association for Chemical Awareness (ASCA) recommends that you do the following:
- Reduce the amount of washing you do.
- When you do wash your clothes, use a product we recommend. (See below.)
- Wear protective gloves when you handle detergents and laundry.

To learn about "clean" laundry detergents, please <u>click here</u> for a special offer.

Chief Researcher

Explanation: The source of the text—bublout.com—is certainly suspicious, as is the only author reference—"Chief Researcher." The information is anything but trustworthy and truthful, listing fictitious chemicals and organizations and making wild claims. Hidden behind all of this gobbledygook is the purpose of the text—to promote a product.

Reading for Organization

Ideas are very important to a piece of writing, but they must be put in the proper order for them to make sense and be of use to the reader.

Knowing the Common Patterns

Listed below are the common patterns of organization that writers use. A writer will often use a combination of patterns—a main pattern plus one or two secondary patterns. Being able to recognize organizational patterns will help you follow the ideas in a text.

Chronological (time order): Autobiographical and biographical texts, science reports, and process papers are usually organized chronologically, explaining events in the order in which they occurred.

Comparison-contrast: Texts that follow this pattern show the similarities and differences between topics. An author may discuss one topic first and then the next; share all the similarities between the topics first and then the differences; or make a point-by-point comparison.

Classification: This pattern, commonly used in science texts, breaks down a subject into groups (*there are three main types of grasslands*) and then discusses each one. *Classification* means "the act of arranging according to classes, groups, or types."

Illustration: Illustrating involves explaining a main idea by giving one detailed example (*Rosa Parks proved that sitting still can be powerful*) or by sharing multiple examples (*Napoli's popularity stems from its signature Sicilian dishes*). *Illustration* means "an example or examples used to prove something."

Cause-effect: This pattern is common in texts that explore a condition (*the causes and effects of deforestation*) or a set of circumstances (*the causes and effects of high gas prices*). Authors will often identify the cause or causes first and then explore the effects.

Problem-solution: Texts following this pattern will often summarize a problem (*school litter*), then discuss possible solutions, and finally focus on the best one.

Order of importance: Texts that support a particular point of view or claim may be organized from the most important argument to the least important, or the other way around.

Logical order: Some texts develop a topic based on the logical flow of ideas. Point A logically leads to point B and so on.

Spatial order: Descriptions may use this pattern, with details ordered from top to bottom, right to left, foreground to background, general (*big picture*) to specific, and so on. Spatial order is almost always used in combination with other patterns.

Understanding the Three-Part Structure

A complete text—such as an essay, article, or textbook chapter—consists of three basic parts: a beginning, a middle, and an ending. Each part plays an important role in the development of a topic, and understanding those roles can guide your reading.

Three-Part Structure

Paragraph Structure	Essay Structure
Topic Sentence ▪ Names the topic and focus	**Beginning Part** ▪ Introduces the topic ▪ Provides background information ▪ Identifies the main idea or thesis
Body Sentences ▪ Provide supporting details ▪ Follow a pattern of organization	**Middle Part** ▪ Supports or develops the main idea ▪ Follows one or more patterns of organization
Closing Sentence ▪ Wraps up the paragraph	**Ending Part** ▪ Summarizes the key ideas ▪ Restates the thesis ▪ Provides final thoughts or analysis

A Closer Look: Reacting to Ideas and Organization

You can react to informational texts on two levels. On one level, you can identify the key information (main idea and evidence). On another level, you can form your own thoughts about the information.

Gathering the Data

Answering the following questions will help you identify the key information in a text. After you have that information, you can form your own thoughts about it.

1. Beginning: What is the main idea?

2. Middle: What does the evidence say about the main idea?

3. Ending: What additional information or conclusion is provided?

Gathering Data About a Paragraph

The paragraph below is taken from an essay about a troublesome plant growing in central Indiana. Questions and answers that reveal the main idea follow the reading.

Bush honeysuckle was originally planted in central Indiana as a food source for wildlife and for erosion control, but it doesn't function very well for either. Birds flock to berries on these bushes because the berries are high in fat and sugar. Dr. Rebecca Dolan, director of the Friesner Herbarium at Butler University, calls them "bird candy." As such, they do not provide migrating birds with effective fuel for long-distant flying. Bush honeysuckle produces a lot of seeds, which berry-eating birds spread, so the plant can easily take over its environment. In addition, the bushes leaf out sooner and for a longer time than other plants, which wipes out the native vegetation. And without the native plants, erosion control suffers. Unfortunately, getting rid of bush honeysuckle requires a great deal of work and patience.

1. Beginning: What is the main idea?

Bush honeysuckle was originally planted in central Indiana as a food source for wildlife and for erosion control, but it does not function very well for either.

2. Middle: What does the evidence say about the main idea?

- The berries on the bush are high in fat and sugar and do not provide quality food for migrating birds.
- The plants take over their environment at the expense of the native plants, so they add to the erosion problem.

3. Ending: What additional information or conclusion is provided?

Getting rid of this plant requires a lot of work and patience.

Summarizing a Text

Writing a summary is another way to identify the main idea in a text. A summary should, for the most part, use your own words and be no more than one-third as long as the original. (See page 294.) The following summary of the paragraph on the previous page contains the main idea and essential information, omitting many of the specific details.

> The bush honeysuckle in central Indiana has failed both as a food source for wildlife and as a means of erosion control. The berries on this bush, high in fat and sugar, do not provide adequate nutrition for migrating birds. Bush honeysuckle also crowds out the native plants, which contributes to erosion. Unfortunately, getting rid of this plant is not easy.

Drawing Inferences

An inference is a logical conclusion that you make about something; it is your own idea. For example, if you go to a movie and say afterward that it "explores the damaging effects of peer pressure," you are drawing an inference based on the actions and events you saw in the movie. Likewise, if you say that your favorite basketball team lacks a go-to scorer, you are drawing an inference based on the team's inability to close out tight games.

To react to an informational text at this level, read the material at least two times, taking notes and annotating the text as needed. Also do the necessary data collecting and summarizing. After taking such care, you will be ready to draw some thoughtful inferences. Questions like the following will prompt your thinking.

- Why was the text written?
- Why does the information matter?
- What have I really learned?
- What is the most important part?

- What seems to be missing?
- What main feeling do I have about the text and why?

Logical Conclusions

Here are two logical conclusions that can be drawn from the paragraph on the previous page.

- **Why does the information matter?**

  Many people just assume that any attempt to improve the environment is a good thing. This text shows that not all attempts are going to work or are based on sound reasoning.

- **What is the most important part?**

  That the attempt failed so completely is the most important part. Why couldn't the planners have known?

Reading for Voice and Point of View

An author's voice is created through word choice and manner of expression. Three common classifications of voice are formal, informal, and satiric.

Formal (academic) voice: Authors use a formal voice when they want to establish a serious tone. Textbooks and thoughtful essays are almost always formal.

> Whether one wind turbine is used by an individual, or a wind farm supplies energy to many people, no air pollutants or greenhouse gases are emitted. California reports that 2.5 billion pounds of carbon dioxide and 15 million pounds of other pollutants have not entered the air because of wind energy.

Explanation: The passage presents facts rather than personal thoughts and feelings, uses words and expressions that sound serious, and exhibits long, somewhat complex sentence structures.

Informal (personal) voice: Authors often use an informal voice when they write personal essays or commentaries.

> It's hard to think of something that is alive like algae not being part of the animal, plant, or fungi kingdoms. How can that be? Seaweed is a type of algae. And it sure looks like a plant to me. Mr. Alvarez calls algae "leftovers" because they don't fit anywhere.

Explanation: The passage shares the author's personal feelings, includes casual words and expressions (*it's* rather than *it is*; *a type of algae* rather than *classified as algae*), and uses short, simple sentences.

Satiric voice: Authors use a satiric voice when they want to criticize or make fun of something. In the example below, Secretary of Education Arne Duncan is compared to a king:

> King Arne graced McHale School with his presence last week, marching down the hallways with his attendants following close behind, ready to assist at a moment's notice. His Excellency seemed impatient with his subjects at McHale because they weren't making enough improvements in their school.

Explanation: This passage exaggerates reality (the Secretary simply visited a school). It includes words and expressions that sound serious but actually aren't, and it uses rather formal sentence structures.

A Closer Look: Understanding Point of View

It is natural to address different people in different ways. For example, you are careful in what you say to someone in authority, such as a school administrator or a city official, and more relaxed when you talk or text with friends.

Authors address readers in different ways as well. Storybook writers use simple, playful words that young children can enjoy. Professional journal writers use sophisticated words and a formal voice to suit a well-educated audience. An author's *point of view*, or approach, depends on the purpose for writing and the intended audience. Recognizing an author's point of view is part of fully understanding a text. Here are some examples of different points of view:

Example 1

This passage comes from a campaign speech delivered by John McCain during his run for president in 2008.

> If I am elected president, I will help to create jobs for Americans in the most effective way a president can do this—with tax cuts that are directed specifically to create jobs, and protect your life savings. I will stand up to the corrupt ways of Washington, the wasteful spending and the abuses of power, and I will end these abuses, whatever it takes. . . . The hour is late and the troubles are getting worse. We have to act immediately. We have to change direction now.

Point of view: An experienced senator campaigning, intent on sounding confident and decisive

Audience: Republican Party members attending the speech

Purpose: To persuade attendees to vote for him and spread the good word

Example 2

This passage comes from Richard Milner's article "Time Traveler" that appeared in a 2012 issue of *Scientific American*.

> You may not know this name, but chances are that you have seen his work. Brooklyn-born artist Charles R. Knight (1874-1953) produced paintings and sculptures of dinosaurs, mammoths, and prehistoric humans that adorn the great natural history museums in the U.S. His dinos have appeared as toys, stamps and comics as well as in books and scientific journals on paleontology. (vol. 306, no. 4, p. 72)

Point of view: An anthropology writer, speaking from a position of authority

Audience: Educated readers interested in science topics

Purpose: To inform readers about a skilled scientific illustrator

Reading for Word Choice

When analyzing an informational text such as Abraham Lincoln's "Gettysburg Address" for word choice, you should (1) interpret the words and phrases, (2) identify and understand the figurative language, and (3) establish how word choice creates tone and meaning.

An older document like this presents a special challenge because of its writing style and word choice, so read it carefully. A word analysis follows.

Gettysburg Address

Four score and seven years ago our fathers brought forth on this continent, a new nation, conceived in Liberty, and dedicated to the proposition that all men are created equal.

Now we are engaged in a great civil war, testing whether that nation, or any nation so conceived, and so dedicated, can long endure. We are met on a great battlefield of that war. We have come to dedicate a portion of it, as a final resting place for those who here gave their lives that that nation might live. It is altogether fitting and proper that we should do this.

But, in a larger sense, we can not dedicate—we can not consecrate—we can not hallow—this ground. The brave men, living and dead, who struggled here, have consecrated it, far above our poor power to add or detract. The world will little note, nor long remember what we say here, but it can never forget what they did here. It is for us the living, rather, to be dedicated here to the unfinished work which they who fought here thus far so nobly advanced. It is rather for us to be here dedicated to the great task remaining before us—that from these honored dead we take increased devotion to that cause for which they gave the last full measure of devotion—that we here highly resolve that these dead shall not have died in vain—that this nation, under God, shall have a new birth of freedom—and that government of the people, by the people, for the people, shall not perish from the earth.

Analysis of Word Choice

- **Interpret words and phrases:** To appreciate the speech, it is essential to understand words like conceived (*created*), consecrated (*to set apart for sacred purposes*), hallow (*honor*), and in vain (*without purpose*).

- **Identify and understand figurative language:** Lincoln uses *conceived*, *new birth*, and *shall not perish* to make the nation sound like a living thing. He also uses repetition to emphasize the ideas of conception, dedication, and consecration.

- **Establish how words create tone and meaning:**
  Lincoln's word choice establishes a fitting formal tone and emphasizes that the war must be won to honor these men.

Reading for Sentences

When analyzing the sentences in an informational text, you should (1) interpret what information they communicate, (2) identify and understand any special features (length, structure, flow), and (3) establish how these sentences help to create tone and meaning.

Analysis of Sentences in the "Gettysburg Address"

- **Interpret what information they communicate:** The sentences explain that the nation is being tested by the war. And while the men slain at the Battle of Gettysburg must be honored, it is up to the living to ensure that they did not die in vain.

- **Identify and understand any special features:** Lincoln uses, almost entirely, lengthy and complex sentences, containing multiple levels of meaning. The use of parallel structure—of the people, by the people, for the people—adds a pleasing, yet sophisticated, rhythm to the speech.

- **Establish how they create tone and meaning:** Lincoln's objectivity and complex sentences help create a formal tone and stress the solemnity and importance of his words.

A Study in Contrast

This passage comes from a famous speech delivered by Sojourner Truth in 1851 at a convention concerning women's rights. Sojourner Truth's words and sentences establish a far different tone than Lincoln's, but they are just as effective.

As you read the passage, notice the common vocabulary, the personal voice, and the easy-to-understand strings of ideas. And above all else, notice how the repetition of the boldface question makes a dramatic point about the inequality she has suffered.

Ain't I a Woman?

That man over there says that women need to be helped into carriages and lifted over ditches, and to have the best place everywhere. Nobody ever helps me into carriages, or over mud-puddles, or gives me any best place. **And ain't I a woman?** Look at me! Look at my arms! I have ploughed and planted, gathered into barns, and no man could head me! **And ain't I a woman?** I could work as much and eat as much as a man—when I could get it—and bear the lash as well! **And ain't I a woman?** I have borne thirteen children, and seen most all sold off to slavery, and when I cried out with my mother's grief, none but Jesus heard me! **And ain't I a woman . . . ?**

(from "Ain't I A Woman," a speech delivered in 1851 at the Women's Convention in Akron, Ohio)

Reading Essays of Argumentation

The dictionary defines argument as a "quarrel, dispute, or heated discussion." In an argument, voices are raised in anger, and emotions rather than good sense dominate the interaction.

But there is a far different form of argumentation in which thorough explanations rather than strong emotions are the priority. Consider a biologist who argues in an essay for increased protection of a certain species. Or consider a judge who is preparing an important decision, or a government official who is preparing a response to an unfolding international crisis. Each will rely on logic, clear thinking, and compelling evidence to present his or her case or argument. In this chapter, you will learn how to read and analyze this type of argument.

Learning Outcomes

Learn the parts of an argument.
Identify argumentative appeals.
Analyze arguments.
Graph an argument.

"Reading furnishes the mind only with materials of knowledge; it is thinking that makes what we read ours."

John Locke

Learning the Parts of an Argument

The parts of an essay of argumentation are listed below. Depending upon the argument, some elements may be arranged differently or omitted altogether.

Background information: The beginning introduces the argument by sharing background or historical information about the topic.

> Cesar Santiago plays the guitar for residents at a rehab facility. Hanna Henderson assists in the food preparation at the local soup kitchen. Riley Odoms helps out at one of the community gardens. Each of these Parkview students is fulfilling a graduation requirement—participating in community service.

Main claim: The main claim is the thesis, or controlling idea, of an argument. It presents a particular belief or point of view and usually appears at the end of one of the beginning paragraphs.

> Parkview's community service requirement (*topic*) gives students life-changing experiences not available in the classroom (*point of view*).

Supporting evidence: The supporting evidence consists of the facts, figures, explanations, quotations, and other details that support the claim. Strong evidence is logical, reasonable, and trustworthy.

- **Facts:** Participating in their community is the first work experience for many Parkview students.
- **Explanation:** Completing this service will help Parkview students learn firsthand how the community works.
- **Quotation:** Ms. Sandra Williams, community service advisor, says, "Working in the community shows students that people need and appreciate their help."

Opposing points of view: Thoughtful arguments often consider opposing points of view. An author may concede or accept another point of view as worthy or counter it by pointing out its weakness.

- **Opposing point of view:** Critics of the community service requirement say students may perceive it as a punishment. They point out how lawbreakers are often required to complete community service hours.
- **Counter:** However, community service work is beneficial to everyone involved. Even the most skeptical students quickly see the experience as pleasurable and rewarding, not a form of punishment.

Confirmation: Arguments often end with an important thought that reinforces the value of the claim and/or calls the reader to action.

> What students gain from this experience far outweighs any time they may have to give up. Their community service gives them a taste of real life at just the right time. Please give your support to the community service requirement.

Remember: While a strong argument may be persuasive, that is not its main purpose. Its real goal is to support a point of view with logic and strong evidence.

An Argument in Action

An *editorial* is a newspaper or magazine article that expresses the opinion of the editor or publisher. If you carefully read the following example and the side notes, you'll have a good feel for what a formal argument sounds like.

Let High School Students Text Outside Class

What's a little H&K (hugs and kisses), HAND (have a nice day), or ILBL (I'll be late) between parents and high school students during the school week?

Background information

Back in the day, parents didn't have to worry as much about coordinating hectic work and school schedules. But life continues to get increasingly complicated—not just with every new after-school activity, but with multiplying job demands on parents.

Main claim

So at the risk of sounding soooo old school in our praise, we think Richardson administrators deserve a gold star for allowing high schoolers to communicate via text messages when they're not in the classroom.

Like most districts, Richardson had banned cell phone use for anything other than teacher-approved instructional purposes during the school day—a restriction that makes it difficult for parents and children to communicate regarding often-changing schedules. Richardson schools still aren't allowed

Supporting evidence

to make phone calls—try to imagine the din generated by that many voices— but at least they have greater freedom to smartly use their smartphones between classes and during lunch.

As long as the texting doesn't interfere with classroom instruction or discipline, this seems like a good experiment. A small number of districts already allow students to use cell phones for calculators and Internet access. The Richardson decision is a sound alternative to students secretly using their phones under their desks or in the bathroom stall as they text, tweet, update Facebook accounts, or stay in contact with their parents.

Most parents want to be able to contact their child during school hours in the event of an emergency or a change in schedule, and students can't use the office phone except in the case of illness or emergency.

Opposing point of view

Sure, some will say that students should be able to put their thumbs, parents, and social media on hold during the school day. But the "no cell

Counter

phone at any time" mandate is probably about as realistic as those apocryphal tales of parents walking to and from school (always uphill both ways!).

"The phone is now a huge part of parenting," says Amanda Lenhart, a senior research specialist with the Pew Research Center Internet and American Life project. "It's how you reach your kids."

Confirmation

If schools can find a way to further family communication without sacrificing academic goals, so much the better. Let the kids go mobile. It's not the end of the world; it's part of the new brave one.

Identifying Argumentative Appeals

A strong argument appeals to the reader's sense of fairness, clear thinking, or common sense. It should not appeal to the reader's fears or biases. The examples below show the difference between worthy and unworthy appeals.

Fact: Every other local high school in the Capitol Conference offers an extensive soccer program.

Fairness appeal: Shouldn't Waterford do the same?

Common sense appeal: Without a complete soccer program, we'll never be able to compete with these schools.

Emotional appeal: Without a better soccer program, our school will look stupid! *(This could weaken the argument.)*

Fact: Because of the Endangered Species Act, 46 species have been removed from the endangered list.

Fairness appeal: The Act's 2010 budget amounts to 9 cents per U.S. citizen, an amount everyone can afford.

Common sense appeal: It takes a long time for a species to earn the endangered tag, so people can expect that it takes a long time to reverse the condition.

Careless appeal: We spend millions trying to help people who are struggling; why can't some of that money be used for animals? *(A plea to use funds intended for needy people weakens the argument.)*

Fact: The Organization for Economic Cooperation and Development (OECD) reports that patients served by the Canadian health-care system wait longer to see specialists and have elective surgery than patients in many other countries.

Logical appeal: With modern management tools, Canadian health-care officials should be able to reduce the wait time.

Moral appeal: Don't patients have a right to timely care, especially when they need to see a specialist?

Exaggerated appeal: Canada shows a complete disregard for the health and well-being of its citizens. *(A statement like this weakens the argument. Overall, Canadians receive excellent health care.)*

Logical Fallacies

Emotional and ill-conceived appeals are considered logical fallacies because they demonstrate fuzzy or shoddy thinking. A fallacy is defined as "a deceptive, misleading, or false belief." The following logical fallacies represent numerous examples of unworthy appeals.

Appeal to ignorance: Maintaining that because no one has ever proved a claim, it must be false

> *Coffee is good for you. Show me one study that proves otherwise.*

Appeal to pity: Begging for leniency or tugging at someone's heart strings

> *Envision what the experience must have been like for her. If anyone deserves a second chance, she does.*

Bandwagon: Appealing to everyone's sense of wanting to belong

> *Everyone is driving hybrid cars. They are the only way to go.*

Broad generalization: Appealing to everything and everyone all at once, without allowing for exceptions

> *All urban dwellers should walk or take public transportation.*

Circular thinking: Assuming the very point you are trying to prove

> *I strongly endorse organic vegetables because that is all I eat.*

Either-or thinking: Reducing a solution to two possible extremes

> *Either we increase the funding significantly or the Endangered Species Act will vanish.*

False cause: Confusing cause and effect

> *Since texting has become popular, math scores have dropped. There has to be some connection.*

Half-truths: Telling only part of the truth

> *The new welfare bill is good because it will get thousands of people off government aid. (It may also cause undue suffering.)*

Red herring: Distracting from the real issue

> *Officer, I know I was speeding, but think what the fine will do to my wife and kids.*

Slated language: Choosing words that carry strong positive or negative connotations to distract from valid arguments

> *How could anyone possibly vote for raising taxes!*

Straw man: Exaggerating or misrepresenting the opponent's position

> *Those who approve euthanasia must believe that the terminally ill deserve to suffer.*

Analyzing Arguments

The analyses of the arguments on the following pages reveal what to look for as you read essays of argumentation. Read each example and analysis carefully.

Example 1

This editorial discusses a serious environmental problem facing the Great Lakes.

Block the Asian Carp by Closing the Canal

The best way to prevent the Asian carp and other invasive species from entering the Great Lakes is to close off their access to the lakes. And the place to start to do that is the Chicago Sanitary and Shipping Canal, which is a critically vulnerable link between the Great Lakes watershed and the Mississippi watershed.

Closing the canal provides a permanent solution to ending the threat posed by invasive species such as the carp, which has been working its way up the Mississippi system and poses a significant threat to the Great Lakes habitat. Given that the Great Lakes comprise the planet's largest freshwater system, this is obviously an important environmental issue. But it is also a key job issue. The carp could wreak havoc on the Great Lakes sport and commercial fishing industry, which has an estimated annual value of $7 billion.

A report issued this week says separation of the two basins can be done, although it will come with a significant cost and will take at least a decade. The report by the Great Lakes Commission and the Great Lakes and St. Lawrence Cities Initiative, which represents dozens of cities, including Milwaukee, lays out three options for blocking the Chicago canal system. . . .

So far, the response by the federal government and the State of Illinois to the spread of the Asian carp has been tepid. The fish have swarmed through much of the river system since escaping from containment ponds in Arkansas in the 1960s. They've been gradually making their way to Lake Michigan through the Illinois River system. An electric barrier in the canal appears to provide insufficient protection. . . .

And beyond that barrier, the federal government has done little. The Army Corps of Engineers is studying the issue and the options, but the study is taking too long.

Cost of the closure is estimated at $3.2 billion to $9.5 billion and could take until sometime between 2022 and 2029 to complete. It's not cheap and will require a massive change in not only the barge industry in Illinois but in the Chicago sewage system, which now drains toward the Mississippi.

But given the threat posed by the carp and other invasives, blocking the canal is cheaper and far more beneficial than dealing with the damage that could result.

A combined effort by the federal, state, and local governments will be needed to meet the challenge. But it's a challenge we must meet. Close the canal.

Analysis

As you read the following analysis of the argument, note that exact statements from the text are in quotation marks; paraphrases of the text are italicized.

▌ What are the basic parts of the argument?

- ▪ **Background information:** *Not included*
- ▪ **Main claim:** "The best way to prevent the Asian carp and other invasive species from entering the Great Lakes *(topic)* is to close off their access to the lakes *(point of view)*."
- ▪ **Supporting evidence:** *Closing the Chicago Sanitary and Shipping Canal provides a permanent solution according to a recent report. A $7 billion fishing industry is in danger. The fish have been making their way to Lake Michigan via the Illinois River. An electric barrier is not doing an adequate job of stopping the fish.*
- ▪ **Opposing point of view:** *The cost of the closure is estimated to be between $3.2 and $9.5 billion. The closure will take time to complete (between 2022 and 2029) and will require changes in the barge industry and the Chicago sewage system.*
- ▪ **Counter:** "But given the threat . . . blocking the canal is cheaper and far more beneficial than dealing with the damage that could result."
- ▪ **Confirmation and call to action:** "A combined effort by the federal, state, and local governments will be needed to meet the challenge. But it's a challenge we must meet. Close the canal."

▌ How do these parts work together to form the argument?

The essay presents a clear case for stopping the Asian carp from entering the Great Lakes. The Great Lakes provide the largest freshwater system in the world and support a $7 billion fishing industry. A solution to the problem, based on reports from more than one source, is proposed.

▌ What questions or concerns do you have about the argument?

Unfortunately, the costs and the time involved to carry out the solution are immense. Before fully accepting this argument, I'd like to know specific details about how the sanitary system and barge industry would cope with the canal closing. I'd also like to know more about Asian carp. Why does this species present such a problem? Is there a less costly and quicker solution?

Example 2

Suffragette Susan B. Anthony delivered this speech after having been tried and fined $100 for casting an illegal vote during the 1872 presidential election.

On Women's Right to Vote

Friends and fellow citizens: I stand before you tonight under indictment for the alleged crime of having voted at the last presidential election, without having a lawful right to vote. It shall be my work this evening to prove to you that in thus voting, I not only committed no crime, but, instead, simply exercised my citizen's rights, guaranteed to me and all United States citizens by the National Constitution, beyond the power of any state to deny.

The preamble to the Federal Constitution says:

"We the people of the United States, in order to form a more perfect union, establish justice, insure domestic tranquility, provide for the common defense, promote the general welfare, and secure the blessings of liberty to ourselves and our posterity, do ordain and establish this Constitution for the United States of America."

It was we, the people; not we, the white male citizens; nor yet we, the male citizens; but we, the whole people, who formed the Union. And we formed it, not to give the blessings of liberty, but to secure them; not to the half of ourselves and the half of our posterity, but to the whole people—women as well as men. For any state to make sex a qualification that must ever result in the disfranchisement of one entire half of the people, is to pass a **bill of attainder**, or, an **ex post facto law**, and is therefore a violation of the supreme law of the land. By it the blessings of liberty are forever withheld from women and their female posterity.

To them this government has no just powers derived from the consent of the governed. To them this government is not a democracy. It is not a republic. It is an odious aristocracy; a hateful oligarchy of sex; the most hateful aristocracy ever established on the face of the globe; an oligarchy of wealth, where the rich govern the poor. An oligarchy of learning, where the educated govern the ignorant, or even an oligarchy of race, where the Saxon rules the African, might be endured; but this oligarchy of sex, which makes father, brothers, husband, sons, the oligarchs over the mother and sisters, the wife and daughters, of every household—which ordains all men sovereigns, all women subjects, carries dissension, discord, and rebellion into every home of the nation. . . .

The only question left to be settled now is: Are women persons? And I hardly believe any of our opponents will have the hardihood to say they are not. Being persons, then, women are citizens; and no state has a right to make any law, or to enforce any old law, that shall abridge their privileges or immunities. Hence, every discrimination against women in the constitutions and laws of the several states is today null and void, precisely as is every one against Negroes.

Analysis

As you read this analysis of Susan B. Anthony's speech, note that exact statements from the text are in quotation marks; paraphrases of the text are italicized.

▌ What are the basic parts of the argument?

- **Background information:** "Friends and fellow citizens: I stand before you tonight under indictment for the alleged crime of having voted at the last presidential election, without having a lawful right to vote."

- **Main claim:** "It shall be my work this evening to prove to you that in thus voting *(topic)*, I not only committed no crime, but, instead, simply exercised my citizen's rights, guaranteed to me and all United States citizens by the National Constitution, beyond the power of any state to deny *(point of view)*."

- **Supporting evidence:** "The preamble to the Federal Constitution says: 'We the people of the United States' . . . not we, the white male citizens . . . but we, the whole people, who formed the union." *How can the liberties identified in the Constitution, including the right to vote, be denied to women then? Citizens are defined as persons in the United States entitled to vote and hold office.* "Are women persons?"

- **Opposing point of view (implied):** *It is up to the individual states to decide on the right to vote.*

- **Counter:** "For any state to make sex a qualification . . . is to pass a bill of attainder, or, an ex post facto law, and is therefore a violation of the supreme law of the land."

- **Confirmation and call to action:** "Being persons, then, women are citizens; and no state has a right to make any law, or to enforce any old law, that shall abridge their privileges or immunities. Hence, every discrimination against women in the constitutions and laws of the several states is today null and void, precisely as is every one against Negroes."

▌ How do these parts work together to form the argument?

Anthony appeals to the rights of citizens spelled out in the Constitution as supreme over any laws passed in any state. And then she asks pointedly: "Are women persons?" Her argument is certainly dramatic and decisive.

▌ What questions or concerns do you have about the argument?

Anthony's confirmation, declaring every state's voting law that disfranchises any citizens (women and Negroes) as null and void, is beyond her legal authority. The states will certainly not agree with her. I'm also wondering if her reference to bills of attainder and ex post facto laws is accurate.

Example 3

This essay of argumentation from an environmental studies textbook claims that the Endangered Species Act, despite its critics, has quite fulfilled its mission.

Accomplishments of the Endangered Species Act

Critics of the Endangered Species Act (ESA) call it an expensive failure because only 46 species have been removed from the endangered list. Most biologists insist that it has not been a failure, for four reasons.

First, species are listed only when they face serious danger of extinction. Arguing that the act is a failure is similar to arguing that a poorly funded hospital emergency room set up to take only the most desperate cases, often with little hope for recovery, should be shut down because it has not saved enough patients.

Second, it takes decades for most species to become endangered or threatened. Not surprisingly, it also takes decades to bring a species in critical condition back to the point where it can be removed from the critical list. . . .

Third, according to federal data, the conditions of more than half of the listed species are stable or improving, and 99% of the protected species are still surviving. A hospital emergency room taking only the most desperate cases and then stabilizing or improving the conditions of more than half of those patients while keeping 99% of them alive would be considered an astounding success.

Fourth, the 2010 budget for protecting endangered species amounted to an average expenditure of about 9 cents per U.S. citizen. To its supporters, it is amazing that the ESA, on such a small budget, has managed to stabilize or improve the conditions of more than half of the listed species.

Its supporters would agree that the act can be improved and that federal regulators have sometimes been too heavy handed in enforcing it. But instead of gutting or doing away with the ESA, some biologists call for it to be strengthened and modified. A study by the U.S. National Academy of Sciences recommended three major changes. . . .

1. Greatly increase the meager funding for implementing the act.
2. Develop recovery plans more quickly. A 2006 study by the Government Accountability Office (GAO), found that species with recovery plans have a better chance of getting off the endangered list. . . .
3. When a species is first listed, establish the core of its habitat as critical for its survival. . . .

Most biologists and wildlife conservationists believe that the United States also needs a new law that emphasizes protecting and sustaining biological diversity and ecosystem functioning rather than focusing mostly on saving individual species.

Analysis

As you read this analysis of the argument, note that exact statements from the text are in quotation marks; paraphrases of the text are italicized.

▌ What are the basic parts of the argument?

- **Background information:** *The opening line of the essay introduces the topic, the Endangered Species Act, and identifies the main opposing viewpoint—critics believe the ESA has been an expensive failure.*

- **Main claim:** "Most biologists insist that it (*topic—the ESA*) has not been a failure, for four reasons (*point of view*)."

- **Supporting evidence:** *The main part of the essay provides four reasons why the act has been a success.*

- **Opposing point of view:** "Critics of the Endangered Species Act (ESA) call it an expensive failure because only 46 species have been removed from the endangered list."

- **Counter and concession:** *The main part of the essay is a counter to the opposing viewpoint. However, the essay also concedes that the act can be improved and that regulators may have been* "heavy handed" *in their enforcement of it. Three sound improvements are proposed.*

- **Confirmation and call to action:** "Most biologists and wildlife conservationists believe that the United States also needs a new law that emphasizes protecting and sustaining biological diversity and ecosystem functioning rather than focusing mostly on saving individual species." *The confirmation suggests another level of care for endangered species.*

▌ How do these parts work together to form the argument?

The beginning clearly states the purpose of the argument—to counter the claim that the ESA is an expensive failure. The reasons supporting the act are clear and logical; the facts and statistics can be checked for accuracy and authenticity. The argument is strengthened by conceding that the act can be improved, and three such improvements are offered.

▌ What questions or concerns do you have about the argument?

The claim states that "most biologists" *believe the act has succeeded. It would be helpful to know if the* "return on investment" *issue is the only one that opposing biologists have.*

Graphing an Argument

Completing a **line diagram** for an argument can help you identify and analyze its main parts. Here's basically how a line diagram is arranged.

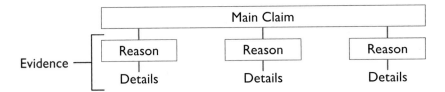

Line Diagram in Action

The line diagram below displays the main parts of "Accomplishments of the Endangered Species Act" found on page 322. This argument is easy to represent graphically because the authors numbered the reasons. Other arguments may take a bit more analysis.

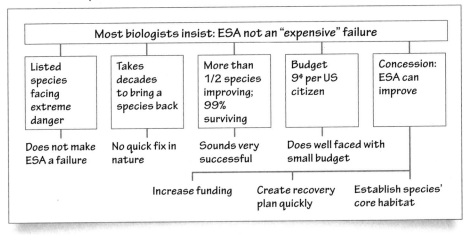

Help File

Another helpful graphic organizer is the web, or cluster. You can use it to display the main parts of most arguments.

Reading Graphics

We live in a world dominated by images. It's hard to imagine an advertisement, a presentation, or a magazine article that does not incorporate graphic images. Graphics are used regularly to clarify, support, and enhance writing at every level—including classroom reports and presentations. "A picture is worth a thousand words," but a carefully planned graphic can be worth even more.

As a reader, you need to know how graphics are used—and how they are sometimes misused. You need to develop the ability to read and interpret the graphics you encounter in the media, in school, and at work. This chapter is designed to help you develop these skills.

Learning Outcomes

Read graphic information.
Understand graphs.
Analyze tables.
Study diagrams.
Read maps.

"Good design is . . . clear thinking made visible."

Edward Tufte

Reading Graphic Information

"Seeing" the big picture is your first priority when looking at a graphic. What is the topic of the graphic? What is your overall impression of it? What is the graphic saying? Here are some guidelines for determining the overall purpose of any graphic you encounter:

- **Scan the graphic as a whole** to get the big picture.
- **Read the title, labels, and column headings** to determine the subject.
- **Read the data within the graphic** to pull out specific details.
- **Read the *key* or any special notes included** to clarify the details.
- **Read the paragraph above or below the graphic** to gather background information.

Help File

Graphics that are used to promote or advertise a product or idea require special attention. Some elements may be purposely skewed to advantage the person or company sponsoring the graphic. Even if the information is true or accurate, it may be incomplete; and presenting some but not all of the essential information can be misleading. This is common in both political and product ads.

Questions to consider . . .

1. Does the graphic address an important topic?
2. What is its purpose? To compare? To promote? To show change?
3. What does the graphic tell you, or *not* tell you?
4. Does it relate well to the surrounding text?
5. Is this the best graphic for displaying this data?
6. What is the source of the information? Is it reliable?
7. Is the graphic out of date or biased in any way?
8. What is the overall message?
9. Are any parts of the message missing?
10. Can the data be used to draw conclusions or make predictions?

Types of Graphics

Words are used to "tell"; graphics are used to "show." More specifically, graphics are used to show patterns and relationships, and each graphic does this in a slightly different way. The following pages contain examples that will help you understand these differences and become a better visual reader.

Understanding Graphs

Graphs show how different pieces of information are related. The most common kinds of graphs are line graphs, pie graphs, and bar graphs.

▌ Line Graph

A line graph shows how things change over time by plotting information on an L-shaped grid. The numbers across the bottom show the passing of time (minutes, years, centuries). The numbers up the side indicate the amounts related to the subject. The line on the graph connects the points where a particular time intersects with a particular amount. It shows change over time and reveals patterns or trends. The line graph below shows the estimated amounts of carbon dioxide emitted into the atmosphere from 1973–2010.

Energy-Related CO2 Emissions in the U.S. (1973–2010)

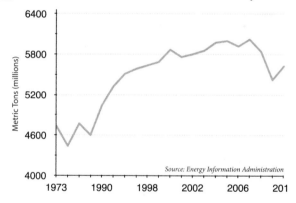

Source: Energy Information Administration

▌ Pie Graph

A pie graph (or pie chart) shows proportions. The reader can see at a glance how the pie is divided and how the pieces relate to each other. Each subject occupies a portion, or percentage, of the total pie. The pie graph to the right shows the carbon dioxide emissions reduction goals for 2020.

Carbon Dioxide Emissions Reduction Goals for 2020

(Million Tons of Carbon)

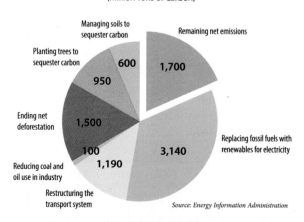

Source: Energy Information Administration

▌ Bar Graph

A bar graph uses bars—sometimes called columns—to show how subjects compare at one particular time. Unlike line graphs, bar graphs do not show how things change over time. The bar graph below compares the CO2 emissions from the use of three different fossil fuels in 1990, 1995, 2005, and 2011.

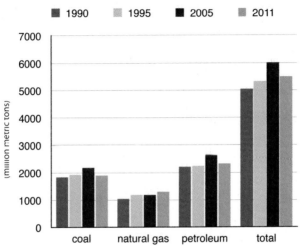

Carbon Dioxide Emissions from Fossil Fuels

Source: Energy Information Administration

▌ Stacked Bar Graph

A stacked bar graph gives more detailed information than a regular bar graph. Besides comparing total amounts with the bars, it compares portions within the bars themselves. The graph below compares total CO2 emissions as well as the portions from fossil and non-fossil fuels for the years 2006 to 2012.

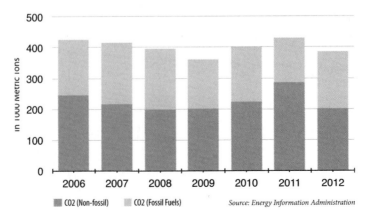

Carbon Dioxide Emissions from 2006–2012

Source: Energy Information Administration

Analyzing Tables

A table presents information in a clear, compact form so the reader can easily use and comprehend it. Most tables have rows (horizontal) and columns (vertical). Rows contain one set of details, while columns contain another.

▌ Schedule

Schedules are often put into table form. Even though they are usually easy to read, it's always a good idea to check them twice and circle the correct times.

Washington, D.C., to New York City Train Schedule

To read this schedule, (1) find the time you want to arrive in New York City in the right-hand column; (2) read across that row, to your left, and stop in the column labeled with your pickup point; (3) circle the time, which is when your train will leave from that point. (Disregard all other times.)

Lv **Washington, D.C.** Union Station	Lv **Baltimore, MD** BWI Airport Station	Lv **Philadelphia, PA** 30th Street Station	Lv **Newark, NJ** North Broad Street	Ar **New York City** Penn Station
5:00 am	5:35 am	6:57 am	7:58 am	8:14 am
6:00 am	5:36 am	7:58 am	8:59 am	9:12 am
7:30 am	8:10 am	10:00 am	11:15 am	11:35 am
8:00 am	8:35 am	9:50 am	10:00 am	10:14 am
1:00 pm	1:35 pm	2:57 pm	4:00 pm	4:20 pm
3:00 pm	3:30 pm	4:45 pm	5:40 pm	5:55 pm
6:00 pm	6:35 pm	7:45 pm	8:45 pm	9:00 pm

▌ Comparison

A comparison table provides information that the reader can use easily to compare different people, places, or things.

American Mobile Wireless Plans

	Premium	Professional	Family	Personal
Cost/Month	$150.00	$125.00	$95.00	$35.00
Contract Term	No Contract	No Contract	1 Year	2 Years
Data	Unlimited	Unlimited	500 MB	200 MB
Minutes	Unlimited	Unlimited	Unlimited	200 min.
Phone Choices	5	5	3	2

Studying Diagrams

A diagram is a drawing designed to show how something is constructed, how it works, or how its parts relate to one another.

▌ Picture Diagram

A picture diagram is just that—a picture or drawing of the subject. The diagram below shows a cross section of a human heart and identifies the important parts. Always study diagrams closely and read the labels carefully.

Anatomy of the Heart

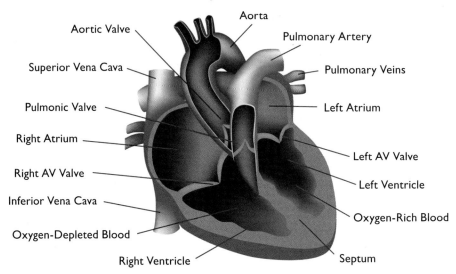

▌ Line Diagram

A line diagram uses lines, symbols, and words to show the relationship between people, places, things, or ideas. The line diagram below shows how various languages that originate from Latin are related.

Latin Origin Languages

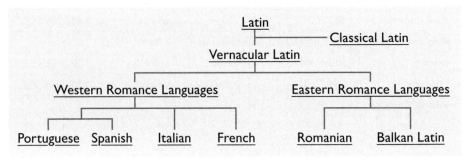

▌ Flowcharts

A flowchart follows a process using a variety of shapes and symbols. Most flowcharts use four basic shapes: *ovals* indicate start and end points, *rectangles* indicate steps, *diamonds* show decision points, and *arrows* indicate relationships or direction. To read a flowchart, begin by looking at the chart as a whole to get a sense of its purpose and main points. Then start at the beginning and follow the arrows from one shape to the next until you reach the end.

Bookstore Shipping and Receiving

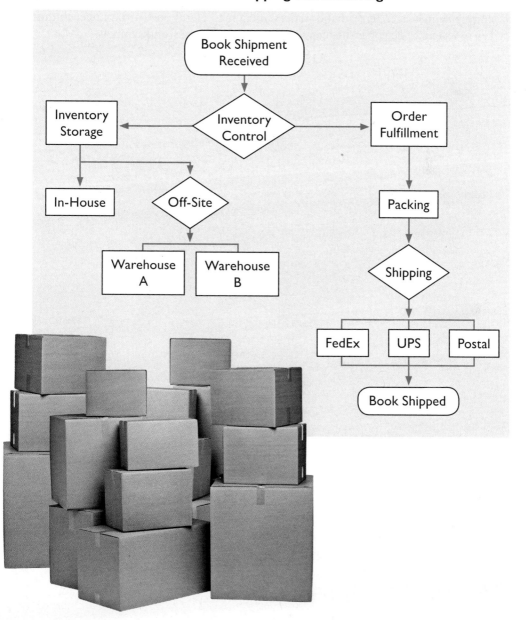

Reading Maps

A map is a visual representation of an area and its features. It may show a continent, a country, a state, a city, or some other geographic area. Different kinds of maps—political, road, topographical, resource, weather, and so on—serve different purposes.

▌ Weather Map

A weather map uses technical language plus symbols, icons, colors, and shading to convey its message. To read and understand a map of any sort, always refer to the key or legend to decipher the map's language, graphic cues, and symbols.

US Weather Map

- Seattle 45/37
- Minneapolis 28/19
- New York 43/36
- Denver 38/15 (H)
- Chicago 35/21
- San Francisco 58/41
- Los Angeles 71/46
- Atlanta 56/47
- Dallas 49/35
- Fairbanks -0/-10
- Miami 83/72
- Anchorage 25/21
- Honolulu 84/73

Conditions
○ Fair ◑ Partly cloudy ● Cloudy | ⧄ Rain
(H) High pressure L Low pressure | ▨ Snow

Fronts
Static
Warm
Cold
Trough

-10s -0s 0s 10s 20s 30s 40s 50s 60s 70s 80s 90s 100s 110s

Improving Graphic Reading Skills | Tips

In addition to the graphics discussed in this chapter, you will find others throughout this handbook, in other texts, and online. To improve your overall reading skill, study each graphic you encounter. Some will simply add color or interest to the topic; others will illustrate a point, arrange details more efficiently, explain a process, and so on.

Reading Literature

The dictionary defines *literature* as "imaginative or creative writing, especially those works of recognized artistic value." The short stories, novels, plays, and poems assigned in your literature classes are likely selected for the valuable representations of life and truth they offer to the reader. According to novelist Ernest Hemingway, if these representations are done right, they become "truer than if they had really happened."

While reading a popular spy thriller or love story may provide a temporary escape, literature, although sometimes challenging, can enlighten and enrich life. To realize this benefit, you must approach your reading very deliberately, armed with the strategies provided in this chapter.

Learning Outcomes

Read and react to fiction.
Understand the elements.
Read and react to poetry.
Understand the elements.

"The test of literature is, I suppose, whether we ourselves live more intensely for the reading of it."

Elizabeth Drew

Reading and Reacting to Fiction

Fiction isn't fact, but good fiction is "true." That is why you can learn so much from reading it. As you read, write down your thoughts and feelings about the story.

Before you read . . .

- **Consider the rhetorical situation.** When did the author write the book? What is the topic of the book? What genre does it reflect (historical fiction, modern drama, quest, etc.)? Is the book similar to other books written by the author? What else do you know about the author?

- **Get a feel for the text.** What do the title, chapter names, and first few pages tell you about the story line and the writer's style?

As you read . . .

- **Follow the action.** What happens in the first part (the exposition), how does the rising action unfold, what is the turning point, and so on? (See page 336.)

- **Pay careful attention to the characters**—their thoughts, feelings, actions, and words. What is the main character like early in the story? What prompts the character's actions? What decision does he or she make?

- **Look for underlying themes.** What messages about life does the story reveal (courage, prejudice, unfairness)?

- **Consider the setting.** Where and when does the story happen? What impact does the setting have on the story?

- **Note the author's style and approach.** What stands out about the author's word choice and manner of expression? From what point of view is the story told? How is the writing figurative or symbolic?

- **Regularly check your understanding.** What are your thoughts about the story? What questions come to mind? What do you expect will happen next?

After you read . . .

- **Reexamine the action.** Does the story line follow a recognized plot type? Were you able to follow the plot from start to finish? What did you like best about the story? What problems did it present?

- **Reflect on the main character.** How does he or she deal with conflict? What change, if any, does the character experience by the end of the story?

- **Consider the main message.** What are the main and secondary themes of the piece? How are they developed throughout the story?

- **Form your final thoughts.** What are your feelings after finishing the book? How would you rate its overall effectiveness?

Reading in Action

The excerpt below comes from Nathaniel Hawthorne's novel *The Scarlet Letter.* The side notes show how one student reacted to this reading. He makes observations, defines unfamiliar words, asks questions, and so on. Whenever you are reading a challenging piece of fiction, you should react to it in the same way.

From *The Scarlet Letter,*
Chapter 2, "The Market-Place"

When the young woman—the mother of this child—stood fully revealed before the crowd, it seemed to be her first impulse to clasp the infant closely to her bosom; not so much by an impulse of motherly affection, as that she might thereby conceal a certain token, which was wrought or fastened into her dress. In a moment, however, wisely judging that one token of her shame would but poorly serve to hide another, she took the baby on her arm, and, with a burning blush, and yet a haughty smile, and a glance that would not be abashed, looked around at her townspeople and neighbours. On the breast of her gown, in fine red cloth, surrounded with an elaborate embroidery and fantastic flourishes of gold thread, appeared the letter A. It was so artistically done, and with so much fertility and gorgeous luxuriance of fancy, that it had all the effect of a last and fitting decoration to the apparel which she wore; and which was of a splendor in accordance with the taste of the age, but greatly beyond what was allowed by the sumptuary regulations of the colony.

The young woman was tall, with a figure of perfect elegance, on a large scale. She had dark and abundant hair, so glossy that it threw off the sunshine with a gleam, and a face which, besides being beautiful from regularity of feature and richness of complexion, had the impressiveness belonging to a marked brow and deep black eyes. She was lady-like, too, after the manner of the feminine gentility of those days; characterized by a certain state and dignity, rather than by the delicate, evanescent, and indescribable grace, which is now recognized as its indication. And never had Hester Prynne appeared more lady-like, in the antique interpretation of the term, than as she issued from the prison. Those who had before known her, and had expected to behold her dimmed and obscured by a disastrous cloud, were astonished, and even startled, to perceive how her beauty shone out, and made a halo of the misfortune and ignominy in which she was enveloped. It may be true, that, to a sensitive observer, there was something exquisitely painful in it. . . .

Side notes:

Hester seems ashamed but still proud.

She makes her mark of shame look gorgeous.

Hawthorne's language sounds "lady-like."

"Evanescent" means "quickly disappearing."

What is a "halo of the misfortune and ignominy?"

Understanding the Elements

Fiction usually follows one of several recognizable plot types. Knowing which is used may help you during your reading. Also note that some stories display characteristics of more than one plot pattern.

Quest: In a quest, the main character goes on a journey into the unknown, overcomes obstacles, and returns either victorious or wiser. This pattern draws on elements from ancient myths. A quest could also be called a "coming of age" story.

Comedy: In a comedy (love story) the establishment tries to block a beautiful young couple from being together. But the couple wins out in the end.

Tragedy: In a tragedy, the main character, a great individual, experiences a downfall caused by a personal failure or flaw. The character and greater society realize what has happened and are reconciled to it.

Choice: The choice pattern involves the main character making a difficult decision. Suspense builds as the decision approaches.

Rite of Passage: In the rite of passage, a difficult experience changes the main character in a significant, lasting way. This pattern can also be called "coming of age."

Reversal: The reversal pattern is one in which the main character follows one course of action until something causes him or her to act in a different way.

Note: A surprising turn in the plot—for example, the hero in a quest suddenly and inexplicably failing—produces irony.

Following Plot Action

Story lines build in a predictable way. This graphic illustrates the usual plot structure. (See pages 214–215 for further explanation.)

Plot Line

Climax
(Crisis)

Rising Action
(Complications)

Falling
Action

Exposition

Resolution
(Denouement)

Considering the Characters

Short stories and plays may include only a few characters. But a novel will almost always include many—usually one or two main characters plus a host of secondary ones. The main character(s) and perhaps one or two others in a story are developed in great detail. They are considered *complex characters*. *Simple characters* are one-dimensional. The reader knows them superficially, as one knows an acquaintance. Here are some tips to help you analyze fictional characters.

- **Consider the characters' actions.** How they act in different situations and interact with other characters will tell you a lot about their personalities.

- **Be alert to the characters' words.** How characters converse also offers insights into their personalities. Are they understanding and sensitive, gruff and uncaring, insecure and indecisive?

- **"Listen" to their thoughts.** A main character's thoughts, if they are provided, can reveal their feelings and beliefs.

- **Note what characters say about each other.** The opinions shared can be used to decipher a character's nature.

- **Consider the narrator's input.** The narrator will often describe the main characters for the reader.

Considering Theme

Themes in fictional pieces are the implicit or hidden messages that a reader draws from the text. You must support your ideas about possible themes with specific evidence (actions and interactions) from the piece itself. Use these tips.

- **Pay careful attention to character development.** What prompts a character's actions? What effect do the actions have?

- **Be alert to the obstacles** blocking the main character and notice how he or she deals with them.

- **Consider the setting's effect** on the plot and on the main character.

- **Note any changes** that the main character undergoes, especially changes that emerge after the character faces the conflict.

- **Pinpoint personal traits**—greed, courage, loyalty, etc.—demonstrated by a character's actions.

- **Complete these sentences:** *This book showed me what it is like to . . . I also learned that . . .*

Important: See page 296 for information about forming personal responses to literature and pages 180–187 for the definitions of literary terms.

Reading and Reacting to Poetry

The poet Robert Fitzgerald believed that "poetry is at least an elegance and at most a revelation." In other words, poetry uses language in special, elegant ways, offering enjoyment even without complete understanding. At its best, though, poetry enlightens and enriches the reader.

Don't expect to fully grasp a poem—especially a complex poem—after one reading. In fact, it often takes two or three careful readings to appreciate a poem. When you read a poem, you must carefully consider its individual words, lines, and stanzas. You need to consider its symbolism and figurative language, and you need to pay special attention to such things as punctuation and line breaks. Use the following strategies to better understand the poetry you read.

First Reading

- Read the poem through once.
- Jot down your first impression, or immediate reaction.

Second Reading

- Read the poem again—out loud, if possible, to hear the sounds of the words and phrases.
- Note examples of alliteration, assonance, rhyme, and other poetic devices. (See pages 230–231.)
- Observe the line breaks, spacing, punctuation, and special treatment of words. These elements are clues to the intended phrasing and rhythm of the poem.
- Ask yourself where the poem is taking you. What overriding feeling or message does it offer?
- Annotate a copy of the poem. (See page 289.)
- Write freely about your thoughts and impressions after this second reading.

Third Reading

- Consider the specific structure of the poem—free verse, blank verse, sonnet, and so on. What does this tell you? Does the poem stray from its main structure?
- Consider the content. What does the poem say to you line by line? Stanza by stanza? Back up your ideas with evidence from the poem. Read it again if you feel you may have missed something.
- Write freely, reflecting on the language, form, and message of the poem.
- Gather your thoughts and write a final statement about what you think the poem is trying to communicate to the reader.

Reading in Action

The poems below—examples of free verse, blank verse, and the sonnet—were written by poets who are often included in anthologies. (The side notes offer one reader's response.

Free Verse

There Was a Child Went Forth

There was a child went forth every day,

Kids like make believe. And the first object he look'd upon, that object he became,

And that object became part of him for the day or a certain part of the day,

Or for many years or stretching cycles of years.

The images are easy to understand. The early lilies became part of this child,

And grass and white and red morning-glories, and white and red clover, and the song of the phoebe-bird,

And the Third-month lambs and the sow's pink-faint litter, and the mare's foal and cow's calf,

mire: wet, swampy ground And the noisy brood of the barnyard or by the mire of the pond-side,

And the fish suspending themselves so curiously below there, and the beautiful curious liquid,

And the water-plants with their graceful flat heads, all became part of him. . . .

—Walt Whitman

Blank Verse

Mending Wall

Word order is odd. Something there is that doesn't love a wall,

That sends the frozen-ground-swell under it

And spills the upper boulders in the sun,

10-syllable lines And makes gaps even two can pass abreast.

The work of hunters is another thing:

I have come after them and made repair

Where they have left not one stone on a stone,

But they would have the rabbit out of hiding,

To please the yelping dogs. The gaps I mean,

sounds flat No one has seen them made or heard them made,

But at spring mending-time we find them there. . . .

—Robert Frost

Understanding the Elements

Review the following information about poetry's form, sound, and meaning to better grasp the significance of the poems you read.

▌ The Form of Poetry

By convention, lines in most traditional English poetry are identified by their meter and length. Groups of lines, called stanzas, are designated according to the number of lines they contain and are comparable to paragraphs in prose. Certain forms like the haiku, limerick, and sonnet require specific line length, meter, rhyme scheme, and stanza length. Some forms even specify the exact number of syllables per line. In contrast, *free verse* has no requirements for line length, meter, or rhyme.

Note: For more on line, meter, length, and form, see pages 223–231.

▌ The Sound of Poetry

- The sense and sound of poetry can be silly:

  I fished up in Saskatchewan—
  Alas, I did not catch a one!

- The sound may seem to imitate nature's sounds:

  Through hiss of spruce, a single drop

- A variety of vowels and consonants can create rich sounds appropriate to the poem's theme:

  Nine bean-rows will I have there, a hive for the honey-bee
  And live alone in a bee-loud glade.   —W. B. Yeats

Note: In each case above, the sound is crafted to evoke the thought. Poets can use rhyme, alliteration, assonance, consonance, repetition, and pause to build patterns of sound. But such patterns should never draw undue attention to themselves.

▌ The Meaning of Poetry

Be aware, however, that a number of false notions about poetry do exist. Here are three common ones:

1. **Poems have no meaning.** This statement is quite obviously false. You will find personal meaning in a poem if you approach it with care and interest.

2. **Poems can mean something completely different to different readers.** Again, this idea is false. A careful reading will very likely evoke similar impressions, feelings, and meanings for different readers.

3. **Every poem should have one basic meaning.** Actually, a well-crafted poem usually sends several messages to the careful reader.

Improving Vocabulary Skills

Learning involves reading about subjects, thinking and writing about them, discussing them—and all of this requires a strong vocabulary. Without a variety of words to express your ideas, your ability to learn, think, and interact with others is limited.

Fortunately, today there are many ways to grow your personal vocabulary. The Internet is full of opportunities, from word-of-the-day Web sites to word-building games. Free apps that list, define, and even pronounce hundreds of words appropriate to each grade level are available for smartphones. And this chapter provides additional solid strategies that can build your vocabulary and boost your power to learn.

Learning Outcomes

Use context clues.
Use a dictionary.
Use a thesaurus.
Use word parts.

"The more words you know, the more clearly and powerfully you will think . . . and the more ideas you will invite into your mind."

Wilfred Funk

Using Context Clues

One of the most practical ways to improve your vocabulary is to read—as often and as much as you can. When you come across an unfamiliar word, try to decipher its meaning by examining its context, the ideas that surround it. By considering the general meaning of the passage so far and looking at familiar words that come before and after an unfamiliar word, it is possible to figure out its meaning. Consider following the **READ-V** method:

Read the passage for its overall meaning.
Examine the words that surround the unfamiliar word.
Apply your overall understanding of the passage and of familiar words nearby.
Determine the meaning of the unfamiliar word based on your discoveries.
Verify the meaning in a dictionary if necessary.

Direct Context Clues

The five types of context clues below can serve as direct links to the meanings of **unfamiliar words.** The example sentences color-code the clues in blue and the unfamiliar words in red.

1. Synonyms and Antonyms

Oftentimes, people living in extremely remote areas are shy and **introverted.** /
We worried the tumor was cancerous, but thankfully it was **benign.**

2. Comparison and Contrast

With storms moving through all evening, Maria was **restive,** while JoAnn sat quietly reading.

3. Definitions

One of the effects of radiation is **genetic mutation,** a change in the DNA sequence that can cause a variety of disorders in adults as well as children.

4. Words in a Series

The **dulcimer,** banjo, and fiddle are very popular among old-time musicians in the Appalachian region.

5. Cause and Effect

After no one volunteered, the principal announced it was **mandatory** for everyone with parking permits to attend Saturday's cleanup.

Help File

A context clue may not appear in the same sentence with the unfamiliar word, so look for clues in surrounding sentences and paragraphs, too.

"All my life I've looked at words
as though I were seeing them for the first time."
Ernest Hemingway

Indirect Context Clues

In some instances, the context clues surrounding an unfamiliar word will be more indirect than direct. While indirect context clues are less obvious than direct clues, they can be just as helpful. Indirect clues can be found in *specific examples,* in the *tone or setting* of a piece, or in *results and consequences.* These kinds of clues often appear a distance away from the unfamiliar words.

▌ **Now you try it.**

After reading the passage below taken from Jack London's *Call of the Wild,* look carefully at the words in red. Then search for direct and indirect context clues to help you figure out the meanings of the words. Even if you already know a certain word, look for the clues that would disclose its meaning to someone who *is* unfamiliar with the word. Double-check the accuracy of your definitions by consulting a dictionary.

They made Sixty Miles, which is a fifty-mile run, on the first day; and the second day saw them booming up the Yukon well on their way to Pelly. But such splendid running was achieved not without great trouble and **vexation** on the part of Francois. The **insidious** revolt led by Buck had destroyed the **solidarity** of the team. It no longer was as one dog leaping in the traces. The encouragement Buck gave the rebels led them into all kinds of petty **misdemeanors.** No more was Spitz a leader greatly to be feared. The old awe departed, and they grew equal to challenging his authority. Pike robbed him of half a fish one night and gulped it down under the protection of Buck. Another night Dub and Joe fought Spitz and made him forego the punishment they deserved. And even Billee, the good-natured, was less good-natured, and whined not half so **placatingly** as in former days. Buck never came near Spitz without snarling and bristling **menacingly.** In fact, his conduct approached that of a bully, and he was given to **swaggering** up and down before Spitz's very nose.

Using a Dictionary

A dictionary, when used effectively, is an invaluable tool for improving your vocabulary.

Spelling ▪ Not knowing how to spell a word can make it difficult, but not impossible, to look it up in the dictionary. Look for the word by using an approximate spelling devised by sounding out the word. If you cannot find an entry for the word, change a letter or two in its spelling and keep looking.

Capitalization ▪ If you're not sure whether a word should be capitalized, check a dictionary.

Syllabication ▪ A dictionary tells you where you can divide a word. The centered dots in the entry word show precisely where you can make an end-of-line division.

Pronunciation ▪ A dictionary tells you how to pronounce a word and also provides a key to pronunciation symbols, usually at the bottom of the page.

Parts of speech ▪ A dictionary tells you what part(s) of speech a word is, using these abbreviations:

n. noun	*v. tr.* transitive verb	*adj.* adjective
pron. pronoun	*interj.* interjection	*adv.* adverb
v. intr. intransitive verb	*conj.* conjunction	*prep.* preposition

Etymology ▪ Many dictionaries give etymologies (word histories) for some words. They tell what language an English word came from, how the word entered our language, and when it was first used.

Special uses ▪ Different kinds of labels tell about special uses of words.

▪ **Usage labels** tell how a word is used: *slang, nonstandard (nonstand.), dialect (dial.),* and so on.

▪ **Geographic labels** tell the region or country in which a word is used: *New England (New Eng.), Canada (Can.), Southern U.S.*

Synonyms and antonyms ▪ Some dictionaries list both synonyms and antonyms of words. (Of course, the best place to look for these is in a thesaurus.)

Illustrations ▪ If a definition is difficult to make clear with words alone, a picture or drawing is provided.

Meanings ▪ Many dictionaries list all the meanings of a word. Some list meanings chronologically, with the oldest meaning first, followed by newer meanings. Other dictionaries list a word's most common meaning first, followed by less common meanings. Read all the meanings listed to be sure you are using the word appropriately.

Sample Dictionary Page

Guide words

Botany Bay An inlet of the Tasman Sea in SE Australia.
botch (bŏch) *tr.v.* **botched, botch•ing, botch•es 1.** To ruin through clumsiness. **2.** To make or perform clumsily; bungle. **3.** To repair or mend clumsily. ❖ *n.* **1.** A ruined or defective piece of work: *"I have made a miserable botch of this description"* (Nathaniel Hawthorne). **2.** A hodgepodge. [ME *bocchen,* to mend.] —**botch′er** *n.* —**botch′y** *adj.*

Synonyms

SYNONYMS *botch, blow, bungle, fumble, muff* These verbs mean to harm or spoil through inept or clumsy handling: *botch a repair; blow an opportunity; bungle an interview; fumbled my chance; muffed the painting job.*

Meaning

bot•fly also **bot fly** (bŏt′flī′) *n.* Any of various stout two-winged flies, chiefly of the genera *Gasterophilus* and *Oestrus,* having larvae that are parasitic on various animals.
both (bōth) *adj.* One and the other; relating to or being two in conjunction: *Both guests came.* ❖ *pron.* The one and the other: *Both are mad.* ❖ *conj.* Used with *and* to link two things in a coordinated phrase or clause: *both he and I.* [ME *bothe* < ON *bādhar.* See **to-** in App.]

Usage

USAGE NOTE *Both* is used to indicate that the action or state denoted by the verb applies individually to each of two entities.

Spelling of related forms

Bo•tha (bō′tə, -tä′), **Louis** 1862–1919. South African general and first prime minister of South Africa (1910–19).
Botha, Pieter Willem b. 1916. South African prime minister (1978–89) who upheld apartheid.
both•er (bŏth′ər) *v.* **-ered, -er•ing, -ers** —*tr.* **1.** To disturb or anger, esp. by minor irritations; annoy. **2a.** To make agitated or nervous; fluster. **b.** To make confused or perplexed; puzzle. **3.** To intrude on without warrant; disturb. **4.** To give trouble to. —*intr.* **1.** To take the trouble; concern oneself. **2.** To cause trouble. ❖ *n.* A cause or state of disturbance. ❖ *interj.* Used to express annoyance or mild irritation. [Prob. < dialectal *bodder,* poss. of Celt. orig.]

Etymology (history)

Pronunciation

both•er•a•tion (bŏth′ə-rā′shən) *n.* The act of bothering or the state of being bothered. ❖ *interj.* Used to express annoyance or irritation.
both•er•some (bŏth′ər-səm) *adj.* Causing bother.
Both•ni•a (bŏth′nē-ə), **Gulf of** An arm of the Baltic Sea between Sweden and Finland.

Spelling and Capital letters

Both•well (bŏth′wĕl′, -wəl, bŏth′-), **4th Earl of.** Title of James Hepburn. 1536?–78. Scottish noble and third husband of Mary Queen of Scots, whose second husband, Lord Darnley, he murdered (1567).
bo tree (bō) *n.* See **pipal.** [Partial transl. of Sinhalese *bo-gaha,* tree of wisdom (because it was the tree under which the Buddha was enlightened) : *bo,* wisdom (< Pali *bodhi* < Skt. *bodhih,* enlightenment; see **bheudh-** in App.) + *gaha,* tree.]
bot•ry•oi•dal (bŏt′rē-oid′l) also **bot•ry•oid** (bŏt′rē-oid′) *adj.* Shaped like a bunch of grapes. Used esp. of mineral formations: *botryoidal hematite.* [< Gk. *botruoeidēs* : *botrus,* bunch of grapes + *-oeidēs,* -oid.] —**bot′ry•oi′dal•ly** *adv.*

Syllabication and Part of speech

bo•try•tis (bō-trī′tĭs) *n.* **1.** Any of various fungi of the genus *Botrytis* responsible for numerous fruit and vegetable diseases. **2.** Noble rot. [NLat., genus name < Gk. *botrus,* bunch of grapes.]
Bot•swa•na (bŏt-swä′nə) Formerly **Bech•u•a•na•land** (bĕch-wä′nə-lănd′, bĕch′ōō-ä′-) A country of S-central Africa; gained independence from Great Britain in 1966. Cap. Gaborone. Pop. 1.443.000. —**Bot•swa′nan** *adj. & n.*

Illustration

Botswana

Using a Thesaurus

A thesaurus is, in a sense, the opposite of a dictionary. You go to a dictionary when you know the word but need the definition. You go to a thesaurus when you know the general definition but need a specific word. For example, you may want to use a word like *fear,* but you are thinking of a specific kind of fear—a kind related to "worrying." You need the word to complete this sentence:

Dana experienced real _____ over the upcoming exam.

If you have a thesaurus in dictionary form, simply look up the word *fear* as you would in a dictionary. If, however, you have a traditional thesaurus, first look up *fear* in the index, and examine the entry:

FEAR **860**
Fearful painful **830**
timid **862**

The numbers in the index entry above are guide numbers, not page numbers. When you find the number 860 in the text of the thesaurus, you will see a long list of synonyms for *fear.* Look up these synonyms in a dictionary before deciding which to use in your sentence. *Anxiety* means "a state of uneasiness, worry, and fear," so it's a good choice for your sentence:

Dana experienced real anxiety over the upcoming exam.

| 259 | PERSONAL AFFECTIONS | 859-861 |

860. FEAR—*N.* **fear**, timidity, diffidence, apprehensiveness, fearfulness, solicitude, anxiety, care, apprehension, misgiving, mistrust, suspicion, qualm, hesitation.

trepidation, flutter, fear and trembling, perturbation, tremor, restlessness, disquietude, funk [*colloq.*].

fright, alarm, dread, awe, terror, horror, dismay, consternation, panic, scare; stampede [*of horses*].

V. **fear**, be afraid, apprehend, dread, distrust; hesitate, falter, wince, flinch, shy, shrink, fly.

tremble, shake, shiver, shudder, flutter, quake, quaver, quiver, quail.

frighten, fright, terrify, inspire (or excite) fear, bulldoze [*colloq.*], alarm, startle, scare, dismay, astound; awe; strike terror, appall, unman, petrify, horrify.

Adj. **afraid**, frightened, alarmed, fearful, timid, timorous, nervous, diffident, fainthearted, tremulous, shaky, apprehensive.

Note: To find the best word for your purpose, review the entire list of synonyms in the thesaurus entry. Also consider a word's connotation, not just its literal meaning.

Using Word Parts

Many of the words in the English language are derived from Greek and Latin, which means they are relatively easy to break into word parts—prefixes, suffixes, and roots. If you know the meaning of each part in a word, you can figure out the meaning of the complete word. The following examples explain how this is done:

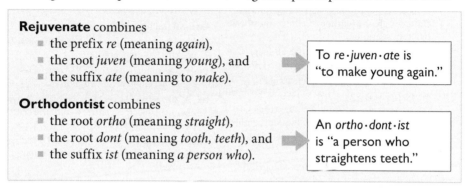

Rejuvenate combines
- the prefix *re* (meaning *again*),
- the root *juven* (meaning *young*), and
- the suffix *ate* (meaning to *make*).

To *re·juven·ate* is "to make young again."

Orthodontist combines
- the root *ortho* (meaning *straight*),
- the root *dont* (meaning *tooth, teeth*), and
- the suffix *ist* (meaning *a person who*).

An *ortho·dont·ist* is "a person who straightens teeth."

Help File

English words that are not a combination of word parts are called *base words*. A base word cannot be divided into parts. However, base words can be combined with other base words and with prefixes and suffixes.

base word	base word + base word	base word + prefix	base word + suffix
ground	background	underground	groundless
hand	handshake	forehand	handful

▌ Prefixes, Suffixes, and Roots

Learning many of the common prefixes, suffixes, and roots is one of the most efficient ways to improve your speaking and writing vocabulary. This is especially true when it comes to new words you encounter in your science classes.

The following pages contain nearly 500 word parts, a number of which you may already know. Scan the pages until you come to a word part that is new to you. Study its meaning and at least one of the sample words listed. Then apply this knowledge as you encounter new words in and out of school. As your understanding of word parts grows, so will your vocabulary. Like solving a puzzle, it can actually be fun to figure out the meanings of the unfamiliar words you encounter each day.

Prefixes

Prefixes are word parts that come before the root of a word. A prefix affects the intent or meaning of the root. As a reader, knowing the meanings of the most common prefixes will help you define unfamiliar words.

a, an [not, without] amoral (without a sense of moral responsibility), atypical, atom (not cuttable), apathy (without feeling), anesthesia (without sensation)

ab, abs, a [from, away] abnormal, abduct, absent, avert (turn away)

acro [high] acropolis (high city), acrobat, acronym, acrophobia (fear of height)

ambi, amb [both, around] ambidextrous (skilled with both hands), ambiguous, amble

amphi [both] amphibious (living on both land and water), amphitheater

ante [before] antedate, anteroom, antebellum, antecedent (happening before)

anti, ant [against] anticommunist, antidote, anticlimax, antacid

be [on, away] bedeck, belabor, bequest, bestow, beloved

bene, bon [well] benefit, benefactor, benevolent, benediction, bonanza, bonus

bi, bis, bin [both, double, twice] bicycle, biweekly, bilateral, biscuit, binoculars

by [side, close, near] bypass, bystander, by-product, bylaw, byline

cata [down, against] catalog, catapult, catastrophe, cataclysm

cerebro [brain] cerebral, cerebrum, cerebellum

circum, circ [around] circumference, circumnavigate, circumspect, circular

co, con, col, com [together, with] copilot, conspire, collect, compose

coni [dust] coniosis (disease that comes from inhaling dust)

contra, counter [against] controversy, contradict, counterpart

de [from, down] demote, depress, degrade, deject, deprive

deca [ten] decade, decathlon, decapod (10 feet)

di [two, twice] divide, dilemma, dilute, dioxide, dipole, ditto

dia [through, between] diameter, diagonal, diagram, dialogue (speech between people)

dis, dif [apart, away, reverse] dismiss, distort, distinguish, diffuse

dys [badly, ill] dyspepsia (digesting badly), dystrophy, dysentery

em, en [in, into] embrace, enslave

epi [upon] epidermis (upon the skin, outer layer of skin), epitaph, epithet

eu [well] eulogize (speak well of, praise), euphony, euphemism, euphoria

ex, e, ec, ef [out] expel (drive out), ex-mayor, exorcism, eject, eccentric (out of the center position), efflux, effluent

extra, extro [beyond, outside] extraordinary (beyond the ordinary), extracurricular, extrovert

for [refusal] forswear (renounce under oath)

fore [before in time] forecast, foretell (to tell beforehand), foreshadow

hemi, demi, semi [half] hemisphere, demitasse, semicircle (half of a circle)

hex [six] hexameter, hexagon

homo [man] Homo sapiens, homicide (killing man)

hyper [over, above] hypersensitive (overly sensitive), hyperactive

hypo [under] hypodermic (under the skin), hypothesis

il, ir, in, im [not] illegal, irregular, incorrect, immoral

in, il, im [into] inject, inside, illuminate, illustrate, impose, implant, imprison

infra [beneath] infrared, infrasonic

inter [between] intercollegiate, interfere, intervene, interrupt (break between)

intra [within] intramural, intravenous (within the veins)

intro [into, inward] introduce, introvert (turn inward)

macro [large, excessive] macrodent (having large teeth), macrocosm

mal [badly, poorly] maladjusted, malady, malnutrition, malfunction

meta [beyond, after, with] metaphor, metamorphosis, metaphysical

mis [incorrect, bad] misuse, misprint

miso [hate] misanthrope, misogynist

mono [one] monoplane, monotone, monochrome, monocle

multi [many] multiply, multiform

neo [new] neopaganism, neoclassic, neophyte, neonatal

non [not] nontaxable (not taxed), nontoxic, nonexistent, nonsense

ob, of, op, oc [toward, against] obstruct, offend, oppose, occur

oct [eight] octagon, octameter, octave, octopus

paleo [ancient] paleoanthropology (pertaining to ancient humans), paleontology (study of ancient life-forms)

para [beside, almost] parasite (one who eats beside or at the table of another), paraphrase, paramedic, parallel, paradox

penta [five] pentagon (figure or building having five angles or sides), pentameter, pentathlon

per [throughout, completely] pervert (completely turn wrong, corrupt), perfect, perceive, permanent, persuade

peri [around] perimeter (measurement around an area), periphery, periscope, pericardium, period

poly [many] polygon (figure having many angles or sides), polygamy, polyglot, polychrome

post [after] postpone, postwar, postscript, posterity

pre [before] prewar, preview, precede, prevent, premonition

pro [forward, in favor of] project (throw forward), progress, promote, prohibition

pseudo [false] pseudonym (false or assumed name), pseudopodia

quad [four] quadruple (four times as much), quadriplegic, quadratic, quadrant

quint [five] quintuplet, quintuple, quintet, quintile

re [back, again] reclaim, revive, revoke, rejuvenate, retard, reject, return

retro [backward] retrospective (looking backward), retroactive, retrorocket

se [aside] seduce (lead aside), secede, secrete, segregate

self [by oneself] self-determination, self-employed, self-service, selfish

sesqui [one and a half] sesquicentennial (150th anniversary, one and a half centuries)

sex, sest [six] sexagenarian (sixty years old), sexennial, sextant, sextuplet, sestet

sub [under] submerge (put under), submarine, substitute, subsoil

suf, sug, sup, sus [from under] sufficient, suffer, suggest, support, suspend

super, supr [above, over, more] supervise, superman, supernatural, supreme

syn, sym, sys, syl [with, together] synthesis, synchronize (time together), synonym, sympathy, symphony, system, syllable

trans, tra [across, beyond] transoceanic, transmit (send across), transfusion, tradition

tri [three] tricycle, triangle, tripod, tristate

ultra [beyond, exceedingly] ultramodern, ultraviolet, ultraconservative

un [not, release] unfair, unnatural, unknown

under [beneath] underground, underlying

uni [one] unicycle, uniform, unify, universe, unique (one of a kind)

vice [in place of] vice president, viceroy, vice admiral

Numerical Prefixes

Prefix	Symbol	Multiples and Submultiples	Equivalent	Prefix	Symbol	Multiples and Submultiples	Equivalent
tera	T	10^{12}	trillionfold	centi	c	10^{-2}	hundredth part
giga	G	10^{9}	billionfold	milli	m	10^{-3}	thousandth part
mega	M	10^{6}	millionfold	micro	u	10^{-6}	millionth part
kilo	k	10^{3}	thousandfold	nano	n	10^{-9}	billionth part
hecto	h	10^{2}	hundredfold	pico	p	10^{-12}	trillionth part
deka	da	10	tenfold	femto	f	10^{-15}	quadrillionth part
deci	d	10^{-1}	tenth part	atto	a	10^{-18}	quintillionth part

Suffixes

Suffixes are word parts that come at the end of a word. A suffix can tell you whether a word is a noun, a verb, an adjective, and so on. For example, words ending in *ly* are usually adverbs.

able, ible [able, can do] capable, agreeable, edible, visible (can be seen)

ade [result of action] blockade (the result of a blocking action), lemonade

age [act of, state of, collection of] salvage (act of saving), storage, forage

al [relating to] sensual, gradual, manual, natural (relating to nature)

algia [pain] neuralgia (nerve pain)

an, ian [native of, relating to] African, Canadian, Floridian

ance, ancy [action, process, state] assistance, allowance, defiance, truancy

ant [performing, agent] assistant, servant

ary, ery, ory [relating to, quality, place where] dictionary, bravery, dormitory

ate [cause, make] liquidate, segregate (cause a group to be set aside)

cian [having a certain skill or art] musician, beautician, magician, physician

cule, ling [very small] molecule, ridicule, duckling (very small duck), sapling

cy [action, function] hesitancy, prophecy, normalcy (function in a normal way)

dom [quality, realm, office] freedom, kingdom, wisdom (quality of being wise)

ee [one who receives the action] employee, nominee (one who is nominated), refugee

en [made of, make] silken, frozen, oaken (made of oak), wooden, lighten

ence, ency [action, state of, quality] difference, conference, urgency

er, or [one who, that which] baker, miller, teacher, racer, amplifier, doctor

escent [in the process of] adolescent (in the process of becoming an adult), obsolescent, convalescent

ese [a native of, the language of] Japanese, Vietnamese, Portuguese

esis, osis [action, process, condition] genesis, hypnosis, neurosis, osmosis

ess [female] actress, goddess, lioness

fic [making, causing] scientific, specific

ful [full of] frightful, careful, helpful

fy [make] fortify (make strong), simplify, amplify

hood [order, condition, quality] manhood, womanhood, brotherhood

ic [nature of, like] metallic (of the nature of metal), heroic, poetic, acidic

ice [condition, state, quality] justice, malice

id, ide [a thing connected with or belonging to] fluid, fluoride

ile [relating to, suited for, capable of] missile, juvenile, senile (related to being old)

ine [nature of] feminine, genuine, medicine

ion, sion, tion [act of, state of, result of] contagion, aversion, infection (state of being infected)

ish [origin, nature, resembling] foolish, Irish, clownish (resembling a clown)

ism [system, manner, condition, characteristic] heroism, alcoholism, Communism

ist [one who, that which] artist, dentist

ite [nature of, quality of, mineral product] Israelite, dynamite, graphite, sulfite

ity, ty [state of, quality] captivity, clarity

ive [causing, making] abusive (causing abuse), exhaustive

ize [make] emphasize, publicize, idolize

less [without] baseless, careless (without care), artless, fearless, helpless

ly [like, manner of] carelessly, quickly, forcefully, lovingly

ment [act of, state of, result] contentment, amendment (state of amending)

ness [state of] carelessness, kindness

oid [resembling] asteroid, spheroid, tabloid, anthropoid

ology [study, science, theory] biology, anthropology, geology, neurology

ous [full of, having] gracious, nervous, spacious, vivacious (full of life)

ship [office, state, quality, skill] friendship, authorship, dictatorship

some [like, apt, tending to] lonesome, threesome, gruesome

tude [state of, condition of] gratitude, multitude (condition of being many), aptitude

ure [state of, act, process, rank] culture, literature, rupture (state of being broken)

ward [in the direction of] eastward, forward, backward

y [inclined to, tend to] cheery, crafty, faulty

Roots

Roots serve as the core of a word. Since the root holds the main meaning of a word, learning the roots below will enable you to define many words.

acer, acid, acri [bitter, sour, sharp] acerbic, acidity (sourness), acrid, acrimony

acu [sharp] acute, acupuncture

ag, agi, ig, act [do, move, go] agent (doer), agenda (things to do), agitate, navigate (move by sea), ambiguous (going both ways), action

ali, allo, alter [other] alias (a person's other name), alibi, alien (from another place), alloy, alter (change to another form)

alt [high, deep] altimeter (a device for measuring heights), altitude

am, amor [love, liking] amiable, amorous, enamored

anni, annu, enni [year] anniversary, annually (yearly), centennial (occurring once in 100 years)

anthrop [man] anthropology (study of mankind), philanthropy (love of mankind), misanthrope (hater of mankind)

anti [old] antique, antiquated, antiquity

arch [chief, first, rule] archangel (chief angel), architect (chief worker), archaic (first, very early), monarchy (rule by one person), matriarchy (rule by the mother)

aster, astr [star] aster (star flower), asterisk, asteroid, astronomy (star law), astronaut (star traveler, space traveler)

aud, aus [hear, listen] audible (can be heard), auditorium, audio, audition, auditory, audience, ausculate

aug, auc [increase] augur, augment (add to, increase), auction

auto, aut [self] autograph (self-writing), automobile (self-moving vehicle), author, automatic (self-acting), autobiography

belli [war] rebellion, belligerent (warlike, hostile)

bibl [book] Bible, bibliography (list of books), bibliomania (craze for books), bibliophile (book lover)

bio [life] biology (study of life), biography, biopsy (cut living tissue for examination)

brev [short] abbreviate, brevity, brief

cad, cas [to fall] cadaver, cadence, caducous (falling off), cascade

calor [heat] calorie (a unit of heat), calorify (to make hot), caloric

cap, cip, cept [take] capable, capacity, capture, reciprocate, accept, except, concept

capit, capt [head] decapitate (to remove the head from), capital, captain, caption

carn [flesh] carnivorous (flesh eating), incarnate, reincarnation

caus, caut [burn, heat] caustic, cauterize (to make hot, to burn)

cause, cuse, cus [cause, motive] because, excuse (to attempt to remove the blame or cause), accusation

ced, ceed, cede, cess [move, yield, go, surrender] procedure, secede (move aside from), proceed (move forward), cede (yield), concede, intercede, precede, recede, success

centri [center] concentric, centrifugal, centripetal, eccentric (out of center)

chrom [color] chrome, chromosome (color body in genetics), chromosphere, monochrome (one color), polychrome

chron [time] chronological (in order of time), chronometer (time measured), chronicle (record of events in time), synchronize (make time with, set time together)

cide, cise [cut down, kill] suicide (killing of self), homicide (human killer), pesticide (pest killer), germicide (germ killer), insecticide, precise (cut exactly right), incision, scissors

cit [to call, start] incite, citation, cite

civ [citizen] civic (relating to a citizen), civil, civilian, civilization

clam, claim [cry out] exclamation, clamor, proclamation, reclamation, acclaim

clud, clus, claus [shut] include (to take in), conclude, recluse (one who shuts himself away from others), claustrophobia (abnormal fear of being shut up, confined)

cognosc, gnosi [know] recognize (to know again), incognito (not known), prognosis (forward knowing), diagnosis

cord, cor, cardi [heart] cordial (hearty, heartfelt), concord, discord, courage, encourage (put heart into), discourage (take heart out of), core, coronary, cardiac

corp [body] corporation (a legal body), corpse, corpulent

cosm [universe, world] cosmic, cosmos (the universe), cosmopolitan (world citizen), cosmonaut, microcosm, macrocosm

crat, cracy [rule, strength] democratic, autocracy

crea [create] creature (anything created), recreation, creation, creator

cred [believe] creed (statement of beliefs), credo (a creed), credence (belief), credit (belief, trust), credulous (believing too readily, easily deceived), incredible

cresc, cret, crease, cru [rise, grow] crescendo (growing in loudness or intensity), concrete (grown together, solidified), increase, decrease, accrue (to grow)

crit [separate, choose] critical, criterion (that which is used in choosing), hypocrite

cur, curs [run] concurrent, current (running or flowing), concur (run together, agree), incur (run into), recur, occur, precursor (forerunner), cursive

cura [care] curator, curative, manicure (caring for the hands)

cycl, cyclo [wheel, circular] Cyclops (a mythical giant with one eye in the middle of his forehead), unicycle, bicycle, cyclone (a wind blowing circularly, a tornado)

deca [ten] decade, decalogue, decathlon

dem [people] democracy (people-rule), demography (vital statistics of the people: deaths, births, and so on), epidemic (on or among the people)

dent, dont [tooth] dental (relating to teeth), denture, dentifrice, orthodontist

derm [skin] hypodermic (injected under the skin), dermatology (skin study), epidermis (outer layer of skin), taxidermy (arranging skin, mounting animals)

dict [say, speak] diction (how one speaks, what one says), dictionary, dictate, dictator, dictaphone, dictatorial, edict, predict, verdict, contradict, benediction

doc [teach] indoctrinate, document, doctrine

domin [master] dominate, dominion, predominant, domain

don [give] donate, condone

dorm [sleep] dormant, dormitory

dox [opinion, belief, praise] orthodox (having the correct, commonly accepted opinion), heterodox (differing opinion), paradox (contradictory)

drome [run, step] syndrome (run-together symptoms), hippodrome (a place where horses run)

duc, duct [lead] produce, induce (lead into, persuade), seduce (lead aside), reduce, aqueduct (water leader, channel), viaduct, conduct

dura [hard, lasting] durable, duration, endurance

dynam [power] dynamo (power producer), dynamic, dynamite, hydrodynamics

endo [within] endoral (within the mouth), endocardial (within the heart), endoskeletal

equi [equal] equinox, equilibrium

erg [work] energy, erg (unit of work), allergy, ergophobia (morbid fear of work), ergometer, ergonomic

fac, fact, fic, fect [do, make] factory (place where workers make goods of various kinds), fact (a thing done), manufacture, amplification, confection

fall, fals [deceive] fallacy, falsify

fer [bear, carry] ferry (carry by water), coniferous (bearing cones, as a pine tree), fertile (bearing richly), defer, infer, refer

fid, fide, feder [faith, trust] confidante, Fido, fidelity, confident, infidelity, infidel, federal, confederacy

fila, fili [thread] filament (a single thread or threadlike object), filibuster, filigree

fin [end, ended, finished] final, finite, finish, confine, fine, refine, define, finale

fix [attach] fix, fixation (the state of being attached), fixture, affix, prefix, suffix

flex, flect [bend] flex (bend), reflex (bending back), flexible, flexor (muscle for bending), inflexibility, reflect, deflect

flu, fluc, fluv [flowing] influence (to flow in), fluid, flue, flush, fluently, fluctuate (to wave in an unsteady motion)

form [form, shape] form, uniform, conform, deform, reform, perform, formative, formation, formal, formula

fort, forc [strong] fort, fortress (a strong place), fortify (make strong), forte (one's strong point), fortitude, enforce

fract, frag [break] fracture (a break), infraction, fraction (result of breaking a whole into equal parts), refract (to break or bend), fragile (easy to break)

gam [marriage] bigamy (two marriages), monogamy, polygamy (many spouses or marriages)

gastr(o) [stomach] gastric, gastronomic, gastritis (inflammation of the stomach)

gen [birth, race, produce] genesis (birth, beginning), genetics (study of heredity), eugenics (well born), genealogy (lineage, descent from a common ancestor), generate, genetic

geo [earth] geometry (earth measurement), geography (earth writing), geocentric (earth centered), geology

germ [vital part] germination (to grow), germ (seed, living substance, as the *germ* of an idea), germane

gest [carry, bear] congest (bear together, clog), congestive (causing clogging), gestation

gloss, glot [tongue] glossary, polyglot (many tongues), epiglottis

glu, glo [lump, bond, glue] glue, agglutinate (make to hold in a bond), conglomerate (bond together)

grad, gress [step, go] grade (step, degree), gradual (step-by-step), graduate (make all the steps, finish a course), graduated (in steps or degrees), progress

graph, gram [write, written] graph, graphic (written, vivid), autograph (self-writing, signature), graphite (carbon used for writing), photography (light writing), phonograph (sound writing), bibliography, diagram, telegram

grat [pleasing] gratuity (mark of favor, a tip), congratulate (express pleasure over success), grateful, ingrate (not thankful)

grav [heavy, weighty] grave, gravity, aggravate, gravitate

greg [herd, group, crowd] gregarian (belonging to a herd), congregation (a group functioning together), segregate (tending to group aside or apart)

helio [sun] heliograph (an instrument for using the sun's rays to send signals), heliotrope (a plant that turns to the sun)

hema, hemo [blood] hemorrhage (an outpouring or flowing of blood), hemoglobin, hemophilia

here, hes [stick] adhere, cohere, cohesion

hetero [different] heterogeneous (different in birth), heterosexual (with interest in the opposite sex)

homo [same] homogeneous (of same birth or kind), homonym (word with same pronunciation as another), homogenize

hum, human [earth, ground, man] humus, exhume (to take out of the ground), humane (compassion for other humans)

hydr, hydra, hydro [water] dehydrate, hydrant, hydraulic, hydraulics, hydrogen, hydrophobia (fear of water)

Hydrophobia

hypn [sleep] hypnosis, Hypnos (god of sleep), hypnotherapy (treatment of disease by hypnosis)

ignis [fire] ignite, igneous, ignition

ject [throw] deject, inject, project (throw forward), eject, object

join, junct [join] adjoining, enjoin (to lay an order upon, to command), juncture, conjunction, injunction

juven [young] juvenile, rejuvenate (to make young again)

lau, lav, lot, lut [wash] launder, lavatory, lotion, ablution (a washing away), dilute (to make a liquid thinner and weaker)

leg [law] legal (lawful, according to law), legislate (to enact a law), legislature, legitimize (make legal)

levi [light] alleviate (lighten a load), levitate, levity (light conversation, humor)

liber, liver [free] liberty (freedom), liberal, liberalize (to make more free), deliverance

liter [letters] literary (concerned with books and writing), literature, literal, alliteration, obliterate

loc, loco [place] locality, locale, location, allocate (to assign, to place), relocate (to put back into place), locomotion (act of moving from place to place)

log, logo, ogue, ology [word, study, speech] catalog, logogram (a symbol representing a word), prologue, dialogue, zoology (animal study), psychology (mind study)

loqu, locut [talk, speak] eloquent (speaking well and forcefully), soliloquy, loquacious (talkative), colloquial (talking together, conversational or informal), locution

luc, lum, lus, lun [light] translucent (letting light come through), lumen (a unit of light), luminary (a heavenly body, someone who shines in his or her profession), luster (sparkle, shine), Luna (the moon goddess)

magn [great] magnify (make great, enlarge), magnificent, magnanimous (great of mind or spirit), magnate, magnitude, magnum

man [hand] manual, manage, manufacture, manacle, manicure, manifest, maneuver, emancipate

mand [command] mandatory (commanded), remand (order back), mandate

mania [madness] mania (insanity, craze), monomania (mania on one idea), kleptomania, pyromania (insane tendency to set fires), maniac

mar, mari, mer [sea, pool] marine (a soldier serving on shipboard), marsh (wetland, swamp), maritime (relating to the sea and navigation), mermaid (fabled sea creature: half fish, half woman)

matri [mother] maternal (relating to the mother), matrimony, matriarchate (rulership of women), matron

medi [half, middle, between, halfway] mediate (come between, intervene), medieval (pertaining to the Middle Ages), Mediterranean (lying between lands), mediocre, medium

mega [great, million] megaphone (great sound), megalopolis (great city, an extensive urban area including a number of cities), megacycle (a million cycles), megaton

mem [remember] memo (a reminder), commemoration (the act of remembering by a memorial or ceremony), memento, memoir, memorable

meter [measure] meter (a metric measure), voltameter (instrument to measure volts), barometer, thermometer

micro [small] microscope, microfilm, microcard, microwave, micrometer (device for measuring small distances), omicron, micron (a millionth of a meter), microbe (small living thing)

migra [wander] migrate (to wander), emigrate (one who leaves a country), immigrate (to come into the land)

mit, miss [send] emit (send out, give off), remit (send back, as money due), submit, admit, commit, permit, transmit (send across), omit, intermittent (sending between, at intervals), mission, missile

mob, mot, mov [move] mobile (capable of moving), motionless (without motion), motor, emotional (moved strongly by feelings), motivate, promotion, demote, movement

mon [warn, remind] monument (a reminder or memorial of a person or an event), admonish (warn), monitor, premonition (forewarning)

mor, mort [mortal, death] mortal (causing death or destined for death), immortal (not subject to death), mortality (rate of death), mortician (one who prepares the dead for burial), mortuary (place for the dead, a morgue)

morph [form] amorphous (with no form, shapeless), metamorphosis (a change of form, as a caterpillar into a butterfly), morphology

multi [many, much] multifold (folded many times), multilinguist (one who speaks many languages), multiped (an organism with many feet), multiply

nat, nasc [to be born, to spring forth] innate (inborn), natal, native, nativity, renascence (a rebirth, a revival)

neur [nerve] neuritis (inflammation of a nerve), neurology (study of nervous systems), neurologist (one who practices neurology), neural, neurosis, neurotic

nom [law, order] autonomy (self-law, self-government), astronomy, gastronomy (art or science of good eating), economy

nomen, nomin [name] nomenclature, nominate (name someone for an office)

nov [new] novel (new, strange, not formerly known), renovate (to make like new again), novice, nova, innovate

nox, noc [night] nocturnal, equinox (equal nights), noctilucent (shining by night)

numer [number] numeral (a figure expressing a number), numeration (act of counting), enumerate (count out, one by one), innumerable

omni [all, every] omnipotent (all-powerful), omniscient (all-knowing), omnipresent (present everywhere), omnivorous

onym [name] anonymous (without name), synonym, pseudonym (false name), antonym (name of opposite meaning)

oper [work] operate (to labor, function), cooperate (work together)

ortho [straight, correct] orthodox (of the correct or accepted opinion), orthodontist (tooth straightener), orthopedic (originally pertaining to straightening a child), unorthodox

pac [peace] pacifist (one for peace only, opposed to war), pacify (make peace, quiet), Pacific Ocean (peaceful ocean)

pan [all] panacea (cure-all), pandemonium (place of all the demons, wild disorder), pantheon (place of all the gods in mythology)

pater, patr [father] paternity (fatherhood, responsibility), patriarch (head of the tribe or family), patriot, patron (a wealthy person who supports, as would a father)

path, pathy [feeling, suffering] pathos (feeling of pity, sorrow), sympathy, antipathy (feeling against), apathy (without feeling), empathy (feeling or identifying with another), telepathy (far feeling, thought transference)

ped, pod [foot] pedal (lever for a foot), impede (get the feet in a trap, hinder), pedestal (foot or base of a statue), pedestrian (foot traveler), centipede, tripod (three-footed support), podiatry (care of the feet), antipodes (opposite feet)

pedo [child] orthopedic, pedagogue (child leader, teacher), pediatrics (medical care of children)

pel, puls [drive, urge] compel, dispel, expel, repel, propel, pulse, impulse, pulsate, compulsory, expulsion, repulsive

pend, pens, pond [hang, weigh] pendant, pendulum, suspend, appendage, pensive (weighing thought), ponderous

phil [love] philosophy (love of wisdom), philanthropy, philharmonic, bibliophile, Philadelphia (city of brotherly love)

phobia [fear] claustrophobia (fear of closed spaces), acrophobia (fear of high places), hydrophobia (fear of water)

phon [sound] phonograph, phonetic (pertaining to sound), symphony (sounds with or together)

photo [light] photograph (light-writing), photoelectric, photogenic (artistically suitable for being photographed), photosynthesis (action of light on chlorophyll to make carbohydrates)

plac [please] placid (calm, peaceful), placebo, placate, complacent

plu, plur, plus [more] plural (more than one), pluralist (a person who holds more than one office), plus (indicating that something more is to be added)

pneuma, pneumon [breath] pneumatic (pertaining to air, wind, or other gases), pneumonia (disease of the lungs)

pod (see "ped")

poli [city] metropolis (mother city), police, politics, Indianapolis, Acropolis (high city, upper part of Athens), megalopolis

pon, pos, pound [place, put] postpone (put afterward), component, opponent (one put against), proponent, expose, impose, deposit, posture (how one places oneself), position, expound, impound

pop [people] population, populous (full of people), popular

port [carry] porter (one who carries), portable, transport (carry across), transportation, report, export, import, support

portion [part, share] portion (a part, a share, as a *portion* of pie), proportion (the relation of one share to others)

prehend [seize] comprehend (seize with the mind), apprehend (seize a criminal), comprehensive (seizing much, extensive)

prim, prime [first] primacy (state of being first in rank), prima donna (the first lady of opera), primitive (from the earliest or first time), primary, primal, primeval

proto [first] prototype (the first model made), protocol, protagonist, protozoan

psych [mind, soul] psyche (soul, mind), psychiatry (healing of the mind), psychology, psychosis (serious mental disorder), psychotherapy (mind treatment), psychic

punct [point, dot] punctual (being exactly on time), punctuation, puncture, acupuncture

reg, recti [straighten] regiment, regular, regulate, rectify (make straight), correct, direction

ri, ridi, risi [laughter] deride (mock, jeer at), ridicule (laughter at the expense of another, mockery), ridiculous, derision

rog, roga [ask] prerogative (privilege, asking before), interrogation (questioning, the act of questioning), derogatory

rupt [break] rupture (break), interrupt (break into), abrupt (broken off), disrupt (break apart), erupt (break out), incorruptible (unable to be broken down)

sacr, sanc, secr [sacred] sacred, sanction, sacrosanct, consecrate, desecrate

salv, salu [safe, healthy] salvation (act of being saved), salvage, salutation

sat, satis [enough] satient (giving pleasure, satisfying), saturate, satisfy (to please, to give as much as is needed)

sci [know] science (knowledge), conscious (knowing, aware), omniscient (knowing everything)

scope [see, watch] telescope, microscope, kaleidoscope (instrument for seeing beautiful forms), periscope, stethoscope

scrib, script [write] scribe (a writer), scribble, inscribe, describe, subscribe, prescribe, manuscript (written by hand)

sed, sess, sid [sit] sediment (that which sits or settles out of a liquid), session (a sitting), obsession (an idea that sits stubbornly in the mind), possess, preside (sit before), president, reside, subside

sen [old] senior, senator, senile (old, showing the weakness of old age)

sent, sens [feel] sentiment (feeling), consent, resent, dissent, sentimental (having strong feeling or emotion), sense, sensation, sensitive, sensory, dissension

sequ, secu, sue [follow] sequence (following of one thing after another), sequel, consequence, subsequent, prosecute, consecutive (following in order), second (following "first"), ensue, pursue

serv [save, serve] servant, service, preserve, subservient, servitude, conserve, reservation, deserve, conservation

sign, signi [sign, mark, seal] signal (a gesture or sign to call attention), signature (the mark of a person written in his or her own handwriting), design, insignia (distinguishing marks)

simil, simul [like, resembling] similar (resembling in many respects), assimilate (to make similar to), simile, simulate (pretend, put on an act to make a certain impression)

sist, sta, stit [stand] persist (stand firmly or unyieldingly, continue), assist (to stand by with help), circumstance, stamina (power to withstand, to endure), status (standing), state, static, stable, stationary, substitute (to stand in for another)

solus [alone] soliloquy, solitaire, solitude, solo

solv, solu [loosen] solvent (a loosener, a dissolver), solve, absolve (loosen from, free from), resolve, soluble, solution, resolution, resolute, dissolute (loosened morally)

somnus [sleep] insomnia (not being able to sleep), somnambulist (a sleepwalker)

soph [wise] sophomore (wise fool), philosophy (love of wisdom), sophisticated

spec, spect, spic [look] specimen (an example to look at or study), specific, aspect, spectator (one who looks), spectacle, speculate, inspect, respect, prospect, retrospective (looking backward), introspective, expect, conspicuous

sphere [ball, sphere] stratosphere (the upper portion of the atmosphere), hemisphere (half of the earth), spheroid

spir [breath] spirit (breath), conspire (breathe together, plot), inspire (breathe into), aspire (breathe toward), expire (breathe out, die), perspire, respiration

string, strict [draw tight] stringent (drawn tight, rigid), strict, restrict, constrict (draw tightly together), boa constrictor (snake that constricts its prey)

stru, struct [build] construe (build in the mind, interpret), structure, construct, instruct, obstruct, destruction, destroy

sume, sump [take, use, waste] consume (to use up), assume (to take, to use), sump pump (a pump that takes up water), presumption (to take or use before knowing all the facts)

tact, tang, tag, tig, ting [touch] contact, tactile, intact (untouched, uninjured), intangible (not able to be touched), tangible, contagious (able to transmit disease by touching), contiguous, contingency

tele [far] telephone (far sound), telegraph (far writing), television (far seeing), telephoto (far photography), telecast

tempo [time] tempo (rate of speed), temporary, extemporaneously, contemporary (those who live at the same time), pro tem (for the time being)

ten, tin, tain [hold] tenacious (holding fast), tenant, tenure, untenable, detention, content, pertinent, continent, obstinate, abstain, pertain, detain

tend, tent, tens [stretch, strain] tendency (a stretching, leaning), extend, intend, contend, pretend, superintend, tender, extent, tension (a stretching, strain), pretense

terra [earth] terrain, terrarium, territory, terrestrial

test [to bear witness] testament (a will, bearing witness to someone's wishes), detest, attest (bear witness to), testimony

the, theo [God, a god] monotheism (belief in one god), polytheism (belief in many gods), atheism, theology

therm [heat] thermometer, therm (heat unit), thermal, thermostat, thermos, hypothermia (subnormal temperature)

thesis, thet [place, put] antithesis (place against), hypothesis (place under), synthesis (put together), epithet

tom [cut] atom (not cuttable, smallest particle of matter), appendectomy (cutting out an appendix), tonsillectomy, dichotomy (cutting in two, a division), anatomy (cutting, dissecting to study structure)

tort, tors [twist] torture (twisting to inflict pain), retort (twist back, reply sharply), extort (twist out), distort (twist out of shape), contort, torsion (act of twisting, as a *torsion bar*)

tox [poison] toxic (poisonous), intoxicate, antitoxin

tract, tra [draw, pull] tractor, attract, subtract, tractable (can be handled), abstract (to draw away), subtrahend (the number to be drawn away from another)

trib [pay, bestow] tribute (to pay honor to), contribute (to give money to a cause), attribute, retribution, tributary

turbo [disturb] turbulent, disturb, turbid, turmoil

typ [print] type, prototype (first printing, model), typical, typography, typewriter, typology (study of types or categories), typify

ultima [last] ultimate, ultimatum (the final or last offer that can be made)

uni [one] unicorn (a legendary creature with one horn), unify (make into one), university, unanimous, universal

vac [empty] vacate (to make empty), vacuum (a space entirely devoid of matter), evacuate (to remove troops or people), vacation, vacant

vale, vali, valu [strength, worth] valiant, equivalent (of equal worth), validity (truth, legal strength), evaluate (find out the value), value, valor (value, worth)

ven, vent [come] convene (come together, assemble), intervene (come between), venue, convenient, avenue, circumvent (come or go around), invent, prevent

ver, veri [true] very, aver (say to be true, affirm), verdict, verity (truth), verify (show to be true), verisimilitude

vert, vers [turn] avert (turn away), divert (turn aside, amuse), invert (turn over), introvert (turn inward), convertible, reverse (turn back), controversy (a turning against, a dispute), versatile (turning easily from one skill to another)

vic, vicis [change, substitute] vicarious, vicar, vicissitude

vict, vinc [conquer] victor (conqueror, winner), evict (conquer out, expel), convict (prove guilty), convince (conquer mentally, persuade), invincible (not conquerable)

vid, vis [see] video, evident, provide, providence, visible, revise, supervise (oversee), vista, visit, vision, television

viv, vivi, vita [alive, life] revive (make live again), survive (live beyond, outlive), vivacious (full of life), vivid, vitality

voc [call] vocation (a calling), avocation (occupation that is not one's calling), convocation (a calling together), invocation, vocal

vol [will] malevolent, benevolent (one of goodwill), volunteer, volition

volcan, vulcan [fire] volcano (a mountain erupting fiery lava), volcanize (to undergo volcanic heat), Vulcan (Roman god of fire)

volvo [turn about, roll] revolve, voluminous (winding), voluble (easily turned about or around), convolution (a twisting)

vor [eat greedily] voracious, carnivorous (flesh eating), herbivorous (plant eating), omnivorous (eating everything), devour

zo [animal] zoo (short for zoological garden), zoology (study of animal life), zodiac (circle of animal constellations), zoomorphism (being in the form of an animal), protozoa (one-celled animals)

The Human Body

capit—head	**gastro**—stomach	**osteo**—bone
card—heart	**glos**—tongue	**ped**—foot
corp—body	**hema**—blood	**pneuma**—breathe
dent—tooth	**man**—hand	**psych**—mind
derm—skin	**neur**—nerve	**spir**—breath

Writers INC

Technology

Using the Internet

What do people use the Internet for? The better question may be, what *don't* people use the Internet for? Just consider some of its functions. It is an encyclopedia, an arcade, a business, a movie theater, a music studio, a social network, a map, a news source, a scoreboard, a critic, a translator, a self-help resource, a dictionary, a weather forecaster, . . . The list goes on and on.

Most of you know your way around an online environment and will be familiar with the tools and technology discussed in this chapter. But as with most things, there's always something more to learn. The instructions and best practices in this chapter will enhance your Internet literacy and help you interact thoughtfully online.

Learning Outcomes

Review the Internet by the numbers.
Communicating on the Internet.
Find and use Internet content.
Evaluate Internet content.

"Cyberspace can give you more homework help than 10 libraries combined, and it's open 24 hours a day."

Preston Gralla

Internet ⊙
by the Numbers

Total world population: 7 billion

Deep Web ⊙
The "deep Web" makes up **99 percent** of Web content.

This part is hidden from view; search engines cannot index it.

Surface Web
The other **1 percent** of Web content resides in the "surface Web."

This part contains **2.07 billion** pages.

⊙ Internet users: **< 3 billion**

Television owners: **1.4 billion**

⊙ Over **6 billion hours** of video are watched each month on YouTube—that's almost an hour for every person on Earth.

80 percent of YouTube traffic comes from outside the U.S.

On average **139,344** new Web sites go live each day.

That's over **96** pages every minute.

1 out of 7 people in the world have an active Facebook account (**1.23 billion people**).

⊙ Percentage of population with access to the Internet

27.5%

78.6%

15.6%

48 percent of Internet users live in Asia.

Highest percentage of population with Internet access in the world.

Internet penetration has grown by more than **3,000 percent** in Africa since 2000.

⊙ By the time you read this, all these numbers will have grown considerably.

Sources: http://www.internetworldstats.com/stats.htm; http://www.worldwidewebsize.com;
http://money.cnn.com/2014/03/10/technology/deep-web; http://www.youtube.com/yt/press/statistics.html; Facebook;
http://www.mediabistro.com/alltwitter/internet-day-stats_b41621; http://www.internetlivestats.com

Communicating on the Internet

Online communication was once primarily text based, but today's applications use video and audio. As the years pass, Internet communications will continue to evolve. The next few pages review some of the most useful current ways of communicating online. (Social media forms are discussed in a separate chapter on pages 377–384.)

Characteristics of Online Communication

As you can see from the infographic on the facing page, the Internet allows you to connect with almost half of the world's population. Because of the potential impact of your online messaging, be responsible and keep in mind these characteristics.

- **Public:** Everything you post online can be seen or forwarded to others, even if you don't intend it to be.
- **Permanent:** Much like a tattoo, the words, photos, and videos you publish online are hard to remove.
- **Consequential:** Your actions can impact your future, positively or negatively.

The Online Communication Situation

When deciding what form to use, consider the importance of the subject, the time you have to communicate, and the audience you wish to reach.

While most online communication options are spontaneous and informal, some are more formal. As the message becomes more formal, more time and thought are required to communicate it. The following chart demonstrates this idea.

The Continuum of Communication

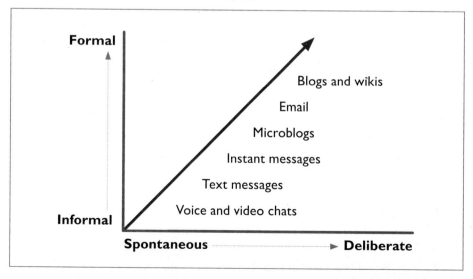

Emailing

Email is a mainstay of online communication. It's been around since the earliest days of the Internet, and its continued popularity is a testament to its usefulness.

Using email effectively will help you transition from school to the workplace, where email remains a workhorse for business correspondence. Remember these best practices when using email (and refer to the writing tips on pages 276–277).

Fit your tone to your purpose. For general messages, use a friendly, conversational writing voice. For serious messages, use a formal voice.

Know your audience. Email may seem private because you choose who receives the message. But what the receiver does with it is out of your control. And as with any Web communication, it never really goes away. Consider how the receiver will react to your words before sending them.

Be respectful and keep "cool." Never write a message when you are angry or emotional and likely to say something you will regret later.

Write meaningful subject lines. Give your reader a subject line that shares the main point of the message. Be clear and descriptive.

Respond promptly. When a message asks you to do something, reply quickly and thoughtfully.

Understand basic functions:
- *Reply* writes back to the sender.
- *Reply all* writes back to the sender and every recipient of the original email.
- *Forward* sends a message you received to other people.
- *Bcc* (blind carbon copy) sends your message to someone else without the primary recipient's knowledge.
- *Cc* (carbon copy) sends the message to someone with whom you wish to share the information, but not as the primary recipient.
- An *attachment* posts a document or other digital file to your message.

Use a readable font and type size. Avoid using bright colors, big type, and odd fonts. A black 10- to 12-point typeface works best.

Text Messaging

Texting is more spontaneous and informal than email. Text messages are short and to the point, making them a quick way to contact a parent or friend.

Texting has spawned a language of its own, characterized by abbreviations and shorthand. Use "text speak" when you are rushed, but only if the receiver is familiar with it.

Remember: Texts do not provide the clues that body language or tone of voice offer. Misunderstandings are common, so be cautious about using sarcasm.

Instant Messaging

Instant messaging (IM) is a real-time text conversation. Most IM programs stay running while you do other work. And some applications like Facebook and Google Docs include their own built-in IM services.

IM communication can be useful for collaborative projects. For instance, you can use IM to discuss your work with team members since multiple users can be included in the same conversation.

Mark_22:
Should we include something about Poe's childhood?
sent 11:03am

KateLady:
G8 idea. Check out this site:
http://www.biography.com/people/edgar-allan-poe-9443160
sent 11:06am

DeJuan.Harris:
Tragedy seemed to follow this guy around, even as a child.
sent 11:11am

Video Chat

Video chat allows for real-time audio and video conversations using computers or smartphones. Most video-chat applications are free, even for international chats. Here are three ways you can use video chat for school projects:

- **Collaborate with other students and classrooms.** Video chat is a valuable tool for collaboration. It allows you to set up video conferences to discuss and plan projects or events with your classmates, even outside of school. You can also connect with students and classrooms from different parts of the country or the world, providing a way to practice a foreign language.

- **Connect with experts and public figures.** In class, you can invite and listen to "guest speakers" via video chat. During research projects, you can conduct interviews with subject-area experts and educators.

- **Take virtual field trips around the world.** Some video-chat applications like Skype partner with museums, zoos, and explorers to plan virtual field trips through video chat. Imagine seeing Mount Everest and the surrounding scenery through the eyes of an actual explorer!

Note: Video and sound quality vary considerably depending upon the connection. Refer to the "Help" section of your video-chat program to set up the best settings.

Help File

Another form of internet communication is VoIP. VoIP stands for voice over Internet protocol. This technology lets you make "phone calls" through an Internet connection, using a computer or smartphone. Although it is an audio-only technology, you can use VoIP in many of the same ways you use video chat.

Finding and Using Internet Content

Software designer Mitchell Kapor compares getting information off the Internet to "taking a drink from a fire hydrant." Indeed, the Internet is saturated with information. By 2015, the indexed Web is expected to host one billion different sites. Searching for the information you need can be a bit overwhelming.

The next few pages describe how to find, use, and evaluate online information.

Surface-Web Research

The "surface Web" refers to all of the sites and pages that are freely available to the public. To find information on this part of the Web, use a search engine.

▌ Using Search Sites

Getting the perfect result on a search engine isn't always easy. Here are some tips to get the most out of your searches.

- **Try different keywords:** Use different combinations of words, and check your spelling.
- **Recognize suggested searches:** These suggestions pop up as you type in your search terms. They may give you new, useful ideas.
- **Browse multiple search pages:** The information you need may be on the second or third page of results, or even later.
- **Use advanced keyword strategies:** See page 414 for a list of strategies.

Deep-Web Research

The "deep Web" is the part of the Internet that is not indexed by ordinary search engines like Google. By some estimates, the deep Web hosts 500 times more content than the surface Web.

Special databases or search engines are needed to access this part of the Web, and almost all sites on it are password protected. However, most libraries allow you to access academic databases hosted on the deep Web.

▌ Using Academic Databases

Publication databases such as EBSCO let you view hundreds of academic journals, magazines, and newspapers. The articles and information in such databases are valuable for school projects for several reasons:

- The articles were written by experts.
- They have been reviewed by educators.
- They are intended for academic readers and communities.
- They are up to date.

Other Sources of Information

Here are some other Internet resources you can use to find information.

Directories Directories list information by subject headings. Instead of searching for a keyword, you choose one broad subject and browse its subheadings, which progressively get more specific.

Online libraries Online libraries include a range of texts and research tools, including primary sources. Three notable online libraries are the Library of Congress (loc.gov), the Internet Public Library (ipl.org), and the Digital Public Library of America (dp.la).

Government sites Government sites give a broad overview of our government's functions and agencies. NASA (nasa.gov) and the National Archives (archives.gov) are two good examples.

Multimedia and social sites Social media allow the exchange of ideas and information among people and communities.

Respecting Copyright Laws

While the Internet provides a depth of freely accessible information and resources, most of it is the property of someone else. When using information, take care to respect the owner's rights.

What is a copyright?

A copyright stems from a federal law that protects the creative works of writers, artists, musicians, and others. Copyright laws give the creators of information the exclusive right to reproduce or distribute their work.

What is fair use?

Fair use is a provision of copyright law that allows you to use portions of copyrighted material for educational purposes. Even though fair use gives you some leeway, never use a copyrighted work in its entirety. As a general rule, use less than 10 percent of an article or written work and no more than 3 minutes of a video, 30 seconds of a song, or 5 photos from a collection.

What are public-domain resources?

After a certain period of time, copyrighted works enter the public domain, and anyone can use them for free. There are many public-domain resources on the Internet, including government works and publications.

"Creative-commons" works are also public. In this case, the creator makes a declaration that the material is free to use and distribute. When using creative-commons media, always credit the creator and follow any conditional terms of use.

Evaluating Internet Content

Not all the information you find online is reliable. Some sources are incorrect, dated, or misleading. Use this checklist to evaluate Internet content.

Web-Reliability Checklist

Creator

___ **Is the creator an authority on the topic?** Use caution with information that does not cite an author.

___ **Does the information reveal a personal or professional bias?** The author should take a fair and balanced approach.

Message

___ **Is the information accurate?** Articles with cited sources are generally reliable, but check the cited sources to determine their reliability as well.

___ **Is the information fair and balanced?** Watch out for one-sided, biased reports that simplify complex concepts or include extreme, emotional language.

___ **Is the information current?** Check the article's date or scroll to the bottom of the page to see when the Web page was last updated.

___ **Is the design clean and professional?** Poor or sloppy design can be a sign of untrustworthy information.

Source

___ **Is the publisher or host of the site reputable?** Academic and government sites (ending in *.edu* or *.gov*) are generally more reputable than commercial sites (ending in *.com*). However, many public sites have established good reputations.

Context

___ **Is the purpose of the information to educate, entertain, or persuade?** Beware of sensational headlines and advertisements disguised as real stories.

___ **Is the content presented as fact or as opinion?** Always fact-check a story portayed as true; and examine the logic of all opinions.

Improving Visual Literacy

Statistics say that you may be watching television, playing video games, and using social media for a combined total of six hours a day. If that's the case, you are looking at thousands of images in a day. How do you make sense of this visual information, and can you always believe what you see?

With today's technology, visuals are easily manipulated, making it difficult to distinguish fact from fiction. That's why being visually literate is so important. The following pages explain this type of literacy and offer guidelines to help you achieve it.

Learning Outcomes

Develop visual literacy.
Apply visual skills.
Appreciate visual art.
View photographs.
Use online media.
View television news and ads.
Use an assessment rubric.

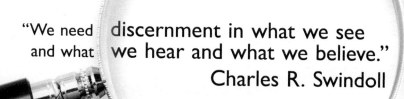

"We need discernment in what we see and what we hear and what we believe."
Charles R. Swindoll

Developing Visual Literacy

More than 90 percent of the information you take in on a daily basis is visual (images) rather than textual (words). That's a lot of images. The good news, according to the experts, is that humans can process visual information 60,000 times faster than they can process text. The challenge is interpreting all that visual information correctly. In short, visual literacy is being able to think and communicate visually.

The Steps in the Process

When using visuals to communicate, the first step is defining the need to use a visual. The second is finding the image. After that, the process turns to inspecting the image, analyzing it, and so on. The diagram below lists these steps and their related concepts. Understanding this process is an important part of improving your visual literacy.

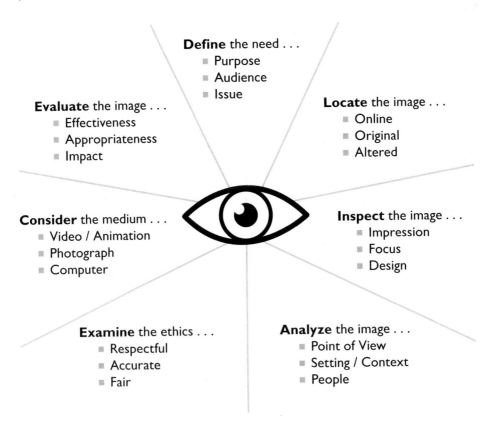

Define the need . . .
- Purpose
- Audience
- Issue

Locate the image . . .
- Online
- Original
- Altered

Evaluate the image . . .
- Effectiveness
- Appropriateness
- Impact

Inspect the image . . .
- Impression
- Focus
- Design

Consider the medium . . .
- Video / Animation
- Photograph
- Computer

Examine the ethics . . .
- Respectful
- Accurate
- Fair

Analyze the image . . .
- Point of View
- Setting / Context
- People

*This diagram is based on the "ACRL Visual Literacy Competency Standards for Higher Education."

Applying Visual Skills

To derive meaning from an image created or shared by someone else, you must examine its parts carefully. Take time to imagine what the author or producer wanted to communicate with this image. Use your physical eyes and your mind's eye to answer the questions below. (Not every question will apply to every visual.)

Follow the Steps

Take a closer look. Look carefully at the image to the right. Then answer the questions below and on the next page. Also consider how you might apply these questions to other images you see or create each day.

africa924 / Shutterstock.com

Define the need . . .

1. What type of image is this? What does it do, say, or show?
2. What is the purpose of this image—to inform, to educate, to persuade?
3. Who is the intended audience?
4. What issues or values does the image promote?

Find the image . . .

1. Where could an image of this sort be found?
2. Is the source or creator of the image credited?
3. Could this image have been created or altered by the author?
4. What other images or sources could have been used?

Inspect the image . . .

1. What is your overall impression of the image?
2. Where are your eyes drawn? What is the focus of the image?
3. Do the design elements (layout, typeface, white space) work well to convey the message of this image?
4. Are any special symbols, sounds, or colors used to enhance the image?

Analyze the image . . .

1. From whose perspective or point of view is the image presented?
2. Who are the people shown, and what are their ages, gender, and ethnicity?
3. Is the image suitable for the intended audience?
4. Is the image placed in an appropriate setting or context?

Evaluate the image . . .

1. Is the image portrayed effectively? What confuses or impresses you about it?
2. Does the image clarify or enhance the intended message?
3. Is the overall tone appropriate for the purpose and audience?
4. How will the image likely impact different viewers?

Consider the medium or format . . .

1. What type of image is it (a video, a computer graphic, a photograph)?
2. Is the medium or format appropriate for the image and the message?
3. Do the images and text work well together in this format?
4. Are animation or other special effects used?

Examine the ethical issues . . .

1. Does the image respect the privacy and integrity of all people?
2. How might a person's age, gender, or culture affect his or her reaction to this image?
3. Does the image convey the message fully and fairly?
4. Does the image accurately reflect the real world as you know it?

Take a closer look. Using the same questions, consider the image to the right. Think about the ways in which this image is the same as (or different from) the one on the previous page. Comparing and contrasting images and how they are used can strengthen your visual literacy.

Appreciating Visual Art

Understanding the traditional elements inherent in all visual art is another important part of becoming visually literate. All artists, from sculptors to architects to design engineers, employ these elements in their work. Learning about them will help you analyze and evaluate the visuals you encounter.

The Elements of Visual Art

Lines create boundaries, establish focus, and influence meaning. Thin lines create a light, airy tone; heavy lines, a serious tone. Various line qualities can produce contrast and emphasis.

Shapes enclose and define spaces. Shapes can be anything from a circle or square to a leaf or seashell. Shapes are often the focal point of visual art.

Value refers to the brightness or darkness of a visual. The contrast between light and dark brings interest and meaning to the art. Lighter images tend to appear closer, and darker images seem farther away.

Color can be looked at from a number of perspectives. For example, consider the categories of color—primary, secondary, tertiary—displayed on a **color wheel.** Studying the relationships of the colors on the wheel will help you understand how colors are used to produce a certain effect.

- **Primary colors** are the pure colors (red, yellow, blue), not a mix of colors.
- **Secondary colors** (orange, green, and violet) are a combination of two primary colors.
- **Tertiary colors** (blue-green, yellow-orange) are a combination of a primary and a secondary color.
- **Complimentary colors** appear opposite one another on the color wheel. When used together, they compliment one another and create energy and harmony.
- **Hot colors** (red, orange, yellow) are bright and eye catching.
- **Cool colors** (green, blue, violet) are calm and soothing.

Color symbolism is a term for the ways in which colors are often used or interpreted. *Red* is associated with love, passion, and energy; *pink* with tenderness, calm, and caring. *Yellow* is sometimes used to represent joy, warmth, or optimism, while *blue* reflects peace, calm, or trust. *White* can signal purity, simplicity, or maturity. *Black* often signals power, death, or fear.

Viewing Photographs

When someone takes a photograph, he or she usually has a specific reason or purpose in mind. It may be to simply capture the moment, or to deliberately preserve an image that could change the world. In either case, the photographer uses certain techniques to create the image, some of which are listed below.

Photographic Elements

Composition is the arrangement of subjects within a photograph. A photograph is "composed" of numerous elements working together to create a compelling image. In addition to the elements listed below, photographers also consider the elements of art and design: line, shape, value, and so on. (See page 371.)

Angle refers to the direction from which a photo is taken. A low angle can make the subject seem larger than reality; a high angle can make the subject seem smaller.

Framing determines where the subject is located within the photograph and what role the foreground and background play. How a photo is "framed" can be used to determine its point or purpose.

Viewpoint is the perspective or vantage point from which the photo is taken.

Focal point is the point in the image to which the viewer's eyes are drawn.

Lighting is used to create a mood or provide contrast in an image.

Assessing a Photograph

Anton Oparin / Shutterstock.com

Observe . . .

1. Study the photograph carefully: What do you see first? Next? Last?
2. What is your overall impression? What details are especially interesting?
3. Is the lighting, framing, and camera angle appropriate for the image?

Analyze . . .

1. What is the focal point of the photo? Is the viewer likely to focus there?
2. From whose viewpoint is this photograph taken?
3. Why do you think this photograph was taken? Who is meant to see it?

Evaluate . . .

1. What impact might this photo have on young people? On older people?
2. Does the image reflect its subject appropriately and fairly?
3. Could another medium present this subject more effectively?

Using Online Media

Like television, online media are popular sources of information and entertainment; and like television, these media sites require critical viewing. When you go online, you need to know what you're getting into. Here are some tips.

Define and inspect the sites . . .
1. What is your overall impression of the site?
2. Who created the site? Does it appear to be current and accurate?
3. What is the purpose of the site? To entertain? To educate? To sell?
4. What audience is attracted to or targeted by this site?

Analyze and evaluate the site's images . . .
1. Is the site appealing and easy to access?
2. Are the pictures and videos up to date and appropriate for the topic?
3. Are the images and language appropriate for the intended audience?
4. What will other less frequent visitors find effective about this site?

Consider how the site uses images . . .
1. Do the persons portrayed on the site represent different ages, ethnic groups, and genders?
2. Are there any stereotypes or inappropriate visuals?
3. Can the information on the site be verified?
4. Does the site cover topics fully and fairly?

Red Flags
- The site is anonymous—no author or organization name is given.
- The content is one sided or includes a great deal of personal commentary.
- The site presents facts and figures but does not name the source of the these details.
- The text is poorly written, or the design and images look unprofessional.
- The site is dominated by ads or pop-ups.

Help File

Remember, many online sites invite the public to contribute information, often anonymously. Always check the reliability of a site's information and images. You can do this by visiting various Web sites, such as FactCheck.org, to double-check any questionable details or images you may find.

Viewing Television News

A recent Pew Research Center project reported that cable news networks, on average, offer straight news 37% of the time and commentary 63% of the time. And although local and network newscasts offer a greater percentage of news, they often include quite a bit of soft news: sports, weather, and lifestyle stories. Clearly, as you sit down to catch the latest cable or network newscast, you need to be a discerning viewer, paying close attention to a story's *completeness, correctness,* and *balance.*

Completeness ▪ A good news story is complete; it tells the whole story.

- **Substance:** A news story should be worthwhile and provide all the relevant facts: who? what? when? where? why? and how?
- **Truthfulness:** A news story must always be true and never contain half-truths. Sometimes, what is reported is true, but something pertinent is left out. Using half-truths is especially deceptive and difficult to detect.
- **Conciseness:** News should be complete but also concise. It should not ramble on with nonessential details that muddle the real story.

Correctness ▪ A good news story states only the known facts; it never speculates.

- **Accuracy:** The words, images, and videos used should be an accurate reflection of the news story and the setting or context in which it occurred; accuracy is honesty.
- **Focus:** The images used should point to the important details of the story and not distract the viewer.
- **Objectivity:** A news story should be objective and unbiased, including only the known facts and featuring only reliable witnesses or experts who can verify that the information is accurate.

Balance ▪ A balanced story covers all sides of an event or issue fairly; it is not one sided.

- **Placement:** Stories ought to be placed appropriately in a newscast—most important first and least important last.
- **Fairness:** A good news story presents all sides, providing adequate time to each witness, expert, or reporter involved.
- **Words and imagery:** The images and words used in a newscast should reflect fairly on all people involved. Just as a newscaster's words, gestures, and tone of voice can slant a news story, so can an altered or specially planned photo or video clip. Watch and listen carefully.

Viewing Television Ads

We probably encounter more television ads on a daily basis than we do any other image-based communication. Surveys have shown that young people view as many as 40,000 ads a year. Unfortunately, many viewers do not think critically about what they are seeing and can be described as passive viewers. We all need to become "active" viewers.

Define the ad . . .

1. What kind of ad are you viewing—realistic, fantasy, animated?
2. What product/service is being sold? What does the ad say?
3. Who is the target audience?

Inspect the ad . . .

1. What ages and genders are depicted in the people who appear in the ad?
2. Notice the people's appearance. How are they dressed?
3. How do the people in the ad relate to the product being sold?

Analyze the ad . . .

1. Are camera angles and close-ups used effectively?
2. How are color and lighting used to enhance the images?
3. Does the ad contain any annoying or distracting elements? Explain.

Evaluate the ad . . .

1. Are the images pleasing? Are they effective messengers?
2. Are the words matched well to the images?
3. Does the ad create unrealistic expectations for the viewers?

Consider the medium's use of device . . .

1. Are any special effects or animation used?
2. Is a slogan or jingle used to highlight the product?
3. Are any special appeals to emotion employed? Which emotions?

Consider the ethics . . .

1. Do the images disrespect anyone based on age, gender, or ethnicity?
2. How might a viewer's age/culture affect how he or she interprets the ad?
3. Is the ad fair and balanced in its attempt to sell its product or service?

Using an Assessment Rubric

Use this rubric as a checklist to evaluate your visual literacy. The rubric is organized according to the steps in the process effectively using visuals to communicate.

I am able to . . .

Define the need.
___ understand the intended audience for the image.
___ recognize the issues or values the image promotes.

Locate the image.
___ identify the source or predict where such images can be found.
___ recognize if the image has been altered or repurposed.
___ suggest other images or sources that could have been used.

Inspect the image.
___ identify the image's design elements (layout, typeface, white space, color, framing, focal point, and so on).

Analyze the image.
___ identify the perspective and context.
___ recognize the age, gender, and ethnicity of people portrayed.

Evaluate the image.
___ discuss the clarity and tone of the image.
___ predict how the image will impact different viewers.

Consider the medium.
___ discuss how the medium affects the image and its message.

Examine the ethics.
___ evaluate the image's appeal and its fairness to the subject.
___ discuss the effectiveness and appropriateness of the image.

Help File

To learn more about communicating with visuals, turn to "Reading Graphics" in this handbook (pages 325–332). The chapter includes an overview of several types of graphics, from tables and charts to diagrams and maps.

Using Social Media

Using social media is probably as much a part of your daily routine as brushing your teeth or choosing something to wear. Applications like Facebook, Twitter, and YouTube give you the power to express yourself and your ideas to people near and far. All you need is a device with access to the Web.

But with power comes responsibility. As you connect with an ever wider audience, you must also commit to using social media for the good of others. This chapter explores how to do that effectively while avoiding the pitfalls that could harm the reputations of others—as well as your own.

Learning Outcomes

Understand the types of social media.
Manage your online brand.
Write microblog posts.
Use social media for learning.
Create social-media campaigns.
Use social media safely.

"Understand your audience and you will understand the impact of your message on each follower in your social media networks."

Matt Gentile

Understanding the Types of Social Media

Social media refers to all of the forms of online communication that allow you to communicate, interact, and share content with others. While social-media services are constantly evolving, they generally fall into one of the following categories.

Social networks allow you to interact with others through messages, pictures, videos, games, and more. Popular social-networking sites include Facebook, Pinterest, and LinkedIn. Users create profiles that include their pictures, interests, and other information.

Microblog services let you broadcast short messages (microblogs) to other subscribers. Twitter, for example, is a service that limits messages to 140 characters.

Blog services host longer messages that are similar to online journal entries. Blogging platforms such as Tumblr and WordPress allow readers to write comments and pose questions to the author of the posted message.

Wikis are Web sites that are built, edited, and managed by many people using a Web browser. Readers can edit the wiki's content at any time. While Wikipedia is the most popular site of this type, specialized wikis about specific subjects also exist. Many high school classrooms have their own wikis.

Message boards are forums where people can post and read messages about specific topics. Each message board focuses on one broad subject (chemistry) while individual conversations relate to specific topics (stabilizing heavy elements). Conversations are called "threads."

Bookmarking services such as Evernote and Instapaper allow you to save important Web links to one central location. Users can then access the links with any device that connects to the Web. Within each bookmarking site, you can organize links into specific categories (John Adams research, must-read list, and so on).

Multimedia-sharing sites allow you to upload and share media, including pictures, podcasts, videos, and music. Users create profiles and rate and comment on others' content. YouTube, Instagram, and Flickr are examples.

Social-news sites such as Reddit let subscribers post and vote on news stories and other media. Entries that receive the most votes are displayed prominently.

Managing Your Online Brand

Each logo on the opposite page represents a particular social-media brand. Just seeing a logo produces a reaction based on your experience with that application— either good or bad. And one bad encounter can tarnish your opinion of the brand. For this reason, successful businesses go to great lengths to establish and maintain positive brands.

In the same way, you ought to manage your own brand by using social media wisely. All the pictures, videos, status updates, and tweets that you share online shape your own unique brand.

Remember: Your online presence can impact your future. Job recruiters and college admissions counselors often evaluate an applicant's social-media activities when deciding whether to hire someone or admit a student. Start managing your online brand by following these tips.

Represent the real you.

Consider your online behavior so far. Does it accurately reflect who you are away from the computer? It should. What you say to others online ought to resemble what you would say to them face-to-face. Don't hide behind your screen name. Be genuine.

Respect others.

Treat others as you want to be treated, and never bully. Friendliness goes a long way online, and it comes back to you. When you compliment other people and promote their work and ideas, they are more likely to return the favor to you.

Consider the situation.

Always think about your subject, audience, and purpose before taking any action on social media. Know who will view your content, and predict how they may react to it. How do you want to be perceived by your audience?

Display your creativity.

Market yourself and your abilities. Post your accomplishments and successful projects. Create videos or short films. Record clips of your work in a school play or musical. Consider creating a digital résumé for employers and colleges.

Pause before you post.

Make smart choices about what you share online. Never post anything that you wouldn't want your parents or teachers to see.

Writing Microblog Posts

Microblogging is the most common social-media writing form. Even though microblog posts are short, they can have real impact. Each post becomes permanent, so be careful about what you write.

▌ Planning and Writing Microblog Posts

To produce thoughtful, engaging microblog posts, follow a condensed version of the writing process.

1. **Prewriting** . . . Think about the rhetorical situation.
   - **Subject:** What are you writing about?
   - **Purpose:** Why are you writing this post?
   - **Audience:** Who will read your message? How might they react? (Consider any unintended readers, including teachers and other adults.)

> **Tip:** Don't post messages when your emotions are running high. You may regret it later.

> I want to share my feelings about an article I read about robots. The message will go to all my followers, so there's a chance my science teacher will read it. I want the post to be entertaining, but I don't want to offend anyone.

2. **Writing** . . . Make your message short and to the point, using conversational language. Readers need to digest the information quickly, so don't waste your words. If you are using Twitter, use hashtags thoughtfully and sparingly.

> **Tip:** A hashtag is # with a keyword: #robotics. Readers search for hashtags to find messages about a particular subject.

> Google is investing stacks of money in robots that can make home deliveries. Will they be capable of drawing Google doodles, too? #robotics

3. **Revising and editing** . . . Reread your message twice before sending it. Cut any unnecessary words, and replace dull words with interesting ones. Finally, correct spelling, capitalization, and punctuation mistakes, especially when you are posting about a serious topic.

> **@BlueKnightEric23**
> 12:22pm via HootSuite
> Google is creating robots that make home deliveries. But can these robots draw Google doodles? #robotics

Using Social Media for Learning

The combination of people, ideas, and technology makes social media a rich environment for learning. Within this environment you can form personalized learning networks (PLN) for school projects, hobbies, and other areas of interest.

A PLN is a network of sources about a subject. Creating your own PLN gives you the chance to do these things:

- Gather information and do research
- Connect with subject-matter experts
- Experience new ideas and ways of thinking
- Receive feedback about your work
- Collaborate with others
- Share your own knowledge and insights

Developing a PLN

Develop your own PLN by considering the resources you already have and then expanding your network's reach to fill in any gaps.

1. Evaluate your current network. Draw a cluster that includes all the people, places, organizations, and media that you learn from. Here is a sample cluster:

2. Fill in the gaps. What other people, places, organizations, or media could offer information about your subject? Identify them and seek them out. Introduce yourself, make a connection, ask questions, and learn.

3. Share your network with others. Your PLN may overlap with the personal learning networks of others. The more people you connect with, the better for all those involved.

Creating Social-Media Campaigns

Imagine that you have a cause or idea that is really important to you. You want others to know about it, too. How can you get the word out to as many people as possible? Using social media may be your best strategy.

A social-media campaign builds awareness about a cause or idea. You may need to raise funds for a school project or inform everyone about an upcoming event or important public issue. Whatever the campaign, follow these principles to be successful.

- **Make it memorable.** Do some branding. Give your campaign an easy-to-remember slogan and incorporate it in your social-media messages.

- **Make it visual.** Give your campaign an eye-catching logo. Ask a classmate who is skilled at graphic design to mock up some options or find an interesting public-domain picture online. If possible, create a short video that grabs the viewer's attention and gives all the important details about the campaign.

- **Use multiple social-media platforms.** Promote your campaign on many different platforms—social networks, multimedia sites, blogs, microblogs, and more. For example, you might create an event page on Facebook, start a Twitter account with a unique username, post a campaign video on YouTube, and post updates and progress reports on Tumblr.

- **Target specific audiences.** Think about who you want to reach with your campaign. How big is the audience? Are you targeting a certain age group or demographic? After establishing your target audience, decide which platforms would reach them best. And always consider the audience as you create messages.

- **Encourage sharing.** The best way to spread your campaign message is to get other people to talk about it. Remind your audience to spread the word about your campaign on their own social-media accounts. Different social-media platforms have different features for sharing. Research how to use them effectively.

- **Post new content regularly.** Time your updates and messages wisely. Consider when your audience regularly checks their social-media sites; post new updates then as well as at other times of the day. However, don't appear pushy by posting messages too often.

▌ Sample Social-Media Campaign

In the following scenario, a high school student writes a personal blog entry about a social-media campaign that she worked on with her school's service club.

Service Club Blog

Home   Comments   Share

Nov 13
2014

The "Dishing Out Delight" Campaign

Background: In September, our service club created the "Dishing Out Delight" campaign to get our school to help at a local soup kitchen. Our first goal was to gather enough unique family recipes to create a week's menu for the soup kitchen. Our second goal was to recruit student volunteers to cook and serve the menu.

Summary: We used social media to raise awareness:

1. We created a "Dishing Out Delight" Facebook event page, which described our cause and included a campaign logo. We used our personal accounts to invite schoolmates to join the event page and asked them to invite their friends. We posted new information and encouraging words as status updates.

2. Next we created a "Dishing Out Delight" board on Pinterest, where we pinned recipes and pictures of food. We also created a campaign Twitter handle, using our personal accounts to find more followers.

3. To add visual appeal, we created a short campaign video, uploaded it to YouTube, pinned it on Pinterest, and embedded it on our Facebook page.

4. We got permission to host an after-school "taste test" of our favorite recipes. Students who attended the taste test could submit their own traditional recipes and sign up to cook or serve. We marketed the taste test through social media.

5. As the week of the service project neared, we collected all of the recipes we had received and created a menu for the week. We used polling features on Facebook to get feedback on our choices.

6. During the weeklong service event, we posted updates on our social-media platforms. We also took pictures and made videos and posted them online.

Conclusion: Using social media, we were able to reach a larger audience than we would have by word of mouth alone. The campaign persuaded other students to join the cause. And after the event was over, our club welcomed 12 new members!

Using Social Media Safely

Social-media platforms give you the power to interact with others. Unfortunately, many people on the Internet abuse this power. They use social media to scam, bully, and steal information from other people. Take care to avoid such unscrupulous users as well as any activities that would put you in a compromising position. Below are tips for using social media safely.

Protect your identity. Review the privacy settings for any social media you use. Never reveal personal details about yourself or others to strangers, including your name, address, or phone number. Likewise, never post information that would reflect poorly on you, your family, or your friends. Think twice before posting personal photos and videos, and do not reveal your current location when you are alone.

Avoid spam. If you feel unsure about a Web link, don't click on it. Spammers often disguise dangerous links by giving them innocent names. Identity thieves use similar techniques by sending emails that claim to be from an official source but include an infected attachment or a link to a dangerous site. Avoid clicking links you receive in your email or links disguised as advertisements on your Web browser. Finally, activate antivirus and anti-spam software to keep your computer safe from intruders.

Beware of bandwagoning. "Bandwagoning" is a logical fallacy that assumes an idea is correct because a lot of people believe it. Bandwagoning occurs often on social networks and microblogging sites, resulting in a "gang" mentality. Unfair or incorrect assumptions can lead to bullying and other harmful consequences. Always think critically about a message before making a judgment about it. And avoid spreading unreasonable or wrong ideas, even if they are popular.

Log out before you leave. Before you stop using a public computer, remember to log out of any accounts you may have open.

Avoid plagiarism. Respect the rights of people who have produced creative works—words, music, videos, photographs, etc.—by reviewing copyright and fair-use laws. Before sharing someone else's work, (1) identify its owner, (2) get permission to use it, (3) give credit to the creator, and (4) if necessary, purchase the work.

Never bully. Do not bully in any way, shape, or form. If you notice someone else bullying, report it to a trusted adult.

Designing Writing with Technology

During a writing project, your computer becomes an all-in-one, indispensable tool. You can use it to conduct research; draft, revise, and edit your writing; and prepare the final copy for publication.

Publishing can take many forms—sharing a report with your class, entering your work in a writing contest, submitting an admission essay to a college, and more. Whatever your purpose, always use the approved format and design. Finally, consider the design guidelines offered in this chapter.

Learning Outcomes

Design academic writing.
Use graphics in academic writing.
Design real-world print projects.

"What's important is to have faith in people . . . and if you give them tools, they'll do wonderful things with them."

Steve Jobs

Designing Academic Writing

The true test of effective page design is that your writing is clear and easy to read. Consider the tips below for designing essays and research papers that are both clear and appealing.

Typography

- **Use an easy-to-read serif font for the main text.** Serif type (like this) has tails on the tops and bottoms of the letters. Consider using sans serif type (like this) for the title and headings. Sans serif type does not have tails.

- **Choose a readable typestyle.** Times New Roman is a commonly used serif font and Helvetica is a common sans serif font.

- **Use a 10- or 12-point type size for the main text** and one or two sizes larger for headings. (If the headings seem lost on the page, make them boldfaced.) The title can be the same size or one or two sizes larger than the headings.

Help File

Most people find sans serif fonts easier to read on-screen, so when publishing online, consider a sans serif font for the main text and a serif font for the title and headings.

Spacing and Margins

- **Maintain a one-inch margin around each page**—top, bottom, left, and right.

- **Indent the first line of each new paragraph five spaces,** unless you are instructed otherwise.

- **Avoid placing a heading or starting a new paragraph on the bottom line of a page.** Also avoid placing a single word in either the bottom or top line of a page, and do not split a hyphenated word between pages.

Design Features

- **Make titles and headings short and to the point.** The title should say something about the topic of the paper. Headings of equal importance should be kept parallel (stated in the same way).

- **Use bulleted lists to highlight important points.** However, be selective; lists lose their effectiveness when used too frequently.

- **Include graphics or visuals when appropriate.** Place a graphic so that it makes sense and connects well with the corresponding text. If necessary, put it on a separate page. (See pages 389–392.)

Special Note: When submitting a paper to a writing contest or publication, check for specific formatting requirements.

Effective Design in Action

The following sample pages (1 and 3) from an explanatory essay display effective design elements.

McGinn 1

Kendall McGinn
Mr. Guilding
American Studies
25 February 2014

The title is 16-point sans serif type.

The Return of the Buffalo

At one point in the early twentieth century, it seemed that the American buffalo would exist only in pictures or on the buffalo nickel. The population of 100 million buffalo in 1700 had been reduced to 1,000 by 1889. Railroad and cattle barons, with the support of the federal government, orchestrated the jaw-dropping decimation of this animal. With the buffalo gone, these barons could use the land for their own purposes. Fortunately, determined individuals and preservation societies saved the buffalo from complete extinction, and remarkably the animals' numbers have increased to nearly 500,000 today (Hodgson 71). Clearly, the buffalo, once endangered, has returned.

Before Europeans came to North America, the native people of the North American plains and the buffalo were one Pte Oyate, or Buffalo Nation. The big bull tatanka was life itself. Native Americans used every part of the buffalo for food, clothing, shelter, religious ceremonies, and medicine. Even the brains were used as a waterproofing agent applied to the hides (History). A Lakota leader summed up the special unity between human and animal in this way: "When the Creator made the buffalo, he put power in them. When you eat the meat, that power goes into you, heals the body and spirit" (qtd. in Hodgson 69).

The main text is 10-point serif type.

Scientists believe that the buffalo originated in Eurasia and migrated to North America over the Bering Strait 10,000 years ago (*Bison*). Similarly, the first Native Americans are believed to have migrated here along the same route. For centuries, hunting buffalo was a hit-or-miss proposition, because Native Americans did not have horses. They had to stampede buffalo over cliffs or, in winter, chase them on ice or into deep snow. With the arrival of Spanish explorers, Native Americans acquired horses, and buffalo hunting became much easier (*History*).

Headings introduce new sections.

Open Season on Buffalo

During the Western expansion of the United States, Europeans practically destroyed the buffalo. By the year 1800, it was reported that there were only about 30 million buffalo left in the United States. Later in the nineteenth century, commercial killers did the most damage. A typical hide would earn a commercial killer about $3.00 (*Bison*). There were also killing contests. One Kansan killed 140 buffalo in 40 minutes. Train companies even allowed riders to shoot buffalo from coach windows (*Spirit*).

388

A graphic visually presents important information.

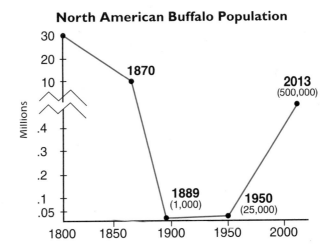

North American Buffalo Population

As the graphic illustrates, the buffalo are returning to North America in ever-increasing numbers. CNN founder and former cable TV mogul Ted Turner raises more than 50,000 on his western ranches. "I guess I've gone buffalo batty," Turner says. He promotes buffalo as an excellent source of low-fat meat and as a way to help save this once-endangered species (Hodgson 75). His Montana Grill restaurants serve buffalo raised on his ranches. Turner claims that his restaurants are showing the way for responsible, sustainable ranching.

Buffalo ranchers are, in fact, learning that raising buffalo has many benefits. It is more cost-effective and more environmentally safe than raising cattle. Other main benefits include the following:

A bulleted list presents information in a digestible format.

- Buffalo don't overeat.
- Their sharp hooves loosen hard soil.
- Buffalo improve grass crops.
- They adapt to any climate.

Buffalo seem well suited for just about every climate. Buffalo living in Florida seem just as happy as those living in Alaska. In Hawaii, they even survived a hurricane. Hawaiian rancher Bill Mowry recalls how the buffalo "loved every minute of it" (qtd. in Allen 105).

The headings use 12-point san serif type.

New Opportunities for Ranchers

Buffalo ranching in Nebraska has created a great deal of public interest. One ranching family provides eco-tours of its operation for a small fee. Last year, more than 4,000 people visited their operation to learn about buffalo, prairie grasses, and chemical-free ranching (*Dixon County*).

Using Graphics in Academic Writing

Bulleted lists, line graphs, bar graphs, pie charts, and time lines are common graphics used in academic writing. When applied thoughtfully in your essays and reports, they can show relationships between ideas and communicate concepts that words alone cannot.

All word-processing programs offer functions for creating graphics. You can easily prepare a graphic and even switch data from one type to another to see which one works best. Check with a tech-support person, your instructor, or a classmate if you need help creating graphics. Also consider the tips below.

Using Graphics Tips

Identify a specific purpose for the graphic. A graphic must support or emphasize key ideas in the main text. The right graphic can make statistics readily available to the reader.

Start with accurate data. A graphic will be only as good as the information it contains. Check and double-check your facts.

Keep the graphic simple. Use color minimally and avoid over-the-top design elements that distract from the main text.

Focus on one main idea. Overly complicated graphics will not serve the reader. Also check that the information is appropriate for your target audience.

Title your graphic and label its parts. Labels should clearly explain the information and be parallel (stated in the same way).

Use the same font for all graphics. Also use upper- and lowercase letters to produce easy-to-read labels. (ALL CAPS can be difficult to read.)

Position the graphic to clearly flow from the information that comes before it.

Size the graphic appropriately, neither too big nor too small for the page. Word-processing programs allow you to modify your graphics.

Credit the source of a borrowed graphic. Using a graphic without listing its source is plagiarism.

Help File

White space is a design element used to make a text more attractive and more readable by drawing attention to the graphic that it frames.

A Closer Look at Graphics

Line Graphs Use a line graph to display a change in quantity over time. The graph's title identifies the subject, the horizontal axis signifies the period of time covered, and the vertical axis measures the quantity. Further explanation is sometimes provided beneath the horizontal axis. The dots, connected by a line, mark points where a particular quantity and a particular point in time meet.

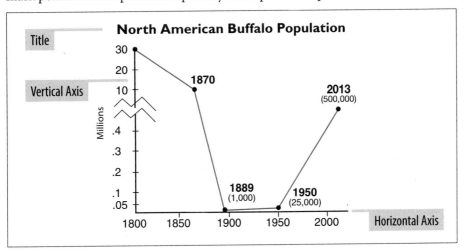

Bar Graphs Use a bar graph to compare amounts, quantities, scores, or other numerical data. The horizontal axis notes the elements being compared, and the vertical axis measures the subject of the comparison (quantity, score, etc.). Labels are provided as needed for each axis. The bars measuring the difference between elements should be uniform except for their height.

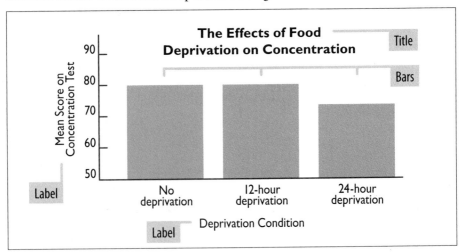

▌ **Pie Charts** Use a pie chart to show how different parts or portions combine to form a whole. A title identifies the subject of the chart. The portions, each a different color, represent slices of the whole pie. Label the portions either within or around the chart. Additional information can be added along the bottom.

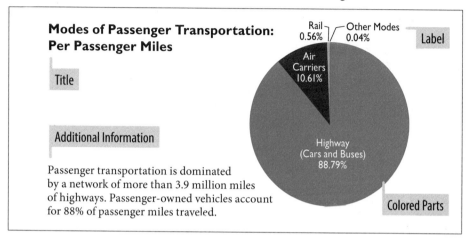

▌ **Time Lines** Use a time line to display the sequence of events related to a subject. A title identifies the subject of the time line, and specific events are listed chronologically. The events listed are of the same type or category and should be stated in a parallel way.

Infographics Create an infographic to present data in a visual way. A title identifies the subject, graphics represent concepts, and text provides key information. Design helps readers navigate the ideas. An infographic may stand alone as its own story, or it may accompany a piece of writing.

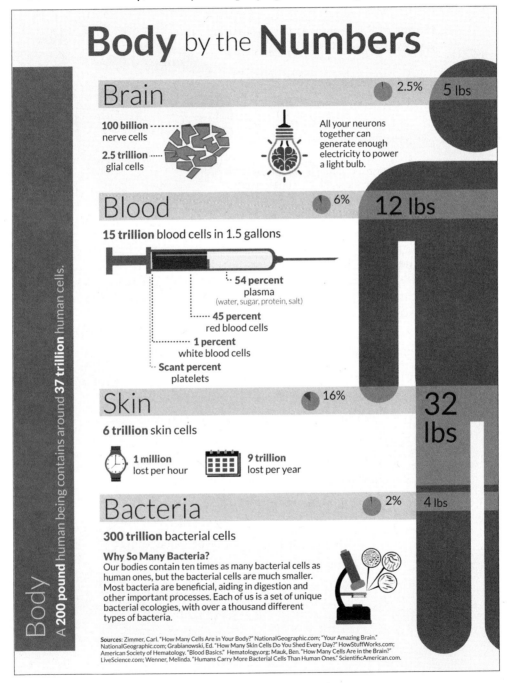

Body by the Numbers

Brain
2.5% 5 lbs

100 billion nerve cells
2.5 trillion glial cells

All your neurons together can generate enough electricity to power a light bulb.

Blood
6% 12 lbs

15 trillion blood cells in 1.5 gallons

54 percent plasma
(water, sugar, protein, salt)

45 percent red blood cells

1 percent white blood cells

Scant percent platelets

Skin
16% 32 lbs

6 trillion skin cells

1 million lost per hour

9 trillion lost per year

Bacteria
2% 4 lbs

300 trillion bacterial cells

Why So Many Bacteria?
Our bodies contain ten times as many bacterial cells as human ones, but the bacterial cells are much smaller. Most bacteria are beneficial, aiding in digestion and other important processes. Each of us is a set of unique bacterial ecologies, with over a thousand different types of bacteria.

Body A **200 pound** human being contains around **37 trillion** human cells.

Sources: Zimmer, Carl. "How Many Cells Are in Your Body?" NationalGeographic.com; "Your Amazing Brain." NationalGeographic.com; Grabianowski, Ed. "How Many Skin Cells Do You Shed Every Day?" HowStuffWorks.com; American Society of Hematology. "Blood Basics." Hematology.org; Mauk, Ben. "How Many Cells Are in the Brain?" LiveScience.com; Wenner, Melinda. "Humans Carry More Bacterial Cells Than Human Ones." ScientificAmerican.com.

Designing Real-World Print Projects

Academic essays and research papers present text with a few graphics. Real-world projects often contain bold graphic elements. Generally speaking, real-world projects are promotional pieces intended to accomplish one of the following:

- Introduce an organization
- Publicize a cause
- Offer a service

- Market a product
- Announce an opportunity
- Educate the reader

Sample Real-World Project

To help students understand how businesses use science, instructor Tim Kamp asked small groups of students to develop brochures encouraging investors to buy stock in a new mining company. During the first phase of the project, each group (1) created a company, (2) researched mineral exploration, (3) analyzed stream-sediment data related to mining, and (4) composed appropriate mining claims. Mr. Kamp established the following requirements for their brochures. (See pages 279–280 for one example.)

- Introduce the company
- Explain briefly the science of mining
- Provide analysis of data

- Offer rationale for selecting claim sites
- Address environmental concerns
- Include contact information

▮ The Basics of a Brochure

Tri-folded

Brochures are usually printed on one sheet of 8.5″ by 11″ or 8.5″ by 14″ paper. The page is turned horizontally and often tri-folded, offering six panels for information. The front panel provides a title, the main point or purpose of the brochure, the name of the organization, and perhaps a logo. The inside panels explain and support the brochure's purpose, provide graphically enhanced information, and may make a call to action. The back panels offer closing comments and contact information, including a mailing address, phone numbers, and email addresses.

Help File

Most word-processing programs such as Microsoft Word contain a design feature that will guide you through the brochure-making process. You can also use a special program such as Adobe InDesign to prepare your work.

A Closer Look at a Brochure

A brochure, like other writing, contains a beginning, a middle, and an ending. **Face 1** introduces the main point or purpose. **Face 2** develops and supports the purpose. **Face 3** offers further information and a conclusion.

Ⓐ The title of the brochure is clear.

Ⓑ Introductory copy explains the purpose.

Ⓒ The company is identified, including its logo.

Ⓓ Information is given in steps for readability.

Ⓔ A graphic provides scientific credibility.

Ⓕ A key point is highlighted.

Ⓖ Photos enhance the copy.

Ⓗ Headings introduce blocks of copy.

Ⓘ Subheadings guide the reader.

Ⓙ A call to action is made.

Face 1 (Front Panel)

Ⓐ Crested Butte
PROJECT

Ⓑ The Moly Mining Co. (MMC) is currently seeking investors to join our team of specialists in developing a new mine near Crested Butte, Colorado. Through careful research and analysis, we have identified in this area what promises to be a large deposit of Molybdenum. Based on our assessment of related costs, we believe that mining the deposit is a great opportunity for a large return on investment.

Ⓒ Moly Mining Co.

Face 2 (Inside Panels)

Science Driven

Step 1 In the Crested Butte area, our specialists first gathered sediments from sites along the river, most of which tested for low concentrations of Molybdenum.

Step 2 The specialists then searched along the west side of Ruby Ridge. Samples taken from that location proved more positive. Concentrations of Molybdenum in sediments in this area were above 10.0 ppb.

Step 3 They then traveled into the mountains near Beartooth Peak and located three specific claims that also showed high concentrations of Molybdenum. On the mining claims map, these claims are numbered 5, 7, and 9.

Ⓕ These three claims indicated levels of Molybdenum that in our other mining operations have produced a high return on investments.

Why Molybdenum?

Molybdenum is a silvery-white, hard transition metal that resists deformation from high heat, making it very valuable in industrial and military applications. Molybdenum is used in steel alloys, electrodes, and catalysts, as well as in many other products.

42
Mo
Molybdenum

A Golden Opportunity

Moly Mining Co. is a growing business with positive goals:

❧ We seek talented and responsible employees.

We continuously aim to improve our company. To that end, we treat our workers with respect and equality in order to strengthen our company and move forward with new ideas.

❧ We protect and restore the environment.

We consider how our actions will affect the environment. Choosing the land for our mines is done carefully in order to ensure that only the land essential to mining is used. In addition, we specialize in minimizing mine waste, fully restoring mine sites, and ensuring that the water quality is as pure or purer than we found it.

❧ We strive to produce strong returns on investments.

The land that we mine and the operations that we conduct are selected to earn your trust and produce a profit for our investors. We appreciate your support and would value your participation in our new venture.

Face 3 (Back Panels)   **Ⓜ**   **(Front Panel)**

Ⓚ

MMC's Process of Mineral Exploration

For our company, mineral exploration begins on paper. We carefully study the area using topographical maps. We factor how the hills, ridges, mountains, lakes, and rivers will influence where the deposit will be most accessible.

We then send teams to gather sediments from likely spots along the river for analysis. Our lab tests help us identify which samples (and related sites) have the highest concentration of Molybdenum.

After analyzing the lab research, we acquire the mineral-rights claims for those sites that are prime spots for mining Molybdenum.

Ⓛ

Our Team

The Moly Mining Co. has excellent employees, all of whom are experienced in their field.

We believe that in order for the environment to benefit us, we must carry out the duties of environmental stewards.

Because we are devoted to the environment, we take many precautions to protect the land, water, and air. We will spare no expense when treating the mine tailings and water needed for the mining process. Our procedures for cleaning the water and mine tailings are unequaled in the industry.

For further information, please contact our specialists:

Tina Snieder President & CEO	970.713.3819 tsnieder@moly.com
Kalee Betcke Vice President for Research & Development	970.713.9287 kbetcke@moly.com
Patrick Franken Director of Operations	970.713.3840 pfranken@moly.com
Sarah Vander Pol Marketing Director	970.713.0281 sarahvp@moly.com

Moly Mining Co.
1243 Main Street
Crested Butte, Colorado 81225

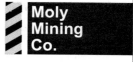

Crested Butte
PROJECT

The Moly Mining Co. (MMC) is currently seeking investors to join our team of specialists in developing a new mine near Crested Butte, Colorado. Through careful research and analysis, we have identified in this area what promises to be a large deposit of Molybdenum. Based on our assessment of related costs, we believe that mining the deposit is a great opportunity for a large return on investment.

Moly Mining Co.

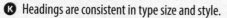

Ⓚ Headings are consistent in type size and style.

Ⓛ Photos frame the copy.

Ⓜ This panel highlights the company and provides contact information.

Additional Real-Word Print Projects

- A **pamphlet** is a small booklet containing information about a single subject.
- A **manual** is a set of instructions for learning about a subject or for operating a device.
- A **poster** is a large printed page publicizing an idea or an event.
- An **infographic** presents a visually appealing combination of information and graphics.
- A **news release** is a written communication announcing a newsworthy item.

Writers INC

Research

Conducting Research

Who, what, when, where, why, and *how* are six very common yet very valuable words in the English language. They are used to ask basic questions about any topic:

- *Who* is Ben Carson?
- *What* is CTE?
- *When* was the first Twitter message sent?
- *Where* can I find information about my ancestors?
- *Why* did males play all the roles in Elizabethan plays?
- *How* did the Allies pull off the D-Day invasion?

Asking questions is the starting point for all types of learning, including the subject of this chapter—conducting research. Questions begin the search for a topic, and questions shape the research that follows. This chapter thoroughly covers the research process—from asking questions to evaluating resources to finding answers.

Learning Outcomes

Ask questions.
Understand resource options.
Select resources.
Evaluate resources.
Carry out research.
Create a working bibliography.
Take notes.

"Research is formalized curiosity. It is poking and prying with a purpose."

Zora Neale Hurston

Asking Questions

Asking questions is an effective way (1) to explore possible topics and (2) to guide your research after choosing one.

Identifying Potential Topics

Suppose you were given this assignment: *In a five-page research paper, examine a critical political or military strategy implemented during World War II.*

Asking questions like those below would lead you to potential writing ideas:

- What was the Lend-Lease Act and how was it implemented?
- What was the strategy behind the German blitzkrieg?
- How did the RAF Bomber Command respond to the indiscriminate German bombing of British cities?
- How did the Allies deceive the Nazis before the D-Day invasion?
- What effect did the *kamikaze* strategy have on the naval war in the Pacific?
- Why did the United States use atomic bombs in Japan?

Guiding Research

After selecting a topic, generating another list of questions can set the course for your research. Suppose you had decided to write about Britain's response to the indiscriminate bombing of London and other cities. Asking the following questions would guide your research. And, you might well use the answers to one or two of these questions as the focus, or thesis, of your paper.

- What prompted Britain's response?
- Who was involved in the decision making?
- Why was that particular strategy implemented?
- What was its effect?
- How did the general population feel about the strategy?
- How did various noteworthy individuals feel about the strategy?

Remember: Posing the journalistic questions—*who? what? when? where? why?* and *how?*—about a topic is always a good way to launch your research.

> "The art and science of asking questions
> is the source of all knowledge."
> Thomas Berger

Understanding Resource Options

Consult a variety of reliable resources—both primary and secondary—to answer your research questions. Be sure always to follow your instructor's requirements. Some instructors may ask you to use at least one primary source during your research. Others may limit your use of online sources.

▍Primary Sources

A primary source is original, giving you firsthand information on a topic. Observing or participating in an activity, interviewing an expert, and reading original documents, speeches, or diaries are examples. A primary source provides information from the author, or "directly from the source."

▍Secondary Sources

Web sites, periodicals, reference books, and nonfiction texts give you secondhand information about a topic. A secondary source can be traced beyond its author to at least one or more other individuals.

Primary Sources	Secondary Sources
A Diary of a WWII British bomber pilot	**A** Article that quotes WWII British bomber pilot
B Manuscript of a House of Commons speech addressing Britain's bombing strategy	**B** Historian's analysis of the House of Commons speech
C Interview with a survivor of the bombing	**C** Documentary about the air war between Germany and Great Britain during WWII

Help File

Some resources are tertiary—that is, thirdhand. They are essentially reports of reports of research and, therefore, are distant from the original information. Examples of tertiary sources would include some articles in popular magazines and entries in Wikipedia or print encyclopedias. Aside from giving you ideas for focusing your topic, tertiary sources should generally not be used in research projects and should not appear in works-cited or reference lists.

Types of Primary Sources

Remember, primary sources inform you directly, not through another person's explanation or interpretation. Here are five basic types of primary sources.

Observing and participating ▪ Observing an event linked to your topic, or participating in it, is a common primary source of information. For example, researching dementia patients and their care may take you to a facility where you can observe your topic firsthand or, if possible, interact with patients and provide some of the care yourself. Testing a hypothesis by conducting an experiment is another primary source of the observation/participation type.

Surveys and questionnaires ▪ Preparing and conducting a survey or a questionnaire can serve very well as a primary source of information. For example, you might survey students in your school about their reading habits. Surveys can be conducted in person, by phone, by email, or by distributing and then collecting the finished surveys later. (See pages 402–403.)

Interviews ▪ Conversing with someone who has expert knowledge of or experience with your topic is another way to collect valuable firsthand information. Interviews can be conducted in person, by phone, by email, or in an online chat. (See the next page.)

Presentations ▪ Attending lectures, visiting museums, and viewing exhibits can provide you with firsthand information about many topics.

Diaries, journals, and letters ▪ Reading diaries, journals, and letters allows you to explore the thoughts of people who are connected in some way to your topic. Look for these writings in autobiographies, in museums, in special library collections, and online.

▌ Using Primary Sources for Research

▪ **Advantages:** Primary sources require your personal analysis and thoughtful involvement, both important components of good research. Also, surveys and interviews that you design and conduct often elicit information that is available nowhere else.

▪ **Disadvantages:** Analyzing the information gleaned from primary sources can be difficult, especially if you have limited background knowledge of the topic. In addition, surveys and interviews are time consuming to prepare, administer, and interpret.

▌ Conducting Interviews

The purpose of an interview is simple. In order to get information, you talk with someone who is an expert on your topic. Use the guidelines below whenever you conduct an interview.

1. Before the interview, do your homework about the topic and your interviewee.

- Arrange the interview in a thoughtful way. Explain your purpose, the process, and the topics to be covered.
- Write questions for each of the specific ideas you want to cover in the interview. The 5 W's and H (who? what? where? when? why? and how?) are important for good coverage.
- Organize your questions in a logical order so that the interview moves smoothly from one subject to the next.
- Write the questions on the left side of a page. Leave room for quotations, information, and impressions on the right side.

2. During the interview, try to relax so that your conversation seems natural and sincere.

- Provide some background information about yourself, your project, and your plans for using the interview information.
- Use recording equipment only if you have the interviewee's permission.
- Jot down key facts, quotations, and impressions.
- Listen actively. Show that you're listening through your body language—eye contact, nods, smiles. Pay attention not only to what the person says but also to how he or she says it.
- Be flexible. If the person looks puzzled by a question, rephrase it. If the discussion gets off track, redirect it. Based on the interviewee's responses, ask follow-up questions. If time allows, ask unplanned questions.

3. After the interview, do the following:

- As soon as possible, review your notes. Fill in responses you remember but couldn't record at the time.
- Document your interview by writing down the interviewee's name, type of interview, and date.
- Thank the interviewee with a note, email, or a phone call.
- If necessary, ask the interviewee to check that your information and quotations are accurate.

Remember: It's always a good idea to offer to send the interviewee a copy of your writing.

Conducting Surveys

One source of information available to all people is the survey. You can use surveys to collect facts and opinions directly from a target audience. To get quality information using a survey, follow these guidelines:

1. Find a focus.
- Limit the purpose of your survey.
- Target a specific audience.

2. Ask clear questions.
- Ask questions that are clear, precise, and complete.
- Use words that are objective (not biased or slanted).
- Make answering relatively easy.
- Offer answer options that are complete and do not overlap.

3. Match your questions to your purpose.
- **Open-ended questions** bring in a wide variety of answers and more complex information, but they take time to complete and the answers are hard to summarize and compile.
- **Closed questions** give respondents easy answer options, and the answers are easy to tabulate. Closed questions can provide two choices (*yes* or *no*, *true* or *false*), multiple choices, a rating or scale (*poor 1 2 3 excellent*), or a blank to fill.

4. Organize your survey so that it's easy to complete.
- In the introduction, state who you are and why you need the information. Explain how to complete the survey and when and where to return it.
- Guide readers with numbers, instructions, and headings.
- Begin with basic questions and end with any necessary complex, open-ended questions. Move in a logical order from one point to the next.
- Give respondents enough room to answer questions.

5. Test your survey.
- Ask a friend or a classmate to read your survey and help you revise it before printing it.
- Check how your survey works with a small test group.

6. Conduct your survey.
- Distribute the survey to a clearly defined group in a way that won't prejudice the sampling (random or cross section).
- Get responses from a good sample (at least 10 percent) of your target group.
- Tabulate responses carefully and objectively.

Sample Survey

<table>
<tr><td>

The introduction provides essential information.

</td><td>

</td></tr>
</table>

Confidential Survey About Learning a Second Language

The introduction provides essential information.

My name is Noelle Green, and I am conducting research about bilingual education in our school. I'd like to hear from you, McKinley High School students. Please answer the questions below by circling or filling in your responses. Then drop your survey in the box outside room 103 by Friday, February 10. Your responses will remain confidential.

The survey begins with clear, basic questions.

1. What is your gender?   **male   female**

2. What grade are you in?   **9   10   11   12**

3. What is your first language?   _____

4. Are you learning a second language?   **yes   no**
   Note: If you circled "no," you may turn in your survey at this point.

The survey covers the topic thoroughly.

5. How long have you been learning the second language?
   1 year   2   3   4   5   6 years or more

6. How are you learning this language?
   foreign language class   bilingual class   tutor   other

7. How would you rate your mastery of the second language?
   very little   1   2   3   4   5   proficient knowledge

The survey asks open-ended questions.

8. Describe the best way to learn a second language.

   _____

   _____

   _____

9. How will you use a second language?

   _____

   _____

   _____

10. How important is it to be bilingual?
    not important   1   2   3   4   5   very important

Note: The results of this survey would add valuable firsthand information to an essay about the merits of bilingual education. (See pages 112–113.)

▌Designing Experiments

The scientific method is an organized way of solving a problem or answering a question. With this method, you make an educated guess, or hypothesis, and then design an experiment to test your idea. The sample responses below are from an experiment conducted by four science students.

Steps in the Scientific Method

1. Ask a question. As you study any topic, questions will occur. Select an especially interesting one.

> Will an invasive species called Eastern red cedar threaten the growth of native prairie grasses?

2. Propose a hypothesis. A hypothesis is a statement that predicts what you suspect is true. Your experiment will test this hypothesis.

> Eastern red cedar and the surrounding soil will negatively affect the germination and growth of native prairie grasses.

3. Research other experiments. Learn about the work other people have already done on the topic.

> Many studies have been conducted on the impact of invasive species in tall-grass prairies, some of which show that the impact is significant.

4. Design and conduct an experiment. Control as many variables as possible so that the results can be attributed to one specific variable or cause.

> - Soil was gathered in a state park from three different locations under three different cedar trees as well as from three non-cedar locations. All of the soils were dried and stored separately.
> - Trays of soil were prepared identically and labeled.
> - Black-eyed Susans and poppies were planted in the soil according to the directions on the packages.
> - Each day, the trays received identical amounts of water, light, and heat.
> - Seed germination was carefully observed and recorded.

5. Analyze the results. Study the data to prove, disprove, or revise your hypothesis.

> Germination differences and survival rates of the seed types planted in the different soils were noted and analyzed.

6. Discuss the results and draw a conclusion. While some experiments may offer a clear yes-or-no answer to the validity of a hypothesis, others will raise new questions or suggest revisions of the same experiment.

> No significant differences were found in the germination or the survival of the two native plants in the prepared soil samples.

Types of Secondary Sources

Secondary sources are those that give you secondhand information. In other words, the person who wrote or recorded this information got it from someone else. Here are basic types of secondary sources of information.

Nonfiction books ▪ Histories, biographies, and how-to books can provide thorough information about topics. The key is finding books that are up to date, adequately researched, and authored by experts.

Periodicals ▪ Magazines, journals, and newspapers published on a regular basis usually contain up-to-date information. Magazines focus on general areas of interest while scholarly journals address professional pursuits.

Government publications ▪ Many government agencies regularly publish guides, reports, pamphlets, and brochures about their work.

Audiovisual resources ▪ Television documentaries, special news shows, and radio interviews can serve as valuable sources of information, although some news sources can be biased.

Electronic sources ▪ Computer technology allows access to a multitude of Web sites brimming with information. The key is learning how to maneuver within the Web and correctly judge the reliability of the information you find. (See pages 364–366 and 411–413.)

Remember: Encyclopedias, atlases, directories, and almanacs are sources of general information. They provide thirdhand or tertiary information by sharing details from secondary sources. Reference books are good starting points for a research project, but they are not necessarily in-depth, comprehensive sources of information.

▌ Using Secondary Sources for Research

▪ **Advantages:** Secondary sources can provide expert perspectives and insights. Peer reviews usually ensure the quality of information in scholarly articles. Also, consulting secondary sources may be more efficient than planning and conducting primary-research strategies.

▪ **Disadvantages:** Finding information applicable to your research topic can be time consuming. And in some cases, that information may be biased or based on faulty research. In addition, secondary sources can quickly become outdated.

"The greatest part of a writer's time is spent in reading. In order to write, a man will turn over half a library to make one book."

Samuel Johnson

Understanding Nonfiction Books

Knowing the parts of a book enables you to use it more effectively in your research project. It is especially important to learn how to make full use of a book's table of contents, index, glossary, and bibliography. The main parts of nonfiction books are listed below and shown on the facing page.

▮ Basic Parts of a Book

Knowing the parts of a book can help you find information easily and quickly. Note that an appendix, a glossary, a bibliography, and an index are typically found only in nonfiction books.

- The **title page** is usually the first printed page in a book. It gives (1) the full title of the book, (2) the author's name, (3) the publisher's name, and (4) the place of publication.

- The **copyright page** follows the title page. Here you will find the year the copyright was issued. When you are looking for up-to-date facts, be sure to check the book's copyright. Remember, though, the copyright date is often the year after a book was actually written.

- The **preface**, **foreword**, or **introduction** come before the table of contents and give an overview of what the book is about and why it was written.

- The **table of contents** lists the names and numbers of the major divisions of the book and the page on which each begins. The table of contents can give you a good overview of what the book is about.

- The **body** is the main text of the book.

- An **epigraph** is a quotation at the beginning of a chapter or a division; an epigraph sets forth the main idea.

- A **footnote** is placed at the bottom of a page and either gives the source of information used in the text or adds useful information. (Endnotes have the same function but appear at the end of a chapter or the end of a book.)

- An **appendix** may follow the body. It provides additional information, often in the form of maps, charts, tables, diagrams, or documents.

- A **glossary** will sometimes follow the appendix. It is an alphabetical listing of key words and definitions related to the topic of the book.

- The **bibliography** will list sources used by the author, suggestions for further reading, or both.

- The **index** is an alphabetical list of all the topics covered in the book along with the page number or numbers on which each topic is covered.

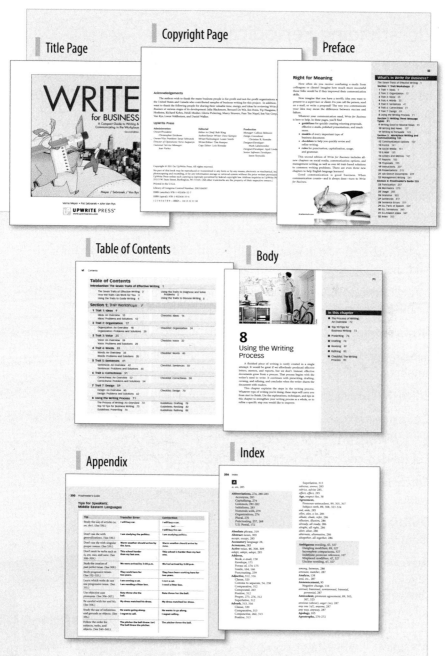

Title Page

Copyright Page

Preface

Table of Contents

Body

8

Using the Writing Process

Appendix

Index

Help File

The index is probably the most useful part of any reference book. It tells you whether the book contains the information you need and, second, where you can find it.

Understanding Periodicals

Most newspapers are published daily, while magazines and journals are published weekly, monthly, quarterly, or at some other regular interval. Almost all periodicals have both print and online versions, although the online version may omit some content provided in the print version.

Basic Parts of a Newspaper

Most print newspapers include the following parts.

- The **front page** includes the nameplate (the paper's designed title), issue date, the most important headlines and news stories, and an index of sections.

- The **masthead**, which is often found on the editorial page, lists the publisher/chairman, editors, officers, and address information.

- Different **sections** separate news, sports, editorial (opinion), entertainment, business and finance, and so on.

- **News stories** are basic stories that explain the day's news.

- **Feature stories** are in-depth stories that discuss important topics from a number of angles.

- **Editorials** are opinion pieces written by an editor of the paper.

- **Columns** are opinion or advice pieces written by syndicated columnists or columnists who work for the paper.

- **Letters to the editor** are opinion pieces from readers.

- **Editorial cartoons** are illustrations that express opinions about current events.

- **Obituaries** are announcements that offer specific information about the deaths of local citizens.

- **Advertisements** are placed within newspapers to generate revenue. Some inside pages will contain advertisements that look and sound like straight news stories. Classified ads appear in a special section and are arranged by category.

antb / Shutterstock.com

▌ Basic Parts of a News Story

Headline

Byline

Lead
paragraph

Explanation
and
amplification

Background
information

Computer Equipment Stolen

by Jamie Siegrist

Early Monday morning, three iPads and a computer printer were reported stolen from the Learning Resource Center, according to Rob Robinson, director of the center.

Robinson said the equipment was worth $2,000. He added that the center received the iPads only a month ago.

Manuals for the equipment were also taken from the LRC circulation desk, leading investigators to believe that the person who stole the equipment knew the center fairly well. Robinson said that to his knowledge no suspects have been identified.

"Truthfully, students would be the last people I would suspect because I know them so well, and they have the most to lose if caught," said Robinson.

There were no signs of a break-in, so it is suspected that someone may have hidden in the center at the end of the day on Friday. It is also possible that someone made a key, according to Robinson. He said a better security system is being discussed.

Last year, two VCRs were stolen from the A-V room adjacent to the computer center. After that theft, locks in the A-V room were changed. All of the electronic equipment in the center was untouched then, so it was thought that the center was safe from burglary.

- The **headline** is a brief descriptive title that announces the topic of the story.

- The **byline** names the writer of the story.

- The **lead paragraph** answers the basic journalistic questions—*who? What? where? when? why?* and *how?* It is most often the first paragraph in the story.

- **Explanation and amplification** occurs in body paragraphs. These body paragraphs provide additional details about the information covered in the lead paragraph.

- **Background information** is provided at the end to provide context for the story.

Basic Parts of Magazines and Journals

Most print magazines and journals include the following parts. (Some online editions may also include videos and links to other sites.)

- The **front cover** of a magazine or journal provides the title, volume and issue numbers, and the publication date. It also announces one or more special articles in the issue, usually with a corresponding graphic. (Each separate printing with a new date marks a new issue of a magazine or journal. A journal volume, especially a scholarly work, may contain a year's worth of issues.)

- The **masthead** is similar to the copyright page of a book. It lists publication information (publisher, editors, directors, and addresses). The masthead appears in small print on one of the magazine's initial pages.

- The **table of contents** lists all of the articles in a particular issue. Some publications may provide more than one table of contents: a "Features" page first, followed by a "Departments" page of other articles.

- An **editor's note** will often appear on the opening page, introducing the issue and providing background for the articles that follow.

- A **letters** page includes print readers' letters about articles in previous issues. In online versions, these messages may appear in a comments list following the article.

- The **body** is the main portion of the publication that contains the articles. (Magazines are usually paginated by issue. That is, each issue begins with page number 1. Journals may be paginated by volume. The first issue each year will begin with page 1, and subsequent issues will begin where the previous issue left off.)

- **Advertisements** may appear as regularly as articles in magazines. Be aware that some advertisers try to make their ads look like articles. Journals generally have fewer advertisements than magazines do.

- **Indexes** sometimes appear in journals. Journal issues may include an index of articles, and volumes often include an index of issues.

Popartic / Shutterstock.com

Selecting Resources

Carefully examine each resource you are considering using. Choosing only reliable sources will establish your own credibility as a researcher.

▌ Consider the Source

Use the tips that follow to help you begin to evaluate sources.

Assess the worthiness of sources by asking these basic questions.

- How closely related to my topic is this source?
- Does the coverage seem too basic, overly complex, or just about right?
- What could this source add to my understanding of the topic?

If you were investigating the first response of the British to indiscriminate German bombing, for example, an in-depth article by a noted WWII historian may prove more valuable than a newspaper story marking the anniversary of the first bombing.

Skim sources before reading them closely.

- Review the author's biography, the preface, and the introduction to determine the source's approach, scope, and quality of research.
- Read the first few paragraphs and skim any headings, graphics, and text summaries.
- For electronic sources, review the site's home page and any of these items: outline, abstract, table of contents, and index.
- Consider marking key pages with sticky notes, tabs, or digital bookmarks.

Approach sources with an open mind.

- Consider the purpose and audience of the text. Was it written to inform or to persuade? Is it addressing the general public or specialists? Is it addressing supporters or opponents of a particular point of view?
- Check for readability. Is the text organized and easy to follow? Relate each source to your research questions. Will it help you find answers?
- Consider how you might use the information in your writing.
- Check the footnotes, references, appendices, and links to additional sources.

Assessing Source Reliability

Judge the worth of each source on its own merit, but understand that sources can also be rated according to authorship, reliability, treatment, and so on. This list can help you determine the merit of various types of resources.

	Source	Description	Examples
Deep, Reliable Sources	Scholarly Works	Peer-reviewed, carefully researched material written by experts	▪ *New England Journal of Medicine* ▪ *Journal of Nutrition*
	Government Publications	Materials created by experts at government agencies and provided for public use	▪ *Federal Register* ▪ *Consumer Action Handbook* ▪ *PubMed.gov*
	Trade Publications	Books and articles created by experts and published for a general educated audience	▪ *National Geographic* ▪ *The Economist* ▪ *Smithsonian*
	Reference Texts	Textbooks and encyclopedias created for general research	▪ *Encyclopedia Britannica* ▪ *The College Writer*
	Official Web Sites	Materials created and posted by reputable organizations	▪ *Redcross.org* ▪ *Stanford.edu*
	News Reports	Articles published in regular news sources to inform the public about current events	▪ *The Washington Post* ▪ *Newsweek* ▪ *NBC Nightly News*
	Popular Magazines	General-interest articles without documentation accompanied by much advertising	▪ *People* ▪ *Us* ▪ *Popular Mechanics*
	Business Sources	Materials published by known businesses to promote products	▪ *Target.com* ▪ *Macys.com*
	General Web Material	Undocumented materials available on the Web through unknown sources	▪ Unknown or personal sites
Shallow, Unreliable Sources	Sensational/ Joke Material	Biased and absurd stories meant to sell advertising	▪ *The Star* ▪ *The National Enquirer* ▪ *The Onion*

Evaluating Resources

To evaluate the reliability and worthiness of a source, check it against the following criteria, including the extra "Web checks."

Authorship ▪ Is the author an expert on the topic? What are his or her credentials? For example, a physician sharing information about a particular treatment is far more credible than a celebrity doing the same in a commercial.
- ▪ *Web check:* Is an author indicated, along with his or her credentials and contact information?

Reliability ▪ Has the information been published by a scholarly or university press, a quality book publisher, or a trusted news source? Did you find the source through a reliable search engine?
- ▪ *Web check:* Which individual or group posted the information? How stable is the site—has it been live for an extended period of time? Check the site's home page and read the mission statement. Look for evidence of the organization's merit and value.

Treatment ▪ Notice any biases in the text. A biased source pushes a particular agenda and is seldom "fair and balanced." Watch, in particular, for bias toward a certain political party or industry. Also be alert to listed financial backers.
- ▪ *Web check:* Is the site published by a reliable group—nonprofit (.org), government (.gov), commercial (.com), educational (.edu), informational (.info), network related (.net), or military (.mil)? Is the organization promoting a particular cause, product, service, or belief? How does advertising affect the site?

Relevancy ▪ Be sure that the text provides relevant information. A three-year-old book about treatment for a flu virus may be outdated, while a thirty-year-old analysis of President Johnson's "War on Poverty" may still be valid.
- ▪ *Web check:* When was the material originally posted and last updated? Are links live or dead?

Accuracy ▪ Be alert for factual errors and questions about documentation. Are sources cited? If so, can you locate them, and are they credible?
- ▪ *Web check:* Does the site contain solid, useful information, or is it thin in content? Is the information unsubstantiated?

Help File

Evaluate visual resources with equal care. Ask yourself the following questions to judge the usefulness of charts, graphs, and photos. (Also see pages 367–376.)
- ▪ Is the graphic informative or decorative?
- ▪ Is it well designed and easy to follow?
- ▪ What does the graphic include or exclude in terms of data?
- ▪ Does it communicate a clear main idea?

Carrying Out Research

For most research projects, you will look either online or in your library. Using either source requires an understanding of search procedures.

Understand the Basics of Electronic Searches

- **Identify a specific topic before conducting a keyword search:** Precisely stated topics will lead to the best results. (You can also use a research question to initiate your search.)

> **Potentially too broad:** German bombing during WWII
> **More specific:** The German Blitz bombing of London

- **Consider other keywords:** Break your topic into parts or terms. Each term is a potential keyword. Also list alternative words or phrases for your search.

> **Examples:** baseball, outside the U.S., approaches
> **Alternatives:** international baseball, baseball in Latin America, in Japan

- **Use Boolean operators to refine your search:** Combining keywords with Boolean operators can improve your search results.

Operator	Examples	Result
and or +	baseball **and** international baseball **+** international	files with both keywords
not or -	international baseball **not** Japanese international baseball **-** Japanese	baseball, but not Japanese
quotation marks (" ")	"international baseball"	files with this exact phrasing
or	Japanese baseball **or** Latin American baseball	files for either term

- **Evaluate your results:** Effective keywords usually bring meaningful results. If you're unhappy with your results, revise your keywords.

- **Go beyond the first page:** You may find your most worthwhile research site on a later page, so keep clicking to the next pages to complete your search.

- **Use multiple search sites:** Different search engines use different algorithms to find and rank results, so go beyond your favorite search engine.

- **Consider advanced search strategies:** If your search program offers a link to an "advanced search" option, take advantage of this feature.

Using the Library

Most print sources—including nonfiction books, reference books, periodicals, and special collections—are housed in school or community libraries. Locating these sources requires an understanding of your library's services.

▊ Staff

Librarians, media specialists, technicians, and assistants can help you find what you need. Their duties may be divided among several desks.

- **Circulation desk:** Here you'll check out materials to be used outside the library.
- **Media services desk:** Here you'll get help with electronic media like videos, audio recordings, computer software, and other devices.
- **Reference desk:** Here you'll find access to almanacs, periodical guides, and archives of periodicals on microfilm. Usually, reference materials cannot be removed from the library.

▊ Resources

- **Computer catalogs:** Every library keeps a catalog of its books and other media, identifying where to find each item. You can search by title, author, or subject.
- **Print books:** Nonfiction books are usually shelved according to the Dewey decimal system, which divides subjects into ten main classes:

000–099 General	**400–499** Languages	**800–899** Literature
100–199 Philosophy	**500–599** Sciences	**900–999** History,
200–299 Religion	**600–699** Technology	Travel, and Geography
300–399 Social Science	**700–799** Arts and Rec.	

  - *Fiction* books are shelved separately, arranged alphabetically by the author's last name.
  - *Biographies* are shelved separately, arranged alphabetically by the subject's last name.

- **Ebooks:** Your library may also lend ebooks and ebook devices.
- **Periodicals:** Libraries subscribe to many types of periodicals. You'll find recent newspapers, magazines, and scholarly journals as well as bound collections of old issues. Some may be stored on computer files or microfilm.
- **Special collections:** Often, libraries house historical documents of local importance. You must ask for permission to view them.
- **Electronic media:** Videos, audio recordings, and computer programs, along with the equipment to use them, are usually available.
- **Personal computers:** Computer stations for public use, often with Internet access, are usually available.

Creating a Working Bibliography

A working bibliography lists sources you intend to use in your research. Making this list is a good way to keep track of your sources, avoid plagiarism, and develop the final works-cited page or bibliography for your research paper. Create your working bibliography on note cards, in a notebook, or on a computer. Arrange your sources alphabetically by the author's last name and number each entry.

▌ What to Include

For each source, include all of the essential publishing information shown here.

- **Books:** author, title and subtitle, publication details (place, publisher, date)
- **Periodicals:** author, article title, journal name, publication information (volume, number, date), page numbers
- **Online sources:** author (if available), document title, site sponsor, database name, publication or posting date, access date, other publication information, URL
- **Primary or field research:** date conducted, name or descriptive title of person interviewed, place observed, survey conducted, document analyzed

Help File

To help you retrace your research footsteps, consider including location details for each source.

- **Books:** Include the call number.
- **Periodical articles:** Note where you accessed them (stacks, current periodicals, online).
- **Web pages:** Record the URL.
- **Field research:** Include a telephone number or an email address.

Sample Bibliography Note Card

> 3
>
> **Internet Source Note**
>
> Gardiner, Judith. "As London Lay Smoking." New Statesman Web site.
> 28 June 2011. Accessed 23 October 2013.
>
> https://www.newstatesman.com/ideas/2011/06/bombing-bell-
> essay-lambeth

Taking Notes

Effective note taking allows you to gather relevant information and record it in a way that will be useful to you later on. It is essential to a research project. Keep your specific topic in mind and use your research questions to stay on track as you take notes. This way you will be able to identify and record the ideas, facts, and quotations that will serve your research in the best way. Here are some additional tips:

- **Use your own words.** Summarize and paraphrase information to show and record your understanding of important ideas.
- **Highlight words and terms.** In your notes, underline the key terms related to your topic.
- **Record useful quotations.** Write down quotations that truly support your own thinking and the main points you will explore in your research report. A well-placed quotation can add authority to your paper. However, be selective, and remember to record quotations exactly.
- **Identify the sources.** Always record the source of the ideas and quotations in your notes for later documentation.

Sample Note Cards

Why did Bishop Bell oppose retaliatory bombing?

- wanted Archbishop of Canterbury to condemn the bombing
- saw German people as separate from Nazis
- questioned policies that limited German options
- worried about "postwar bitterness"

Gardiner, Judith. "As London Lay Smoking." New Statesman Web site. 28 June 2011.

What was the response to Bell?

- Archbishop Temple wanted to "disassociate" himself from Bell
- Churchill infuriated by him
- Bell: "There were moments during the war, when people thought I went too far pleading against obliteration either of city or of nation."

Gardiner, Judith. "As London Lay Smoking." New Statesman Web site. 28 June 2011.

A Closer Look

Two-column notes. In this system of note taking, reserve two-thirds of the page for source notes and one-third for your own thoughts and reflections. Include the source's essential publishing information either at the top of the page before your research question, or at the end of that portion of notes.

Why did Bishop Bell oppose retaliatory bombing?

The distinction between the German people and the Nazi Party valid.	• wanted Archbishop of Canterbury to condemn the bombing • saw German people as separate from Nazis
Was that belief held by others?	• questioned policies that limited German options; they had to fight to finish

Gardiner, Judith. "As London Lay Smoking." <u>New Statesman</u> Web site. 28 June 2011.

Electronic notes. With a portable computer—or Internet access to a personal account—you can take notes with a word-processing program or note-taking application. The notes can be easily edited and reorganized, making them a good launching point for writing. With a touch screen, drawing pad, or mouse, you may be able to add simple sketches to your notes.

Printouts. Printouts of Web pages, other Internet files, and microfilm documents can enhance your notes. You can write directly on printouts. Remember to write documentation details in the margins.

Photocopies. Copying a few pages from a print source allows you to highlight important points and write your own thoughts as well as documentation information in the margins.

Audio and video recordings. Recordings are useful for interviews and other events. Portions of such recordings can be embedded in multimedia projects. Finally, a pocket voice recorder is a handy tool for saving your own thoughts and ideas.

Snapshots and OCR. Digital cameras—including those on cell phones and on portable media devices and computers—can capture a printed page, a computer screen, a work of art, and so on. If your device has Internet access, you can upload the photos to a file-saving site, email them to yourself, or save them to a note-taking application. Optical-character-recognition (OCR) apps and services can even convert photographed text to a document you can edit.

Writing the Research Paper

A research paper is a carefully documented essay resulting from the thorough investigation of a topic. You may gather information from secondary sources such as books and Web sites as well as from primary sources such as interviews and diaries. In the end, however, it's your own thoughts and observations about the topic that truly count.

The combination of searching, analyzing, and writing involved in meaningful research requires time. That is why instructors often assign a research project far in advance of the due date. They may also establish a timetable to help you manage the workload. Typically, research papers contain five or more pages of text plus a works-cited page. This chapter offers step-by-step guidelines for writing a research paper.

Learning Outcomes

Plan your research.
Write the first draft.
Revise and edit your writing.

"He who would search for pearls must dive below."

John Dryden

Planning Your Research

The initial steps in the research process may be the most important. Among other things, you must identify a topic, gather information about it, and establish a thesis for your writing.

Understanding the Assignment

1. **Analyzing the rhetorical situation . . .** To begin, identify the rhetorical elements (*subject, purpose, audience,* etc.) of the assignment. You can do this by answering the **STRAP** questions.

   Suppose your history instructor hands out this assignment: *In a five-page research paper, examine a critical political or military strategy implemented during World War II. Follow the MLA documentation style for your paper.*

   > **S**ubject: A critical political or military strategy during WWII
   > **T**ype: Research paper following MLA guidelines
   > **R**ole: History student studying WWII
   > **A**udience: Instructor and classmates
   > **P**urpose: To examine, which means to investigate and analyze

2. **Noting other aspects of the assignment . . .** Be clear about the assignment's requirements, including the number and types of sources that you must consult, due dates for different parts, whether you need to include a title page and outline, and so on. Your instructor may establish a timetable to help you pace your work. Here is an example:

Research Timetable

Prewriting: *(two to three weeks)*
- Select a specific topic.
- Generate a working bibliography.
- Establish a thesis.
- Organize your research.

Due Date: _____

Revising: *(one week)*
- Ask for two peer reviews.
- Prepare a clean revised draft.
- Attach all earlier revisions to the clean draft.

Due Date: _____

Writing the First Draft:
(one week)

Due Date: _____

Editing: *(one week)*
- Check for proper documentation.
- Prepare a final copy according to guidelines.
- Proofread this copy before submitting it.

Due Date: _____

Selecting a Topic

3. **Searching for a specific topic . . .** Start by reviewing your class textbook and notebook for writing ideas. You may also talk with your classmates about the assignment, write freely about World War II in your notebook, or search the Web. Your instructor may suggest effective starting points for a Web search.

4. **Evaluating a possible topic . . .** A potential topic is worth exploring if you can answer yes to each of the following questions:
   - Am I truly interested in the topic?
   - Does it meet the requirements of the assignment?
   - Do I have access to enough information about it?
   - Is the topic limited enough to cover in a single report?

   The last question is crucial. You couldn't, for example, write about World War II air strategies, a topic that spans several years and many developments, in a five-page paper. Even focusing on German air strategies alone is too general. However, a specific topic such as the British response to the German Blitz of London in 1940–1941 would be limited enough to cover effectively in a research paper.

5. **Focusing your efforts . . .** After choosing a specific topic, research it to learn more about the topic in general. Then decide on a particular part of the topic that truly interests you. That focus will drive the rest of your research. The chart below shows how the focusing process works.

The Focusing Process

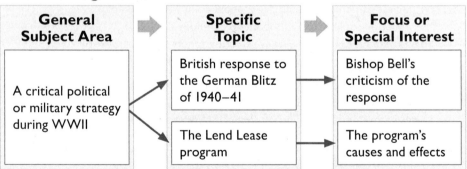

General Subject Area	Specific Topic	Focus or Special Interest
A critical political or military strategy during WWII	British response to the German Blitz of 1940–41	Bishop Bell's criticism of the response
	The Lend Lease program	The program's causes and effects

6. **Writing a thesis statement . . .** Once you have established the focus for your research, you are ready to write a thesis statement, or controlling idea. The thesis is the main idea that you will examine or prove in your paper. (See the next page for guidelines and examples.)

   Note: At this point, you have a working thesis statement. As you learn more about your topic, you may change your mind about it. If this happens, revise your thesis accordingly.

Thesis Statement Writing Tips

An effective thesis statement tells the reader exactly what you plan to write about in your paper. It also focuses your continued research of your topic.

The Process at Work

A thesis statement may express a specific feeling about your topic, point to a particular feature of it, or take a stand. Write as many versions as it takes to find the one that sets the right tone for your writing. Use this formula:

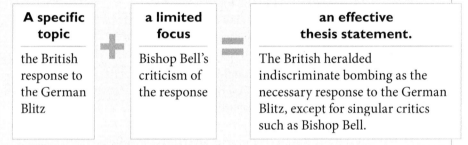

A specific topic		a limited focus		an effective thesis statement.
the British response to the German Blitz	✚	Bishop Bell's criticism of the response	═	The British heralded indiscriminate bombing as the necessary response to the German Blitz, except for singular critics such as Bishop Bell.

Sample Thesis Statements

Writing assignment: Analysis of a novel
    Specific topic: *Frankenstein* by Mary Shelley
    Thesis statement: Mary Shelley's novel *Frankenstein (topic)* focuses on the theme of friendship *(feature)*.

Writing assignment: Research paper about computer technology
    Specific topic: Current robotics technology
    Thesis statement: Engineers are creating robots *(topic)* capable of sophisticated human thinking *(feature)*.

Writing assignment: Research paper about energy
    Specific topic: Wind power
    Thesis statement: Wind power *(topic)* is cleaner and more cost effective than nuclear power *(stand)*.

Thesis Checklist

Your thesis statement must . . .

- ____ identify a specific topic;
- ____ express a particular feeling about or feature of the topic, or take a stand;
- ____ share a clear, coherent idea;
- ____ be supported with convincing facts and details; and
- ____ meet the requirements of the assignment.

Searching for Information

7. Using a working bibliography . . . A working bibliography lists sources you intend to use in your research. With this bibliography, you can keep track of your sources, avoid plagiarism, and develop your final works-cited page. Record bibliography entries on note cards, in a notebook, or on a computer. Arrange the sources alphabetically by the author's last name, number each entry, and include details about the location of each source.

Sample Bibliography Note Card

Internet Source Note   3

Gardiner, Judith. "As London Lay Smoking." New Statesman Web site. 28 June 2011. Accessed 23 October 2013.

https://www.newstatesman.com/ideas/2011/06/bombing-bell-essay-lambeth

Sample Note Card

Why did Bishop Bell oppose retaliatory bombing?   3

- wanted Archbishop of Canterbury to condemn the bombing
- saw German people as separate from Nazis
- questioned policies that limited German options
- worried about "postwar bitterness"

Gardiner, Judith. "As London Lay Smoking." New Statesman Web site. 28 June 2011.

---

8. Taking notes . . . As you consult secondary sources, take notes and write out useful quotations related to your thesis. Your notes should identify relevant information and record it in a way that is useful to you later on.

- Keep notes on cards of the same size (four-by-six-inch cards are recommended), in a notebook, or on a computer.
- Record important details along with the page numbers where the information can be found. Also place the number of the related bibliography card in the upper right-hand corner.
- Place quotations marks around word-for-word quotations.
- Use an ellipsis (. . .) in place of words you omit from a quotation. Place brackets [ ] around words you add to quotations.
- Look up unfamiliar words and copy their definitions onto the note cards where they appear.
- Give each card a descriptive heading, either an appropriate phrase or question.

Searching Tips

To organize your research and note taking, write a series of questions that you would like to answer. When you find information that answers a question, take notes on it.

Sample Questions

1. What prompted the British response?
2. Who was involved in the decision making?
3. How was the strategy implemented?
4. How was the response received by the general population?
5. Why was Bishop Bell critical of the decision?

9. Using primary sources . . . Collect firsthand information if possible. Consider writing e-mails or letters to experts, taking surveys, conducting interviews, and so on.

Designing a Writing Plan

10. Organizing your research . . . After you have completed your research, plan your writing by listing or outlining the main points you want to cover in your paper. Use the headings on your note cards or your list of research questions to form your plan. Here is a plan for the sample research paper on pages 457–462. An outline for the paper appears on page 456.

Sample Writing Plan

1. Introduction—presents topic and thesis
2. Background information—establishes the setting
3. Examination of the decision making
4. Specifics of the response
5. Bishop Bell's criticism and reaction to it
6. Conclusion—sums up main points

11. Continuing your research as needed . . . If necessary, search for additional information to develop your thesis. Revise your thesis and writing plan if the new details change your mind about the topic and prompt more research.

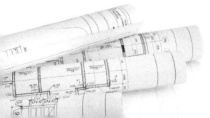

Writing the First Draft

In a first draft, you connect your information and thoughts about the topic for the first time. Write this draft in one sitting, if possible, while the research is fresh in your mind. Here are some additional tips.

Writing Tips

- Revisit the rhetorical situation so you are clear about your *purpose, audience, role*, and so on. (See page 420.)
- Use your own words as much as possible. Include the ideas of others (paraphrases) or direct quotations only when they add significant support to your thesis. (See pages 434–436.)
- Present your ideas honestly and clearly. If you feel strongly about your research and have something meaningful to say, you are more likely to write an interesting paper.
- Work to achieve a formal to semiformal style. Avoid fragments, abbreviations, informal expressions, and slang.
- Present only ideas that you can support with facts and details.

I. Developing the introduction . . . The opening accomplishes two objectives. You must (a) introduce your topic, gaining the reader's attention and paving the way for your thesis, and (b) identify the thesis of your research.

Starting Strategies
- Start with a revealing story or quotation.
- Give important background information.
- Offer a series of interesting or surprising facts.
- Introduce an important concept.
- State your reason for choosing this topic.

Sample Introduction

No one argues the idea that Hitler needed to be stopped. His fascist regime was so shocking that even controversial decisions by the "good guys" during WWII—dropping two atomic bombs, for example—cannot make him seem any less evil. If this is still the case in 2014, then how much more evil must he have appeared to the citizens of Great Britain, an island nation who trembled beneath the force of the hellish German bombing?

2. **Writing the body . . .** The body of your paper presents information that supports or proves your thesis. You can either write freely, relying on the thoughts and ideas that you have processed during your research, or you can work systematically, carefully following your notes and writing plan.

> **Writing Freely** To proceed in this way, put your writing plan and note cards aside and write as much as you can on your own. Refer to your note cards only when you need a quotation, specific facts, or figures. After you have completed this first writing, review your plan and your note cards to see if you have missed or misplaced any important points. Then continue writing, filling in or reorganizing ideas as you go along.
>
> **Writing Systematically** To work in a systematic fashion, carefully follow your writing plan and note cards right from the start. Begin by laying out the first section of note cards (those covering the first main point in your plan). Then write a general statement that covers the first main point. Using the note cards you have in front of you, add supporting facts and details. Repeat this process until you have dealt with all the main points in your plan.

Remember: Each main supporting point (the phrase or question at the top of each set of notes) should be developed in a separate paragraph.

3. **Writing the conclusion . . .** Your paper's ending should leave the reader with a clear understanding of your research topic. You can accomplish this by summarizing your main points and presenting a conclusion or, using a more personal voice, you can discuss how your research has either strengthened or changed your thinking about the topic.

Sample Conclusion

> We naturally support actions that put history on "our side," but we can't really afford to view these actions with an uncritical eye. Otherwise, we may repeat mistakes of the past. For example, some say that the drone bombing in Pakistan is a huge mistake because of the civilian casualties it can cause. Of course, if we were victims of the Blitz in 1940, we may have had a hard time siding with Bishop Bell. The shock and horror of the bombing would have been too much. In retrospect, however, his controversial stand has merit, both morally and militarily. We should study it, and learn from it.

"A conclusion is the place where you got tired of thinking."
Martin Henry Fischer

Revising and Editing Your Writing

Your first draft is the end product of your researching and planning, but it also holds the raw material that you will revise and edit as you develop your finished paper. (See page 464 for a rubric that can serve as a revising and editing guide.)

Improving Your Writing

1. **Taking a break . . .** If possible, set your paper aside for a day or two before you revise and edit it. Taking a break from your work enables you to return to it with a fresh, objective attitude.

2. **Reviewing your writing . . .** To begin the revising process, read your work carefully at least two times: once silently and once aloud.

   - **First look at the big picture.** Decide if you have effectively developed your thesis, or if you have changed your mind about the thesis. Ask yourself questions like these:

     - *Have I effectively developed the thesis?*
     - *Are my main points clear and complete?*
     - *Do I address the reader's most likely questions about the topic?*
     - *Have I presented the information in a logical order?*

   - **Then look at specific parts**—the introduction, the body paragraphs, and the conclusion.

3. **Seeking advice . . .** Ask at least one other person (writing peer, instructor, family member) to review your first draft. Share your own concerns about the writing, and ask the reviewer to look for parts that are unclear or evoke questions.

4. **Making changes . . .** Focus your attention on cleanly developing your thesis. Add, cut, move, or rework parts as necessary to improve the clarity and coherence of your writing.

5. **Documenting your sources . . .** Give credit for the ideas and direct quotations taken from your sources. Also prepare the works-cited section, which lists all the sources you have cited in the text of your paper. (See pages 442–454, 463, and 470–477.)

6. **Checking for accuracy . . .** After you are satisfied with the content of your paper, carefully edit your writing for accuracy. First check the accuracy of your documentation. Then look for spelling, grammar, usage, and mechanics errors. Also ask a trusted peer or instructor to check your writing for errors.

Completing Your Final Copy

7. Following the appropriate style . . . Refer to pages 456–463 for MLA formatting guidelines, and to page 466 for APA guidelines.

8. Setting up the first page . . . If you are following MLA guidelines, type your name, the name of the instructor, the course title, and the date in the upper left-hand corner. (Begin one inch from the top and double-space.) In the upper right-hand corner, type your last name and the page number 1. Center the title beneath the date (double-space before and after the title); then type the first line of your paper. (Also see "Help File" below.)

9. Setting up the other pages . . . Double-space your entire paper, including the works-sited section. Do not justify the right margins and leave a one-inch margin on all sides. Repeat your last name and the appropriate page number on all pages, including the works-cited page. (See pages 456–463 for a formatted research paper.)

10. Proofreading your final copy . . . Check the final draft from beginning to end, working diligently to submit an error-free paper.

Help File

If your instructor requires a title page, center the title one-third of the way down from the top of the page; then center your name, the name of your instructor, course title, and date two-thirds of the way down. If you need to submit an outline, prepare or revise it to follow the final version of your paper. (See page 456.)

A Thorn Beneath the Shining Armor:
Area Bombing and Bishop Bell

Robert Minto
Mr. Sewell
World History
30 January 2014

Minto 1

rn Beneath the Shining Armor:
ea Bombing and Bishop Bell
at Hitler needed to be stopped. His fascist regime
troversial decisions by the "good guys" during
bombs, for example—cannot make him seem
ase in 2014, then how much more evil must he
f Great Britain, an island nation who trembled
German bombing?
the fight against him and his Nazi Party could
usade. When the citizens of London suffered
e good guys—in this case, Winston Churchill
nd—responded with their own area bombing of
mbing was a necessary response to the German
such as Bishop Bell who questioned this
grounds.

er Command authorized its first operation
bers carried pamphlets urging the German
Garrett 9). Eight months passed before
ing more lethal than literature against
Neville Chamberlain believed that bombs
d not help the cause. In a parliamentary
following:

Minto 7

Works Cited

ates. Vol. 125. London: British House of Lords,

in Greatness. London: Oxford University

dern History of International Law of Armed
ess, 1983. Print.

ry Debates. Vol. 337. London: British House

ars, and Sweat: The Great Speeches. Ed.
guin Books, 2002. Print.

. New York: W.W. Norton and Co.,

moking." New Statesman. New Statesman,

wer in World War II: The British Bombing
Martin's Press, 1997. Print.

l." Great Lives. BBC Radio 4, 5

p of Chichester. Oxford University Press,

History Learning Site. History Learning

nd the Strategic Bombing Offensive,
Press, 1984. Print.

mburg. London: Allen Lane Publishers,

artacus Education

Writing Responsibly

Philosopher Kenneth Burke described life as an ongoing conversation. Of course, by the time you arrive, the conversation has already begun. You listen, think, and eventually say something. Others may agree with you, disagree, or perhaps think a moment before adding their own comments. And the conversation keeps moving.

The research paper is a smaller model of that process. You research a topic to find out what others have said about it. Eventually, you share your thoughts in writing. However, to do this responsibly, you must give credit to the people whose ideas influenced your own. Otherwise, you are robbing them and your reader, who will not have the opportunity to find these sources and learn even more. It is important not only to keep the "conversation" moving, but also to keep it genuine.

Learning Outcomes

Use sources for research.
Avoid plagiarism.
Write paraphrases.
Use quoted material.

"If a creative person steals your idea . . . it won't create the impact you could have created, because it wasn't from the right source."

Michael Bassey Johnson

Using Sources for Research

What does *research* mean? Simply put, research means "searching out answers to your questions."

Beginning Your Research

- **Start early.** Give yourself plenty of time to do your research project. The sooner you start, the more you can relax and enjoy the process, and the easier it will be to find sources.
- **Consider your topic.** What do you already know about your topic? If you had to write your paper right now, what would you write?
- **Ask questions.** What do you wonder about your topic? Make a list of questions; then think about sources for finding answers.
- **Begin with the basics.** For most topics, an encyclopedia or Web search will turn up basic information. Use these sources to get an overview.

Reflecting on Your Research

- **Think about what you have read.** How has your initial research affected your thinking about the topic?
- **Ask more questions.** What new, more informed questions do you have as a result of your reading?
- **Refine your topic, if necessary.** What new ideas occur to you regarding the topic? Do you need to adjust your topic?

Doing Further Research

- **Focus your efforts.** Look for more answers to your informed questions.
- **Use the best sources.** Look for trustworthy books, periodicals, and Web pages that specifically answer your questions. Also, remember to consider using personal surveys, interviews, and letters to experts.

Presenting Your Results

- **Make the topic your own.** Your research paper should not just repeat other people's ideas. First and foremost, it should present your own thoughts and understanding of the topic.
- **Paraphrase or quote appropriately.** To support your ideas, paraphrase or quote credible sources as needed. But remember: References to other sources should only be used to enhance or support your own thinking. (See page 436.)
- **Credit your sources.** Let your reader know the source of each idea you summarize or quote.

Avoiding Plagiarism

You owe it to your sources and your reader to give credit for anyone else's ideas or words that you use in your research paper. If you don't, you may be guilty of *plagiarism*—the act of presenting someone else's ideas as your own. (See pages 432–433 for examples.)

Forms of Plagiarism

Submitting another writer's paper: The most blatant form of plagiarism is to put your name on someone else's work (another student's paper, an essay bought from a "paper mill," or the text of an article from the Internet) and turn it in as your own.

Using copy-and-paste: It is unethical to copy phrases, sentences, or larger sections from a source and paste them into your paper without giving credit for the material. Even if you change a few words, this is still plagiarism.

Neglecting necessary quotation marks: Whether it's just a phrase or a larger section of text, if you use the exact words of a source, they must be put in quotation marks and identified with a citation.

Paraphrasing without citing a source: Paraphrasing (rephrasing ideas in your own words) is an important research skill. However, paraphrased ideas must be credited to the source, even if you reword the material entirely.

Confusing borrowed material with your own ideas: While taking research notes, it is important to identify the source of each idea you record. That way, you won't forget whom to credit as you write your paper.

Other Source Abuses

Using sources inaccurately: Make certain that your quotation or paraphrase accurately reflects the meaning of the original. Do not misrepresent the original author's intent.

Overusing source material: Your paper should be primarily your words and thoughts, supported by outside sources. If you simply string together quotations and paraphrases, your voice will be lost.

"Plunking" source material: When you write, smoothly incorporate any information from an outside source. Dropping in or "plunking" a quotation or paraphrased idea without comment makes your writing seem choppy and disconnected.

Relying too heavily on one source: If your writing is dominated by one source, the reader may doubt the depth and integrity of your research.

Original Article

The excerpt below about the German blitz is an original source article. Take note of the examples of plagiarism that follow the article.

The British and the Blitz by Ernest Kay

Total war came to London on September 7, 1940, when **German bombs deliberately targeted civilians in Great Britain's largest city. Initially, the Luftwaffe bombers carried 40 SC50 bombs, each packed with 50 kilograms of TNT** that could severely damage its target plus spray deadly shrapnel moving at 7,000 miles per hour. Then the Luftwaffe dropped larger bombs carrying 250 kg of TNT combined with incendiary bombs. The goal of the Blitz, a German word for lightning, was to break the morale of the people and force the British government to surrender.

There were 22,000 deaths after the first four months of the bombing. If a direct hit or shrapnel wasn't enough, other bombing victims succumbed to suffocating "blast lung," a deadly condition caused by sucking the air out of the lungs and causing them to malfunction. In addition, more than a quarter of a million people were left homeless.

At first, the common citizenry had no way to escape the constant, brutal bombing. However, they soon went underground, enduring the nightly raids in the vast London subway system. They did so against the wishes of the government, which was afraid that the citizenry would acquire a bunker mentality and want to remain underground, rather than contribute to the war effort.

Eventually, however, the government provided bedding supplies and other basic accommodations in the subway system. The government also built eight other deep shelters that were connected to the underground system. Thousands of people came to rely on the subway system and shelters during the Blitz. While the German Blitz inflicted a devastating blow, it never fulfilled its intended goal. After bombing Coventry and important port cities in addition to London, Hitler suddenly turned his attention to the Soviet Union, perhaps with the realization that the British were not going to surrender.

The Blitz may have been the result of the following accident: **In an August 24, 1940, bombing raid, the Luftwaffe had targeted oil depots in East London, but a number of the bombers missed the depots and hit homes in the area.** Hitler was furious when informed of this deadly error. In retaliation, the British Bomber Command carried out an indiscriminate bombing mission on Germany, an action that infuriated Hitler even more. In response, he promised to drop one million kilograms of bombs on London. The first of this Blitz bombing then took place on September 7. . . .

Examples of Plagiarism

Below are the three common types of plagiarism, sometimes committed on purpose and sometimes by accident. The plagiarized text is shown in bold type.

Using copy-and-paste

- In this example, the writer pastes in two sentences from the original text without using quotation marks or a citation.

> The British people had no preparation for the type of bombing inflicted upon them starting in September of 1940. **German bombs deliberately targeted civilians in Great Britain's largest city of London. Initially, the Luftwaffe bombers carried 40 SC50 bombs, each packed with 50 kilograms of TNT.** Wave after wave of bombers hit the city. Never before had air warfare like this been carried out.

Paraphrasing without citing a source

- Here the writer accurately paraphrases (restates) a passage from the original text, but he includes no citation.

> **Citizens had no way to escape the nightly bombing. Desperate for safe shelter, they flocked en masse into the London subway system. They did this despite the concern by the government that once underground, citizens would want to stay there, a move that would significantly hinder the war effort.**

Neglecting necessary quotation marks

- In this example, the writer cites the source of the exact words that he uses from the original text, but he doesn't enclose these words in quotation marks or capitalize the first word (In) of the quoted material.

> Ironically, the Blitz may never had occurred if it wasn't for a German error. In "The British and the Blitz," Ernest Kay states **in an August 24, 1940, bombing raid, the Luftwaffe had targeted oil depots in East London, but a number of the bombers missed the depots and hit homes in the area.** Hitler was infuriated by this deadly error. The destruction of civilian areas prompted a British bombing mission in Germany, which then led to the Blitz bombing in 1940-1941.

Writing Paraphrases

There are two ways to share information from another source: (1) quote the source directly or (2) paraphrase the source. When you quote directly, you include the exact words of the author and put quotation marks around them. When you paraphrase, you use your own words to restate someone else's ideas. In either case, you must cite your source. To paraphrase, follow the steps below.

1. **Skim the selection first** to get the overall meaning.

2. **Read the selection carefully**; pay attention to key words and phrases.

3. **List the main ideas** on a piece of paper, without looking at the selection.

4. **Review the selection again.**

5. **Write your paraphrase**; restate the author's ideas in your own words.
   - Stick to the essential information (drop anecdotes and details).
   - State each important idea clearly and concisely.
   - Put quotation marks around ideas taken directly from the source.
   - Arrange the ideas into a smooth, logical order.

6. **Check your paraphrase for accuracy** by asking these questions:
   - Have I kept the author's ideas and viewpoints clear in my paraphrase? Have I quoted where necessary?
   - Have I cut out enough of the original? Too much?
   - Could another person understand the author's main idea by reading my paraphrase?

Help File

A quotation, a paraphrase, and a summary are all ways of referencing a source.

Quoting: A quotation states the words of a source exactly. Quoting should be used sparingly in a research paper so that your writing doesn't sound like a patchwork of other people's statements. Use a quotation only when the exact words of the source are essential.

Paraphrasing: In a paraphrase, you recast an idea from a source into your own words. Paraphrasing demonstrates that you understand the idea, and it maintains your voice within your paper. In a research paper, paraphrasing is more commonly used than quoting or summarizing.

Summarizing: A summary is a condensed version of an entire source. In a research paper, there is seldom any need to summarize an entire work unless that work is the subject of the paper. For example, you might summarize the plot of *King Lear* in a research paper about that play.

█ Sample Paraphrases

Following the original passage below from a book by Travis Taylor, you'll find two sample paraphrases, both properly cited.

Original Passage

Kyudo, which means "the way of the bow" in Japanese, is the Zen martial art of archery. It was adapted into traditional Buddhist practice from medieval Japanese archers who used seven-foot asymmetrical bows called yumi. Although kyudo lacks the widespread popularity of karate or judo, it is often regarded as one of the most intensive martial arts in existence, taking an estimated 30 years to master.

The standard execution of kyudo involves a series of specific actions, including assuming the proper posture, approaching the intended target, nocking the arrow, drawing it, releasing it, and then repeating the process. After the second arrow has been released, the archer approaches the target, withdraws the arrows, and thus completes the exercise.

There is far more to kyudo, however, than simply shooting arrows. For every movement, the archer must maintain a specific posture, inhaling and exhaling at predetermined points throughout the exercise. The repetitive action and deep breathing greatly relaxes the archer—heightening his alertness and lowering his stress.

Basic Paraphrase with Quotation

Kyudo is the Zen martial art of archery. It was adapted from medieval traditional Japanese archery into a spiritual and physical exercise. "The standard execution of kyudo involves a series of specific actions, including assuming the proper posture, approaching the intended target, nocking the arrow, drawing it, [and] releasing it . . . " (Taylor 26). An archer's sense of balance comes from focused breathing and balanced posture, which lessen stress and increase the archer's ability to concentrate (Taylor 26).

Basic Paraphrase

Kyudo is the Zen martial art of archery. It was adapted from medieval Japanese archery into a spiritual and physical exercise. Through a series of specific actions, the archer prepares and shoots an arrow into a target and then repeats the action one more time. The archer's sense of balance comes from focused breathing and balanced posture, which lessen stress and increase the archer's ability to concentrate (Taylor 26).

Using Quoted Material

A quotation can be a single word or an entire paragraph. Choose quotations carefully, keep them as brief as possible, and use them only when they are necessary. When you do quote material directly, be sure that the capitalization, punctuation, and spelling are the same as that in the original work. Clearly mark changes for your readers: (1) changes within the quotation are enclosed in brackets [like this]; (2) explanations are enclosed in parentheses at the end of the quotation before closing punctuation (like this).

Short Quotations

If a quotation is four typed lines or fewer, work it into the body of your paper and put quotation marks around it.

Long Quotations

Quotations of more than four typed lines should be set off from the rest of the writing by indenting each line 10 spaces and double-spacing the material. When quoting two or more paragraphs, indent the first line of each paragraph three additional spaces. Do not use quotation marks. (See page 567.2.)

Note: *After* the final punctuation mark of the set-off quotation, include the parenthetical reference. Generally, a colon is used to introduce quotations set off from the text. (See page 561.1.)

Quoting Poetry

When quoting up to three lines of poetry (or lyrics), use quotation marks and work the lines into your writing. Use a diagonal (/) to show where each line of the poem ends. For quotations of four lines or more, indent each line 10 spaces and double-space (the same as the rest of the text). Do not use quotation marks.

Note: To show that you have left out a line or more of verse in a longer quotation, make a line of spaced periods the approximate length of a complete line of the poem.

Partial Quotations

If you want to leave out part of the quotation, use an ellipsis to signify the omission. An ellipsis (. . .) is three periods with a space before and after each one.

"In the garden of literature, the highest and most charismatic flowers are always the quotations."

Mehmet Murat ildan

MLA Documentation Style

The Modern Language Association first published the *MLA Handbook for Writers of Research Papers* in 1977. It covers all aspects of research writing for students in history, language, literature, philosophy, and other humanities classes. MLA's style of documenting sources is commonly required in high school and college papers. This chapter provides a summary of the style and offers example entries.

Learning Outcomes

Make in-text citations.
Understand the works-cited section.
Entries for books
Entries for periodicals
Entries for online sources
Entries for other sources

"Adam was the only man who, when he said a good thing, knew that nobody had said it before him."

Mark Twain

Making In-Text Citations

The most efficient way to credit a source is to use "parenthetical citation." This means identifying the author and page number in parentheses at the end of words, facts, or ideas you borrow from the source. Each citation must refer to a specific entry in your works-cited list, telling your readers how to find that source for themselves.

▌ Points to Remember

- Clearly indicate a particular works-cited entry with each parenthetical reference you insert. Use the word or words by which the entry is alphabetized in your list of works cited. Typically this is the author's last name.
- Keep citations as brief as possible. Sometimes you may identify the author in your text and the page number alone in parentheses.
- Integrate source material and citations smoothly into your writing.
- When paraphrasing instead of quoting, make it clear where your borrowing begins and ends. Use stylisic cues to distinguish a source's thoughts ("Kalmbach points out . . .") from your own ("I believe . . .").
- For inclusive page numbers larger than ninety-nine, give only the last two digits of the second number (113–14, not 113–114).
- Place your parenthetical citation before the sentence's final punctuation.
- Use italics (not underlining) for titles of books, movies, and other major works.

Model In-Text Citations

One Author: A Complete Work

When citing a complete work, you must give the author's last name in a parenthetical citation unless it is already mentioned in the text; no page numbers are needed. (The same applies to articles in alphabetized encyclopedias, one-page articles, and unpaginated sources.)

- **With Author in Parentheses**

    Changing the Face of Hunger describes the causes of, and working solutions for, famine in third-world countries (Hall).

- **With Author in the Text**

    In *Changing the Face of Hunger*, Ambassador Tony Hall describes the causes of, and working solutions for, famine in third-world countries.

One Author: Part of a Work

If you quote words or borrow ideas from a particular part of a work, include a page number. (Leave a space between the author's last name and the page reference.)

- **With Author in Parentheses**

    Genetic engineering was dubbed "eugenics" by a cousin of Darwin's, Sir Francis Galton, in 1885 (Bullough 5).

- **With Author in the Text**

    Bullough writes that genetic engineering was dubbed "eugenics" by a cousin of Darwin's, Sir Francis Galton, in 1885 (5).

Two or More Works by the Same Author(s)

When your works-cited list includes two or more works by the same author(s), add a shortened version of the title to your in-text citation.

- **With Author in Parentheses**

    Though mistakes are inevitable, "The secret of life . . . is to fall seven times and to get up eight times" (Coelho, *The Alchemist* xiii).

- **With Author in the Text**

    Coelho admits that mistakes are inevitable but says, "The secret of life . . . is to fall seven times and to get up eight times" (*The Alchemist* xiii).

Note: When including both author(s) and title in a parenthetical reference, separate them with a comma, as shown above.

A Work by Two or Three Authors

Give the last names of every author in the same order that they appear in your works-cited list. (The correct order can be found on the work's title page.)

One common effect of divorce is that the youngest child often grows up feeling lonely (Wallerstein, Lewis, and Blakeslee 176).

A Work by Four or More Authors

Give the first author's last name as it appears in the list of works cited, followed by *et al.* (meaning *and others*).

Communication on the job is more than talking: it is "inseparable from your total behavior" (Culligan et al. 111).

A Work by an Agency, a Committee, or Another Organization

If a book or other work was written by an organization, it is said to have a *corporate author*. If the corporate name is long, include it in the text to avoid disrupting the flow of your writing. After the full name has been used at least once, use a shortened form in subsequent references.

- **First Time**

    The European Society of Human Reproduction and Embryology argues that reproductive assistance is a basic medical right (I).

- **Subsequent References**

    ESHRE explains that "infertility may be a serious handicap that prevents people from realizing an important life goal" (2).

An Anonymous Work

When no author is listed, give the title or a shortened version of the title as it appears in the works-cited section.

Statistics indicate that 20 percent of a person's total exposure to lead comes from drinking water (*Information* 572).

Two or More Works Included in One Citation

To cite multiple works within a single parenthetical reference, separate the references with a semicolon.

In medieval Europe, Latin translations of the works of Rhazes, a Persian scholar, were a source of medical knowledge (Albala 22; Lewis 266).

A Work Referred to in Another Work

If you must cite an indirect source—a source that quotes information from another source—use the abbreviation *qtd. in* (quoted in) before the indirect source in your reference.

Paton improved the conditions in Diepkloof (a prison) by "removing all the more obvious aids to detention. The dormitories are open at night: the great barred gate is gone" (qtd. in Callan xviii).

Quoting Verse

Do not use page numbers when referencing classic verse plays and poems. Instead, cite them by division (act, scene, canto, book, part) and line, using Arabic numerals for the various divisions, unless your instructor prefers Roman numerals. Use periods to separate the various numbers.

In the first act of the play named after him, Hamlet comments, "How weary, stale, flat and unprofitable, / Seem to me all the uses of this world" (1.2.133-34).

Note: A slash, with a space on each side, shows where a new line of verse begins.

Quoting Verse *(continued)*

If you are citing lines only, use the word *line* or *lines* in your first reference and numbers only in additional references.

> In book 5 of Homer's *Iliad*, the Trojans' fear is evident: "The Trojans were scared when they saw the two sons of Dares, one of them in fright and the other lying dead by his chariot" (lines 22–24).

Set off verse quotations of more than three lines by indenting them one inch (ten spaces). Do not add quotation marks; begin each line of the poem or play on a separate line, double-spacing between them. Place the parenthetical citation outside of the end punctuation mark of the quotation.

> In "Song of Myself," poet Walt Whitman claims to belong to everyone:
> > I am of old and young, of the foolish as much as the wise,
> > Regardless of others, ever regardful of others,
> > Maternal as well as paternal, a child as well as a man,
> > Stuffed with the stuff that is coarse, and stuffed with the stuff
> > > that is fine. (16.326-29)

Quoting Prose

To cite fiction prose, list more than the page number if the work is available in several editions. Give the page reference first and then add a chapter, section, or book number, if appropriate.

> In *The House of the Spirits*, Isabel Allende describes Marcos, "dressed in a mechanic's overalls, with huge racer's goggles and an explorer's helmet" (13; ch. 1).

When a prose quotation (either fiction or nonfiction) requires more than four typed lines, indent each line one inch (ten spaces) and double-space between them. Do not add quotation marks, and place the parenthetical citation outside of the end punctuation mark of the quotation.

> Allende describes the flying machine that Marcos has assembled:
> > The contraption lay with its stomach on terra firma, heavy and sluggish and looking more like a wounded duck than like one of those newfangled airplanes they were starting to produce in the United States. There was nothing in its appearance to suggest that it could move, much less take flight across the snowy peaks. (12; ch. 1)

Understanding the Works-Cited Section

The works-cited section lists all of the sources you have referred to in your paper. It does not include sources you may have read but did not use in your writing. Begin your list on a new page and number it as if it were the next page of text. Follow these guidelines:

1. Type the page number in the upper-right corner, one-half inch from the top of the page, with your last name before it.

2. Center the title *Works Cited* (not in italics) one inch from the top; then double-space before the first entry.

3. Begin each entry flush with the left margin. If the entry runs more than one line, indent additional lines one-half inch (five spaces) or use the hanging indent function on your computer.

4. Double-space lines within each entry and between entries.

5. List each entry alphabetically by the author's last name. If there is no author, use the first word of the title (disregard *A, An, The*). Italicize titles of complete works; place titles of articles and chapters in quotation marks.

6. End each entry with the medium of publication (print, Web, television, DVD, and so on). For Web sources, also include your date of access.

Basic entry for a book:

Author's last name, First name. *Book Title*. City: Publisher, date. Medium.

Morris-Suzuki, Tessa. *Exodus to North Korea: Shadows from Japan's Cold War*. Lanham: Rowman & Littlefield, 2007. Print.

Basic entry for a periodical:

Author's last name, First name. "Article Title." *Periodical Title* volume.issue (publication date): page numbers. Medium.

Cullen, Chris. "Aaron Rodgers." *Current Biography* 73.11 (Nov. 2012): 70–79. Print.

Basic entry for an online source:

Author's last name, First name. Title of Work (quotation marks or italics, as appropriate). *Site Title*. Site Sponsor, date of publication. Medium. Date of access.

Ghose, Tia. "10 Coolest Archaeology Discoveries of 2013." *Live Science*. Tech Media Network, 31 Dec. 2013. Web. 3 Jan. 2014.

Note: Do not include the source's URL unless your reader cannot locate the source without it or your instructor requires it.

Entries for Books

The entries on the following pages illustrate how to cite certain print items: books, sections of a book, pamphlets, and government publications. The possible components of these entries are listed in their usual order here:

1. Author's name

2. Title of a part of the book (an article in a reference book, a foreword, a preface, an afterword, etc.)

3. Title of the book (in italics)

4. Editor's or translator's name

5. Edition

6. Volume number

7. Series name

8. City of publication: publisher, year published

9. Page numbers (when citing part of the book; see item 2)

10. Medium (Print)

Note: In general, if any of these components do not apply, they are not included in a works-cited entry. However, in the rare case that a book is missing certain publication information, use the following abbreviations instead:

N.p.   No place of publication given

n.p.   No publisher given

n.d.   No date of publication given

N. pag.   No pagination given

Additional Guidelines

- List only the city for the place of publication. If several cities of publication are listed, use only the first.

- Publisher names should be shortened by omitting articles (*A, An, The*), business abbreviations (Co., Ltd., Inc., Corp.), and descriptive words (Books, Press, House, Publishers).

- Cite the surname alone if the publisher's name includes the name of one person. If it includes the names of more than one person, cite only the first surname.

- Abbreviate University Press as UP. Also use standard abbreviations whenever possible. (See pages 579 and 580.)

A Work by One Author

> Bhagwati, Jagdish. *In Defense of Globalization.* New York: Oxford UP, 2004. Print

Two or More Books by the Same Author

List the books alphabetically according to title. After the first entry, substitute three hyphens for the author's name.

> Dershowitz, Alan M. *Rights from Wrongs.* New York: Basic, 2005. Print.
>
> ---. *Supreme Injustice: How the High Court Hijacked Election 2000.* Oxford: Oxford UP, 2001. Print.

A Work by Two or Three Authors

List the authors in the same order as they appear on the title page. Reverse only the name of the first author.

> Chen, Xinyin, and Kenneth H. Rubin. *Socioemotional Development in Cultural Context.* New York: Guilford, 2011. Print.

A Work by Four or More Authors

List the first author, followed by "et al." (You may instead choose to list all names in full, in the order they are listed on the title page.)

> Gallagher, Karen Symms, et al. *Urban Education: A Model for Leadership and Policy.* New York: Routledge-Taylor & Francis Group, 2011. Print.

A Work Authored by an Agency, a Committee, or Another Organization

In this case treat the organization as the author.

> National Research Council. *Abrupt Impacts of Climate Change: Anticipating Surprises.* Washington, D.C.: Natl. Academies, 2013. Print.

An Anonymous Book

If no author is listed, use the title of the book at the front of the entry.

> *Babylon on Hudson.* New York: Harper, 1932. Print.

A Single Work from an Anthology

An anthology contains a variety of texts, usually from different authors. When citing a single work from an anthology, begin with the author and title of that work, followed by the anthology's title, editor's name, and other publication details, including the page numbers of the work cited.

> Mitchell, Joseph. "The Bottom of the Harbor." *American Sea Writing.* Ed. Peter Neill. New York: Library of America, 2000. 584–608. Print.

Two or More Works from the Same Anthology or Collection

Cite the collection once, with complete publication information (see *Rothfield* below). Cite individual entries by listing the author, the title of the piece, the editor of the collection, and page numbers (see *Becker* below).

> Becker, Carol. "The Brooklyn Controversy: A View from the Bridge." Rothfield 15–21.
>
> Rothfield, Lawrence, ed. *Unsettling "Sensation": Arts-Policy Lessons from the Brooklyn Museum of Art Controversy.* New Brunswick: Rutgers UP, 2001. Print.

One Volume of a Multivolume Work

When citing a single volume of many, list that volume number immediately after the title.

> Cook, Jacob Ernest, and Milton M. Klein, eds. *North America in Colonial Times.* Vol. 2. New York: Scribner's, 1998. Print.

If you cite more than one volume of a multivolume work, list the total number of volumes instead. Within your parenthetical reference of a volume, list volume and page numbers as follows: (5:112–14).

> Salzman, Jack, David Lionel Smith, and Cornel West. *Encyclopedia of African-American Culture and History.* 5 vols. New York: Simon, 1996. Print.

An Introduction, a Preface, a Foreword, or an Afterword

To cite the introduction, preface, foreword, or afterword of a book, list the author of the part first. Then identify the part by type, without quotation marks or underlining. Next name the book's title, and after that, the book's author, using the word *By.* (If both the book and part have the same author, give just the last name after *By.*) For a book that gives cover credit to an editor instead of an author, identify the editor as usual. Just before the medium, list page numbers for the part being cited.

> McCourt, Frank. Foreword. *Eats, Shoots & Leaves: The Zero Tolerance Approach to Punctuation.* By Lynne Truss. New York: Gotham, 2003. xi–xiv. Print.
>
> Atwood, Margaret. Introduction. *Alice Munro's Best: Selected Stories.* By Alice Munro. Toronto: McClelland, 2006. vii–xviii. Print.

Second and Subsequent Editions

When you have used a later edition of a particular work (2nd ed., Rev. ed., 2012 ed.), add that information to your citation.

> Schulte-Peevers, Andrea, et al. *Germany.* 5th ed. Victoria: Lonely Planet, 2007. Print.

An Edition with Author and Editor

The term edition can also refer to a writer's work that is prepared by an editor.

> Shakespeare, William. *A Midsummer Night's Dream.* Ed. Jane Bachman. Lincolnwood: NTC, 1994. Print.

A Translation

When citing a translation, identify the translator (*Trans.*) after the title of the work.

>Lebert, Stephan, and Norbert Lebert. *My Father's Keeper.* Trans. Julain Evans. Boston: Little, 2001.

An Article in a Familiar Reference Book

It is not necessary to give full publication information for familiar reference works (encyclopedias, dictionaries). List the edition and publication year. If citing an article that is initialed, check the index of authors for the author's full name.

>Lum, P. Andrea. "Computed Tomography." *World Book.* 2000 ed. Print.

A Government Publication

State the name of the government (country, state) followed by the name of the agency. Most federal publications are published by the Government Printing Office (GPO).

>United States. Dept. of Labor. Bureau of Labor Statistics. *Occupational Outlook Handbook 2000–2001.* Washington: GPO, 2000. Print.

When citing the *Congressional Record*, give only the date and page numbers.

>*Cong. Rec.* 5 Feb. 2002: S311–15. Print.

A Book in a Series

Give the series name and number (if any) after the medium of publication.

>Paradis, Adrian A. *Opportunities in Military Careers.* Lincolnwood: VGM Career Horizons, 1999. Print. VGM Opportunities Series.

A Book with a Title Within Its Title

If the title contains a title normally in quotation marks, keep the quotation marks, and place the entire title in italics.

>Stuckey-French, Elizabeth. *"The First Paper Girl in Red Oak, Iowa" and Other Stories.* New York: Doubleday, 2000. Print.

If the title contains a title that is normally italicized, do not italicize that internal title.

>Harmetz, Aljean. *The Making of* The Wizard of Oz: *Movie Magic and Studio Power in the Prime of MGM.* New York: Hyperion, 1998. Print.

A Pamphlet, Brochure, Manual, or Other Workplace Document

Treat any such publication as you would a book.

>Grayson, George W. *The North American Free Trade Agreement.* New York: Foreign Policy Assn., 1993. Print.

If publication information is missing, list what you know [in square brackets] to show that it did not come from the source. Use *n.p.* (no place) if the place or the publisher is unknown and *n.d.* if the date is unknown, just as you would for a book.

>*Pedestrian Safety.* [United States]: n.p., n.d.

Entries for Periodicals

The possible components of periodical entries are shown below in the order in which they would be listed.

1. Author's name

2. Title of article (in quotation marks)

3. Name of the periodical (in italics)

4. Series number or name (if relevant)

5. Volume number (for a scholarly journal)

6. Issue number

7. Date of publication (abbreviate all months but May, June, July)

8. Page numbers (preceded by a colon, without "p." or "pp.")

9. Medium (Print)

10. Supplementary information, as needed

Note: If any of these components do not apply, they are not included in a works-cited entry.

An Article in a Weekly or Biweekly Magazine

List the author (if identified), article title (in quotation marks), publication title (italicized), full date of publication, and page numbers for the article. Do not include volume and issue numbers. End with the medium.

> Green, Andy. "U2, Neil Young Films Rock Sundance." *Rolling Stone* 7 Feb. 2008: 20. Print.

An Article in a Monthly or Bimonthly Magazine

As for a weekly or biweekly magazine, list the author (if identified), article title (in quotation marks), and publication title (in italics). Then identify the month(s) and year of the issue, followed by page numbers for the article. Do not give volume and issue numbers. End with the medium.

> Mead, Walter Russel. "Born Again." *Atlantic Monthly* Mar. 2008: 21–24. Print.

An Article in a Scholarly Journal Paginated by Issue

Rather than month or full date of publication, scholarly journals are identified by volume number. If each issue is numbered from page 1, your works-cited entry should identify the issue number, as well. List the volume number immediately after the journal title, followed by a period and the issue number, and then the year of publication (in parentheses). End with the page numbers of the article, followed by the medium, as usual.

> Sanchez, Melissa E. "Seduction and Service in *The Tempest*." *Studies in Philology* 105.1 (Winter 2008): 50–82. Print.

An Article in a Scholarly Journal with Continuous Pagination

For scholarly journals that continue pagination from issue to issue, no issue number is needed in the works-cited entry.

> Tebble, Nicola J., David W. Thomas, and Patricia Price. "Anxiety and Self-Consciousness in Patients with Minor Facial Lacerations." *Journal of Advanced Nursing* 47 (2004): 417–26. Print.

A Printed Interview

Begin with the name of the person interviewed.

> Cantwell, Maria. "The New Technocrat." By Erika Rasmusson. *Working Woman* Apr. 2001: 20–21. Print.

Note: If the interview is untitled, *Interview* (no italics) follows the interviewee's name.

A Newspaper Article

A newspaper article is listed much like an article in a magazine. When citing the edition of a major daily newspaper, list it after the date.

> Segal, Jeff, and Lauren Silva. "Case of Art Imitating Life?" *Wall Street Journal* 3 Mar. 2008, Eastern ed.: C9. Print.

Note: If a local paper's name does not include the city of publication, add it in square brackets (no italics) after the name.

A Newspaper Article in a Lettered Section

To cite an article in a lettered section of the newspaper, list the section followed by the page number (A4). If the sections are numbered, however, use a comma after the year (or the edition); then indicate sec. 1, 2, 3, and so on, followed by a colon and the page number (sec. 1: 20). An unsigned newspaper article follows the same format:

> "Bombs—Real and Threatened—Keep Northern Ireland Edgy." *Chicago Tribune* 6 Dec. 2001, sec. 1: 20. Print.

A Newspaper Editorial

If an article in the newspaper is identified as an editorial, put *Editorial* (no italics) after the title.

> "Hospital Power." Editorial. *Bangor Daily News* 14 Sept. 2004: A6. Print.

A Letter to the Editor

To identify a letter to the editor, put *Letter* (no italics) after the author's name.

> Sory, Forrest. Letter. *Discover* July 2001: 10. Print.

A Review

Begin with the author (if identified) and title of the review. Use the notation *Rev. of* (no italics) between the title of the review and that of the original work. Identify the author of the original work with the word *by* (no italics). Then follow with the publication date for the review.

> Dillon, Brian. "Onion Pilfering." Rev. of *Divisadero*, by Michael Ondaatje. *London Review of Books* 13 Dec. 2007: 19–20. Print.

Note: If you cite the review of a work by an editor or a translator, use *ed.* or *trans.* instead of *by*.

An Unsigned Article in a Periodical

If no author is identified for an article, list the entry alphabetically by title among your works cited (ignoring any initial *A, An,* or *The*).

> "Feeding the Hungry." *Economist* 8 May 2004: 74. Print.

An Article with a Title or Quotation Within its Title

If the internal title would normally be italicized, use italics as usual. If the internal title would normally be set off by quotation marks, use single quotation marks for that title, instead.

> Morgenstern, Joe. "Sleeper of the Year: *In the Bedroom* Is Rich Tale of Tragic Love." *Wall Street Journal* 23 Nov. 2001: W1. Print.

> Lams, Victor J. Jr. "Ruth, Milton, and Keat's 'Ode to a Nightingale.' " *Modern Language Quarterly* 34.4 (Dec. 1973): 417–36. Print.

An Article Reprinted in a Loose-Leaf Collection

The entry begins with original publication information and ends with the name of the loose-leaf volume (*Youth* in the example below), the editor, the volume number, publication information including the name of the information service (SIRS), and the article number.

> O'Connell, Loraine. "Busy Teens Feel the Beep." *Orlando Sentinel* 7 Jan. 1993: E1+. Print. *Youth*. Ed. Eleanor Goldstein. Vol. 4. Boca Raton: SIRS, 1993. Art. 41.

An Article with Pagination That Is Not Continuous

For articles that are continued on a nonconsecutive page, whatever the publication type, add a plus sign (+) after the first page number.

> Garrett, Robyne. "Negotiating a Physical Identity: Girls, Bodies and Physical Education." *Sport, Education and Society* 9 (2004): 223+. Print.

Entries for Online Sources

Citations of online sources are similar to print sources, with a few exceptions to reflect the changeable nature of the Internet. The usual components are listed below. However, if the work you are citing also appears in print, you may need to include the print information first and then the electronic details.

1. **Author's name** (if identified)
2. **Title of article, posting, or page** (if any, in quotation marks)
3. **Title of Web site, project, or book** (in italics)
4. **Version or edition** (if applicable)
5. **Publisher or site sponsor** (or *N.p.* if not available, without italics)
6. **Date of publication** (or *n.d.* if unknown, without italics)
7. **Medium** (Web)
8. **Date of access**
9. **URL** (if needed to find the resource, or if your instructor requires it)

Note: If any of these items do not apply, they are not included in a works-cited entry.

A Web Site

When citing an entire Web site, no article or page title is needed.

> *The Purdue OWL Family of Sites.* The Writing Lab and OWL at Purdue and Purdue U, 2008. Web. 22 Jan. 2014.

A Page or an Article on a Web Site

Place the title of the page or article in quotation marks.

> Le Guin, Ursula K. "A Sketchy Introduction to Copyright and Contracts." *The official web site of author Ursula K. Le Guin.* Ursula K. Le Guin, 13 July 2008. Web. 19 May 2014.

A Site with a URL

If you must include a URL, place it in angle brackets at the end of the entry. Line breaks in the URL must occur only after a double or single slash.

> "Fort Frederica." *National Parks Service.* US Department of the Interior, n.d. Web. 6 Jan. 2012. <http://www.cr.nps.gov/nr/twhp/wwwlps/lessons/31frederica/31frederica.htm>.

An Article in a Web Magazine

Often the publishing date will be listed at the beginning of the article. If not, check the bottom of the Web page.

> Ehrenreich, Barbara. "It Is Expensive to Be Poor." *The Atlantic.* The Atlantic Monthly Group, 13 Jan. 2014. Web. 3 Feb. 2014.

An Article in a Scholarly Journal

MLA style calls for a page range in citations of articles from scholarly journals. If an online journal is unpaginated, list *n. pag.* (without italics).

> Lanson, Jerry. "It's time to make the Web an equal partner." *Online Journalism Review* 30.2 (2000): n. pag. Web. 23 Jan. 2013.

An Article in a Scholarly Project or Information Database

Include the name of the information database in italics.

> Bujak, Nick. "Form and Generic Interrelation in the Romantic Period: Walter Scott's Poetic Influence on Jane Austen." *Narrative* 22.1 (2014): 45–67. *Academic Search Premier, EBSCOhost*. Web. 22 Jan. 2014.

An Online Posting of Art, Other Media, and Manuscripts

Follow the guidelines for other types of sources (see pages 452–453). Instead of the original medium of publication, however, list the title of the database or Web site (in italics), followed by the medium (Web) and date of access.

> Goya, Francisco de. *Saturn Devouring His Children*. 1819–1823. Fresco. Museo Nacional del Prado, Madrid. *Museodelprado.es*. Web. 13 Dec. 2011.

A Posting on a Blog, Discussion Group, or Listserv

Treat such an entry as you would a page or an article on a Web site. If necessary, identify the poster by username, as in the example that follows.

> jreitzprr. "Signal light on turnout." *Lionel_PostwarTrains*. Yahoo Groups, 2 Aug. 2011. Web. 6 Jan. 2014.

A Tweet

Cite the author's name, then the user name in parentheses. Begin with the username (no parentheses) if the author's name is unknown. Include the entire message in quotation marks, and end with the date, time, and medium (Tweet).

> Berman, Dan (@DHBerman). "White House launches new political office, puts David Simas in charge." 24 Jan. 2014, 2:01 p.m. Tweet.

Note: In the body of your paper, quote the entire tweet or paraphrase it. Include the author's name in the text or cite it in parentheses as shown here (Berman).

An Email (Including an Interview by Email)

List the message author, the subject line, and the addressee, followed by the date sent and the medium (Email). In the following example, the addressee is the author of the paper in which the email is cited.

> Barzinji, Atman. "Update on Frog Populations in Wisconsin Wetlands." Message to the author. 1 May 2013. Email.

Entries for Other Sources

Research often involves sources other than books, periodicals, and online sources. That might include interviews, speeches, works of art, recordings, and even a film or movie. Guidelines for many additional resources are provided below and on the next two pages.

An Interview

For a **personal interview** (one you conducted), list the person interviewed, the descriptor "Personal interview" (without quotation marks), and the date.

Biccum, Jon. Personal interview. 25 July 2013.

For a **published or broadcast interview**, follow the interviewee's name by either the title of the interview in quotation marks or (if the interview is untitled) the descriptor "Interview by" and the interviewer's name. End with the usual information for the medium (print, Web, radio, television) in which the interview was published or broadcast.

Elliott, Jane. "An Unfinished Crusade." *Frontline*. WGBH Educational Foundation, 19 Dec. 2002. Web. 12 Apr. 2014.

An Oral Presentation

Cite a lecture, speech, reading, or other such oral presentation by the speaker's name, the presentation title, the meeting and the sponsoring organization, the location, and the date. End with a descriptive label such as *Address, Lecture, Reading,* or *Speech.*

Annan, Kofi. "Acceptance of Nobel Peace Prize." Oslow City Hall, Oslow, Norw. 10 Dec. 2001. Speech.

Published Conference Proceedings

Treat a presentation in the published proceedings of a conference as you would a titled section from a book. If the conference date and location are not part of the publication title, add that information after the title.

Zarkowski, M. "Identification-Driven Emotion Recognition System for a Social Robot." *MMAR 2013: 18th International Conference on Methods and Models in Automation and Robotics.* 26–29 Aug. 2013, Miedzyzdroje, Poland. Ed. Faculty of Electrical Engineering. Szczecin, Poland: West Pomeranian U of Technology, 2014. 138-43. Print.

A Work of Art on Display

List the artist, the title (in italics), the date of composition (if known), and a descriptor identifying the type of artwork. Follow with the location and city of display.

Titian. *The Entombment of Christ.* c. 1520. Oil on canvas. Louvre, Paris.

A Film or Movie

List the title, director, distributor, and year, followed by *Film* (no italics) as medium. You may also include information such as performers if desired.

> *The Aviator.* Dir. Martin Scorsese. Perf. Leonardo
> DiCaprio. Miramax, 2004. Film.

If the film is on physical media—Blu-ray, DVD, or VHS, for example—list that in place of *Film*.

> *Beyond the Da Vinci Code.* A&E Home Video, 2005. DVD.

To emphasize an actor or director, begin the entry with that person's name and role.

> Hood, Gavin, dir. *Ender's Game.* Perf. Harrison Ford, Asa Butterfield.
> Lionsgate Home Entertainment, 2014. Blu-ray.

A Radio or Television Program

For a broadcast program, place the episode title (if part of a series) in quotation marks, followed by the series title in italics. Next, list the network name and the call letters of the specific station, followed by the city and the broadcast date. End with the medium (Television, Radio). Other information (director, writers, performers, etc.) may be added if desired. (In the example below, the *Foyle's War* series was rebroadcast as part of another series, *Masterpiece Theater,* so both are listed.)

> "Eagle Day." *Foyle's War.* Dir. Jeremy Silberston. *Masterpiece Theater.* PBS.
> WGBH, Boston, 23 Feb. 2003. Television.

A Radio or Television Recording

For a television or radio recording, follow the format of a film or movie (above). Add the episode title (if part of a series) in quotation marks at the beginning. Include abbreviations for director (dir.), writer (writ.), performer (perf.), composer (comp.), conductor (cond.), and such, as needed. End with the publisher and date, followed by the medium.

> Wand, Günter, cond. "Vier letzte Lieder." Comp. Richard Strauss. Perf.
> Kölner Rundfunk-Sinfonie-Orchester. *Günter Wand: The Radio Recordings.*
> Profil Medien GmbH, 2013. Audio CD.

A Sound Recording

For music and spoken-word recordings, give whatever information your reader will need to locate the source. You may list the performer's or writer's name, followed by the selection title in quotation marks (if citing a specific selection) and recording title in italics, then publisher, date, and medium. If the recording date and publishing date are different, you may include the recording date before the publisher's name.

> Jacobs, W. W. *The Monkey's Paw.* LibriVox, 2 Mar. 2007. MP3 file.

A Map or Chart

When citing a map or chart, follow the format for an anonymous book, adding *Map* or *Chart* (no italics).

Wisconsin Territory. Map. Madison: Wisconsin Trails, 1988. Print.

A Cartoon or Comic Strip (in Print)

Follow the format for an article in a periodical or a book, as appropriate. Include the descriptive term *Cartoon* (no italics).

Hands, Phil. "Dragon guards Wisconsin's treasure horde." Cartoon. *Wisconsin State Journal* 24 Jan. 2014: B2. Print.

Computer Software

For a general publication on DVD or CD-ROM, use the citation format below. If available, include publication information for the printed source.

Microsoft Encarta Deluxe 2005. Redmond: Microsoft, 2005. CD-ROM.

A Periodically Published Database on CD-ROM or DVD-ROM

Citations of periodical materials (magazines, newspapers, periodically updated reference works) gathered in a database on CD-ROM or DVD-ROM are treated similarly to those of print sources. Note however that database contents may vary from one medium to another, as well as from one update to another. For this reason, try to list the publication dates of both the material cited and of the database itself. Also note that if the publisher of the material and the vendor of the database are separate entities, it is necessary to identify both.

"Bunker Hill Monument to Get $3.7M Makeover." *Boston Business Journal* 13 June 2005. *Business Dateline.* CD-ROM. ProQuest. July 2005.

Malleron, Jean-Luc, and Alain Juin. *Database of Palladium Chemistry.* CD-ROM Version 1.1. Burlington, MA: Academic Press, 2002.

"'Google' is not a synonym for 'research.'"

Dan Brown

Sample MLA Research Paper

There is no substitute for interest or passion when it comes to developing effective writing. This is especially true when it comes to research writing because of its demanding requirements. As you will see, Robert Minto, the writer of the paper shared in this chapter, feels strongly about his topic and, consequently, takes care to be clear and convincing.

To fully appreciate Minto's paper, first skim it for a general look at its content. Then read it carefully—at least twice—examining its title page, outline, introduction, thesis, and supporting paragraphs. In addition, review the side notes that highlight important features in the paper and the assessment rubric at the end of the chapter.

Learning Outcomes

Review the title page and outline.
Study a research paper.
Use an assessment rubric.

"The guiding question in research is 'so what?'
Answer that question in every sentence you write."

Donald W. McClosky

Reviewing the Title Page and Outline

MLA style does not require a title page or an outline. However, if your instructor asks you to include these items in your research paper, use the following samples as a guide.

Title Page

Center the title one-third of the way down the page; center author information two-thirds of the way down.

A Thorn Beneath the Shining Armor:

Area Bombing and Bishop Bell

Robert Minto

Mr. Sewell

World History

30 January 2014

Research Paper Outline

Center the title one inch from the top of the page. Double-space throughout.

A Thorn Beneath the Shining Armor:

Area Bombing and Bishop Bell

Introduction—During World War II, the British responded to the German Blitz with area bombing of their own; but one religious leader, Bishop Bell, questioned the response on religious and moral grounds.

   I. Early Actions

      A. "Pamphlet" bombing

      B. German bombing mistakes

      C. British response

      D. Resulting German Blitz

  II. British Area Bombing

      A. Churchill-backed reprisal

      B. More aggressive over time

      C. "Out-blitzed" the Blitz

 III. Bishop Bell's Response

      A. Singular voice in opposition

      B. Humanitarian activist

      C. Area-bombing speech

      D. Effect of opposition

Conclusion—If we had been victims of the Blitz, we may have had a hard time siding with Bishop Bell. But his stance has merit, and we should study it and learn from it.

speedimaging / Shutterstock.com

Studying a Research Paper

Minto 1

A complete heading is provided.

Robert Minto

Mr. Sewell

World History

30 January 2014

The title is centered.

A Thorn Beneath the Shining Armor:

Area Bombing and Bishop Bell

No one argues the idea that Hitler needed to be stopped. His fascist regime was so shocking that even controversial decisions by the "good guys" during WWII—dropping two atomic bombs, for example—cannot make him seem any less evil. If this is still the case in 2014, then how much more evil must he have

Double spacing is used throughout the paper.

appeared to the citizens of Great Britain, an island nation who trembled beneath the force of the hellish German bombing?

Hitler appeared so evil that the fight against him and his Nazi Party could be considered a modern-day crusade. When the citizens of London suffered from German area bombing, the good guys—in this case, Winston Churchill and the British Bomber Command—responded with their own area bombing of

The writer introduces his subject and states his thesis (underlined).

Germany. The British felt this bombing was a necessary response to the German Blitz, yet there were a few critics such as Bishop Bell who questioned this response on religious and moral grounds.

EARLY ACTIONS

On September 3, 1939, Bomber Command authorized its first operation in World War II. The British bombers carried pamphlets urging the German people to rebel against Nazi rule (Garrett 9). Eight months passed before Bomber Command sent out anything more lethal than literature against German citizens. Prime Minister Neville Chamberlain believed that bombs were too inaccurate and thus could not help the cause. In a parliamentary debate on July 21, 1938, he said the following:

Minto 2

A quotation longer than four lines is indented.

> We can strongly condemn any declaration on the part of anybody, wherever it be made, that it should be part of a deliberate policy to try to win a war by the demoralization of the civilian population through the process of [area] bombing from the air. This is absolutely contrary to international laws, and I would add that, in my opinion, it is a mistaken policy from the point of view of those who adopt it, but I do not believe that deliberate attacks upon a civilian population will ever win a war for those who make them. (Chamberlain)

A title is included in this citation because two sources by the same author are used.

According to Geoffrey Best, Chamberlain based his opposition to bombing on a declaration signed at the Hague Conference in 1907, which "prohibited the discharge of projectiles and explosives from balloons or by other new methods of similar nature." However, this was only a "declaration," and became nothing more than a curiosity (*Humanity in Warfare* 262).

On August 24, 1940, German bombers targeted oil depots in East London, but a number of these bombers missed their targets and hit homes. It is reported that Hitler was furious about this mistake. Winston Churchill then sent the British Bomber Command to Germany on a retaliation mission. This infuriated Hitler even more, and he ordered the Luftwaffe to drop one million kilograms of bombs on London ("Impact of the Blitz"). In September 1940, an aerial bombardment of London known as the Blitz began, and it would last for 57 days, killing nearly 50,000 civilians.

A second source is cited by the same author.

What becomes of international law when one party violates it so viciously as did Germany? Nations bring out their enforcers. Winston Churchill, who was chosen to replace Chamberlain as Prime Minister, was England's enforcer. Churchill felt at the time that it was "as if [he] were walking with destiny" (Best, *Churchill* 65). He advanced the war on Germany, not just to protect England, but for far more. In his very first public speech as Prime Minister, Churchill delivered these aggressive words in the House of Commons:

> You ask, what is our aim? I can answer in one word: Victory—victory at all costs, victory in spite of all terror, however long and hard the road may be,

Minto 3

for without victory, there is no survival. Let that be realized; no survival for the British Empire; no survival for all that the British Empire has stood for; no survival for the urge and impulse of the ages, that mankind will move forward toward its goal. But I take up my task with buoyancy and hope. I feel sure that our cause will not be suffered to fail among men. At this time I feel entitled to claim the aid of all, and I say, "Come, then, let us go forward together with our united strength." (Churchill 149)

The spirit that Churchill prods to life—the spirit of British nationalism—demonstrates how his appointment as prime minister was a fire-against-fire measure. In this sense, the war was initially one of German nationalism versus British nationalism. Churchill seemed just as successful in rallying Great Britain through his rhetoric and statesmanship as was Hitler in his promotion of the Third Reich in Germany.

> **The writer offers his own analysis.**

BRITISH AREA BOMBING

In that House of Commons speech, Churchill also set up the British Empire as the guardian over the future of mankind. So with a clear conscience, his administration approved area bombing in the name of the Empire and the greater good of the world. In 1940, Churchill addressed his war cabinet with these words: ". . . the civilian populations around the target areas must be made to feel the weight of the war" (Messenger 40). Geoffrey Best states that reprisals or retaliation are not uncommon in war, even though they may be criminal according to international law:

> **Subheadings help the reader follow the organization.**

> The short and easy [way] to avert criticism was to admit to the illegality of the whole thing at once by announcing it plainly as a reprisal; as was often done by all the bombing powers in both world wars. Reprisals by definition are unlawful acts deliberately done to punish and deter an unlawfully behaving enemy. Wars being what they are, and the business of propaganda being what it is, there was never much difficulty in finding pretexts for reprisals. (*Humanity in Warfare* 267-268)

> **A longer quotation explains a technical term: *reprisals*.**

On February 14, 1942, Churchill moved beyond the excuse of reprisal into the realm of specific aggression. *Directive N. 22* stated that the bombing offensive was to be "focused on the morale of the enemy civil population and in particular of the industrial workers" (Colville 311). Over the next three years, about three-quarters of the bombs dropped in Germany by Great Britain were dropped on densely populated civilian targets (Garrett 11-12). Support for Bomber Command's actions was strong because of the suffering and death experienced by the British people, especially at a time when no other military strategy was working.

Eventually, other factors contributed to the area-bombing decision. For example, Lord Cherwell, in a memo to the prime minister on March 30, 1942, stated that according to one analysis, housing damage caused by area bombing was even more demoralizing than the death of relatives. So the idea of "shattering the German people's morale, and thus of Germany's will or ability to continue her war" was further justified and became one of the Bomber Command's guiding principles (Garrett 13). Ironically, this rationale ignored the nearest example of the effect of area bombing upon national morale. The Blitz, far from shattering the British spirit, became the source of their fighting spirit.

British area bombing served up more destruction than the German Blitz did; it is estimated that more than 500,000 German civilians died in these bombardments (Garrett 21). Perhaps the biggest and most deceptive rationale for area bombing involved secondary damage to factories and military installations. Martin Middlebrook describes the public relations of the British bomber offensive in this way:

> In some ways, area bombing was a three-year period of deceit practiced upon the British public and upon world opinion. . . . The impression usually given was that the industry was the main target and that any bombing of workers' housing was an unavoidable necessity. Charges of "indiscriminate bombing" were consistently denied. The deceit lay in the concealment of the fact that the areas most heavily bombed were nearly always either city centers or densely populated residential areas, which rarely contained any industry. (343-344)

The writer demonstrates a thorough understanding of the topic.

Quotations add authenticity to the research.

BISHOP BELL'S RESPONSE

> The final section specifically addresses the focus of the thesis.

One might expect the Church of England to have had something to say about the area-bombing strategy. For the most part, they were swept up in the general atmosphere of British nationalism and anti-German sentiment. One churchman, however, stood apart. Bishop Bell, an Anglican clergyman, questioned the approach of his contemporaries with respect to Germany and feared the outcome of the war, even if the British won. He stated that the actions by Allied bombers would "reap a whirlwind" of postwar bitterness (Gardiner).

> A variety of reliable sources are cited.

Bell was a humanitarian activist in many ways. He made area bombing his own issue, and he always tried to make a distinction between the German people and the Nazis (Gardiner). He visited German refugee camps, lobbying for better conditions for them, and chaired the Famine Relief Committee. He also supported Dietrich Bonhoeffer, who was part of a group conspiring to overthrow Hitler from within the Fuhrer's own ranks (Simkin).

> A formal style is maintained throughout.

All of this prepared Bell for his biggest stand—a stand against British area bombing. In a speech to the House of Lords on February 11, 1943, he addressed the inhumanity of the strategy:

> To line up the Nazi assassins in the same row with the people of Germany whom they have outraged is to make for more barbarism, possibly to postpone peace, and to make certain an incredible worsening of the conditions of all Europe when at last peace comes. . . . The remedy is to tell those inside Germany who are anti-Fascists that we want their help, that we are willing to help them in getting rid of the common enemy, and that we intend that a Germany delivered from Hitlerism shall have fair play and a proper place in the family of Europe. (Bell 31)

> The writer compares Bell's position with Churchill's.

Churchill built up the British spirit with a nationalistic plea; Bell took a moral position based on religious principles. He was clearly aware of the church and its commitment: British Christians could not abandon German Christians, and certainly they could not accept the massacre of German citizens by the area bombing. In the January 1940 *Chichester Diocesan Gazette*, Bell wrote the

Minto 6

An indirect source is cited—quoting information in another source.

following: "It is our task to make the European tradition, a tradition animated by the Christian spirit, prevail: to interpret its character, to show it reintegrating a dying civilization, by a rekindling of the old strength at the ancient sources" (qtd. in Jasper 259).

Bell's stance infuriated Churchill as well as almost all members of the government and the general British citizenry. Even important church members opposed Bell. The Archbishop of Canterbury Cosmo Lang did not approve of the speech. The Archbishop also opposed Bell's call for negotiations between Churchill and Hitler because he felt that such a meeting would tell Hitler that his Blitz bombing was a success (Simkin). In the end, Bell's pleas were never acted upon.

No parenthetical citation is needed here because the source is mentioned in the text.

In a recent BBC Radio special about George Bell, journalist Peter Hutchins said that Bell's controversial position cost him any chance of becoming Archbishop of Canterbury himself. The Archbishop of Canterbury is the principal leader of the Church of England. But Bell didn't care what other people thought. He simply could not condone area bombing on religious grounds. Hutchins also said that Bell wasn't a complete pacifist; it was the random civilian deaths that sickened him. The special also reported that Bell may have been correct about the flaw in the strategy, because it did not break the German spirit. Instead, it may have caused them to fight for their lives.

A connection to the present is made in the conclusion.

We naturally support actions that put history on "our side," but we can't really afford to view these actions with an uncritical eye. Otherwise, we may repeat mistakes of the past. For example, some say that the drone bombing in Pakistan is a huge mistake because of the civilian casualties it can cause. Of course, if we were victims of the Blitz in 1940, we may have had a hard time siding with Bishop Bell. The shock and horror of the bombing would have been too much. In retrospect, however, his controversial stand has merit, both morally and militarily. We should study it, and learn from it.

"Works Cited" is centered one inch from the top.

Works Cited

Bell, George. *Parliamentary Debates.* Vol. 125. London: British House of Lords, 1943. Print.

Best, Geoffrey. *Churchill: A Study in Greatness.* London: Oxford UP, 2003. Print.

---. *Humanity in Warfare: The Modern History of International Law of Armed Conflicts.* Bristol: Methuen, 1983. Print.

Sources are listed in alphabetical order.

Chamberlain, Neville. *Parliamentary Debates.* Vol. 337. London: British House of Commons, 1938. Print.

Churchill, Winston. *Blood, Toil, Tears, and Sweat: The Great Speeches.* Ed. David Cannadine. London: Penguin, 2002. Print.

Colville, John. *The Fringes of Power.* New York: Norton, 1985. Print.

Double spacing is used throughout.

Gardiner, Judith. "As London Lay Smoking." *New Statesman.* New Statesman, 28 June 2011. Web. 23 Oct. 2013.

Garrett, Stephen A. *Ethics and Air Power in World War II: The British Bombing of German Cities.* New York: St. Martin's, 1997. Print.

"The Great Life of Bishop George Bell." *Great Lives.* BBC Radio 4, 5 Apr. 2013. Radio.

Second and third lines are indented five spaces.

"The Impact of the Blitz on London." *History Learning Site.* History Learning Site, May 2010. Web. 7 Nov. 2013.

Jasper, Ronald C. D. *George Bell, Bishop of Chichester.* Oxford UP, 1967. Print.

Messenger, Charles. "Bomber" *Harris and the Strategic Bombing Offensive, 1939-45.* London: Arms & Armour, 1984. Print.

Middlebrook, Martin. *The Battle of Hamburg.* London: Lane, 1980. Print.

Simkin, John. "Bishop George Bell." *Spartacus Educational.* Web. 10 Nov. 2013.

Using an Assessment Rubric

Use this rubric as a checklist to evaluate your research writing. The rubric is arranged according to important standards of effective writing.

The writing . . .

Ideas

____ focuses on an important part or feature of a subject, expressed in a thesis statement.

____ effectively supports or develops the thesis with reliable evidence from a variety of sources.

____ gives credit, when necessary, for ideas from other sources.

Organization

____ forms a meaningful whole with a clearly developed beginning, middle, and ending.

____ presents supporting information in an organized manner (one main point per paragraph).

____ uses linking words and transitions to connect ideas.

Voice

____ speaks in an objective tone appropriate for the purpose.

____ demonstrates the writer's understanding of the topic and evidence.

Word Choice

____ uses specific nouns and verbs.

____ explains or defines any unfamiliar terms.

____ uses words with the appropriate level of formality.

Sentence Fluency

____ flows smoothly from one idea to the next.

____ uses sentences with an appropriate level of formality.

Conventions

____ adheres to the rules of grammar, spelling, and punctuation.

____ follows MLA or APA guidelines for documentation.

APA Documentation Style

The *Publication Manual of the American Psychological Association* (APA) provides research guidelines for behavioral and social science writers. To become familiar with scientific communication practices, you may be asked to follow the APA documentation style in some of your research reports.

This chapter explains basic APA style and offers example citations and reference entries. You can find additional information, including a sample APA research paper, at www.thewritesource.com/apa.htm.

Learning Outcomes

Understand APA format.
Make in-text citations.
Understand the reference list.
    Entries for books
    Entries for periodicals
    Entries for online sources
    Entries for other sources

"If I have seen further than others, it is by standing upon the shoulders of giants."

Isaac Newton

Understanding APA Format

Title Page ▪ (1) Include your paper's title, your name, and your school's name centered on three separate lines, double-spaced, in the top half of the first page. *Do not include the instructor's name or course title unless your instructor requires it.* (2) Flush left in the top margin, include the words *Running head:* (no italics) followed by a short version of your title in all capital letters. (3) Flush right in the top margin, include the page number, 1.

Abstract ▪ (1) On the second page, include an abstract: a 150– to 250–word summary of your paper, one paragraph long with no indentation. (2) Center the word *Abstract* (no italics) about one inch from the top of the page. (3) Flush left in the top margin, repeat your shortened title but without the words *Running head* preceding it. (4) Flush right in the top margin, include the page number, 2.

Body ▪ Follow this format for the body of your paper:

▪ **Running head:** Include your shortened title in the top margin, flush left without the words *Running head* preceding it.

▪ **Page numbers:** Continue numbering your pages, beginning with 3, flush right in the top margin.

▪ **Full title:** Include your full title, centered, at the top of page 3.

▪ **Margins:** Leave a one-inch margin on all four sides of each page (adjust the left margin to remain uniform if the paper will be bound).

▪ **Line spacing:** Double-space your entire paper unless your instructor allows single spacing for tables and figures to improve legibility.

▪ **Internal headings:** Section headings (level 1) and subheadings (levels 2–5)

Level 1	**Centered, Boldface, Uppercase and Lowercase**
Level 2	**Flush Left, Boldface, Uppercase and Lowercase**
Level 3	**Indented, boldface, lowercase, ending with a period.** Followed by the paragraph's text . . .
Level 4	***Indented, boldface, italicized, lowercase, ending with a period.*** Followed by the paragraph's text . . .
Level 5	*Indented, italicized, lowercase, ending with a period.* Followed by the paragraph's text . . .

In-Text Citations ▪ Within your paper, cite sources by author and date. If citing specific parts of a source, add location information, such as page or paragraph.

References ▪ Place full publication information for all sources cited in your paper in an alphabetized list of references at the end of your paper. (See page 470.)

Making In-Text Citations

In-text citations must include the author and date of the sources, either within the paper's running text or in parentheses. Each citation must be matched to an entry in the alphabetized list of references at the end of your paper.

According to a 2014 essay by Gabri . . .

According to a recent essay by Gabri (2014) . . .

According to a recent essay (Gabri, 2014) . . .

For a **short quotation**, also indicate the page where it is found in the source.

According to Madeira (2008), "Left and right brain share many tasks" (p. 36).

Madeira (2008) found that "left and right brain share many tasks" (p. 36).

She stated, "Left and right brain share many tasks" (Madeira, 2008, p. 36).

Note: Place **quotations of 40 or more words** in block style, indented five to seven spaces from the left margin. Include the necessary source information in parentheses *after* the final punctuation mark of the block quotation. If the quotation is more than one paragraph, indent the first line of subsequent paragraphs another five to seven spaces.

Model In-Text Citations

A Work by One Author

Identify the source by the author's last name and date, as shown above. If citing a quotation or a specific part of a work, give location information, such as the page, paragraph, or chapter number. In the parenthetical citation, that information is designated as follows: (p. or pp., para., Chapter).

Bush's 2002 budget was based on revenue estimates that "now appear to have been far too optimistic" (Lemann, 2003, p. 48).

Two or More Works by One Author Published in the Same Year

Arrange the works alphabetically by title in the reference list, and add a small *a* (no italics) after the date of the first work, a small *b* after the date of the second, and so on. Then use these letters in your in-text citations.

Gene therapy holds great promise for the future (Gormann, 2000a).

A Work by Two Authors

If a work has two authors, identify both in every citation of that work. Separate their names with an ampersand in a parenthetical reference.

A rise in global temperature and a decrease in atmospheric oxygen led to the mass extinction during the Late Permian Period (Huey & Ward, 2005).

A Work by Three to Five Authors

Mention all authors—up to five—in your first citation of a work.

> Love changes not just who we are, but who we can become (Lewis, Amini, & Lannon, 2000).

After the first citation, list only the first author followed by *et al.* (no italics).

> These discoveries lead to the hypothesis that love actually alters the brain's structure (Lewis et al., 2000).

A Work by Six or More Authors

If your source has six or more authors, refer to the work by the first author's name followed by *et al.* (no italics) in all parenthetical citations. However, be sure to list all of the authors (up to seven) in your reference list.

> Among children 13 to 14 years old, a direct correlation can be shown between cigarette advertising and smoking (Lopez et al., 2004).

A Work Authored by an Agency, a Committee, or Another Organization

Treat the organization name as the author name. If the organization has a well-known abbreviation, list the full name when first citing it in your paper, and provide the abbreviation in parentheses. (If citing the full name of the organization in parentheses, use square brackets for the abbreviation.) For subsequent citations, use just the abbreviation.

▪ **First Citation of an Organization, in a Signal Phrase**

> The National Institute of Mental Health (NIMH, 2014)) states that the fight-or-flight response is natural in fearful situations.

▪ **First Citation of an Organization, in Parentheses**

> Fearful situations naturally cause the fight-or-flight response (National Institute of Mental Health [NIMH], 2014).

▪ **Subsequent Citations**

> The NIMH (2014) says that post-traumatic stress disorder need not involve personal danger; it can result from seeing another person in a life-threatening situation.

A Work with an Unidentified Author

If your source lists no author, use the first two or three words of the title (capitalized normally) instead.

> . . . including a guide to low-fat diets and low-impact exercises ("Staying Healthy," 2004).

A Work Referred to in Another Work

Whenever possible, find the original source. If that can't be done, credit the source by adding "as cited in" within the parentheses.

> . . . theorem given by Ullman (as cited in Hoffman, 1998).

Note: In the reference list, an entry for Hoffman (not Ullman) would be included.

Two or More Works in One Citation

When citing two or more works within one parenthetical reference, list the sources in alphabetical order, separated with semicolons.

> These near-death experiences are reported with conviction (Rommer, 2000; Sabom, 1998).

Note: Arrange two or more works by the same author(s) by year of publication, separated by commas. (McIntyre & Ames, 1992, 1995)

An Electronic Source

Whenever possible, cite electronic sources like any other source.

> Legerski (2012) demonstrated that . . .

An Electronic Source with No Author

It is not uncommon for an electronic source to list no author. As with any other work with an unidentified author, use instead a shortened version of the title by which the entry is alphabetized in your reference list.

> The Webinar discussed how "games can engage students in learning and encourage application of critical skills like creativity, problem solving, persistence, resilience, and collaboration" ("Play, Mod, Design," 2013).

An Electronic Source with No Date

If an electronic source lists no date of publication, use the abbreviation *n.d.* (do not italicize).

> While some experts have argued that "fun" has no place in the discipline of learning, others have noted that "even in nature, young animals learn by play" (Arenz, n.d.).

Personal Communications

Cite personal letters, email messages, and phone conversations as a "personal communication" with their full date. Do not list your personal communications in your reference list.

> The management team expects to finish hiring this spring (R. Fouser, personal communication, December 14, 2004).

Understanding the Reference List

The reference list includes all of the retrievable sources cited in a paper. It begins on a separate page and follows the format below.

Running head ▪ Flush left, in the upper margin of the page, continue the running head (shortened title) from the body of your paper.

Page numbers ▪ Flush right, in the upper margin of the page, continue the numbering scheme of your paper. (For example, if the last page of the body is page 9, the first page of the reference list is page 10.)

Title ▪ Place the title *References* (no italics) approximately one inch from the top of the page and center it.

Entries ▪ List the entries alphabetically by the author's last name. If no author is given, then list by the title (disregarding *A, An,* or *The*).

- Double-space after the title *References* and between all lines thereafter.
- Leave a single space after the periods that separate parts of a reference entry.
- Capitalize only the first word (and any proper nouns) of book and article titles; capitalize the names of periodicals in the usual uppercase and lowercase style.
- Italicize titles of books and periodicals; but do not place the titles of articles, reference book entries, or book chapters in quotation marks.
- Use "hanging indentation": Begin each entry at the left margin and indent any additional lines of an entry five to seven spaces.

Format for a Book Entry

> Author's last name, Initials for first name and middle name. (year).
> *Book title.* Location: Publisher.

Note: For "Location," give the city and state, using the two-letter U.S. Postal abbreviation; for international publishers, give the city and country (spelled out). Omit the terms *Publishers, Co., Inc.* from publishers' names, but retain the terms *Press* and *Books.*

Format for a Periodical Entry

> Author's last name, Initials for first and middle names. (year, Month day). Article title. *Periodical Title, volume*(issue), pages.

Format for an Online Periodical Entry

> Author's last name, Initials for first and middle names. (year, Month day). Article title. *Periodical Title, volume*(issue), pages. DOI or URL

Entries for Books

A Book by One Author

After the author name and date, include the book title in italics, capitalizing only the first word, the first word after a colon, and any proper nouns.

> Kuriansky, J. (2007). *Beyond bullets and bombs: Grassroots peacebuilding between Israelies and Palestinians.* Westport, CT: Praeger Press.

A Book by Two or More Authors

Follow the first author's name with a comma; then join the two authors' names with an ampersand (&) rather than "and."

> Dustin, C. A., & Ziegler, J. E. (2007). *Practicing mortality: Art, philosophy, and contemplative seeing.* New York, NY: Palgrave Macmillan.

Note: You can list up to seven authors in a reference entry.

An Anonymous Book

If an author is listed as "Anonymous," treat it as the author's name. Otherwise, begin the reference with the book's title:

> *American Medical Association essential guide to asthma.* (2003). New York, NY: American Medical Association.

A Chapter from a Book

List the chapter title without quotation marks, followed by "In" and the book title.

> Tattersal, I. (2002). How did we achieve humanity? In *The monkey in the mirror* (pp. 138–168). New York, NY: Harcourt.

A Single Work from an Anthology

After the usual author, date, and entry title, list editors' names—initials first, then surname, and the identifier "Eds." in parentheses—followed by the anthology title.

> Nichols, J. (2005). Diversity and stability in language. In B. D. Joseph & R. D. Janda (Eds.), *The handbook of historical linguistics* (pp. 283–310). Malden, MA: Blackwell.

One Volume of a Multivolume Edited Work

To cite an entire volume, place the editors' names in the author position. For a multivolume work, identify the volume in parentheses after the title.

> Salzman, J., Smith, D. L., & West, C. (Eds.). (1996). *Encyclopedia of African-American culture and history* (Vol. 4). New York, NY: Simon & Schuster Macmillan.

A Group Author as Publisher

List the group as author, and in the publisher spot list "Author."

> Amnesty International. (2007). *Maze of injustice: The failure to protect indigenous women from sexual violence in the USA*. New York, NY: Author.

Note: If the publication is a brochure, identify it as such in brackets after the title [Brochure].

A Single Work within a Volume of a Series

For the book title, make a two-part title of the series and the particular volume you are citing.

> Marshall, P. G. (2002). The impact of the cold war on Asia. In T. O'Neill (Series Ed.), *World history by era: Vol. 9. The nuclear age* (pp. 155–162). San Diego, CA: Greenhaven Press.

An Edition Other Than the First

If the edition you use is not a first edition, include the edition number in parentheses after the book title.

> Trimmer, J. (2009). *The new writing with a purpose* (14th ed.). Boston, MA: Cengage Learning.

An Article in a Reference Book

When citing an article included in a reference book, begin with the author's name, if identified. Otherwise start with the entry title.

> Lewer, N. (1999). Non-lethal weapons. In *World encyclopedia of peace* (pp. 279–280). Oxford, England: Pergamon Press.

A Technical or Research Report

Follow the usual guidelines for a book or similar print document.

> Ball, J., & Evans, C., Jr. (2001). *Safe passage: Astronaut care for exploration missions*. Washington, DC: National Academies Press.

A Government Publication

Generally, list the government agency as the author. When possible, include an identification number for the document in parentheses after the title.

> National Renewable Energy Laboratory. (2003). *Statistical wind power forecasting for U.S. wind farms* (NREL Publication No. CP-500-35087). Springfield, VA: US Department of Commerce.

Note: If the document is not available from the Government Printing Office (GPO), the publisher would be either "Author" or the separate government department that published it.

Entries for Periodicals

An Article in a Scholarly Journal, Consecutively Paginated

After the author's name, list the year of publication. For journals that continue pagination from issue to issue, no issue number is needed.

> Epstein, R., & Hundert, E. (2002). Defining and assessing professional competence. *JAMA, 287,* 226–235.

A Journal Article, Paginated by Issue

When each issue starts with page 1, include the issue number (not italicized) in parentheses after the volume number.

> Carnegie, E., & Jones, A. (2013). Improving the management of asthma in older adults. *Nursing Standard, 28*(13), 50–58.

A Journal Article, Up to Seven Authors

List all the authors, separated by commas, and add an ampersand (&) before the last.

> Yuste, R., & Church, G. M. (2014). The new century of the brain. *Scientific American, 310*(3), 38–45.

A Journal Article, More Than Seven Authors

List the first six authors as usual, followed by an ellipsis, and then the last.

> Yamada, A., Suzuki, M. [Miyoshi], Kato, M., Suzuki, M. [Mei], Tanaka, S. Shindo., T., . . . Furukawa, T. A. (2007). Emotional distress and its correlates among parents of children with pervasive developmental disorders. *Psychiatry & Clinical Neurosciences, 61*(6), 651–657.

Note: Within your paper, cite the authors as follows: (Yamada et al., 2007).

An Abstract of a Scholarly Article (from a Secondary Source)

To reference an abstract published separately from the article it summarizes, list the article publication details first, followed by the abstract's publication information.

> Yamamoto, S., & Nakamura, A. (2000). A new module of continuous dust production from the lunar surface. *Astronomy & Astrophysics, 356,* 1112–1118. Abstract taken from the CDS Bibiliographic Service, 2005.

Note: When the dates of the article and the secondary-source abstract differ, cite both dates in your text, the original first, separated by a slash (2001/2002). When the abstract is obtained from the original source, place the description [Abstract] in brackets following the title (but before the period).

A Magazine Article, Author Given

After the author's name, list the full date (as much as is identified in the magazine). Also list volume (in italics) and issue number (in parentheses, no italics), if those are identified. End with the page or pages of the article.

Silberman, S. (2001, December). The geek syndrome. *Wired, 9*(12), 174–183.

A Magazine Article, No Author Given

Place the article title in the author position, followed by the publication date.

Arctic ozone wiped out by solar storms. (2005, March 12). *New Scientist, 185*(2490), 17.

A Review in a Journal

After the title of the review, identify the original work and its author(s) in brackets, preceded by the phrase *Review of,* as shown here.

Hutcheon, L., & Hutcheon, M. (2008). Tuning into the mind [Review of the book *Musicophilia: Tales of music and the brain,* by O. Sacks]. *Canadian Medical Association Journal, 178,* 441.

A Newspaper Article

For newspapers, list the author, date, title, name of the publication, and the page number(s). Identify page numbers with the abbreviation "p." (for a single page) or "pp." (for more than one page). If the article is not on continuous pages, give all the page numbers, separated by commas.

Stolberg, S. C. (2002, January 4). Breakthrough in pig cloning could aid organ transplants. *The New York Times,* pp. 1A, 17A.

Note: The "A" means that the letter appeared in the newspaper's section A. Also, if no author is listed, begin with the title followed by the date, publication, and page number(s).

A Newsletter Article, No Author Given

A reference entry for a newsletter article is arranged in the same way as an entry for a magazine article is arranged.

Teaching mainstreamed special education students. (2002, February). *The Council Chronicle, 11,* 6–8.

Entries for Online Sources

The flexible nature of the Internet is both a strength and a weakness. On the one hand, you can find the most recent information there. On the other, the information that you find and cite today may have changed or moved by tomorrow.

For that reason, the APA recommends using the version of record, also known as the "archival" version of a source: the print version; the final electronic version with a digital object identifier (DOI); or an electronic version with a "Retrieved from" statement and URL if neither of the previous options is possible.

URL Note: If you must break a URL across lines, do not add hyphens. Breaking only after "http://" and before other punctuation marks in the URL. Do not add a retrieval date unless the material may change over time.

A Journal Article with a Digital Object Identifier (DOI)

End the entry with the abbreviation "doi" (lowercase) followed by a colon, and then the DOI itself. Do not place a space after the colon.

> Bibel, W. (2014). Artificial intelligence in a historical perspective. *AI Communications, 27*(1), 87-102. doi:10.3233/AIC-130576

A Journal Article without a DOI

If the source is relatively stable and can be accessed directly via the URL, end the entry with a "Retrieved from" statement. Do not include a period after the URL.

> Tysiac, K. (2014, February 24). How real work experience can help students, businesses. *Journal of Accountancy.* Retrieved from http://www .journalofaccountancy.com/News/20149652.htm

Note: For sources that require a subscription or that must be located by on-site search, use the term "Available from" and the site URL.

> Greven, D. (2009). Contemporary Hollywood masculinity and the double-protagonist film. *Cinema Journal, 48*(4), 22–43. Available from http:// www.scribd.com/doc/168294895/Contemporary-Hollywood -Masculinity-and-the-Double-protagonist-Film

An Article from a Database

Include the database information only if the article cannot be easily found elsewhere.

> Bell, J. B., & Nye, E. C. (2007). Specific symptoms predict suicidal ideation in Vietnam combat veterans with post-traumatic stress disorder. *Military Medicine, 172,* 1144–1147. Available from http://www.ebscohost.com

A Newspaper Article

Include the full date of the article and a "Retrieved from" statement.

> Hotz, R. L. (2014, February 26). NASA scientists discover 715 new planets. *Wall Street Journal.* Retrieved from http://online.wsj.com

An Abstract

When refering to an abstract for which the full text is available, include [Abstract] after the source title.

> Aguilar, R. (2013). Old, female and homeless [Abstract]. *Nation, 296*(6), 24–26.

Note: If the full text is not available, include the database in which you found the abstract, and the accession number identifying it.

> Callanan, P. (2001, November). Characteristics of street gangs. *Campus Safety Journal, 9*(10), 16. Abstract retrieved from National Criminal Justice Reference Service Abstracts. (Accession No. 192019)

An Electronic Book

In general, reference an electronic book or audio book only if no print version is available. Include the specific version you are referencing (e.g. [ePub version]).

> US Office of Civil Defense. (1968). *In time of emergency: A citizen's handbook on nuclear attack, natural disasters* [MP3 audiobook]. Retrieved from https://librivox.org

Note: If citing a chapter or other section of an electronic document, provide the URL to the specific section when possible.

A Book Review

Follow the format for a print book review, but add a "Retrieved from" statement if the review is generally available or an "Available from" statement if it must be acquired by subscription or purchase.

> Shapiro, K. (2007). Mystic chords. [Review of the book *Musicophilia: Tales of music and the brain*, by Oliver Sacks]. *Commentary, 124*(5), 73–77. Available from http://www.ebscohost.com

An Entry in an Online Encyclopedia or Dictionary

If no author is identified, start with the entry name. If no publication date is given, list (n.d.). Use "In" to indicate the source itself. Avoid wikis, as their information is usually not peer reviewed and changes often.

> Stockholm. (2014). In *Encyclopaedia Britannica*. Retrieved from http://www.britannica.com/EBchecked/topic/566797/Stockholm

Content on a Nonperiodical Website

For multipage documents, provide a URL to the first page. You may have to search the site to find needed publication information.

> Gaskill, M. (2014, February 28). *Tackling tumors with space station research.* Retrieved from http://www.nasa.gov/mission_pages/station/research/news/tackling_tumors

A Post on a Newsgroup, an Online Forum, or a Discussion Group

List the poster's screen name if the actual name is not available. Do not italicize the subject line of the message, which serves as the post title. Supply the URL where the post can be read, and include an "archived at" notation if applicable.

> O'Brien, E. (2011, September 15). Untitled post [Online forum comment]. Retrieved from http://www.edweb.net/.59c2d36b/17, archived at http://www.edweb.net/?230@@.59c2d36b

An Email Message

Email messages are not included in the reference list. Instead, they are identified as a "personal communication" in the body of the paper. (See page 469.)

Entries for Other Sources

A Television or Radio Broadcast

Identify the program as a broadcast in brackets immediately after the title.

> Crystal, L. (Executive Producer). (2005, February 11). *The newshour with Jim Lehrer* [Television broadcast]. New York and Washington, DC: Public Broadcasting Service.

An Audio Recording

Begin with the writer and copyright year, followed by the title of the specific selection. Next list the performer (if different from the writer), the title of the overall work, the medium (CD, cassette, etc.), and the publisher. Finish with the recording date in parentheses if it differs from the copyright date.

> Fullerton, G. S. (1906). Common thought, science, and reflective thought [Narrated by M. Mosely]. On *Introduction to philosophy* [MP3 file]. Newark: Audible. (2012, February 28)

A Motion Picture

Give the name and function of the director, producer, or both. If the motion picture's circulation was limited, provide the distributor's name and complete address in parentheses.

> Jackson, P. (Director). (2003). *The lord of the rings: Return of the king* [Motion picture]. United States. New Line Productions, Inc.

A Published Interview

Begin with the author and continue with the usual publication information. Include the title of the interview and follow with the description "Interview" and the names of the person interviewed in brackets.

> Fussman, C. (2002, January). What I've learned [Interview with Robert McNamara]. *Esquire, 137*(1), 85.

Writers
INC

Speaking
and Listening

Speaking Effectively

Have you ever heard someone speaking so well that you actually stopped to listen? Good speakers are able to influence and inspire us. Some have been powerful enough, in fact, to change the world.

While it is true that some speakers are better than others, all of them use the same skills to prepare and present a speech. From choosing a topic to researching, writing, practicing, and presenting, you can learn how to speak effectively. This chapter will help.

Learning Outcomes

Plan a speech.
Write a speech.
Present a speech.
Assess a speech.
Prepare a multimedia presentation.

"There are always three speeches . . . . The one you practiced, the one you gave, and the one you wish you gave."

Dale Carnegie

Planning a Speech

Giving a speech is an opportunity both to learn and to teach. You will learn as you plan and write your speech, and you will teach as you present it. Speaking will often require you to demonstrate, inform, or persuade.

As you begin to think about a speech assignment, analyze the rhetorical situation by answering the **STRAP** questions.

> **STRAP Questions**
> **S**ubject: What subject am I considering?
> **T**ype: What type of speech am I giving? How long will I talk? What format will I follow?
> **R**ole: Am I speaking as myself, as a representative of a group, as a character from history or fiction, . . . ?
> **A**udience: Who will hear my speech? What do they likely know about this subject? What do they need to know about it?
> **P**urpose: What is my purpose —to inform, to persuade, to demonstrate?

Selecting Your Topic

After briefly analyzing the rhetorical situation, you must select a suitable topic. Follow these guidelines:

1. Choose a subject that meets the requirements of the assignment and will interest your audience.

2. Narrow the subject to a specific topic that you can cover in the time allotted for your speech.

General Subject		**Specific Topic**
Credit cards	Credit card debt	Credit card debt among young people

3. Write a thesis statement that will serve as the focus for your speech by completing this formula:

Formula
My purpose is [to convince, to show] my audience [add your specific topic].

Thesis Statement
"My purpose is to convince my audience that credit cards must be used wisely in order to avoid long-lasting debt and credit issues."

Researching Your Topic

After you have selected a specific topic, you are ready to begin your research. Depending on the kind of speech you are planning, the sources of information explained below will prove useful.

Search your memory. If you are basing your speech on a personal experience, ask yourself *who? what? when? where? why?* and *how?* about it. Record the sensory details related to your experience—sights, sounds, smells, flavors, and textures.

Talk to others. Ask others who have had the same or similar experience what they learned from it and how it changed them. If necessary, speak to an expert on your topic.

Get firsthand experience. Learn about your topic firsthand, especially if you are giving a demonstration. Visit a lab, a field station, or a job site to make observations. Tour a local historical site or museum, or attend a reenactment.

Explore the Internet. Use the Internet to gather facts, figures, dates, examples, quotations, and similar information. Watch videos or listen to podcasts and radio shows. Make sure the sources offer current, reliable information.

Search the library. Search the library for books, magazines, pamphlets, videos, and other types of media. Remember that librarians are media experts who can help you find additional material you may have overlooked.

Help File

It is usually a good idea to begin your research by looking at the big picture. Understanding the history or background of a particular topic can give you a useful perspective. Once you have a good overview of your topic, begin to search for details that support your focus and add interest and credibility to your speech.

Writing a Speech

After gathering enough information, it's time to analyze and organize it. Begin by constructing a list or a working outline of the key points you plan to cover in your presentation, keeping in mind your purpose and audience.

A short talk on a current topic may require only a few notes or a brief list of points to cover. A full-length report for history class, on the other hand, may require an essay or manuscript that must be handed in afterward.

Once you've determined what sort of written form is necessary, you can begin to select and arrange your details. Whether you make a list, write an outline, or prepare a word-for-word manuscript, keep the three key parts of your speech in mind—the introduction, the body, and the conclusion.

Writing Your Introduction

The introduction sets the tone and direction of your speech. It also includes an attention-getting element. One way to spark interest is to connect the content of your speech to the lives of your listeners. Consider the following suggestions:

1. **Grab attention** with a series of thoughtful questions, a short demonstration, a personal connection, or a surprising fact or statistic.

2. **Provide background information** with a short history or story (anecdote) related to the topic. (See page 486.)

3. **Present the thesis or focus statement** of your speech and explain why the topic is important to your audience.

4. **Ask a rhetorical question:** "You may be asking, 'Why should I care about . . . ?'"

5. **Ask a real question:** "How many of you have ever seen . . . ?"

Help File

Some experts suggest writing your speech from *finish to start*—the conclusion first, then your main points, and last, the introduction. This approach allows you to consider the content carefully, in preparation for writing an introduction.

Organizing Your Details

When planning the body of your speech, choose an organizational pattern that suits your purpose (to inform, to persuade, to demonstrate). Each pattern explained below is further defined with an example.

Order of importance: Arrange details according to importance—from most important to least important or from least to most.

> A persuasive speech on the benefits of buying a hybrid car

Chronological order: Arrange details according to time—the order in which events (or steps in a process) take place.

> A demonstration of how a solar panel works to produce electricity

Spatial order: Provide information according to the location of the different parts of the topic.

> An informative speech, including some demonstration, about the working parts of a cell phone

Comparison/contrast: Present details by comparing subjects (showing how they are alike) and by contrasting them (showing how they are different).

> An informative speech comparing the workings of the U.S. Congress with those of England's Parliament

Cause and effect: Provide information that reveals the causes and effects of a situation, a problem, or a process.

> A lab report explaining your science experiment and its results

Problem-solution: Describe a problem and offer a solution.

> A report about elderly shut-ins and a new student visitation program

Choosing a Form

Once you have written your introduction and considered the appropriate organization for your speech, turn your attention to the body, or main points. The form you use—whether a list, an outline, or a full manuscript—will depend on the rhetorical situation and your teacher's instructions.

List ▪ Use a list for a brief, informal speech—the kind you might be asked to give in class on short notice. Think about your purpose and then list the following items:

- Your opening sentence (or two)
- A summary phrase for each main point
- Your closing sentence (or two)

Outline ▪ Use an outline for a longer, more formal speech, such as a thoroughly researched classroom report. An outline organizes material in greater detail and provides more reminders of what you plan to say. Include these items:

- Opening statement as a sentence
- Main points in sentence form
- Quotations written word for word
- Sources, supporting numbers, and technical details listed precisely
- Closing statement as a sentence
- Notes [in brackets] for visual aids

Manuscript ▪ Use the guidelines below if you plan to write out your presentation word for word. (See page 486–487 for a sample manuscript.)

- Write your manuscript using a style that fits your purpose and audience.
- Write in an appropriate tone; what you write is going to be heard—not read.
- Use short sentences and avoid running sentences from one page to the next.
- Double-space your lines and number each page.
- Spell out difficult words phonetically [FO-NET-IC-LEE].
- Mark your script for emphasis, key pauses, and visual aids. (See page 488.)

List

1. Opening sentences
2. Summary phrase 1
   Summary phrase 2
   Summary phrase 3
3. Closing sentences

Outline

  I. Opening statement
    A. Point (purpose or thesis)
    B. Point [show visual]
  II. Body (with 3-5 main points)
    A. Main point
      1. Supporting detail
      2. Supporting detail
    B. Main point
      1. Supporting detail
      2. Supporting detail
    C. Main point
      1. Supporting detail
      2. Supporting detail
  III. Closing statement
    A. Point (restated thesis)
    B. Point (call to action)

Developing the Body

When preparing a speech, always use a voice appropriate to your topic, purpose, and audience. A natural, sincere voice works well in most situations. Never mislead your audience with half-truths, slanted language, or other logical fallacies. (See pages 110–111.) Instead, select trustworthy details to achieve your purpose. Note the following objectives for using different types of details in presentations:

Facts and statistics . . . . present specific, measurable ideas.
Definitions and examples. . clarify information.
Stories and anecdotes . . . . . connect personally with listeners.
Visuals and videos . . . . show rather than merely tell the audience.
Quotations . . . . offer expert or firsthand ideas.
Demonstrations . . . . show the audience just what to do.

Writing Your Conclusion

The conclusion, like the introduction, is critical to the success of any speech. The introduction captures attention, sets the tone, and identifies the focus or main point. Almost in reverse, the conclusion reviews key points, restates the main idea, and reminds the audience of the topic's importance. Together, these parts define a presentation and put the message in perspective for the audience.

Concluding Strategies
  1. Come full circle, reinforcing your opening thoughts.
  2. Connect your topic to the bigger picture.
  3. Remind the audience of how this topic affects them. (See page 487.)
  5. End with a thoughtful summary, question, or challenge.

Help File

For a speech that moves smoothly from start to finish, arrange your main points and details into compact, well-organized segments. Also make a clean break between the segments, giving the audience time to absorb ideas and follow your line of thinking. To separate main points, use transitions (*first, second, next; another key point; remember what I said earlier; and so on*).

Sample Manuscript Speech

Mark a manuscript with dashes, underlining, and boldface to show where you will pause, add emphasis, or adjust your voice. Use brackets to indicate visual aids.

1

Avoid the Crunch

The speaker begins with an anecdote.

Let's say that you decide to buy a pair of jeans, and the cashier says, "That will be $30, please. Or, if you prefer, you can just pay a little each month for the next 17 years." Sound ridiculous? Teenagers do it every day, creating credit card debt that will follow them into adulthood.

Credit card companies are hoping to cash in by targeting <u>students</u>. Plush toys, T-shirts, and snacks are freebies intended to lure potential customers. Sociologist Robert Manning states, "The credit card marketers sign high school kids at college fairs. They get paid by the number of applications they turn in." Many students sign up without considering the fine print. [hold up credit card application form] Can you see what's written here? No? Let me read from a typical credit card application form. "Introductory rate of **0%**." That means you pay nothing on the balance of your credit card. <u>Sounds great, right</u>? Let me keep reading. "After the promotional period of six months, the standard rate of **15%** will be applied. However, if you default or fail to pay, the rate will be raised to **30%**."

He holds up a credit application.

What does this mean to you? Let's say you spend $2,000 during the first six months. Then the interest rate zooms up to 15%. You decide to start paying off the balance, but you don't have enough money to pay the whole thing, because you work only weekends at Big Burger. So you pay the monthly minimum of 2% or at least $25 a month. How long do you think it would take to pay off the original $2,000 balance? [ask for guesses] Not only would it take **almost 12 years**, but you would also end up spending about **$4,000**! [show visual aid]

A visual aid emphasizes the point.

You charged . . .

You paid . . .

2

As radio talk-show host Clark Howard says, "What you really need to know is that you are ripping yourself off because you are not paying off that balance."

The speaker points out the importance of the topic.

Some students are so overwhelmed by debt that they file for bankruptcy, which is a legal cancellation of debt. Writer Cindy Landrum gathered the following statistics: "Bankruptcy filings for people ages 18–25 were at an all-time high in 2000, numbering almost 150,000, a **tenfold increase** in just five years. More young adults filed for bankruptcy than graduated from college in 2001." For up to 10 years, bankruptcy will be a nasty stain on your credit report.

He quotes an expert to support his argument.

"Your credit report is often called your second résumé," according to Dr. Flora Williams in her book *Climbing the Steps to Financial Success*. A credit report covers your history of borrowing, bill payment, and debt owed. If you use your credit card irresponsibly, your credit card company will make negative comments on your credit report. And banks, college loan officers, employers, and landlords often request credit reports.

So how do you maintain a positive credit report? Here are four key points:

1. **Use your credit card wisely.** Keep track of what you are buying. Know how long it will take you to pay for each item. Don't be tempted by the latest laptop or video game system that you can't afford.

2. **Know your credit limit.** Going over the limit may result in fines or even cancellation of your account.

3. **Pay off the balance**, or at least more than the minimum.

4. **Pay on time.** This is the simplest way to avoid late fees and credit damage.

The closing paragraph encourages the audience to reflect on the subject.

What is the lesson here? As a teenager, making bad decisions with a credit card can have a negative impact on student loans, future jobs, and even the purchase of your first home. It takes common sense and hard work to avoid the pitfalls of credit card debt, but if you read the fine print, spend wisely, and pay promptly, you'll be on your way to building a **solid** financial foundation.

Presenting a Speech
Rehearsing Your Speech

After you are finished writing your speech, it's time to practice, practice, practice. Rehearse your presentation until you feel completely comfortable with it. Even then, ask a friend or family member to listen and provide some feedback. Here are 10 suggestions for both practicing and actually presenting your speech.

1. Be in the moment. Focus entirely on what you are doing.
2. Be prepared to handle any audiovisual equipment or visual aids you are using.
3. Walk to the front of the room and connect with your audience by offering a smile and a greeting.
4. Stand up straight and avoid slouching or shifting from one leg to the other.
5. Speak up—and speak clearly—right from the beginning.
6. Speak in a natural, conversational voice but also be energetic and compelling.
7. Don't rush. Take your time and pause to look at your notes whenever necessary.
8. Think about what you are saying, adding appropriate feeling to your words so the audience remains interested.
9. Communicate with your audience in a visual way by using your eyes and facial expressions.
10. Avoid these vocal pitfalls: "Uh . . . um . . . y'know . . . okay."

Marking Your Copy

As you rehearse your speech, you may think of ways to improve your delivery. For example, you may decide to emphasize different words, pause in certain places, use a visual aid you hadn't thought of before, and so on. Mark your final presentation copy using the suggestions below. Also spell out difficult words phonetically [FO-NET-IC-LEE].

Boldface	for emphasizing key points
Underlining	for additional feeling or emotion
Dash—	for a dramatic pause
[Brackets]	for visual aids [show chart] or actions [raise hand]

Using Presentation Aids

Visual aids can be helpful for holding the attention of your audience and getting your message across in a convincing manner. Here are some tips.

1. Prepare visuals that are large enough and clear enough to be seen and understood by everyone in the audience.

2. Put just enough information in your graphic to be useful; remember, white space provides balance and emphasis.

3. Keep visual aids hidden until they are needed so they don't become a distraction.

4. Introduce each visual ("As you can see on this chart . . .") and point out its key details; then go back to talking directly to your audience.

5. Practice using any technology, such as white-board projectors.

Screen shot courtesy Federal Trade Commission

Overcoming Stage Fright

Even though stage fright is inevitable, you do need to control it. The best remedy for stage fright is practice. Here are some suggestions.

1. Know your subject thoroughly and rehearse your presentation frequently.

2. Mark your copy to make it easy to follow. (See page 488.)

3. Use visual aids whenever appropriate.

4. Visualize yourself finishing your speech successfully.

5. Remember, no presentation is perfect; if you make a mistake, move on.

6. Take a deep breath, and begin your speech with an icebreaker, perhaps a rhetorical question ("How many of you . . .?").

7. Keep your delivery slow and under control.

Assessing a Speech

Use this rubric as a checklist to evaluate your speeches. The rubric is arranged according to important standards of effective speech making.

The speech . . .

Ideas

___ focuses on an important and interesting topic.

___ presents the main points clearly from beginning to ending.

Organization

___ has an easy-to-follow story or line of reasoning.

___ moves smoothly from one point to the next.

___ includes accurate and appropriate facts and figures.

___ comes full circle, tying everything together in the conclusion.

___ feels complete and effective.

The speaker . . .

Voice

___ speaks loudly and clearly enough to be heard by everyone.

___ uses plain, conversational language.

Delivery

___ presents material with energy and purpose.

___ avoids distracting mannerisms or vocal issues.

___ uses effective eye contact throughout.

___ uses visual aids to clarify or emphasize information.

___ holds the audience's attention from start to finish.

Preparing a Multimedia Presentation

With a few guidelines and tips, you can turn your oral report or speech into a multimedia presentation. In most cases, you will use a computer to help you organize and present the slides, music, video, and other graphic devices. The computer allows you to move from slide to slide, reinforcing and clarifying information for your audience.

▌ Prewriting

  1. **Selecting a topic . . .** Choose a topic that is right for your audience and appropriate for a multimedia presentation.
  2. **Gathering details . . .** Collect and organize information about your topic in the same manner you would if you were writing a report or speech. (See page 481.)

▌ Writing and Revising

  3. **Creating a design . . .** Use an appealing graphic design for your pages. Consider whether it is a good fit for your topic and your audience. It should be formal or businesslike for a serious topic; more casual or informal for a less serious topic. Also choose a typestyle and size that is easy to read from the back of the room.
  4. **Creating pages . . .** Prepare a new page for each main idea in your presentation. (See the storyboard on page 492.) If an idea has several parts, present them separately on that page. Also use transitions to move smoothly from one point to the next. Transitional effects (dissolves, fades, wipes) may also be available on your computer.
  5. **Fine-tuning your presentation . . .** Practice delivering your speech several times, clicking through the prepared pages. Try it with a sample audience, if possible, and ask for their input. Insert separate pages for quotations or statements that need special emphasis.
  6. **Revising for style and accuracy . . .** Include clear, concise, and correct key words to share your message on each screen.

▌ Editing and Proofreading

  7. **Preparing a final version . . .** Create a final version that runs smoothly and is free of any glitches or mechanical errors. Remember, on-screen errors are especially obvious. When your presentation is completely satisfactory, protect your investment of time and effort by making a backup copy.

Creating a Storyboard

A storyboard shows what each screen or page in your report will look like. The storyboard below demonstrates one way to turn the model speech on pages 486–487 into either a multimedia presentation or an interactive report. The light green boxes show notes for pages in a simple step-by-step order. The white boxes show added links and pages. To view the final versions of the presentation and report, visit www. thewritesource.com/multimedia_reports.

Sample Storyboard

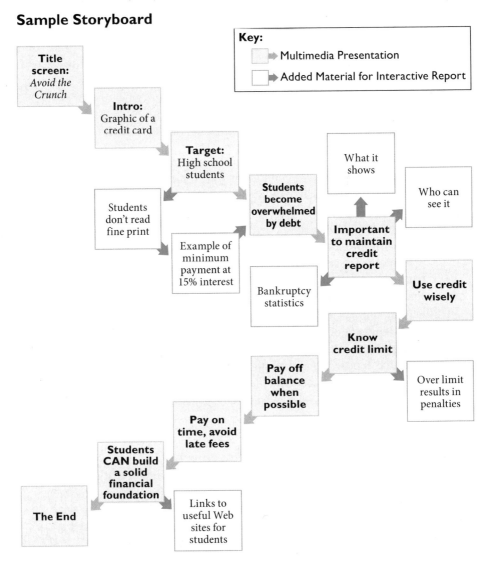

Key:
- Multimedia Presentation
- Added Material for Interactive Report

Title screen: *Avoid the Crunch*

Intro: Graphic of a credit card

Target: High school students

Students don't read fine print

Example of minimum payment at 15% interest

Students become overwhelmed by debt

Bankruptcy statistics

What it shows

Important to maintain credit report

Who can see it

Use credit wisely

Know credit limit

Over limit results in penalties

Pay off balance when possible

Pay on time, avoid late fees

Students CAN build a solid financial foundation

Links to useful Web sites for students

The End

Participating in Discussions

It is almost always a good idea to listen more than you speak. This is especially true when working in a group—large or small. Whether you and a classmate are planning a project or your entire class is discussing an assigned reading, you need to be a listener first and a talker second.

In all discussions, start by listening carefully. Only after doing so should you speak up. This chapter provides some helpful guidelines for successfully participating in group discussions. If you follow these guidelines, you will be listening with both ears and speaking with one clear voice.

Learning Outcomes

Prepare for discussions.
Listen attentively.
Respond appropriately.
Cooperate with others.
Clarify unclear statements.
Reflect on the discussion.
Assess your participation.

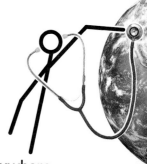

"A good listener is not only popular everywhere, but after awhile he gets to know something."

Wilson Mizner

Preparing for Discussions

A discussion is a conversation among a group of people who gather together to share ideas. During an effective discussion, the group members present and consider all sides of an issue. Their goal is to reach a consensus, perhaps by making a decision, solving a problem, or resolving a conflict.

Preparing Effectively

To be an effective member of a discussion group, come prepared. At a basic level this means you are ready to talk, listen, cooperate with others, and consider everyone's ideas.

Come prepared. Do the necessary research to be informed about the topic and know what you think about it.

Set the guidelines. Be ready to set or follow the established rules, goals, and deadlines for the discussion. Understand the roles of individual participants: leader, note taker, timer, and so on.

Set the proper tone. Determine to discuss matters in a civil, democratic way. Do not dominate the discussion but rather encourage others to share their thoughts. Promote a fair, productive discussion.

Leading a Discussion

Although all members of a discussion group are equal participants, a leader can ensure that the group stays on task and remains objective. A discussion leader has these responsibilities:

1. State the purpose or goal of the discussion.
2. Get the conversation started.
3. Stay on the topic.
4. Keep members from dominating the conversation.
5. Encourage everyone to participate.
6. Ask that only one person speaks at a time.
7. Remind members to speak loudly and clearly enough for all to hear.
8. Clarify ideas as necessary.
9. Move the group toward a consensus.
10. Summarize the discussion.

Listening Attentively

Group participants must listen attentively and objectively for the discussion to reach its goal. Being a good listener takes both concentration and restraint.

Listen actively. Listen with an open mind. Make eye contact with the speaker, nodding your head, asking good questions, and offering insightful comments.

Listen for specific details. Rather than being swept along by the general drift of the conversation, listen for answers to the 5 W's and H about the topic—*who? what? when? where? why?* and *how?*

Listen for signal words. Be on the lookout for signal words that indicate where the speaker is headed (Let me emphasize . . . ; Other people may say . . . but I say . . . ; What it all comes down to is . . .). These words serve as signposts to help you find the main ideas.

Listen critically. Remain somewhat skeptical when listening to others. Sometimes opinions are presented as facts, misleading information is shared, or logical fallacies are applied. (See pages 110–111.) Be ready to challenge ideas that don't quite ring true.

Listen between the lines. Pay attention not only to what a person says, but also to how he or she says it. Watch for body language, gestures, facial expressions, and other forms of nonverbal communication.

Good Listeners . . .

- listen with an open mind.
- make eye contact and think about what the speaker is saying.
- stay focused so that they are ready to respond thoughtfully.
- pay attention to the speaker's tone of voice and emphasis.
- watch for gestures and facial expressions.
- interrupt only when necessary to ask for clarification.

Good Speakers . . .

- speak loudly and clearly.
- maintain eye contact with their listeners.
- explain and clarify information for the audience.
- emphasize their main points by changing the tone and volume.
- use gestures and body language to communicate effectively.
- provide time for listeners to ask questions or make observations.

Avoid Listening Pitfalls

When you listen in groups, avoid the following pitfalls.

1. **Multitasking.** When you listen to someone, give the person your full attention. Put down the cell phone. Put down the game device. Stop checking Facebook or email. Turn off the TV. Forget about yesterday or next hour or what's for lunch. Focus on the person and what he or she is saying.

2. **Thinking instead of listening.** Don't try to formulate your own response while the other person is speaking. Pay full attention to what the person is actually saying. Then respond.

3. **Listening *without* thinking.** Listen critically, weighing and testing concepts rather than mindlessly accepting everything as stated. Test concepts in your mind and aloud, politely of course.

4. **Taking too many notes.** Jot down important ideas, but avoid taking too many notes. If you record everything you find interesting or debatable, you may miss the big picture, and losing track of the discussion makes it hard to contribute intelligently.

5. **Talking too much.** People talking *at* each other rather than *with* each other does not make a good conversation or a fruitful discussion. Speak only when you have something to contribute. Otherwise, listen and think.

6. **Becoming upset.** Remain invested in your ideas without becoming overly emotional. Participants can disagree, but remember to focus on ideas, not on personalities; and keep the group's goal in mind at all times.

Responding Appropriately

Responding is an important element in a discussion. Only when a participant responds do others know what he or she is thinking. Without thoughtful, back-and-forth exchanges, a discussion is not really a discussion.

Respond at the right time. Listen carefully to the discussion and recognize when it is appropriate to speak. Don't interrupt unless you have something significant to offer, something that can clarify a point or avoid confusion. Never speak over the top of another person.

> Could I add one point to what Tamara just said?

Respond in a positive manner. If you disagree, challenge the ideas, not the people. Try beginning your comments with "Yes, and . . ." rather than "Yes, but . . . ." Strike a balance between how much you add and how much you listen.

> Which of these two ideas seems more practical?

State your case. When you do decide to speak, state your position confidently without sounding pushy. Provide concrete examples and convincing evidence, and don't change the topic unless it's necessary to clarify a point.

> I'd like to propose an alternative approach.

Cooperating with Others

Participants ought to value and encourage the responses of others. Without cooperation, the discussion is unlikely to meet its goal.

Contribute your ideas. Share your thoughts when the time is right and try to build on what others have already said. Discussions work best when participants create ideas collaboratively.

> Let's build on Eduardo's suggestion.

Encourage others to participate. Keep the tone positive, welcoming everyone's comments. Consider asking quieter group members what they think about something that was just said.

> Sasha, what do you think about this concept?

Keep the discussion moving forward. Summarize what others have said before you add your own thoughts. Also speak up when you think the discussion is getting off track.

> Let's keep our goal in mind here.

Clarifying Unclear Statements

A key part of any discussion is the give-and-take among its members. If a comment is unclear, misleading, or distracting, it is best to ask for clarification.

Ask questions. Clarifying means listening closely and asking good questions. If you're not sure you understand something, summarize the idea and then ask if you have it right. If a group gets bogged down, a good question can help members refocus.

> Could we have an example of that idea?

Explain or clarify. If you've shared a long or complex thought, end by asking for questions. Try to recognize confusion in others and offer to explain. If someone contradicts a key point, either clarify it or resolve the contradiction.

> It seems we have two different suggestions.

Verify evidence. Be alert for facts and figures that don't add up. Ask the speaker for evidence or offer details that you know are credible and can be verified. Listen for opinions masquerading as facts.

> What facts support that opinion?

Reflecting on the Discussion

To end a discussion successfully, participants think about what they've discussed and come to a consensus or fair conclusion about it.

Distinguish between logic and emotion. Participants will often use both logic and emotion to get their points across; but in the end, decisions need to be based on evidence and logic—not on emotion.

> Let's think logically about this.

Review key ideas. As the discussion wraps up, summarize the main points. Evaluate them and consider how each relates to the larger idea or solution you have been discussing. Come to an agreement about the summary.

> Do we agree on these key points?

Draw conclusions and move ahead. After reaching an agreement, it is time to consider the next steps. Discuss the actions members should take and help the group decide who is doing what and by what time.

> We need volunteers for the following tasks.

Assessing Your Participation

Use this rubric as a checklist to evaluate your participation in a discussion. The rubric reflects important elements of effective participation.

To participate in a discussion, I . . .

Preparing

____ research the issue/topic.

____ arrive with an important insight or perspective to share.

____ bring a positive attitude and helpful focus.

Listening

____ listen closely to what everyone has to say.

____ keep an open mind about ideas.

____ discriminate between facts and opinions.

____ listen for bias, prejudice, and faulty logic.

Responding

____ wait for appropriate times to offer ideas.

____ challenge and question ideas, not people.

____ respond politely, calmly, and succinctly.

Cooperating

____ encourage others to participate.

____ build on group members' contributions.

____ guide the discussion to keep it on track.

Clarifying

____ ask questions to clarify ideas when appropriate.

____ test ideas and study evidence for reliability.

Reflecting

____ reflect on the logical and emotional arguments presented.

____ help bring the discussion to a fitting conclusion.

Writers
INC

Thinking Skills

Thinking Critically

Thinking has always been an important part of the learning process, but it's even more important today. To navigate the sea of information floating in and out of our lives, we need to think both critically and creatively; we need to ask the right questions. And being able to do that requires a closer look at thinking itself.

We need to remember, too, that the way we think has changed over time. The way our brains worked when we were six is very different from the way they work now. Now, we need to use our brains more often and more efficiently. In short, we need new strategies to help us think through the challenges we face every day—both in and out of school. This chapter will provide some of those strategies.

Learning Outcomes

Understand critical thinking.
Use critical-thinking strategies.
Remember and understand information.
Apply and analyze information.
Evaluate and create information.
Assess your critical thinking.

"Asking the right questions takes as much skill as giving the right answers."

Robert Half

Understanding Critical Thinking

Putting forth the effort to become a clear, critical thinker will benefit you in several important ways.

Critical thinking . . .

1. enables you to delve deeply into topics and sort through ideas.

2. helps you to recognize and solve problems systematically.

3. improves your ability to use language accurately and effectively.

4. allows you to carefully consider issues and form well-reasoned opinions.

5. helps you to evaluate evidence and draw logical conclusions.

So how do you go about improving your critical-thinking skills? First, you must remember to think logically each time you speak, write, or listen. Here are some helpful tips.

Be focused ▪ Block out all distractions. Make it your goal to concentrate on the topic or issue in front of you. Approach thinking with the same determination you bring to any other important activity in your life.

Be patient ▪ Don't rush, especially with complex issues. Ask yourself, "Am I taking the time I need to really think this through?"

Be curious ▪ Ask *why? how?* and *what if?* Ask questions about what you see, hear, and read—both inside and outside of the classroom.

Be flexible ▪ Be open to new ideas. Realize that some issues have more than one answer or solution. Consider all the possibilities. What you're looking for may not be a simple fact or clear reason; it may lie somewhere in between.

Be connected ▪ Stay on top of things. Follow the news, watch documentaries, talk to people, listen to others and read what they write or post.

Be critical ▪ Test your ideas, especially the information you find on popular media or the Internet. Ask questions: "Is the information up to date?" "Is it logical?" "Can I trust the author?"

Using Critical-Thinking Strategies

Thinking can be as simple as recalling a name, or as complex as analyzing a poem. To better understand the levels of thinking, refer to the chart below. Arranged from simple to complex tasks, the chart was developed by researcher Benjamin Bloom. Together with the strategies on the pages that follow, this information will put you on the path to becoming a critical thinker.

Bloom's Revised Taxonomy		**Critical-Thinking Strategies**
Remembering is recalling basic information. (*What is this?*)		Use **lists**, **questions**, and **journals** to collect, organize, and recall what you have learned.
Understanding is knowing what the information means. (*What does it mean?*)		Use **summaries** and **graphic organizers** to comprehend the significance of ideas or issues.
Applying is putting the information to use. (*What can I do with it?*)		Use **instructions** and **flowcharts** to generate a set of directions or a plan of action.
Analyzing is looking at the parts and figuring out how they work or fit together. (*What are its parts?*)		Use **line diagrams** and **picture diagrams** to compare, classify, and visualize the parts.
Evaluating is determining the value or worth of something. (*What is its worth?*)		Use the **ALU strategy** and **pro-con charts** to judge the importance, accuracy, strengths, and weaknesses of a claim or issue.
Creating is putting ideas together in new ways and forms. (*What else could I do with it?*)		Use **problem solving** and **engineering design** to develop new solutions with the information.

Simple ... *Complex*

"We can't solve problems by using the same kind of thinking we used when we created them."

Albert Einstein

Remembering Information

Critical thinking begins with remembering. Think about the information you have gathered and choose a strategy for arranging and organizing it. The better your information is organized, the easier it will be to remember.

▌ Think about it . . .

- *Do I have all the information I need? (Answer who? what? when? where? why? and how?)*
- *How can I arrange this information to make it easier to remember?*
- *Do I recognize any patterns in the information?*
- *Does any of this information remind me of things I already know?*

▌ Use a strategy . . .

One of the best strategies for organizing information and key details is filling in a **5W's and H chart**. This strategy gives you a system for both recording and remembering details. Another useful strategy is keeping a **learning log**—a notebook in which you take notes, explore ideas, and personalize important information. In a learning log, you can record and ask questions about your class work, draw pictures or graphics, start a glossary of important terms, and more. (See page 235.)

5 W's and H Chart:

The Velvet Revolution

Who? Czechoslovakian protesters

What? The peaceful overthrow of a Communist government

Where? Prague, Czechoslovakia

When? 1989

Why? Widespread dissatisfaction with 41 years of Communist rule, sparked by the suppression of a peaceful demonstration by students

How? A series of protests followed by a 2-hour strike by almost all citizens of Czechoslovakia

Learning Log

- Take notes.
  - Explore ideas.
- Personalize information.
  - Ask questions.
- Draw pictures.
  - Describe things.
- Define terms.
  - Draw conclusions.
- Assess your progress.

Understanding Information

Understanding goes beyond remembering facts and details. It is knowing what the facts and details mean, why the information is important, and how it relates to other ideas. Understanding requires that you read and listen carefully to gather information, think about it, and organize it thoughtfully.

Think about it . . .

- *Why is this information important? What does it mean?*
- *How does the information relate to what I already know?*
- *How can I arrange the information to show its meaning and importance?*
- *Can I use deductive or inductive reasoning to make sense of it? (See page 99.)*
- *Would I be able to explain this information to someone else?*

Use a strategy . . .

One of the best ways to test and improve your understanding of information is to **summarize** it. A summary is a concise expression of ideas using your own words. Begin by stating the main idea and then follow with other sentences, each containing an important supporting idea. Finally, add a personal conclusion or reaction. Graphic organizers are also useful for seeing the big picture. A **classifying chart,** for example, allows you to sort a topic into categories and sub-categories so that you can better understand the material.

Summarizing
• Be concise and use your own words.
• Clearly state the main idea.
• Stick to the essential details.
• State each important idea in a single sentence or two.
• Write a concluding statement.

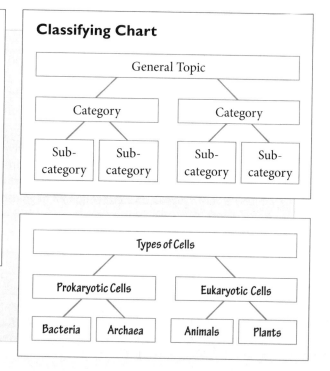

Classifying Chart

General Topic

Category — Category

Sub-category | Sub-category | Sub-category | Sub-category

Types of Cells

Prokaryotic Cells — Eukaryotic Cells

Bacteria | Archaea | Animals | Plants

Applying Information

When you apply information, you use it for a specific purpose. For example, writing instructions or making a plan requires that you (1) learn and understand a body of ideas/information, (2) sort out the most important facts and details, (3) organize the information in a way that will fulfill your purpose, and (4) act . . . either by following the plan or offering the instructions. This deeper level of thinking demonstrates your ability to connect ideas to real situations.

▌ Think about it . . .

- *What information or ideas are you considering?*
- *Could the information be used to make something better or to instruct?*
- *How might you apply this information to a process or problem?*
- *Which facts and details are most important to your plan?*
- *How will you organize your ideas to best fulfill your purpose?*

▌ Use a strategy . . .

When you want to *apply* information, consider creating a **flowchart** or a set of **instructions** that others could follow. To create either of these, list the steps in time order. Provide all the necessary details and use transition words to make your plan easy to follow. Also use command verbs as appropriate to add clarity and direction.

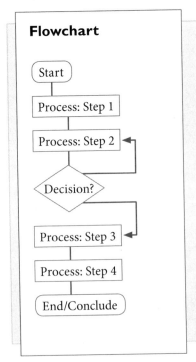

Flowchart

Start → Process: Step 1 → Process: Step 2 → Decision? → Process: Step 3 → Process: Step 4 → End/Conclude

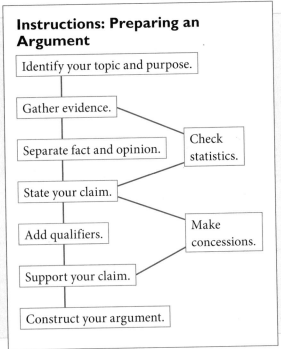

Instructions: Preparing an Argument

Identify your topic and purpose.

Gather evidence. — Check statistics.

Separate fact and opinion.

State your claim.

Add qualifiers. — Make concessions.

Support your claim.

Construct your argument.

Analyzing Information

When you analyze, you study something closely to learn about its parts and how they work together. You may also relate what you learn to other ideas or objects in the same class, or compare your findings to a more familiar idea or item to see how the two are similar or different.

▌ Think about it . . .

- ▪ *What parts or features does the object or idea exhibit?*
- ▪ *How does it work or function?*
- ▪ *What group or class does it fit into?*
- ▪ *How is it similar to or different from other examples in the group?*
- ▪ *How is this object or idea ranked within its group?*

▌ Use a strategy . . .

Filling in a **Venn diagram** is a popular strategy for analyzing ideas by comparing them. The diagram presents two overlapping circles, each labeled for one of the two topics being compared. The similarities are recorded in the overlapping space, and the differences are recorded in the outer portions of the circles. This visual offers a clear look at the relationship between the topics. (If you are comparing three topics, you may add a third overlapping circle.)

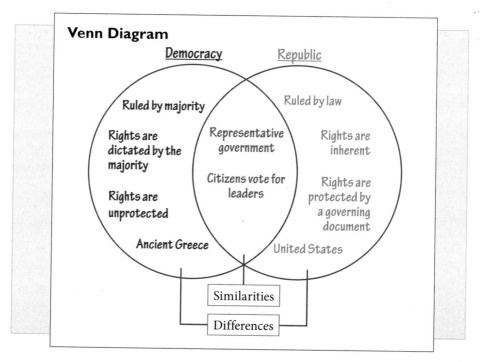

Venn Diagram

Democracy — Republic

- Ruled by majority
- Rights are dictated by the majority
- Rights are unprotected
- Ancient Greece

- Representative government
- Citizens vote for leaders

- Ruled by law
- Rights are inherent
- Rights are protected by a governing document
- United States

Similarities

Differences

Evaluating Information

When you evaluate something, you determine its value or worth, deciding whether it is useful, meaningful, or accurate. Determining the trustworthiness of the information you find about a topic, or selecting the best information to support your idea or opinion, are two examples of evaluating.

▌ Think about it . . .

- *What information (statements, facts, ideas) am I evaluating?*
- *Can I trust the information? How can I test its accuracy?*
- *What are its strengths and weaknesses?*
- *What previous experience or attitude do I bring to this topic?*
- *How would I rate the information or idea. What advice would I give?*

▌ Use a strategy . . .

To effectively evaluate information, use an assessment tool such as an **ALU chart** (advantages, limitations, unique features). After considering the ALU of a topic, you are in a good position to evaluate its worth or importance. Another evaluation strategy is the **pro-con chart**. Use it to list the positives and negatives of an idea. Seeing both sides spelled out in front of you can make it easier to judge the pros and cons of an idea or argument.

ALU Chart

Water Treatment Methods

Method	Advantages	Limitations	Unique Features
Filtering			
Chlorine			
Boiling			
Iodine			

Pro-Con Chart

Water Treatment: Filtering

Pro: *Positives*	Con: *Negatives*
• Eliminates parasites	• Bulky and heavy
• Filters most bacteria	• Expensive
• Doesn't alter taste	• May clog
• Works quickly	• Need 2nd method for total purification

Creating New Information

Creating means putting ideas together in new ways. You may come up with an original idea, rework an existing one, make an insightful prediction, or find a solution to a problem. Creating is the most complex and perhaps the most rewarding form of critical thinking.

Think about it . . .

- *What new or interesting things can I do with these ideas?*
- *How can I connect or combine them to improve them?*
- *What potential solutions or alternatives can I devise?*
- *What are my predictions concerning these ideas?*
- *What are my next steps?*

Use a strategy . . .

The **engineering-design** approach is one way to create a new idea or solve a problem. This strategy offers a systematic method for creating or modifying a basic design. Step-by-step you will find new ways to improve the quality of a product or the efficiency of a process.

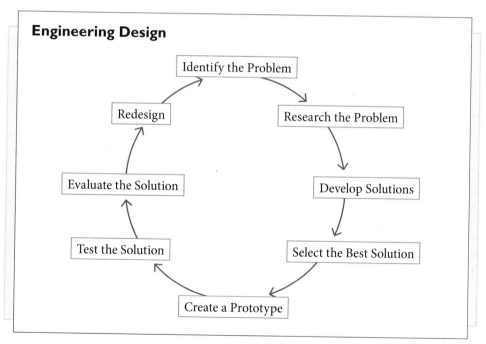

Engineering Design

Identify the Problem

Research the Problem

Develop Solutions

Select the Best Solution

Create a Prototype

Test the Solution

Evaluate the Solution

Redesign

Assessing Your Critical Thinking

Use the statements below to assess your critical-thinking skills. In your mind, answer *always, usually, sometimes,* or *never* to each statement. Then think about why you do (or do not) use these critical-thinking skills regularly.

Critical-Thinking Checklist

____ **1.** I enjoy using my imagination, especially when it involves finding creative solutions to a problem.

____ **2.** I enjoy brainstorming for creative ideas with others.

____ **3.** I am able to visualize a problem or situation in my mind.

____ **4.** I keep a journal where I write down or draw my most creative ideas.

____ **5.** I ask "What If . . .?" when I'm thinking to myself.

____ **6.** I'm good at finding alternatives or exceptions to the rule.

____ **7.** I listen carefully to the ideas of others and am able to add to what they say.

____ **8.** I can think quickly and contribute new ideas to group discussions.

____ **9.** I recognize the creative people around me, and I watch and listen to them.

____ **10.** I enjoy exploring the other side of an issue.

____ **11.** I try to imagine what life is like for other people.

____ **12.** I make connections between things I know and things I wonder about.

____ **13.** I use thinking strategies to help me think more creatively.

____ **14.** I recognize that there may be several solutions to any problem.

____ **15.** I enjoy explaining things to other people.

Thinking Creatively

You may have heard that creative thinking is seeing what everybody else has seen, but thinking what nobody else has thought. That's true. You may also have heard that artists and musicians are creative, but scientists and historians are not. That's not true. Success in all subjects requires creative thinking. Even Albert Einstein once said, "Imagination is more important than knowledge."

Creative thinking and critical thinking work in tandem. When you think critically, you narrow your focus on a specific issue ("Yes, but . . ."). When you think creatively, you open yourself to possibilities ("Yes, and . . ."). Combined with critical thought, creative thinking enhances your learning and problem-solving experiences in all course work.

Learning Outcomes

Understand creative thinking.
Use creative-thinking strategies.
Remember and understand information.
Apply and analyze information.
Evaluate and create information.
Assess your creative thinking.
Think to solve problems.

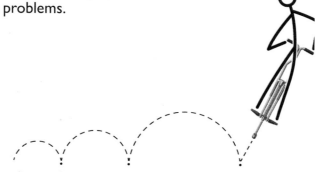

"Creativity makes a leap, then looks to see where it is."
Mason Cooley

Understanding Creative Thinking

Creative thinking leads to new insights, fresh perspectives, novel approaches, possible solutions, and different ways of understanding everything from literature to technological innovations.

Creative thinking . . .

1. expands your curiosity and your imagination.

2. allows you to apply knowledge to new situations.

3. helps you to find connections between seemingly unrelated ideas.

4. turns you into a visual thinker.

5. helps you to focus on the big picture.

You can improve your creative-thinking skills by practicing them. Follow these guidelines whenever you must work with ideas, consider a topic, or solve a problem.

Be focused ▪ Block out all distractions. Make it your goal to fully concentrate on the issue. Observe closely and study the topic until it tells you something about itself, even if it seems to be "off the topic."

Be patient ▪ Don't rush. Sometimes your best ideas will come to you when you least expect them. Be willing to take detours and unexpected side trips.

Be curious ▪ Ask *why? how?* and *what if?* Ask questions about everything. Consider what you already know, and then ask questions about the unknown, the unlikely, or the unexpected.

Be flexible ▪ Be open and innovative. Realize that many issues have more than one answer or solution. Consider all the possibilities. What you're looking for may not be a simple fact or a clear reason; it may lie somewhere in between.

Be connected ▪ Stay on top of things. Follow the news, watch documentaries, talk and listen to those around you, and read interesting blogs and posts.

Be critical ▪ Challenge your thinking. Don't settle for the first thought or solution that pops into your head. Realize that many possibilities exist. Look for alternatives and exceptions to the rule.

Using Creative-Thinking Strategies

While computers can calculate, analyze, estimate, and more, only people can imagine and create. The list below provides an overview of creative thinking and the strategies (from simple to complex) you can use to become a more imaginative thinker.

Bloom's Revised Taxonomy	Creative-Thinking Strategies
Remembering is recalling basic information. *(That's a car?)*	Use **mind maps** and **drawings** to collect, organize, and remember what you have learned.
Understanding is knowing what the information means. *(That's a hybrid car.)*	Use **metaphorical thinking** and **off-beat questions** to comprehend and explain the significance of ideas or issues.
Applying is putting the information to use. *(This is how a hybrid works.)*	Use **manipulative verbs** and **square pegging** to generate a plan of action or alternate solutions to a problem.
Analyzing is looking at the parts and figuring out how they work or fit together. *(That's a hybrid, not a plug-in.)*	Use **Socratic questions** and **reverse thinking** to compare, classify, and examine parts.
Evaluating is determining the value or worth of something. *(Hybrids are a great value.)*	Use **SCAMPER** and **manipulative verbs** to judge the importance, accuracy, and strengths and weaknesses of a claim or issue.
Creating is putting ideas together in new ways or new forms. *(Hybrids may soon be fueled by solar panels.)*	Use **brainstorming** and **predicting** to develop ways of looking at or using information in unique ways.

Simple → *Complex*

"Microsoft is a company that manages imagination."

Bill Gates

Remembering Information

Your creative mind actually is your best ally when it comes to remembering important facts and details. Finding creative ways to store information gives you a better chance of recalling it later on.

▍ Think About It

- ▪ *What unique way can I devise to remember this information?*
- ▪ *Can I draw a picture of it?*
- ▪ *Can I visualize the information in my mind?*
- ▪ *Can I think of a memorable way to map or cluster this information?*
- ▪ *Can I use a rhyme or story to help me remember?*

▍ Use a Strategy

One of the most effective memorization strategies is **visualization**. (A picture is worth a thousand words.) Simply picture the image in your mind, using all of your senses—see it, hear it, touch it, color it, exaggerate it.

Another effective strategy is **mind mapping,** a graphic strategy for organizing material. Mind maps use both sides of the brain and force you to be more than a passive recorder of information.

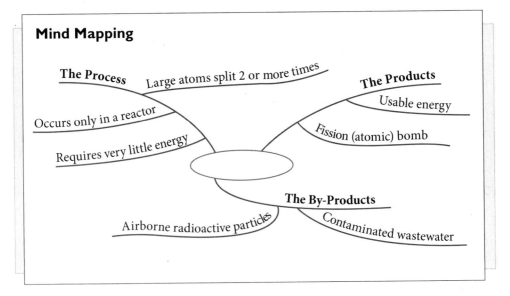

Mind Mapping

The Process — Large atoms split 2 or more times — The Products

Occurs only in a reactor

Usable energy

Fission (atomic) bomb

Requires very little energy

The By-Products

Airborne radioactive particles

Contaminated wastewater

Understanding Information

To understand information, you must think carefully about it. Metaphorical thinking is a creative strategy that can help you understand ideas.

▌ Think About It

- ▪ *What type of issue or problem is this? Why is it important?*
- ▪ *What are the main features and functions of this idea?*
- ▪ *What person am I reminded of by this subject?*
- ▪ *What object, thing, place, word, or sport is this subject like?*
- ▪ *What phrase or word expresses this idea for me?*

▌ Use a Strategy

Metaphorical thinking is a form of creative thought that connects two different ideas by showing how they are similar. The comparison will not be exact, but the slight mismatch will add a new dimension to your understanding. The most common types of metaphorical thinking are *similes*, *metaphors*, and *symbols*.

Creating and answering **off-beat questions** is another strategy for improving your understanding of information. Consider answering each question with a mini freewriting (2–3 minutes).

Metaphorical Thinking	Off-beat Questions
Simile: An electron is like an energetic kid running around her parents. **Metaphor:** The proton and neutron are the parents in the atom. **Analogy:** The force that binds a nucleus resembles the marriage that binds a couple. **Symbol:** This binding force could be represented with a marriage certificate.	• What does this object or idea look like upside down? • Where does it go for advice? • What type of clothing does it wear? • What machine does it resemble? • What club would it join? • What is its favorite song? • What would you find in its garbage can? • Would it take the stairs or the elevator?

Applying Information

When you apply an idea, you put it to work in a specific situation. By using a creative-thinking strategy, you can discover applications you may otherwise not have imagined.

▌Think About It

- ▪ *What can I do with this information?*
- ▪ *What else is needed to make this idea work?*
- ▪ *What other ways could the information be used?*
- ▪ *What alternative answers or solutions can I imagine?*
- ▪ *What questions about this idea would I ask an expert?*

▌Use a Strategy

One creative strategy for applying the knowledge you've gained is **square pegging**. Usually, "you can't put a square peg in a round hole," but forcing something to be used in a whole new way may produce a workable solution or idea. Use the formula below to create a "square peg" question; then answer it in as many ways as you can.

Manipulative verbs present another strategy for applying knowledge. These command verbs are used to apply actions to an object or idea in order to change or improve a situation.

Square-Pegging

How can ___*water pollution*___ ___*be turned into something beneficial?*___
               (your topic)   (do something or become something unexpected)

Manipulative Verbs

| accelerate | amplify | break | isolate | multiply | shrink |
| automate | freeze | divide | reverse | twist | stretch |

Sample Manipulation

    Information: *The world's oceans are filling up with islands of garbage.*

            Verb: *isolate*

  Manipulation: *Isolate these islands of garbage and incinerate them in an environmentally safe manner.*

Analyzing Information

Someone once said that our heads are round so that our thinking can change directions. As you analyze ideas, your thinking may do just that. Examining the parts of an idea requires that you move back and forth between them, exploring connections.

▌ Think About It

- ▪ *What are the parts or elements of this topic?*
- ▪ *What connections can I make between the parts? What connections do I see between this and other objects or ideas?*
- ▪ *What does this object or idea symbolize?*
- ▪ *How does this idea work? How could it be made to work better?*
- ▪ *What if . . . ?*

▌ Use a Strategy

An age-old strategy for thinking creatively (outside the box) is the **Socratic method**. First used by the philosopher Socrates, this method involves asking questions and engaging students in a conversation rather than lecturing them. You can use Socratic questions to analyze problems, arguments, and other ideas.

Another strategy worth considering is **word analysis**. Examining a topic's key words (considering the parts of each and their combined meaning) may offer new insight into the greater concept you are analyzing. (See pages 348–357.)

Using Socratic Questions

Clarification:	*How could we summarize this point?*
	What's another way of saying that?
Assumption:	*What are the assumptions underlying this idea?*
	How can we verify or disprove those assumptions?
Reason:	*What causes this situation to occur?*
	What is this situation similar to and how is it similar?
Perspective:	*What would others say about this idea?*
	What is another way to look at it?
Consequence:	*What will result from this assumption?*
	How can this idea be applied in a new way?
Recursion:	*What is the point of this question?*
	How does this question apply to the situation?

Evaluating Information

When you evaluate information, you judge it or give it a value. You may compare it to similar ideas or to concepts that are familiar. You must also consider the information's practical worth and the value it holds for others.

▮ Think About It

- *What practical worth does this idea have?*
- *What is its social or artistic value?*
- *How can the idea be improved?*
- *How do other people view the idea or feel about it?*
- *How do I feel about it?*

▮ Use a Strategy

SCAMPER is an evaluation tool created by researcher Bob Eberle. This strategy's name is an acronym for seven tasks that can be applied to a concept in order to assess its worth. The questions that follow each of the verbs in the chart below offer a creative way to evaluate/improve an idea or process.

SCAMPER Evaluation

Substitute: *What alternatives to this idea can I discover?*
What other ideas, materials, or goals would be useful?

Combine: *How can this concept be combined with another?*
How can the idea connect with other people?

Adapt: *What changes or modifications would improve the idea?*
How can the idea be made more appealing?

Magnify: *How can the idea become bigger or more powerful?*
How can I improve the outcome or performance of this idea?

Put to other uses: *What other uses are there for this idea? Who else could use it?*
What other problem could it solve?

Eliminate: *What other sequence or arrangement would work here?*
Could the idea be used at a different time? In a different place?

Rearrange: *What other sequence or arrangement could work for this?*
Could this happen at a different time or place?

Creating New Information

Creating new information involves putting existing ideas together to present novel concepts, unique inventions, even predictions of things that do not, as yet, exist.

▌Think About It

- *How could this idea be modified or put to other uses?*
- *What other ideas does it bring to mind?*
- *What is the exact opposite of this concept?*
- *Can I think of an original way to . . . ?*
- *What would happen if . . . ?*

▌Use a Strategy

One of the most effective strategies for creating new ideas is **brainstorming**, or freewriting. Brainstorming, often done in groups or with another person, is expressing as many ideas or solutions as you possibly can—without judging or criticizing them.

Another creative strategy is **predicting.** You can do this by simply stopping at any point in a book, lesson, or discussion and writing down what you think will happen next or proposing a solution to a problem. Later, you can test your prediction.

Brainstorming (Freewriting)

1. *Identify the problem or issue.*

2. *Write down everything that comes to mind.*

3. *Don't stop to judge or change anything.*

4. *Encourage all the possibilities.*

5. *When you run out of details, jot down "I wonder . . ." and begin writing again, using all of your senses.*

6. *Review your freewriting and underline the ideas you like.*

7. *Begin writing again about these underlined ideas.*

8. *Look for ways to combine or improve your ideas.*

9. *Consider how these ideas might be modified or adapted.*

10. *Listen to and learn from the brainstorming of others.*

Assessing Your Creative Thinking

Use the statements below to test your overall awareness of the thinking process and your creative thinking skills. In your mind, answer *always, usually, sometimes,* or *never* to each statement. Then think about why you do (or do not) use these creative thinking skills on a regular basis.

_____ **1.** I enjoy using my imagination, especially when it involves finding creative solutions to a problem.

_____ **2.** I enjoy brainstorming for creative ideas with others.

_____ **3.** I am able to visualize a problem or situation in my mind.

_____ **4.** I keep a journal in which I write about or draw my creative ideas.

_____ **5.** I ask *what if . . . ?* when I'm thinking about an idea.

_____ **6.** I'm good at finding alternatives or exceptions to the rule.

_____ **7.** I listen carefully to the ideas of others and am able to add to what they say.

_____ **8.** I can think quickly and contribute new ideas to group discussions.

_____ **9.** I recognize the creative people around me, and I watch and listen to them.

_____ **10.** I enjoy exploring the other side of an issue.

_____ **11.** I try to imagine what life is like for other people.

_____ **12.** I make connections between ideas I know about and those I wonder about.

_____ **13.** I use thinking strategies to discover and use my creativity.

_____ **14.** I recognize that there may be several solutions to any problem.

_____ **15.** I enjoy explaining things to other people.

"Imagination is everything. It is the preview of life's coming attractions."

Albert Einstein

Thinking to Solve Problems

The key to problem solving is, of course, thinking. Study the diagram below, which explains the process of moving back and forth between critical and creative thinking to solve problems.

Critical Thinking

Creative Thinking

Analyze the Problem

To solve any problem, you must first analyze it. That means investigating all aspects of it, especially its causes and effects.

Imagine Solutions

Next, imagine as many ways as you can to solve the problem. Think of all the possibilities, and don't hold back.

Choose a Solution

After gathering possible solutions, choose the best one for the situation. Consider your goal and the time and resources available.

Plan the Solution

Once you have chosen the best solution, plan it. Imagine following through with your ideas, anticipating surprises and setbacks, without losing focus.

Evaluate the Solution

Next, consider how well your solution will work. Check it against the initial problem and your analysis of it. Is the solution solid?

Make Improvements

After evaluating your solution and marking its issues and weak spots, revise your plan before putting it into practice.

Implement the Solution

Finally, put your solution to work. If all goes well, your problem will be solved, and you can move on to the next one.

Writers
INC

Test Taking

Test-Taking Skills

What's the secret to doing well on tests? Preparation. It's true of any test—from a small-stakes quiz to a high-stakes assessment. And to be well prepared, you must have an effective test-taking plan.

A good plan includes a number of key parts—organizing the test material, reviewing it, remembering it, and, finally, using it on the test itself. Having such a plan will reduce test anxiety and give you the best chance to succeed. The guidelines and example test questions in this chapter will help you create such a plan and improve your test-taking skills.

Learning Outcomes

Understand test types.
Prepare for tests.
Answer objective questions.
Answer essay questions.
Write paragraph and essay responses.
Understand key words.
Write timed responses.

"Give me six hours to chop down a tree, and I
will spend the first four sharpening the axe."

Abraham Lincoln

Understanding Test Types

In your high school career, you'll take many types of tests. Here's a quick overview.

Classroom Tests ▪ Daily and weekly, your instructors will measure your learning with quizzes and tests. These tests involve objective questions and provide a score that is combined with other measures to create your grade.

Exams ▪ At the end of a unit, semester, course, or year, you'll likely take an exam that covers all of the material in that period. Exams strongly influence your grade and often include both objective and essay questions.

State-Level Exams ▪ You may also take a test that the state uses to measure your learning against state standards. If your state has adopted the Common Core, you may take the PARCC or Smarter Balanced assessment. These tests use objective and essay questions to test deeper knowledge.

College Entrance Exams (SAT/ACT) ▪ If you plan to go to a two- or four-year college, you will also take a college entrance exam such as the SAT or ACT. These tests assess verbal and math reasoning ability. Colleges consider scores on these tests along with high school performance, extracurricular activities, and recommendations when they process college applications. Each test takes about three hours to complete.

Advanced Placement (AP) Exams ▪ If you have taken any advanced placement courses, you will take AP exams to determine whether you receive college credit for the courses.

Armed Services Vocational Aptitude Battery (ASVAB) ▪ If you enlist in the military, you will take the ASVAB test. It has nine subtests: General Science, Arithmetic Reasoning, Word Knowledge, Paragraph Comprehension, Mathematics Knowledge, Electronic Information, Auto & Shop, Mechanical Comprehension, and Assembling Objects.

College Placement Tests ▪ Once you are accepted to a community college or four-year college, you'll take placement tests in various subjects to determine the course level you are qualified to enter. Often students take college placement tests in reading and math, which are core subjects; but they may also take tests in specific majors, such as biology or music composition.

Preparing for Tests

Cramming for a test is not the best way to prepare. It puts information into your short-term memory, where it is quickly forgotten. Cramming may also cause you to lose sleep and become stressed. Instead, follow these steps to prepare well for a test.

1. Organize your study sessions.

- Ask your instructor what will be on the test.
- Ask how the material will be tested (multiple choice, short answer, essay).
- Review your class notes and recopy important sections.
- Get any missed notes from your teacher or other students.
- Set up specific study times and stick to them.
- Review quizzes and tests you took earlier in the class.
- Predict test questions and write sample answers.
- Make a list of questions to ask your instructor or other students.

2. Review your material.

- Begin reviewing early. Don't wait until the night before the test.
- Look for patterns in the material (cause/effect, comparison, time).
- Use maps, lists, diagrams, acronyms, rhymes, or other memory aids.
- Use flash cards or note cards to review material.
- Recite material out loud when possible.
- Study first by yourself and then with others.
- Teach the subject to someone else to deepen your understanding.
- Review difficult material the night before and the morning of the test.
- Connect personally or emotionally to the test material to help you remember it.

3. Take the test.

- Listen to the instructions and read all directions—carefully.
- Look over the test and plan your time so you are sure to finish.
- Answer the easy questions first; then return to the harder ones.
- In a multiple-choice test, read all the choices before selecting one.
- Make an educated guess when you aren't sure of an answer.
- Double-check your answers before submitting your test.

Answering Objective Questions

Objective test questions require specific answers. These questions may be multiple choice, true/false, fill in the blank, or matching.

▌Multiple Choice

Multiple-choice questions begin with a stem—a question, a command, or a sentence starter—and end with a set of options. Follow these tips:

- Read the directions carefully.
- Find out if questions can have more than one correct answer.
- Read each stem.
- Watch for negative words like *not, never, except,* and *unless.*
- Try to complete the stem in your mind before reading the options.
- Read all the choices before selecting one.
- Watch for phrases such as *all of these* or *all of the above.*

14. Select all infinitives below:
- Ⓐ to walk
- Ⓒ seeing
- Ⓑ walking
- Ⓓ to see

21. Which are not plural verbs?
- Ⓐ walks
- Ⓒ walking
- Ⓑ walk
- Ⓓ to walk

32. Which are personal pronouns?
- Ⓐ he
- Ⓒ they
- Ⓑ she
- Ⓓ all of these

▌True-False

True/false questions provide a statement and ask you to indicate whether it is true or not. Follow these tips:

- Read the entire question before answering.
- Make sure the whole statement is true before you mark "true."
- If any part of the statement is false, mark "false."
- Carefully consider each fact— name, date, number, detail—to be sure it is correct.
- Watch for words like *all, every, always,* and *never.* These words can make a statement false because few conditions are *always* or *never* true.
- Watch for and track negative words (two negatives equal a positive).

12. Mark Twain was the *nom de plume* of Samuel Clemens.
True False

23. Twain worked as a riverboat captain and a sportscaster.
True **False**

35. After publishing *Huckleberry Finn,* Twain never had to worry about finances again.
True **False**

▍ Fill in the Blanks

Fill-in-the-blank questions provide an open spot in a sentence for inserting the appropriate word or phrase. Use the following tips:

- If *an* precedes the blank, insert a singular word that starts with a vowel sound.
- If *a* precedes the blank, insert a singular word that starts with a consonant sound.
- Look at related words in the sentence to choose between a singular or plural answer.
- If there are multiple blanks, provide a word for each blank.
- Read the completed sentence to see if your answer makes sense.

10. A noun is modified by an ___adjective___ .

25. An adverb can modify a ___verb___ , an ___adjective___ , or another ___adverb___ .

37. A compound sentence consists of two ___independent___ ___clauses___ joined by a comma and a coordinating conjunction.

▍ Matching

Matching questions ask you to connect items in one list to items in another. These tips will help:

- Read through both lists quickly before answering.
- Note similar terms so that you don't mix them up.
- When matching words, connect nouns with nouns, verbs with verbs, and so on.
- When matching words to phrases, start with the phrases and work backward.
- Check off each item as you match it, unless answers can be used more than once.
- If you must write the letters of your answers, use capitals, which are less likely to be misread.

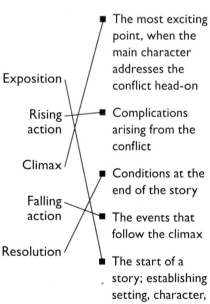

Exposition

Rising action

Climax

Falling action

Resolution

- The most exciting point, when the main character addresses the conflict head-on
- Complications arising from the conflict
- Conditions at the end of the story
- The events that follow the climax
- The start of a story; establishing setting, character, and plot

Focusing on Question Types

Tests that measure your skill in English and language arts use the following types of questions:

▌ Vocabulary

Vocabulary questions ask you to select synonyms or antonyms for words. Synonyms are words with the same meaning; antonyms are words with the opposite meaning.

Synonym: **BIBLIOPHILE**

    Ⓐ soldier   Ⓑ artist   **Ⓒ** book lover   Ⓓ music lover   Ⓔ bricklayer

Antonym: **PROTAGONIST**

    Ⓐ hero   **Ⓑ** foe   Ⓒ comrade   Ⓓ conflict   Ⓔ resolution

▌ Sentence Completion

Sentence-completion questions test your understanding of how words work in a sentence. The blanks indicate omissions, and you must choose the answer that best fits the meaning of the sentence. Consider all choices before marking your answer, and reread the sentence to see if your answer makes sense.

16. In an effort to _____ their controversial decision, the committee _____ an open meeting where the public could ask questions.

    Ⓐ explain . . . canceled   Ⓒ disavow . . . suggested

    Ⓑ clarify . . . scheduled   Ⓓ ignore . . . proposed

▌ Sentence Revision

Sentence-revision questions cover such skills as combining sentences, fixing ambiguous wording, creating parallel structure, correcting dangling modifiers, and eliminating sentence errors.

21. The weather which consisted of seven straight days of rain. It ruined our vacation.

    Ⓐ The weather, which consisted of seven straight days of rain, ruined our vacation.

    Ⓒ The weather that consisted of seven straight days of rain. It ruined our vacation.

    Ⓑ The weather consisted of seven straight days of rain. And it ruined our vacation.

    Ⓓ NO CHANGE

Paragraph Revision

Paragraph-revision questions ask you to improve paragraphs by selecting the best additions, deletions, and changes. Here is an example:

(1) Are dogs more moral than cats? (2) A bad dog often exhibits a "hangdog" look of guilt, but a bad cat usually wears a "So what?" expression. (3) Perhaps dogs' sense of right and wrong stems from their understanding of pack hierarchy. (4) They recognize that someone else is the master, and to disobey the master is wrong. (5) Cats have no master but themselves, so they are always right. (6) Cats also are easier to care for.

41. Which transition would be most appropriate at the beginning of sentence 5?

  Ⓐ Furthermore,   Ⓒ By contrast,

  Ⓑ As a result,   Ⓓ Due to the fact that

42. Which sentence in this paragraph is off topic and should be deleted?

  Ⓐ Sentence 1   Ⓒ Sentence 4

  Ⓑ Sentence 3   Ⓓ Sentence 6

Grammar Rules

Some writing tests assess your editing skills by asking you to find an error in usage or grammar.

In the following sentences, choose the underlined section that contains an error. If there is no error, choose D.

1. Inez heard the phone ringing, answered it, and has taken the message.
           Ⓐ   Ⓑ   Ⓒ

Ⓓ NO ERROR

2. Sam, an apprentice, he was afraid he would lose his job.
         Ⓐ   Ⓑ   Ⓒ

Ⓓ NO ERROR

Reading Comprehension

Reading-comprehension questions determine whether you understand the information presented in a reading selection.

11. In the Gettysburg Address, what does the line "Four score and seven years ago" refer to?

  Ⓐ Eighty-seven years ago   Ⓒ The country's founding

  Ⓑ The Declaration of Independence   Ⓓ All of these

Answering Essay Questions

Unlike objective questions, which elicit "right" or "wrong" answers, essay questions, or prompts, seek your thoughts about a specific subject. The best responses are thorough, thoughtful, and well developed. Follow these tips:

1. Analyze the prompt using STRAP.

A writing prompt is a set of directions that sets up the writing situation. In order to write an on-target response, you must carefully analyze and understand the prompt. You can do so by asking and answering the **STRAP** questions.

Subject........What is my subject?
Type.............What type of writing is required?
Role.............What role do I have in writing?
Audience.....What audience will read my work?
Purpose.......What is the purpose of my writing?

Sample Essay Question

Virginia Woolf wrote, "For most of history, Anonymous was a woman." What does this quotation mean for female writers such as herself? Write a letter to a literary magazine, providing a reader's perspective on the historical barriers female writers have faced.

STRAP Analysis

Subject: historical barriers female
          writers have faced
Type: letter
Role: reader
Audience: magazine readers
Purpose: to provide a reader's
          perspective

2. Plan your response.

If your response will be longer than a paragraph, take a moment to write a simple outline. Start with your thesis statement, which should restate the topic and focus of the prompt. Then write your first main point (I.) and provide details beneath (A., B., C.). Move on to your second main point (II.) and details, continuing until you have outlined your whole response.

Outline

Pioneering female writers such as the Brontë sisters overcame many barriers in order to succeed.

I. Women who wrote as men
  A. George Elliot
  B. Brontë sisters
  C. J. K. Rowling
II. Female protagonists
  A. Heroines of Jane Austen
  B. Miss Marple vs. Poirot
III. Women in publishing

3. Create an opening, a middle, and a closing.

To write your response, expand your outline into opening, middle, and closing paragraphs. Follow these tips:

Opening: Begin the first paragraph with a sentence that introduces your topic and captures the reader's attention. Follow with sentences that lead to your thesis statement.

Middle: Create middle paragraphs for the main points in your outline. Begin each paragraph with a topic sentence that identifies the main point. Then follow with details that support the topic sentence. Use transition words and phrases to guide the reader through your ideas.

Closing: Write a closing paragraph that reflects on your thesis, sums up your ideas, and gives the reader a final thought.

If you walk through a bookstore these days, you'll notice as many books by women as by men. That wasn't always the case, though. Like many other things in society, novel writing used to be a career dominated by men. Pioneering female writers such as the Brontë sisters overcame many barriers in order to succeed.

In the early days, aspiring female writers had to adopt male pseudonyms just to get their works published. . . .

A second barrier took the form of subject matter. Most novels focused on male protagonists doing typically masculine things. . . .

Female writers have overcome many obstacles to take their rightful place beside male writers on the bookshelves of the nation.

---

4. Revise and edit your response.

After drafting your response, reread the prompt and the response. Then make any necessary changes.

- Does your response specifically answer the prompt?
- Is your thesis statement clear and effective?
- Does each middle paragraph support the thesis statement?
- Do you end with a strong summary and a final thought?
- Have you corrected all errors in punctuation, capitalization, spelling, and grammar?

5. Pace yourself.

Use a compressed version of the writing process when you respond to a prompt: take 5 minutes to analyze the prompt and create a quick list or outline, use most of the allotted time to draft your response, and take the last 5 minutes to revise and edit your work.

Writing Paragraph and Essay Responses

Below you will find two sample essay questions, the first calling for a paragraph response, and the second, an essay response. Note the STRAP analysis of each question and the student's organization of each response.

Paragraph Response

Sample Essay Question

In a brief paragraph, define *soliloquy*. Include a short history of the term and an example.

STRAP Analysis

Subject: soliloquy
Type: brief paragraph
Role: student responder
Audience: test grader
Purpose: to define

Response

The paragraph defines the term, gives its origin, and provides an example.

A soliloquy is a speech made by a literary character who is speaking while alone. It is not intended for others to hear. The word is formed from *solus*, which means "alone," and *loqui*, which means "to speak." Shakespeare's plays feature many soliloquies, such as Hamlet's "To be or not to be" speech. A soliloquy helps the audience know what a character is thinking, thoughts he or she would not likely share publicly.

Essay Response

Sample Essay Question

Some playwrights, such as Shakespeare, are fond of soliloquies. Others prefer dramatic monologues. Write an essay that explains the different uses of soliloquy and dramatic monologue within a play.

STRAP Analysis

Subject: uses of soliloquy and dramatic monologue
Type: essay
Role: student responder
Audience: test grader
Purpose: to explain

Outline

Soliloquy and dramatic monologue have different purposes and effects.
I. Explanation + Examples
   A. Soliloquy: *Romeo and Juliet*
   B. Dramatic monologue: "My Last Duchess"
II. Uses
   A. Soliloquy: Reveals a character's thoughts
   B. Dramatic monologue: Shows how characters relate to each other

Response

The opening paragraph shares the thesis.	We know that Hamlet is struggling with the death of his father because of his "To be or not to be" soliloquy. Those words are spoken by Hamlet to himself. What if, instead, they had been spoken in a dramatic monologue to another character? Although both techniques involve a single speaker, soliloquy and dramatic monologue have different purposes and effects in literature.
Each middle paragraph deals with a different main point.	In a soliloquy, the speaker thinks out loud and is usually alone. Many of Shakespeare's characters deliver soliloquies. One of the most famous occurs in *Romeo and Juliet* when Juliet speaks from her heart near the start of the balcony scene. During a dramatic monologue, however, a character speaks to someone who remains silent, a situation like hearing a person talking on the phone. In Robert Browning's poem "My Last Duchess," the duke talks about his former wife to another man, whose reactions we do not hear.
The response expands on the outline.	Writers often use soliloquies to reveal a character's thoughts. In the balcony scene, Juliet is unaware that Romeo can hear her, so she says things to herself that she would not tell anyone else. It's clear that she has strong feelings for Romeo, and she is embarrassed when he speaks and reveals his presence. Juliet wishes she could take back her words, but the soliloquy has done its job: We (and Romeo) know her true thoughts, and the romance picks up speed.
	A dramatic monologue shows how a character relates to others. The duke in "My Last Duchess" is talking to a man who has been sent to find out whether the duke would be a good husband. The duke should show how considerate he is. Instead, he brags about how he dominated his first wife and thus is a totally unlikable character.
The final paragraph reflects on the message of the essay.	Literary characters are interesting for what they do, but even more so for what they say. Soliloquy and dramatic monologue are two methods used by writers to reveal who their characters are. In both cases, a single character speaks, but for different reasons and effect.

Understanding Key Words

Since writing prompts use command verbs that tell you exactly what you must do in a response, it is important to understand the meaning of each of these verbs. Note the explanations and examples below.

Common Command Verbs

Classify To classify is to group things by how they are alike, or similar. Classification questions are often used on science tests. Organize your response so that the groups are clearly identified.

> Classify the following forms of water according to the three physical states: clouds, steam, snow, drizzle, dew, water vapor, and frost.

Compare To compare is to show how things are similar and different, with the greater emphasis on similarities.

> Compare England's Bill of Rights with the United States' Bill of Rights.

Contrast To contrast is to show how things are different in one or more important ways.

> Contrast how a writer might use dramatic monologue and soliloquy.

Defend To defend a position is to support it with evidence and answer the main objections of opponents.

> Defend the National Security Administration's use of data mining and meta-analysis to track potential terror suspects.

Define To define is to give a clear definition or meaning for a term. A definition often identifies how one thing is different from other things in the same category or class.

> Define deductive reasoning. (Your definition might point out how deductive reasoning differs from inductive reasoning.)

Demonstrate To demonstrate is to show how something works. A demonstration often uses examples or leads the reader through a process.

> Demonstrate how a main character's greatest strength can also be his or her greatest weakness. Use examples from novels you have read.

Describe To describe is to tell how something looks or to give a general impression of it.

> Describe Scout's appearance on the night of the Halloween party.

Diagram To diagram is to explain something using a flowchart, a map, or some other graphic device, with the important parts or details labeled.

> Draw a diagram of the skin, showing its layers.

Discuss To discuss is to talk about an issue from all sides.

> Discuss the various attempts to introduce democracy to the Middle East.

Evaluate To evaluate is to judge the value or worth of something by comparing its qualities against a standard of excellence.

> Evaluate the United States' current economic strength, factoring in its productivity, joblessness, and debt.

Explain To explain is to make clear, to analyze, to show a process. Although it is similar to the term *discuss*, *explain* places more emphasis on cause-effect relationships and step-by-step sequences.

> Explain the greenhouse effect on Earth's atmosphere.

Illustrate To illustrate means to share information about a topic through specific examples and instances. A drawing or graphic may be part of the answer.

> Illustrate how a bill becomes a law in your state.

Justify To justify is to defend a position or point of view. A justification stresses the advantages over the disadvantages.

> Justify the position that presidents should be elected for one six-year term.

Outline To outline is to organize a set of facts or ideas by listing main points and subpoints. An effective outline shows how topics or ideas fit together.

> Outline the events in the Tom Robinson affair.

Predict To predict is to forecast future outcomes based on current conditions.

> Predict how the information age will change the reading habits of Americans.

Prove To prove means to bring out the truth by giving evidence, facts, and examples to back up your point.

> Attempt to prove that capital punishment is not an effective deterrent to crime.

Rank To rank is to put items in order from least to most important or from most to least important, giving reasons for the rankings.

> Rank the top three American writers in terms of their impact on literature.

Review To review is to reexamine or to summarize the major points of a topic, usually in chronological (time) order or in order of importance.

> Review the events leading to the beginning of World War I.

State To state means to present a concise statement of a position, fact, or point of view.

> State your position on the current health-care debate.

Summarize To summarize is to present the main points of an issue in a shortened form. Details, illustrations, and examples are usually omitted.

> Summarize the main reasons for the French Revolution.

Writing Timed Responses

Use the topics below to practice writing timed responses.

Think and write about . . .

world/local problems
notable people
occupations and
   professions
nature
education and learning

places and events
art or music
food and drink
cars and travel
language and
   communication

manners and morals
laws and justice
social concerns
money and costs
government and politics
the media

Read and respond to . . .

short magazine or
   Internet articles
song lyrics and poems

quotations, or
   short stories

classroom literature

Listen and respond to . . .

news broadcasts
interviews

music videos
short films

recited poetry

Analyze and write about . . .

unusual statistics
quotations

proverbs
clichés

euphemisms

Describe . . .

your favorite place
a flock of birds
   in flight
a person you admire

a gritty workplace
an unusual hobby or
   collection
yourself in twenty years

a concert or play
a ride on a bus or train

Compare . . .

original vs. imitation
middle school vs.
   high school
winter vs. summer
like vs. love

one course vs. another
2000s vs. now
musicians or musical
   groups
movies or TV programs

bad days vs. good days
alligator vs. crocodile
wisdom vs. knowledge
opinion vs. belief

Analyze causes and effects of . . .

misunderstandings
cancer
sunburn

violence
prejudice
war

schools
towns
emotion

Taking Exit and Entrance Exams

Many school districts and states use high school exit exams to determine whether students will graduate. Other schools have students take the PARCC or Smarter Balanced assessment to measure their college and career readiness. In addition, the SAT and ACT tests help colleges and universities determine which students they will admit.

Whether you are taking a test to leave high school or to enter college, the tips in this chapter can help. You'll find sample questions, prompts, and responses that demonstrate how to do well on these exams.

Learning Outcomes

Understand high-stakes tests.
Prepare for exams.
Answer reading questions.
Answer revising questions.
Answer vocabulary questions.
Answer editing questions.
Respond to readings.
Write argumentative responses.

"The results you achieve will be in direct proportion to the effort you apply."

Denis Waitley

Understanding High-Stakes Tests

High-stakes tests are tests that matter, and your personal results matter even more. For example, if a test determines whether you graduate from high school, get into the college you want, or otherwise move forward with your plans for the future, it is a high-stakes test.

Most high-stakes tests focus on core knowledge and often use multiple-choice questions. Still others require you to write responses to prompts. In short, you need to be ready to respond to whatever the test throws your way. Some tests still use bubble sheets, requiring you to shade in the letter of the correct answer. Others are administered online so that your answers are automatically logged and graded.

Exit Exams ▪ A standardized exit exam is a statewide assessment that a student must pass in order to graduate from high school. For example, the California High School Exit Examination (CAHSEE) determines which students graduate in that state. About half of the states in the United States use exit exams.

PARCC ▪ The PARCC assessment evaluates whether student learning matches the requirements of the Common Core State Standards. PARCC stands for the Partnership for Assessment of Readiness for College and Careers, one of two organizations that won Race-to-the-Top funds to develop assessments to measure the Common Core. The PARCC assessment has been adopted in about half of the states.

Smarter Balanced ▪ The Smarter Balanced assessment has been adopted in most of the other states. This assessment also measures student learning against the Common Core.

SAT ▪ The SAT is a college entrance exam that tests students' abilities in reading, math, and writing. This test is created and administered by the College Board, a not-for-profit organization.

ACT ▪ The ACT test is another college entrance exam. It tests students' abilities in English, math, reading, science, and writing.

Preparing for Exams

To perform well on a high-stakes test, don't wait for the night before to prepare. Instead, work carefully and persistently for weeks and even months before the test. The following tips will help you do well on these high-stakes tests:

1. Develop strong learning habits.

- Apply yourself in class.
- Take accurate notes and review them regularly.
- Read and analyze your school texts with these tests in mind.
- Think analytically about key ideas in all your classes.
- Write at length about what you read.
- Routinely compare two or more documents.
- Develop the habit of curiosity.

2. Prepare for the exam.

- Find out as much as you can about the exam.
- Arrange to take a practice version of the exam.
- Practice writing on-demand responses.
- Attend a preparation course.
- Involve multiple senses—sight, sound, touch—as you study.
- Study in different locations and at different times to commit information to your long-term memory.
- Write about topics covered in math and science courses.
- ***Remember:*** It's very important that you get a good night's sleep the night before the exam and eat a good breakfast the day of the exam.
- Relax and stay focused during the exam.

3. Take the exam.

- Listen carefully to all verbal instructions.
- Ask about anything that is unclear to you.
- Read through all the written directions.
- Use close-reading strategies to gain the most from texts.
- Pace yourself.
- Mark answers clearly and write legibly.
- Answer easy questions first and more difficult ones later.
- Make an educated guess when you don't know the answer.
- Review your responses before handing in your exam.
- Use all the time allotted.

Answering Reading Questions

Some exams ask you to read selections and then answer questions that test your comprehension. Your answers must show that you understand what you have read and that you can draw logical inferences from it. These tips will help:

I. Read the selection.

- Use **SQ3R**, a close-reading strategy, to analyze the text:

Survey......Survey the material from start to finish, looking at headings, illustrations, captions, and lists.

Question ...Question what you expect to learn from the reading.

Read ....Read the text quickly to get a sense of the whole.

Recite ......Recite the main points of each paragraph to yourself and the main point of the entire reading after completing it.

Review .....Review the text again to reinforce your understanding.

- If it's permitted, annotate the text, or take notes on a separate piece of paper as you work through the reading.

2. Work through each question.

- Read each question carefully.
- Note references to specific paragraphs or lines from the selection.
- Watch for multiple-choice answers that paraphrase the text, because such answers are often correct.
- Answer questions you are sure of first; then return to tackle more difficult ones.
- Consider the purpose of each type of question:

> **Main-point questions** focus on the overall point of the reading.
>
> **Support questions** focus on the facts, statistics, examples, definitions, and other details that support the main point.
>
> **Inference questions** ask you to determine unstated ideas from the information contained in the document.
>
> **Vocabulary questions** ask you to identify the meanings of key terms based on their context.
>
> **Style questions** focus on the author's sentence construction and use of stylistic features such as irony, metaphor, understatement, and so on.

3. Review your answers.

- Check to see that you have answered all the questions and that your answers make sense.
- Look again at the difficult questions and consider your educated guesses.

Sample Reading

Responsibility in the Media Age

People like to tell us that the media are ruining our lives. The 24/7 news cycle polarizes public opinion, fashion magazines indoctrinate teenagers into the cult of beauty, and Facebook replaces real people with profile pics. But are modern media truly to blame for so many of society's ills?

To answer that question, we first need to understand what the term *media* means. *Media* is the plural of *medium*, which means a "transmitting agent or substance." News media transmit news, popular media transmit entertainment, and social media transmit messages between people.

The media that plague us are just messengers, but don't we love to blame the messenger? Politicians on both sides of the aisle complain that the media are biased against them. Parents criticize movies and video games for promoting violence, perpetuating stereotypes, and pandering to our basest nature. And all of us regret the real human relationships that have withered while we busily "liked" statuses and tended our FarmVille cabbages.

For all their shortcomings, these media are just the way that messages, good and bad, reach us in the information age. As voters, consumers, and human beings, we need to take responsibility for the messages we heed and those we ignore. We have not only the right but also the obligation to master the media in our lives rather than letting them master us.

So turn off that ranting radio. Close the fashion magazine. Step away from the pulsing screen. Take responsibility for the media you use and the messages you receive.

1. Which of the following best expresses the writer's position about media?
Ⓐ The media are responsible for society's ills.
Ⓒ The media are not responsible for society's ills.
🅑 We are responsible for the media messages we heed.
Ⓓ None of these

2. Which definition of *medium* is closest to the one the writer uses?
Ⓐ An option that is between two extremes
🅒 Something that transmits information
Ⓑ A spiritualist who contacts the "other side"
Ⓓ All of these

3. Which of the following words from paragraph 3 have negative connotations?
Ⓐ love, both sides of the aisle, good, human relationships
Ⓒ stereotypes, pandering, basest nature, regret
Ⓑ blame, complain, biased, criticize, violence
🅓 Both B and C

4. The author implies that some forms of media should be outlawed.
True (**False**)

Answering Revising Questions

Some exams include questions that test your revising skills. First you read a sample article, and then you answer multiple-choice questions about ways to improve the piece.

Sample Essay

(1) A dog has a wet nose. (2) Whether you think of that nose as annoying or cute, it is much more complex than it seems. (3) A dog's nose is part of a highly developed system that is good for the dog but even better for humankind.

(4) The dog's acute sense of smell serves humans in many ways. (5) Tracker dogs have a long history of tracing escaped criminals and missing children. (6) Some dogs focus on finding people trapped alive in avalanches and collapsed buildings, while others are trained to hunt for the corpses of those who have not survived. (7) Patrol dogs sniff around border checkpoints for things like explosives and illegal drugs. (8) But the most amazing canine contributions are emerging in medicine. (9) Medical companion dogs can detect oncoming epileptic seizures, high blood pressure, heart attacks, migraines, and low blood sugar. (10) The most recent medical "miracle" is that dogs seem to be able to smell certain kinds of cancer before they are measurable by lab tests.

(11) The anatomy or structure of a dog's nose helps explain its sophisticated sense of smell. (12) The wetness itself is important. (13) It improves the dog's sense of smell by strengthening odors. (14) Then behind the nose itself, there are two other important olfactory organs— the receptors and the brain. (15) Inside the dog's nose is a very large number of smell receptors—25 times more than in humans. (16) These receptors are not active in the dog's normal breathing but come into play during sniffing. (17) The sensations from the receptors go to a part of the dog's brain that is four times larger than the corresponding part in a human brain. (18) These organs together give the dog the ability to sense odor in concentrations 100 million times lower than humans can. (19) But although canine noses sense much more than human noses do, dogs are not overwhelmed; they can sort out many layers of odor at the same time.

(20) For a long time, dogs have been thought of as humans' best friends. (21) They wag their tails and enjoy human company. (22) Their personalities are only part of the story, though. (23) Sometimes dogs need obedience lessons. (24) Scientists are probably only beginning to understand the power of dogs' olfactory sense.

This item focuses on openings, or introductions.

1. Which replacement for the first sentence would be the most engaging?
   Ⓐ On a sleepy Saturday morning, you suddenly wake up because you feel your dog's cold, wet nose on your hand—a signal that it's time to let him outside.
   Ⓑ I'd like to talk about a dog's nose.
   Ⓒ A dog's nose is perceptive.
   Ⓓ NO CHANGE

This item focuses on paragraph unity.

2. Which of the following sentences should be deleted?
   Ⓐ Sentence 8
   Ⓑ Sentence 13
   Ⓒ Sentence 23
   Ⓓ NONE

This item focuses on transitions.

3. Which of the following would be the best addition to the beginning of sentence 12?
   Ⓐ On the other hand,
   Ⓑ First of all,
   Ⓒ Likewise,
   Ⓓ In other words,

This item focuses on the main idea, or thesis.

4. Which sentence best paraphrases the focus of the essay?
   Ⓐ Medical science is learning more and more about how dogs can help humans.
   Ⓑ Humans cannot get along without the help of dogs.
   Ⓒ Dogs should be given greater respect.
   Ⓓ A dog's keen sense of smell has wide-ranging benefits to humans.

This item focuses on endings and tone.

5. If you were to add a sentence to the end of the essay, which of the following would best reflect the way the writer feels about the topic?
   Ⓐ Dogs can be pretty goofy, but sometimes they're a big help.
   Ⓑ The preponderance of evidence indicates that dogs are beneficial.
   Ⓒ Different breeds of dogs have different levels of intelligence.
   Ⓓ With their keen noses, canines can improve human lives in many ways.

Answering Vocabulary Questions

Some exams ask questions about words and their meanings. You must figure out what a word means by looking at its context. Use the following clues:

1. Consider embedded definitions.

Watch for words that rename or explain the word you are considering.

> The pilot passed the first *pylon*, rounding the tall metal tower.
> (A **pylon** must be a tall metal tower.)

2. Look for synonyms and antonyms.

See if nearby words mean the same or the opposite of the word in question.

> His so-called *infallible* reasoning actually resembled faulty logic.
> ("Faulty" is likely an antonym for **infallible**, which must mean "faultless.")

3. Use comparisons and contrasts.

Infer meaning using nearby words that are similar to or different from the term.

> The surgeon asked for a scalpel, a *lancet*, and a drill.
> (If a scalpel is a surgical instrument for cutting, and a drill is a surgical instrument for boring holes, a **lancet** must be a surgical instrument for another purpose, perhaps slicing or lancing.)

4. Infer categories from items in a series.

If a word appears in a series with other words, determine what all the items have in common, and then you should be able to figure out the word's meaning.

> He sported manicured nails, *coiffed* hair, and a pressed suit.
> ("Manicured" nails and pressed suits are neat, so **coiffed** hair must be combed, or neat.)

5. Use prefixes, suffixes, and roots.

Analyze the word according to its parts.

> She consumes an *immoderate* amount of coffee each day.
> (If "moderate" means "reasonable," then **im-moderate** must mean "unreasonable.")

6. Track causes and effects.

Infer a definition by considering the causes or effects of the word.

> Because we are planning to be out of the country on election day, we completed a *provisional* ballot.
> (A **provisional** ballot must be a ballot you can use to cast your vote before an election.)

Answering Editing Questions

Some exams include questions to assess your editing skills. These questions require you to find a usage, grammatical, or stylistic error somewhere (A, B, C) in a sentence.

This item focuses on pronoun-antecedent agreement.

1. Everyone should remember to bring their notebook.
   (A)   (B)   **C**
 (D) NO ERROR

This item focuses on subject-verb agreement.

2. One of my friend's favorite books are *To Kill a Mockingbird*.
     (A)   **B** (C)
 (D) NO ERROR

This item focuses on double subjects.

3. Sam, an apprentice, he was afraid he would lose his job, but he didn't.
        A   (B)   (C)
 (D) NO ERROR

This item focuses on comma errors.

4. Four questions, followed the reading selection.
   (A) **B**   (C)
 (D) NO ERROR

This item focuses on usage errors.

5. She had a habit of speaking two softly.
   (A)   (B) **C**
 (D) NO ERROR

This item focuses on indefinite pronoun reference.

6. As she swung her bat at the ball, it whistled through the air.
     (A)   **B** (C)
 (D) NO ERROR

This item focuses on ineffective expressions, or "deadwood."

7. We recommend that you institute new rules at this point in time.
      (A)   (B)   **C**
 (D) NO ERROR

Responding to Readings

Some exams ask you to respond to literature. First you read the prompt and the piece of literature, which may be fiction or nonfiction. Then you outline the key points and compose an appropriate response. Here are some tips:

1. Read the prompt and text.

- Read the prompt and analyze it using the **STRAP** questions. (See page 30.)
- Read the text as thoroughly and carefully as time allows. (For nonfiction, you may find SQ3R helpful. See page 288.)
- Highlight or jot down important details about the subject.

2. Plan and write your response.

- Plan your response quickly (5 minutes or so).

> **1. Write a thesis statement** that takes into account the prompt and what it is asking of you. Include the subject and the main idea you will share about it.
>
> **2. Outline the main points** that support your thesis statement.

- Using your outline, draft your response.

> **1. Develop an opening** that introduces the topic and leads to your thesis.
>
> **2. Create a middle** with a paragraph for each supporting point.
>
> **3. Write a closing** that sums up your thesis and observations.

- Use these strategies as they apply to your writing situation.

> **1. Offer your insights** on the reading. Don't just summarize text.
>
> **2. Use key details** from the reading to support your thesis.
>
> **3. Quote or paraphrase** important excerpts to add credibility to your main points.

3. Revise and edit your response.

- Review the prompt to make sure that you have answered it correctly.
- Read your response to check that you have fully developed each point.
- Add, cut, rearrange, and rewrite as needed to improve your work.
- Check for correct conventions and fix any errors that you find.

Sample Prompt

Many poets have written about the role leaders play in history. The two poems that follow are examples. In "Ozymandias," Percy Bysshe Shelley describes a monument created to commemorate the Egyptian king Ramesses II (Ozymandias in Greek texts), who lived from 1304–1213 B.C.E. In "O Captain! My Captain!" Walt Whitman writes about the legacy of U.S. President Abraham Lincoln, who was assassinated in 1865.

Read both poems. Then, in an essay, reflect on what these poems have to say about the role of a leader. Use evidence from both readings to support the main point of your response.

First Poem

STRAP Analysis

Subject: the role of a leader
Type: essay
Role: reader/responder
Audience: test graders
Purpose: to reflect on what the readings say about leaders

Ozymandias

I met a traveller from an antique land
Who said: Two vast and trunkless legs of stone
Stand in the desert. Near them, on the sand,
Half sunk, a shattered visage lies, whose frown,
And wrinkled lip, and sneer of cold command,
Tell that its sculptor well those passions read
Which yet survive, stamped on these lifeless things,
The hand that mocked them and the heart that fed;
And on the pedestal these words appear:
"My name is Ozymandias, king of kings:
Look on my works ye mighty, and despair!"
Nothing beside remains. Round the decay
Of that colossal wreck, boundless and bare
The lone and level sands stretch far away.

—Percy Bysshe Shelley (1792–1822)

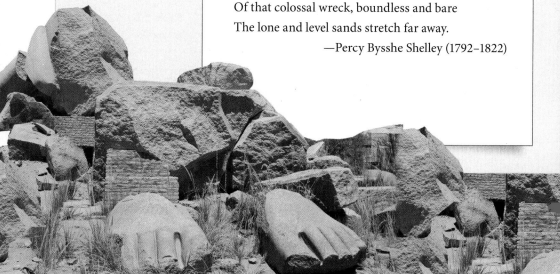

Second Poem

O Captain! My Captain!

O Captain! my Captain! our fearful trip is done,
The ship has weather'd every rack, the prize we sought is won,
The port is near, the bells I hear, the people all exulting,
While follow eyes the steady keel, the vessel grim and daring;
　　But O heart! heart! heart!
　　　　O the bleeding drops of red,
　　　　　　Where on the deck my Captain lies,
　　　　　　　Fallen cold and dead.

O Captain! my Captain! rise up and hear the bells;
Rise up—for you the flag is flung—for you the bugle trills,
For you bouquets and ribbon'd wreaths—for you the shores a-crowding,
For you they call, the swaying mass, their eager faces turning;
　　Here Captain! dear father!
　　　　This arm beneath your head!
　　　　　　It is some dream that on the deck,
　　　　　　　You've fallen cold and dead.

My Captain does not answer, his lips are pale and still,
My father does not feel my arm, he has no pulse nor will,
The ship is anchored safe and sound, its voyage closed and done,
From fearful trip the victor ship comes in with object won;
　　Exult O shores, and ring O bells!
　　　　But I with mournful tread,
　　　　　　Walk the deck my Captain lies,
　　　　　　　Fallen cold and dead.

—Walt Whitman (1819–1892)

Sample Response Plan

Taken together, these two poems suggest that effective leadership is not about power and authority, but instead about the ability to inspire people.

I. Ozymandias' achievements have turned to dust.
　A. Only wreckage and "lifeless things" remain.
　B. Emptiness and desert lie all around.
　C. This king's inscription is now ironic.
II. The Captain's achievements live on in his people.
　A. The "ship" has survived the dangerous voyage.
　B. People crowd the shore and bells ring.
　C. The Captain's legacy is heroism.

Sample Response

In the response below, the student opens by introducing the topic, which leads, in turn, to a thesis statement. The middle paragraphs develop that statement with ideas from the outline, and the ending revisits the thesis.

True Leadership

The opening shares a question and answers it in the thesis statement (underlined).

History is filled with tales of leaders—some great, and some terrible. What does it take to be a great leader? In the poems "Ozymandias" and "O Captain! My Captain!" Percy Bysshe Shelley and Walt Whitman describe two very different types of leaders and their effects on the world. <u>Taken together, the poems suggest that effective leadership is not about power and authority, but instead about the ability to inspire people.</u>

One middle paragraph discusses the first poem.

"Ozymandias" describes an authority figure with the power to have an enormous stone statue raised in his honor. This ruler declared himself the "king of kings" and flaunted his strength in the face of other rulers, telling them to "look on my works ye mighty, and despair!" Shelley uses images of fear and domination to describe Ozymandias. His "sneer of cold command" keeps people in line during his life, but in death, his greatness fades. Ironically, all that now remains of his monument are a few ruined pieces in the emptiness of a vast desert. The word "despair" now reflects the fleeting quality of the king's power.

Another middle paragraph discusses the second poem.

By contrast, the leader in "O Captain!" has devoted himself to guiding the ship of state through troubled times to safety. "The prize we sought is won," the poet says, and the people cheer the return of their "dear father!" They crowd the shore with "bouquets and ribbon'd wreaths," and "the bugle trills." The Captain has inspired his people, and they love him because of it. The Captain has given his very life in service. Despite the state's victory, the leader is lost, and the poet weeps—a very different reaction than we see for Ozymandias. Despite his death, the Captain's legacy will live on. In fact, the poem itself becomes a memorial to this great leader.

The closing paragraph expands on the thesis statement.

As long as the United States survives, its people will remember Lincoln's sacrifice. He held the country together through a great crisis and became one of our best-loved heroes. On the other hand, Ramesses II is most remembered for the ruins he left behind. In Shelley's poem, this great ruler is mocked by his own inscription. The lesson would seem to be that the best leader is one who sacrifices for others, not one who commands others for his own glory.

Writing Argumentative Responses

Some writing prompts require you to construct an argument that uses logic and persuasive techniques to convince the reader. For an argumentative response, follow these guidelines:

1. Read the prompt and analyze it using STRAP.

The prompt below deals with the issue of rules in education.

STRAP Analysis

Subject: rules vs. freedom in education

Type: position essay

Role: student

Audience: educators

Purpose: to convince others of my opinion

Some educators feel that students need very specific rules to guide them. Others maintain that students can grow only when they are allowed to make most of their own decisions. As a student, how do you feel about this debate? Do students thrive when they are given strict rules to live by, or are they better off learning by trial and error? Write a position essay to convince educators of your opinion about this issue.

2. Write a position statement.

Name the topic and state your position. Then fashion a position statement.

Topic	My Position	Position Statement
rules or freedom for students	**+** needless rules distract from learning, but some rules are necessary	**=** Needless rules distract from learning, but rules that help students focus and plan for the future are necessary.

3. Outline your response, including support.

Write your position statement and then add key supporting details.

Needless rules distract from learning, but rules that help students focus and plan for the future are necessary.

A. Avoid rules that have no long-term value.

B. Promote rules that help students focus on the future.

C. Dad made a rule that helped me.

4. Write your response.

Using your outline as a guide, write a thoughtful, detailed response to the prompt.

A Ruling on Rules

The opening question leads up to the position statement (underlined).

Do students learn better with clearly defined rules, or should they be free to find out for themselves what works and what doesn't? It all depends on what the rules are intended to accomplish. <u>Needless rules distract from learning, but rules that help students focus and plan for the future are essential.</u>

Each middle paragraph develops one main point.

Some of the most frustrating rules are those that don't matter in the long term. Unreasonable dress and grooming codes are particularly annoying. What lasting benefit do they provide? Should boys with long hair be sent home? Should their participation in class, and therefore their learning, be sacrificed for the sake of good grooming? School rules should focus on education, not fashion. Yes, students who fail to groom themselves appropriately are at risk of having embarrassing yearbook photos, but these aren't truly "at risk" students. School rules should not put needless burdens on students.

On the other hand, most students respect rules and requirements that help them stay focused on their schoolwork and their future. Though students may complain about having to take required courses, do community service, and read books during summer vacation, most of them recognize that these requirements improve their lives over the long term. The future depends much more on what students learn and on how they relate to others than on the clothes they wear during high school.

The writer uses a personal anecdote to support a main idea.

My own lesson in rules happened when I was in eighth grade. Because I got all C's on my first-quarter report card, my dad said that I was limited to one hour of TV on school nights. Of course, I was upset and said my freedom was being taken away. Dad stood firm, I spent more time studying, and my grades improved dramatically. More importantly, I got out of the habit of wasting time when I should have been doing something more useful. I probably wouldn't have come up with the TV rule on my own, and, as a result, my life may have been much different.

The closing paragraph concedes an opposing viewpoint.

I realize that educators who create rules mean well. They are trying to remove distractions and smooth the way for students to succeed. But the rules ought to focus on real learning, not on personal preferences. The best school rules help students learn now and in the future.

Writers

INC

Proofreader's Guide

"Cut out all those exclamation marks.
An exclamation mark is like laughing at your own joke."

F. Scott Fitzgerald

Marking Punctuation

▌ Period

553.1 At the End of a Sentence

Use a period at the end of a sentence that makes a statement, requests something, or gives a mild command.

(Statement) The man who does not read good books has no advantage over the man who can't read them.
—Mark Twain

(Request) Please bring your laptop to class.

(Mild command) Listen carefully so that you don't make the same mistake again.

Note: It is not necessary to place a period after a statement that has parentheses around it and is part of another sentence.

The first college game had taken place twelve years earlier, and that initial contest between Rutgers and Princeton (Rutgers won 6–4) more resembled a street fight than a sporting event.
—Lars Anderson, *Carlisle vs. Army*

553.2 After an Initial or an Abbreviation

Place a period after an initial or an abbreviation.

Ms.   Sen.   D.D.S.   M.F.A.   M.D.   Jr.   U.S.   p.m.   a.m.
Edna St. Vincent Millay   Booker T. Washington   D. H. Lawrence

Note: When an abbreviation is the last word in a sentence, use only one period at the end of the sentence.

Jaleesa eyed each door until she found the name Fletcher B. Gale, M.D.

553.3 As a Decimal Point

A period is used as a decimal point.

New York City has a population of 8.3 million people. The proposed budget for 2013 is $70.1 billion.

Question Mark

554.1 Direct Question

Place a **question mark** at the end of a direct question.

> What can I know? What may I hope?
>
> —Immanuel Kant

> Where did my body end and the crystal and white world begin?
>
> —Ralph Ellison, *Invisible Man*

When a question ends with a quotation that is also a question, use only one question mark, and place it within the quotation marks.

> On road trips, do you remember driving your parents crazy by asking, "Are we there yet?"

Note: Do *not* use a question mark after an indirect question.

> Out on the street, I picked out a friendly looking old man and asked him where the depot was.
>
> —Wilson Rawls, *Where the Red Fern Grows*

554.2 To Show Uncertainty

Use a question mark within parentheses to show uncertainty.

> This summer marks the 35th season (?) of the American Players Theatre.

554.3 Short Question Within a Sentence

Use a question mark for a short question within parentheses.

> We crept so quietly (had they heard us?) past the kitchen door and back to our room.

Use a question mark for a short question within dashes.

> Maybe somewhere in the pasts of these humbled people, there were cases of bad mothering or absent fathering or emotional neglect—what family surviving the '50s was exempt?—but I couldn't believe these human errors brought the physical changes in Frank.
>
> —Mary Kay Blakely, *Wake Me When It's Over*

Exclamation Point

554.4 To Express Strong Feeling

Use the exclamation point (sparingly) to express strong feeling. You may place it after a word, a phrase, or a sentence.

> "That's not the point," said Wangero. "These are all pieces of dresses Grandma used to wear. She did all this stitching by hand. Imagine!"
>
> —Alice Walker, "Everyday Use"

❚ Comma

555.1 Between Two Independent Clauses

Use a **comma** between two independent clauses that are joined by a coordinating conjunction (*and, but, or, nor, for, yet, so*).

> I wanted to knock on the glass to attract attention, but I couldn't move.
>
> —Ralph Ellison, *Invisible Man*

Note: Do not confuse a sentence containing a compound verb for a compound sentence.

> I had to burn her trash and then sweep up her porches and halls.
>
> —Anne Moody, *Coming of Age in Mississippi*

555.2 To Separate Adjectives

Use commas to separate adjectives that *equally* modify the same noun.

> Bao's eyes met the hard, bright lights hanging directly above her.
>
> —Julie Ament, student writer

Note: Do not use a comma between the last adjective and the noun.

A Closer Look: To determine whether adjectives modify equally—and should, therefore, be separated by commas—use these two tests:

1. Shift the order of the adjectives; if the sentence is clear, the adjectives modify equally. (In the example below, *hot* and *smelly* can be shifted and the sentence is still clear; *usual* and *morning* cannot.)

> Matty was tired of working in the hot, smelly kitchen and decided to take her usual morning walk.

2. Insert *and* between the adjectives; if the sentence reads well, use a comma when *and* is omitted. (The word *and* makes sense when it is inserted between *hot* and *smelly*, but *and* does not make sense between *usual* and *morning*.)

555.3 To Separate Contrasted Elements

Use commas to separate contrasted elements within a sentence.

> Since the stereotypes were about Asians, and not African Americans, no such reaction occurred.
>
> —Emmeline Chen, "Eliminating the Lighter Shades of Stereotyping"

▌ Comma (continued)

556.1 To Enclose Parenthetical Elements

Use commas to separate parenthetical elements, such as an explanatory word or phrase, within a sentence.

> They stood together, away from the pile of stones in the corner, and their jokes were quiet, and they smiled rather than laughed.
>
> —Shirley Jackson, "The Lottery"
>
> Allison meandered into class, late as usual, and sat down.

556.2 To Set Off Appositives

A specific kind of explanatory word or phrase called an **appositive** identifies or renames a preceding noun or pronoun.

> Benson, our uninhibited and enthusiastic Yorkshire terrier, joined our family on my sister's fifteenth birthday.   —Chad Hockerman, student writer

Note: Do not use commas with *restrictive appositives*. A restrictive appositive is essential to the basic meaning of the sentence.

> Twenty-one-year-old student Edna E. Rivera almost had a nose job but changed her mind.   —Andrea Lo and Vera Perez

556.3 Between Items in a Series

Use commas to separate individual words, phrases, or clauses in a series. (A series contains at least three items.)

> I'd never known anything about having meat, vegetables, and a salad all at the same meal. (Three nouns in a series)
>
> I took her for walks, read her stories, and made up games for her to play. (Three phrases in a series)   —Anne Moody, *Coming of Age in Mississippi*

Note: Do not use commas when all the words in a series are connected with *or, nor,* or *and.*

> Her fingernails are pointed and manicured and painted a shiny red.
>
> —Carson McCullers, "Sucker"

556.4 After Introductory Phrases

Use a comma after an introductory participial phrase.

> Determined to finish the sweater by Thanksgiving, my grandmother knits night and day.

Use a comma after an introductory prepositional phrase.

> In the oddest places and at the strangest times, my grandmother can be found knitting madly away.

Note: You may omit the comma if the introductory phrase is short.

> Before breakfast my grandmother knits.

557.1 After Introductory Clauses

Use a comma after an introductory adverb (subordinate) clause.

> After the practice was over, Tina walked home.

Note: A comma is also used if an adverb clause follows the main clause and begins with *although, even though, while,* or another conjunction expressing a contrast.

> Tina walked home, even though it was raining very hard.

However, a comma is not used if the adverb clause following the main clause is needed to complete the meaning of the sentence.

> Tina practiced hard because she feared losing.

557.2 To Set Off Nonrestrictive Phrases and Clauses

Use commas to set off **nonrestrictive** (unnecessary) clauses and participial phrases. A nonrestrictive clause or participial phrase adds information that is not necessary to the basic meaning of the sentence. For example, if the clause or phrase (in **red**) were left out in the two examples below, the meaning of the sentences would remain clear. Therefore, commas are used to set them off.

> The Altena Fitness Center and Visker Gymnasium, which were built last year, are busy every day. (nonrestrictive clause)
>
> Students and faculty, improving their health through exercise, use both facilities throughout the week. (nonrestrictive phrase)

Important Note: Do not use commas to set off **restrictive** (necessary) clauses and participial phrases. A restrictive clause or participial phrase adds information that the reader needs to know in order to understand the sentence. For example, if the clause and phrase (in **red**) were dropped from the examples below, the meaning wouldn't be the same. Therefore, commas are *not* used.

> The handball court that has a sign-up sheet by the door must be reserved.
> The clause identifies which handball court must be reserved. (restrictive clause)
>
> Individuals wanting to use this court must sign up a day in advance.
> (restrictive phrase)

A Closer Look: That and Which Use *that* to introduce restrictive (necessary) clauses; use *which* to introduce nonrestrictive (unnecessary) clauses. When the two words are used in this way, the reader can quickly distinguish necessary information from unnecessary information.

> The treadmill that monitors heart rate is the one you must use.
> (The reader needs the information to find the right treadmill.)
>
> This treadmill, which we got last year, is required for your program.
> (The main clause tells the reader which treadmill to use; the other clause gives additional, unnecessary information.)

▌Comma (continued)

558.1 To Set Off Dates

Use commas to set off items in a date.

> He began working out on December 1, 2013, but quit by May 1, 2014.

However, when only the month and year are given, no commas are needed.

> He began working out in December 2013 but quit by May 2014.

558.2 To Set Off Items in Addresses

Use commas to set off items in an address. (No comma is placed between the state and ZIP code.)

> Mail the box to Friends of Wildlife, Box 402, Spokane, Washington 20077.

When a city and state (or country) appear in the middle of a sentence, a comma follows the last item in the address.

> Several charitable organizations in Juneau, Alaska, pool their funds.

558.3 To Set Off Dialogue

Use commas to set off the speaker's exact words from the rest of the sentence.

> "It's like we have our own government," adds Tanya, a 17-year-old squatter.
> —Kyung Sun Yu and Nell Bernstein, "Street Teens Forge a Home"

558.4 To Set Off Interjections

Use a comma to separate an interjection or a weak exclamation from the rest of the sentence.

> Hey, how am I to know that a minute's passed?
> —Nathan Slaughter and Jim Schweitzer, *When Time Dies*

> Boy, those pigs dove right in, snout first, feet to follow.
> —Michael Perry

558.5 To Set Off Interruptions

Use commas to set off a word, a phrase, or a clause that interrupts the movement of a sentence. Such expressions usually can be identified through the following tests: (1) They may be omitted without changing the meaning of a sentence. (2) They may be placed nearly anywhere in the sentence without changing its meaning.

> For me, well, it's just a good job gone!
> —Langston Hughes

> As a general rule, the only safe way to cross this street is with the light.

559.1 In Numbers

Use commas to separate numerals in large numbers in order to distinguish hundreds, thousands, millions, and so forth.

   1,101   25,000   7,642,020

559.2 In Direct Address

Use commas to separate a noun of direct address from the rest of the sentence. A noun of *direct address* is the noun that names the person(s) spoken to.

> "But, Mother Gibbs, one can go back; one can go back there again. . . . "
> —Thornton Wilder, *Our Town*

559.3 To Enclose Titles or Initials

Use commas to enclose a title or initials and names that follow a surname.

> Until Martin, Sr., was 15, he never had more than three months of schooling in any one year.   —Ed Clayton, *Martin Luther King: The Peaceful Warrior*
>
> Hickok, J. B., and Cody, William F., are two popular Western heroes.

559.4 For Clarity or Emphasis

You may use a comma for clarity or for emphasis. There will be times when none of the traditional rules call for a comma, but one will be needed to prevent confusion or to emphasize an important idea.

> It may be that those who do most, dream most. (emphasis)
> —Stephen Leacock
>
> What the crew does, does affect our voyage. (clarity)

▌ Semicolon

559.5 To Join Two Independent Clauses

Use a **semicolon** to join two or more closely related independent clauses that are not connected with a coordinating conjunction. (Independent clauses can stand alone as separate sentences.)

> I did not call myself a poet; I told people I wrote poems.
> —Terry McMillan, *Breaking Ice*
>
> Silence coated the room like a layer of tar; not even the breathing of the 11 Gehad made any sound.   —Gann Bierner, "The Leap"

Note: When the related independent clauses are especially long or contain commas, a semicolon plus a coordinating conjunction may be used to separate them.

> We waited all day in the crowded concourse with other tired, disgruntled travelers; and now and then I squeezed my way to the cafeteria, returning with coffee or sandwiches.

▮ Semicolon (continued)

560.1 With Conjunctive Adverbs

A semicolon is used *before* a conjunctive adverb (with a comma after it) when the word connects two independent clauses in a compound sentence. (Common conjunctive adverbs are *also, besides, finally, however, indeed, instead, meanwhile, moreover, nevertheless, next, still, then, therefore,* and *thus.*)

> Sonia arrived early for her interview; however, she was dressed completely wrong for the occasion.

560.2 To Separate Groups That Contain Commas

A semicolon is used to separate groups of words that already contain commas.

> My favorite foods include runny eggs; peanut butter and banana sandwiches; Hawaiian pizza with cheese, pineapple, and ham; and diet ginger ale. Does that make me weird?

▮ Colon

560.3 After a Salutation

Use a colon after the salutation of a business letter.

> Dear Judge Parker: Dear Governor Whitman:

560.4 Between Numerals Indicating Time

Use a colon between the hours, minutes, and seconds of a number indicating time.

> 8:30 p.m.   9:45 a.m.   10:24:55

560.5 For Emphasis

Use a colon to emphasize a word, a phrase, a clause, a sentence, or a question that explains or adds impact to the main clause.

> His guest lecturers are local chefs who learn a lesson themselves: Homeless people are worth employing.
> —Beth Brophy, "Feeding Those Who Are Hungry"

> Here is the thing: how do you get a skunk out of a horse stall? Clearly the direct approach was no good.
> —Michael Perry, "From the Top"

561.1 To Introduce a Quotation

Use a colon to formally introduce a quotation, a sentence, or a question.

Directly a voice in the corner rang out wild and clear: "I've got him! I've got him!"
—Mark Twain, *Roughing It*

561.2 To Introduce a List

A colon is used to introduce a list.

I got all the proper equipment: scissors, a bucket of water to keep things clean, some cotton for the stuffing, and needle and thread to sew it up.
—Joan Baez, *Daybreak*

A Closer Look: Do not use a colon between a verb and its object or complement, or between a preposition and its object.

Incorrect: Min has: a snowmobile, an ATV, and a canoe.

Correct: Min has plenty of toys: a snowmobile, an ATV, and a canoe.

Incorrect: Dad watches a new show about: cooking wild game.

Correct: Dad watches a new show about his latest interest: cooking wild game.

561.3 Between a Title and a Subtitle

Use a colon to distinguish between a title and a subtitle, volume and page, and chapter and verse in literature.

Writers INC: A Student Handbook for College-and-Career Readiness
Encyclopedia Americana IV: 211   Psalm 23:1-6

▌Hyphen

561.4 In Compound Words

Use the hyphen to make compound words.

great-great-grandfather   maid-in-waiting   three-year-old
It was taller than my-dad-and-me-on-his-shoulders tall.
—Kristen Frappier, "The Corn"

Note: A dash is indicated by two hyphens--without spacing before or after--in all handwritten material. Don't use a single hyphen when a dash is required.

561.5 To Join Letters and Words

Use a hyphen to join a capital letter or lowercase letter to a noun or participle. (Check your dictionary.)

T-shirt   Y-turn   G-rated   x-axis

▌Hyphen (continued)

562.1 Between Numbers and Fractions

Use a hyphen to join the words in compound numbers from *twenty-one* to *ninety-nine* when it is necessary to write them out.

twenty-five   forty-three   seventy-nine   sixty-two

Use a hyphen between the numerator and denominator of a fraction, but not when one or both of those elements are already hyphenated.

four-tenths   five-sixteenths   (7/32) seven thirty-seconds

562.2 In a Special Series

Use hyphens when two or more words have a common element that is omitted in all but the last term.

The ship has lovely two-, four-, or six-person cabins.

562.3 To Join Numbers

Use a hyphen to join numbers indicating the lifespan of a person or the score in a contest or a vote.

We can thank Louis Pasteur (1822–1895) for pasteurized milk.

In November, Grinnell College defeated Crossroads College 173–123.

562.4 To Divide a Word

Use a hyphen to divide a word (only between syllables) at the end of a line of print. Always place the hyphen after the syllable at the end of the line—never before a syllable at the beginning of the following line.

Guidelines for Dividing with Hyphens

1. When you divide a word, leave enough letters at the end of the line to help the reader identify the word easily.

2. Never divide a one-letter syllable from the rest of the word: **omit-ted**, not **o-mitted**.

3. When a vowel is a syllable by itself, divide the word after the vowel: **epi-sode**, not **ep-isode.**

4. Always divide a compound word between its basic units: **sister-in-law**, not **sis-ter-in-law.**

5. Avoid dividing a word of five or fewer letters: **paper, study, July.**

6. Never divide a one-syllable word: **rained, skills, through.**

7. Never divide abbreviations or contractions: **shouldn't**, not **should-n't.**

8. Never divide the last word in more than two lines in a row.

9. Avoid dividing the last word in a paragraph.

563.1 To Prevent Confusion

Use a hyphen with prefixes or suffixes to avoid confusion or awkward spelling.

re-create (not *recreate*) the image   re-cover (not *recover*) the sofa

563.2 To Create New Words

Use a hyphen to form new words beginning with the prefixes *self-*, *ex-*, *all-*, and *half-*. Also use a hyphen to join any prefix to a proper noun, a proper adjective, or the official name of an office. Use a hyphen before the suffix *-elect*.

self-contained	ex-governor	all-inclusive	half-painted
pre-Cambrian	mid-December	president-elect	

Use a hyphen to join the prefix *great* to names of relatives, but do not use a hyphen to join *great* to other words.

great-aunt, great-grandfather (correct)   great-hall (incorrect)

563.3 To Form an Adjective

Use a hyphen to join two or more words that serve as a single adjective (a single-thought adjective) before a noun.

In real life I am a large, big-boned woman with rough, man-working hands.

—Alice Walker, "Everyday Use"

Note: Use common sense to determine whether a compound adjective might be misread if it is not hyphenated. Generally, hyphenate these kinds of compound adjectives:

Noun + Adjective

oven-safe handles   book-smart student

Noun + Participle (*ing* or *ed* form of a verb)

line-dried clothes   bone-chilling story

Phrase

heat-and-serve meal   off-and-on relationship

A Closer Look: When words forming the adjective come after the noun, do not hyphenate them.

In real life I am large and big boned.

When the first of these words is an adverb ending in *ly*, do not use a hyphen; also, do not use a hyphen when a number or a letter is the final element in a single-thought adjective.

delicately prepared pastry (adverb ending in *ly*)

class B movie (letter is the final element)

▌Apostrophe

564.1 In Contractions

Use an **apostrophe** to show that one or more letters have been left out of a word group to form a contraction.

hadn't (*o* is left out)   they'd (*woul* is left out)   it's (*i* is left out)

Note: Use an apostrophe to show that one or more numerals or letters have been left out of numbers or words in order to show special pronunciation.

class of '99 (*19* is left out)   g'day (*ood* is left out)

564.2 To Form Plurals

Use an apostrophe and *s* to form the plural of a letter, a number, a sign, or a word discussed as a word.

B – B's   C – C's   8 – 8's   + – +'s   *and – and's*

Ms. D'Aquisto says our conversations contain too many *like's* and *no way's.*

Note: If two apostrophes are called for in the same word, omit the second one.

Be sure to follow closely the do's and don'ts (not *don't's*) on the life jacket checklist.

564.3 To Form Singular Possessives

Add an apostrophe and *s* to form the possessive of most singular nouns.

Marley's bark   Benson's toy   the dog's bed

Note: When a singular noun ends with an *s* or a *z* sound, you may form the possessive by adding just an apostrophe. When the singular noun is a one-syllable word, however, you usually add both an apostrophe and an *s* to form the possessive.

San Carlos' government (or) San Carlos's government (two-syllable word)

Ross's essay (one-syllable word) The class's field trip (one-syllable word)

564.4 To Form Plural Possessives

The possessive form of plural nouns ending in *s* is usually made by adding just an apostrophe.

students' homework   bosses' orders

A Closer Look: When punctuating possessive nouns, remember that the word immediately before the apostrophe is the owner.

girl's guitar (*girl* is the owner)   boss's order (*boss* is the owner)

girls' guitar (*girls* are the owners)   bosses' order (*bosses* are the owners)

565.1 ▌ In Compound Nouns

Form the possessive of a compound noun by placing the possessive ending after the last word.

> the secretary of the interior's (singular) agenda
>
> her lady-in-waiting's (singular) day off

If forming the possessive of a plural compound noun creates an awkward construction, you may replace the possessive with an *of* phrase, as shown here:

> their fathers-in-law's (plural) birthdays
> (or) the birthdays of their fathers-in-law
>
> the ambassadors-at-large's (plural) plans
> (or) the plans of the ambassadors-at-large

565.2 ▌ With Indefinite Pronouns

Form the possessive of an indefinite pronoun by placing an apostrophe and an *s* on the last word. (See 626.2.)

> everyone's   anyone's   somebody's   no one's

565.3 ▌ To Express Time or Amount

Use an apostrophe and an *s* with an adjective that is part of an expression indicating time or amount.

> a penny's worth   today's business   this morning's meeting
> yesterday's news   a day's wage   a month's pay

565.4 ▌ To Show Shared Possession

When possession is shared by more than one noun, use the possessive form for the last noun in the series.

> Hoshi, Linda, and Nakiva's water skis (All three own the same skis.)
> Hoshi's, Linda's, and Nakiva's water skis (Each owns her own skis.)

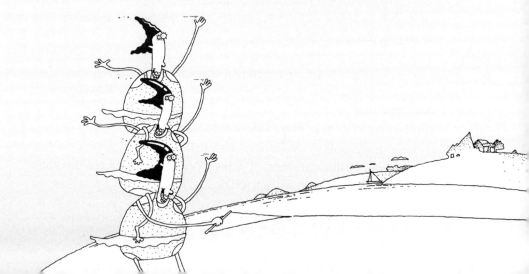

▌Quotation Marks

566.1 To Punctuate Titles

Use **quotation marks** to punctuate titles of songs, poems, short stories, one-act plays, lectures, episodes of radio or television programs, chapters of books, unpublished works, electronic files, and articles found in magazines, newspapers, encyclopedias, or online sources. (For punctuation of other titles, see 568.2.)

"Santa Lucia" (song)

"The Chameleon" (short story)

"Twentieth-Century Memories" (lecture)

"Affordable Adventures" (magazine article)

"Dire Prophecy of the Howling Dog" (chapter in a book)

"Dancing with Debra" (television episode)

"Miss Julie" (one-act play)

566.2 For Special Words

You may use quotation marks (1) to distinguish a word that is being discussed, (2) to indicate that a word is unfamiliar slang, or (3) to point out that a word is being used in a special way.

(1) A commentary on the times is that the word "honesty" is now preceded by "old-fashioned."   —Larry Wolters

(2) I . . . asked the bartender where I could hear "chanky-chank," as Cajuns called their music.   —William Least Heat-Moon, *Blue Highways*

(3) In order to be popular, she works at being "cute."

Note: You may use italics (underlining) in place of quotation marks in each of these three situations. (See 568.3.)

566.3 Placement of Punctuation

Always place periods and commas inside quotation marks.

"Dr. Slaughter wants you to have liquids, Will," Mama said anxiously. "He said not to give you any solid food tonight."

              —Olive Ann Burns, *Cold Sassy Tree*

Place an exclamation point or a question mark *inside* quotation marks when it punctuates the quotation and *outside* when it punctuates the main sentence.

"Am I dreaming?"

Had she heard him say, "Here's the key to your new car"?

Always place semicolons or colons outside quotation marks.

I wrote about Wallace Stevens' "Thirteen Ways of Looking at a Blackbird"; I found it enlightening.

Quick Guide

▌Marking Quoted Material

567.1 To Set Off Quoted Passages

Place quotation marks before and after the words in direct quotations.

"Just come to a game," he pleads. "You'll change your mind."

—Sandra Lampe, "Batter UP!"

In a quoted passage, put brackets around any word or punctuation mark that is not part of the original quotation.

(Original) Conservative pundits point to it as the classic example of the impossibility of providing good government service.

(Quotation) "Conservative pundits point to it [the U.S. Postal Service] as the classic example of the impossibility of providing good government service."

—Brad Branan, "Dead Letter Office?"

Note: If you quote only part of the original passage, be sure to construct a sentence that is both accurate and grammatically correct.

Much of the restructuring of the Postal Service has involved "turning over large parts of its work to the private sector."

567.2 For Long Quotations

If you quote more than one paragraph, place quotation marks before each paragraph and at the end of the last paragraph (example A). If a quotation has more than four lines on a page, you may set it off from the text by indenting 10 spaces from the left margin (block form). Do not use quotation marks either before or after the quoted material, unless they appear in the original. Double-space the quotation (example B).

Example A

"
_____
_____
_____ .
"
_____
_____ .
"
_____ "
_____ .

Example B

_____ .
_____
_____
_____
_____
_____
_____ .
_____ .

567.3 For Quoting a Quotation

Use single quotation marks to punctuate a quotation within a quotation. Use double quotation marks in order to distinguish a quotation within a quotation within a quotation.

"For tomorrow," said Mr. Botts, "read 'Unlighted Lamps.'"

Sue asked, "Did you hear Mr. Botts say, 'Read "Unlighted Lamps"'?"

❚ Italics (Underlining)

568.1 Handwritten and Printed Material

Italics is a printer's term for a style of type that is slightly slanted. In this sentence, the word *happiness* is printed in italics. In material that is handwritten, underline each word or letter that should be in italics.

> My Ántonia is the story of a strong and determined pioneer woman.
> (printed)
> Willa Cather's My Ántonia describes pioneer life in America.
> (typed or handwritten)

568.2 For Titles

Use italics to indicate the titles of magazines, newspapers, pamphlets, books, full-length plays, films, videos, radio and television programs, book-length poems, ballets, operas, paintings, lengthy musical compositions, albums, CD's, legal cases, and the names of ships and aircraft. (For punctuation of other titles, see 566.1.)

> Newsweek (magazine)
> Saving Mr. Banks (film)
> Caring for Your Cat (pamphlet)
> Chicago Tribune (newspaper)
>
> Cold Sassy Tree (book)
> Iron Chef (television program)
> Hedda Gabler (full-length play)

Note: Punctuate one title within another title as follows:

> "Is Grey's Anatomy Reality Trustworthy?" (title of TV program in article title)

568.3 For Special Uses

Use italics for a number, letter, or word that is being discussed or used in a special way. (Sometimes quotation marks are used for this reason. See 566.2.)

> I hope that this letter I stands for incredible and not incomplete.

568.4 For Foreign Words

Use italics for foreign words that have not been adopted into the English language; also use italics for scientific names.

> The voyageurs—tough men with natural bonhomie—discovered the shy Castor canadensis, or North American beaver.

▌ Parentheses

569.1 To Set Off Explanatory Material

You may use **parentheses** to set off explanatory or added material that interrupts the normal sentence structure.

> Benson (our dog) sits in on our piano lessons (on the piano bench), much to the teacher's surprise and amusement.
>
> —Chad Hockerman, student writer

Note: Place question marks and exclamation points within the parentheses when they mark the added material.

> Ivan at once concluded (the rascal!) that I had a passion for dances, and . . . wanted to drag me off to a dancing class.
>
> —Fyodor Dostoyevsky, "A Novel in Nine Letters"

569.2 To Set Off a Full Sentence

When using a full sentence within another sentence, do not capitalize it or use a period inside the parentheses.

> Since your friend won't have the assignment (he was just thinking about calling you), you'll have to make a couple more calls to actually get it.
>
> —Ken Taylor, "The Art and Practice of Avoiding Homework"

When the parenthetical sentence comes after the main sentence, capitalize and punctuate it the same way you would any other complete sentence.

> They kiss and hug when they say "hello," and I love this. (In Korea, people are much more formal; they just shake hands and bow to each other.)
>
> —Sue Chong, "He Said I Was Too American"

Note: For unavoidable parentheses within parentheses (. . . [. . .] . . .), use brackets. Avoid overuse of parentheses by using commas instead.

▌ Diagonal

569.3 To Show a Choice

Use a **diagonal** (also called a *slash*) between two words, as in *and/or*, to indicate that either word is applicable.

> Press the load/eject button.
>
> Don't worry; this is indoor/outdoor carpet.

569.4 When Quoting Poetry

When quoting more than one line of poetry, use a diagonal to show where each line of poetry ends. (Insert a space on each side of the diagonal.)

> I have learned not to worry about love; / but to honor its coming / with all my heart.
>
> —Alice Walker, "New Face"

❚ Dash

570.1 ❚ To Indicate a Sudden Break

Use a **dash** to indicate a sudden break or change in the sentence.

> Near the semester's end—and this is not always due to poor planning—
> some students may find themselves in a real crunch.

Note: Dashes are often used in place of commas. Use dashes when you want to give special emphasis; use commas when there is no need for emphasis.

570.2 ❚ To Set Off an Introductory Series

Use a dash to set off an introductory series from the clause that explains the series.

> A good book, a cup of tea, a comfortable chair—these things always saved
> my mother's sanity.

570.3 ❚ To Set Off Parenthetical Material

You may use a dash to set off parenthetical material—material that explains or clarifies a word or a phrase.

> A single incident—a tornado that came without warning—changed the face
> of the small town forever.

570.4 ❚ To Indicate Interrupted Speech

Use a dash to show interrupted or faltering speech in dialogue.

> SOJOURNER: Mama, why are you—
>
>   MAMA: Isabelle, do as I say!
>
>   —Sandy Asher, *A Woman Called Truth*

570.5 ❚ For Emphasis

Use a dash to emphasize a word, a series, a phrase, or a clause.

> After years of trial and error, Belther
> made history with his invention—the
> unicycle.

Quick Guide

■ Ellipsis

571.1 To Show Omitted Words

Use an **ellipsis** (three periods/points with one space before and after each) to show
that one or more words have been omitted in a quotation.

> (Original) We the people of the United States, in order to form a more
> perfect Union, establish justice, insure domestic tranquility, provide for the
> common defense, promote the general welfare, and secure the blessings
> of liberty to ourselves and our posterity, do ordain and establish this
> Constitution for the United States of America.
>
> —Preamble, U.S. Constitution
>
> (Quotation) "We the people . . . in order to form a more perfect Union . . .
> establish this Constitution for the United States of America."

571.2 At the End of a Sentence

If words from a quotation are omitted at the end of a sentence, place the ellipsis after
the period that marks the conclusion of the sentence.

> "Five score years ago, a great American, in whose symbolic shadow we stand,
> signed the Emancipation Proclamation. . . . But one hundred years later, we
> must face the tragic fact that the Negro is still not free."
>
> —Martin Luther King, Jr., "I Have a Dream"

Note: If the quoted material is a complete sentence (even if it was not complete in
the original), use a period and then an ellipsis.

> (Original) I am tired; my heart is sick and sad. From where the sun now
> stands I will fight no more forever.   —Chief Joseph of the Nez Percé
>
> (Quotation) "I am tired. . . . From where the sun now stands I will fight no
> more forever." (or) "I am tired. . . . I will fight no more. . . ."

571.3 To Show a Pause

Use an ellipsis to indicate a pause.

> I brought my trembling hand to my focusing eyes. It was oozing, it was red, it
> was . . . it was . . . a tomato!
>
> —Laura Baginski, student writer
>
> I heard Ray Wylie Hubbard talking about the late Lightnin' Hopkins the other
> day, and how Lightnin' played the twelve-bar blues . . . and the thirteen-bar
> blues . . . and the thirteen-and-a-half-bar blues. . . .
>
> —Michael Perry, "From the Top"

▮ Brackets

572.1 To Set Off Clarifying Information

Use **brackets** before and after words that are added to clarify what another person has said or written.

> "They'd [the sweat bees] get into your mouth, ears, eyes, nose. You'd feel them all over you."
> —Marilyn Johnson and Sasha Nyary, "Roosevelts in the Amazon"

Note: The brackets indicate that the words *the sweat bees* are not part of the quotation but were added for clarification.

572.2 To Set Off Added Words

Place brackets around comments that have been added to a quotation.

> "Congratulations to the astronomy club's softball team, which put in, shall we say, a 'stellar' performance." [groans]

572.3 Around an Editorial Correction

Place brackets around an editorial correction inserted within quoted material.

> "Brooklyn alone has 8 percent of lead poisoning [victims] nationwide," said Marjorie Moore.
> —Donna Actie, student writer

Note: Place brackets around the letters *sic* (Latin for "as such"); the letters indicate that an error appearing in the quoted material was made by the original speaker or writer.

> "When I'm queen," mused Lucy, "I'll show these blockheads whose [sic] got beauty and brains."

Punctuation Marks

´ Accent, acute	, Comma	(−) Parentheses
` Accent, grave	† Dagger	. Period
' Apostrophe	— Dash	? Question mark
* Asterisk	/ Diagonal/Slash	"_" Quotation marks
{ } Brace	(ü) Dieresis	§ Section
[ ] Brackets	... Ellipsis	; Semicolon
^ Caret	! Exclamation point	~ Tilde
(ç) Cedilla	_ Hyphen	_____ Underscore
ˆ Circumflex	... Leaders	
: Colon	¶ Paragraph	

"English spelling is weird . . . or is it wierd?"

Irwin Hill

Checking Mechanics

▌ Capitalization

573.1 Proper Nouns and Adjectives

Capitalize proper nouns and proper adjectives (those derived from proper nouns). The chart below provides a quick overview of capitalization rules. The pages following explain some specific rules of capitalization.

Capitalization at a Glance

Names of people . . . . Alice Walker, Matilda, Jim, Mr. Roker

Days of the week, months . . . . Sunday, Tuesday, June, August

Holidays, holy days . . . . Thanksgiving, Easter, Hanukkah

Periods, events in history . . . . Middle Ages, the Battle of Bunker Hill

Official documents . . . . Declaration of Independence

Special events . . . . Elgin Community Winter Carnival

Languages, nationalities, religions . . . . French, Canadian, Buddhism

Political parties . . . . Republican Party, Socialist Party

Trade names . . . . Oscar Mayer hot dogs, Chevrolet Volt

Official titles used with names . . . . Senator Baldwin, Justice Ginsburg

Formal epithets . . . . Alexander the Great

Geographical names

    Planets, heavenly bodies . . . . Earth, Jupiter, the Milky Way

    Continents . . . . Australia, South America

    Countries . . . . Ireland, Grenada, Sri Lanka

    States, provinces . . . . Ohio, Utah, Nova Scotia

    Cities, towns, villages . . . . El Paso, Burlington, Wonewoc

    Streets, roads, highways . . . . Park Avenue, Route 66, Interstate 90

    Landforms . . . . the Rocky Mountains, the Sahara Desert

    Bodies of water . . . . Yellowstone Lake, Pumpkin Creek

    Buildings, monuments . . . . Elkhorn High School, Gateway Arch

    Public areas . . . . Times Square, Sequoia National Park

---

▌ Capitalization (continued)

574.1 First Words

Capitalize the first word of every sentence, including the first word of a full-sentence direct quotation.

> The boy came awkwardly through the crowd. Someone said, "Don't be nervous, Jack," and Mr. Summers said, "Take your time, son."
> —Shirley Jackson, "The Lottery"

574.2 Sentences in Parentheses

Capitalize the first word in a sentence enclosed in parentheses, but do not capitalize the first word if the parenthetical appears within another sentence.

> Shamelessly she winked at me and grinned again. (That grin! She could have taken it off her face and put it on the table.)
> —Jean Stafford, "Bad Characters"

> Damien's aunt (she's an active woman) plays bingo every Saturday night.

574.3 Sentences Following Colons

Capitalize the first word in a complete sentence that follows a colon when (1) you want to emphasize the sentence or (2) the sentence is a quotation.

> When we quarreled and made horrible faces at one another, Mother knew what to say: "Your faces will stay that way, and no one will marry you."

574.4 Sections of the Country

Capitalize words that indicate particular sections of the country; do not capitalize words that simply indicate direction.

> Mr. Johnson is from the Southwest. (section of the country)
> After moving north to Montana, he had to buy winter clothes. (direction)

574.5 Certain Religious Words

Capitalize nouns that refer to the Supreme Being, the title Bible, the books of the Bible, and the names of other holy books.

> God   Jehovah   the Lord   the Savior
> Allah   Bible   Genesis   Koran   Talmud

574.6 Titles

Capitalize the first word of a title, the last word, and every word in between except articles (*a, an, the*), short prepositions, and coordinating conjunctions. Follow this rule for titles of books, newspapers, magazines, poems, plays, songs, articles, films, works of art, photographs, and stories.

> *The Women of Brewster Place*   *Washington Post*   "Nothing Gold Can Stay"
> *A Midsummer Night's Dream*   "The Diary of a Madman"

575.1 Letters

Capitalize the letters used to indicate form or shape.

U-turn   I-beam   S-curve   T-shirt   V-shaped

575.2 Organizations

Capitalize the name of an organization, an association, or a team.

Lake Ontario Sailors   American Indian Movement   Democratic Party

575.3 Abbreviations

Capitalize abbreviations of titles and organizations. (Some other abbreviations are also capitalized. See pages 579–580.)

AAA   CEO   NAACP   M.D.   Ph.D.

575.4 Words Used as Names

Capitalize words like *father, mother, uncle,* and *senator* when they are used as titles with a personal name or when they are substituted for proper nouns (especially in direct address).

We've missed you, Aunt Lucinda! (*Aunt* is part of the name.)

I hope Mayor Bates arrives soon. (*Mayor* is part of the name.)

A Closer Look To test whether a word is being substituted for a proper noun, simply read the sentence with a proper noun in place of the word. If the proper noun fits in the sentence, the word being tested should be capitalized; if the proper noun does not work in the sentence, the word should not be capitalized.

Did Mom (Sue) say we could go? (*Sue* works in this sentence.)

Did your mom (Sue) say you could go? (*Sue* does not work here.)

Note: Usually the word is not capitalized if it follows a possessive pronoun—*my, his, your*—as it does in the second sentence above.

575.5 Titles of Courses

Capitalize words like *sociology* and *history* when they are used as titles of specific courses; do not capitalize these words when they name a field of study.

Who teaches History 202? (title of a specific course)

It's the same professor who teaches my sociology course. (a field of study)

Note: The words *freshman, sophomore, junior,* and *senior* are not capitalized unless they are part of an official title.

Rosa is a senior this year and is in charge of the Senior Class Banquet.

▌Plurals

576.1 Most Nouns

Form the **plurals** of most nouns by adding *s* to the singular.

    cheerleader – cheerleaders   wheel – wheels   crate – crates

576.2 Nouns Ending in *sh, ch, x, s,* and *z*

Form the plurals of nouns ending in *sh, ch, x, s,* and *z* by adding *es* to the singular.

    lunch – lunches   dish – dishes   mess – messes   fox – foxes

576.3 Nouns Ending in *y*

The plurals of common nouns that end in *y*—preceded by a consonant—are formed by changing the *y* to *i* and adding *es*.

    fly – flies   jalopy – jalopies

The plurals of nouns that end in *y* and are preceded by a vowel are formed by adding only *s*.

    donkey – donkeys   monkey – monkeys

Note: Form the plurals of all proper nouns ending in *y* by adding *s*.

    We have three Kathys in our English class.

576.4 Nouns Ending in *o*

The plurals of nouns ending in *o*—preceded by a vowel—are formed by adding *s*.

    radio – radios   rodeo – rodeos   studio – studios   duo – duos

The plurals of most nouns ending in *o*, preceded by a consonant, are formed by adding *es*.

    echo – echoes   hero – heroes   tomato – tomatoes

Exception: Musical terms ending in *o*, preceded by a consonant, form plurals by adding only *s*.

    alto – altos   banjo – banjos   solo – solos   piano – pianos

576.5 Nouns Ending in *f* or *fe*

Form the plurals of nouns that end in *f* or *fe* in one of two ways: If the final *f* sound is still heard in the plural form of the word, simply add *s*; but if the final *f* sound becomes a *v* sound, change the *f* to *ve* and add *s*.

    Plural ends with *f* sound: roof – roofs; chief – chiefs

    Plural ends with *v* sound: wife – wives; loaf – loaves

Note: Several words are correct with either ending.

    Plural ends with either sound: hoof – hooves/hoofs; wharf – wharves/wharfs

577.1 Irregular Spelling

A number of words form a plural by taking on an irregular spelling.

| crisis – crises | child – children | radius – radii |
| criterion – criteria | goose – geese | die – dice |

Note: Some of these words are now acceptable with the commonly used *s* or *es* ending.

index – indices/indexes   cactus – cacti/cactuses

Some nouns remain unchanged when used as plurals.

deer   sheep   salmon   aircraft   series

577.2 Words Discussed as Words

The plurals of symbols, letters, numbers, and words being discussed as words are formed by adding an apostrophe and an *s*.

Mom yelled a lot of *wow*'s and *yippee*'s when she saw my A's and B's.

Note: You may omit the apostrophe if it does not cause any confusion.

the three R's or Rs   YMCA's or YMCAs

577.3 Nouns Ending in *ful*

Form the plurals of nouns that end in *ful* by adding *s* to the end of the word.

two tankfuls   three pailfuls   four mouthfuls

Note: Do not confuse these examples with three *pails full* (when you are referring to three separate pails full of something) or two *tanks full*.

577.4 Compound Nouns

Form the plurals of most compound nouns by adding *s* or *es* to the important word in the compound.

brothers-in-law   maids of honor   secretaries of state

577.5 Collective Nouns

A collective noun may be singular or plural depending upon how it's used. A collective noun is singular when it refers to a group considered as one unit; it is plural when it refers to the individuals in the group.

The class was on its best behavior. (group as a unit)

The class are preparing for their final exams. (individuals in the group)

If it seems awkward to use a plural verb with a collective noun, add a clearly plural noun such as *members* to the sentence.

The class members are preparing for their final exams.

You may also change the collective noun into a possessive followed by a plural noun that describes the individuals in the group.

The class's students are preparing for their final exams.

▌Numbers

578.1 Numerals or Words

Numbers from one to nine are usually written as words; numbers 10 and over are usually written as numerals.

    two   seven   nine   10   25   106   1,079

Exception: Numbers being compared or contrasted should be kept in the same style.

    8 to 11 years old   eight to eleven years old

You may use a combination of numerals and words for very large numbers.

    1.5 million   3 billion to 3.2 billion   6 trillion

If numbers are used infrequently in a piece of writing, you may spell out those that can be written in no more than two words.

    ten   twenty-five   two hundred   fifty thousand

578.2 Numerals Only

Use numerals for the following forms: decimals, percentages, chapters, pages, addresses, phone numbers, identification numbers, and statistics.

    26.2   8 percent   Highway 36   chapter 7
    pages 287-89   July 6, 1945   44 B.C.E.   a vote of 23 to 4

Always use numerals with abbreviations and symbols.

    8%   10 mm   3 cc   8 oz   90°C   24 mph   76.9%

578.3 Words Only

Use words to express numbers that begin a sentence.

    Fourteen students "forgot" their assignments.

Note: Change the sentence structure if this rule creates a clumsy construction.

    Clumsy: Six hundred thirty-nine teachers were laid off this year.

    Better: This year, 639 teachers were laid off.

Use words for numbers that come before a compound modifier if that modifier includes another number.

    They made **twelve** 10-foot sub sandwiches for the picnic.

578.4 Time and Money

If time is expressed with an abbreviation, use numerals; if it is expressed in words, spell out the number.

    4:00 A.M. (or) four o'clock

If an amount of money is spelled out, so is the currency; if a symbol is used, use a numeral.

    twenty dollars (or) $20

■ Abbreviations

579.1 Formal and Informal Abbreviations

An **abbreviation** is the shortened form of a word or phrase. Some abbreviations are always acceptable in both formal and informal writing:

   Mr.   Mrs.   Jr.   Ms.   Dr.   a.m. (A.M.)   p.m. (P.M.)

Note: In most of your writing, ***do not*** abbreviate the names of states, countries, months, days, or units of measure. Do not abbreviate the words *Street, Road, Avenue, Company,* and similar words, especially when they are part of a proper noun (name). Also, do not use signs or symbols (%, &, #, @) in place of words. The dollar sign, however, is appropriate with numerals ($325).

579.2 Correspondence Abbreviations

United States

	Standard	Postal
Alabama	Ala.	AL
Alaska	Alaska	AK
Arizona	Ariz.	AZ
Arkansas	Ark.	AR
California	Calif.	CA
Colorado	Colo.	CO
Connecticut	Conn.	CT
Delaware	Del.	DE
District of Columbia	D.C.	DC
Florida	Fla.	FL
Georgia	Ga.	GA
Guam	Guam	GU
Hawaii	Hawaii	HI
Idaho	Idaho	ID
Illinois	Ill.	IL
Indiana	Ind.	IN
Iowa	Iowa	IA
Kansas	Kan.	KS
Kentucky	Ky.	KY
Louisiana	La.	LA
Maine	Maine	ME
Maryland	Md.	MD
Massachusetts	Mass.	MA
Michigan	Mich.	MI
Minnesota	Minn.	MN
Mississippi	Miss.	MS
Missouri	Mo.	MO
Nebraska	Neb.	NE
Nevada	Nev.	NV
New Hampshire	N.H.	NH
New Jersey	N.J.	NJ
New Mexico	N.M.	NM
New York	N.Y.	NY
North Carolina	N.C.	NC
North Dakota	N.D.	ND
Ohio	Ohio	OH
Oklahoma	Okla.	OK
Oregon	Ore.	OR
Pennsylvania	Pa.	PA
Puerto Rico	P.R.	PR

	Standard	Postal
Rhode Island	R.I.	RI
South Carolina	S.C.	SC
South Dakota	S.D.	SD
Tennessee	Tenn.	TN
Texas	Texas	TX
Utah	Utah	UT
Vermont	Vt.	VT
Virginia	Va.	VA
Virgin Islands	V.I.	VI
Washington	Wash.	WA
West Virginia	W.Va.	WV
Wisconsin	Wis.	WI
Wyoming	Wyo.	WY

Canadian

	Standard	Postal
Alberta	Alta.	AB
British Columbia	B.C.	BC
Labrador	Lab.	NL
Manitoba	Man.	MB
New Brunswick	N.B.	NB
Newfoundland	N.F.	NL
Northwest Territories	N.W.T.	NT
Nova Scotia	N.S.	NS
Nunavut		NU
Ontario	Ont.	ON
Prince Edward Island	P.E.I.	PE
Quebec	Que.	QC
Saskatchewan	Sask.	SK
Yukon Territory	Y.T.	YT

Addresses

	Standard	Postal
Apartment	Apt.	APT
Avenue	Ave.	AVE
Boulevard	Blvd.	BLVD
Circle	Cir.	CIR
Court	Ct.	CT

	Standard	Postal
Drive	Dr.	DR
East	E.	E
Expressway	Expy.	EXPY
Freeway	Fwy.	FWY
Heights	Hts.	HTS
Highway	Hwy.	HWY
Hospital	Hosp.	HOSP
Junction	Junc.	JCT
Lake	L.	LK
Lakes	Ls.	LKS
Lane	Ln.	LN
Meadows	Mdws.	MDWS
North	N.	N
Palms	Palms	PLMS
Park	Pk.	PK
Parkway	Pky.	PKY
Place	Pl.	PL
Plaza	Plaza	PLZ
Post Office Box	P.O. Box	PO BOX
Ridge	Rdg.	RDG
River	R.	RV
Road	Rd.	RD
Room	Rm.	RM
Rural	R.	R
Rural Route	R.R.	RR
Shore	Sh.	SH
South	S.	S
Square	Sq.	SQ
Station	Sta.	STA
Street	St.	ST
Suite	Ste.	STE
Terrace	Ter.	TER
Turnpike	Tpke.	TPKE
Union	Un.	UN
View	View	VW
Village	Vil.	VLG
West	W.	W

■ Abbreviations (continued)

580.1 Other Common Abbreviations

abr. abridged; abridgment
AC, ac alternating current
ack. acknowledge; acknowledgment
ACV actual cash value
A.D. in the year of the Lord (Latin *anno Domini*)
aka also know as
AM amplitude modulation
A.M., a.m. before noon (Latin *ante meridiem*)
ann. annual
anon. anonymous
ann. annual
ASAP as soon as possible
assoc. Association
avg., av. average
BBB Better Business Bureau
B.C. before Christ
B.C.E. before the Common Era
bibliog. bibliographer; bibliography
biog. biographer; biographical; biography
C 1. Celsius 2. centigrade 3. coulomb
c. circa (about) 2. cup
cc 1. cubic centimeter 2. carbon copy
CDT, C.D.T. central daylight time
C.E. of the Common Era
chap. chapter
cm centimeter
c.o., c/o care of
.com commercial
co-op cooperative
CST, C.S.T. central standard time
cu., c cubic
D.A. district attorney
d.b.a. doing business as
DC, dc direct current
dept. department
dob date of birth
DST, D.S.T. daylight saving time
dup. duplicate
DVD digital video disc
ea. each
ed. edition; editor
EDT, E.D.T. eastern daylight time
.edu education
e.g. for example (Latin *exempli gratia*)
EST, E.S.T. eastern standard time
ETA estimated time of arrival
etc. and so forth (Latin *et cetera*)
ex. example
F Fahrenheit
FYI for your information
FM frequency modulation
F.O.B., f.o.b. free on board
ft foot

g 1. gram 2. gravity
gal. gallon
GNP gross national product
.gov government
GPA grade point average
hdqrs, HQ headquarters
HIV human immunodeficiency virus
Hon. Honorable (title)
hp horsepower
HTML hypertext markup language
Hz hertz
ibid. in the same place (Latin *ibidem*)
id. the same (Latin *idem*)
i.e. that is (Latin *id est*)
illus. illustration
inc. incorporated
info information
IQ, I.Q. intelligence quotient
IRS Internal Revenue Service
ISBN International Standard Book Number
Jr., jr. junior
K 1. kelvin (temperature unit) 2. Kelvin (temperature scale)
kc kilocycle
kg kilogram
km kilometer
kn knot
kw kilowatt
l liter
lat. latitude
lb, lb. pound (Latin *libra*)
l.c. lowercase
lit. literary; literature
log logarithm
long. longitude
Ltd., ltd. limited
m meter
M.A. master of arts (Latin *Magister Artium*)
M.C., m.c. master of ceremonies
M.D. doctor of medicine (Latin *medicinae doctor*)
mdse. merchandise
mfg. manufacturing
mg milligram
mi. 1. mile 2. mill (monetary unit)
misc. miscellaneous
ml milliliter
mm millimeter
mpg, m.p.g. miles per gallon
mph, m.p.h. miles per hour
Ms., Ms title of courtesy for a woman
MST, M.S.T. mountain standard time

nav navigate
nc no charge
neg. negative
N.S.F., n.s.f. not sufficient funds
oz, oz. ounce
PA 1. public-address system 2. Pennsylvania
pct. percent
pd. paid
PDT, P.D.T. Pacific daylight time
Pfc, Pfc. private first class
pg., p. page
P.M., p.m. after noon (Latin *post meridiem*)
pop. population
POW, P.O.W. prisoner of war
pp. pages
ppd. 1. postpaid 2. prepaid
PR, P.R. 1. public relations 2. Puerto Rico
P.S. 1. postscript 2. public school
psi, p.s.i. pounds per square inch
PST, P.S.T. Pacific standard time
PTA, P.T.A. Parent-Teachers Association
qt. quart
RN registered nurse
R.P.M., rpm revolutions per minute
R.S.V.P., r.s.v.p. please reply (French *répondez s'il vous plaît*)
SASE self-addressed stamped envelope
SCSI small computer system interface
SOS 1. international distress signal 2. any call for help
ST standard time
St. 1. saint 2. strait 3. street
std. standard
syn. synonymous; synonym
TBA to be announced
TBD to be determined
tbs, tbsp tablespoon
TM trademark
tsp teaspoon
UHF, uhf ultra high frequency
UPC universal product code
UV ultraviolet
V 1. *Physics:* velocity 2. *Electricity:* volt 3. volume
V.A., VA Veterans Administration
VIP *Informal:* very important person
vol. 1. volume 2. volunteer
vs. versus
whse., whs. warehouse
wkly. weekly
w/o without
wt. weight
yd yard (measurement)

▌Acronyms and Initialisms

581.1 Acronyms

An **acronym** is a word formed from the first (or first few) letters of words in a phrase. Even though acronyms are abbreviations, they require no periods.

radar	radio detecting and ranging
CARE	Cooperative for American Relief Everywhere
NASA	National Aeronautics and Space Administration
VISTA	Volunteers in Service to America
LAN	local area network

581.2 Initialisms

An **initialism** is similar to an acronym except that the initials used to form this abbreviation are pronounced individually.

CIA	Central Intelligence Agency
FBI	Federal Bureau of Investigation
FHA	Federal Housing Administration

581.3 Common Acronyms and Initialisms

ACT	American College Testing Service		LAN	Local Area Network
ADD	attention deficit disorder		LCD	liquid crystal display
AIDS	acquired immunodeficiency syndrome		LLC	limited liability company
			MADD	Mothers Against Drunk Driving
AP	Advanced Placement		MRI	Magnetic Resonance Imaging
ATM	automatic teller machine		NASA	National Aeronautics and Space Administration
BA	Bachelor of Arts			
BS	Bachelor of Science		NATO	North Atlantic Treaty Organization
CD	compact disc		OPEC	Organization of Petroleum-Exporting Countries
DMV	Department of Motor Vehicles			
ETS	Educational Testing Service		OSHA	Occupational Safety and Health Administration
FAA	Federal Aviation Administration			
FTC	Federal Trade Commission		PAC	political action committee
FCC	Federal Communications Commission		PDF	portable document format
			PIN	personal identification number
FDA	Food and Drug Administration		PSA	public service announcement
FDIC	Federal Deposit Insurance Corporation		PSAT	Preliminary Scholastic Aptitude Test
FEMA	Federal Emergency Management Agency		RSS	Rich Site Summary
			SADD	Students Against Destructive Decisions
GPS	global positioning system			
HTML	Hyper-Text Markup Language		SAT	Scholastic Aptitude Test
INS	Immigration and Naturalization Service		SNN	Social Security Number
			VA	Veterans Administration
IRS	Internal Revenue Service		VOIP	Voice Over Internet Protocol
IT	information technology		WLAN	Wireless Local Area Network
JPEG	Joint Photographic Experts Group			

Quick Guide

▮ Spelling Rules

582.1 Write *i* before *e*

Write *i* before *e* except after *c*, or when sounded like *a* as in *neighbor* and *weigh*.

    relief   receive   perceive   reign   freight   beige

Exceptions: There are a number of exceptions to this rule.

    neither   leisure   seize   weird   species   science

582.2 Words with Consonant Endings

When a one-syllable word (*bat*) ends in a consonant (*t*) preceded by one vowel (*a*), double the final consonant before adding a suffix that begins with a vowel (*batting*).

    bat—batter   sum—summary   god—goddess

Note: When a multisyllable word (*control*) ends in a consonant (*l*) preceded by one vowel (*o*), and the accent is on the last syllable (*con trol´*), and the suffix begins with a vowel (*ing*)—the same rule holds true: double the final consonant before adding a suffix that begins with a vowel (*controlling*).

    control—controlled   begin—beginning
    forget—forgettable   admit—admittance

582.3 Words with a Silent *e*

If a word ends with a silent *e*, drop the *e* before adding a suffix that begins with a vowel. Do not drop the *e* when the suffix begins with a consonant.

    state—stating—statement   like—liking—likeness
    use—using—useful   nine—ninety—nineteen

Exceptions: There are a number of exceptions to this rule.

    judgment   truly   argument   ninth

582.4 Words Ending in y

When *y* is the last letter in a word and the *y* is preceded by a consonant, change the *y* to *i* before adding any suffix except those beginning with *i*.

    fry—fries—frying   hurry—hurried—hurrying   lady—ladies
    ply—pliable   happy—happiness   beauty—beautiful

When *y* is the last letter in a word and the *y* is preceded by a vowel, do not change the *y* to *i* before adding a suffix.

    play—plays—playful   stay—stays—staying   employ—employed

Important reminder: Never trust your spelling to even the best spell-checker. Use a dictionary for words your spell-checker may not cover.

■ Commonly Misspelled Words

A

abbreviate
abrupt
abscess
absence
absolute (ly)
absorbent
absurd
abundance
accede
accelerate
accept (ance)
accessible
accessory
accidentally
accommodate
accompany
accomplice
accomplish
accordance
according
account
accrued
accumulate
accurate
accustom (ed)
ache
achieve (ment)
acknowledge
acquaintance
acquiesce
acquired
actual
adapt
addition (al)
address
adequate
adjourned
adjustment
admirable
admissible
admittance
advantageous
advertisement
advertising
advice (n.)
advisable
advise (v.)
aerial
affect

affidavit
again
against
aggravate
aggression
agreeable
agreement
aisle
alcohol
alignment
alley
allotted
allowance
all right
almost
already
although
altogether
aluminum
always
amateur
amendment
among
amount
analysis
analyze
ancient
anecdote
anesthetic
angle
annihilate
anniversary
announce
annoyance
annual
anoint
anonymous
answer
antarctic
anticipate
anxiety
anxious
anything
apartment
apologize
apparatus
apparent (ly)
appeal
appearance
appetite

appliance
applicable
application
appointment
appraisal
appreciate
approach
appropriate
approval
approximately
architect
arctic
argument
arithmetic
arouse
arrangement
arrival
article
artificial
ascend
ascertain
asinine
assassin
assess (ment)
assignment
assistance
associate
association
assume
assurance
asterisk
athlete
athletic
attach
attack (ed)
attempt
attendance
attention
attitude
attorney
attractive
audible
audience
authority
automobile
autumn
auxiliary
available
average
awful

awfully
awkward

B

bachelor
baggage
balance
balloon
ballot
banana
bandage
bankrupt
bargain
barrel
basement
basis
battery
beautiful
beauty
become
becoming
before
beggar
beginning
behavior
being
belief
believe
beneficial
benefit (ed)
between
bicycle
biscuit
blizzard
bookkeeper
bough
bought
bouillon
boundary
breakfast
breath (n.)
breathe (v.)
brief
brilliant
Britain
brochure
brought
bruise
budget
bulletin

buoyant
bureau
burglar
bury
business
busy

C

cafeteria
caffeine
calendar
campaign
canceled
candidate
canister
canoe
can't
capacity
capital
capitol
captain
carburetor
career
caricature
carriage
cashier
casserole
casualty
catalog
catastrophe
caught
cavalry
celebration
cemetery
census
century
certain
certificate
cessation
challenge
changeable
character (istic)
chauffeur
chief
chimney
chocolate
choice
choose
Christian
circuit

circular
circumstance
civilization
clientele
climate
climb
clothes
coach
cocoa
coercion
collar
collateral
college
colloquial
colonel
color
colossal
column
comedy
coming
commence
commercial
commission
commit
commitment
committed
committee
communicate
community
comparative
comparison
compel
competent
competition
competitively
complain
complement
completely
complexion
compliment
compromise
concede
conceive
concerning
concert
concession
conclude
concrete
concurred
concurrence
condemn
condescend
condition

conference
conferred
confidence
confidential
congratulate
conscience
conscientious
conscious
consensus
consequence
conservative
considerably
consignment
consistent
constitution
contemptible
continually
continue
continuous
control
controversy
convenience
convince
coolly
cooperate
cordial
corporation
correlate
correspond
correspondence
corroborate
cough
couldn't
council
counsel
counterfeit
country
courage
courageous
courteous
courtesy
cousin
coverage
creditor
crisis
criticism
criticize
cruel
curiosity
curious
current
curriculum
custom

customary
customer
cylinder

D

daily
dairy
dealt
debtor
deceased
deceitful
deceive
decided
decision
declaration
decorate
deductible
defendant
defense
deferred
deficit
definite (ly)
definition
delegate
delicious
dependent
depositor
depot
descend
describe
description
desert
deserve
design
desirable
desirous
despair
desperate
despise
dessert
deteriorate
determine
develop
development
device
devise
diamond
diaphragm
diarrhea
diary
dictionary
difference
different

difficulty
dilapidated
dilemma
dining
diploma
director
disagreeable
disappear
disappoint
disapprove
disastrous
discipline
discover
discrepancy
discuss
discussion
disease
dissatisfied
dissipate
distinguish
distribute
divide
divine
divisible
division
doctor
doesn't
dominant
dormitory
doubt
drudgery
dual
duplicate
dyeing
dying

E

eagerly
earnest
economical
economy
ecstasy
edition
effervescent
efficacy
efficiency
eighth
either
elaborate
electricity
elephant
eligible
eliminate

ellipse
embarrass
emergency
eminent
emphasize
employee
employment
emulsion
enclose
encourage
endeavor
endorsement
engineer
English
enormous
enough
enterprise
entertain
enthusiastic
entirely
entrance
envelop (v.)
envelope (n.)
environment
equipment
equipped
equivalent
especially
essential
establish
esteemed
etiquette
evidence
exaggerate
exceed
excellent
except
exceptionally
excessive
excite
executive
exercise
exhaust (ed)
exhibition
exhilaration
existence
exorbitant
expect
expedition
expenditure
expensive
experience
explain

explanation
expression
exquisite
extension
extinct
extraordinary
extremely

F

facilities
fallacy
familiar
famous
fascinate
fashion
fatigue (d)
faucet
favorite
feasible
feature
February
federal
feminine
fertile
fictitious
field
fierce
fiery
finally
financially
foliage
forcible
foreign
forfeit
forgo
formally
formerly
fortunate
forty
forward
fountain
fourth
fragile
frantically
freight
friend
fulfill
fundamental
furthermore
futile

G

gadget
gangrene
garage
gasoline
gauge
genealogy
generally
generous
genius
genuine
geography
ghetto
ghost
glorious
gnaw
government
governor
gracious
graduation
grammar
grateful
gratitude
grease
grief
grievous
grocery
grudge
gruesome
guarantee
guard
guardian
guerrilla
guess
guidance
guide
guilty
gymnasium
gypsy
gyroscope

H

habitat
hammer
handkerchief
handle (d)
handsome
haphazard
happen
happiness
harass
harbor

hastily
having
hazardous
height
hemorrhage
hesitate
hindrance
history
hoarse
holiday
honor
hoping
hopping
horde
horrible
hospital
humorous
hurriedly
hydraulic
hygiene
hymn
hypocrisy

I

iambic
icicle
identical
idiosyncrasy
illegible
illiterate
illustrate
imaginary
imaginative
imagine
imitation
immediately
immense
immigrant
immortal
impatient
imperative
importance
impossible
impromptu
improvement
inalienable
incidentally
inconvenience
incredible
incurred
indefinitely
indelible
independence

independent
indictment
indispensable
individual
inducement
industrial
industrious
inevitable
inferior
inferred
infinite
inflammable
influential
ingenious
ingenuous
inimitable
initial
initiation
innocence
innocent
inoculation
inquiry
installation
instance
instead
institute
insurance
intellectual
intelligence
intention
intercede
interesting
interfere
intermittent
interpret (ed)
interrupt
interview
intimate
invalid
investigate
investor
invitation
iridescent
irrelevant
irresistible
irreverent
irrigate
island
issue
itemized
itinerary
it's (it is)

J

janitor
jealous (y)
jeopardize
jewelry
journal
journey
judgment
justice
justifiable

K

kitchen
knowledge
knuckle

L

label
laboratory
lacquer
language
laugh
laundry
lawyer
league
lecture
legal
legible
legislature
legitimate
leisure
length
letterhead
liability
liable
liaison
library
license
lieutenant
lightning
likable
likely
lineage
liquefy
liquid
listen
literary
literature
livelihood
living
logarithm
loneliness

loose
lose
losing
lovable
lovely
luncheon
luxury

M

machine
magazine
magnificent
maintain
maintenance
majority
making
management
maneuver
manual
manufacture
manuscript
marriage
marshal
material
mathematics
maximum
mayor
meanness
meant
measure
medicine
medieval
mediocre
medium
memorandum
menus
merchandise
merit
message
mileage
millionaire
miniature
minimum
minute
mirror
miscellaneous
mischief
mischievous
miserable
misery
missile

missionary
misspell
moisture
molecule
momentous
monotonous
monument
mortgage
municipal
muscle
musician
mustache
mysterious

N

naive
naturally
necessary
necessity
negligible
negotiate
neighborhood
nevertheless
nickel
niece
nineteenth
ninety
noticeable
notoriety
nuclear
nuisance

O

obedience
obey
oblige
obstacle
occasion
occasionally
occupant
occur
occurred
occurrence
offense
official
often
omission
omitted
operate
opinion
opponent

opportunity
opposite
optimism
ordinance
ordinarily
original
outrageous

P

pageant
paid
pamphlet
paradise
paragraph
parallel
paralyze
parentheses (pl.)
parenthesis (s.)
parliament
partial
participant
participate
particularly
pastime
patience
patronage
peculiar
perceive
perhaps
peril
permanent
permissible
perpendicular
perseverance
persistent
personal (ly)
personnel
perspiration
persuade
phase
phenomenon
philosophy
physician
piece
planned
plateau
plausible
playwright
pleasant
pleasure
pneumonia

politician
possess
possession
possible
practically
prairie
precede
precedence
preceding
precious
precisely
precision
predecessor
preferable
preference
preferred
prejudice
preliminary
premium
preparation
presence
prevalent
previous
primitive
principal
principle
priority
prisoner
privilege
probably
procedure
proceed
professor
prominent
pronounce
pronunciation
propaganda
prosecute
protein
psychology
publicly
pumpkin
purchase
pursue
pursuing
pursuit

Q

qualified
quantity
quarter

questionnaire
quiet
quite
quotient

R

raise
rapport
realize
really
recede
receipt
receive
received
recipe
recipient
recognition
recognize
recommend
recurrence
reference
referred
rehearse
reign
reimburse
relevant
relieve
religious
remember
remembrance
reminisce
rendezvous
renewal
repetition
representative
requisition
reservoir
resistance
respectably
respectfully
respectively
responsibility
restaurant
rheumatism
rhyme
rhythm
ridiculous
route

S

sacrilegious
safety
salary
sandwich
satisfactory
Saturday
scarcely
scene
scenery
schedule
science
scissors
secretary
seize
sensible
sentence
sentinel
separate
sergeant
several
severely
shepherd
sheriff
shining
siege
significance
similar
simultaneous
since
sincerely
skiing
soldier
solemn
sophisticated
sophomore
sorority
source
souvenir
spaghetti
specific
specimen
speech
sphere
sponsor
spontaneous
stationary
stationery
statistic
statue
stature

statute
stomach
stopped
straight
strategy
strength
stretched
studying
subsidize
substantial
substitute
subtle
succeed
success
sufficient
summarize
superficial
superintendent
superiority
supersede
supplement
suppose
surely
surprise
surveillance
survey
susceptible
suspicious
sustenance
syllable
symmetrical
sympathy
symphony
symptom
synchronous

T

tariff
technique
telegram
temperament
temperature
temporary
tendency
tentative
terrestrial
terrible
territory
theater
their
therefore

thief
thorough (ly)
though
throughout
tired
tobacco
together
tomorrow
tongue
tonight
touch
tournament
tourniquet
toward
tragedy
traitor
tranquilizer
transferred
treasurer
tried
truly
Tuesday
tuition
typical
typing

U

unanimous
unconscious
undoubtedly
unfortunately
unique
unison
university
unnecessary
unprecedented
until
upper
urgent
usable
useful
using
usually
utensil
utilize

V

vacancies
vacation
vacuum
vague

valuable
variety
various
vegetable
vehicle
veil
velocity
vengeance
vicinity
view
vigilance
villain
violence
visibility
visible
visitor
voice
volume
voluntary
volunteer

W

wander
warrant
weather
Wednesday
weird
welcome
welfare
where
whether
which
whole
wholly
whose
width
women
worthwhile
worthy
wreckage
wrestler
writing
written
wrought

Y

yellow
yesterday
yield

▌ Steps to Becoming a Better Speller

1. Be patient.
Becoming a good speller takes time.

2. Check the correct pronunciation of each word you are attempting to spell.
Knowing the correct pronunciation of a word can help you remember its spelling.

3. Note the meaning and history of each word as you are checking the dictionary for pronunciation.
Knowing the meaning and history of a word provides you with a better notion of how the word is properly used, and this can help you remember its spelling.

4. Before you close the dictionary, practice spelling the word.
Look away from the page and try to "see" the word in your mind. Then write it on a piece of paper. Check your spelling in the dictionary; repeat the process until you are able to spell the word correctly.

5. Learn some spelling rules.
This handbook contains four of the most useful rules. (See page 582.)

6. Make a list of the words that you often misspell.
Select the first 10 and practice spelling them.

STEP A: Read each word carefully; then write it on a piece of paper. Check to see that you've spelled it correctly. Repeat this step for the words that you misspelled.

STEP B: When you have finished your first 10 words, ask someone to read them to you as you write them again. Then check for misspellings. If you find none, congratulations! (Repeat both steps with your next 10 words, and so on.)

7. Write often—and use your spell checker.

"There is little point in learning to spell if you have little intention of writing."

Frank Smith

"The difference between the right word and the nearly right word is the same as that between lightning and the lightning bug."

Mark Twain

Using the Right Word

a lot ▪ *A lot* (always two words) is a vague descriptive phrase that should be used sparingly.

"You can observe a lot just by watching."

— Yogi Berra

accept, except ▪ The verb *accept* means "to receive" or "to believe"; the preposition *except* means "other than."

The principal accepted the boy's story about the broken window, but she asked why no one except him saw the ball accidentally slip from his hand.

adapt, adopt ▪ *Adapt* means "to adjust or change to fit"; *adopt* means "to choose and treat as your own" (a child, an idea).

After a lengthy period of study, Malcolm X adopted the Islamic faith and adapted to its lifestyle.

affect, effect ▪ The verb *affect* means "to influence"; the verb *effect* means "to produce, accomplish, complete."

Ming's hard work effected an "A" on the test, which positively affected her semester grade.

The noun *effect* means the "result."

Good grades have a calming effect on parents.

aisle, isle ▪ An *aisle* is a passage between seats; an *isle* is a small island.

Many airline passengers on their way to the Isle of Capri prefer an aisle seat.

all right ▪ *All right* is always two words (not *alright*).

allusion, illusion ▪ *Allusion* is an indirect reference to someone or something; *illusion* is a false picture or idea.

My little sister, under the illusion that she's movie-star material, makes frequent allusions to her future fans.

already, all ready ▪ *Already* is an adverb meaning "before this time" or "by this time." *All ready* is an adjective meaning "fully prepared."

Note: Use *all ready* if you can substitute *ready* alone in the sentence.

> Although I've already had some dessert, I am all ready for some ice cream from the street vendor.

altogether, all together ▪ *Altogether* means "entirely." The phrase *all together* means "in a group" or "all at once."

> "There is altogether too much gridlock," complained the Democrats. All together, the Republicans yelled, "No way!"

among, between ▪ *Among* is used when speaking of more than two persons or things. *Between* is used when speaking of only two.

> The three of us talked among ourselves to decide between going out or eating in.

amount, number ▪ *Amount* is used for bulk measurement. *Number* is used to count separate units. (See also *fewer, less*.)

> A number of soft drinks contain a substantial amount of caffeine.

annual, biannual, semiannual, biennial, perennial ▪ An *annual* event happens once every year. A *biannual* or *semiannual* event happens twice a year. A *biennial* event happens every two years. A *perennial* event is one that is persistent or constant.

> Dad's annual family reunion gets bigger every year.
> We're going shopping at the department store's semiannual white sale.
> Due to dwindling attendance, the county fair is now a biennial celebration.
> A perennial plant persists for several years.

anyway ▪ Do not add an *s* to *anyway*.

ascent, assent ▪ *Ascent* is the act of rising or climbing; *assent* is "to agree to something after some consideration" (or such an agreement).

> The group's ascent of the butte was completed with the assent of the landowner.

bad, badly ▪ *Bad* is an adjective. *Badly* is an adverb.

> This apple is bad, but one bad apple doesn't ruin the whole bushel.
> In today's game, Ross passed badly.

base, bass ▪ *Base* is the foundation or the lower part of something. *Bass* is a deep sound or tone. *Bass* (when pronounced like *class*) is a fish.

beside, besides ▪ *Beside* means "by the side of." *Besides* means "in addition to."
> Mother always grew roses beside the trash bin. Besides looking nice, the flowers smelled sweet and masked odors.

board, bored ▪ *Board* is a piece of wood. *Board* is also an administrative group or council.
> The school board approved the purchase of fifty 1- by 6-inch pine boards.

Bored is the past tense of the verb "bore," which may mean "to make a hole by drilling" or "to become weary out of dullness."
> Joe bored a hole in the wall where he could hang his new photograph. Photography never bored him.

brake, break ▪ *Brake* is a device used to stop a vehicle. *Break* means "to separate or to destroy."
> I hope the brakes on my car never break.

bring, take ▪ *Bring* suggests the action is directed toward the speaker; *take* suggests the action is directed away from the speaker.
> I'll bring home some garbage bags so you can take the trash outside.

can, may ▪ *Can* suggests ability, while *may* suggests permission.
> "Can I go to the mall?" means "Am I physically able to go to the mall?"
> "May I go to the mall?" asks permission to go.

capital, capitol ▪ The noun *capital* refers to a city or to money. The adjective *capital* means "major or important." *Capitol* refers to a building.
> The state capital is home to the capitol building for a capital reason. The state government contributed capital for its construction.

cent, sent, scent ▪ *Cent* is a coin; *sent* is the past tense of the verb "send"; *scent* is an odor or a smell.
> For forty-nine cents, I sent my girlfriend a mushy love poem in a perfumed envelope. She adored the scent but hated the poem.

cereal, serial ▪ *Cereal* is a grain, often made into breakfast food. *Serial* relates to something in a series.
> Mohammed enjoys reading serial novels while he eats a bowl of cereal.

chord, cord ▪ *Chord* may mean "an emotion" or "a combination of musical tones sounded at the same time." A *cord* is a string or a rope.
> The guitar player strummed the opening chord to the group's hit song, which struck a responsive chord with the audience.

chose, choose ▪ *Chose* (chōz) is the past tense of the verb *choose* (chüz).

Last quarter I chose to read Martin Luther King's *Strength to Love*—a book that says it takes strength to choose a nonviolent response to injustice.

coarse, course ▪ *Coarse* means "rough or crude"; *course* means "a path or direction taken." *Course* also means "a class or a series of studies."

Fletcher, known for using coarse language, was barred from the coffee shop until he took an etiquette course.

complement, compliment ▪ *Complement* refers to that which completes or fulfills. *Compliment* is an expression of admiration or praise.

Kimberly smiled, thinking she had received a compliment, when Carlos said that her new chihuahua complemented her personality.

continual, continuous ▪ *Continual* refers to something that happens again and again with some breaks or pauses; *continuous* refers to something that keeps happening, uninterrupted.

Sunlight hits Iowa on a continual basis; sunlight hits Earth continuously.

counsel, council ▪ When used as a noun, *counsel* means "advice"; when used as a verb, it means "to advise." *Council* refers to a group that advises.

The student council counseled all freshmen to join at least one school activity. That's good counsel.

desert, dessert ▪ The noun *desert* (dez'ert) refers to a barren wilderness. *Dessert* (di zûrt') is food served at the end of a meal.

The scorpion scampered through the moonlit desert, searching for dessert.

The verb *desert* (di zûrt') means "to abandon"; the noun *desert* (di zûrt') means "deserved reward or punishment."

The burglar's hiding place deserted him when the spotlight swung his way; his subsequent arrest was his just desert.

die, dye ▪ *Die* (dying) means "to stop living." *Dye* (dyeing) is used to change the color of something.

different from, different than ▪ Use *different from* in a comparison of two things. *Different than* should be used only when followed by a clause.

Yassine is quite different from his brother.

Life is different than it used to be.

farther, further ▪ *Farther* refers to a physical distance; *further* refers to additional time, quantity, or degree.

Alaska extends farther north than Iceland does. Further information can be obtained in an atlas.

fewer, less ▪ *Fewer* refers to the number of separate units; *less* refers to bulk quantity.

Because we have fewer orders for cakes, we'll buy less sugar and flour.

flair, flare ▪ *Flair* refers to style or natural talent; *flare* means "to light up quickly" or "burst out" (or an object that does so).

Ronni was thrilled with Josie's flair for decorating—until one of her designer candles flared, marring the wall.

good, well ▪ *Good* is an adjective; *well* is nearly always an adverb. (When *well* is used to describe a state of health, it is an adjective: He was happy to be well again.)

The strange flying machines worked well and made our team look good.

heal, heel ▪ *Heal* means "to mend or restore to health." A *heel* is the back part of a foot.

Achilles died because a poison arrow pierced his heel and caused a wound that would not heal.

healthful, healthy ▪ *Healthful* means "causing or improving health"; *healthy* means "possessing health."

Healthful foods build healthy bodies.

hear, here ▪ You *hear* with your ears. *Here* means "the area close by."

heard, herd ▪ *Heard* is the past tense of the verb "hear"; *herd* is a large group of animals.

hole, whole ▪ A *hole* is a cavity or hollow place. *Whole* means "complete."

idle, idol ▪ *Idle* means "not working." An *idol* is someone or something that is worshipped.

The once-popular actress, who had been idle lately, wistfully recalled her days as an idol.

immigrate, emigrate ▪ *Immigrate* means "to come into a new country or environment." *Emigrate* means "to go out of one country to live in another."

Martin Ulferts immigrated to this country in 1882. He was only three years old when he emigrated from Germany.

imply, infer ▪ *Imply* means "to suggest or express indirectly"; *infer* means "to draw a conclusion from facts." (A writer or speaker implies; a reader or listener infers.)

Dad implied by his comment that I should drive more carefully, and I inferred that he was concerned for his new car.

insure, ensure ▪ *Insure* means "to secure from financial harm or loss." *Ensure* means "to make certain of something."

> To ensure that you can legally drive that new car, you'll have to insure it.

it's, its ▪ *It's* is the contraction of "it is." *Its* is the possessive form of "it."

> It's hard to believe, but the movie *Pride and Prejudice* still holds its appeal for many people.

later, latter ▪ *Later* means "after a period of time." *Latter* refers to the second of two things mentioned.

> Later that year, my sister had her second baby and also adopted a stray kitten. The latter was far more welcomed by her toddler.

lay, lie ▪ *Lay* means "to place." *Lay* is a transitive verb. (See 605.3.)

> Lay your books on the big table.

Lie means "to recline," and *lay* is the past tense of *lie. Lie* is an intransitive verb. (See 605.3.)

> In this heat, the young children must lie down for a nap. Yesterday they lay down without one complaint. Sometimes they have lain in the hammocks to rest.

lead, led ▪ *Lead* (lēd) is the present tense of the verb meaning "to guide." The past tense of the verb is *led* (lĕd). The noun *lead* (lĕd) is a metal.

> We were led along the path that leads to an abandoned lead mine.

learn, teach ▪ *Learn* means "to acquire information." *Teach* means "to give information."

> I learn better when people teach with real-world examples.

leave, let ▪ *Leave* means "to allow something to remain behind." *Let* means "to permit."

> Would you let me leave my car at your house?

lend, borrow ▪ *Lend* means "to give for temporary use." *Borrow* means "to receive for temporary use."

> I told Mom I needed to borrow twenty dollars, but she said she could not lend me any money until tomorrow.

like, as ▪ When *like* is used as a preposition meaning "similar to," it can be followed only by a noun, pronoun, or noun phrase; when *as* is used as a subordinating conjunction, it introduces a subordinate clause.

> If you want to be a gymnast like her, you'd better practice three hours a day as she does.

medal, meddle ▪ *Medal* is an award. *Meddle* means "to interfere."

Helicopter parents meddle in the awards process to make sure that their kids receive medals.

metal, mettle ▪ *Metal* is a chemical element like iron or gold. *Mettle* is "strength of spirit."

Grandad's mettle during battle left him with some metal in his shoulder.

miner, minor ▪ A *miner* digs for valuable ore. A *minor* is a person who is not legally an adult. A *minor* problem is one of no great importance.

The use of minors as miners is no minor problem.

moral, morale ▪ A *moral* is a lesson drawn from a story; as an adjective, it relates to the principles of right and wrong. *Morale* refers to someone's attitude.

Ms. Ladue considers it her moral obligation to help those in need.

The students' morale sank after their defeat in the forensics competition.

past, passed ▪ *Passed* is a verb. *Past* can be used as a noun, an adjective, or a preposition.

That old pickup truck passed my sports car! (verb)

Many senior citizens hold dearly to the past. (noun)

Tilly's past life as a circus worker must have been . . . interesting. (adjective)

Who can walk past a bakery without looking in the window? (preposition)

peace, piece ▪ *Peace* means "tranquility or freedom from war." *Piece* is a part or fragment.

Grandpa treats himself to a piece of pie or cake during the peace and quiet of the evening.

peak, peek, pique ▪ A *peak* is a high point. *Peek* means "brief look" (or "look briefly"). *Pique*, as a verb, means "to excite by challenging"; as a noun, it is a feeling of resentment.

The peak of Dr. Fedder's professional life was her ability to pique students' interest in her work.

"Take a peek at this slide," the doctor urged her students.

pedal, peddle, petal ▪ A *pedal* is a foot lever; as a verb, it means "to ride a bike." *Peddle* means "to go from place to place selling something." A *petal* is part of a flower.

Don Miller paints beautiful petals on his homemade birdhouses. Then he pedals through the flea market every weekend to peddle them.

personal, personnel ▪ *Personal* means "private." *Personnel* are people working at a particular job.

plain, plane ■ *Plain* means "an area of land that is flat or level"; it also means "clearly seen or clearly understood."

It's plain to see why settlers of the Great Plains had trouble moving west.

Plane means "flat, level"; it is also a tool used to smooth the surface of wood.

I used a plane to make the board plane and smooth.

pore, pour, poor ■ A *pore* is an opening in the skin. *Pour* means "to cause to flow in a stream." *Poor* means "needy or pitiable."

Tough exams on late spring days make my poor pores pour sweat.

principal, principle ■ As an adjective, *principal* means "primary." As a noun, it can mean "a school administrator" or "a sum of money." *Principle* means "idea or doctrine."

His principal gripe is lack of freedom. (adjective)
The principal expressed his concern about the open-campus policy. (noun)
During the first year of a loan, you pay more interest than principal. (noun)

The principle of *caveat emptor* is "Let the buyer beware."

quiet, quit, quite ■ *Quiet* is the opposite of "noisy." *Quit* means "to stop." *Quite* means "completely or entirely."

quote, quotation ■ *Quote* is a verb; *quotation* is a noun.

The quotation I used was from Woody Allen. You may quote me on that.

real, really, very ■ Do not use *real* in place of the adverbs *very* or *really*.

Mother's cake is usually very (not *real*) tasty, but this one is really stale!

right, write, wright, rite ■ *Right* means "correct or proper"; it also refers to that which a person has a legal claim to, as in *copyright*. *Write* means "to inscribe or record." A *wright* is a person who makes or builds something. *Rite* refers to a ritual or ceremonial act.

Write this down: It is the right of the shipwright to perform the rite of christening—breaking a bottle of champagne on the stern of the ship.

ring, wring ■ *Ring* means "encircle" or "to sound by striking." *Wring* means "to squeeze or twist."

At the beach, my aunt would ring her head with a large scarf. Once, it blew into the lake, so she had me wring it out.

scene, seen ■ *Scene* refers to the setting or location where something happens; it also may mean "sight or spectacle." *Seen* is a form of the verb "see."

Serena had seen her boyfriend making a scene; she cringed.

seam, seem ▪ *Seam* (noun) is a line formed by connecting two pieces. *Seem* (verb) means "to appear to exist."

The ragged seams in his old coat seem to match the creases in his face.

set, sit ▪ *Set* means "to place." *Sit* means "to put the body in a seated position." *Set* is transitive; *sit* is intransitive. (See 605.3.)

How can you just sit there and watch as I set all these chairs in place?

sight, cite, site ▪ *Sight* is the act of seeing; a *sight* is what is seen. *Cite* means "to quote," "to summon" (as before a court), or "to call to another's attention." *Site* means "location."

In her report, the general contractor cited several problems at the downtown job site. For one, the loading area was a chaotic sight.

sole, soul ▪ *Sole* means "single, only one"; *sole* also refers to the bottom surface of the foot. *Soul* refers to the spiritual part of a person.

As the sole inhabitant of the island, he put his heart and soul into his farming.

stationary, stationery ▪ *Stationary* means "not movable"; *stationery* refers to the paper and envelopes used to write letters.

steal, steel ▪ *Steal* means "to take something without permission"; *steel* is a metal.

than, then ▪ *Than* is used in a comparison; *then* tells when.

Abigail shouted that her big brother was bigger than my big brother. Then she ran away.

their, there, they're ▪ *Their* is a possessive personal pronoun. *There* is an adverb used to point out location. *They're* is the contraction of "they are."

They're a well-dressed couple. Do you see them over there, with their matching jackets?

threw, through ▪ *Threw* is the past tense of "throw." *Through* means "from beginning to end."

Through seven innings, Egor threw just seven strikes.

to, too, two ▪ *To* is a preposition that can mean "in the direction of." *To* is also used to form an infinitive. (See 606.3.) *Too* means "also" or "very." *Two* is the number.

vain, vane, vein ▪ *Vain* means "valueless or fruitless"; it may also mean "holding a high regard for oneself." *Vane* is a flat piece of material set up to show which way the wind blows. *Vein* refers to a blood vessel or a mineral deposit.

The vain prospector, boasting about the vein of silver he'd uncovered, paused to look up at the turning weather vane.

vary, very ▪ *Vary* means "to change." *Very* means "to a high degree."
Though the weather may vary from day to day, generally, it is very pleasant.

vial, vile ▪ A *vial* is a small container for liquid. *Vile* is an adjective meaning "foul, despicable."
It's a vile job, but someone has to clean these lab vials.

waist, waste ▪ *Waist* is a part of the body. The verb *waste* means "to use carelessly" or "to wear away or decay"; the noun *waste* refers to material that is unused.
Her waist is small because she wastes no opportunity to exercise.

wait, weight ▪ *Wait* means "to stay somewhere expecting something." *Weight* refers to a degree or unit of heaviness.

ware, wear, where ▪ *Ware* refers to a product that is sold; *wear* means "to have on"; *where* asks the question *in what place* or *in what situation.*
The designer boasted, "Where can one wear my ware? Anywhere."

way, weigh ▪ *Way* means "path or route." *Weigh* means "to measure weight" or "to have a certain heaviness."
My dogs weigh too much. The best way to reduce is a daily run in the park.

weather, whether ▪ *Weather* refers to the condition of the atmosphere. *Whether* refers to stated or implied alternatives.
Because of the weather forecast, Coach Pennington wondered whether he should reschedule the practice.

which, that ▪ Use *which* to refer to objects or animals in a nonrestrictive clause (set off with commas). Use *that* to refer to objects or animals in a restrictive clause. (For more information about these types of clauses, see 557.2.)
The birds, which stay in the area all winter, know exactly where the feeders are located. The food that attracts the most birds is sunflower seed.

who, whom ▪ Use *who* to refer to people. *Who* is used as the subject of a verb in an independent clause or in a relative clause. *Whom* is used as the object of a preposition or as a direct object.
To whom do we owe our thanks for these pizzas? And who ordered that one with pepperoni and pineapple?

who's, whose ▪ *Who's* is the contraction of "who is." *Whose* is a pronoun that can show possession or ownership.
Cody, whose car is new, will drive. Who's going to read the map?

your, you're ▪ *Your* is a possessive pronoun. *You're* is the contraction of "you are."
Put on your boots if you're going out in that snow.

"Don't be afraid to throw more than one verb in a sentence. I think 'She twisted and fell' is more exciting than 'She twisted. She fell to the ground.'"

Martyn Godfrey

Using the Parts of Speech

▌Noun

A **noun** is a word that names something: a person, a place, a thing, or an idea.

governor   Oregon   hospital   Hinduism   love

Classes of Nouns

The five classes of nouns are *proper, common, concrete, abstract,* and *collective.*

`599.1` Proper Noun

A **proper noun** names a particular person, place, thing, or idea. Proper nouns are always capitalized.

Jackie Robinson   Brooklyn   Ebbets Field   World Series   Christianity

`599.2` Common Noun

A **common noun** does not name a particular person, place, thing, or idea. Common nouns are not capitalized.

person   woman   president   park   baseball   government

`599.3` Concrete Noun

A **concrete noun** names a thing that is tangible (can be seen, touched, heard, smelled, or tasted). Concrete nouns are either proper or common.

child   Grand Canyon   music   aroma   pizza   Adele

`599.4` Abstract Noun

An **abstract noun** names an idea, a condition, or a feeling—in other words, something that cannot be touched, smelled, tasted, seen, or heard.

New Deal   greed   poverty   progress   freedom   hope

`599.5` Collective Noun

A **collective noun** names a group or a unit.

United States   Portland Trail Blazers   team   crowd   community

▌Noun (continued)

Forms of Nouns

Nouns are grouped according to their *number, gender,* and *case.*

600.1 Number of a Noun

Number indicates whether the noun is singular or plural.

■ A singular noun refers to one person, place, thing, or idea.

    actor   stadium   Canadian   bully   truth   child   person

■ A plural noun refers to more than one person, place, thing, or idea.

    actors   stadiums   Canadians   bullies   truths   children   people

600.2 Gender of a Noun

Gender indicates whether a noun is masculine, feminine, neuter, or indefinite.

   Masculine: uncle   brother   men   bull   rooster   stallion

   Feminine: aunt   sister   women   cow   hen   filly

   Neuter (without gender): tree   cobweb   locomotive   closet

   Indefinite (masculine or feminine): president   plumber   doctor   parent

600.3 Case of a Noun

Case tells how nouns are related to other words used with them. There are three cases: *nominative, possessive,* and *objective.*

■ A **nominative case** noun can be the *subject* of a clause.

> Patsy's heart was beating very wildly beneath his jacket. . . . That black horse there owed something to the orphan.
> —Paul Dunbar, "The Finish of Patsy Barnes"

A nominative noun can also be a predicate noun (or predicate nominative), which follows a "be" verb (*am, is, are, was, were, be, being, been*) and renames the subject. In the sentence below, *type* renames *Mr. Cattanzara.*

> Mr. Cattanzara was a different type than those in the neighborhood.
> —Bernard Malamud, "A Summer's Reading"

■ A **possessive case** noun shows possession or ownership.

> Like the spider's claw, a part of him touches a world he will never enter.
> —Loren Eiseley, "The Hidden Teacher"

■ An **objective case** noun can be a direct object, an indirect object, or an object of the preposition.

> Marna always gives Mylo science-fiction books for his birthday.
> (*Mylo* is the indirect object and *books* is the direct object of the verb "gives." *Birthday* is the object of the preposition "for.")

▌Pronoun

A **pronoun** is a word used in place of a noun.

I, you, she, it, which, that, themselves, whoever, me, he, they, mine, ours

601.1 Types of Pronouns

There are three types of pronouns: *simple, compound,* and *phrasal.*

Simple: I, you, he, she, it, we, they, who, what
Compound: myself, someone, anybody, everything, itself, whoever
Phrasal: one another, each other

601.2 Antecedent

All pronouns have antecedents. An **antecedent** is the noun that the pronoun refers to or replaces. (Below, *Ambrosch* is the antecedent of *him, he,* and *his.*)

Ambrosch was considered the important person in the family. Mrs. Shimerda and Ántonia always deferred to him, though he was often surly with them and contemptuous toward his father.   —Willa Cather, *My Ántonia*

Note: Each pronoun must agree with its antecedent. (See page 627.)

601.3 Classes of Pronouns

The six classes of pronouns are *personal, reflexive* and *intensive, relative, indefinite, interrogative,* and *demonstrative.*

Personal
I, me, my, mine / we, us, our, ours
you, your, yours / they, them, their, theirs
he, him, his, she, her, hers, it, its

Reflexive and Intensive
myself, yourself, himself, herself, itself, ourselves, yourselves, themselves

Relative
what, who, whose, whom, which, that

Indefinite

all	both	everything	nobody	several
another	each	few	none	some
any	either	many	no one	somebody
anyone	everybody	most	one	someone
anything	everyone	neither	other	something

Interrogative
who, whose, whom, which, what

Demonstrative
this, that, these, those

▌Pronoun (continued)

602.1 Personal Pronoun

A **personal pronoun** can take the place of any noun.

> Our coach made her point loud and clear when she raised her voice.

- A **reflexive pronoun** is formed by adding *self* or *selves* to a personal pronoun. A reflexive pronoun can be a direct object, an indirect object, an object of the preposition, or a predicate nominative.

> Miss Sally Sunshine loves herself. (direct object of *loves*)

> Tomisha does not seem herself today. (predicate nominative)

- An **intensive pronoun** is a reflexive pronoun that intensifies or emphasizes the noun or pronoun it refers to.

> Leo himself taught his children to invest their lives in others.

> The dessert the children had baked themselves tasted . . . interesting.

602.2 Relative Pronoun

A **relative pronoun** relates an adjective clause to the noun or pronoun it modifies.

> Students who study regularly get the best grades. Surprise!

> The dance, which we had looked forward to for weeks, was canceled.

(The relative pronoun *who* relates the adjective clause to *students*; *which* relates the adjective clause to *dance*.)

602.3 Indefinite Pronoun

An **indefinite pronoun** often refers to unnamed or unknown people or things.

> I don't know if you've known anybody from that far back; if you've loved anybody that long. . . . (The antecedent of *anybody* is unknown.)
> —James Baldwin, "My Dungeon Shook: Letter to My Nephew"

602.4 Interrogative Pronoun

An **interrogative pronoun** asks a question.

> "Then, who are you? Who could you be? What do you want from my husband?" —Elie Wiesel, "The Scrolls, Too, Are Mortal"

602.5 Demonstrative Pronoun

A **demonstrative pronoun** points out people, places, or things without naming them.

> This shouldn't be too hard. That looks about right.

> These are the best ones. Those ought to be thrown out.

Note: When one of these words precedes a noun, it functions as an adjective, not as a pronoun. (See 611.1.)

> That movie bothers me. (*That* is an adjective.)

Forms of Personal Pronouns

The form of a personal pronoun indicates its *number* (singular or plural), its *person* (first, second, third), its *case* (nominative, possessive, or objective), and its *gender* (masculine, feminine, or neuter).

603.1 Number of a Pronoun

Personal pronouns are singular or plural. The singular personal pronouns include *my, him, he, she, it.* The plural personal pronouns include *we, you, them, our.* (*You* can be singular or plural.) Notice in the caption below that the first **you** is singular and the second **you** is plural.

> Larry, you need to keep all four tires on the road when turning. Are you still with us back there?

603.2 Person of a Pronoun

The **person** of a pronoun indicates whether the person, place, thing, or idea represented by the pronoun is speaking, is spoken to, or is spoken about.

- **First person** pronouns are used in place of the name of the speaker or speakers.

> "We don't do things like that," says Pa. "We're just and honest people. . . . I don't skip debts."
>
> —Jesse Stuart, "Split Cherry Tree"

- **Second person** pronouns name the person or persons spoken to.

> "If you hit your duck, you want me to go in after it?" Eugie said.
>
> —Gina Berriault, "The Stone Boy"

- **Third person** pronouns name the person or thing spoken about.

> She had hardly realized the news, further than to understand that she had been brought . . . face to face with something unexpected and final. It did not even occur to her to ask for any explanation.
>
> —Joseph Conrad, "The Idiots"

Forms of Personal Pronouns (continued)

604.1 Case of a Pronoun

The **case** of each pronoun tells how it is related to the other words used with it. There are three cases: *nominative, possessive,* and *objective.*

- A **nominative case** pronoun can be the subject of a clause. The following are nominative forms: *I, you, he, she, it, we, they.*

    I like life when things go well.
    You must live life in order to love life.

    A nominative case pronoun can be a *predicate nominative* if it follows a "be" verb (*am, is, are, was, were, be, being, been*) and renames the subject.

    "It's only she who impresses me just now," said the drama coach.
    "Yes, it is I," said Mai in a superior tone.

- **Possessive case** pronouns show possession or ownership. Apostrophes, however, are not used with personal pronouns.

    But as I placed my hand upon his shoulder, there came a strong shudder over his whole person.
    —Edgar Allan Poe, "The Fall of the House of Usher"

- An **objective case** pronoun can be a direct object, an indirect object, or an object of the preposition.

    The kids loved it! We lit a campfire for them and told them old ghost stories. (*It* is the direct object of the verb *loved. Them* is the object of the preposition *for* and the indirect object of the verb *told.*)

Number, Person, and Case of Personal Pronouns			
	Nominative	Possessive	Objective
First Person Singular	I	my, mine	me
Second Person Singular	you	your, yours	you
Third Person Singular	he she it	his her, hers its	him her it
	Nominative	Possessive	Objective
First Person Plural	we	our, ours	us
Second Person Plural	you	your, yours	you
Third Person Plural	they	their, theirs	them

604.2 Gender of a Pronoun

Gender indicates whether a pronoun is masculine (he, him, his), feminine (she, her, hers), or neuter (without gender: it, its).

▌ Verb

A **verb** is a word that expresses action (*run, carried, declared*) or state of being (*is, are, seemed*).

Classes of Verbs

605.1 Linking Verbs

A **linking verb** links the subject to a noun or an adjective in the predicate.

> On his skateboard, the boy felt confident. He was the best skater around.

			Common Linking Verbs				
is	are	was	were	be	been	am	smell
seem	grow	become	appear	sound	taste	feel	remain
stay	look	turn	get				

605.2 Auxiliary Verbs

Auxiliary verbs, or helping verbs, are used to form some of the **tenses** (608.3), the **mood** (610.1), and the **voice** (607.1) of the main verb. (In the example below, the auxiliary verbs are red; the main verbs are blue.)

> The long procession was led by white-robed priests, their faces streaked with red and yellow and white ash. By this time the flames had stopped spurting, and the pit consisted of a red-hot mass of burning wood, which attendants were leveling with long branches.
>
> —Leonard Feinberg, "Fire Walking in Ceylon"

			Common Auxiliary Verbs				
is	was	being	did	have	would	shall	might
am	were	been	does	had	could	can	must
are	be	do	has	should	will	may	

605.3 Action Verbs: Transitive and Intransitive

An **intransitive verb** communicates an action that is complete in itself. It does not need an object to receive the action.

> The boy flew on his skateboard. He jumped and flipped and twisted.

A **transitive verb** (red) is an action verb that needs an object (blue) to complete its meaning.

> The city council passed a strict noise ordinance.

Some action verbs can be either transitive or intransitive, depending on how they are used.

> He finally stopped to rest. (intransitive)
> He finally stopped the show. (transitive)

Classes of Verbs (continued)

606.1 Objects with Transitive Verbs

- A **direct object** receives the action of a transitive verb directly from the subject. Without it, the transitive verb's meaning is incomplete.

    The boy kicked his skateboard forward. (*Skateboard* is the direct object.)

- An **indirect object** also receives the action of a transitive verb, but indirectly. An indirect object names the person *to whom* or *for whom* something is done. (It can also name the thing *to what* or *for what* something is done.)

    Then he showed us his best tricks. (*Us* is the indirect object.)

Note: When the word naming the indirect receiver of the action is in a prepositional phrase, it is no longer considered an indirect object.

    Then he showed his best tricks to us. (*Us* is the object of the preposition *to*.)

Verbals

A **verbal** is a word that is derived from a verb but acts as another part of speech. There are three types of verbals: *gerunds, infinitives,* and *participles.* Each is often part of a verbal phrase.

606.2 Gerunds

A **gerund** is a verb form that ends in *ing* and is used as a noun.

    Swimming is my favorite pastime. (subject)
    I began swimming at the age of six months. (direct object)
    Swimming in chlorinated pools makes my eyes red. (gerund phrase as subject)

606.3 Infinitives

An **infinitive** is a verb form that is usually introduced by *to*; the infinitive may be used as a noun, an adjective, or an adverb.

    Most people find it easy to swim. (adverb)
    To swim the English Channel must be a thrill. (infinitive phrase as noun)
    The urge to swim in tropical waters is more common. (infinitive phrase as adjective)

606.4 Participles

A **participle** is a verb form ending in *ing* or *ed* that acts as an adjective.

    The farmhands harvesting corn are tired and hungry. (participial phrase modifies *farmhands*)
    The cribs full of harvested cobs are evidence of their hard work. (participle modifies *cobs*)

Forms of Verbs

A verb has different forms depending on its *voice* (active, passive); *number* (singular, plural); *person* (first, second, third); *tense* (present, past, future, present perfect, past perfect, future perfect); and *mood* (indicative, imperative, subjunctive).

607.1 Voice of a Verb

Voice indicates whether the subject is acting or being acted upon.

- **Active voice** indicates that the subject of the verb is, has been, or will be doing something.

    Baseball great Walter Johnson pitched 50 consecutive scoreless innings.

    For many years Lou Brock held the base-stealing record.

Note: Use the active voice as much as possible because it makes your writing more direct and lively.

- **Passive voice** indicates that the subject of the verb is being, has been, or will be acted upon.

    Fifty consecutive scoreless innings were pitched by baseball great Walter Johnson.

    For many years the base-stealing record was held by Lou Brock.

Note: With a passive verb, the person or thing creating the action is not always stated.

    The ordinance was overturned. (It is not clear who did the overturning in this example.)

Tense	Active Voice		Passive Voice	
	Singular	Plural	Singular	Plural
Present	I see you see he/she/it sees	we see you see they see	I am seen you are seen he/she/it is seen	we are seen you are seen they are seen
Past	I saw you saw he saw	we saw you saw they saw	I was seen you were seen it was seen	we were seen you were seen they were seen
Future	I will see you will see he will see	we will see you will see they will see	I will be seen you will be seen it will be seen	we will be seen you will be seen they will be seen
Present Perfect	I have seen you have seen he has seen	we have seen you have seen they have seen	I have been seen you have been seen it has been seen	we have been seen you have been seen they have been seen
Past Perfect	I had seen you had seen he had seen	we had seen you had seen they had seen	I had been seen you had been seen it had been seen	we had been seen you had been seen they had been seen
Future Perfect	I will have seen you will have seen he will have seen	we will have seen you will have seen they will have seen	I will have been seen you will have been seen it will have been seen	we will have been seen you will have been seen they will have been seen

Forms of Verbs (continued)

608.1 Number of a Verb

Number indicates whether a verb is singular or plural. In a clause, the verb and its subject must both be singular or both be plural.

- **Singular**
     One large island floats off Italy's "toe."
     Italy's northern countryside includes the spectacular Alps.
     The Po Valley stretches between the Alps and the Apennines.

- **Plural**
     Five small islands float inside Michigan's "thumb."
     The Porcupine Mountains rise above the shores of Lake Superior.
     High bluffs and sand dunes border Lake Michigan.

608.2 Person of a Verb

Person indicates whether the subject of the verb is first, second, or third person (is speaking, is spoken to, or is spoken about). Usually, the singular third-person present-tense verb changes form by adding an *s,* as shown in these examples: **he sniffs/the dog sniffs/Addie sniffs..**

Person of a Verb	Singular	Plural
First Person	I sniff	we sniff
Second Person	you sniff	you sniff
Third Person	he/she/it sniffs	they sniff

608.3 Tense of a Verb

Tense indicates time. Each verb has three principal parts: the present, past, and past participle. All six tenses are formed from these principal parts. The past and past participle of regular verbs are formed by adding *ed* to the present form. The past and past participle of irregular verbs are usually different words; however, a few have the same form in all three principal parts. (See page 609.)

- **Present tense** expresses action that is happening at the present time, or action that happens continually or regularly.
     We arrive at 8:00 a.m. and bring our books.

- **Past tense** expresses action that is completed at a particular time in the past.
     We arrived at 8:00 a.m. and brought our books.

- **Future tense** expresses action that will take place in the future.
     We will arrive at 8:00 a.m. and will bring our books.

Common Irregular Verbs and Their Principal Parts

Present Tense	Past Tense	Past Participle	Present Tense	Past Tense	Past Participle
be	was, were	been	lie (deceive)	lied	lied
begin	began	begun	ride	rode	ridden
bite	bit	bitten	ring	rang	rung
blow	blew	blown	rise	rose	risen
break	broke	broken	run	ran	run
bring	brought	brought	see	saw	seen
catch	caught	caught	shake	shook	shaken
choose	chose	chosen	shine (light)	shone	shone
come	came	come	shine (polish)	shined	shined
dive	dove	dived	show	showed	shown
do	did	done	shrink	shrank	shrunk
drag	dragged	dragged	sing	sang, sung	sung
draw	drew	drawn	sink	sank, sunk	sunk
drink	drank	drunk	sit	sat	sat
drive	drove	driven	slay	slew	slain
drown	drowned	drowned	speak	spoke	spoken
eat	ate	eaten	spring	sprang, sprung	sprung
fall	fell	fallen			
fight	fought	fought	steal	stole	stolen
flee	fled	fled	strive	strove	striven
fly	flew	flown	swear	swore	sworn
forsake	forsook	forsaken	swim	swam	swum
freeze	froze	frozen	swing	swung	swung
get	got	gotten	take	took	taken
give	gave	given	teach	taught	taught
go	went	gone	tear	tore	torn
grow	grew	grown	throw	threw	thrown
hang (execute)	hanged	hanged	wake	waked, woke	waked, woken
hang (suspend)	hung	hung			
hide	hid	hidden, hid	weave	weaved, wove	weaved, woven
know	knew	known			
lay	laid	laid	wring	wrung	wrung
lead	led	led	write	wrote	written
lie (recline)	lay	lain			

Note: These verbs are the same in all principal parts: *costs, cut, hurt, let, put, set,* and *spread.*

- **Present perfect tense** expresses action that began in the past but continues in the present or is completed in the present.

  Our boat has weathered worse storms than this one.

- **Past perfect tense** expresses an action in the past that occurs before another past action.

  They reported, wrongly, that the hurricane had missed the island.

- **Future perfect tense** expresses action that will begin in the future and be completed by a specific time in the future.

  By this time tomorrow, the hurricane will have smashed into the coast.

Forms of Verbs (continued)

610.1 Mood of a Verb

Mood of a verb indicates the tone or attitude with which a statement is made.

- **Indicative mood** is used to state a fact or to ask a question.

   Sometimes I'd yell questions at the rocks and trees, and across gorges, or yodel, "What is the meaning of the void?" The answer was perfect silence, so I knew.

   —Jack Kerouac, "Alone on a Mountain Top"

- **Imperative mood** is used to give a command.

   "Whatever you do, don't fly your kite during a storm."

   —Mrs. Abiah Franklin

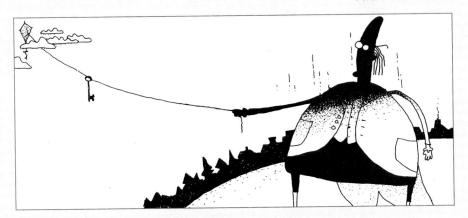

- **Subjunctive mood** is no longer commonly used; however, careful writers may choose to use it to express the exact manner in which their statements are meant.

   Use the subjunctive *were* to express a condition that is contrary to fact.

   If I **were** finished with my essay, I could go to the movie.

   Use the subjunctive *were* after *as though* or *as if* to express an unreal condition.

   Mrs. Young acted as if she **were** sixteen again.

   Use the subjunctive *be* in "that" clauses to express necessity, legal decisions, or parliamentary motions.

   "It is moved and supported that no more than 6,000,000 quad **be used** to explore the planet Earth."

   "Ridiculous! Knowing earthlings is bound to help us understand ourselves! Therefore, I move that the sum **be amended** to 12,000,000 quad."

   "Stupidity! I move that all missions **be postponed** until we have living proof of life on Earth."

▌Adjective

An **adjective** describes or modifies a noun or a pronoun. The articles *a, an,* and *the* are also adjectives.

> The young driver peeked through the big steering wheel. (*The* and *young* modify *driver; the* and *big* modify *steering wheel.*)

611.1 Types of Adjectives

A **proper adjective** is created from a proper noun and is capitalized.

> In Canada (proper noun), you will find many cultures and climates.
>
> Canadian (proper adjective) winters can be harsh.

A **predicate adjective** follows a form of the "be" verb (or other linking verb) and describes the subject.

> Late autumn seems grim to those who love summer. (*Grim* modifies *autumn.*)

Note: Some words can be either adjectives or pronouns (*that, these, all, each, both, many, some,* etc.). These words are adjectives when they come before the nouns they modify; they are pronouns when they stand alone.

> Jiao made both goals. (*Both* modifies *goals;* it is an adjective.)
>
> Both were scored in the final period. (*Both* stands alone; it is a pronoun.)

611.2 Forms of Adjectives

Adjectives have three forms: *positive, comparative,* and *superlative.*

- The **positive form** describes a noun or a pronoun without comparing it to anyone or anything else.

  > The first game was long and tiresome.

- The **comparative form** (*-er, more,* or *less*) compares two persons, places, things, or ideas.

  > The second game was longer and more tiresome than the first.

- The **superlative form** (*-est, most,* or *least*) compares three or more persons, places, things, or ideas.

  > The third game was the longest and most tiresome of all.

Note: Use *more* and *most* (or *less* and *least*)—instead of adding a suffix—with adjectives of two or more syllables.

Forms of Adjectives		
Positive	Comparative	Superlative
big	bigger	biggest
helpful	more helpful	most helpful
painful	less painful	least painful

▮ Adverb

An **adverb** describes or modifies a verb, an adjective, or another adverb.

> She sneezed loudly. (*Loudly* modifies the verb *sneezed*.)
> Her sneezes are really dramatic. (*Really* modifies the adjective *dramatic*.)
> The sneeze exploded very noisily. (*Very* modifies the adverb *noisily*.)

An adverb usually tells *when, where, how,* or *how much*.

612.1 Types of Adverbs

Adverbs can be categorized in four basic ways: *time, place, manner,* and *degree*.

- **Time** (These adverbs tell *when, how often,* and *how long*.)

    today, yesterday   daily, weekly   briefly, eternally

- **Place** (These adverbs tell *where, to where,* and *from where*.)

    here, there   nearby, beyond   backward, forward

- **Manner** (These adverbs often end in *ly* and tell *how* something is done.)

    precisely   effectively   regally   smoothly   well

- **Degree** (These adverbs tell *how much* or *how little*.)

    substantially   greatly   entirely   partly   too

Note: Some adverbs are correct with or without the *ly* ending. When in doubt, use the *ly* form.

    slow, slowly   loud, loudly   fair, fairly   tight, tightly   quick, quickly

612.2 Forms of Adverbs

Adverbs of manner have three forms: *positive, comparative,* and *superlative*.

- The **positive form** describes a verb, an adjective, or another adverb without comparing it to anyone or anything else.

    Model X vacuum cleans well and runs quietly.

- The **comparative form** (*-er, more,* or *less*) compares how two things are done.

    Model Y vacuum cleans better and runs more quietly than model X does.

- The **superlative form** (*-est, most,* or *least*) compares how three or more things are done.

    Model Z vacuum cleans best and runs most quietly of all.

Forms of Adverbs

Positive	Comparative	Superlative
well	better	best
fast	faster	fastest
remorseful	more remorsefully	most remorsefully

▌ Preposition

A **preposition** is the first word (or group of words) in a prepositional phrase. It shows the relationship between its object (a noun or a pronoun that follows the preposition) and another word in the sentence. The first noun or pronoun following a preposition is its object.

> To make a mustache, Natasha placed the hairy caterpillar under her nose. (*Under* shows the relationship between the verb, *placed*, and the object of the preposition, *nose*.)

> The drowsy insect clung obediently to the girl's upper lip. (The first noun following the preposition *to* is *lip*; *lip* is the object of the preposition.)

613.1 ▌ Prepositional Phrase

A **prepositional phrase** includes the preposition, the object of the preposition, and the modifiers of the object. A prepositional phrase functions as an adverb or as an adjective.

> Some people run away from caterpillars. (The phrase functions as an adverb and modifies the verb *run*.)

> However, little kids with inquisitive minds enjoy their company. (The phrase functions as an adjective and modifies the noun *kids*.)

Note: A preposition is always followed by an object; if there is no object, the word is an adverb, not a preposition.

> Natasha never played with caterpillars before. (The word *before* is not followed by an object; therefore, it functions as an adverb and modifies the verb *played*.)

Common Prepositions

aboard	before	from	of	save
about	behind	from among	off	since
above	below	from between	on	subsequent to
according to	beneath	from under	on account of	together with
across	beside	in	on behalf of	through
across from	besides	in addition to	onto	throughout
after	between	in back of	on top of	till
against	beyond	in behalf of	opposite	to
along	by	in front of	out	toward
alongside	by means of	in place of	out of	under
along with	concerning	in regard to	outside of	underneath
amid	considering	inside	over	until
among	despite	inside of	over to	unto
apart from	down	in spite of	owing to	up
around	down from	instead of	past	up to
aside from	during	into	prior to	upon
at	except	like	regarding	with
away from	except for	near	round	within
because of	for	near to	round about	without

▌Conjunction

A **conjunction** connects individual words or groups of words. There are three kinds of conjunctions: *coordinating, correlative,* and *subordinating.*

614.1 Coordinating Conjunctions

Coordinating conjunctions usually connect a word to a word, a phrase to a phrase, or a clause to a clause. The words, phrases, or clauses joined by a coordinating conjunction are equal in importance or are of the same type.

> I could tell by my old man's eyes that he was *nervous* and *wanted to smooth things over,* but Syl didn't give him a chance.　　—Albert Halper, "Prelude"
> (*And* connects the two parts of a compound predicate; *but* connects two independent clauses that could stand on their own.)

614.2 Correlative Conjunctions

Correlative conjunctions are conjunctions used in pairs.

> They were not only exhausted by the day's journey but also sunburned.

614.3 Subordinating Conjunctions

Subordinating conjunctions connect two clauses that are *not* equally important, thereby showing the relationship between them. A subordinating conjunction connects a dependent clause to an independent clause in order to complete the meaning of the dependent clause.

> A brown trout will study the bait before he eats it. (The clause *before he eats it* is dependent. It depends on the rest of the sentence to complete its meaning.)

Kinds of Conjunctions

Coordinating: and, but, or, nor, for, yet, so

Correlative: either, or; neither, nor; not only, but also; both, and; whether, or

Subordinating: after, although, as, as if, as long as, as though, because, before, if, in order that, provided that, since, so that, that, though, till, unless, until, when, where, whereas, while

---

Note: Relative pronouns (see 602.2) and conjunctive adverbs (see 560.1) can also connect clauses.

▌Interjection

An **interjection** communicates strong emotion or surprise. Punctuation (often a comma or an exclamation point) is used to set off an interjection from the rest of the sentence.

> Oh no! The TV broke.　Good grief! I have nothing to do!　Yikes, I'll go mad!

Quick Guide

▌ Parts of Speech

Words in the English language are used in eight different ways. For this reason, there are eight parts of speech.

Noun
A word that names a person, a place, a thing, or an idea
> Governor Smith-Jones   Oregon   hospital   religion

Pronoun
A word used in place of a noun
> I   you   she   him   who   everyone   these
> neither   theirs   themselves   which

Verb
A word that expresses action or state of being
> float   sniff   discover   seem   were   was

Adjective
A word that describes a noun or a pronoun
> young   big   grim   Canadian   longer

Adverb
A word that describes a verb, an adjective, or another adverb
> briefly   forward   regally   slowly   better

Preposition
The first word or words in a prepositional phrase (which functions as an adjective or an adverb)
> away from   under   before   with   for   out of

Conjunction
A word that connects other words or groups of words
> and   but   although   because   either, or   so

Interjection
A word that shows strong emotion or surprise
> Oh no!   Yikes!   Good grief!   Well, . . .

Note: Many words in the English language function in different ways depending upon how they're used in a sentence. A word might be a noun in one instance, an adjective in another, and—at times—even a verb.

"A sentence should read as if its author, had he held a plough instead of a pen, could have drawn a furrow deep and straight to the end."

Henry David Thoreau

Using the Language

❚ Constructing Sentences

A **sentence** is made up of one or more words that express a complete thought. A sentence begins with a capital letter; it ends with a period, a question mark, or an exclamation point.

What should we do for our vacation this year? We could go camping.
No, I hate bugs!

Using Subjects and Predicates

A sentence usually has a **subject** and a predicate. The subject is the part of the sentence about which something is said. The predicate, which contains the verb, is the part of the sentence that says something about the subject.

Like the pilot, the writer must see faster and more completely than the ordinary viewer of life.

—Paul Engle, "Salt Crystals, Spider Webs, and Words"

616.1 The Subject

The **subject** is the part of the sentence about which something is said. The subject is always a noun; a pronoun; or a word, clause, or phrase that functions as a noun (such as a gerund or a gerund phrase or an infinitive).

Wolves howl. (noun)   They howl for a variety of reasons. (pronoun)
To establish their turf may be one reason. (infinitive phrase)
Searching for "lost" pack members may be another. (gerund phrase)
That wolves and dogs are similar animals seems obvious. (noun clause)

- A **simple subject** is the subject without its modifiers.
  Most wildlife biologists disapprove of crossbreeding wolves and dogs.

- A **complete subject** is the subject with all of its modifiers.
  Most wildlife biologists disapprove of crossbreeding wolves and dogs.

- A **compound subject** is composed of two or more simple subjects.
  Wise breeders and owners know that wolf-dog puppies can display unexpected, destructive behaviors.

617.1 Delayed Subject

In sentences that begin with *There* or *It* followed by a form of the "be" verb, the subject comes after the verb. The subject is also delayed in questions.

> There was nothing in the refrigerator. (The subject is *nothing*; the verb is *was*.)
>
> Where is my sandwich? (The subject is *sandwich*; the verb is *is*.)

617.2 The Predicate

The **predicate** is the part of the sentence that shows action or says something about the subject.

> Giant squid do exist.

- A **simple predicate** is the verb without its modifiers.

  > One giant squid measured nearly 60 feet long.

- A **complete predicate** is the simple predicate with all its modifiers.

  > One giant squid measured nearly 60 feet long.
  > (*Measured* is the simple predicate; *nearly 60 feet long* modifies *measured*.)

- A **compound predicate** is composed of two or more simple predicates.

  > A squid grasps its prey with tentacles and bites it with its beak.

Note: A sentence can have a **compound subject** and a **compound predicate**.
> Both sperm whales and giant squid live and occasionally clash in the deep waters off New Zealand's South Island.

- A **direct object** is part of the predicate and receives the action of the verb. (See 606.1.)

  > Sperm whales sometimes eat giant squid. (The direct object *giant squid* receives the action of the verb *eat* by answering the question *whales eat what?*)

Note: The **direct object** may be compound.
> In the past, whalers harvested oil, spermaceti, and ambergris from slain sperm whales.

617.3 Understood Subject and Predicate

Either the subject or the predicate may be "missing" from a sentence, but both must be clearly **understood**.

> Who is making supper?
> (*Who* is the subject; *is making supper* is the predicate.)
> No one.
> (*No one* is the subject; the predicate *is making supper* is understood.)
> Put on that apron.
> (The subject *you* is understood; *put on that apron* is the predicate.)

Using Phrases

A **phrase** is a group of related words that function as a single part of speech. The sentence below contains a number of phrases.

Finishing the race will require running down several steep slopes.

finishing the race (This gerund phrase functions as a noun used as a subject.)

will require (This phrase functions as a verb.)

running down several steep slopes (This gerund phrase functions as a noun used as a direct object.)

618.1 Types of Phrases

There are several types of phrases: *verb, verbal, prepositional, appositive,* and *absolute.*

- A **verb phrase** consists of a main verb preceded by one or more helping verbs.

   The snow has been falling for three straight days.
   (*Has been falling* is a verb phrase.)

- A **verbal phrase** is a phrase based on one of the three types of verbals: *gerund, infinitive,* or *participle.* (See 606.2, 606.3, and 606.4.)

A **gerund phrase** consists of a gerund and its modifiers. The whole phrase functions as a noun.

Spotting the tiny mouse was easy for the hawk.
(The gerund phrase is used as the subject of the sentence.)

The mouse escaped by ducking under a rock.
(The gerund phrase is the object of the preposition *by.*)

An **infinitive phrase** consists of an infinitive and its modifiers. The whole phrase functions either as a noun, an adjective, or an adverb.

To shake every voter's hand was the candidate's goal.
(The infinitive phrase functions as a noun used as the subject.)

Your efforts to clean the kitchen are appreciated.
(The infinitive phrase is used as an adjective modifying *efforts.*)

Please watch carefully to see the difference.
(The infinitive phrase is used as an adverb modifying *watch.*)

A **participial phrase** consists of a past or present participle and its modifiers. The whole phrase functions as an adjective.

Following his nose, the beagle stayed on the scent.
(The participial phrase modifies the noun *beagle.*)

The raccoons, warned by the rustling, took cover.
(The participial phrase modifies the noun *raccoons.*)

- A **prepositional phrase** is a group of words beginning with a preposition and ending with a noun or a pronoun. They function mainly as adjectives or adverbs.

   Zach won the wheelchair race **in record time.** (The prepositional phrase *in record time* is used as an adverb modifying the verb *won*.)

   Reach for that catnip ball **behind the couch.** (The prepositional phrase *behind the couch* is used as an adjective modifying *catnip ball*.)

- An **appositive phrase**, which follows a noun or a pronoun and renames it, consists of a noun and its modifiers. An appositive adds new information about the noun or pronoun it follows.

   The Trans-Siberian Railroad, **the world's longest railway,** stretches from Moscow to Vladivostok. (The appositive phrase renames *Trans-Siberian Railroad* and provides new information.)

- An **absolute phrase** consists of a noun and a participle (plus the participle's object, if there is one, and any modifiers). An absolute phrase functions as an adjective that adds information to the entire sentence. Absolute phrases are always set off with commas.

   Its wheels clattering rhythmically over the rails, the train rolled into town. (The noun *wheels* is modified by the present participle *clattering*. The entire phrase modifies the rest of the sentence.)

Using Clauses

A **clause** is a group of related words that has both a subject and a predicate.

619.1 Independent and Dependent Clauses

An **independent clause** presents a complete thought and can stand alone as a sentence; a **dependent clause** (also called a *subordinate clause*) does not present a complete thought and cannot stand alone as a sentence.

   Sparrows make nests in cattle barns (independent clause) **so that they can stay warm during the winter** (dependent clause).

619.2 Types of Dependent Clauses

There are three basic types of dependent clauses: adverb, noun, and adjective.

- An **adverb clause** is used like an adverb to modify a verb, an adjective, or an adverb. Adverb clauses begin with a subordinating conjunction. (See 614.3.)

   If I study hard, I will pass. (The adverb clause modifies the verb *will pass*.)

- A **noun clause** is used in place of a noun.

   The teacher said **that the essay questions are based on the last two chapters.** (The noun clause functions as a direct object.)

- An **adjective clause** modifies a noun or a pronoun.

   Tomorrow's test, **which covers the entire book,** is part essay and part short answers. (The adjective clause modifies the noun *test*.)

▮ Forming Correct Sentences

Avoiding the common sentence errors requires careful attention. This section looks at errors in construction, clarity, and usage.

Errors in Construction

The most common sentence errors are errors in construction: fragments, comma splices, rambling sentences, and run-ons.

620.1 Sentence Fragment

A **sentence fragment** is a group of words used as a sentence. It is not a sentence, though, because it lacks a subject, a verb, or some other essential part. Because of the missing part, the thought is incomplete.

Fragment: Spaghetti all over the table. (This fragment lacks a verb.)

Sentence: Spaghetti flew all over the table.

Fragment: When Aneko opened the box. (This fragment has a subject and a verb, but it does not convey a complete thought. We need to know what happened "when Aneko opened the box.")

Sentence: When Aneko opened the box, spaghetti flew all over the table.

Fragment: Laughing and scooping up a pile of spaghetti. Kate remarked, "Now, that's what I call a spaghetti mess!" (The fragment is followed by a complete sentence. This fragment, a participial phrase, can be combined with the sentence to form a complete thought.)

Sentence: Laughing and scooping up a pile of spaghetti, Kate remarked, "Now, that's what I call a spaghetti mess!"

620.2 Comma Splice

A **comma splice** results when two independent clauses are connected (spliced) with only a comma. The comma is not enough: a period, a semicolon, or a conjunction is needed. (**Note:** An independent clause presents a complete thought and can stand alone as a sentence.)

Splice: The concertgoers had been waiting in the hot sun for two hours, many were beginning to show their impatience by chanting and clapping.

Corrected: The concertgoers had been waiting in the hot sun for two hours, and many were beginning to show their impatience by chanting and clapping. (A coordinating conjunction has been added.)

Corrected: The concertgoers had been waiting in the hot sun for two hours; many were beginning to show their impatience by chanting and clapping. (The comma has been changed to a semicolon.)

621.1 Rambling Sentence

A **rambling sentence** seems to go on and on in a monotonous fashion (often because of too many *and*'s). To correct this error, remove some of the *and*'s, fix the punctuation, and reword different parts if it results in a better passage.

> **Rambling:** The intruder entered through the window and tiptoed down the hall and stood under the stairwell and waited in the shadows.

> **Corrected:** The intruder entered through the window. He tiptoed down the hall and stood under the stairwell, waiting in the shadows.

> **Corrected:** The intruder, who had entered through the window, tiptoed down the hall. He stood under the stairwell and waited in the shadows.

621.2 Run-On Sentence

A **run-on sentence** is two (or more) sentences joined without adequate punctuation or a connecting word.

> **Run-on:** I thought the ride would never end my eyes were crossed, and my fingers were numb.

> **Corrected:** I thought the ride would never end. My eyes were crossed, and my fingers were numb.

Errors in Clarity

It can be frustrating for a reader who must reread a sentence several times in order to understand it. Avoiding the five common errors explained in this section will improve the clarity of your sentences.

621.3 Incomplete Comparison

An **incomplete comparison** occurs when a writer leaves out a word or words that are needed to explain exactly what is being compared to what.

> **Incomplete:** I get along with Rosa better than my sister. (Do you mean that you get along with Rosa better than you get along with your sister, or that you get along with Rosa better than your sister does?)

> **Clear:** I get along with Rosa better than my sister does.

621.4 Ambiguous Wording

Ambiguous wording is unclear because it has two or more possible meanings.

> **Ambiguous:** Mike decided to take his brother's new scooter to the movie, which turned out to be a real horror story. (What turned out to be a real horror story—Mike's taking the scooter or the movie?)

> **Clear:** Mike decided to take his brother's new scooter to the movie, a decision that turned out to be a real horror story.

Errors in Clarity (continued)

622.1 Indefinite Reference

An **indefinite reference** is caused by the careless use of pronouns. As a result, the reader is not sure who or what the pronoun is referring to.

Indefinite: In *To Kill a Mockingbird*, she describes the problems faced by Atticus Finch and his family. (Who is *she*?)

Clear: In *To Kill a Mockingbird*, the author, Harper Lee, describes the problems faced by Atticus Finch and his family.

Indefinite: As he pulled his car up to the service door, it made a strange rattling sound. (Which rattled, the car or the door?)

Clear: His car made a strange rattling sound as he pulled up to the service door.

622.2 Misplaced Modifiers

Misplaced modifiers are placed in a way that makes the sentence unclear. (A modifier should be placed as close as possible to the word it modifies.)

Misplaced: We have an assortment of combs for physically active people with strong teeth. (People with unbreakable teeth?)

Corrected: For physically active people, we have an assortment of combs with strong teeth. (Corrected by rearranging the sentence.)

622.3 Dangling Modifiers

Dangling modifiers seem to modify the wrong word, and the correct word often does not even appear in the sentence. (Rewording is necessary to fix a dangling modifier.)

Dangling: Trying desperately to get under the fence, Chan's mother called her. (The phrase *trying desperately to get under the fence* appears to modify *Chan's mother*.)

Corrected: Trying desperately to get under the fence, Chan heard her mother call her. (Corrected by rewording and adding *Chan*, the person being referred to by the modifier.)

Dangling: After standing in line for five hours, the manager announced that all the tickets had been sold. (In this sentence, it appears as if the manager had been *standing in line for five hours*.)

Corrected: After I stood in line for five hours, the manager announced that all the tickets had been sold. (Corrected by rewording the sentence.)

Errors in Usage

In your academic writing, remember to follow accepted, standard usage. A number of common usage errors are discussed below.

623.1 Nonstandard Language

Nonstandard language is often acceptable in everyday conversation, but seldom in formal writing.

Colloquial: Avoid using colloquial language such as *go with* or *wait up*.
Hey, wait up! Cam wants to go with. (Nonstandard)
Hey, wait! Cam wants to go with us. (Acceptable)

Double Preposition: Avoid using certain double prepositions: *off of, off to, in on*.
Reggie went off to the movies. (Nonstandard)
Reggie went to the movies. (Acceptable)

Substitution: Avoid substituting *and* for *to* in formal writing.
Try and get here on time. (Nonstandard)
Try to get here on time. (Acceptable)

Avoid substituting *of* for *have* when combining with *could, would, should,* or *might*.
I should of studied for that test. (Nonstandard)
I should have studied for that test. (Acceptable)

Slang: Avoid using slang or any other "in" words.
The museum trip was way cool. (Nonstandard)
The museum trip was great. (Acceptable)

623.2 Double Negative

A **double negative** wrongly uses two negative words to perform the same function in a sentence. In standard English, use only one negative word in a sentence.

Double Negative: The relief pitcher couldn't get none of his pitches across the plate.

Corrected: The relief pitcher couldn't get any of his pitches across the plate.

Note: Using the words *hardly, barely,* or *scarcely* with the words *no, not, or none* also results in a double negative.

Errors in Usage (continued)

624.1 **Shifts in Construction**

A **shift in construction** is a change in the structure or style midway through a sentence. (See 628.2.)

Shift in number: When a person has the flu, they ought to stay at home.
Corrected: When people have the flu, they ought to stay at home.

Shift in person: When you are well again, you can do all the things a person loves to do.
Corrected: When you are well again, you can do all the things you love to do.

Shift in voice: Marcia is playing soccer again, and many new skills are being learned by her. (The verbs shift from *active* to *passive voice*. See 607.1.)
Corrected: Marcia is playing soccer again and learning many new skills. (Both verbs display the *active voice*.)

Shift in tense: Marcia drinks juice and got plenty of rest.
Corrected: Marcia drinks juice and gets plenty of rest.

Note: A tense shift is acceptable when one action happens before another action.
I think (present tense) he completed (past tense) his assignment last night.

624.2 **Unparallel Construction**

Unparallel construction uses different grammatical forms for ideas that ought to be stated in a similar form in order to be clear. (See 628.2.)

Unparallel: In today's world, common construction projects include repairing roads, building apartment houses, and to expand medical complexes. (The sentence switches from gerunds, *-ing* words, to an infinitive phrase.)
Parallel: In today's world, common construction projects include repairing roads, building apartment houses, and expanding medical complexes. (Now the three ideas are expressed in similar form.)

Unparallel: For the open house, teachers prepare handouts for parents and are organizing the students' work for display. (In this sentence, the verbs *prepare* and *are organizing* are unparallel.)
Parallel: For the open house, teachers prepare handouts for parents and organize the students' work for display. (Now both verbs are stated in the same way.)

▌Considering Sentence Agreement

Agreement of Subject and Verb

A verb must agree in number (singular or plural) with its subject.

> The student was proud of her quarter grades.

Note: Do not be confused by words that come between the subject and verb.

> The coach, as well as the players, is required to display good sportsmanship. (*Coach*, not *players*, is the subject.)

625.1 Singular Subjects

Singular subjects joined by *or* or *nor* take a singular verb.

> Neither Bev nor Kendra is going to the street dance.

Note: When one of the subjects joined by *or* or *nor* is singular and one is plural, the verb must agree with the subject nearer the verb.

> Neither Yoshi nor his friends are playing in the band anymore. (The plural subject *friends* is nearer the verb, so the plural verb *are* is correct.)

625.2 Compound Subjects

Compound subjects connected with *and* require a plural verb.

> Strength and balance are necessary for gymnastics.

625.3 Delayed Subjects

A delayed subject occurs when the verb comes before the subject. In these inverted sentences, the delayed subject must agree with the verb.

> There are many hardworking students in our schools.
> There is present among many young people today a will to succeed.
> (*Students* and *will* are the true subjects of these sentences, not *there*.)

625.4 "Be" Verbs

When a sentence uses a form of the "be" verb followed by a predicate noun (subject complement), the verb must agree with the subject, not the subject complement.

> The car's worst problem was the bad brakes.
> The bad brakes were the car's worst problem.

625.5 Special Cases

Some nouns that are **plural in form but singular in meaning** take a singular verb: *mumps, measles, news, mathematics, economics, gallows, shambles.*

> Measles is still considered a serious disease in many parts of the world.

Some nouns that are plural in form but singular in meaning take a plural verb: *scissors, trousers, tidings.*

> The scissors are missing again.

Agreement of Subject and Verb (continued)

626.1 Collective Nouns

Collective nouns (*faculty, committee, team, congress, species, crowd, army, pair, squad*) take a singular verb when they refer to a group as a unit; collective nouns take a plural verb when they refer to the individuals within the group.

> The home team is losing, and the crowd is getting restless. (Both *team* and *crowd* are considered units in this sentence, requiring the singular verb *is*.)

> The pair were finally reunited after 20 years apart. (Here, *pair* refers to two individuals, so the plural verb *were* is required.)

626.2 Indefinite Pronouns

Some **indefinite pronouns** are singular: *each, either, neither, one, everybody, another, anybody, everyone, nobody, everything, somebody,* and *someone.* They require a singular verb.

> Everybody is invited to the cafeteria for refreshments.

Some **indefinite pronouns** are plural: *both, few, many,* and *several.*

> Several like chocolate cake. Many ask for ice cream, too.

Note: Do not be confused by words or phrases that come between the indefinite pronoun and the verb.

> One of the participants is (not *are*) going to have to stay late to clean up.

A Closer Look: Some **indefinite pronouns** can be either singular or plural: *all, any, most, none,* and *some.* These pronouns are singular if the number of the noun in the prepositional phrase is singular; they are plural if the noun is plural.

> Most of the food complaints are coming from the seniors.
> (*Complaints* is plural, so *most* is plural.)

> Most of the tabletop is sticky with melted ice cream.
> (*Tabletop* is singular, so *most* is singular.)

626.3 Relative Pronouns

When a **relative pronoun** (*who, which, that*) is used as the subject of a clause, the number of the verb is determined by the antecedent of the pronoun. (The antecedent is the word to which the pronoun refers.)

> This is one of the books that are required for geography class. (The relative pronoun *that* requires the plural verb *are* because its antecedent *books* is plural.)

Note: To test this type of sentence for agreement, read the "of" phrase first.

> Of the books that are required for geography class, this is one.

Agreement of Pronoun and Antecedent

A pronoun must agree in number, person, and gender with its *antecedent*. (The *antecedent* is the word to which the pronoun refers.)

Cal brought his guitar to school. (The antecedent of *his* is *Cal.* Both the pronoun and its antecedent are singular, third person, and masculine; therefore, the pronoun is said to "agree" with its antecedent.)

627.1 Agreement in Number

Use a **singular pronoun** to refer to such antecedents as *each, either, neither, one, anyone, anybody, everyone, everybody, somebody, another, nobody,* and *a person.*

Neither of the brothers likes his (not their) room.

Two or more singular antecedents joined by *or* or *nor* are also referred to by a singular pronoun.

Either Connie or Sue left her smartphone in the library.

If one of the antecedents joined by *or* or *nor* is singular and one is plural, the pronoun should agree with the nearer antecedent.

Neither the manager nor the players were crazy about their new uniforms.

Use a **plural pronoun** to refer to plural antecedents as well as compound subjects joined by *and.*

Jared and Carlos are finishing their assignments.

627.2 Agreement in Gender

Use a **masculine** or **feminine pronoun** depending upon the gender of the antecedent.

Is either Connor or Grace bringing his or her baseball glove?

When *a person* or *everyone* is used to refer to both sexes or either sex, you will have to choose whether to offer optional pronouns or rewrite the sentence.

A person should be allowed to pursue his or her interests. (optional pronouns)
People should be allowed to pursue their interests. (rewritten in plural form)

▌Using Sentence Variety

A sentence may be classified according to the kind of statement it makes, the way it is constructed, and its arrangement of words.

628.1 Kinds of Statements

Sentences can make five basic kinds of statements: *declarative, interrogative, imperative, exclamatory,* or *conditional.*

- **Declarative sentences** make statements. They tell us something about a person, a place, a thing, or an idea.

  The Statue of Liberty stands in New York Harbor.

  It has greeted many immigrants and visitors to America.

- **Interrogative sentences** ask questions.

  Did you know that the Statue of Liberty is made of copper and stands over 150 feet tall?

- **Imperative sentences** make commands. They often contain an understood subject (you) as in these examples.

  Visit the Statue of Liberty.

  Climb its 168 stairs.

- **Exclamatory sentences** communicate strong emotion or surprise.

  Climbing 168 stairs is not a dumb idea!

  Just muster some of that pioneering spirit!

- **Conditional sentences** express wishes ("if . . . then" statements) or conditions contrary to fact.

  If you were to climb to the top of the statue, then you could share in the breathtaking feeling experienced by many hopeful immigrants.

628.2 Types of Sentence Construction

A sentence may be *simple, compound, complex,* or *compound-complex.* It all depends on the relationship between independent and dependent clauses.

- A **simple sentence** can have a single subject or a compound subject. It can have a single predicate or a compound predicate. However, a simple sentence has only one independent clause, and it has no dependent clauses.

  My back aches. (single subject; single predicate)

  My teeth and my eyes hurt. (compound subject; single predicate)

  My throat and nose feel sore and look red. (compound subject; compound predicate)

  I must have caught the flu from the sick kids in class. (independent clause with two prepositional phrases: *from the sick kids* and *in class*)

■ A **compound sentence** consists of two independent clauses. The clauses must be joined by a comma and a coordinating conjunction or by a semicolon.

> I usually don't mind missing school, but this is not fun.
>
> I feel too sick to watch TV; I feel too sick to eat.

Note: The comma can be omitted when the clauses are very short.

> I slept and I slept and I slept.

■ A **complex sentence** contains one independent clause and one or more dependent clauses.

> When I get back to school, I'm actually going to appreciate it.
> (one dependent clause; one independent clause)
>
> I won't even complain about math class when I return, even though I'll be so far behind. (one independent clause; two dependent clauses)

■ A **compound-complex sentence** contains two or more independent clauses and one or more dependent clauses.

> Yes, I have a bad flu, and because I need to get well soon, I won't think about school just yet. (two independent clauses; one dependent clause)

629.1 Arrangement of Words

Depending on how words are arranged and ideas are emphasized, a sentence may be classified as *loose, balanced, periodic*, or *cumulative*.

■ A **loose sentence** expresses the main thought near the beginning and adds explanatory material as needed.

> We hauled out the boxes of food and set up the camp stove, all the while battling the hot wind that would not stop.

■ A **balanced sentence** is constructed so that it emphasizes a similarity or a contrast between two or more of its parts (words, phrases, or clauses).

> He goes out onto his baseball field, spins around second base, and looks back at the academy.   —from *The Headmaster* by John McPhee

■ A **periodic sentence** is one that postpones the crucial or most surprising idea until the end.

> While gasoline and diesel engines are the prime movers for many types of machines, the simplest mover is human muscle power.

■ A **cumulative sentence** places the general idea in the middle of the sentence with modifying clauses and phrases coming before and after.

> With careful thought and extra attention to detail, I wrote out my plan for being a model teenager, a teen who cared about neatness and reliability.

▌Diagramming Sentences

A **graphic diagram** of a sentence is a picture of how the words in that sentence are related and how they fit together to form a complete thought.

630.1 Simple Sentence with One Subject and One Verb

Chris fishes.

| Chris | fishes | | subject | verb |

630.2 Simple Sentence with a Predicate Adjective

Fish are delicious.

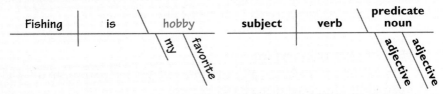

630.3 Simple Sentence with a Predicate Noun and Adjectives

Fishing is my favorite hobby.

Note: When possessive pronouns (*my, his, their,* etc.) are used as adjectives, they are placed on a diagonal line under the word they modify.

630.4 Simple Sentence with an Indirect and a Direct Object

My grandpa gave us a trout.

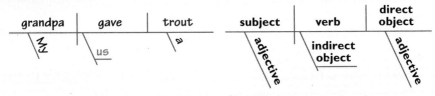

Note: Articles (*a, an, the*) are adjectives and are placed on a diagonal line under the word they modify.

631.1 Simple Sentence with a Prepositional Phrase

I like fishing by myself.

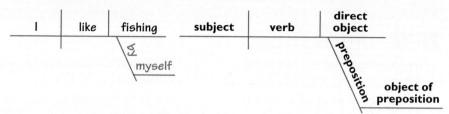

631.2 Simple Sentence with a Compound Subject and Compound Verb

The team and fans clapped and cheered.

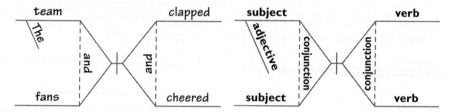

631.3 Compound Sentence

The team scored, and the crowd cheered wildly.

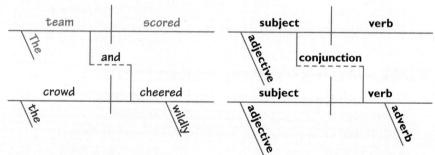

631.4 Complex Sentence with One Dependent Clause

Before Erin scored, the crowd sat quietly.

▌Using Fair Language

When depicting individuals or groups according to their differences, always use language that implies equal value and equal respect for all people.

632.1 Addressing Ethnicity

Acceptable General Terms	Acceptable Specific Terms
American Indians, Native Americans	Cherokee, Inuit, Navaho
Asian Americans (not Orientals)	Chinese Americans
Hispanic or Latino	Mexican Americans

African Americans, blacks
> *African American* has come into wide acceptance, though the term *black* is preferred by some individuals.

Anglo-Americans (English ancestry), European Americans
> Avoid the notion that *American*, used alone, means *white*.

Note: Also avoid using *Americans* to mean just *people from the U.S.*

632.2 Addressing Age

General Age Group	Acceptable Terms
Up to age 12	boys, girls
Between 13 and 19	youth, young people, teens, adolescents
Late teens and 20's	young adults
30's and older	adults, men, women
70 and older	older adults, older people (not *elderly*)

632.3 Addressing Disabilities and Impairments

Not Recommended	Preferred
handicapped	disabled
birth defect	congenital disability
an AIDS victim	person with AIDS
stutter, stammer, lisp	speech impairment (impaired)
deaf	hearing impairment (impaired)
blind	visual impairment (impaired)

632.4 Putting People First

Refer to people *with* various conditions, not as the condition itself (*quadriplegics*).

Not Recommended	Preferred
the retarded	people with mental health conditions
neurotics	patients with neuroses
quadriplegics	people who are quadriplegic

633.1 Avoiding Sexism

- **Don't** use masculine-only pronouns (*he, his, him*) to refer to a human being in general:

     A politician can kiss privacy good-bye when he runs for office.

  Do use one of the several ways to avoid sexism:

  > **Reword the sentence:** Running for office robs a politician of privacy.
  >
  > **Express in the plural:** Politicians can kiss privacy good-bye when they run for office.
  >
  > **Offer optional pronouns:** A politician can kiss privacy good-bye when he or she runs for office.

- **Don't** use a male word in the salutation of a business letter to someone you do not know:

     Dear Sir: Dear Gentlemen:

  Do address both if you're not sure whether the reader is male or female . . .

     Dear Madam or Sir:

     Dear Ladies and Gentlemen:

  or address a position:

     Dear Personnel Officer:

     Dear Members of the Big Bird Fan Club:

- **Don't** give special treatment to one of the sexes:

     The men and the ladies came through in the clutch.

     Mr. Bubba Gumm, Mrs. Bubba Gumm

  Do use equal language for both sexes:

     The men and the women came through in the clutch.

     Mr. Bubba Gumm, Mrs. Lotta Gumm

633.2 Avoiding Gender Typecasting

- **Don't** typecast either gender.

  Do show both women and men as doctors and nurses, principals and teachers, breadwinners and housekeepers, bosses and secretaries, grocery-store owners and cashiers, pilots and plumbers, etc.

- **Don't** associate particular qualities (courage, strength, brilliance, creativity, independence, persistence, seriousness, emotionalism, passivity, or fearfulness) with one or the other gender.

  Do portray people of both sexes along the whole range of potential human strengths and weaknesses.

▌Using Fair Language (continued)

634.1 Avoiding Unfair References

- **Don't** refer to women according to their physical appearance and to men according to their mental abilities or professional status:

    The admirable Dr. William Hicks and his wife Sareena, a former model, both showed up at the party.

    Do refer to both on the same plane:

    Bill and Sareena Hicks showed up at the party.

- **Don't** take special notice when a woman does a "man's job" or vice versa:

    lady doctor   male nurse   coed   steward   policewoman

    Do treat men's or women's involvement in a profession in the same way:

    doctor   nurse   student   flight attendant   police officer

Not Recommended	Preferred
chairman	chair, presiding officer, moderator
salesman	sales representative, salesperson
mailman	mail carrier, postal worker, letter carrier
fireman	firefighter
businessman	executive, manager, businessperson
congressman	member of Congress, representative, senator
policeman	police officer

634.2 Avoiding Demeaning Portrayals

- **Don't** portray women as the possessions of men:

    Fred took his wife and kids on a vacation.

    Do portray women and men, husbands and wives, as equal partners:

    Fred and Wilma took their kids on a vacation.

- **Don't** use demeaning or sexually loaded labels:

    the weaker sex   chick, fox   jock
    the little woman   stud, hunk   the old man

    Do use respectful terms rather than labels; consider what the person might wish to be called:

    women, females   attractive woman   athletic man
    mother, wife   handsome man   father, husband

> "Learning another language is . . . learning another way to think."
>
> —Flora Lewis

Learning English

As you practice writing and speaking English, your native-speaking friends may sometimes remark that "no one says it that way" or "something doesn't sound right." They may not be able to explain why, either. After all, they have spoken English for a long time. They probably follow the rules without actually being aware of them. This section explains some of these rules for people who are new to English, perhaps learning it as a second, third, or fourth language.

▮ Noun

635.1 Count Nouns

Most nouns name things that can be counted: *student, classroom, pencil, dream.* Count nouns have a plural form (*students*) and can be preceded by articles (*a, an, the*) or numbers (*one, two, three, seven*).

635.2 Noncount Nouns

Some nouns name things that cannot be counted: *flour, water, homework, health.* Noncount nouns do not have a plural form and cannot be preceded by the indefinite articles (*a, an*) or by numbers.

Common Noncount Nouns					
Classes	**Materials**	**Languages**	**Activities**	**Items**	**Ideas**
biology	water	Chinese	swimming	luggage	publicity
history	ice	French	soccer	clothes	advice
poetry	wood	Latin	hockey	furniture	harm
math	plastic	Finnish	boating	equipment	health
economics	steel	Farsi	reading	furniture	honesty
English	aluminum	Spanish	photography	baggage	homework

635.3 Two-Way Nouns

Some nouns can be used as either count nouns or as noncount nouns.

This water glass (count noun) is made of plastic, not glass (noncount noun).

▌ Articles and Adjectives

Articles—*a, an,* and *the*—and other adjectives provide information about nouns.

636.1 Indefinite Articles

The words *a* and *an* mark nonspecific nouns. They tell you that the writer is not thinking of a specific person, place, thing, or idea. Use *a* before words that start with a consonant *sound*, and use *an* before words that start with a vowel *sound*.

a restaurant	a house	a European	a one-time fee
an eatery	an hour	an eggplant	an orange

Do not use *a* or *an* with plural nouns or noncount nouns.

I have ideas. (**Not** "I have an ideas.")

I am doing homework. (**Not** "I am doing a homework.")

I study English. (**Not** "I study an English.")

636.2 Definite Article

The word *the* marks specific nouns. It tells you that the writer is thinking of a specific person, place, thing, or idea. You can use *the* with most count and noncount nouns.

the mall	the news	the homework	the performance
the stores	the dogs	the oxygen	the government

Do not use *the* with most proper nouns (unless *the* is part of an official title).

I met Susan Sarandon. (**Not** "I met the Susan Sarandon.")

I visited Washington, D.C. (**Not** "I visited the Washington, D.C.")

I read the *Washington Post*. (**Not** "I read *Washington Post*.")

636.3 Indefinite Adjectives

Indefinite adjectives show that a noun does not refer to a specific person, place, thing, or idea. (Think of indefinite adjectives as more descriptive versions of the indefinite articles *a* and *an*.)

Any person can watch either movie.

Each film received much praise.

With Count Nouns

each	either	every	few	many	neither	several

With Noncount Nouns

much

With Count or Noncount Nouns

all	any	more	most	some

637.1 Demonstrative Adjectives

Demonstrative adjectives show that a noun refers to a specific person, place, thing, or idea. (Think of demonstrative adjectives as more descriptive versions of the definite article *the*.)

These movies won those awards.

That director gave this advice: "Follow your dreams."

With Count Nouns	With Count or Noncount Nouns
these those	this that

637.2 Possessive Nouns

Possessive nouns show ownership and **function as adjectives**. They are formed by adding an apostrophe and an *s* ('s) to a singular noun or by adding just an apostrophe (') to a plural noun ending in *s*.

Javin's song played on the theater's sound system.

The movers' van held the Kings' furniture.

Note: If a singular noun ends in *s*, add *'s*.

We read Kansas's constitution.

It was our history class's first assignment.

637.3 Possessive Pronouns

Possessive pronouns show ownership and **function as adjectives**. One form of the pronoun appears before the noun, and a different form appears after the noun. (See the chart below.)

My car is new. That old car is not mine.

Their yard is always perfect. That overgrown yard can't be theirs.

	Possessive Pronouns			
	Singular Before the Noun	After the Noun	Plural Before the Noun	After the Noun
First Person	my	mine	our	ours
Second Person	your	yours	your	yours
Third Person	his	his	their	theirs
	her	hers	their	theirs
	its	its	their	theirs

▌Placing Articles and Adjectives

When more than one adjective appears before a noun, you need to place them in a specific order. Generally, the stronger or more descriptive adjectives are placed closer to the noun. Follow the order explained in this chart:

Start with . . .

1. articles . . . . a, an, the
   demonstrative adjectives . . . . that, this, these, those
   possessives . . . . my, our, your, her, their, Jill's

Next, place adjectives that tell . . .

2. time/order . . . . first, beginning, next, third, final
3. how many . . . . several, some, few, many
4. value . . . . costly, cheap, expensive, affordable
5. size . . . . puny, gigantic, miniature, gargantuan
6. shape . . . . oblong, triangular, spheric, bumpy
7. condition . . . . fresh, tattered, dirty, polished
8. age . . . . young, old, classic, new
9. color . . . . blue, yellow, maroon, amber
10. nationality . . . . Australian, French, Persian, Korean
11. religion . . . . Islamic, Christian, Hindu
12. material . . . . iron, cotton, plastic, woolen

Finally, place . . .

13. nouns used as adjectives . . . . sport [coat], window [shade]

Note: Here's an example of how this works.

an expensive Persian rug
(1 +   4   +   10   + noun)

Avoid using too many modifiers, which can make a sentence difficult to read.

Don't write: The first few tiny new yellow silken blooms pushed
            through the snow.

Do write: The first yellow blooms pushed through the snow.

638.1 ▌Punctuating Adjectives

If two adjectives equally modify a noun, place a comma between them.

the round, bumpy fruit

Adjectives equally modify a noun if they come from the same category in the chart above. You can test whether adjectives are equal by switching their order or by putting the word *and* between them. If they still sound okay, they are equal.

the bumpy, round fruit   the round and bumpy fruit

▌ Verbs

In their base form, most present-tense verbs are plural. (As a general guide, if a subject noun ends in *s*, the verb probably shouldn't.)

> The cars race. The mothers shop locally.

639.1 Forming Present-Tense Singular Verbs

Create the singular form of most present-tense verbs by adding *s*. (As a general guide, if a subject noun does not end in *s*, the verb probably should.)

> The car races. Dave King shops locally.
>
> A fan cheers. The store sells fresh produce.

1. If the base form of the verb ends in *s, x, z, sh,* or *ch,* add *es.*

> Juan fixes cars. The snow crunches underfoot.

2. If the verb is *go* or *do,* add *es.*

> Sheila goes to Chicago. That dog does whatever it wants.

3. If the base form ends in a consonant plus *y* (*fly, try*), change the *y* to *i* and add *es.*

> Time flies on Saturdays. He tries harder than others.

639.2 Forming Past-Tense Verbs

Form the past tense of most verbs by adding *ed* to a base form that . . .

> - ends in two consonants: jump—jumped   start—started
> - ends in two vowels and a consonant: peer—peered   look—looked
> - ends in one vowel plus *y*: play—played   enjoy—enjoyed
> - ends in one vowel plus a consonant, and the syllable is not stressed: water—watered   brighten—brightened

1. If the base form ends in one vowel plus a consonant, and the syllable is stressed, double the final consonant and add *ed.*

> stop—stopped submit—submitted

2. If the base form ends in a consonant plus *y*, change the *y* to *i* and add *ed.*

> fry—fried supply—supplied

3. If the base form ends in *e* or *ie,* add *d.*

> live—lived lie—lied

639.3 Forming Tenses with Irregular Verbs

Some of the oldest verbs in the English language do not simply add *ed* but change their form to create the past and other tenses. These verbs came into English before the tense rules were established. If a verb states an action that you can imagine someone doing a thousand years ago, it is probably an irregular verb.

> swim—swam speak—spoke draw—drew see—saw

▌ **Verbs** (continued)

640.1 Forming Progressive Tenses

Progressive-tense verbs express action that is continuous or ongoing.

> We are cleaning today.
> We were cleaning yesterday.
> We will be cleaning tomorrow.

1. Form the present progressive with *am, is,* or *are* before the *ing* form.

> I am requesting a ride tonight.
> My brother is planning to drive me.

2. Form the past progressive with *was* or *were* before the *ing* form.

> The choir was practicing when the fire alarm sounded.
> They were singing too loudly to hear the alarm.

3. Form the future progressive with *will be* before the *ing* form.

> We will be traveling to Dallas tomorrow.
> My favorite basketball team will be competing in the final four.

640.2 Creating the *ing* Form of Verbs

The *ing* verb form is used along with helping verbs to create progressive tenses. To create the *ing* form of most verbs, add *ing* to a base form that . . .

- ends in two consonants: dump—dumping   lend—lending
- ends in two vowels and a consonant: read—reading   look—looking
- ends in one vowel plus *y*: stray—straying   toy—toying
- ends in one vowel plus a consonant, and the syllable is not stressed: fidget—fidgeting   flutter—fluttering

---

1. If the base form ends in one vowel plus a consonant, and the syllable is stressed, double the final consonant and add *ing.*

> top—topping   admit—admitting

2. If the base form ends in *e,* drop the *e* and add *ing.*

> dive—diving   rove—roving

3. If the base form ends in *ie,* change the *ie* to *y* and add *ing.*

> tie—tying   lie—lying

641.1 Using Modal Helping Verbs

Some helping verbs work with the main verb to express a mode—such as a possibility, a necessity, an ability, and so on. The following chart lists meanings and the modals that express them.

Meaning	Modal + Base Verb	Modal + Past Participle
possibility	*may, might, could*	*may have, might have, could have*
	We may take the boat. We might see whales. They could sing for us.	You may have seen dolphins. You might have taken a picture. You could have invited me.
advisability	*should*	*should have*
	You should go to college.	You should have gone to college.
expectation	*should*	*should have*
	The letter should arrive soon.	The letter should have arrived last week.
necessity	*have to, must*	**(certainty)** *must have*
	You have to finish by noon. You must finish by noon.	You must have finished by noon.
request	*may, might, would, could, will, can*	
	May I help you? Might I change my order? Would you prefer toast? Could I have a bagel? Will you pay cash? Can I use a debit card?	
ability	*can, could*	*could have*
	I can meet you at the park. I could arrive by 8:00 p.m.	I could have met you earlier.
intent	*shall, will*	*would have*
	We shall finish on Saturday. We will finish on Saturday.	We would have finished on Saturday.
assumption	*must*	*must have*
	I must be mistaken.	I must have been mistaken.
repeated action	*would*	*would have*
	We would watch TV.	We would have watched TV.

▌Verbs (continued)

642.1 Using Phrasal Verbs

Some verbs consist of two or more words, a base verb plus a preposition or an adverb. These phrases have special meanings far different from the meanings of the separate words. The following chart will explain.

Phrasal Verb	Meaning	Example
ask out	invite on a date	Did you ask out Megan?
back up	reverse/support	Back up your car./Back me up.
blow up	add air/enlarge	Blow up the ball./Blow up the photo.
break down	stop working/ get upset	Old cars often break down./Grandma may break down in tears.
call off	cancel	Let's call off practice.
care for	like	I care for you. I don't care for peas.
clean up	tidy	Clean up your room.
clear out	empty	Clear out your email in-box.
cross out	delete	Please cross out my name.
cut back on	use less of	We should cut back on the salt.
cut off	separate/interrupt	The prisoner is cut off from family./ Do not cut off the other debater.
drop off	take and leave	Drop off the kids at school.
drop out	quit	Don't drop out of school.
figure out	decipher, solve	Can you figure out the crossword?
fill in	complete	Please fill in the blanks.
find out	discover	Find out who owns this computer.
get away with	do without penalty	He always gets away with cheating.
get over	recover from	Soon I will get over this cold.
give away	reveal/ provide for free	Don't give away the story's ending./ I will give away my couch.
give back	return	I will give the book back after school.
give up	abandon	Don't give up hope.
go after	try to get	This year I will go after good grades.
go out with	date	I want to go out with you.
hang out	spend time	Let's hang out at the park.
hang up	end a phone call	Don't hang up yet.
hold back	stop/keep secret	Don't hold back./Hold back those facts.

Phrasal Verb	Meaning	Example
hold on	wait	Please hold on while I tie my shoe.
keep on	continue	Keep on stirring.
keep out	exclude	Keep the cat out of the bedroom.
leave out	omit	Leave out the unnecessary details.
log in/on	access program	I should log in to Facebook.
log out/off	leave program	When you leave Facebook, log out.
look down on	mark as inferior	Don't look down on the elderly.
look forward to	anticipate	I look forward to the concert.
look out	be vigilant	Look out for deer crossing the road.
look up	find	Look up his batting average.
look up to	admire	I look up to my older sister.
make up	invent/reconcile	Fiction writers make up stories./After an argument, they always make up.
mix up	confuse, switch	Don't mix up the salt and sugar.
pass away	die	My grandfather will pass away one day.
pass out	faint	You may pass out when you see the bill.
pick out	select	Pick out your favorite song.
point out	indicate	Let me point out two benefits.
put off	delay	I put off applying for a loan.
put out	extinguish	Put out the candle.
put together	assemble	The bicycle must be put together.
put up with	tolerate	I put up with the elevator music.
run out of	use till it's gone	We often run out of hand soap.
run over	review/drive a vehicle over	Let's run over the report again./Don't run over the tulips with the mower.
set up	prepare/trap	Set up an account./You set me up!
shop around	compare deals	Let's shop around for phones.
show off	be flashy	He likes to show off with magic tricks.
sort out	organize/fix	Sort out the seed packs./We need to sort out the problem.
take after	resemble	I take after my mother.
take apart	disassemble	Don't take apart the remote control.
turn down	reduce/refuse	Turn down the heat./Turn down the job.
turn up	increase/appear	Turn up the volume./I'll turn up to eat.

▌ Verbs (continued)

644.1 Creating Direct Objects

Sometimes the subject performs the action of the verb, and a direct object receives the action.

$$\underset{\text{verb (action)}}{\text{Javin }\underline{\text{throws}}}\;\text{the ball.}$$

subject — Javin   object — the ball   verb (action) — throws

- **Infinitives** can be used as direct objects. An infinitive phrase begins with *to* followed by the base form of a verb plus any objects or modifiers. The infinitive phrase functions as a noun.

  subject — Javin   infinitive (object) — to take long walks   verb (action) — likes

  Javin likes to take long walks.

- **Gerunds** can be used as direct objects. A gerund phrase begins with the *ing* form of a verb and includes any objects or modifiers. The gerund phrase functions as a noun.

  subject — Javin   gerund (object) — taking long walks   verb (action) — likes

  Javin likes taking long walks.

Sometimes the meaning of a sentence changes depending on whether an infinitive or a gerund is used as the direct object:

Javin stopped to think. (He began thinking.)

Javin stopped thinking. (He ended his thinking.)

You can use infinitives or gerunds after these verbs:

begin	hate	love	remember	stop
continue	like	prefer	start	try

644.2 Verbs That Take Infinitives

Some verbs take infinitives but not gerunds as direct objects.

Javin decided to attend college. (*Not* "Javin decided *attending college*.")

I hope to see him. (*Not* "I hope *seeing him*.")

Use infinitives but *not* gerunds after these verbs:

agree	claim	expect	offer	seem
appear	consent	fail	plan	tend
ask	decide	hesitate	prepare	venture
attempt	demand	hope	pretend	volunteer
bother	deserve	intend	promise	want
choose	endeavor	need	refuse	wish

645.1 Verbs That Take Gerunds

Some verbs take gerunds but not infinitives as direct objects.

Javin avoids arguing. (*Not* "Javin avoids to *argue*.")

I keep bothering him. (*Not* "I keep to *bother him*.")

Use gerunds but *not* infinitives after these verbs:

admit	consider	finish	practice	suggest
appreciate	delay	imagine	recall	tolerate
avoid	deny	keep	recommend	
be worth	discuss	miss	resist	
can't help	enjoy	postpone	risk	

645.2 Participles as Modifiers

Participles are formed by adding *ing* or *ed* to base verbs. The present participle ends in *ing* and describes a cause:

The confusing map sent the tourists in the wrong direction.

The **past participle** usually ends in *ed* and describes an effect.

The confused tourists circled the block three times.

Present (Cause)	Past (Effect)
amazing	amazed
amusing	amused
appalling	appalled
boring	bored
confusing	confused
compelling	compelled
convincing	convinced
depressing	depressed
exciting	excited
fascinating	fascinated
haunting	haunted
misleading	misled
opposing	opposed
shocking	shocked

645.3 Nouns as Modifiers

Sometimes nouns function as adjectives to modify other nouns. Use the noun's singular form as a modifier:

My boot laces are knotted. (*Not* "My *boots* laces are knotted.")

▌ Prepositions

A preposition is placed before a noun to create a prepositional phrase. The prepositions *in, on, at,* and *by* are commonly used in the following ways:

In refers to . . .

- **the inside of something:** in the drawer, in the closet, in a parking spot
- **a geographical location:** in Seattle, in the U.S., in the Midwest
- **paper media:** in the report, in the article, in the book, in *The Great Gatsby*
- **a unit of time:** in an hour, in a month, in a moment, in a year

On refers to . . .

- **the surface of something:** on the floor, on the counter, on the earth
- **electronic media:** on the flash drive, on the hard drive, on the computer
- **a day or date:** on January 9, on the 9th of January, on Memorial Day

At refers to . . .

- **a specific place:** at the grocery store, at the corner, at the peak of the roof
- **a specific time:** at 7:00 p.m., at noon, at the changing of the guard

By means . . .

- **next to a certain place:** by the bookshelf, by the ballpark, by the lake
- **before a certain time:** by midnight, by morning, by Monday, by 2:30 p.m.

646.1 Phrasal Prepositions

Some prepositions consist of two or more words. A phrasal preposition is placed before a noun to form a prepositional phrase (***due to** the storm,* **on top of** *the fridge*).

according to	because of	in back of	on account of
across from	by means of	in behalf of	on behalf of
ahead of	contrary to	in case of	on top of
alongside of	down from	in front of	out of
along with	due to	in place of	outside of
apart from	except for	in regard to	over to
as for	from among	inside of	owing to
aside from	from between	in spite of	prior to
away from	from under	instead of	round about
back of	in addition to	near to	subsequent to

▌Avoiding Transfer Errors

When you learn a new language, you naturally apply what you know about grammar from your native language. Occasionally this can create "transfer errors." The following pages list common transfer errors and how to correct them.

647.1 **Help for Spanish Speakers**

Rule	Transfer Error	Correction
Use just a noun or a pronoun as the subject, not both (a double subject).	Jose, he got the job.	Jose got the job.
Use just one negative instead of two (a double negative).	Maria doesn't have no homework.	Maria doesn't have any homework. *(or)* Maria has no homework.
Use a subject in each sentence (including the pronoun *it*).	Was the funniest thing I ever heard. Is too hot.	That story was the funniest thing I ever heard. It is too hot.
When a subject is delayed, start with *here* or *there*.	Is my locker. Are my friends.	Here is my locker. There are my friends.
Position most subjects before the verb.	Ordered we pancakes.	We ordered pancakes.
Negate a verb with *don't* or *doesn't* (instead of *no*).	I no enjoy tennis. He no want snow.	I don't enjoy tennis. He doesn't want snow.
Do not make adjectives plural.	We had three beautifuls days.	We had three beautiful days.
Avoid placing an adverb between a verb and a direct object.	Carlos created carefully a plan.	Carlos carefully created a plan.
Don't use *which* to refer to people (use *who*).	My friend which loves to read gave me the book.	My friend who loves to read gave me the book.
Do not confuse *his* and *her*.	Lupita brought his purse.	Lupita brought her purse.
Use just a noun or a pronoun as the subject, not both (a double subject).	Darla, she finished her research paper.	Darla finished her research paper.

▌Avoiding Transfer Errors (continued)

Help for English Dialect Speakers

Rule	Transfer Error	Correction
Do not place an indefinite-pronoun subject between parts of a verb.	Hasn't nobody done the dishes.	Nobody has done the dishes.
Use *an* before a vowel sound and *a* before a consonant sound.	I need a answer. We want an report.	I need an answer. We want a report.
Use an article or demonstrative adjective before a general noun.	Girl can act. Dog can sense fear.	That girl can act. A dog can sense fear.
Use *their,* not *they,* to show ownership.	I like the color of they car.	I like the color of their car.
Form possessives by adding *'s* or *'* to nouns.	Did you see Jim email?	Did you see Jim's email?
After a plural number, use a plural noun.	We have two cat.	We have two cats.
Do not use *be* to express habitual action (use *is, am, are, was, were* instead).	We be working hard every day. He be working now.	We are working hard every day. He is working now.
Use just one negative instead of two (a double negative).	He doesn't have no ticket.	He doesn't have a ticket. *(or)* He has no ticket.
Negate a verb with *don't* or *doesn't* (instead of *no*).	I no like that movie.	I don't like that movie.
Do not use *ain't* (use *isn't/ aren't, hasn't/haven't* instead).	The bus ain't here yet. We ain't finished our project.	The bus isn't here yet. We haven't finished our project.
Don't use *hisself* (use *himself* instead).	He solved the problem hisself.	He solved the problem himself.

Credits

Image Credits:

Shutterstock: v, vi, vii, viii, ix, 1, 3, 5, 9, 10, 11, 13, 19, 23, 25, 29, 33, 35, 41, 44, 47, 52, 58, 61, 66, 69, 72, 81, 83, 90, 93, 99, 107, 112, 113, 115, 123, 128, 131, 135, 136, 141, 144, 150, 157, 159, 173, 189, 193, 197, 204, 211, 216, 224, 233, 237, 242, 243, 252, 259, 263, 265, 269, 277, 279, 283, 288, 293, 297, 303, 306, 311, 313, 322, 325, 330, 331, 333, 341, 343, 347, 359, 360, 367, 370, 371, 375, 377, 380, 381, 385, 392, 393, 394, 395, 397, 400, 404, 408, 410, 419, 424, 429, 431, 437, 439, 451, 453, 455, 456, 465, 474, 479, 481, 483, 486, 489, 493, 496, 501, 504, 511, 519, 523, 525, 534, 537, 547

Wikimedia: 162, 163, 165, 167, 197, 255, 332, 369, 372

Index

Y